HIGH TREASON

HIGH TREASON

The Assassination of JFK
& the Case for Conspiracy

Harrison Edward Livingstone
and Robert J. Groden

CARROLL & GRAF PUBLISHERS, INC.
NEW YORK

First Carroll & Graf edition 1998

Carroll & Graf Publishers, Inc.
19 West 21st Street
New York, NY 10010-6805

Library of Congress Cataloging-in-Publication Data is available.
ISBN: 0-7867-0578-7

Manufactured in the United States of America

For the young people of our country
Within whom lies the future.
They were the inspiration for this book
Without them it could not have been written.
They must learn the truth and care about the past
Without the truth, we are lost.

– Harrison Edward Livingstone

Dedicated to my wife Christine Groden for her love and support, and my children, Robbie, John, Melanie and Michael, who have put up with so much and given only love. To my parents Charles and Augusta Groden for their love and guidance. And to Dick Gregory and former Rep. Thomas N. Downing, D. Virginia. And finally to the memory of President John F. Kennedy, our last real President, for his vision and compassion.

– Robert Groden

TABLE OF CONTENTS

Acknowledgments.. ix

Preface.. xiii

Introduction... 1

PART I   The Tragedy

1. Murder... 11

PART II   The Medical Evidence

2. The President's Head Wounds and the New Evidence
   of Forgery 25
3. The Magic Bullet Theory and the Wounds
   of Kennedy and Connally 54
4. The Fragments and the X-rays 62
5. The Autopsy and the Autopsy Photographs 73

PART III – Conspiracy

6. Tampering with the Evidence 101
7. Strange Deaths 110
8. The Secret Service Protection............................. 127
9. Lee Harvey Oswald 138

PART IV   The Case

10. Fake Photographs... 171
11. Evidence... 181
12. Acoustics.. 206
    Some Basic Conclusions.................................. 226

PART V   Political Affairs

13. People and Sinister Connections 235

14. Deadly Politics 257
15. From Dallas to Watergate 272

PART VI   The House Assassinations Committee

16. The Investigation Begins 291
17. How the Investigation Foundered 310
18. The End of the Investigation 322

PART VII   The Bay of Pigs and National Security

19. Why Kennedy Was Killed: The War Party in Power 348
20. Special Operations and the Secret Team 368

      Afterword 386

      Addendum 403

      Bibliography 563
      Sources and Notes 567
      Subject Index 601
      General Index 613

ACKNOWLEDGMENTS

There are many loyal people who have worked long and hard in this investigation conducted by private citizens, with no other client than truth. They have done the job that the government could not do, dare not do. Few could face what really happened to John Kennedy.

First and foremost were Harold Weisberg, Sylvia Meagher, Vincent Salandria, Penn Jones Jr. and Mary Ferrell and the ladies of the Housewives' Underground. They broke the ground. They were not known in the media because these were the real critics. The people who wouldn't quit. They were more interested in the truth than publicity.

We are indebted personally to Penn Jones, Victor Marchetti, Harold Weisberg, Fletcher Prouty, Josiah Thompson, George O'Toole, and Judge Jim Garrison, for their encouragement and friendship. These people all wrote seminal books and did crucial investigation and research. Congressmen Thomas Downing, Henry Gonzalez, and Louis Stokes were at one time or another greatly helpful. Many others such as Gary Shaw, Larry Harris, Jim Marrs, Raymond Marcus, Richard E. Sprague, Jack White, Mort Sahl, Dr. Jack Gordon, Robert Saltzman, Donald Freed, Gary Mack, Earl Golz, David Lifton, Andy Liddell, Bernard Fensterwald, William Turner, Gaeton Fonzi, Robert Sam Anson, and the members of the Assassination Information Bureau, all who contributed greatly. We would like to thank Paul Hoch, Geraldo Rivera, Peter Dale Scott, Jerry Rose, Moses Weitzman, Dorothy E. Price, Liz and Rick Tonge, Michael Susko, Jamie Patterson, Dr. Charles Wilber, Dr. Donald Siple, Dr. Raymond Beazley, Dr. Paul Peters, and numerous others among the Dallas doctors who freely spoke to us, despite their anger and cynicism at the manner in which the official investigatory bodies had treated them. More than anything else they wanted to set the record straight. We would also like to acknowledge Eugene Scheiman and Lanny Sinkin, for their encouragement and help. There are so many other courageous, decent people, appalled by the prospect of their nation in the grip of gangsters and wheeler-dealers, of a military ruined by the CIA, of a government corrupted by the wealthy and powerful. These people refused to be discouraged or intimidated.

In particular co-author Harrison Livingstone would like to thank John Adams and the Playwright and Franciscan, William Alfred (the Author of "Hogan's Goat" and "Agamemnon") at Harvard University. Mr. Alfred talked Livingstone into writing this book. In addition, he would like to thank members of his family, especially Marianne and Milton, for their great assistance, without which this book never would have advanced to the point where a publisher took an interest.

The Authors particularly wish to thank Dr. Cyril H. Wecht for all his assistance and support, and for his courage through the years. We would like to thank Ali Jiron and John Barrie, Ray and Lois Machinest, Ezra Greenberg, Christine Schneimann, Stanhope Gould, Jacqueline Hall-Kallas, Jerrol Custer, Floyd Riebe, Paul O'Conner, Dennis David, Aubrey Rike, Jim Mustard, John Stupack, Rod Daniels, WBAL, Diane Raymond and WWDB.

They know who they are. We have many other friends who helped us stay alive to research and to write. Those who helped us write this book – and there are many – believed above all else, in their country. They believed in truth and were willing to risk all to achieve it. They could not accept that the sovereignty of the American people could be seized by a handful of assassins. What we lost on November 22nd, 1963, cannot be measured. On that terrible day in Dallas we forfeited our innocence, idealism and confidence. We cannot begin to restore these until we have exposed the truth.

In the end, the truth will emerge. Slowly, painfully perhaps, but *it will emerge*. And when it does, we will owe a debt of gratitude to those who make it possible, to all of these we extend our thanks.

U.S. AS A MATTER OF POLICY CANNOT CONDONE
ASSASSINATION

> – Cable to U.S. consul from President Kennedy, 1961

"In the eyes of posterity it will inevitably seem that, in safeguarding
our freedom, we destroyed it; that the vast clandestine apparatus we built
up to probe our enemies' resources and intentions only served in the
end to confuse our own purposes; that the practice of deceiving others
for the good of the state led infallibly to our deceiving ourselves; and
that the vast army of intelligence personnel built up to execute these purposes were soon caught up in the web of their own sick fantasies, with
disastrous consequences to them and us."

> – Malcolm Muggeridge, May, 1966

"In psychological warfare the intelligence agencies of the democratic
countries suffer from the grave disadvantage that in attempting to
damage the adversary they must also deceive their own public."

> – *Washington Post*, November 15, 1965

"There is no federal agency of our government whose activities receive
less scrutiny and control than the CIA."

> – Senator Stuart Symington, Committee for CIA Oversight

AUTHOR'S PREFACE TO THE 1998 EDITION

On July 31, 1998, the Assassination Records Review Board (ARRB) released major new interviews with autopsy or photographic witnesses just as this book was going to press. The reader will find a distillation of the important points in these interviews in a new article by me in the addendum of this book, along with the findings of Dr. David Mantik that the Zapruder film is fake and my findings that the so-called original in the National Archives cannot possibly be the original, but is a reframed, altered version.

The important point of the new interviews is the insistence of all witnesses that things they saw are not in the autopsy photographs, that several X-rays are missing including one that showed much or all of a bullet broken up at the top of the spinal column, and flat denials by some that the pictures showing the back of the head are accurate. James W. Sibert, one of the FBI men present at the autopsy, insists that there was a large hole in the back of the head and that the scalp was missing and doesn't recognize the official picture. One of the key differences between the picture and the body he saw was that the hair in the photo has been cleaned. This was not done before photographs were taken and there would be no reason to do this. In fact, an effort would have been made to document the entry hole in the scalp that would show in the photographs, but this was not done. The reader is reminded of the massive discrepancies I point out in four of my books, including this one, between what all medical witnesses saw and what is shown in the back of the head photographs. Readers should restudy the chapter "The Faked Autopsy Photographs from the Secret Documents" and "The Forged Autopsy X rays" in my fourth book, *Killing Kennedy and the Hoax of the Century*, published by Carroll & Graf in 1995. This book extensively documented what the doctors secretly told the House Select Committee on Assassinations, especially Dr. Pierre Finck's strong denunciation of the pictures of the back of the head.

The doctors are not going to come out and say the pictures are fake—it's too risky. Instead, they continue to dispute what is shown on the back of the head and the change in the position of the entry hole there, a discrepancy that was first raised by the Ramsey Clark Panel after they studied the photos and X rays now in the official evidence. From the ARRB's new interviews, we now know there is no chain of evidence on the official photos and everything in the record is a lie. Testimony of the Navy corpswoman at Anacostia Naval Processing Center, who processed the photos for Secret Service Agent James K. Fox and Robert L. Knudsen, a White House photographer who accompanied Fox, shows that the film he brought and the prints he left with were not the ones we have today. So where did the official evidence come from and who put it into the record?

This new evidence represents a massive vindication of my previously stated theories.

One final word of caution prior to the issuance of the report of the ARRB in September 1998: Do not trust official, "expert," or "scientific" analysis of visual evidence. Put far more trust in what witnesses say. *Weigh* the evidence. Keep in mind at all times that the JFK and related cases are political assassinations and the evidence is therefore politicized. Too many people have too much at stake to allow the truth to come out, even though it has been squeezed out drop by drop over the years. The cover-up is kept in place to this day by those with interests that are threatened by the truth of a political assassination. Nobody, in any official capacity is going to rock the boat and declare any or all of the visual evidence in the case the obvious fake it is. Nobody is going to say that the Zapruder film is fake. Kodak isn't going to say it and the National Archives aren't going to say it when they have so much at stake. Many had a hand in shaking down millions from the taxpayer for this fake film from the government after it was seized in early 1998. The media swallowed the film all over again, hook line and sinker.

Strange that the Associated Press story from Washington put a gloss on the release, emphasizing that Dr. James J. Humes had destroyed the first draft of his autopsy report, something we suspected but did not know, and distorting the release with their lead paragraph: "Records of the 1963 autopsy performed on John F. Kennedy are incomplete, and the doctors who conducted it undermined the integrity of their work by trying to protect 'the privacy and the sensibilities of the president's family' a government review board says" (AIP story, August 31 1998). This was not at all what the interviews were about. The autopsy was not accurate because the doctors did not bother to check with Dallas and find out that there was a bullet hole in the throat, or because they had X-rays, now gone, which showed that metal had struck the spine, evidently from behind, just beneath the skull, and probably came from the bullet that hit him near the hairline. The entry for that rear head wound is something that the government evidently intends to cover up at all costs, in spite of the doctor's insistence upon it. Certainly it is not reported in the press.

Instead, statements by Dr. Humes to the ARRB about Kennedy's Addison's disease (if in fact that was his condition), ignoring that President Kennedy had no adrenals at all and the confirmation of my findings about that in the *New York Times* in 1992, direct attention away from the key issues. The Associated Press throws only one sop to us, perhaps alerting the public that something might be wrong with the pictures: "In testimony to the board, photographer John T. Stringer questioned whether the pictures he took at a 'supplemental autopsy' of Kennedy's brain are the ones preserved at the National Archives." George Lardner at the *Washington Post* was more on target when he described testimony recently taken that indicates the entire set of photographs is not in fact authentic. The media continues to ignore the vast weight of the evidence demonstrating a faked case and fake evidence. Or do they even want to know about that evidence? After all, they can't afford to be proved wrong, can they?

Just a bit more of the truth began to emerge in an Associated Press dispatch printed in many newspapers July 3, 1997: "Conspiracy theorists seize on Ford change in Warren Report." The article stated that former president Gerald Ford, the only surviving member of the Warren Commission, had changed language in the report, according to new documents released by the Assassination Records Review Board. "Ford's changes tend to support the single-bullet theory by saying the bullet entered Kennedy's body at the back of his neck rather than in his uppermost back, as the Commission staff originally wrote." Ford's editing suggested that a bullet struck Kennedy in the neck—raising the wound some six inches from where the autopsy report and other accounts placed it. "Without that alteration," one researcher said, "they could never have hoodwinked the public as to the true number of assassins."

HIGH TREASON

The bullet could not have gone through both men and struck Connally in the way the Commission stated if the bullet had hit Kennedy lower on the back. There would have had to be two assassins to fire the shots that hit both men. Ford's revision made it possible to cover up the conspiracy.

John J. McCloy, another Commission member, was quoted in an article in *Newsday* (August 11, 1997) that in June 1964, he had expressed in a memo to Commission chief counsel J. Lee Rankin serious doubts about the "controversial conclusion" the Commission was coming to. "I think too much effort is expended on attempting to prove that the first bullet, which hit the President, was also responsible for all of Connally's wounds," McCloy wrote. "The evidence against this is not fully stated." This meant that four of the seven committee members (McCloy, Senator John Sherman Cooper, Senator Richard Russell, Congressman Hale Boggs) were on record as not believing their own conclusion of a single gunman. Evidently, Ford didn't believe it either.

McCloy also questioned the account that the bullet found on a stretcher at Dallas Parkland Hospital—where Kennedy and Connally were treated after being shot—was the "magic bullet." This put him at loggerheads with Commission counsel Arlen Specter, and Allen Dulles, a member of the Warren Commission, whom President Kennedy had fired as CIA director. Clearly, these men put Earl Warren in a corner, and got the "no conspiracy" result they wanted to prevent a domestic uproar over the violent overthrow of the administration.

On November 28, 1997, another article in *Newsday* about a secret document released by the Assassination Records Review Board bolstered the "contention that Lee Harvey Oswald was seen in Dallas with a U.S. intelligence agent about two months before the killing. . . . Those reports center on a shadowy figure called Maurice Bishop—likely a pseudonym—said to have been an intelligence agent during the early 1960's." The article then revisits information about one Antonio Veciana and his statements that he had met with Bishop more than one hundred times over thirteen years, and that one of these meetings was in Dallas with Lee Harvey Oswald present some two months prior to the assassination.

G. Robert Blakey, chief counsel to the House Committee (1977–79), was quoted in the 1997 article, saying, "We decided not to credit Veciana's claim" because there was no proof that Maurice Bishop existed.

"But the document released by the (ARRB) supports the contention that Bishop existed and otherwise backs Veciana's story." The document was a U.S. Army intelligence report dated October 17, 1962, describing a man who fit the profile of Bishop. "He used a different name, but we believe this man fits Bishop's profile very closely," one government official said. The report was from Col. Jeff W. Boucher, an Army intelligence officer, to Brig. General Edward Lansdale, an assistant to Secretary of Defense Robert S. McNamara, "a controversial figure in the Vietnam War."

The article said that "that issue has long been connected with unproved reports that a violent Cuban exile group—perhaps with the help of a U.S. intelligence agency—was involved in the assassination."

Martin Shackelford calls *High Treason* the best introduction to the evidence in the assassination of President John F. Kennedy. *High Treason* introduced major new evidence in the case when it questioned the authenticity of the autopsy photographs and analyzed the physical disparity found years before by the Clark Panel, and confirmed by the House Select Committee on Assassinations (HSCA), between the entry hole of a bullet in the back of the president's head, and where it is placed in the photographs and X rays. No one had made an issue of this before, but, as we have now learned *eighteen years later*, the autopsy doctors had not only denied the point of entry, but vigorously resisted the HSCA autopsy photographic evidence ostensibly found in the National Archives.

High Treason was the most comprehensive synthesis of the evidence up to 1989, and may still be. It was also the first book to give forum to the findings of the HSCA, other than that fine book by Anthony Summers, *Conspiracy*. Summers, like Peter Dale Scott, another writer whom I have great respect for, ignored the conflicts in the medical evidence and therefore did not have a sound foundation for assuming conspiracy. This did not negate their work, however. My book had an entirely different critique of the HSCA than that of Summers and, in addition, contained an extensive history of the Assassinations Committee and its foibles (chapters 16–18).

High Treason was also readable, something that could not be said for some of the other books. Today we are graced with many lightweights in the JFK case who achieve their moment of fame and influence—and then recede into the obscurity they so richly deserve. These people are troubling because they muddy the waters and confuse the issues, not to speak of preventing others with important research to be heard. I have tried in my books to bring forward and credit many unsung and otherwise obscure researchers with important work.

In 1995, I published for the first time a major amount of material from the HSCA interviews with the autopsy pathologists in my fourth book, *Killing Kennedy, and the Hoax of the Century*. This book had followed two massive volumes: *High Treason 2* and *Killing the Truth*, all published by Carroll & Graf. *Killing Kennedy* was perhaps the most important, because it brought to fruition both my research and synthesis of the case. I had concluded that it was clear that *all of the evidence*, including the famous Zapruder film, *was fake*, and I sought to prove as much in *High Treason 2* where I offered my evidence for the probable alteration of the film. Following this preface the reader will find a list of additional reasons suggesting alteration—from the observations of David Mantik, M.D., a physicist and physician with whom I work closely on the scientific evidence in the case.

I had stumbled into the one area that those who sought to cover up the conspiracy had to keep warded off. That was an area where researchers and investigators dared not question the physical and visual evidence in the case. There would be a heavy price to pay for questioning the Zapruder film and its entrepreneurs. We had blundered out of the labyrinth into a field of intense psychological warfare. The guards then tried to close the gate, and harsh retaliation and harassment ensued for daring to question the establishment.

We had found the key.

The four JFK case books I wrote and co-wrote show a progression of thought and some inconsistencies. I changed my mind on some issues and on points of evidence as more information became known. But not much that is persuasive changed, and I stick by my overview of what happened and why. Where I have thought I was mistaken, I say so, as in the acoustic chapter. For the record, the acoustical chapter in *High Treason* is incomplete and is better represented by Chapter 12 in *Killing The Truth*. I was wrong in my acceptance of the findings of the House Assassinations Committee, and I feel that the testimony and evidence as presented in *Killing the Truth* is conclusive. I also believe that the false evidence was deliberately planted on the HSCA.

Is there any reason to believe that the autopsy evidence is authentic as the latest developments reveal themselves? Not at all. Yet the pressure to cave in on this issue from those who cannot accept the weight of the evidence of forgery is enormous.

In addition, after this book was written and first published, quite a few people came to me and mentioned almost off-hand that the Zapruder film was fake. This gave me a lot to think about, though no published work questioned its authenticity. In addition, I had come to question the veracity of some of those connected with it and so began to take a closer look at the film myself. I found much wrong with it. It quickly became apparent that the film had to be fake, and a sort of animation. As soon as I published these thoughts in *High Treason 2* and the succeeding books, I found that by 1996 research community belief was widespread that the film was false. And soon I had the uneasy sensation that the whole issue was being co-opted by those who had opposed me. When I heard them taking up my position and not having anything to do with me, I knew I had won.

High Treason was also notable for pounding at the issue of whether there was a large hole in the back of the head, and whether President Kennedy's body was stolen and altered, as David Lifton maintained. I discounted the later idea in the text in a hastily written afterword as we were going to press but gave some credence to that author's autopsy witnesses—whose statements seemed so believable if taken at face value. As always, we were faced with a mass of contradictions from the establishment critics.

My later research, with tremendous difficulty finding those same witnesses, tended to discount the body theft story, but not entirely. Today, I feel that the root of the problem lies in semantics and distortion of the facts. These men all described the same wounds that were seen in Dallas. This was backed up when I was able to publish drawings in *Killing Kennedy* made by some of the autopsy witnesses for the HSCA that all showed a large hole in the back of the head and nowhere else. The conclusion to the years of confusion and misinformation on the body theft issue was that the body was not altered.

I've never discounted the possibility that someone did get at the body and dug bullets out of it. That might have been essential to the conspiracy. The conspirators would have been certain to have someone close to the body at all times, and they would have never lost control of it. Part of the plan would have had to include the removal of extra bullets.

Other key issues cannot be resolved entirely, and what we are left with is a reasonable certainty that the doctors lied on some issues because they were forced to, and told the truth on others, and that all the medical witnesses in Dallas and Bethesda were discredited at the start so that they would not be a worry to the conspirators.

That was a key to where the conspiracy came from, and I went into this in far greater detail in the chapters on Dallas in *Killing the Truth*. That book also argued that the JFK case had not been solved because the Texas conspirators were running a major disinformation operation among our amateur investigation and research community. That operation ensured that none of the evidence was clear, and that the media and the authorities were thoroughly confused.

Later, having smoked out some of the disinformation agents, we were finally fighting on an open field. The smiles to battle and war are appropriate. The viciousness of this in-fighting had no limits, and "anything goes" was the way they played it—just like politics.

One could say this disunity and factionalism was counterproductive, but it could not be avoided. The alternative, which we had lived with for three decades, was far worse. At least this way, other voices could be heard, and we had a chance to establish alternative views of the case and the evidence. It was necessary, as any political reformer knows, to expose the wolves in sheep's clothing among us and try to purge them. Very hard fighting ensued.

After writing *High Treason*, I located the missing British nurse, Diana Bowron, who had washed Kennedy's body at Parkland Hospital, and after signing an agreement with British police not to reveal her whereabouts, I obtained a series of stunning interviews. There were many more major interviews, including one with Dr. Robert Frederick Karnei, who had participated throughout the autopsy, and who was simply unknown as a witness. I interviewed many others from the autopsy and published all of this, including a chapter on my talks with Marina Oswald, and one on Kennedy's secret medical problems *High Treason 2*, later acknowledged as solving the mystery of his adrenal glands in *the New York Times*, 6 October 1992, Science Section by Dr. Lawrence Altman. Unfortunately, this was all the medical community and Dr. Altman seemed interested in.

They were not interested in the real state of development of the medical evidence[a] which overturned the findings of the Warren Report, and, instead, Altman parroted what they thought the autopsy doctors were saying, as regurgitated by the *Journal of the American Medical Association.*

In that same book I argued that it was "prima facie crazy" to suppose that Lyndon Johnson was "behind" the plot to kill President Kennedy. "It is unreasonable to suppose that Johnson planned Kennedy's murder or ordered it," and I quoted Jon Margolis of the *Chicago Tribune*: "To remember Lyndon Johnson is not to love him. But the suggestion that Johnson would stoop to murder, stupidly plotting with men he knew enough to distrust, is even less credible than was Johnson at his worst" (page 528 of *High Treason 2*). I said that Johnson *had* to be privy to the plot beforehand and would have had to participate in it in order for the cover-up to work. He was part of a committee of conspirators that coalesced almost by accident. I think enough evidence was there, from the string of murders that followed him from the time of the Billie Sol Estes case, to understand that he was ruthless and capable of ordering such violence. Estes gave evidence after Johnson's death that he had ordered the murder of a witness. And there were more killings in the Estes case, as is explained in Madeleine Brown's *Texas in The Morning* (p. 190), which I published.

Crimes of State were committed in the past for a king or a leader by his men and supporters. In this case, I have no doubt but that Johnson had guilty knowledge—and the assassination of JFK was with his approval. The evidence is clear that the murder was done by close supporters of Johnson, and that they could not have proceeded without his knowledge and help, even if he did not personally order the death of Kennedy. I don't think that is something he could have done without the agreement of powerful people with the capacity and methods for killing Kennedy as well as covering it up. J. Edgar Hoover and the oilmen had made LBJ their captive.

One of the most hurtful experiences in my life was the aftermath of my trip to Dallas in 1979. I achieved much there, but found myself abandoned when I returned, and in great fear. I was terrified when I left Dal-

---

[a]With the help of Kathleen Fitzgerald, I prepared a major encyclopedia of the medical evidence as it was then known in Appendix J of *Killing the Truth*, pp. 664–747.

las with the story that the doctors who treated Kennedy as he lay dying knew that the autopsy photographs of his head were completely false. I taped these interviews and was absolutely sure of what they meant. It was four or five years before anyone else tried to do the same thing.

But I could not get this story out, try as I might. I called important newspapers and magazines to ask them to take my story. But I was a nobody. Several long months would pass before the *Baltimore Sun* revealed the results of their own communications with the Dallas doctors, which corroborated my story. At that time, Robert Groden offered to combine his autopsy photographs, both black-and-white and color, with my story, if I could get someone to publish it. He said that the photographs would help sell my article.

The main force of my research began to establish itself. I simply had to find the strength from my religious faith to survive the onslaught of character assassination, slander, and libels in national magazines. And go on writing and interviewing witnesses, some of whom were poisoned against me by competing researchers.

The emotional and financial cost of involvement in these investigations is vast. It is not a healthy climate in which to conduct research. As in politics, one comes under vicious attack—often with lies and slander. I'm not perfect, but I've tried to be forthright and conduct my affairs honestly. Many false things have been written and said about me, as well as other well-meaning, honest people. The evidence in the JFK case is politicized because the assassination was a political murder. So the Left and Right battle, and those in the middle are eaten alive. At times, this work is a killing thing and we pay the price that John Kennedy paid for defending his memory in the face of vicious smears.

It is my belief that lately we are beset by military types and their stooges, often unwitting, who are trying to direct attention away from the Pentagon, Military Intelligence, Bethesda Naval Hospital, and toward the CIA—everyone's favorite fall guy. Some CIA men appear to have been involved in the assassination, but certainly the agency, which was run by a friend and appointee of John Kennedy, had nothing to do with it.

I also believe that there is a major mind control operation at work, not only with the visual evidence planted in this case, but with some of the key operatives in the research community. One sign of it are the conflicting theories. That is, some researchers hold views that contradict each other, thus negating the truth of either. There are many examples of this. I feel that some of the organizations that entered the case have a hidden agenda to co-opt the issues and the community so that they are positioned to speak for the entire community and its research. In one sense, this might be better than the free-for-all that existed before, but it is also threatening to the flow of ideas. Certainly the establishment of COPA as the "opposite number" and foil for the ARRB pushed many individuals out of the way. The appearance of new writers and their books of "research" also tended to displace major work that had gone before.

Anything I have to say about anything or anyone is the truth as best as I can know it. Ultimately, this book that I co-wrote and paid such a heavy price for has triumphed, and I'm very proud of it—like a father with his child, now eighteen years old since it was first written at Harvard and in the home of friends. They all looked over my shoulder as every word went down.

Little did I imagine what I was getting into and the journey I would take.

—Harrison Livingstone
Baltimore, August 1998

"The CIA's strategy, according to these sources is to stymie the House Assassination probe. Too close scrutiny of the tragedy might embarrass the CIA, which withheld crucial facts from the Warren Commission. It was a mistake, we believe, for the CIA to operate at the KGB level."

– Jack Anderson and Les Witten

INTRODUCTION

When President Kennedy died, much of the world believed that a conspiracy was involved. The first reports from Dallas told of a second gunman on a grassy knoll at Dealey Plaza, a large hole in the back of the President's head, and a fusillade of shots. A few days later, the Warren Commission was established under the Chief Justice of the Supreme Court, Earl Warren, to inquire into the assassination. Many witnesses had said that someone had fired from the knoll,[1] which was to the right and front of the President's car. The Commission denied that a gunman was on the knoll, but years later a committee in the U.S. House of Representatives was forced to admit the existence of the second gunman, and the probable existence of a conspiracy,[2] when it was demonstrated that police sound recordings made during the shooting contained a gunshot which could only have come from the Grassy Knoll.* This was one more shot than the Warren Commission admitted to.

The Warren Commission was composed of the ideological enemies of the murdered liberal northern Democrat, five Republicans and two conservative southern Democrats. The Commission chose to ignore

1

much of the hard evidence in the case, kept much of it a secret, and in the end, published a theory known as the Warren Report.

THE "SINGLE BULLET" THEORY

This theory held that there was only one gunman, that he was in a sixth floor window of the Texas School Book Depository, and that only three shots were fired at the President.[3] The Commission said that Lee Harvey Oswald was the assassin, and they found no evidence of conspiracy. The media then made it a certainty, and convicted Oswald in the press. One of the bullets, according to the Commission, struck the President in the back of the neck, came out the front of his throat and badly wounded former Democratic Governor John Connally. This theory was invented by Warren Commission counsel (now Republican Senator from Pennsylvania) Arlen Specter, and former President Gerald Ford, a member of the Commission at the time he was in Congress. This theory had no basis in fact, as it contradicted the evidence. Insofar as the theory relies upon the bullet which was recovered in the hospital, the theory is "impossible," as one of the doctors (Lt. Col. Pierre Finck) who conducted the autopsy said, "for the reason that there are more grains of metal still in Governor Connally's wrist than there are missing from that bullet. That bullet could not have done it."[4]

A second bullet, allegedly fired from behind, was claimed to have struck President Kennedy in the back of the head near the hairline, about 2.5 cm from the occipital protuberance,[5] exploding the head and blowing out a large part of the skull – killing him. The Report simply suppressed the exact location of the large blow-out, which was in fact in the back of the head just above an entry wound. Was the President struck twice in the head, first from behind near the hairline, and then from in front? Was he also struck in his throat from the front, and then six inches down from the neck in his back from behind, rather than in the rear of the neck? Was John Connally hit with still another bullet, as the FBI and Connally originally said, rather than the single bullet Specter and Ford claimed hit both men?

According to the Warren Commission, a third shot missed, and a bystander, James Tague, was struck with debris from the cement curb it hit.[6]

The assumption that a single bullet allegedly struck both Kennedy and Connally became known as the "magic" or "single bullet theory."[7] Three of the seven members of the Commission did not actually believe this theory.[8] It appears now that most of the Commission's conclusions were in error.

A STRANGE AUTOPSY

The autopsy at the Naval Military Hospital in Bethesda was not really an autopsy at all. Many standard autopsy procedures were not followed.[9] The doctors did not explore the wounds in the throat to see if a bullet had passed through the body, because they didn't know that there was a wound in the throat, as a tracheotomy had been performed in Dallas by enlarging the hole.[10] All of the evidence was that the wound was not in the back of the neck, but six inches down in the back, and that the bullet did not traverse the chest at all.[11] In fact, it appears the President was struck by two separate shots from behind. These shots from the rear struck him in the back and head, while two more frontal shots struck him in the throat and head. Additional shots struck Connally and Tague. Contrary to the Warren Report, there was no evidence that the President was shot in the back of the neck. In addition, the President's brain was never sectioned (a standard autopsy procedure) to determine the number and trajectories of the missiles,[12] and the brain later *disappeared*.

For two years beginning in the fall of 1976, Congress investigated the assassinations of President Kennedy and Martin Luther King. The House Select Committee on Assassinations delivered a devastating critique of the autopsy, the photographs and X-rays,[13] and began the painful process of rewriting history. Deciding that America was ready for a little more of the truth, but not the whole truth, Congress admitted, albeit reluctantly, that it was likely there were conspiracies in the murders of both President Kennedy and Dr. Martin Luther King, Jr.

TRAVELING WOUNDS

The Parkland Hospital doctors and nurses in Dallas were not allowed to see the X-rays and photographs alleged to be of the body.[14] They were quite amazed more than a decade later when co-author Harrison Livingstone, *The Baltimore Sun*, Ben Bradlee, Jr. and his *Boston Globe* team (both newspapers motivated by and acting under Livingstone's direction) separately showed the pictures to these medical witnesses.[15] In addition, when the Bethesda Naval Hospital autopsists were shown the photographs and X-rays by the House Select Committee on Assassinations, they strongly denounced them as not accurately depicting the wounds. The autopsists found that one of the head wounds had *moved* four inches toward the top of the head.[16] They denied strongly that there originally had been such a wound.[17] This wound, and the large hole in the back of the head described by many witnesses, which is missing from the official pictures, are the subject of Chapter 2. The fact that the autopsists questioned these pictures at all indicates something is seriously amiss with the official autopsy photographs.

The early controversy over the evidence first culminated in the investigations of the former District Attorney of New Orleans, Jim Garrison, who put one of the autopsy doctors (Dr. Pierre Finck) on the stand. This doctor testified that high-ranking officers prevented them from performing the autopsy properly,[18] and that the wound in the back did not pass through the body.[19] The Attorney General of the U.S. at the time, Ramsey Clark – who was from Texas (as was President Lyndon Johnson, Kennedy's successor) – sought to stymie Garrison's inquiry, and constituted a panel of four doctors who were allowed to see the alleged autopsy photos and X-rays.[20]

Upon observing these photographs and X-rays, the Clark panel of doctors found that the wounds had mysteriously traveled. The head entry wound moved four inches toward the top of the head from the base of the hairline where the autopsists had seen it,[21] and the neck wound began to gravitate down the back.

TOO MANY MISTAKES

Originally, police officers with expert knowledge of rifles testified that they had found a German Mauser by the "sniper's nest."[22] The gun soon changed into an Italian Mannlicher-Carcano, despite the fact that it would have been impossible to confuse the two. Gerald Ford, a long-time supporter of the CIA and a member of the Warren Commission, was later appointed by Nixon as Vice President to replace Spiro Agnew, who resigned in disgrace. Nixon was himself then forced to resign in the face of almost certain impeachment. President Ford then pardoned Nixon in advance (an unheard of legal procedure) of possible criminal prosecution in the Watergate affair. Ford was not re-elected. He had gone to some pains to publish classified (Top Secret) material from the Warren Commission without permission in his book on Oswald, in order to suppress information that Oswald was a government agent[23] and to scotch implications that Oswald had worked for the Office of Naval Intelligence. Oswald had many connections to government operatives.[24] In his book on the case, Ford said the policemen were "mistaken" about the type of rifle that was found. "Mistake" is the operative word in all the cover-ups that followed. It was said that the autopsists were mistaken. The Warren Commission said that the Dallas doctors and nurses and Jacqueline Kennedy were mistaken, and that the witnesses to a gunman on the Grassy Knoll made a mistake.

Allen Dulles, also a member of the Warren Commission, whom President Kennedy had *fired* as head of the CIA, made it clear that if Oswald was a government agent, it would never be known.[25] "Not in our time," Chief Justice Warren said, "will all of the facts be revealed."

Since then, evidence has piled up that intelligence operatives were involved in the crime, that Oswald himself was an agent – but was set up as the patsy, and did not shoot anyone.

Many witnesses and others connected with the case – the biggest mystery of the century – have died under strange circumstances.[26] A handful of researchers and critics who continued to pursue the case were placed under surveillance ordered by Chief Justice Warren. They experienced destabilization and harassment. The critics were often reviled as scavengers or Communists.[27] The CIA and FBI sent out directives on how to counteract criticism of the Report.[28] Oswald was considered a pro-Castro Communist, and anyone who said Oswald didn't murder President Kennedy was stigmatized as a leftist. Today, critics of the Warren Report are called "buffs" to make them appear like hobbyists who play with model trains or collect coins.

THE FACTS ABOUT OSWALD

Oswald, it would appear, was not remotely what he was made out to be after the assassination and his own murder.[29] He had become fluent in Russian while a U.S. Marine, and it is not credible that he would be stationed at the CIA base at Atsugi, Japan (the base from which U-2 flights were flown over the Soviet Union), as an admitted "Marxist" speaking fluent Russian without being a trusted agent. Many facts make it clear that his much publicized defection to the Soviet Union was staged. He was probably sent to the Soviet Union by the Office of Naval Intelligence or the CIA, and then repatriated.[30]

In 1987, evidence began to surface that an extra-legal organization of government agents and officers can operate independently in foreign affairs, as in President Reagan's Iran-Contra Affair, even functioning from the White House itself, perhaps without the entire knowledge or consent of the President. Such a group or *secret team* put Oswald together and controlled him from the beginning.

It should finally be clear, when all the evidence is heard, that Oswald probably never went to Mexico City and visited the Cuban and Soviet Embassies there shortly before the assassination as alleged in the Warren Report. This evidence was deliberately fabricated by the people who set Oswald up as the patsy in the assassination of President Kennedy. The House of Representatives continues to hold secret a major report on this. Why?

The 1976 House Assassinations Committee, walking the most terrible and highest of all tightropes, found after two years that "there probably was a conspiracy" in the murders of both President Kennedy and Dr. Martin Luther King, Jr.[31] They appeared determined at first not to find any conspiracy, but were trapped by two of their Members into admitting evidence of conspiracies at the very end, on almost the last day of the investigation. They then had to rewrite their conclusions, which took another six and a half months.

FABRICATED EVIDENCE

The Assassinations Committee admitted sixteen years after the crime that there was an assassin on the Grassy Knoll firing, as some 50 witnesses had said all along.[32] A police recording made during the assassination has the sounds of the shots on it. There were at least six shots – probably seven – on the tape, but the House Committee confirmed only four. There is considerable photographic evidence of the sniper on the knoll as well.[33] But the Dictabelt recording of the shots made by the Dallas Police was never essential to prove the conspiracy. The tape only corroborated "what we already knew," as Congressman Louis Stokes, the last Chairman of the Assassinations Committee, said on national TV.

The recent Congressional Committee decided to tell us of four shots, which is one more than the 1964 Warren Commission admitted; but they claim, after long confusion and debate, that the Grassy Knoll sniper's bullet missed.[34] They have to cover up the rest, because otherwise it would reveal that the autopsy evidence is fabricated, and the Committee had in fact evidence of that fabrication from the beginning.

This book will provide evidence of that forgery, and evidence of a third sniper and a probable fourth: two in front and two behind. Congressman Christopher Dodd (now Senator) believed it was clear that there were two snipers firing from behind the President, in addition to the Grassy Knoll sniper. In fact, the whole world believed there was a conspiracy in the assassination. President Johnson believed it right up to the time of his death, and he believed that the CIA was involved in the murder.[35]

The 1980 book by Anthony Summers, *Conspiracy*, goes a long way towards saying what really happened on that terrible day in November, 1963. But even Summers' work leaves many questions unanswered. *High Treason* picks up where Summers' work left off.

The Committee, as with all of the other investigative bodies before it, could not conduct a clean, honest investigation, and it was doomed from the start. Considering the forces ranged against the inquiry, it is extraordinary that anything at all was achieved.

The key to understanding who killed President Kennedy lies with the autopsy photographs. Those photographs may tell us more about the assassination than all of the official investigations. Perhaps the single most important question in the investigation was never asked: Why were the autopsy photographs and X-rays never officially shown to the numerous doctors and nurses in Dallas who treated President Kennedy?

Had this question been pursued, the true nature of the conspiracy would then have been exposed, because the crucial pictures allegedly of the back of the President's head are forged! That forgery is one of the keys to the conspiracy. Who would have had that kind of *access* to the evidence in order to alter it? Who had the *capability* to alter it?

The vital autopsy photos of the back of the President's head were altered immediately after the autopsy in order to cover up the fact that the President received two bullets in the head, one from the rear and one from the front, and this second shot blew out the back of his head, as Jackie Kennedy testified to the Warren Commission. Nobody, including the Warren Commission, saw these pictures for years.

The Groden enhancement of the Zapruder film taken during the assassination clearly shows the President rocketed backwards by this frontal shot, and the back of his head blowing out. Subsequent frames of the film show that the shape of the President's head has changed and is elongated after the explosion, with the back of the head stretched out, a large ring apparent where the hole in the back of the head is, beneath a shock of hair. Part of the President's skull and brains were blown backwards and to the left onto a motorcycle policeman, and onto the grass beside the road.[36]

"There was nothing Robert Kennedy could do about... the cover-up that he knew Allen Dulles was perpetrating on the Warren Commission..." Harris Wofford wrote in his book *Of Kennedys and Kings*. President Kennedy was killed because of his policies, and because he was too "liberal," because he would have been re-elected, and, specifically, because he had begun the complete withdrawal from Vietnam three weeks before he died.

"That's why he was killed," writes Col. Fletcher Prouty, former liaison between the CIA and the General Staff.

The War Party that took America into Vietnam killed him. They are still in power, and still calling the shots.

PART I   The Tragedy

"If a prospective agent cannot be recruited by an appeal to patriotism, he is bribed. If he cannot be bribed, he is blackmailed. If he refuses to be blackmailed, he is 'programmed.' If all these fail, he is killed, for it must not be known that he had ever been approached – so important is 'national security.' "

– W.H. Bowart, *Operation Mind Control*

"Private CIA's-for-hire have metastasized across the landscape. Whether it's computers, hamburgers, newspapers, or jets, America's paladin spooks are increasingly likely to have a hand in it (and sometimes a strong arm as well). More often the public is their target and... justice is often undone, subverting federal agencies and the courts... industry's intelligence agents often labor in a moral vacuum: Profit, rather than patriotism, is their assignment. Laws *are* broken: smears, bag jobs, bribes, wiretaps, deception operations, currency scams, industrial espionage, tax frauds, and even assassination programs have been planned and carried out by contract agents of the business world."

– Jim Hougan, *Spooks*

"I will smash the CIA into a thousand pieces."

– President John F. Kennedy

CHAPTER 1

MURDER

President Kennedy came to Texas in late November of 1963 to mend political fences between liberal and conservative Democrats. Perhaps we can say that he was lured to Dallas, driven into an ambush in a well planned plot to overthrow the government and control it without the public learning what had happened.

The conspirators had to place the President in a situation where the murder could be easily committed, and where a cover-up could start on the spot with the help of a few policemen. The plotters had to have a place where the conditions were right.*

A patsy had to be prepared and ready to be blamed for the crime. And they had to be able to kill him so that he could not prove his innocence. That patsy was Lee Harvey Oswald.

Dallas was filled with hatred at the time of the murder. The Right Wing vilified Kennedy, and the country seethed with plots and murderous groups of Cubans, radical and violent Right Wingers,

*As related at the end of the book, Miami Police had recorded Joseph Milteer, a Right Wing extremist, who apparently had inside knowledge of the plot to kill President Kennedy in Dallas. He described the plot to a police informant in amazing detail. In addition, a Secret Service agent, Abraham Bolden, reported that four Cuban gunmen planned to assassinate Kennedy in Chicago in early November.[1] It is deeply troubling that the Federal authorities to whom the Miami police gave the information did nothing, and the Chicago affair seems to be covered up. If true, taken together with the apparent luring of the President's Secret Service guards to a bar in the early morning hours of the day of assassination, it would appear that elements of the Secret Service might have been involved. See the end of the chapter (8) on the Secret Service for a further discussion.

Organized Crime, and dangerous, out-of-control intelligence agency operatives of all kinds. Dallas was a nightmare: "... a city of mixed emotions," Chief of Police Jesse Curry wrote in the first sentence of his book. "As the tension mounted the small and violent minority were in danger of upsetting the stability of the whole city."[2]

The morning the President arrived, a black bordered ad was placed in the paper by the American Fact-Finding Committee, a Right Wing extremist outfit, which tried to make out that Kennedy was a Fellow Traveler.[3] And along the parade route, handbills were distributed which said "Wanted For Treason," beneath pictures of Kennedy arranged like police mug shots on a Wanted poster in the post office.

There was a strange confluence of events at the time of the assassination. Almost all of the Administration was removed from Washington. Six members of the Cabinet were on a plane far out over the Pacific, with the notable exception of the President's brother Robert, who remained in Washington.[4] Robert Blakey, later chief counsel of the Assassinations Committee, was with him. Richard Nixon, later to be President, and J. Edgar Hoover – perhaps the most powerful man or the second most powerful man in Washington – were both in Dallas with oil baron Clint Murchison the night before the killing,[5] and Vice President Lyndon Johnson was there with the President.

We know where the Secret Service was the night before: At midnight, when they were technically on duty, nine of them went out for a drink. Seven of them were still drinking at 2 A.M. and most of them until 3 A.M. at Pat Kirkwood's "Cellar"; one was still at it at 5 A.M. They all had to report for duty at 8 A.M. Recalling that Lincoln's guard also slipped out for a drink on that fatal evening when another President was murdered, we should ask: Were these men lured?[6]

The bubble was removed from the President's car so that he, his wife, Governor John Connally of Texas and his wife sitting just in front of the President, and the driver and guard in the front seat were open and unprotected. The driver was fifty-five years old, and his reactions were slow.

The President had spent the early morning of November 22, 1963 in Fort Worth, and then was flown the short distance to Dallas. He was gratified by the reception he received, though not forgetting that Adlai Stevenson, a liberal and former presidential candidate whom Kennedy had appointed as America's ambassador to the United Nations, had been cursed, struck, and spit at during his visit to Dallas shortly before.

The route of the motorcade through downtown Dallas had been publicized, and very large crowds turned out to wish the President well. But the original route had been changed slightly, so that the whole motorcade had to make a difficult and slow series of turns in Dealey Plaza.

At 12:30 in the afternoon, the President's car made the last, fatal turn. The limousine was slowed by the cars and motorcycles in front of it, which blocked the way. They had come to the end of the large crowds lining Main Street in the center of downtown. The car turned left onto Elm Street, past the Texas School Book Depository, and headed down the slight grade that would take the car through Dealey Plaza and beneath the triple underpass onto Stemmons Freeway. Governor Connally, who had invited Kennedy to Texas and who was his official host, sat with his wife in the jump seats of the limousine in front of the President and his wife.

The terrible shots began to ring out, one after another.

Amateur photographer Abraham Zapruder trained his camera on the President's car and photographed the assassination as it happened. The first bullet missed. Zapruder was startled by the shot and his camera jumped, blurring the film at around frame 155. His film would again blur with each subsequent shot.

The next shot from the front struck the President in the throat, and his hands clutched his throat in a defensive motion. His wife turned to look at him and reached for his wrists, concern and terror on her face. No-one else reacted.

Then another bullet struck the President in his back six inches below the shoulder line and just to the right of the spinal column. Mr. Kennedy still sat up straight, held in place by his back brace.

Governor Connally heard the shots and first turned around to his right to try to see what was happening to the President. Then Connally started to turn to his left, but was stopped by a bullet in his back near the right armpit. He held his hat in his right hand. The bullet nearly killed him as it transited his chest and came out at the right nipple. He insisted it wasn't the same bullet that hit the President in the back.

The driver of the limousine was startled. Instead of reacting and speeding off, he turned to look in the back of the car.

In the follow-up car, filled with Secret Service agents, the men did nothing at all throughout the ten seconds of shooting. Secret Service Agent Emory Roberts ordered the others not to move.[7]

But in the next car behind the Secret Service agents, Vice President Johnson ducked down out of harm's way.

Shot after shot rang out, echoing among the buildings lining the plaza. One bullet struck the inside chrome above the windshield of the President's car. Another hit the sidewalk alongside the car. The shots and their echoes were recorded at the central police station by an open microphone transmitting from a policeman's motorcycle.

Bystanders said there was a fusillade of shots fired, and they appeared to come from several directions all around the car. Senator Ralph Yarborough, who was riding with Vice President Lyndon Johnson two cars back, swore that he smelled and saw gun smoke coming from the fence on the Grassy Knoll to the right front of the motorcade, and many witnesses said that there was a gunman there.

Then the President was struck in the head, twice, nearly simultaneously, first from behind – pushing his head forward a bit – and then from the front, throwing his head and body rearward and to the left at great speed. His head exploded all over a motorcycle policeman to the left rear of the nearly stopped limousine. This happened at frames 312 and 313 of the Zapruder film.

After the President received the shots to his head – six-tenths of a second later – another bullet smashed Governor Connally's wrist, and entered his thigh.

Still another bullet struck the curb down the street and a bystander – James Tague – was hit on the left cheek with debris flying up from the sidewalk.

Jacqueline Kennedy crawled out of the still slowly moving car and onto the trunk to retrieve part of the head.[8] A Secret Service agent, Clint Hill, ran forward, jumped on the car and pushed Mrs. Kennedy back into her seat as the car finally began to accelerate. "Just about as I reached it," Hill said, "there was another sound, which was different than the first sound. I think I described it in my statement as though someone was shooting a revolver into a hard object – it seemed to have some type of an echo ... the second noise that I had heard had removed a portion of the President's head, and he had slumped noticeably to his left. Mrs. Kennedy had jumped up from the seat and was, it appeared to me, reaching for something coming off the right rear bumper of the car, the right rear tail, when she noticed that I was trying to climb on the car. She turned towards me and I grabbed her and put her back in the back seat, crawled up on top of the back seat and lay there. I noticed a portion of the President's head on the right rear side was missing and he was bleeding profusely. Part of his brain was gone."[9] Bones were later retrieved from the street and grass. One of these is known as the Harper fragment, identified in Dallas as being from the back of the head – occipital bone.[10]

Jacqueline said, "And in the motorcade, you know, I usually would be waving mostly to the left side and he was waving mostly to the right, which is one reason why you are not looking at each other very much. And it was terribly hot. Just blinding all of us...

"You know, there is always noise in a motorcade and there are always motorcycles beside us, a lot of these backfiring. So I was looking to the left, I guess there was a noise, but it didn't seem like any different noise really because there is so much noise, motorcycles and things. But then suddenly Governor Connally was yelling, 'Oh, no, no, no.'

"... I was looking this way, to the left, and I heard these terrible noises. You know. And my husband never made any sound. So I turned to the right. And all I remember is seeing my husband, he had this sort of quizzical look on his face, and his hand was up, it must have been his left hand. And just as I turned and looked at him, I could see a piece of his skull and I remember it was flesh colored. I remember thinking he just looked as if he had a slight headache. I just remember seeing that. No blood or anything.

"And then he sort of did this, put his hand to his forehead and fell in my lap." Jackie cried: "They have killed my husband. I have his brains in my hand.

"And then I just remember falling on him and saying 'Oh, no, no, no.' I mean 'Oh, my God, they have shot my husband,' and 'I love you, Jack.' I remember I was shouting. And just being down in the car with his head in my lap. And it just seemed an eternity.

"You know, then, there were pictures later on of me climbing out the back, but I don't remember that at all."

"Do you remember Mr. Hill coming to try to help on the car?"

"I don't remember anything. I was just down like that. And finally I remember a voice behind me, or something, and then I remembered the people in the front seat finally or somebody knew something was wrong, and a voice yelling, which must have been Mr. Hill, 'get to the hospital,' or maybe it was Mr. Kellerman, in the front seat. But someone yelling." The following is her secret testimony concerning the wounds: "I was trying to hold his hair on. But from the front there was nothing. I suppose there must have been. But from the back you could see, you know, you were trying to hold his hair on, and his skull on." [11]

The problem is, the large hole in the back of the head described by these and many more witnesses doesn't show in the secret autopsy evidence.

When the shooting stopped, the motorcade finally speeded up and headed for Parkland Hospital, where there was a chaotic scene when the car arrived with its bloody contents.

The Chief of Police in Dallas, Jesse Curry, wrote, "Agent Hill finally convinced her to let go of the President. Apparently she didn't want anyone to see that the back of the President's head was partially blown off. He gave her his coat which she used to carefully wrap the President's head and neck as five or six Secret Service men lifted him toward the stretcher. His body was limp like a dead man's; they struggled to get him on the stretcher." [12] "... A small neat wound was in the throat. The back of the head was massively damaged and blood from this wound covered the floor and the aluminum hospital cart.

"Dr. Perry examined the throat wound and assessed it as the entrance wound. He was no amateur at assessing wounds. By his later testimony he stated he had previously treated from 150 to 200 gunshot wounds. ... Dr. Perry insisted that the President was shot from in front." [13] "... the motorcycle officers on each side of the rear of the Presidential car knew that he was hurt and hurt badly. No one knew any more forcefully than motorcycle officer Bobby Hargis. He had been following close, just behind the left rear fender of the limousine. A red sheet of blood and brain tissue exploded backward from Kennedy's head into the face of Officer Hargis. The trajectory must have appeared to Hargis to have come from just ahead and to the right of the motorcade. He parked his motorcycle and started running in that direction." [14] Along with many others, he ran up the Grassy Knoll.

We learned that the telephone system in Washington went dead 2.5 minutes after the last bullet was fired, and that it took one hour to restore service. It was later explained that the breakdown was caused by overloaded phone lines.[15] Since this occurred almost at the moment that the shots were fired, it seems unlikely that a lot of people, let alone enough to knock out the phone system of a whole city – if that ever would be possible under any circumstances – would have been making calls at that time.

In Dallas, in the motorcade, the press telephone was immobilized. "At 12:34 the radiotelephone in a press car carrying representatives of the wire services was rendered inoperative." Merriman Smith got out the first word of the shooting, but the phone went immediately dead.[16]

The only other means of communication from the motorcade, the police radio, Channel One, went dead. This occurred at 12:29; for the next four minutes, someone blocked the channel by keeping his microphone open. This appeared to be a motorcycle policeman, as the only sound that could be heard was that of a motorcycle engine.[17]

"Abroad, a teletype machine aboard a military aircraft carrying Cabinet members to Japan began chattering the first report that shots had been fired at the Presidential motorcade in Dallas. There was a moment of panic; fearing an international plot, and with specific codes and procedures for such an emergency, Secretary of State Dean Rusk and Press Secretary Pierre Salinger attempted to contact the White House to verify the report. They reached the Situation Room but were prohibited from authenticating the data because *the official code book was missing* from its special place aboard the plane."[18]

Shortly after the assassination, that afternoon, when the plane carrying the new President, Lyndon Johnson, was in the air flying back to Washington with the body of Kennedy, Johnson and the others were told that a message had come from the Situation Room at the White House saying that there was no conspiracy, and that only one person had committed the crime.[19] This message came from either McGeorge Bundy or Commander Oliver Hallet.[20] Colonel Fletcher Prouty told the authors that it was Bundy. "The Situation Room was manned by military personnel and receiving much of its information from the Defense Intelligence Agency (DIA) in the Pentagon."[21]

Jim Bishop wrote in *The Day Kennedy Was Shot,* "Officials at the Pentagon were calling the White House switchboard at the Dallas-Sheraton Hotel asking who was now in command. An officer – a member of the Presidential party – grabbed the phone and assured the

Pentagon that Secretary of Defense Robert McNamara and the Joint
Chiefs of Staff 'are now the President.' "[22]

The Bagman, the man carrying a suitcase with an apparatus that
would allow the President to set in motion the nation's war machine,
and Major General Chester Clifton were separated from first Kennedy
and then Johnson, and left behind at the airport.[23]

Dallas Police Chief Jesse Curry tells us, "The physical security
arrangements provided by the Dallas Police Force for the Secret Service
were carried out exactly as they requested. In my opinion, all police
officers involved gave their complete and whole-hearted co-operation.
Yet the Dallas Police Department was never given any information or
asked to co-operate with the FBI or Secret Service in any attempt to
locate possible conspirators. The Dallas Police Department was never
informed of the presence of Lee Harvey Oswald in Dallas."[24]

Although there is some doubt about the last statement that they had
no information on Oswald, the Texas authorities did have a file on him
with an address at Elsbeth Street. Oswald had not lived at Elsbeth Street
for some time.[25] But the point of what Curry said is that the investigation became so compartmentalized from the start that it was doomed.
The Secret Service, as the Assassinations Committee found, had some
important information on the violent Cuban groups which may have
been involved, but the FBI steered them away from the investigation.[26]

THE SECRET TEAM

Before we go on, the concept of what Colonel Prouty calls the
"Secret Team" should be introduced. Prouty, the liaison between the
Pentagon and the CIA, was in a position to know many or most of the
nation's secrets, if not all, for a number of years. He wrote a book, *The
Secret Team* . According to Prouty, "The Secret Team is a group of men
who can orchestrate the activities of the United States government. They
are not always the same men. But they are always from the same areas
of interest – industry, big business, the military, big banks, big lawyers.
Through their ability to direct the activities of key people, they
manipulate government policy and have probably done so since 1959 or
1960. Certainly since the murder of Jack Kennedy in 1963."[27] This
"Secret Team" played a pivotal role in the assassination of President

Kennedy. Their presence is felt in Dealey Plaza and in every stage of the murder and the cover-up which followed.

SLOW MOVING TARGET

James L. Simmons, who was standing on the railroad overpass during the assassination, as the motorcade came towards him, was asked, "Did the car speed up?" "No, in fact the car stopped, or almost stopped." "Then did the car speed up?" "Yes, after they got the motorcycle policeman out of the way."[28]

This, perhaps, is why the car did not take evasive action. We are told that the motorcycle policemen directly in front of the car were Ellis, Gray, Brewer, Lumpkin, and Freeman. Three more were in front of them: Bellah, Garrick, and McBride.[29]

But we know that Bill Greer, the driver of the limousine, stared over his shoulder at Kennedy for a long time, with his foot on the brakes, during the shooting, until the *fatal headshots were fired*.[30] It is difficult to forget the laugh on Greer's face as he left his questioning by the Warren Commission, with Clint Hill and Roy Kellerman. That laugh was captured for all time by the camera.

AFTERMATH

As the echoes of the shots died in Dealey Plaza, policemen dashed up the slope of the Grassy Knoll, where they were met by men flashing Secret Service badges, and turned away.[31] Later, it was established that no Secret Service agents were present anywhere in that area,[32] so clearly, men had been provided with false identification and were in place during the shooting to turn back the police, giving the gunmen time to escape. One of these gunmen was seen running west across the railroad tracks.[33]

Nevertheless, a number of men were shortly arrested in the yard area behind the Plaza;[34] this further occupied the time of the policemen, helping the gunmen to escape, climb into the trunks of cars, or escape down the sewers. Photographs known as the "tramp photos" were taken of some of the arrested men,[35] and incredibly, almost no record was made of their arrests. The alleged tramps were peculiarly clean shaven, with good shoes and clothing, though arranged in such a way as to disguise them.

An officer dashed into the Texas School Book Depository within a moment of the shots, and there, along with the manager of the building, found Oswald drinking a Coke by the Coke machine on the second floor.[36] Oswald would have had to have dashed down the stairs from the sixth floor, and they would have noticed if he had been winded. Later, when others tried to duplicate the feat of coming down from the sixth floor, it was found to be impossible in the time span available.

That wasn't the only impossible time span in the scenario making out Lee Harvey Oswald to be the killer. The timing of the shots on the recording made by the police during the shooting was also impossible for the alleged rifle used. No lone gunman could load, aim and fire a weapon several times in those few seconds.[37]

And it would seem impossible for Oswald to have performed all the movements he was accused of in the next hour. He left the Depository and started home. He was supposed to have got onto a bus, then left it because of the traffic and taken a taxi, then gone to his house some miles away, changed his shirt, got his revolver, walked a mile to where he allegedly shot to death Officer J. D. Tippit, and finally entered a movie theater, where he was shortly captured.[38]

How come they went after *him*? A very vague description of the killer was broadcast moments after the shots ended – a description that could have fit many young men.[39] No-one knows to this day how the police obtained this description. It therefore seems likely that Oswald was privately identified to the police by the conspirators, and told where he could be found.

Shortly after the murder, a police car was seen by Oswald's landlady stopping in front of their house,[40] which was not far from the home of Jack Ruby – the man who was shortly to kill Oswald in the central police station. The driver of the car blew its horn and then moved on. This may have been Officer Tippit, who is thought to have known both Ruby and Oswald.

THE COVER-UP BEGINS

Although the police were directed to the movie house by someone in a store nearby who saw a person he felt was suspicious enter the movie house, it would appear that Oswald had been directed to that particular place as part of what he thought was an intelligence operation.

Secret Service agents and members of the President's party struggled with the Dallas County Medical Examiner, and took the body illegally from Parkland Hospital in Dallas.[41] From that moment forward, the observations of all witnesses at Parkland and to the murder itself, including those of the President's wife, were ignored. A series of murders began to take the lives of numerous witnesses, and the Big Lie soon overwhelmed the truth.

In John Kennedy's murder, the footprints of intelligence and of Prouty's Secret Team are clear. The case has a pattern of forged, planted, and missing evidence that could only come from a covert action capability equipped to do these things.

The body was flown to Washington shortly after the murder, but not before the new President (Johnson) was sworn in on the same plane. The plane was filled with the mourners, the President's widow in shock, his staff and Secret Service men, the new President's staff and Secret Service men, and newspaper reporters. Kennedy's coffin was never unattended for even a second by friends so close to him in life that they would have laid down their lives had the wrong persons tried to get near. The authors have personally investigated this matter, and it is simply impossible that the body might have been removed from its coffin at any time, or tampered with, as some have claimed.

The body was rushed to Bethesda Naval Hospital, where the autopsy was being hastily organized. That autopsy, as we shall see later, was inadequate and unprofessional. Even common criminals had better.

The conspirators had someone present in the morgue in a position to observe and control events. The cover-up would have to take shape around the findings of that autopsy, and some of those findings would have to be changed or altered. This was done, and the autopsists were threatened with courts-martial and ordered not to speak.

The President's body was taken to the rotunda of the Capitol, where it lay in state in a closed coffin for days. His funeral was one of the saddest events in recent history. Kings and Queens, Presidents and leaders from everywhere on the planet, including leaders or representatives from America's adversaries, walked down Pennsylvania Avenue in the cortege. Most Americans old enough to remember can recall the funeral and interment in Arlington National Cemetery in Virginia that sad day in November, 1963.

Later on, Chief of Police Curry wrote, "Investigators were awaiting the results of the autopsy with the naive assurance that the government would release a detailed autopsy report which could be used in the investigation. The photographs and autopsy evidence were never released by the government. Apparently portions of the material have even been destroyed. The Warren Commission itself yielded to political pressure and never examined the autopsy photographs."[42] The cover-up had begun. As Stanley Keeton has written, if evidence can disappear from the National Archives, it can be fabricated.[43]

Neil Sheehan wrote in the *New York Times* after reading the Pentagon Papers that there was an inner government in the United States, "a centralized state, far more powerful than anything else, for whom the enemy is not simply the Communists but everything else, its own press, its own judiciary, its own Congress, foreign and friendly governments – all these are potentially antagonistic. It had survived and perpetuated itself," Sheehan continued, "often using the issue of anti-Communism as a weapon against the other branches of government and the press, and finally, it does not function necessarily for the benefit of the Republic but rather for its own ends, its own perpetuation; it has its own codes which are quite different from public codes. Secrecy was a way of protecting itself, not so much from threats by foreign governments, but from detection from its own population on charges of its own competence and wisdom."

PART II   The Medical Evidence

There is an inscription chiseled onto the CIA building in Langley, Virginia, a quote from Jesus Christ:

> *Ye shall know the truth*
> *and the truth shall make you free.*

"I didn't mind putting people through hard times as long as the truth came through. I gave the Saigon military a lot of names of people I wanted killed. But I found out that the truth wasn't going to make anybody free because it wasn't getting back to Washington."

– Former CIA agent and author Frank Snepp

"We cannot, as a free nation, compete with our adversaries in tactics of terror (and) assassination."

– President John F. Kennedy, November, 1961

"One of the most profound changes that has come to the presidency has resulted from a new factor in American life – assassination as a political instrument."

– George E. Reedy, former Special Assistant to President Lyndon Johnson, in *The Twilight of the Presidency*

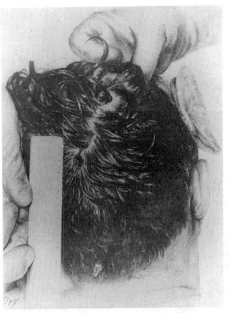

The official picture of the back of the President's head, though the government only released the above, which is an exact tracing. This picture disagrees with all accounts of the head wounds by the Dallas medical staff and autopsists.

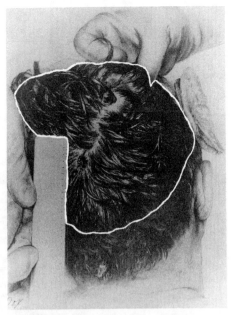

The same photo with an outline of the matte line. This shows where a composite photo was made by combining two different photos to make the forgery. The matte line is visible to the naked eye.

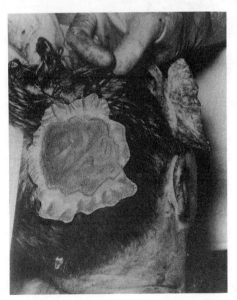

How the wounds actually looked.

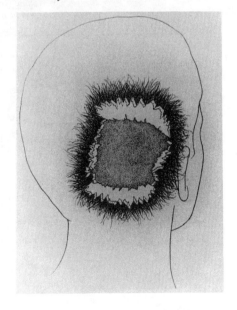

A pictorial representation of President Kennedy's head wound as described by Dr. Robert N. McClelland of Parkland Hospital. It was verified by every doctor, nurse and eyewitness as accurate. The exit wound was described as being almost squarely in the back of the head (the occiput).

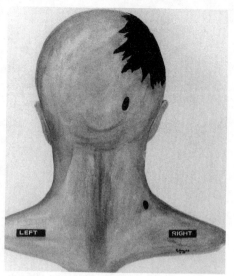

This drawing published by the Warren Commission shows the rear exit wound partially to the rear of the head, almost as described in the autopsy report written at Bethesda Naval Hospital and in the Dallas doctors' description. It explains why autopsist Dr. James Humes told the Warren Commission that there was an exit wound there. Note also the very low entry wound in the back of the head, and a wound in the neck-shoulder.

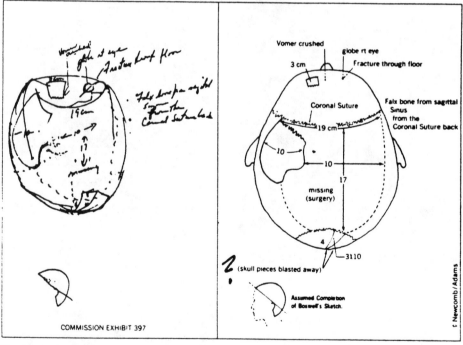

COMMISSION EXHIBIT 397

© Newcomb/Adams

The autopsy face sheet (reverse) showing an apparent entry wound near the left eye 3 cm across. A redrawing (left) of the head wounds from the autopsy face sheet. The autopsists were never asked what they meant by "missing," but a dotted line points to the triangular pieces of bone at the back of the head, one of which corresponds to the Harper fragment found on the grass near where the car had passed.

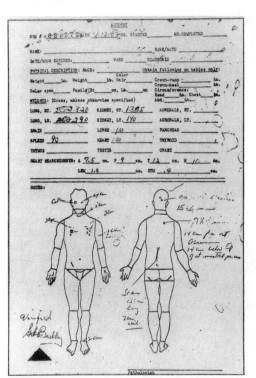

The JFK autopsy face sheet, showing the wounds.

The autopsy face sheet drawn by Dr. Boswell, showing the wounds on the body. Note that he has drawn an entry wound on the back well down from the neck.

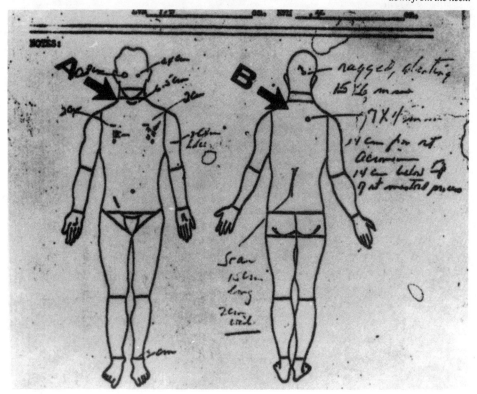

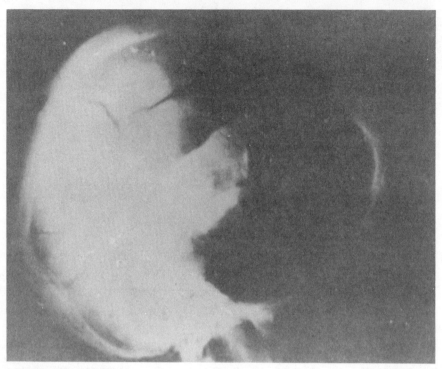

X-ray of JFK's skull, lateral view unenhanced. Note that the right front face and eye is missing in all the X-rays.

Unenhanced photo of JFK head X-ray.

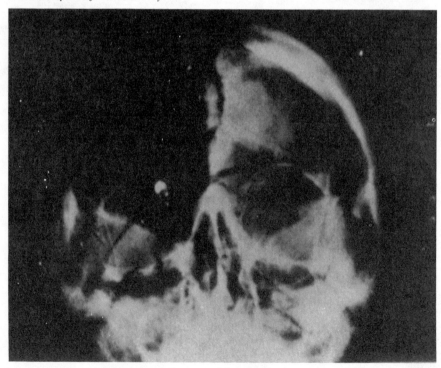

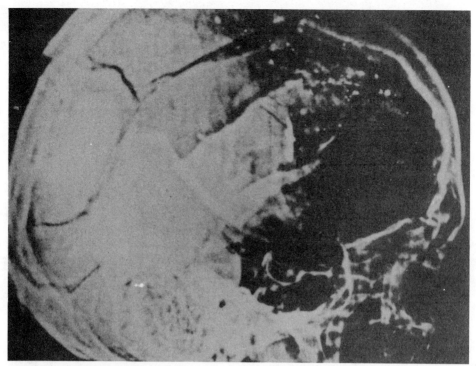

Enhanced photo of JFK's skull X-ray.

A-P (front to back) view.

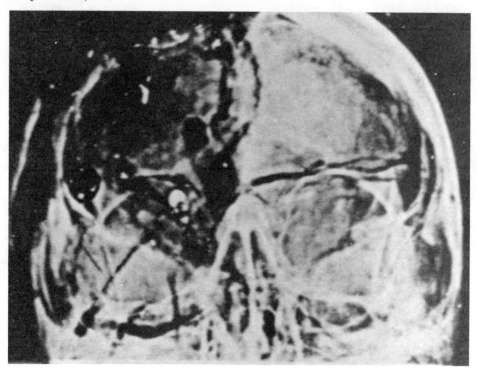

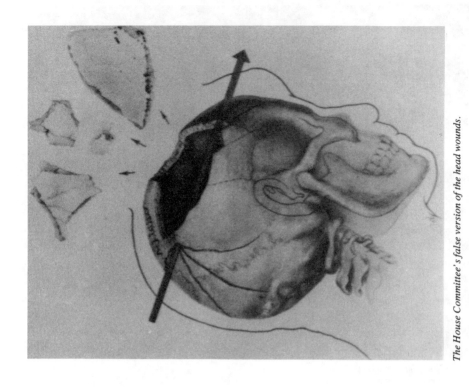

The House Committee's false version of the head wounds.

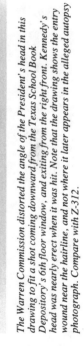

The Warren Commission distorted the angle of the President's head in this drawing to fit a shot coming downward from the Texas School Book Depository's 6th floor window, and exiting from the right front. Kennedy's head was nearly erect when it was hit. Note that the drawing shows the entry wound near the hairline, and not where it later appears in the alleged autopsy photograph. Compare with Z-312.

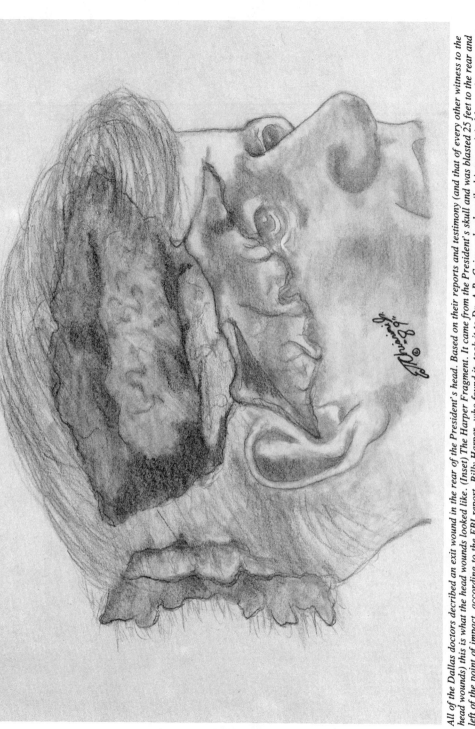

All of the Dallas doctors decribed an exit wound in the rear of the President's head. Based on their reports and testimony (and that of every other witness to the head wounds) this is what the head wounds looked like. (Inset) The Harper Fragment. It came from the President's skull and was blasted 25 feet to the rear and left of the point of impact, according to the FBI report. Billy Harper, who found it, took it to Dr. A.B. Cairns who described it as occipital bone, from the back of the head.

DEPARTMENT OF SURGERY
Division of Urology
Paul C. Peters, M.D.
   Professor & Chairman
Terry D. Allen, M.D.
   Professor

SOUTHWESTERN MEDICAL SCHOOL
5323 Harry Hines Blvd.
Dallas, Texas 75235
(214) 688-3546

August 7, 1979

Mr. H. E. Livingston
30 West 25th Street
Baltimore, Maryland   21218

Dear Mr. Livingston:

I have marked an "X" on the picture which more accurately depicts the wound, although neither is quite accurate in my opinion. There was a large hole in the back of the head through which one could see the brain.

Sincerely yours,

Paul Peters

Paul C. Peters, M. D.
Professor and Chairman
Division of Urology

PCP:pl

Dr. Peter's letter to co-author Livingstone describing the head wounds, which said that there was a large hole in the back of the head.

A pictorial representation of President Kennedy's head wound as described by Dr. Robert N. McClelland of Parkland Hospital.

tissue, posterior cerebral tissue and some of the cerebellar tissue had been blasted out (6H33).

This is the clearest description we have of the Kennedy head wound.[11] In reading it we can understand quite readily why neurosurgeon Clark called the wound "tangential." For Dr. McClelland is quite clearly describing an impact on the right side of the head that blasted backward, springing open the parietal and occipital bones [see diagram] and driving out a mass of brain tissue. The precise character of the brain tissue is also important, for only a deep-ranging shot could have blown out cerebellar tissue, which is located very low in the brain. Dr. Marion Jenkins of Parkland remembers how "there was herniation and laceration of great areas of the brain, even to the extent that the cerebellum had protruded from the wound" (17H15; cf. 6H48), and Dr. James Carrico speaks of how the head wound "had avulsed [exploded] the calvarium [skull]" (17H4). A nurse, Pat Hutton, later recalled how "a doctor asked me to place a pressure dressing on the head wound. This was of no use, however, because of the massive opening on the back of the head" (21H216).

140

Dr. Paul Peters was given a copy of the official picture of the back of the head, and a copy of the above drawing showing a rear exit wound. He marked the later as more accurately depicting the way the head looked.

Government recreation of the shooting.
Note: 1) Location of the rear head entry is near
the hair line and four inches lower than where
the alleged autopsy photograph shows it.

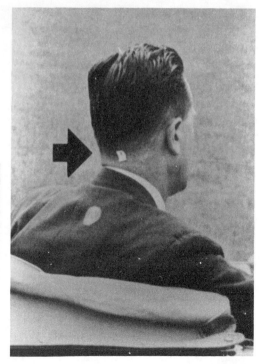

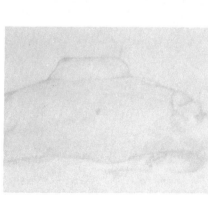

2) The back wound is placed well down from
the neck.

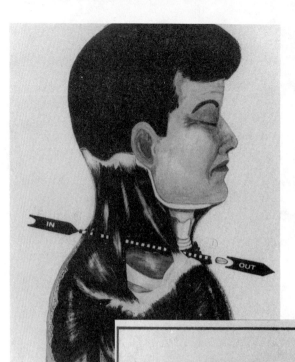

The Warren Commission's version of the back and throat wounds. The back wound is represented too high and the throat entrance wound is shown as an exit wound.

Receipt from the FBI for a missile (or bullet), not a fragment, removed from JFK during the autopsy. The bullet was never turned in as evidence.

The President's death certificate signed by Dr. Burkley, stating "a second wound occurred in the posterior back at about the level of the third thoracic vertebra." (The third thoracic vertebra is about six inches down from the shoulderline).

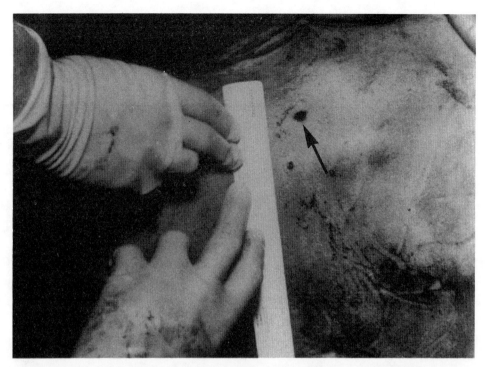

The back wound, in a distorted perspective. Although this view cannot show how far down the back the wound actually is, it clearly shows that the wound was not in the back of the neck. The picture is distorted by the angle of the photograph because the body was lifted off its back and not turned over to take the picture.

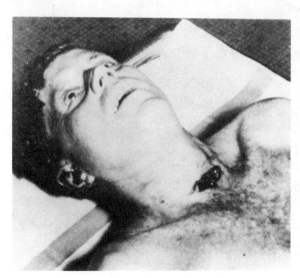

The throat wound, showing the tracheotomy obliterating it. Because of this operation, the autopsists missed the fact that there was a missle wound there, but the Dallas Doctors called it a small, neat wound of entrance, 3 to 5 mm in size.

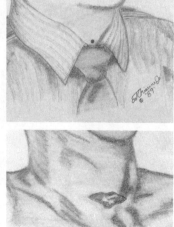

The frontal neck entry wound as described by the Dallas doctors.

The President's jacket and shirt showing bullet holes 5 3/4 to 6 inches down from the collar. If the frontal neck wound had been an exit wound as the Warren Commission and the House Assassinations Committee said, it would have been travelling on an upward trajectory and could not possibly have been fired from any sixth floor window.

The frontal damage to the President's shirt collar is a slit caused by the scalpal used to cut away the necktie NOT a bullet hole! This confirms the testimony of Dr. Charles Carrico (one of the Parkland doctors) that the neck wound was above the shirt collar. This places the frontal neck wound far ABOVE the back wound, thus destroying the single bullet theory.

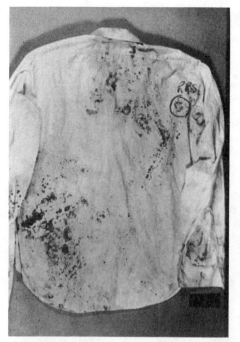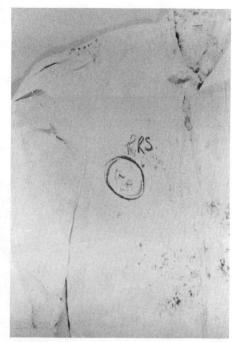

Governor Connally's shirt showing the rear entry and front exit wounds.

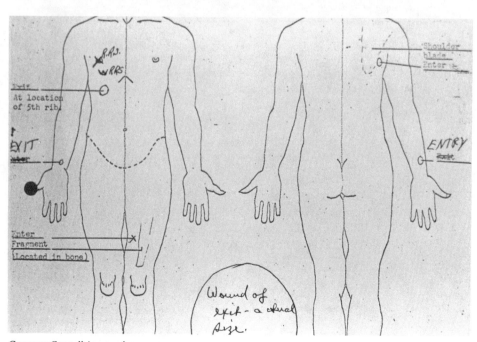

Governor Connally's wounds

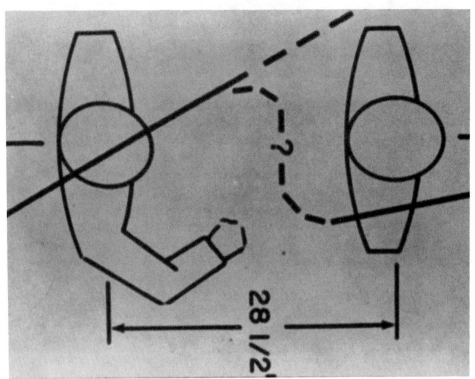

The "magic" or single bullet theory.

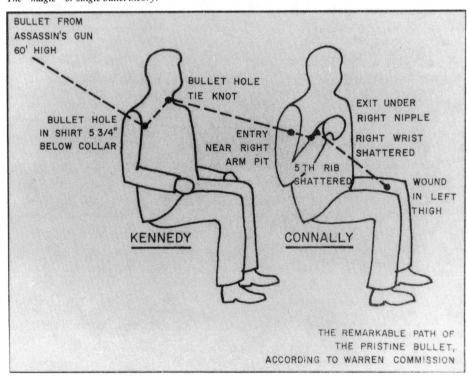

BULLET FROM
ASSASSIN'S GUN
60' HIGH

BULLET HOLE
TIE KNOT

BULLET HOLE
IN SHIRT 5 3/4"
BELOW COLLAR

ENTRY
NEAR RIGHT
ARM PIT

EXIT UNDER
RIGHT NIPPLE

RIGHT WRIST
SHATTERED

5TH RIB
SHATTERED

WOUND
IN LEFT
THIGH

KENNEDY

CONNALLY

THE REMARKABLE PATH OF
THE PRISTINE BULLET,
ACCORDING TO WARREN COMMISSION

Another diagram of the single bullet theory.

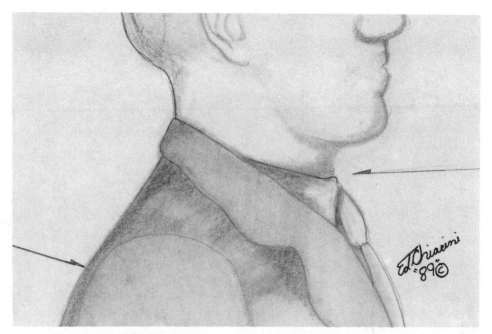

The true locations and directions of the President's non-fatal wounds.

Line up of the back wounds leaves no chance that the President's frontal neck wound was caused by a single bullet. The bullet would have exited far too low.

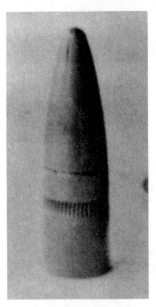

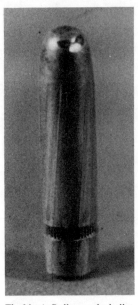

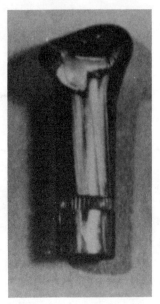

The type of bullet found by the stretcher in Parkland Hospital. It had a pointed nose, whereas the alleged murder bullets had rounded noses, as does the "Magic Bullet."

The Magic Bullet, or the bullet alleged to have struck Kennedy and Connally.

Test bullet fired into a wrist bone shows far more damage than the "magic bullet" which was alledged to have caused seven separate wounds in two men, and shattering a dense bone in Governor Connally's right wrist.

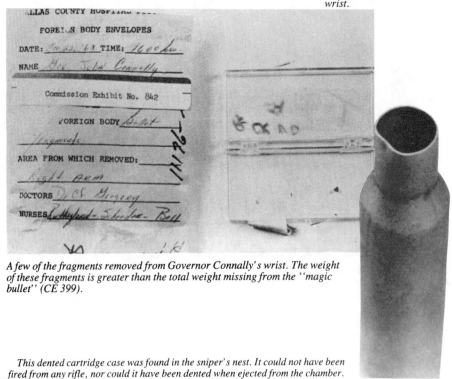

A few of the fragments removed from Governor Connally's wrist. The weight of these fragments is greater than the total weight missing from the "magic bullet" (CE 399).

This dented cartridge case was found in the sniper's nest. It could not have been fired from any rifle, nor could it have been dented when ejected from the chamber.

"The panel continued to be concerned about the persistent disparity between its findings and those of the autopsy pathologists and the rigid tenacity with which the prosecutors maintained that the entrance wound was at or near the external occipital protuberance."

– VII House Select Committee on Assassinations,
p. 115 (308)

CHAPTER 2

THE PRESIDENT'S HEAD WOUNDS AND THE NEW EVIDENCE OF FORGERY

Dr. James J. Humes and Dr. Thornton Boswell – the Bethesda Naval Hospital autopsists – insisted to the panel of doctors interviewing them for the House Assassinations Committee in 1977 that the entrance wound they found on President Kennedy's head was at or near the occipital protuberance – the bump on the back of the head – stating that there was a large hole above it "through which one could see the brain." They knew that there could not be a bullet entrance wound in an otherwise intact scalp and skull where we now see it in the official autopsy photographs, which the doctors were looking at while being questioned.

"Was the head lifted up from the table? Did someone look at it?"

"Yeah… in fact we shined a light in the cranial vault there, and noticed a large amount of brain missing," Dr. Adolphe Giesecke told co-author Harrison Livingstone. Dr. Giesecke looked at a copy of the official autopsy picture of the head for the first time when Livingstone showed it to him. Livingstone pointed to the back of the head: "Was this blown out here?"

"Yes. It was missing."[1]

Dr. Giesecke was an anesthesiologist at Parkland Hospital in

25

Dallas, where President Kennedy was brought moments after he had
been mortally wounded.

Dr. Robert G. Grossman, another of the Parkland doctors, also
described the head being picked up by Dr. Kemp Clark. Grossman told
The Boston Globe's Ben Bradlee, Jr., that he had noted a large, separate
wound, located squarely in the occiput.[2]

The Parkland doctors had in fact conducted a close enough examination to report the same large hole in the back of the head. *All* the
doctors and nurses at Parkland Hospital who saw the body described
a large exit wound in the back of the President's head. It is unlikely that
so many trained medical personnel could be in error regarding the nature
of the wounds.

The Warren Report states that "Dr. Clark, who most closely
observed the head wound, described a large, gaping wound in the right
rear part of the head..."[3] The Report of the Assassinations Committee
states that "The Warren Commission based its findings primarily upon
the testimony of the doctors who had treated the President at Parkland
Memorial Hospital in Dallas and the doctors who performed the autopsy
on the President at the Naval Medical Center in Bethesda, Md."[4]
Since the most important observations of the Parkland doctors were a
large hole in the back of the head and an entry wound in the throat, it
should be clear that the testimony of the *Dallas doctors was never taken
into account.* In addition, the Warren Commission ignored the testimony
of the autopsists locating the entry wound well down on the President's
back, and instead gave the impression with an inaccurate drawing that
the other wound of entry was in the back of the neck. This made it easier
for the Warren Commission to claim that the same bullet also hit Governor John Connally.

ORWELLIAN STATEMENT

Yet the major investigation of the case conducted by the House of
Representatives in 1976-9 claimed that the Parkland doctors must have
been mistaken about the large wound in the back of the head since it
did not show up in the photographs. In a blatant Orwellian statement,
the Committee wrote: "In disagreement with the observations of the
Parkland doctors are the 26 people present at the autopsy. All of those

interviewed who attended the autopsy corroborated the general location of the wounds as depicted in the photographs; none had differing accounts."[5] This is an outright fabrication. Twenty-two of the 26 people at the autopsy were not shown any of the autopsy photographs or X-rays, which were only seen by the four doctors. In fact, *none* of the doctors even remotely agreed with the photographs or X-rays. Dr. Finck believed strongly that the observations of the autopsy pathologists were more valid than those of individuals who might subsequently examine the photographs.[6] The government then says that the autopsy report was mistaken: "It is probably misleading in the sense that it describes 'an actual absence of scalp and bone.' The scalp was probably virtually all present; but torn and displaced: probably only the separately recovered bone fragments were absent."[7] This is the only way the Committee tries to discount the major discrepancy the autopsists found with the photographs. Even if the head was in some way reconstructed to make this picture, nothing can discredit the unanimity with which the autopsists insisted that the photographs did not show the entrance wound remotely near where they had seen it. The doctors have many times repeated that there was a corresponding small entrance hole in the skull near the hairline, and this does not show in the present X-rays, either.

The Committee "assumed that if the Parkland doctors are correct, particularly with respect to the gaping hole in the back of the President's head, then it would mean: (1) the autopsy photographs and X-rays had been doctored to conceal this hole; (2) the body itself had been altered, either before its arrival at Bethesda or during the autopsy so that the hole was not obvious in the photographs and X-rays; or (3) the photographs and X-rays were not of President Kennedy. Further, if the Parkland doctors are correct, then the autopsy personnel are incorrect and either lying or mistaken. It did not seem plausible to the committee that 26 persons (at the autopsy) would be lying... If the autopsy doctors are correct, then the Parkland doctors are incorrect and either lying or mistaken. It does not seem probable that they are lying, because it would be difficult to maintain a conspiracy of lying among the approximately 14 persons involved for 15 years. On the other hand, it does seem possible, that the Parkland personnel could be mistaken..."[8]

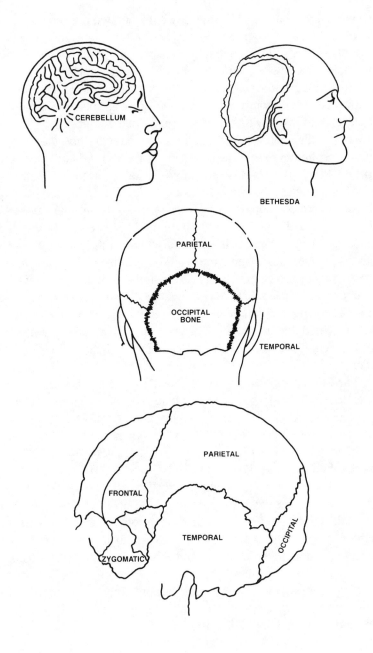

IGNORING THE EVIDENCE

Both they and the Warren Commission overlooked the fact that the autopsists described just such a large hole in the *back* of the head in their report; they ignored the insistence by the autopsists that the photographs did not show the entry wound anywhere near where they had seen it, and they ignored the possibility that the photographs might be forged. In other words, the findings of some 23 doctors and nurses in Dallas and Washington were simply ignored or lied about. Furthermore, the doctors (like many other witnesses, including co-author Robert Groden) were subject to threats, coaching, and other forms of manipulation to force them to cooperate. For many years the autopsists and all other military personnel involved were threatened with court martial.[9]

The observations of the Dallas doctors were consistently disregarded on the pretense that they were mistaken. Moreover, the findings of the Bethesda Naval Hospital autopsists themselves were disregarded by the official panels on the pretext that they too were mistaken. It was never understood that the autopsists agreed with the Parkland doctors on some crucial observations. Perhaps this is why they were also ignored. When it suited them, the official bodies repeatedly lied and distorted the facts.

Each of the four doctors at the autopsy was asked individually to locate the entrance wound after reviewing the photographs, X-rays, and the autopsy report. The Committee's volume on medical evidence goes on to say "They identified the approximate location of the entrance wound on a human skull and within the photographs as being in a position perceived by the panel to be below that described in the autopsy report."[10] For instance, in Brazil and other Iberian countries military courts kept careful records of testimony about torture, because they never thought it would get out, so our official bodies can make conflicting statements within a few pages of the same book because it is "for the use of the Assassinations Committee" only. They state what the final line will be, in total disregard for the facts as they just stated them. This has been the pattern in this case from the time of the assassination.

The autopsy report placed a small wound of entry corresponding to the diameter of a bullet "slightly above" the external occipital protuberance or bump on the back of the head, four inches below the position of a bullet entry wound seen in the official photographs. The autopsists insisted to the Committee's panel that it was in fact *below* that, which put an entry wound an additional inch below the four inches beneath the wound in the photograph. More than four inches below is a great difference. "I have a little trouble with that; 10 centimeters is a significant – four inches," Dr. James Humes said.[11] In fact, the autopsists have added another inch, making it about five inches below where we see the wound now, by saying that the entry was below the protuberance.

In other words, the responses of two autopsists (Dr. Humes and Dr. Boswell) indicated that not only were the photographs and X-rays false, but their own report itself was either inaccurate or had been altered. (Dr. Charles Wilber, in his important book on the subject, repeatedly suggests that the autopsy report was altered and that the autopsists were afraid. He details extensive bullying of the witnesses, and an investigation by the Warren Commission that was also dishonest in other respects.) It is noteworthy that the Committee refused to print a single word of its interviews with the other autopsist, Dr. Pierre Finck, and the radiologist at the autopsy, Dr. John H. Ebersole. Both of these doctors have also at one time or another exploded some of the official suppositions in the case.

The autopsy report described a large hole in the back of the head: "There is a large irregular defect of the scalp and skull on the right involving chiefly the parietal bone but extending somewhat into the temporal and occipital regions. In this region there is an actual absence of scalp and bone producing a defect which measures approximately 13 cm. in greatest diameter... situated in the posterior scalp approximately 2.5 cm. laterally to the right and slightly above the external occipital protuberance is a lacerated wound measuring 15 x 6 mm. In the underlying bone is a corresponding wound through the skull."[12]

Dr. Humes further clarified this when he testified before the Warren Commission by answering Allen Dulles' question as to where the bullet that struck President Kennedy might have exited. "Scientifically, sir, it is impossible for it to... have exited from other than behind," Dr. Humes said.[13] Allen Dulles, the former head of the CIA whom President Kennedy had fired, was a member of the Warren Commission investigating Kennedy's death. This was not at all the answer Dulles was looking for. The question he asked was: "Am I correct in assuming from what you have said that this wound is entirely inconsistent with a wound that might have been administered if the shot were fired from in front or the side of the President: it had to be fired from behind the President?" Humes' answer to this confusing, greatly circumlocutious question was to say that the bullet exited from behind. This is a seeming impossibility unless there was a second, frontal shot to the head.

The Assassinations Committee based its findings – which contradict all the doctors in the case – upon the alleged autopsy photographs and X-rays. What do they show? There is an apparent entry wound in the cowlick, and a flap of scalp and skull in the right temple area which has been reflected back. This flap had apparently been more or less closed, perhaps by Jacqueline Kennedy, except that Dr. Grossman noticed it in Dallas.[14] The Committee noted "There is a large skin flap in the right frontal region anteriorly and laterally, with two fragments of an anterior compound fracture of the calvarium of the skull deflected outward and toward the right ear."[15] The Committee and others assume that this flap represents the only exit wound in the head. After this wound was opened up to observe and remove the brain, the edges revealed evidence that a bullet fragment had exited there.[16] The back of the head is otherwise clearly intact in the alleged autopsy photographs.

A TOTALLY FABRICATED THEORY

The Warren Commission did not deal with the hard evidence in the case, instead putting forward a theory that bore no relationship to the facts. Humes, under written threat of court-martial,[17] tried to stick to some of the facts, while often speaking with double meanings. In this case, he is backing up the Dallas doctors and nurses insofar as he adheres to what he wrote in the autopsy report.

An exit wound in the skull is much larger than an entry wound, and it is scored out around the edges in a widening conical effect in the direction of the missile's forward movement. Material is pushed out along the edges of the wound, with the direction of the shot.[18] The second wound described is an elliptical entry wound into the skull measuring 15 x 6 mm. Dr. Humes originally wrote that the entry wound was a "puncture" wound rather than a "lacerated" wound, and *puncture* was changed to *lacerated* several times in the record.[19]

Yet in 1968 when a panel of doctors, led by the Medical Examiner of Maryland, Dr. Russell Fisher, reviewed the autopsy photographs and

X-rays of President Kennedy for Attorney General Ramsey Clark, they found this entry hole to be much rounder, rather than greatly elliptical, and 8 mm. in diameter.[20] Not only was the rear head entry wound changed in size and shape, but it was placed 4 to 5 inches higher than it was said to be by the autopsists. In addition, this new entry position is in the center of where the much larger exit wound had been, but no longer was. *Both wounds had moved.*

The basic conflict then, is clear: Where was the large hole in the head, and where was the rear entry wound in the head?

All of the many medical and other witnesses in Dallas who saw the body placed the large hole in the very back of the head, or a little to the right, but basically in the occipital area of the head. The autopsists described this wound as being in the same place but larger. In Dallas, Dr. Robert McClelland (who was called to the Emergency Room when Kennedy was brought to Parkland Hospital) wrote that the "cause of death was due to a massive head and brain injury from a gunshot wound of the left temple."[21] Such a shot could blow out the back of the head, just as described by all of the witnesses. The Warren Commission disregarded this evidence. Other evidence which will be outlined later in this book indicates that the President was shot twice in the head, once from behind and once from the front, which would explain the conflict over the head wounds.

The Assassinations Committee in the U.S. House of Representatives, following a 1978 break-in of their safe and the removal of the autopsy photographs,[22] published what they called a drawing of the back of the head made from the photo.[23] This was actually a precise tracing, accurate to the hair, as established by artist Ida Dox in her testimony before the House Assassinations Committee. Indistinguishable from the actual autopsy photograph, it shows an apparent entry wound in the cowlick of the head, but the large defect which should be there is not.

The picture of the back of the head may be found in 7 HSCA p. 104, and also in 1 HSCA p. 234, as well as in several books published since. It is reproduced in this book.

CLEARLY FAKED PHOTOS

Co-author Harrison Livingstone wanted to show the picture of the back of the President's head to the medical witnesses in Dallas who had seen the body. The authors have seen the actual autopsy photos, and thus possessed knowledge that had been denied even to the doctors who treated the President at Parkland. In 1979, Livingstone traveled to Dallas on a trip paid for by Steve Parks of *The Baltimore Sun* and was the first person to show some of the Dallas doctors copies of the autopsy pictures. Since then, Livingstone, *The Baltimore Sun*, and Ben Bradlee, Jr. of *The Boston Globe* have compiled the testimony of a number of additional witnesses, and the startling conclusion of their work is clear: *The autopsy pictures are fake*, and hold the key to the true nature of the plot which took the life of the President. (The research conducted by the *Globe* and the *Sun* was subsequently turned over to Livingstone and placed in the JFK Library in Boston.)

Two facts may be offered which, independent of the wealth of testimony given below, add weight to this startling conclusion. First, the fact that the autopsists could have insisted to a panel of expert doctors that the alleged autopsy pictures of the back of the head did not show the entry wound in the place where they had described it, but in the area where they said the large hole extended, should be sufficient to demonstrate the fraudulent nature of the pictures.[24] Secondly, the fact that neither the House Assassinations Committee nor the government had ever shown these pictures to the Dallas medical witnesses demonstrates the existence of a cover-up. If the evidence still being kept secret in the case proved the government's theory, then they would have shown that evidence to everyone involved.

Each medical witness in Dallas had told the Warren Commission that there was a large hole in the rear of the head, and all of them believed it was an exit wound. Upon seeing the official government autopsy photograph of the back of the head for the first time, each witness independently denounced it.

Just prior to Ben Bradlee's *Boston Globe* trip to Dallas, the evidence he was about to gather was subject to a powerful negative influence, which changed the results he might otherwise have collected. A book was published by David Lifton – *Best Evidence* – which revolved around the question we are dealing with in this book: Why the alleged autopsy photograph does not show the wounds as they were described by all of the witnesses.

In addition to the theory which it propounded, the book gave the erroneous impression that there was a flap of scalp on the President's head which covered up the large hole in the back. This book promptly became a best seller for five months. The flap of scalp story convinced some of the doctors co-author Livingstone and *The Baltimore Sun* had interviewed to change their feelings about the picture, as will be explained below. (See discussion at the top of page 393).

Lifton puts forward in his book the theory that President Kennedy's body was stolen from its coffin in the rear of the plane in the first few minutes directly after it was brought on board in Dallas. "The critical period was 2:18 to 2:32 PM (CST). It appeared, from the public record, that the coffin was then unattended." He says that removal of the body by an unspecified person or persons, "in a body bag seemed the only remaining possibility. Disguised as luggage, it might have been put in the baggage hold, or in the forward galley area."

He says that the body was hidden until the plane landed, then it was somehow brought forward and removed from the right front door of the plane within 90 seconds of the plane's landing, put onto a helicopter, flown to Walter Reed Hospital where a hasty inspection of the body was conducted, the brain removed, the real wounds covered up, other wounds created, the head reconstructed, and the photographs of the wounds taken. He says the body became a medical forgery to cover up the direction from which the shots came.

There was never any evidence for the existence of such a flap on the back of the head. Clearly, given the explicit description in the autopsy report of the missing scalp and of the stellate fractures and tears in the scalp, the autopsists would have noted any flap of scalp. The apparent flap on the side of the head in the photograph was where the scalp and bone were reflected back, in order to inspect the interior of the cranium. But that temporary flap obviously could not cover the large hole in the back of the head, which doesn't show in the autopsy photograph. Forensic scientists say that a reconstruction of this nature would be impossible since the scalp is shredded and destroyed, blown away entirely by the exiting bullet. The autopsy report stated that the scalp was absent over the large defect, an observation that was also made by many of the doctors and nurses in Dallas. Morticians state that it would have taken hours to reconstruct the head and scalp with artificial matter to make such a picture, which was taken before such a cosmetic effort could have occurred.

Mandatory to this hypothesis is the necessity for the coffin to have been left unattended by Kennedy's aides, or by his wife during the first fifteeen minutes after it was brought on board Air Force One, the Presidential jet – in order for the body to have been secretly removed. The evidence indicates that the coffin was never unattended. President Kennedy's entire party, including several of his closest long-time friends and his wife, were crowded into the rear of the plane, since the new President and his party were also on board, filling the plane tightly.

Dave Powers, a long-time friend and close aide of President Kennedy, told co-author Harrison Livingstone on June 23, 1987 that "the coffin was never unattended. Lifton's story is the biggest pack of malarkey I ever heard in my life. I never had my hands or eyes off of it during that period he says it was unattended, and when Jackie got up to go to her stateroom where Lyndon Johnson was, Kenny O'Donnell went with her, but we stayed right there with the coffin and never let go of it. In fact several of us were with it through the whole trip, all the way to Bethesda Naval Hospital. It couldn't have happened the way that fellow said. Not even thirty seconds. I never left it. There was a general watch. We organized it."

Dave Powers rode in the Secret Service back-up car just behind the President and saw the whole shooting, to his horror. He stayed with the body from the hospital to the plane, and helped carry it in, with Larry O'Brian, Kenneth O'Donnell, Godfrey McHugh and others.

There has for many years been a "public record" consisting of personal interviews with the President's party by the media, in William Manchester's *Death of a President* (a book upon which Lifton relies heavily) and other records.

TESTIMONY OF PARKLAND DOCTORS AND NURSES

At Parkland Hospital in Dallas, there were approximately 19 doctors and nurses present at the President's final agony, plus other witnesses such as the President's wife, Secret Service men, the Dallas Chief of Police, and Congressman Henry Gonzalez, who years later was briefly Chairman of the Assassinations Committee.

The following is a documentation of the new testimony co-author Livingstone has collected from the doctors and nurses, which is the *best evidence* in the case.

Only Dr. Kemp Clark and Nurse Diana Bowron have not been re-interviewed. Nurse Bowron cannot be found, and Dr. Clark refuses to be interviewed. He testified strongly to the Warren Commission that the large defect was in the back of the head. Clark wrote that there was "a large wound in the right occiput extending into the parietal region."[25] In another report, he said that the large hole was "in the occipital region of the skull" and "There was a large wound in the right occipital-parietal region... There was a considerable loss of scalp and bone tissue."[26] He told the Warren Commission that he "examined the wound in the back of the President's head. This was a large, gaping wound in the right posterior part, with cerebral and cerebellar tissue being damaged and exposed."[27] Clark is currently Professor and Chairman of the Southwestern Medical School's Division of Neurological Surgery in Dallas. He was the senior physician in Trauma Room 1 and the doctor who pronounced the President dead.

Nurse Bowron first saw the President in the limousine, and helped wheel him into the Emergency Room. Describing the President's condition, Nurse Bowron testified to the Warren Commission that "He was moribund. He was lying across Mrs. Kennedy's knee and there seemed to be blood everywhere. When I went around to the other side of the car, I saw the condition of his head... the back of his head... it was very bad... I just saw one large hole."[28]

Dr. Robert McClelland is Professor of Surgery at the University of Texas' Southwestern Medical School (Parkland). At the time of the assassination he was an Assistant Professor. He told the Warren Commission that he stood at the head of the table in the Emergency Room in "such a position that I could very closely examine the head wound, and I noted that the right posterior portion of the skull had been extremely blasted. It had been shattered, apparently, by the force of the shot so that the parietal bone was protruded up through the scalp and seemed to be fractured along its right posterior half, as well as some of the occipital bone being fractured in its lateral half, and this sprung open the bones that I mentioned in such a way that you could actually look down into the skull cavity itself and see that probably a third or so, at least, of the brain tissue, posterior cerebral tissue and some of the cerebellar tissue, had been blasted out."[29] Dr. McClelland went on to say that the bullet went "out the rear of the skull."[30]

Some time later, Dr. McClelland approved a drawing showing the large gaping hole in the back of the head, which was then used in the book *Six Seconds in Dallas* by Professor Josiah Thompson. McClelland has since repeated to *The Baltimore Sun*[31], *The Boston Globe*[32] and others that the drawing is accurate and what he "vividly" remembers. Co-author Livingstone was the first to query Dr. McClelland concerning the autopsy photo; he rejected it. He later reiterated his repudiation of the photo to the *Sun* and the *Globe*. It should be noted that in a drawing of the head wounds made during the autopsy by Dr. Thornton Boswell, there appear to be bones fractured and missing at the very rear of the head, precisely in the trapezoidal shape of the "Harper fragment" identified as occipital in 1963.[33] According to the FBI report, this piece of bone was found "25 feet south" of where the President was at the moment of the fatal shot.

Dr. Richard Dulany, a Resident on call in the Emergency Room, gave a deposition to the Warren Commission.[34] The copy of the autopsy photograph was shown to him by the *Globe* and he stated that it was not accurate. When shown the official picture, he said that there was a "definite conflict" and "that's not the way I remember it."[35]

Nurse Patricia (Hutton) Gustafson had told the Warren Commission that there was a "...massive opening in the back of the head."[36] She had gone out to the limousine and helped wheel President Kennedy to the Emergency Room. She was asked to put a pressure bandage on the head wound. "I tried to do so but there was really nothing to put a pressure bandage on. It was too massive. So he told me just to leave it be." She said the large wound was at "the back of the head." "Definitely in the back?" she was asked. "Yes." She strongly rejects the official picture. This testimony was taken by Ben Bradlee, Jr. of *The Boston Globe*.[37]

Dr. Ronald Coy Jones, now a Professor of Surgery, was the Chief Resident in Surgery at Parkland in 1963. He told the Warren Commission of "what appeared to be an exit wound in the posterior portion of the skull." He told Arlen Specter, "There was a large defect in the back side of the head as the President lay on the cart with what appeared to be some brain hanging out of this wound with multiple pieces of skull noted next with the brain and with a tremendous amount of clot and blood."[38] Note that he states that the large hole in the back of the head was an exit wound.

Dr. Jones viewed the official picture shown to him by the *Globe* team and stated that the wound was not the same as what he saw in 1963. He outlined with his finger a large hole in the very back of the head. He said that the McClelland drawing was "close."[39]

Nurse Doris Nelson was the Supervisor of the Emergency Room at the time of the tragedy, and is now the Nursing Supervisor at Parkland Hospital. She assisted in treating the President, and helped prepare his body to be placed in the coffin. Nurse Nelson drew a picture of the head wound, mostly in the parietal area, but well towards the rear of the head. Her drawing conflicts strongly with the official autopsy photograph. When she saw that picture she said immediately "It's not true... There wasn't even hair back there. It was blown away. All that area (on the back of the head) was blown out."[40]

Dr. Paul Peters, Professor and Chairman of the Urology Department at Southwestern Medical School, was an Assistant Professor when he assisted at the death of the President. Dr. Peters told reporters that the large defect was in both the occipital and parietal area of the head. When shown the official picture, he stated: "I don't think it's consistent with what I saw."[41] He said of the McClelland drawing, "It's not too far off. It's a large wound, and that's what we saw at the time."

THE HOLE IN THE BACK OF THE HEAD

Co-author Livingstone first showed the official picture to Dr. Peters in 1979, along with the sketch approved by Dr. McClelland. He returned them, marking with an X the sketch of the large exit wound in the back of the head as being accurate, and rejected the official picture. He wrote that "There was a large hole in the back of the head through which one could see the brain." He reconfirmed this in long phone conversations, and in talks with fellow researcher Gary Mack, Ben Bradlee of the *Globe* and others. Dr. Peters told the Warren Commission, "We saw the wound of entry in the throat and noted the large occipital wound, and it is a known fact that high velocity missiles often have a small wound of entrance and a large wound of exit."[42]

Dr. Gene Akin was an Anesthesiologist at Parkland at the time. He told the Warren Commission that "the back of the right occipital-parietal portion of (Kennedy's) head was shattered, with brain substance extruding."[43] "I assume that the right occipital parietal region (right rear) was the exit."[44] Akin reaffirmed this to the *Globe* team and basically did not accept the official picture. On seeing the sketch, he said, "Well in my judgment at the time, what I saw was more parietal. But on the basis of this sketch, if this is what Bob McClelland saw, then it's more occipital."[45] Akin further said that Dr. Kemp Clark saw the entry wound in the temple.

Dr. Fouad Bashour, an Associate Professor of Medicine in Cardiology at the time, was the subject of an article in the *Texas State Journal of Medicine* in January, 1964, along with some of the other doctors present in the Emergency Room. Livingstone interviewed Dr. Bashour in 1979 in his office in the presence of his secretary, Lee, and others. He was most insistent that the official picture was not representative of the wounds, and he continually laid his hand both on the back of Livingstone's head and his own to show where the large hole was. "Why do they cover it up?" he repeated numerous times. "This is not the way it was!" he kept repeating, shaking his head no.[46]

On the same day in 1979, Livingstone interviewed Dr. Charles Baxter in a lengthy taped conversation. He had told the Warren Commission that there was a "large gaping wound in the back of the skull."[47] He told Livingstone that without question, the back of the head was blown away: "It was a large gaping wound in the occipital area."[48] He did think it might have been a tangential wound of some kind. But he could not have been more clear when he rejected the official picture. When the *Globe* interviewed him later, he again did not fully support the picture.[49]

Baxter also insisted that the wound in the throat was "no more than a pinpoint. It was made by a small caliber weapon. And it was an entry wound."[50] Now a Professor of Surgery at Parkland, he was an Assistant Professor at the time of the assassination.

Margaret Hood, whose name was Henchcliffe at the time, had been an Emergency Room nurse for twelve years when the President was brought in. She helped wheel him in and helped prepare the body for the coffin. Interviewed by reporters in 1981, she drew a picture of the large wound on a model of a skull. She sketched a gaping hole in the occipital region which extended only slightly into the parietal area, thereby rejecting out of hand the official picture.[51] She also insisted the President had an "entry" wound in his throat.

Livingstone taped an interview with Dr. Marion Jenkins in 1979 in the presence of 13 witnesses. Dr. Jenkins stared at the official picture for a long time and then said: "No, not like that. Not like that. No. You want to know what it really looked like?"[52] It was Dr. Jenkins who picked up the head of the President to show Dr. Dulany that the back of it was completely gone.

Dr. Jenkins had told the Warren Commission, "There was a great laceration of the right side of the head... (temporal and occipital) even to the extent that the cerebellum had protruded from the wound." "I would interpret it (as) being a wound of exit."[53] In 1979, when shown the official photograph, he told Livingstone: "Well, that picture doesn't look like it from the back." Jenkins continually demonstrated on his head and Livingstone's where the large exit wound was, in the rear and slightly to the side, covering the cowlick area where it would certainly show in the autopsy photograph. "You could tell at this point with your fingers that it was scored out, that the edges were blasted out." He emphasized the word "out" twice. He continually beat on the back of the author's head with the palm of his hand to demonstrate where the large hole was.

There were many people standing in Dr. Jenkins' office watching, and there was no question about what he was saying when these pictures were first shown to him, or any of the other doctors. They had never been permitted to see them before. Jenkins was the Chief Anesthesiologist at Parkland at the time, and is now Chairman of the Southwestern Medical School's Department of Anesthesiology. Why did the Committee not show Dr. Jenkins (or any of the other Parkland doctors) the autopsy photographs? Had they pre-ordained that the doctors were mistaken about the wounds? If so, why interview them at all?

Dr. Adolph Giesecke, Jr., currently Professor and Vice-Chairman of the Southwestern Medical School's Department of Anesthesiology, was an Assistant Professor there in 1963. Livingstone first showed him these pictures in 1979, and taped his responses. When Livingstone read the statements of each witness before the Warren Commission describing a large blowout in the back of the head, Giesecke said very emphatically "Right!" Livingstone showed him the picture Dr. McClelland approved, showing the hole in the back of the head: "Would you say that this picture on page 140 of Thompson's book (paperback ed.) is an accurate representation?" "From what I saw, I think that's a reasonable representation," Dr. Giesecke replied.[54]

In 1979, Dr. Malcolm Perry – one of the most important witnesses among the Parkland doctors – who refused to be interviewed by Ben

Bradlee, Jr., was shown copies of the alleged autopsy photos by Jeff Price of *The Baltimore Sun*.

It was an emotional encounter and Dr. Perry was moved almost to tears. He said the pictures of the back of the head were not accurate.

In an article in *The Baltimore Sun* headlined **"The Bullets Also Destroyed Our Confidence"**[55] Steve Parks wrote: "Why were the doctors at Parkland Hospital who tried to save the president's life and who declared him dead never consulted about the autopsy (conducted by military authorities), and why have the autopsy photos never been shown to these doctors? Earlier this year, during an investigation by the *Sun*, one doctor who had been given access to copies of the photos said the president's head wounds in the pictures were not consistent with what he recalled seeing that day 16 years ago." This was Dr. Malcolm Perry.

Dr. Perry, now a Professor of Surgery and a General Surgeon at the time, performed the tracheotomy on the President when he was brought into the Emergency Room. He appeared twice before the Warren Commission and described "a large wound of the right posterior parietal area in the head exposing lacerated brain,"[56] and "a large avulsive wound of the right occipital parietal area in which both scalp and portions of skull were absent, and there was severe laceration of underlying brain tissue..."[57] The Associated Press dispatch on November 22 stated that Dr. Perry "said the entrance wound was in the front of the head." This is a long way from the cowlick. All the AP wires that day stated that the President had a large hole in the "back" of his head.

THE GLOBE REPORT

On June 21, 1981, the *Globe* published an article based on taped testimony basically corroborating the authors' findings. It appears that the *Globe* editors attempted to water down this powerful evidence discrediting the secret autopsy pictures by quantifying their results on a scale of 1 to 10. They had to literally change – or loosely interpret – the testimony of some witnesses. Although the *Globe* found overwhelming evidence that the pictures are false, the evidence they claim supports the autopsy photographs appears very weak when we realize that *all* the doctors they cite as supporting the picture had previously denounced it.

Ben Bradlee, Jr. wrote co-author Livingstone, "Dear Harry: Here is the story as it appeared yesterday. It is not as I wanted it, as the enclosed copies of my original drafts will attest. There was so much haggling over the piece, however, I was glad just to be done with it and get it in the paper. Note your acknowledgement at bottom left. Thanks for the book. Best regards, Ben."

Of all the many witnesses, the *Globe* counted four who they felt supported the picture.[58] Three of the four had made strong statements denouncing the picture at one time.

The *Globe* wrongly interpreted the data on doctors Giesecke, Jenkins, Perry, and Carrico, for they all had been led to believe – after their interviews with the author and the *Sun* – that there was a flap of scalp on the back of the head which was pulled down to show an alleged entry wound. We have already seen that the autopsists hotly denied that there had been an entry wound in that region, and they said, like many other Dallas witnesses, that there was no scalp there to be pulled down.[59]

Dr. Giesecke confirmed to the *Globe* that the back of the head was missing, but he had been told – after Livingstone had spoken to him and before the *Globe's* visit – about the alleged flap of scalp. the *Globe* erroneously interpreted this as meaning that he no longer felt there was a large hole in the back of the head. Trying to explain this, Dr. Giesecke later wrote co-author Livingstone: "in doing so (pulling down the flap), the underlying bony defect is obscured,"[60] making clear that the large hole was still there.

The Boston Globe completely ignored the evidence co-author Livingstone had obtained from Dr. Jenkins, and claimed that the doctor agreed with the autopsy photographs (without being shown them by the *Globe*). Dr. Jenkins is not quoted or mentioned in the *Globe* article, but the following statement of his is used to discredit what Jenkins had said before: "I thought it was cerebellum, but I didn't examine it." Bradlee wrote in his notes that Jenkins was therefore mistaken in his statements concerning the hole in the back of the head, and they presumed that he had never looked at the back of the head. It was this, and only this, that the *Globe* used in their rejection of Jenkins' clear position that the large hole was above and posterior to the right ear, which he in fact pointed out to Bradlee, whom he made lie down for the demonstration.

The House Assassinations Committee interviewed Dr. Jenkins in November 1977. He told the investigator that he "was the only one who knew the extent of the head wound." "His location was customary for an anesthesiologist. He was positioned at the head of the table so that he had one of the closest views of the head wound. Regarding the head wound, Dr. Jenkins said that only one segment of bone was blown out – it was a segment of occipital or temporal bone. He noted that a portion of the (lower rear brain) cerebellum was hanging out from a hole in the right – rear of the head."[61] They did not show him the autopsy photographs.

The *Sun* published the fact that Dr. Malcolm Perry hotly denounced the picture, but the *Globe*, although they did not interview him, said that he supported the autopsy photograph. They did not print the denial or any reference to this doctor.[62] In any event, the *Sun's* intensive interview with Dr. Perry was conducted in front of witnesses, and the results corroborated the testimony of every other witness who had been interviewed up to that time.

The Assassinations Committee interviewed Dr. Perry in 1978, but did not show him the autopsy photographs. Perry told the interviewer that he had looked at the head wound and that it "was located in the 'occipital parietal' region of the skull and that the right posterior aspect of the skull was missing."[63] It does not make sense that Dr. Perry and the only other two Parkland doctors (Jenkins and Carrico) the Committee interviewed would have somehow changed their observation that the back of the head was missing – for *The Boston Globe*.

In addition, the testimony of Dr. Perry to the Warren Commission, and his extensive first-hand experience with the wounds, makes any later retraction attributed to him not credible.

The fourth witness, Dr. Carrico, made such contradictory statements to the *Globe* that it would be inaccurate to count him as supporting the picture. Dr. Carrico was the first physician to see the dying President. He told the Warren Commission: "The wound that I saw was a large gaping wound, located in the right occipitoparietal area. I would estimate it to be about 5 to 7 cm. in size, more or less circular, with avulsions of the calvarium and scalp tissue. As I stated before, I believe there was shredded macerated cerebral and cerebellar tissues both in the wounds and on the fragments of the skull attached to the dura."[64]

When interviewed in January 1978 by the House Assassinations Committee, Dr. Carrico repeated the same thing: "The other wound was a fairly large wound in the parietal, occipital area. One could see blood and brains, both cerebellum and cerebrum fragments in that wound... The head wound was a much larger wound than the neck wound. It was five by seven centimeters, something like that, 2 1/2 by 3 inches, ragged, had blood and hair all around it, located in the part of the parietal occipital region... above and posterior to the ear, almost from the crown of the head,"[65] that is, just where the small entry wound shows in the alleged autopsy photograph. It would have been impossible for this to be true without showing on the photograph.

Dr. Carrico was not interviewed by the *Globe,* but he wrote them two contradictory letters.[66] In nearly all other cases, the witnesses have just as clear a picture of the events of November 22, 1963 today in 1988 as they did then.

The first spontaneous, emotional response of a witness is the most credible. In legal terms, such evidence bears the indicia of truth and reliability, before the witness has a chance to be subjected to conflicting influences and pressures, and/or reflect on his own self-interest. Eyewitnesses can be very wrong, depending on the circumstances, but the medical witnesses at Parkland, the President's wife – who held his head in her lap – and other officials and agents present in Dallas cannot all be wrong.

Dr. Robert Grossman, now a Professor and Chairman of the Department of Neurosurgery at the Baylor College of Medicine in Houston, had just joined the staff at Parkland at the time of the assassination as an Instructor in Neurosurgery. He never testified to the Warren Commission or to the Assassinations Committee. He said that he saw two large holes in the head, as he told the *Globe,* and he described a large hole squarely in the occiput,[67] far too large for a bullet entry wound, which would have shown in the disputed picture. It does not.

Since the *Globe* did not take into account the previous testimony taken by Livingstone and *The Baltimore Sun,* it would seem that by their own standards, any testimony or position on the issue of the validity or lack of validity of the autopsy photographs should be discounted if they did not actually speak to the witness. The *Globe* and Ben Bradlee, Jr. had no contact whatsoever with Dr. Kemp Clark or Nurse Diana Bowron, yet the *Globe* placed them on their chart ranking as 9s on a scale of 1 to 10, ten meaning total disagreement with the autopsy photographs.

Dr. David Stewart wrote Livingstone on December 11, 1981: "I enjoyed our phone conversation and I appreciate your sending the material. I'll try to answer your questions as well as I can.

"On the Joe Dolan radio show, I meant to indicate that there was no controversy concerning the wounds between the doctors in attendance. I was with them either separately or in groups on many occasions over a long period of time.

"Concerning exhibit F-48, there is no way the wound described to me by Dr. Perry and others could be the wound shown in this picture. The massive destructive wound could not remotely be pulled together well enough to give a normal contour to the head that is present in this picture." We would have to say that if Dr. Stewart did not actually see the wound, then this is hearsay evidence insofar as what he saw or did not see. What is admissible in evidence here is what he was told by Dr. Perry, the wound described to him.

Dr. Jackie Hunt, like Dr. Bashour, was not interviewed by the *Globe*, but Livingstone showed her the picture in 1979 and she instantly denounced it. She did not see the back of the head because she was standing directly over the President, but she insisted that the back part of the head was blown out and rejected the official picture. "That's the way it was described to me," she said, saying that the back of the head was gone.[68] Had the large defect been anywhere else, she would have seen it and described it. Dr. Akin said that if you looked directly down on Kennedy, you could not see the large hole.[69] Therefore, Dr. Hunt's testimony is significant.

Dr. Hunt responded to Livingstone's question: "So, the exit wound would be in the occipital-parietal area?" "Yeah, uh-huh. It would be somewhere on the right posterior part of it..." She pointed to the sketch from *Six Seconds In Dallas*: "That's the way it was described to me. I went around this way and got the equipment connected and started – but I saw the man's face like so, and I never – the exit wound was on the other side – and what was back there, I don't know. That is the way it was described to me," she said, pointing to the sketch showing the large hole in the back of the head. "I did not see that. I did not see this part of his head. That would have been here," she said, and put the palm of her hand on the back of Livingstone's head. She did this before Livingstone showed her the sketch from Thompson.[70]

THE ISSUES AND THE EVIDENCE

The main issues, then, are whether or not there was a large hole in the back of the head, whether it would show in the autopsy photographs, whether it was covered by a flap of scalp, and where the entry wound or exit wounds were located. (The rear entry hole in the official photo now appears where the large hole in the back of the head originally was.)

The overwhelming weight of the evidence appears to demonstrate that the official picture of the back of the President's head does not show the wounds as they were, and that the photographs were tampered with in some way so as to conceal the existence of other shots and snipers and change the evidence of the direction from which the shot entered the back of the head. A shot striking the President where the autopsy report placed it, at or near the hairline of the back of the head, would not, and indeed could not, have blown out the portion of the head which was in fact blown away. The fact remains that the autopsists themselves seriously questioned the photos. The common denominator among *every* witness interviewed was their denunciation of the official autopsy photograph.

This conclusion must be taken together with the fact that there are many more anomalies in the case, with similar questions, each one compelling the conclusion that evidence had been planted, fabricated, faked, destroyed or forged. Perhaps one way of resolving the questions, short of exhumation, is to gather all the Dallas witnesses in one room, together with those who were in the autopsy room in Maryland, and show them the secret pictures. This should be done immediately.

In addition, Dr. Robert Grossman told the *Globe*, "It was clear to me... that the right parietal bone had been lifted up by a bullet which had exited."[71] Thus, one of the doctors who saw President Kennedy before he died observed two large holes in the head, though the hole in the right temple area was largely closed. Dr. James J. Humes, the autopsist, in effect described both of these large wounds as wounds of exit. Co-author Robert Groden found in the films made during the shooting clear, strong evidence of two separate shots to the President's head, the first from behind and the second from in front. Each of these shots blew out a portion of skull. The shot from the rear created a flap of skin and bone over the right temple area, which appeared closed until reflected back at the autopsy; and the second shot destroyed the rear of his head, throwing the President backwards at great speed. The opened flap is visible on the right side of the head in the alleged autopsy photographs.

GRODEN'S REPORT

The House Assassinations Committee published the following report by co-author Robert Groden: "My visual inspection of the autopsy photographs and X-rays reveal evidence of forgery in four of the photographs," showing the back of the head. "Within the circumference of the President's head, there is an irregular line. Within this line the hair appears black and wet. On the outside of the line it is auburn and completely dry. In later generations of these photographs, a large degree of contrast buildup becomes apparent at the line's edge and the line becomes clearly defined. This phenomenon is characteristic of crop lines in matte insert processes used for retouching and recomposition of photographs. It is my opinion that these two photographs are forgeries, composites manufactured to eliminate evidence of an exit wound in the rear of the President's head. The only method I am aware of that could have been used to create these composites is known as 'soft edge matte insertion.'"[72]

Groden was not allowed to talk about this when he was interviewed on national television during the first day of the Committee's public hearings. He was carefully coached as to what he could or could not say. "Don't volunteer anything," he was told. "Just answer the questions." They lied and told him that he would have another opportunity to appear and present whatever else was on his mind, which never happened.

The Warren Commission's staff often simply rewrote witnesses' testimony, if they didn't want it to go into the record, or ignored it altogether. Coaching of witnesses in our judicial and legislative process is common. In the chapter on acoustics, we will discuss the other major findings the Committee did not want Groden to talk about.

Livingstone asked Colonel Fletcher Prouty, former liaison between the CIA and the Pentagon, who has written about the conspiracy and who describes it as a domestic *coup,* "How could the autopsy photos be faked?"

"Now you are getting to the core of the problem. That is where the solution lies!" he told us.[73]

EYE-WITNESS ACCOUNTS

The Secret Service agents who were in the limousine when it arrived at Parkland, in the trauma room, and in the autopsy room at Bethesda, testified, beginning with Clint Hill: "The right rear portion of his head was missing. It was lying in the rear seat of the car. His brain was exposed. There was blood and bits of brain all over the entire rear portion of the car. Mrs. Kennedy was completely covered with blood. There was so much blood you could not tell if there had been any other wound or not, except for the one large gaping wound in the right rear portion of the head."[74]

The driver of the limousine, William Greer, said: "His head was all shot, this whole part was all a matter of blood like he had been hit."[75] The examiner asked Greer if the part of the head that was gone was "the top and right rear side of the head?"

"Yes, sir; it looked like that was all blown off." Another Secret Service agent, Roy Kellerman, was shown a picture of a head, indicating the rear portion: "Yes." "More to the right side of the head?"

"Right. This was removed." "When you say, 'This was removed,' what do you mean by this?" "The skull part was removed." "All right." Representative – later President – Gerald Ford asked him, "Above the ear and back?"

"To the left of the ear, sir, and a little high; yes. About right here." "When you say 'removed,' by that do you mean that it was absent when you saw him, or taken off by the doctor?" "It was absent when I saw him." "Fine. Proceed."

"Entry into this man's head was right below that wound, right here," Kellerman said. "Indicating the bottom of the hairline immediately to the right of the rear about the lower third of the ear?" "Right. But it was in the hairline, sir." "In his hairline?" "Yes, sir." "Near the end of his hairline?" "Yes, sir." "What was the size of that aperture?" "The little finger." "Indicating the diameter of the little finger." "Right."

"Now, what was the position of that opening with respect to the portion of the skull which you have described as being removed or absent?" "Well, I am going to have to describe it similar to this. Let's say part of your skull is removed here; this is below." "You have described a distance of approximately an inch and a half, 2 inches, below." "That is correct; about that, sir," Kellerman said.[76]

THE "DAMN RECORD"

In 1978, Dr. Humes was shown the photographs and X-rays, and he told the Assassinations Committee panel of experts that the wounds were not in the right place. Dr. Petty, the Medical Examiner of Dallas County, asked him, "I am now looking at X-ray No. 2. Is this the point of entrance that I'm pointing to?" referring to the cowlick area.[77] "No." "This is not?" "No," both Drs. Humes and Boswell, the autopsists, replied. Who should know better than they?

"Then this is the entrance wound. The one down by the margin of the hair in the back?" "Yes, sir." "Well, in terms of the inshoot, my impression when I first looked at those films was that the inshoot was higher," Dr. Davis said. "No, no, that's no wound," Dr. Humes said, pointing to the newly discovered apparent bullet hole in the cowlick area.[78] The autopsists continually repeat this denunciation.

How could the head wounds (and back wounds) move? The front page stories in 1963 asked: How could the President be shot from in front from behind?[79]

Later on, discussion was silenced by Dr. Loquvam: "I don't think this discussion belongs in this record... We have no business recording this... This is for us to decide between ourselves; I don't think this belongs on this record..."

Dr. Humes attempted to go on and was again interrupted: "I don't think this belongs on the damn record... You guys are nuts writing this stuff. It doesn't belong in that damn record." What was it? It's not in the damn record.

When Humes emerged from his interview with the Committee's panel of doctors, he told George Lardner, Jr. of *The Washington Post*, "They had their chance, and they blew it. They didn't ask the right questions."[80]

On February 5, 1988, co-author Livingstone spoke to both Dr.

James J. Humes, and Dr. J. Thornton Boswell, the U.S. naval officers who conducted the autopsy in the death of President Kennedy on the evening of November 22, 1963.

To the author's knowledge, no-one has ever been able to interview these doctors as to specific details of evidence in the case, due to the threat of courts-martial laid on the doctors by the Navy, or other forms of intimidation.

The authors are also investigating the death by gunshot of Lt. Cmdr. William Bruce Pitzer, who was found dead in his office at Bethesda Naval Hospital on October 29, 1966. We believe (along with his family) that Bruce Pitzer was murdered. The authors believe that Pitzer was murdered as part of the cover-up in the death of President Kennedy, and that his death in Bethesda Hospital was meant as a warning to other witnesses in that hospital. His family was told that his death was a suicide, and no-one in his family believes it. The government refuses to give up a copy of the autopsy report or of any investigation of his death, if there was one. His widow stated to the authors that Pitzer left her and everyone notes for the smallest thing, and would have left a suicide note. All persons close to him said that he was happy and had far too much to live for to take his life. His widow said that his left hand was so mangled that they could not remove his wedding ring to give to her, but he was right-handed. The question is, if he had shot himself in his office with his right hand, how could his left hand be mangled?

Nevertheless, the authors were able to obtain a small piece of very important information from the autopsy doctors. After refreshing Dr. Boswell's memory as to the placement in the autopsy report of the entry wound at or near the occipital protuberance at the back of the head, and then describing the fact that when the alleged autopsy photos and X-rays were examined sometime later by the Clark Panel of doctors, they found that the entry wound had moved some four to five inches up on the head to the cowlick area, Dr. Boswell stated quickly and emphatically: "It didn't move!" This is the same position both he and Dr. Humes insisted upon to the panel of doctors who interviewed them for the House Assassinations Committee, when both doctors insisted that the photos and X-rays did not show the entry wound remotely near where they saw it.

Dr. Boswell repeated this twice more during a continuing presentation of those facts by the author. That makes a total of three reaffirmations that the entry wound was low down on the head near the hairline.

But when the author then attempted to ask if there was in fact a large hole in the head where the entry wound now shows in the alleged photos of the body, the doctor would not answer, and terminated the discussion. Both doctors hung up as soon as they could when this crucial question was broached with them.

Dr. Boswell described the morgue where the autopsy was conducted. When asked about the death of Pitzer in the hospital, both doctors became hostile. "What business is that of yours?" Dr. Humes demanded. Years ago, the author had spoken with Dr. Humes on two occasions, once for about an hour and once for a half an hour. During all that time, Dr. Humes would not discuss a single issue pertinent to the case.

STONEWALLING

In the most recent discussion, Dr. Humes stated, "We have nothing to hide. Go ahead and call Dr. Boswell. He has nothing to hide. He is in the Washington phone book." Moments later, when asked whether or not there was a large hole in the back of the head, Dr. Humes became hostile, and said, "What business is it of yours?" Later he said, "I'm sorry, I can't discuss this with you. These things don't concern you."

The clear impression was that this evidence was U.S. Navy business, and that it was not anyone's right to know. It is everybody's business. The author felt a steel door slamming shut at those key points in the conversations; he had come face to face with what *The New York Times* has called "The Inner Government." Boswell said, "I can't talk about it" or "I don't remember." Dr. Boswell could recall very precisely and give a description of the morgue where the autopsy was conducted, but he could not remember where the large hole in the President's head was and what it looked like.

Boswell also said that Pitzer was not present at the autopsy (he is not on the list of those officially present), despite several reports that he was not only there but filmed the autopsy.

The overall impression in speaking with these doctors over the years is that they are covering up. It is not just that they were ordered a long time ago not to talk about the case. If the government had nothing to hide with regard to the autopsy, why would they refuse to discuss a simple point of evidence concerning the condition of the back of the head?

In the past, the authors have tried to give these doctors the benefit of the doubt, but their position seems highly questionable. It is clear that something of major importance is being hidden. Nevertheless, the evidence already on the record is important enough. On balance, it is clear that the crimes of murder and obstruction of justice were committed within the jurisdiction of the states of Maryland and Texas. The Federal government does not now have and never has had jurisdiction in the case, but they usurped this authority. For instance, Cmdr. Pitzer may have actually been murdered elsewhere and brought into Bethesda where he was found dead to make it far more difficult for the Maryland authorities to investigate his murder, even though they have jurisdiction over crimes committed on Federal property and military bases within Maryland. The fact that Pitzer's autopsy report has never been released to his widow and family indicates that another murder has been covered up.

THE RIGHT QUESTIONS

What were the right questions which should have been asked of the autopsists? "Where, exactly, was the large exit defect in the head? Did you find a whole bullet? Did you note a large bullet fragment imbedded on the outside of the skull near the alleged entry hole shown in the present X-rays and photos, or another large bullet fragment behind the forehead inside the skull? Were there two large exit defects? Could a bullet have entered the hole on the right forward side of the head and blown out the back of the head? Was there any scalp in the back of the head which could have been pulled down to make this picture? Why did your report state that the entrance hole was slightly above the occipital protuberance when you now state that it was slightly below it? Did you make a mistake, or was your report altered? Did anyone tell you what to write? Why was the word 'puncture' changed to 'lacerated' in several places in the handwritten copy of your report? Was the brain severed from its root? How many entry wounds did you see? Exactly where was the wound in the back and how deep did it go? Was there another wound of entry in the front of the head or in the left eye or temple? What does Dr. Boswell's drawing of an apparent wound there mean? Why do you think the autopsy photographs are inaccurate? Did the large hole in the rear of the head cover the cowlick area, where we now see an apparent entry wound? Was there surgery to the head when you received the body? Was the brain in the skull when you received it?"

Some of these questions may have secretly been asked. If so, the answers aren't in the "damn record."

CHAPTER 3

THE MAGIC BULLET THEORY AND
THE WOUNDS OF KENNEDY AND CONNALLY

The House Assassinations Committee concluded that the President was struck by a bullet that entered in the upper right of the back and exited from the front of the throat.[1] The Committee adjusted this evidence somewhat, but they did it in an interesting fashion. They moved the wound down to the "upper right of the back" from the back of the neck where the Warren Commission seemed to have placed it. This additional traveling wound demonstrates the difficulty the Committee had in upholding the original Warren Commission finding, when all the evidence, including the President's clothing, proved that he was struck six inches down on his back.

But to admit the real location of the wound in the President's back makes the "magic bullet theory" all the more implausible, for the bullet would then have to have turned upwards, without striking any bone, come out the throat, made some right and left turns, gone up and then down to find Governor John Connally, and then gone downward through his body at a 25 degree angle.[2]

The Committee's Report went on to say: "The forensic pathology panel determined that Governor Connally was struck by a bullet from the rear, one that entered just below the right armpit and exited below

54

the right nipple of the chest. It then shattered the radius bone of the Governor's right wrist and caused a superficial wound to the left thigh."[3]

The question raised by both Connally and others is: Did two bullets do all this to him, rather than one? He was still holding on to his Stetson hat long after the "pristine" or "magic" bullet supposedly shattered his wrist and the bone and tendon in it, and the trajectory through his chest made it highly unlikely that the same bullet could have hit him in all three parts of his body, ending up in his thigh.[4]

It is almost impossible for any bullet to travel through two men, smashing numerous bones, and end up in nearly perfect shape: "Based on its examination of the nature and alignment of the Governor's wounds, the panel concluded that they were all caused by a single bullet that came from the rear. It concluded further that, having caused the Governor's wounds, the bullet was dislodged from his left thigh." (See Dr. John Nichols' important article on this subject.[5])

"The panel determined that the nature of the wounds of President Kennedy and Governor Connally was consistent with the POSSIBILITY (emphasis added by the authors) that one bullet entered the upper right back of President Kennedy and, after emerging from the front of the neck, caused all of the Governor's wounds."[6] This is the "magic bullet" theory.

If the above shot passed through both men and came out in nearly perfect condition, another bullet, supposedly fired from the same gun, would have to have entered the President's head and behaved as though it was a frangible bullet; that is, it broke up or exploded upon entry into the skull. This is extremely unlikely. It is also unlikely for an assassin to use two different types of bullets in succession. Dr. Jenkins wrote, "...there was also obvious... chest damage,"[7] meaning Kennedy was shot in the chest, either in the front or back, which is why the surgeons inserted drainage tubes. Later, the government implied that the professors/doctors were liars or incompetents.

AUTOPSISTS PROTEST SINGLE BULLET THEORY

Arlen Specter, the author of the "single bullet" theory, along with Gerald Ford – while they were working with the Warren Commission – asked Dr. Humes, the autopsist, whether the magic or pristine bullet could have been the one that ended up in the Governor's thigh. "I think that extremely unlikely. The reports (from Parkland Memorial Hospital in Texas) tell of an entrance wound on the lower midthigh of the Governor and X-rays taken there are described as showing metallic fragments in the bone, which apparently by this report were not removed and are still present in Governor Connally's thigh, I can't conceive of where they came from this missile," Dr. Humes said.[8] Dr. Finck and Dr. Boswell, his fellow autopsists, agreed.

Dr. Charles F. Gregory, one of the doctors who treated Governor Connally, said that the bullet "behaved as though it had never struck anything except him."[9] Dr. George Shires was also there. Specter asked him if the pristine bullet could have gone through both men and come out nearly whole: "I assume that it would be possible. The main thing that would make me think that this was not the case is that he remembers so distinctly hearing a shot and having turned prior to the time he was hit, and in the position he must have been – I think it's obvious that he did turn rather sharply to the right and this would make me think that it was a second shot..."[10]

Another of Connally's doctors, Robert Shaw, said then and still says of Connally's wounds: "As far as the wounds of the chest are concerned, I feel that this bullet could have inflicted those wounds. But the examination of the wrist both by X-ray and at the time of surgery showed some fragments of metal that make it difficult to believe that the same missile could have caused these two wounds."[11]

Governor Connally said, "It is not conceivable to me that I could have been hit by the first bullet, and then I felt the blow from something which was obviously a bullet, which I assumed was a bullet, and I never heard the second shot – didn't hear it. I didn't hear but two shots. I think I heard the first shot and the third shot."[12]

Connally has repeatedly said since then that he was not hit with the same shot that struck the President.[13] Dallas Police Chief Jesse Curry agreed and stated Connally wasn't hit until frame number 236 of the Zapruder film.[14]

Specter asked Dr. Finck: "And could it have been the bullet which inflicted the wound on Governor Connally's right wrist?," referring again to the pristine bullet. The autopsist replied, "No; for the reason that there are too many fragments described in that wrist."[15]

"A factor that influenced the panel significantly was the ovoid shape of the wound in the Governor's back, indicating that the bullet had begun to tumble or yaw before entering. An ovoid wound is characteristic of one caused by a bullet that has passed through or glanced off an intervening object."[16] If a bullet strikes leaves, it can yaw and cause a slightly ovoid wound, like this one. Secondly, any bullet striking at any angle does not make a perfectly round hole, but an ovoid one. Third, the position of the muscles at the moment of impact may not be relaxed or the position they end up in after the shot, and the shape of the hole is stretched or changed accordingly. Fourth, the Governor's wound wasn't very ovoid, indicating the bullet had not struck anything beforehand. Dr. Shaw told the Warren Commission that the longest diameter of the hole was 6/10 of an inch [17] which is corroborated by the hole in his coat, which measured .25 by .65 inches.

"Based on the evidence available to it, the panel concluded that a single bullet passing through both President Kennedy and Governor Connally would support a fundamental conclusion that the President was struck by two, and only two, bullets, each fired from behind. Thus, the forensic pathology panel's conclusions were consistent with the so-called single bullet theory advanced by the Warren Commission."[18]

Dr. Milton Helpern, who was at one time the Chief Medical Examiner of New York City, said, "The original, pristine weight of this bullet before it was fired was approximately 160-161 grains. The weight of the bullet recovered on the stretcher in Parkland Hospital was reported by the Commission at 158.6. This bullet wasn't distorted in any way. I cannot accept the premise that this bullet thrashed around in all that bony tissue and lost only 1.4 to 2.4 grains of its original weight. I cannot believe either that this bullet is going to emerge miraculously unscathed, without any deformity, and with its lands and grooves intact... You must remember that next to bone, the skin offers greater resistance to a bullet in its course through the body than any other kind of tissue... This single bullet theory asks us to believe that this bullet went through seven layers of skin, tough, elastic, resistant skin. In addition... this bullet passed through other layers of soft tissue; and then shattered bones! I just can't believe that this bullet had the force to do what (the Commission) have demanded of it; and I don't think they have really stopped to think out carefully what they have asked of this bullet."[19]

The New York Times wrote, "He (Dr. Helpern) knows more about violent death than anyone else in the world." He had conducted more than 10,000 autopsies on people killed with bullets. Where did CE 399 – the magic bullet – come from if it hadn't struck both men? Either it came from another sniper's rifle, or it was planted. The man who found it in the hospital insisted it did not come from the stretcher of either President Kennedy or John Connally. The evidence indicates that a bullet was found on the stretcher of a little boy[20] but both Darrell Tomlinson and O.P. Wright, the hospital security director, "declined to identify it (CE 399) as the bullet they each handled on November 22."[21]

"...The time between the observable reactions of the President and of the Governor was too short to have allowed, according to the Commission's test firings, two shots to have been fired from the same rifle. FBI marksmen who test fired the rifle for the Commission employed the telescopic sight on the rifle, and the minimum firing time between shots was approximately 2.25 to 2.3 seconds. The time, between the observable reactions of the President and the Governor, according to the Commission, was less than two seconds."[22] Again, the Committee did not consider that there were two separate snipers behind the limousine. Further, it would have been simply impossible for any marksman in the world to fire two shots in less than two seconds at a moving target at such a distance and hit anything. The conclusions of the official bodies are preposterous in view of the weight of the evidence from all these doctors and witnesses.

Not one single witness to the shooting ever suggested that both men were hit at the same time, and in fact all the witnesses in Dealey Plaza who had anything to say about it indicated that the victims were hit by separate bullets.

Nearly half the members of the Warren Commission never accepted the single bullet theory, but the conservative Senators Russell, Cooper, and Congressman Hale Boggs were overwhelmed by the CIA connected persons on the panel: Allen Dulles, former Director of the CIA, whom Kennedy had fired; Gerald Ford, known as the CIA's man in the House; and John McCloy, Rockefeller's lawyer.[23] Boggs at first believed the theory, but later changed his mind.

"Senator Richard Russell reportedly said that he would not sign a Report which concluded that both men were hit by the same bullet."[24] Researchers and authors Gary Shaw and Larry Harris write: "Russell later told Harold Weisberg that he had asked Chairman Earl

Warren to include a footnote at the bottom of the page saying, 'Senator Russell dissents,' but that Warren refused, insisting on unanimity. According to author-researcher Harold Weisberg, Russell was satisfied that there had been a conspiracy, that no one man could have done the known shooting, and that 'we have not been told the truth about Oswald' by Federal agencies. Russell encouraged Weisberg to challenge and disprove the Commission's findings.

"Senator John Cooper said, 'I, too, objected to such a conclusion; there was no evidence to show both men were hit by the same bullet.' Representative Hale Boggs said, 'I had strong doubts about it (the single-bullet theory),' adding that he felt the question was never resolved."[25]

In an internal FBI memorandum from Cartha D. DeLoach to Clyde Tolson, J. Edgar Hoover's assistant and living mate, DeLoach writes: "the President (Lyndon Johnson) felt that CIA had something to do with this plot."[26]

Plot!

TWO SEPARATE WOUNDS

It is crucial to understand that no autopsists saw the throat wound in the President, since it was slit open for a tracheotomy, but that the doctors in Dallas all stated that the throat wound prior to the tracheotomy was an entry wound, that is, it was very small;[27] they repeated this to co-author Livingstone in 1979. This evidence, overlooked by the official bodies, indicates that the President was shot from in front, in the throat; taken together with massive testimony on the back wound going nowhere, i.e. not transiting the body and being too far down on the back, this shows that these were two separate gunshot wounds, which could not be responsible for Governor Connally's wounds.

Doctor McClelland, who assisted in the tracheotomy, said: "I was standing at the end of the stretcher on which the President was lying, immediately at his head, for purposes of holding a tracheotom, or a retractory in the neckline." He described the neck wound as less than 0.25 inches in diameter, far too small to be an exit wound.[28]

Doctor Perry, who actually performed the tracheotomy, said that it was "a very small injury, with clearcut, although somewhat irregular margins of less than a quarter inch with minimal tissue damage surrounding it on the skin." Dr. Perry insisted that it was an entry wound, as did Dr. McClelland.[29]

Nurse Henchcliffe, when asked by Arlen Specter, "And what did that appear to you to be?," answered "an entrance bullet hole." Specter asked, "Could it have been an exit bullet hole?" She answered, "I have never seen an exit bullet hole... that looked like that."[30]

Every witness has consistently identified the throat wound as an entrance wound.[31]

The House Assassinations Committee in 1979 admitted that there was a gunman on the Grassy Knoll to the right front of the President. Why are they sticking with the single bullet theory? The answer is that there were *two* gunmen *behind* the President, not just one, in addition to the gunman the Committee found on the Grassy Knoll. They can't admit it because that would indicate an official cover-up, fabricated evidence, and a much larger conspiracy. The only recourse was to use more phoney drawings, doubletalk, and magic code words to delude us like "scientific," "medical," and "neutron activation analysis."

"In addition to the conclusions reached by the committee's forensic pathology panel, the single bullet theory was substantiated by the findings of a neutron activation analysis performed for the committee. The bullet alleged to have caused the injuries to the Governor and the President was found on a stretcher at Parkland Hospital... Neutron activation analysis, however, established that it was highly likely that the injuries to the Governor's wrist were caused by the bullet found on the stretcher in Parkland Hospital."[32] Not very likely. The main problem with this test was that Dr. Guinn stated afterwards that none of the fragments he tested weighed the same as any listed as evidence by the Warren Commission. That is, along with the many missing fragments, it would appear that his evidence had been switched before he got it. (Certainly, many bullets could have come from the same lot of lead.) Guinn couldn't validate the genuineness of the specimens given to him, assuming they were genuine.

"Further, the committee's wound ballistics expert concluded that the bullet found on the stretcher – Warren Commission exhibit 399 (CE 399) – is of a type that could have caused the wounds to President Kennedy and Governor Connally without showing any more deformity than it does."[33] (It could have, but it didn't.) "In determining whether the deformity of CE 399 was consistent with its having passed through both the President and Governor, the committee considered the fact that it is a relatively long, stable, fully jacketed bullet, typical of ammunition often used by the military. Such ammunition tends to pass through body tissue more easily than soft nose hunting bullets. Committee consultants with knowledge in forensic pathology and wound ballistics concluded that it would not have been unusual for such a fully jacketed bullet to have passed through the President and the Governor and to have been only minimally deformed."[34] All this speculation doesn't measure up against the weight of the evidence that these were three separate shots, rather than one.

The bullet that hit President Kennedy in the head fragmented into many pieces. It was clearly not a military jacketed bullet.

It would be unusual for a bullet to pass through a President and be only minimally deformed, and another bullet to enter the President from the same gun a moment later and explode into fragments in his head, as happened in this case.

"The committee also considered photographic evidence in its analysis of the shots... The panel concluded there is clear photographic evidence that two shots, spaced approximately 6 seconds apart, struck the occupants of the limousine... The panel found that the alignment of the President and the Governor during this period was consistent with the single bullet hypothesis."[35] Again, as with the Warren Commission's Report, there is no evidence to support this hypothesis. There was no way to line up the wounds and get the results quoted here.

> *"If the Gonzalez affidavit is to be believed,
> the United States is a police state run by a dangerous
> consortium of CIA officers, private intelligence
> agencies, and White House entrepreneurs."*
>
> – *"Spooks"* by Jim Hougan

CHAPTER 4

THE FRAGMENTS AND THE X-RAYS

"The forensic pathology panel concluded that there was no evidence that the President or Governor was hit by a bullet fired from the grassy knoll and that only two bullets, each fired from behind, struck them."[1]

The Committee never seriously questioned this evidence, nor did they properly question the neutron activation analysis data: "Further, neutron activation analysis indicated that the bullet fragments removed from Governor Connally's wrist during surgery, those removed from the President's brain during the autopsy, and those found in the limousine were all very likely fragments from Mannlicher-Carcano bullets."[2] There is no such thing as Mannlicher-Carcano bullets; Mannlicher-Carcano was a rifle manufacturer. Secondly, this test is precise: The molecular structure of the metal either matches or it doesn't. There is no "very likely." Third: The above sentence intends to leave the loophole that the fragments came from some bullet, but not necessarily the ones the Warren Commission indicated: "It was also found that there was evidence of only two bullets among all the specimens tested – "[3] (much of the evidence was found to be missing) "the fragments removed from Governor Connally's wrist during surgery were very likely from the almost whole bullet found on the stretcher at Parkland Hospital, and the fragments removed from the President's brain during the autopsy very likely matched bullet fragments found in the limousine."[4] Not very likely. The fragments from the Governor's wrist exceeded in weight the amount lost by the "pristine bullet" found on the stretcher. CE 399, or the "pristine bullet," lost only about 1.4 to 2.4 grains, and none of this was from being fired.[5] That amount was removed by the FBI for the original test. For a bullet to emerge in such perfect condition, it would have to have been test fired into water. The fact that it was in such perfect condition would not be related to its military jacket. The Committee claimed, without foundation, that such a jacketed bullet could smash bone and flesh and emerge undamaged. This does not explain how a similar bullet to the President's skull broke up into small bits. And thereby, both the Warren Commission's and the House Committee's theories collapse, because there can be no such fragmentation from that type of military bullet, nor can there be fragments weighing more than the weight missing from the bullet.

The point is that there were more than three grains of metal in Connally's wrist wounds alone, which exceeded what CE 399 lost, and there was also a portion of bullet which remains lodged in his thigh.[6]

What the Committee had to say here was simply untrue. Further, the writer of the Report is trying to draw our attention to the "almost whole bullet" in each sentence: "The neutron activation analysis findings, when combined with the finding of the committee that the almost whole bullet found on the stretcher at Parkland Hospital as well as the larger fragment found in the limousine were fired from Oswald's Mannlicher-Carcano rifle."[7] The aim of the investigation was not to seek out the truth but to "establish that only two bullets struck the President and the Governor, and each was fired from the rifle found on the sixth floor of the Texas School Book Depository and owned by Oswald." Oswald may have owned the rifle, but no-one ever established that he fired it, or was the assassin. The above sentence states simply that Oswald owned the rifle. The bullets may have been fired from the rifle, but not necessarily by Oswald. It is far more likely that the bullets came from other guns, in particular Mausers. Originally, the police found only a Mauser in the building, but this was covered up.[8] It is unlikely that any sniper would have used such a poor weapon as the Mannlicher-Carcano. The rifle, like so much other evidence, appears to have been planted and the evidence linking it to Oswald fabricated.

What the public is getting here is an extraordinary amount of double-talk. The Committee was all but trapped, and they knew it. The supervising operating room nurse at Parkland Hospital, Audrey Bell, stated she had looked at and handled "four or five bullet fragments" taken from Governor Connally's wrist. She put them in an envelope and gave it to government agents. She said that "the smallest was the size of the striking end of a match and the largest at least twice that big. I have seen the picture of the magic (pristine) bullet, and I can't see how it could be the bullet from which the fragments I saw came."[9]

Dr. Guinn, who conducted the neutron activation analysis, found that one of the fragments recovered from the floor of the limousine was gone.[10] He found that a can which had contained fragments that had apparently struck the windshield of the limousine was empty.[11]

One fragment specimen, CE 569, could not be tested because it was only the "copper bullet jacket with no lead inside."[12] The Committee believed that it had been fired from the Oswald rifle, but couldn't prove it.

The Warren Commission indicated that two or three bullet fragments they had could have come from the magic bullet, but this was unlikely because of their weight. All of this is indicative of the destruction of evidence over the years. A secret letter to the Warren Commission from J. Edgar Hoover on July 8, 1964, concerning the spectrographic analysis, said that there were "minor variations" between the fragments. *Any* variation indicates that different bullets were involved. Again, we must ask why these results have been kept secret.

There is no significance to the neutron activation tests that were conducted in this case, because some of the known fragments have disappeared and Guinn was unable to test one of the fragments he had. For him to say that it was "highly probable" that the fragments and missile he had represented only two bullets is ridiculous in view of the other evidence that the fragments weighed more than was lost from the pristine bullet, but of course, in any intelligence operation, the idea is to keep each operative compartmentalized away from the next guy with his conflicting information or evidence.

If you take one lump of lead and make 50 bullets from it, they will all have the same atomic structure. The bullets cannot be distinguished from any other bullet made from the same lot. Therefore, more than one rifle using bullets from the same batch could not necessarily be distinguished. Weisberg writes: "Unless the metal from Connally has *the same* composition as Bullet 399, poof! and the Report goes up in smoke. If there is *any* variation in the lead composition of *everything else* – the erroneously accounted for fragments removed from the President's head, the fragments found in the car, the scrapings from the windshield, the traces from the curbstone – all other lead of which there is any relic – then this Report is revealed as a lie. *All this lead must be of exactly the same composition* or it cannot be claimed that the fatal bullet was fired from 'Oswald's rifle.'" Dr. Charles Wilber wrote that "The precise characterization of a given bullet is still not feasible... It is doubtful that significant information can come from the analytical work done on the Kennedy-Connally bullets and fragments."[13]

The ballistics experts said that the fragments found in the car were fired by the alleged "Oswald gun." How can a fragment be determined to have come from anywhere, in this instance? It can't. In addition, there is certainly no way to determine that those fragments came from a rifle fired from the "Oswald window" on the sixth floor of the School Book Depository.

The final proofs relied upon by the Committee are that the make-up of the fragments found in Connally's wrist (CE 842) was the same as that of the pristine bullet, which is of course possible, except that the fragments weighed more than the lost weight from the "pristine bullet" (CE 399).[14]

The X-rays of the President's head, which are reproduced in Vol. I & VII, p. 112 & 110 of the House Committee Report, show (this is actually a left lateral view reversed; see *The Continuing Inquiry*, Gary Mack, p. 5 June, 1980), as Dr. Humes testified to the Warren Commission, "30 or 40 tiny dustlike particle fragments" of metal.[15] Humes said that the "dust particles"[16] on the X-rays would actually have been smaller because "X-ray pictures... have a tendency to magnify these minute fragments somewhat in size."[17]

The Assassinations Committee showed the X-rays to Dr. Norman Chase, who noted that the head wound "was massive, not the kind he would expect from a single, jacketed bullet hitting straight on; it was possibly tumbling or hit on an angle."[18]

Commander John H. Ebersole examined the X-rays of the neck at the time of the autopsy, and reported the absence of fractures and metal particles in the neck, which was confirmed by the autopsists.[19]

As well, the bullet which is alleged to have struck President Kennedy in the back of the neck, CE 399, we are told by the Clark Panel, left particles of lead in the neck,[20] and again, the bullet we have – CE 399 – is nearly whole, with its jacket intact, and could not have broken up in such a manner.

In reporting the above, Dr. John Nichols writes, "In this writer's experience, identical and similar jacketed bullets do not leave metal fragments in soft tissues when bone is not struck. Even unjacketed lead bullets do not leave metal fragments in soft tissues when bone is not struck."[21]

This means that at the time of the autopsy, no metal fragments were seen in the neck. Further, there was no knowledge or evidence of any wound in the back of the neck from a bullet. Had there been a wound, surely the radiologist, Dr. Ebersole, would have seen the fragments. In 1968, the Clark Panel saw fragments for the first time, just as for the first time the wounds were seen in far different places from where they were reported in 1963.[22] When the House Committee interviewed Dr. Chase, he noted the presence of a metal fragment or artifact in the area of the transverse process – definitely not a bone fragment.[23]

MISTAKE OR FABRICATION?

The Clark Panel found that "Films #8, 9, 10 allowed visualization of the lower neck. Subcutaneous emphysema is present just to the right of the cervical spine immediately above the apex of the right lung. Also several small metallic fragments are present in this region."(p. 13) Stanley Keeton says, "Why Humes was able to discern dustlike metallic particles in the head, but unable to recognize fragments in the President's neck remains a mystery."[24] Humes had stated under oath to the Warren Commission that the X-rays of the neck did not reveal metallic fragments: "...We examined carefully the bony structures in this vicinity as well as the X-rays, to see if there was any evidence of fracture or of deposition of metallic fragments in the depths of this wound, and we saw no such evidence, that is no fracture of the bones of the shoulder girdle, or of the vertical column, and no metallic fragments were detectable by X-ray examination."[25] Humes here gives the impression he saw the X-rays during the autopsy. We already know that he never knew the President was shot in the neck, and so his description of the wound as an exit wound in his undated report was obviously fabricated after the fact. Either Humes made a mistake in not seeing fragments, or he made it up.

"One can believe in innocent coincidence, but not when it reaches epidemic proportions and works persistently in favor of the Commission's fixed lone assassin thesis," writes Sylvia Meagher, one of the first people to research this case.[26]

Art Smith writes, concerning his interview with Dr. Ebersole, "At this point I must now state publicly that the autopsy doctors, Humes, Boswell, Finck, Ebersole and others deliberately falsified their reports and their testimony pertaining to the throat and the head wound." Ebersole had told Gil Delaney of *The Lancaster* (PA) *Intelligencer Journal* that "He knew... the back of the head was blown off."[27]

Dr. Ebersole was then forced to retract his statement when someone from the Navy Department called "to remind him that he was still under secrecy not to discuss the case."[28]

Gary Mack writes: "It's inconceivable that no X-rays were taken from the back or right side of Kennedy's head. Surely there are others which have never been acknowledged. As for the Committee's misrepresentation of this evidence, I can only believe the Committee conclusions based on those two X-rays are, in fact, not probable."[29] For these reasons, the work of the Committee is highly suspect.

When co-author Livingstone showed these X-rays to a radiologist, he noted that an orbit is missing and the whole face is gone. He asked, "Did they blow away his face? Did they sever the head from the body?" and noted that there appeared to be surgery in the area of the temple.

We have to ask why these X-rays were cropped for presentation to the public by the Assassinations Committee. The cropping removes the jaw – the mandible and the odontoid process – which would have made possible identification by the teeth. The vertebrae that ought to fit into the skull appear to be missing.

Regarding the circular temporal bone area, Chase said it appeared to represent normal skull thinning at that point, but said there could be bone missing, noting the area was "...awfully lucent."[30]

You can see an air space through the skull in the occipital protuberance area, just where the Warren Commission placed an entry wound. But the hole is too big for just an entry wound. And that wound was moved in 1968 four inches above where it shows on the X-rays.

Doctors whom the authors consulted spotted this "large defect" instantly. This is what the doctors began to point out when they were interviewing Dr. Humes, the autopsist, for the Assassinations Committee.

The X-ray that purports to show the face has an apparent air space below an eye which radiologists stated almost instantly to Livingstone was not normal. We are given the impression that this is the right eye, but if this X-ray is also reversed, it is therefore beneath the left eye. This X-ray is JFK exhibit F-55.[31] In the picture shown on page 111 of volume 7, a radiologist immediately said that there appeared to be an entry wound in the left eye-temple area. In any event, these X-rays show damage to the skull which is nowhere clarified by the evidence.

The Clark Panel found that there was a large fragment at the base of the skull. "There is, embedded in the outer table of the skull close to the lower edge of the (entrance) hole, a large metallic fragment which... lies 25 mm. to the right of the midline. This fragment... is round and measures 6.5 mm. in diameter."[32]

This very large piece was not mentioned in the autopsy report, although such a large fragment would have been seen on the X-ray had it been there at the time of the autopsy – as were "multiple minute metallic fragments," and "...from the surface of the disrupted right cerebral cortex two small irregularly shaped fragments of metal" measuring "7 x 2 mm. and 3 x 1 mm." mentioned in the autopsy report.

It would also appear that this fragment was probably the base of a bullet. If we also have the base of a bullet in the front seat of the limousine, we have to add yet another bullet fired at the President. This is far more bullets than can be explained as having been fired from the Mannlicher-Carcano found on the TSBD's sixth floor. The fact that this fragment was not noted in the autopsy report is more than strange, and another indication that the X-rays are forged.

A little-known but fine book by Howard Roffman entitled *Presumed Guilty*, published by Fairleigh Dickenson University Press, and in London by the Associated University Presses, 1975, makes some telling points that should have been addressed by the Assassinations Committee. The fact that they were not demonstrates a major flaw in the House Committee's investigation, and points to a deliberate intent to avoid dealing with the true nature of the conspiracy.

6.5 mm. is the diameter of the bullets allegedly fired by the assassin. Howard Roffman says, "The bullet from which was shaved this substantial fragment upon entrance could not have been covered with a hard metal jacket, such as copper alloy. Such a fragment is, in fact, a not infrequent occurrence from a *lead bullet*. Rowland Long, in his book *The Physician and the Law*, speaks of the penetration of lead bullets into the skull and asserts: 'Not infrequently a collar shaped fragment of lead is shaved off around the wound of entrance and is found embedded in the surrounding scalp tissues.'[33]

"The Commission's case against Oswald requires full-jacketed ammunition to have been used to inflict the wounds of President Kennedy. The presence of the 6.5 mm. metallic fragment in the margin of the skull entrance eliminates the possibility that a full-jacketed bullet entered through this hole. Such a fragment located at that site is indicative of a lead or soft-nosed bullet," Roffman writes.[34]

Forensic pathologist Halpert Fillinger said, "You can appreciate the fact that a jacketed projectile is going to leave very little on the (bone) margins because it's basically a hardened jacket, and it's designed so that it will not scrape off when it goes through a steel barrel. One can appreciate the fact that going through bone, which is not as hard as steel, may etch or scratch it, but it's not going to peel off much metal. In contrast to this a softer projectile might very well leave metallic residues around the margins..."[35]

Nowhere is there any evidence of copper in the skull or the limousine. When a copper-jacketed bullet breaks up, it leaves fairly large fragments, but it does not leave dust-like particles. The lead core is chemically hardened to prevent just that from happening.[36]

Roffman points out that perhaps more of the dust-like fragments of metal were lost from the head when brain matter was blasted away and later oozed out in the car and at Parkland.

We find no lateral X-rays of the neck, so there is no accurate way to see the alleged fragments in that area. But the very fact that the Clark Report alleges that there are fragments in the neck shows that they could not have come from the magic bullet found on the stretcher – CE 399. The copper jacket of that bullet was intact.[37]

EVIDENCE OF SUBSTITUTION

"Pathologists could present no evidence to substantiate the 'conclusion' that the gaping defect was an exit wound." By this, Roffman means that the large hole across the right side of the head may or may not have been an exit wound. It would appear that a bullet may have entered from the front in the same place. "The evidence does not establish that it was the rear-entering bullet that produced the explosive wound to the right-front of the head, nor is there currently any evidence to preclude the possibility that the head was in fact struck by two separate bullets from different directions."[38]

The skull was extensively damaged, with numerous fractures, and "Dr. J. Thornton Boswell, assistant to Dr. Humes at the autopsy, has confirmed to a private researcher that a large area of skull was present in the mid- and low-temple region, although none of these fractures had broken the skin."[39]

Roffman writes, "The size and extent of the gaping defect, and the associated fracturing and fragmentation of the skull, are indicative of a high-velocity bullet's having struck the head to produce this damage."[40] Many researchers and doctors have agreed.

"FBI ballistics expert Robert Frazier called the velocity low."[41] Two thousand feet per second is considered medium velocity, and 3000 is a high velocity bullet, which can go up to 4100 fps. The Mannlicher-Carcano was probably travelling at 1800 fps. "To produce this kind of effect (there was great damage to the head and extensive bullet fragmentation in the brain), you have to have a very high-velocity projectile, and the Carcano will not stand very high bolt pressures," Dr. Fillinger told Roffman.[42]

The Warren Report (p. 83 of the *N.Y. Times* edition) tells us that both the nose and the base of a bullet were found in the front seat of the limousine. These fragments weighed 44.6 grains and 21 grains respectively (a whole bullet weighed 160 grains). Where did they come from? This certainly wasn't the magic bullet which had allegedly struck both victims and came out in pristine condition, without any blood or other matter, which it would have to have collected had it passed through a body. The two fragments were covered with blood and gore and had to be cleaned. Did they have a military jacket?

Had the nose of this bullet found in the front seat passed through the head of the President, struck the chrome over the windshield of the car and fallen into the front seat, as appeared to be the case, it could not have described such a trajectory if it came from the sixth floor window. The shot had to have come from a low level in relation to the car.

The Clark Panel found a large shimmering object in the brain which would seem to be a bullet. Why was this not noted at the time of the autopsy?

The autopsy report notes that 30 or 40 dust-like fragments of metal are seen on the X-rays of the skull and brain, as well as two larger pieces measuring 7x2 mm and 3x1 mm. No other fragments are mentioned. All of the above were in the brain, and the two larger pieces were on the surface of the "disrupted right cerebral cortex." Nowhere is there any mention of the two very large fragments first seen in the X-rays available to the Clark Panel, both embedded in the skull. These large fragments in the skull simply could not have been there without being commented upon and removed, and could not have been missed on any X-ray. During an examination of the scalp, we should think the large fragment on the outside of the skull would have been seen and removed for analysis. Ordinarily, the scalp is carefully combed in the search for wounds during an autopsy.

The proof in this case lies here: A military jacketed bullet cannot shave off such a collar-shaped fragment as is now claimed to be imbedded in the President's skull. This fragment was not seen at the autopsy or in the X-rays at the time, and such a bullet will not leave a trail of metal particles as is now seen in X-rays of the neck. Only lead bullets will do this. For this reason, the slides of the margins of the wounds are missing from the evidence, because a military jacketed bullet will not leave a residue around the edges of a wound, and if a lead residue was in fact present, then the bullets could not have come from the alleged murder weapon.

All this demonstrates conclusively that the X-rays have been substituted or otherwise tampered with.

Newsweek (August 15, 1964) wrote of the frustration of journalists and researchers concerning the autopsy evidence even then: "The whereabouts of these photographs and X-rays remains one of Washington's most puzzling mysteries. A diligent two-month inquiry... has failed to turn up a single government official who can, or will, give a simple answer to the question: 'Where are the Kennedy autopsy photos?'"

Jacob Cohen, writing in *The Nation* at that time, said that no-one with any interest or involvement in the case could see the photos.

The pictures were probably missing because they were being switched. They wouldn't turn up again until the conspirators could claim that the memories of witnesses had faded or were mistaken. Fortunately, what the witnesses saw then they will never forget.

The X-rays of both the neck and the head are fake. They are not of President Kennedy. The X-rays of the head are completely incompatible with the photographs, which show the face undamaged.

The X-rays of the head show the right eye and forehead missing. No witness described any such massive wound, and the surviving photographs refute it. All the medical witnesses interviewed have ridiculed the X-rays of the head, Dr. Robert McClelland of Parkland Hospital, and Jerrol Custer, the Bethesda autopsy X-ray technician who took the X-rays, among them.

We believe that the reason why there is such a wide discrepancy between the X-rays and the photographs is that the conspirators had a look at the films on the night of the assassination and got the idea that the face was blown away. They faked the X-rays to show this. The photographs of the face survive, which contradict the X-rays. The photographs were taken prior to the autopsy. No Y incision is present.

The conspirators did not expect anyone to see all of the photographs at that time, including the real ones of the face published in this book. They did not dare destroy all of them for fear of a Presidential or Congressional order asking to see them. Earl Warren was shown only the photo of the back of the head and X-rays. They needed to preserve some of the actual evidence in the event of an investigation in the future, or that someone would have access to the evidence. They were in a position to control which pictures and X-rays were shown to Earl Warren, and to redirect the U.S. government.

The photo of the back of the head was forged at a different time from the faking of the X-rays, which were made by shooting a body in the manner in which they wished to have it appear the President was killed – shot from behind with a large blow-out in the front of the head, and taking an X-ray of it. It was not possible to co-ordinate perfectly what the two efforts produced in the short time available. No one among the conspirators realized the photographs were incompatible with the forged X-rays.

This was the "greasy thumbprint," the one deliberate or unintentional mistake the conspirators made. The X-rays are totally incompatible with the photographs, and a key to the case.

"John Kennedy wasn't a virtuous man; he just looked towards virtue and they shot his head off. America became an 'anything goes' country with his death."

– Mort Sahl

CHAPTER 5

THE AUTOPSY AND THE AUTOPSY PHOTOGRAPHS

We have been leading up, obliquely, to the Assassinations Committee's problem of the "Authentication of the Kennedy autopsy photographs and X-rays."[1] The three autopsists signed an autopsy report that was undated, meaning that it could have been written at any time after the original autopsy notes were destroyed. It was written by Dr. J. J. Humes, Commander U.S.N., who signed it.[2] What we are concerned with here is the veracity of the official witnesses, the official evidence, and the integrity of the government and its panels, which have consistently been in question since November 22, 1963. The Warren Report, the Gulf of Tonkin incident, Vietnam, Watergate, El Salvador, the Libyan hit squad, the Iran-Contra Affair and many other events have all called into question that integrity.

DR. HUMES TESTIFIES

Arlen Specter questioned Commander (Dr.) Humes regarding the photographs and X-rays for the Warren Commission. Humes stated, "...the photographs and the X-rays were exposed in the morgue of the Naval Medical Center on this night, and they were not developed, neither the X-rays or the photographs. They were submitted to... either the Federal Bureau of Investigation or to the Secret Service. I am not sure..." "Did you submit those yourself immediately after they were taken, Dr. Humes?" "Again, one of the senior people present, I believe my own Commanding Officer, Captain Stover, took care of turning this material over to these authorities, and receiving a receipt... I supervised the positioning of the body for various of these examinations but as far as beyond that, I did not consider that my responsibility."(Humes Warren Commission testimony, *supra*).

Arlen Specter was interviewed by *U.S. News & World Report* on October 10, 1966. He was asked if he had seen the pictures. "The complete set of pictures taken at the autopsy was not made available to me or to the Commission. I was shown one picture of the back of a body which was represented to be the back of the President, although it was not technically authenticated. It showed a hole in the position identified in the autopsy report. To the best of my knowledge, the Commission did not see any photographs or X-rays... The photographs and X-rays would, in the thinking of the Commission, not have been crucial, because they would have served only to corroborate what the autopsy surgeons had testified to under oath as opposed to adding any new facts for the Commission."

WHERE WAS THE EVIDENCE?

It would seem that the evidence at this point was being co-opted by other agencies, either the Secret Service or the FBI. In an adversary hearing, the best evidence rule would exclude any testimony about the photographs and X-rays without actually introducing these materials into evidence.

One member of the Warren Commission, John McCloy, asked Commission Counsel Rankin "about this raw material business that is here. What does it consist of? Does it consist of the raw materials of the autopsy? They talk about the colored photographs of the President's body – do we have those?"

Mr. Rankin: "Yes, it is part of it, a small part of it." Mr. McCloy: "Are they here?"

Rankin's reply: "Yes. But we don't have the minutes of the autopsy, because we wanted to see what doctor said about something while he was saying it, to see whether it is supported by the conclusions in the autopsy and so forth, and then we have volumes of material in which people have purported to have said, or say to various agents certain things, they are not sworn..."[3]

FILM SEIZED

A Secret Service statement claims that "the X-ray films were used for the briefing of the Warren Commission staff on the autopsy procedure and results,"[4] and that the evidence was turned over to the National Archives and/or the Commission.

The autopsists said, "One roll of 120 film (processed but showing no recognizable image) which we recall was seized by Secret Service agents from a Navy medical corpsman whose name is not known to us during the autopsy and immediately exposed to light."[5]

Other witnesses at Bethesda stated that the Naval photographer had taken photographs of the autopsy room itself and those present. Somebody didn't want that kind of a record: Texas Highway Patrolman Hurchel Jacks, in his statement of November 28, 1963, said, "We were assigned by the Secret Service to prevent any pictures of any nature to be taken of the President's car or the inside." We will learn in a later chapter that on the following day, the President's limousine, a crucial piece of evidence since it had been struck in several places by bullets or fragments, was taken to Detroit, torn apart, and rebuilt, thus deliberately destroying the evidence. The boundary between coincidence and deliberate action seems to have again been overstepped.

"I, James J. Humes, certify that I have destroyed by burning certain preliminary draft notes relating to Naval Medical School Autopsy Report A63-272 and have officially transmitted all other papers related to this report to higher authority." (24 November 1963). This certificate was apparently required by the President's personal physician, Admiral George Burkley, who wrote on it "accepted and approved this date."[6] Burkley, a crucial eyewitness present at both Parkland and Bethesda, was *never* called to answer any questions about anything. *Why not?*

In a separate certificate signed the same day by Humes, again apparently required by Burkley, who again wrote "accepted and approved," Humes wrote: "I, James J. Humes, certify that all working papers associated with Naval Medical School Autopsy Report

A63-272 have remained in my personal custody at all times. Autopsy notes and the holograph draft of the final report were handed to Commanding Officer (J. H. Stover, Jr.), U. S. Medical School, at 1700, 24 November 1963. No papers relating to this case remain in my possession." Why two separate certificates when one would suffice? Humes first certifies that he destroyed his notes, and then says he handed them to his commanding officer.

COURT-MARTIAL THREATS

The autopsists were threatened with courts-martial as follows: "You are reminded that you are under verbal orders of the Surgeon General, U.S. Navy, to discuss with no one events connected with official duties on the evening of 22 November – 23 November, 1963.

"This letter constitutes official notification and reiteration of these verbal orders. You are warned an infraction of these orders makes you liable to Court Martial proceedings under appropriate article of the Uniform Code of Military Justice."[7] This order applied to all officers and enlisted men concerned. Apparently it still binds them after retirement.

Although the Dallas doctors presented evidence that two shots hit the President from in front, the Secret Service claimed they "obtained a reversal of their original view that the bullet in his neck entered from the front.

"The investigators did so by showing the surgeons a document described as an autopsy report from the United States Naval Hospital at Bethesda. The surgeons changed their original view to conform with the report they were shown."[8]

TESTIMONY IGNORED

In fact none of the doctors, with one possible exception, changed their opinion when they later testified to the Warren Commission. What they had to say was simply ignored. The possible exception was Dr. Marion Jenkins, who has a consistent track record of waffling. Specter asked him, "Have you ever changed any of your original opinions in connection with the wounds received by President Kennedy?"

Dr. Jenkins: "I guess so. The first day I had thought because of his pneumo-thorax, that his wound must have gone – that the one bullet must have traversed his pleura, must have gotten into his lung cavity, his chest cavity, I mean, and from what you say now, I know it did not go that way. I thought it did." *Something* must have gotten into the chest cavity, because chest tubes were inserted in the President to drain all the blood that was collecting there. The transcripts make it clear that Specter bullied all these doctors and anyone else with testimony contradicting the theory he was about to invent. The government was in serious trouble because the evidence demonstrated far too many shots from too many directions, and far too many gunmen.

The New York Times reported on December 5, 1963, "Most private citizens who had cooperated with newsmen reporting the crime have refused to give further help after being interviewed by agents of the Federal Bureau of Investigation."

At this point, the FBI report on the assassination had been leaked out to the press long before the Warren Report was issued. It said that John Connally was not hit by the same bullet that hit the President in the throat, meaning that at least four shots had been fired: two hitting Kennedy and one hitting Connally. They ignored the missed shot and James Tague's wound from a cement fragment. Only later did they discover that this was impossible with the alleged weapon.

A NEW STORY

When the limitations of the Mannlicher-Carcano became public knowledge, the known facts had to undergo change and a new story had to be invented. On December 6, 1963, *Life Magazine*, which owned the Zapruder film, reported that "the 8 mm. film shows the President turning his body far around to the right as he waves to someone in the crowd. His throat is exposed – towards the sniper's nest – just before he clutches it." Few outside of the government and Time/Life Inc. had seen the film until years later, and the Warren Commission knew that this description was not true. But *Life Magazine* is admitting, still, that the throat wound is an entry wound. The Warren Commission reversed the frames of the film to have the frontal head shot coming from behind, and Dan Rather stated on television that the President was thrown forward. Next, Gerald Ford had Kennedy waving at the crowd in order to bunch up his coat and shirt so that Ford could explain the holes so far down on his clothes. This invention didn't work either, because there were too many photographs taken during the shooting. Note the FBI-SS reenactments of the crime and where they have the entries pinned on the victim in the illustration.

When news of the autopsy conclusions was originally leaked, around December 18, 1963, Nat Haseltine wrote, "President Kennedy was shot twice, both times from the rear, and could readily have survived the first bullet which was found deep in his shoulder." The Associated Press admitted on the same day that this bullet "penetrated two or three inches." *The New York Times* also said "that bullet lodged in his shoulder." As some newspapers noted, why was the President not thrown down and protected when his life could have been so easily saved? Why didn't the car drive off at top speed upon the first shot?

Haseltine went on to write: "The second bullet to hit the President, however, tore off the right rear portion of his head so destructively as to be 'completely incompatible with life.' A fragment was deflected and passed out the front of the throat creating the erroneous belief he may have been shot from two angles." *The New York Times* repeated this on January 25, 1964.

This lie didn't work either, because there were too many photographs to show that the President was struck long before he was hit in the head.

Secret Service Agent Glenn Bennett, who was just behind the President in the next car, said: "I looked at the back of the President. I heard another firecracker noise and saw the shot hit the President about four inches down from the right shoulder."

Haseltine continued: "These are the findings of the as yet unofficial report of the pathologists who performed the autopsy on the President's body the night of Nov. 22... The disclosure that a bullet hit the President in the back shoulder, 5 to 7 inches below the collar line ..." They tried this out on us until they found that the bullet would have had to go upwards through the President's body at much too high an angle to also strike John Connally, so the entry place on the back was moved upwards by six inches.

AN EXIT WOUND?

Dr. Humes wrote in the autopsy report: "2. The second wound presumably of entry is that described above in the upper right posterior thorax... The missile path through the fascia and musculature cannot be easily probed. The wound presumably of exit was that described by Dr. Malcolm Perry of Dallas in the low anterior cervical region. When observed by Dr. Perry, the wound measured 'a few millimeters in diameter,' however it was extended as a tracheotomy incision and thus its character is distorted at the time of autopsy."[9] The thorax is the chest, not the neck. We have massive testimony from the doctors in Dallas that the throat wound was an entry wound, and they insist on it today.[10] Where did Dr. Humes get the idea that the throat wound was "the wound presumably of exit" when he never saw that wound at all,[11] had no idea how many shots were fired unless he was told that the President was hit only twice, and when he had been told only after the body was taken away from him that there was a wound in the throat and that it was an entry wound?

What kind of an autopsy was this? Dr. Perry certainly never told him that the throat wound was a wound of exit. In fact, all the doctors who saw the throat wound said that it was an entry wound, and that it was very small, even made by a small caliber weapon.[12] An entry wound closes up somewhat so that its diameter is smaller than the diameter of the transiting bullet, because of the elasticity of the skin.

It is of crucial importance here to know that the autopsists really had no way to judge how many shots had been fired. They fixed the brain in preserving solution and did not section all of it. They would not have known if a frangible or exploding bullet had also struck the President in the head, which would not appear so obvious to them, without much more of an examination than the one they performed.

DR. FINCK TESTIFIES

One of the autopsists previously testified in New Orleans, before District Attorney Jim Garrison. His testimony offered a fascinating insight into how the autopsy was conducted. It also reveals the sort of pressure the autopsy doctors were under to arrive at the "official" predesignated conclusions.

Q. "Did you have an occasion to dissect the track of that particular bullet in the victim as it lay on the autopsy table?" Dr. Pierre Finck was asked, about the bullet in the back.

A. "I did not dissect the track in the neck."

Q. "Why?"

A. "This leads into the disclosure of the medical records."

"You should answer, doctor," the judge said.

A. "We didn't remove the organs of the neck."

Q. "Why not, doctor?"

A. "For the reason that we were told to examine the head wounds, and that the – "

Q. "Are you saying someone told you not to dissect the track?"

A. "I was told that the family wanted an examination of the head, as I recall, the head and chest, but the prosecutors in this autopsy didn't remove the organs of the neck, to my recollection."

Q. "You have said they did not, I want to know why didn't you as an autopsy pathologist attempt to ascertain the track through the body which you had on the autopsy table in trying to ascertain the cause or causes of death? Why?"

A. "I had the cause of death."

Q. "Why did you not trace the track of the wound?"

A. "As I recall I didn't remove these organs from the neck."

Q. "I didn't hear you," Mr. Oser said.

A. "I examined the wounds but I didn't remove the organs of the neck."

Q. "Why did you not dissect the track of the bullet wound that you have described today and you saw at the time of the autopsy at the time you examined the body? Why?"

A. "As I recall I was told not to, but I don't remember by whom."

Q. "You were told not to but you don't remember by whom?"

A. "Right."

Q. "Could it have been one of the Admirals or one of the Generals in the room?"

A. "I don't recall."

    After a couple of days of this, Colonel Finck, in the trial of Clay Shaw for conspiracy in the murder of President Kennedy, was asked, "Can you give me the name of the General that you said told Dr. Humes not to talk about the autopsy report?"

A. "This was not a General, it was an Admiral."

    Finck had originally said, "I heard an Army General. I don't remember his name, stating 'I am! (in charge).'"

Q. "Colonel, did you feel that you had to take orders from this Army General that was there directing the autopsy?"

A. "No, because there were others, there were Admirals."

Q. "There were Admirals?"

A. "Oh, yes, there were Admirals, and when you are a Lieutenant Colonel in the Army you just follow orders, and at the end of the autopsy we were specifically told – as I recall it, it was by Admiral Kenney, the Surgeon General of the Navy – this is subject to verifications – we were specifically told not to discuss the case." [13]

Secret Service agent Roy Kellerman told the Warren Commission: "A Colonel Finck – during the examination of the President, from the hole that was in his shoulder, and with a probe, and we were standing right alongside of him, he is probing inside the shoulder with his instrument and I said 'Colonel, where did it go?' He said 'There are no lanes for an outlet of this entry in this man's shoulder.'" [14]

At this point, we must conclude that someone is lying, and that this is where the cover-up begins.

DISTORTED PERSPECTIVE

The alleged autopsy photo of the President's back was taken, not by turning him over and photographing the wound, but by lifting up the head and shoulders so that there is a distorted perspective of how far down the back wound lies. That wound has been placed all the way from the back of the neck, as in the official Warren Commission illustration shown by the Committee as JFK Exhibit F-47, [15] to six inches down from the shoulder, as the holes in the President's suit and shirt clearly show.

FBI Document 7 states, "During the latter stages of this autopsy, Dr. Humes located an opening which appeared to be a bullet hole which was below the shoulders and two inches to the right of the middle line of the spinal column. This opening was probed by Dr. Humes with the finger, at which time it was determined that the trajectory of the missile entering at this point had entered at a downward position of 45 to 60 degrees. Further probing determined that the distance traveled by this missile was a short distance inasmuch as the end of the opening could be felt with the finger." Where was the bullet? We have a receipt for "one missile" recovered during the autopsy signed by FBI agents. "We hereby acknowledge receipt of a missle (sic) removed by Commander James J. Humes, MC, USN on this date... . (signed) Francis

X. O'Neill, Jr. and James W. Sibert." [16] What happened to this bullet? Since four large "fragments" were also recovered, the "missle" (sic) must be a bullet. The FBI and other authorities later denied that any bullet had been found.

So far, this bullet, entering at a downward angle, could not have turned upward and come out of the neck. Note that they state the bullet was two inches to the right of the spinal column, but do not say how many inches down it is from the shoulders.

The important thing is that this entry wound in the back could not have come out of the throat, because it did not go anywhere. "The end of the opening could be felt with the finger."

All three doctors at the autopsy probed the wound in the back with their fingers up to the first or second knuckle – a penetration of one or two inches. They used a metal probe as well. But this wound was never dissected.

"I did not dissect the track in the neck," Dr. Finck tells us. "We didn't remove the organs of the neck." Why not? Because they did not know that there was a wound in the neck.

Dr. Humes wrote of the neck wound, "When observed by Dr. Perry (of Parkland Hospital) the wound measured 'a few millimeters in diameter,' however it was extended as a tracheotomy incision and thus its character is distorted at the time of autopsy." Humes does not tell us that he did not know that there was a bullet wound in the throat, that he did not speak to Dr. Perry until after the autopsy. The wound of "a few millimeters in diameter" meant that it was very small. Dr. Perry said that it was "3 to 5 millimeters in diameter." "No more than a pinprick," Dr. Baxter told co-author Livingstone in 1979. Nevertheless, the missile did tear open the President's trachea.

Close examination of the Zapruder film and other photographs indicates that the President was first struck in the throat at about frame 189 of the Zapruder film, which is now where the Committee places the second shot fired. Co-author Robert Groden says that the President was shot in the back at frame 230 of the film, when he is propelled forward.

UNDER ORDERS?

At the end of Dr. Humes' testimony before the panel of doctors at the Assassinations Committee, he says something very strange: That he will not talk about the case to anyone inappropriate.[17] Is he still acting under orders? Have these men been intimidated? They ought to have been. The Assassinations Committee published a list of the names of everyone supposedly in the autopsy room. They list the names of the men they say took the autopsy photographs. But among the names missing from this list is Lieutenant William Pitzer, who, according to an article printed after his alleged suicide, was in fact the man who took the photographs. Pitzer's family and friends believed that he had been murdered, that he had no reason to commit suicide, and had been badly frightened by repeated threats because of what he knew.[18]

The bullet wound in the neck was never examined. "This meant that there was a very real possibility that the bullet even yet was lodged in the thick extension of the spine which forms the center of the neck," Jim Garrison writes. "A probe of the neck wound by the pathologists in the Bethesda autopsy room would have revealed which way the truth lay. In retrospect, it is easy to see that this is precisely why no such probe was allowed."[19] How credible are the autopsists? Is the autopsy report credible when part of it was clearly fabricated, invented on the basis of hearsay, and clearly speculative with regard to the neck wound? We have to weigh the facts and give credence to what is sufficiently corroborated by other evidence.

ABOVE OR BELOW?

The autopsy report tells us that "situated in the posterior scalp approximately 2.5 cm. laterally to the right and slightly above the external occipital protuberance is a lacerated wound measuring 15 x 6 mm. In the underlying bone is a corresponding wound through the skull which exhibits bevelling of the margins of the bone when viewed from the inner aspect of the skull."[20] Did this originally read "slightly *below*" the external occipital protuberance? When former Commander Humes testified before the panel of doctors at the Assassinations Committee, he was asked about the head wound: "Where is the point of entrance? That doesn't show?"

"It doesn't show. It's below the external occipital protuberance."

"It's below it?" Dr. Petty asked, incredulously.

"Right."

"Not above it?"

"No. It's to the right and inferior to the external occipital protuberance. And when the scalp was reflected from there, there was virtually an identical wound in the occipital bone."

Somebody changed "below" to "above" in the report, just as "puncture" became "laceration," and Jacqueline Kennedy's testimony was altered. This is apparently a common practice in intelligence operations. A classic example of this is the manner in which FBI reports are written two ways, one for the public and one for the file.

"Then this is the entrance wound. The one down by the margin of the hair in the back?" Petty asked.[21] Looking at the illustration, note the white spot on the hair at the top of the neck, just above the hairline.[22] This is what they are referring to, where a white tab was fixed to the back of a man's head at his hairline in the re-enactment of the crime.

(The government's placement of the inshoot wound in the back of the head had moved five inches, up to the cowlick area, from where Humes saw it. It moved by 1968, when Attorney General Ramsey Clark convened a secret panel of doctors headed by the Medical Examiner of Maryland, Dr. Russell S. Fisher, who was closely connected to the Armed Forces Institute of Pathology. That panel was shown the fake autopsy photos and X-rays and reported what they saw. Again, the wound on the head *had* to be "moved" because the trajectory back to the "assassin's window" was wrong.)

"Well, in terms of the inshoot, my impression when I first looked at these films was that the inshoot was higher," Dr. Davis said.

"No, no, that's no wound," Dr. Humes said, pointing to the newly discovered apparent bullet hole in the cowlick.

"I interpret that as a wound, and the other, lower down in the neck, as just being a contaminant, a piece of brain tissue," Dr. Davis said.

Humes: "No, that was a wound, and the wound on the skull precisely coincided with it."

"But they describe, some of them, the entrance wound they feel being 10 centimeters above the occipital protuberance," Dr. Coe said.

"Well, there have been all sorts of changes from the original – I mean, right and left and up and down,"[23] Dr. Petty said. Clearly the doctors were seeing different things, different pictures, different evidence.

"STRUCK IN THE HEAD"

As we discuss the credibility of the witnesses and the evidence upon which this whole cover-up hangs, let us examine the death certificate signed by Admiral George G. Burkley, President Kennedy's personal doctor.* Unbelievably, he simply says that the President "was struck in the head." Then he says, "A second wound occurred in the posterior back at about the level of the third thoracic vertebra."[24] This is almost six inches below where the Warren Commission finally moved the wound. We note that the Assassinations Committee has now moved the wound several inches closer to this back position than it previously was with the Warren Commission.

Humes had placed the wound roughly in the same location where Burkley placed it: "Situated on the upper right posterior thorax just above the upper border of the scapula there is a 7 x 4 millimeter oval wound. This wound is measured to be 15 cm. from the tip of the right acromion process and 14 cm. below the tip of the right mastoid process."[25] These are not the landmarks of autopsy protocol. The mastoid process is on the head.

Under pressure during his interview with the medical panel, from which Dr. Cyril Wecht had been expressly excluded, Humes would not retract his statement about the entry wound in the head. Afterwards Dr. Humes was prepped for his public national TV appearance during the hearings on September 7, 1978: "Yes, I think that I do have a different opinion. No. 1, it was a casual kind of a discussion that we were having with the panel members, as I recall it... We described the wound of entrance in the posterior scalp as being above and to the right of the external occipital protuberance, a bony knob on the back of the head... and it is obvious to me as I sit here now with this markedly enlarged drawing of the photograph that the upper defect to which you pointed (in the cowlick area) or the upper object is clearly in the location of where we said approximately where it was, above the external occipital protuberance; therefore, I believe that is the wound entry." This is a movement of some four inches from where he placed it in 1963, and not "slightly above the occipital protuberance" as the autopsy report said.

---

*The death certificate was found by Harold Weisberg during his search of the files in the National Archives.

"It (sic) relative position to bony structure underneath it is somewhat altered by the fact that there were fractures of the skull under this and the President's head had to be held in this position thus making some distortion of anatomic structures to produce this picture."[26] Why did they not turn the body over to take the picture? Now we are beginning, but only just beginning, to find out what the skull really looked like back there. "Do you want to know what it really looked like?" Dr. Marion Jenkins, one of the Dallas doctors, said to co-author Livingstone when he saw the government picture. *"No, no, not like that!"*

"By the same token," Dr. Humes went on, "the object in the lower portion, which I apparently and I believe now erroneously previously identified before the most recent panel, is far below the external occipital protuberance and would not fit with the original autopsy findings."[27] It wasn't "far below," perhaps half an inch at most. At the time of the autopsy, he and Dr. Boswell had seen only one gunshot wound between them.

Gary Cornwall, Deputy Chief Counsel of the Assassinations Committee, asked: "Your initial autopsy report indicated that, as you have just stated, the wound was, indeed, above, I believe the report is worded in terms of 'slightly above' the external occipital protuberance. The testimony today indicates that the panel places that at approximately 10 centimeters above the external occipital protuberance. Would that discrepancy be explainable?"

"Well. I have a little trouble with that; 10 centimeters is a significant – 4 inches," Dr. Humes said.

Then Cornwell begins leading the witness: "To determine whether we can understand how such a discrepancy might have occurred. The autopsy was completed late at night; is that correct?"

"That's correct." Humes is led through more questions showing that they were up until 5 A.M. after the autopsy, and then the next day "Spoke with Dr. Perry and learned of the wound in the front of the neck and things became a lot more obvious to us as to what had occurred." That is, there were wounds they missed. "...Was the distance between the wound and the external occipital protuberance noted on those notes?"

"It was not noted, in any greater detail than appears in the final report."

"So, the exact distance, then, above the external occipital pro-tuberance was not noted – "

"Was not noted, with the feeling, of course, that the photographs and X-rays that we had made would, of themselves suffice to accurately locate this wound."[28] Humes told the Warren Commission that he didn't know whether or not he would be allowed to see the autopsy photographs and X-rays before or when he testified. "When apprised of the necessity for our appearance before this Commission, we did not know whether or not the photographs, which we had made, would be available to the Commission."[29] He wasn't, of course, allowed to see them. Some greater power was controlling the evidence, even keeping it from the Commission, and when necessary, destroying it.

For TV and in the public hearings, the doctor was made to say that the position of the "entry" wound in the back of the head was not noted. But of course, Humes had noted it precisely in the autopsy report: "Situated in the posterior scalp approximately 2.5 cm. laterally to the right and slightly above the external occipital protuberance..."

PHONEY EVIDENCE

"I only have one final question... the notes are no longer in existence; is that correct?"

"The original notes which were stained with the blood of our late President, I felt, were inappropriate to retain..."[30] Humes replied. But the sketches with the blood on them were kept, and we have seen above that the notes may not have actually been destroyed.

During Humes' interview with the Assassinations Committee's panel of doctors, Humes caught himself as he was beginning to get mixed up about the wounds. Dr. Michael Baden asked: "Now, for example, not exploring the wound from the back to the neck, that was not done. I mean, cutting it open completely, that wasn't done specifical-ly. Was that because somebody said don't do it?"

Dr. Humes: "Now wait a minute, that wound was excised."

Dr. Baden: "The back wound?"

Humes: "Yes, sir. The back of the neck, and there are microscopic slides of that wound?"

Baden: "I see. The skin was taken out. And then was it – "

Humes: "It was probed."

Baden: "Was it opened up?"

Humes: "It was not laid open."

Baden: "Now, that was your decision as opposed to somebody else's decision?"

Humes: "Yes, it was mine."

Baden: "With everything else going on at the time?"

Humes: "Yes. Our collective decisions, I suppose."[31]

AUTHENTICATION

Were the photographs and X-rays altered? The focus of the previous section was the Committee's attempt at "AUTHENTICATION OF THE KENNEDY AUTOPSY PHOTOGRAPHS AND X-RAYS." The very first note in this section says, "Because the Department of Defense was unable to locate the camera and lens that were used to take these photographs, the panel was unable to engage in an analysis similar to the one undertaken with the Oswald backyard pictures that was designed to determine whether a particular camera in issue had been used to take the photographs that were the subject of inquiry."[32]

We can add this to our long list of missing, altered or destroyed evidence and dead witnesses.

"Conclusion: the postmortem photographs and X-rays in the custody of the National Archives purporting to depict Kennedy do, in fact, depict him.

"2. There is no evidence that either the Kennedy autopsy photographs or X-rays have been altered."[33] Yet the Committee did in fact gather evidence of forgery, as we have seen.

THE GRODEN ANALYSIS

Co-author Robert Groden, long a critic of the official cover-up, was a consultant to the Committee; his views were published at the end of Vol. VI. He says, after describing how a soft edge matte insertion forgery of a photograph is done: "The final result is what appears to be the rear of the President's head with a small wound of entry near the top. The same thing (was) done to the other original in register and the result is a pair of virtually undetectable forgeries of the finest possible quality.

The technique would allow the near integrity of stereo views."[34] The Committee had allowed Groden to test the pictures, and then printed his results as above. Commercial photographers often make composites in advertising. We see them all the time.

Groden viewed the autopsy photographs in stereo pairs, after reduction to 35 mm. The matte line clearly stood out from the rest of the photograph, demonstrating that the pictures are forgeries. The rest of the background area matched, but not the matte line. The forgeries are extremely good, and to the untrained observer might appear as perfect pairs, but the edge of the matte seems to stand out closer to the observer. They do not match perfectly, and for those who know what to look for, the discrepancy can easily be spotted. The pictures are taken an inch or two apart without using a tripod. "There is a discomfort to the eyes," Groden finds.

The autopsy photographs are not the only example of forged photographs in the Kennedy case. Considerable doubt has been cast on the Oswald "backyard" photos as well.

Leading European experts say that some of the material in the JFK case is forged. When asked "Would you be prepared to produce yourself those photographs as evidence in court?" about the Oswald "backyard photos": "After having examined them – definitely not. I couldn't resort to producing anything in court which was other than just the original print from the original negative, even to the point if there was a flaw in the negative..."[35] So said Detective Superintendent Thompson of Great Britain. While citizens of other countries may consider the possibility, it just is not in the American mind to consider that evidence might be fabricated, especially by the authorities.

The Assassinations Committee does admit that the autopsy photographs "are generally of rather poor photographic quality. 2. Some, particularly close-up views, were taken in such a manner that it is nearly impossible to orient anatomically the direction of view. 3. In many, scaler references are entirely lacking, or when present, were positioned in such a manner to make it difficult or impossible to obtain accurate measurements of critical features (such as the wound in the upper back) from anatomical landmarks. 4. None of the photographs contain information identifying the victim; such as his name, the autopsy case number, and the date and place of examination. 5...In fact, in a criminal trial, the defense would probably raise many objections to an attempt to introduce such poorly made and documented photographs as evidence."[36]

Dr. Wilber writes that the autopsy photographs are "unverified and may have no probative value" in a court of law.

The Clark Panel of doctors also noted the poor quality of the photographs. "Due to lack of contrast of structures portrayed and lack of clarity of detail in these photographs, the only conclusion reached by the Panel from study of this series was that there was no exiting bullet defect in the supraorbital region of the skull."[37]

EVIDENCE IGNORED

According to the House Committee studying the assassination, "The Warren Commission based its findings primarily upon the testimony of the doctors who had treated the President at Parkland Memorial Hospital in Dallas and the doctors who performed the autopsy on the President at the Naval Medical Center in Bethesda, Md." On the contrary, this evidence was *completely* ignored.

The House Committee goes on to say, "In forming this conclusion, neither the members of the Warren Commission, nor its staff, nor the doctors who had performed the autopsy, took advantage of the X-rays and photographs of the President that were taken during the course of the autopsy. The reason for the failure of the Warren Commission to examine these primary materials is that there was a commitment to make public all evidence examined by the Commission."[38]

So says the House Committee. What are they claiming? That had the Warren Commission seen the autopsy evidence, the result would have been different? This is unlikely. The Commission placed in the National Archives hundreds of documents at least up to the number of Commission Document 1552 which were classified and to be withheld from the public until the year 2039. Many of these documents, if not all, were reviewed by the Commission. They included dental reports, Jack Ruby's tax return, Oswald's tax return – which would be interesting to see – and countless other items. It is hard to see how any of this can or should be withheld from the public. Some of it has now been released, thanks to the efforts of researcher Harold Weisberg and his suits under the Freedom of Information Act. This information has gone a long way towards resolving many questions surrounding the case.

Why has the Assassinations Committee bothered to repeat the theories of the Warren Commission, when they did not investigate the basic findings of the Commission themselves? "The (Warren) Commission was concerned that publication of the autopsy X-rays and photographs would be an invasion of the privacy of the Kennedy family."[39] This did not deter the Assassinations Committee from publishing precise copies of some of the alleged autopsy materials, so real that they do not appear to be copies at all. The Warren Commission and the Assassinations Committee had access to mountains of crucial evidence which did not infringe upon the "privacy of the Kennedy family" but much of this was also withheld from the public – much of it remains inaccessible even today.

The Assassinations Committee repeated many of the findings of the Warren Commission without conducting a proper new investigation. They stated, for example, that "(a) Reliance on scientific analysis... the Committee believed from the beginning of its investigation that the most reliable evidence upon which it could base determinations as to what happened in Dealey Plaza on November 22, 1963, was an analysis of hard scientific data... (1) The medical evidence... The committee also employed experts to authenticate the autopsy photographs... The committee, in light of the numerous issues that had arisen over the years with respect to autopsy X-rays and photographs, believed authentication to be a crucial step in the investigation. ... Two questions were put to these experts:

"Could the photographs and X-rays stored in the National Archives be positively identified as being of President Kennedy?

Was there any evidence that any of these photographs and X-rays had been altered in any manner?"[40]

PROCEDURES NOT FOLLOWED

The Committee's experts, for whom panel member Dr. Cyril Wecht had scathing words, found that the pictures were of Kennedy.[41] But proper procedures were not followed in taking the pictures of the back of the head, and it cannot in fact be identified as that of Kennedy.[42]

They also concluded that there was no evidence of the photographic or radiographic materials being altered."[43] How did they arrive at these sweeping conclusions?

The evidence presented by the Committee to say that it is authentic is invalid. Further, since it is believed by several researchers that Navy Lt. Cmdr. William Bruce Pitzer – who had been trained as an X-ray technician and may have filmed the autopsy – was apparently murdered in the same hospital, not many will stick their necks out to say that the pictures are fake.

Of course the Committee found that the pictures were of the President. They ignored certain facts, because each hand was shielded from the other.

The panel of "photographic experts" did not know what to look for, and they did not know what the issues in question were. They did not run tests on the questionable photographs. (They had no reason to raise the question of whether they were forged, so they did not look at them with this question in mind.)* Co-author Robert Groden, a consultant to the Assassinations Committee, asked to see and test the pictures. This test consisted simply of making successive generations of prints which brought out a matte line – where another picture was inserted to cover over a large hole in the back of the head.[44] Some of the official pictures are composites, if not simply pictures of someone else's head. Clever composites are made all the time by photographic technicians and the advertising industry.

Had the experts consulted with the doctors and nurses at Parkland or read their testimony, they would have learned of this large hole.

A SECRET BREAK-IN

One week after Groden's study and initial report, the CIA's liaison with the Assassinations Committee, Regis Blahut, broke into their safe and removed the photos, specifically the photographs of the back of the head.[45] The fact that this man once worked for James McCord,[46] who Jim Hougan maintains entrapped Howard Hunt and his Cubans in Watergate,[47] may be of great significance.

---

*Although he was their photographic consultant, co-author Robert Groden was not allowed to raise this question in front of the Photographic Panel nor in front of the Committee members.

But no-one knew about that break-in until the summer of 1979, long after the Committee and co-author Groden had their shot at the pictures. Only investigators from the FBI, CIA, Washington, D.C. Police, and the Committee Chief Counsel, G. Robert Blakey, knew about it, and they kept it a secret.

"Consequently, the committee determined that the autopsy X-rays and photographs were a valid basis for the conclusions of the committee's forensic pathology panel."[48] This is how the Assassinations Committee covered up: Nobody asked the right questions.*

"The forensic pathology panel concluded that President Kennedy was struck by two, and only two, bullets, each of which entered from the rear."[49] In other words, they had a photograph that apparently showed a small hole in the back of the head at the cowlick. The fact was, they weren't too sure if it was at the hairline where the autopsists had placed it, and where they could now see a bit of "dried brain tissue," or somewhere else – at the cowlick. These fabricated pictures were the basis for the conclusion that there was only one bullet which struck the President's head.

"THAT'S NO WOUND"

Dr. James Humes, the autopsist, was shown the pictures and cried "What's that?" at the new point of entry. Both he and Dr. Boswell insisted that the neat little mark at the cowlick was not the point of entry, but that it was four inches away, near the hairline. "No, no, that's no wound," he said.[50] His evidence, and that of his colleague, Dr. Boswell, was ignored by the distinguished panel of doctors. There was one exception: Dr. Cyril Wecht who, interestingly, was not told about the meeting with Humes, and so wasn't there. The first microscopic footnote of the un-indexed report appears: "In many of its conclusions, the forensic pathology panel voted 8 to 1, with the dissenting vote being consistently that of Cyril H. Wecht, M.D., coroner of Allegheny County, PA. In all references to conclusions of the panel,

---

*During the questioning of Richard Helms, the former Director of the CIA, the issue of Oswald's "201" or CIA personnel file came up. Helms stated that the file was a "dummy file" and not actually a CIA employee file. The file had been emptied but the folder itself remained (4 HSCA 5-250; 11 HSCA 64). No-one ever asked Helms why of all the people on earth the CIA would carry a personnel file on a "nobody" like Oswald.

unless it is specifically stated that it was unanimous, it should be assumed that Dr. Wecht dissented."[51]

The *autopsists* didn't go quietly, either. But almost no-one heard them. The "expert" panel of doctors failed to ask the autopsists where the large hole was, what Dr. Boswell's drawing meant, or any of the other questions that would have shed light on the real location of the wounds.

TROUBLING DISCREPANCIES

On January 12, 1982, Dr. Cyril Wecht wrote co-author Livingstone about the autopsy pictures he saw: "The massive head wound does not involve the occipital region in the photographs that I studied. It involves the right parietal-temporal zones with slight extension into the right frontal area. In other words, the 'back of the skull' was not blown away or shattered." These are the same pictures that Dr. Lattimer and the Clark Panel saw in 1968.

On January 19, 1982, Dr. Wecht insisted to Livingstone over the phone that the large defect he saw in the pictures and X-rays did not extend back behind the ear. This agrees with what the authors saw. The pictures Dr. Wecht, the authors and others have seen do not depict the massive defect extending behind the ear. Neither of these two positions shows the massive defect where it was in Dallas and Bethesda: Dr. Jenkins insisted to the Assassinations Committee that "only one segment of bone was blown out – it was a segment of occipital or temporal bone... a portion of the cerebellum (lower rear brain) was hanging out from a hole in the right – rear of the head."[52] Dr. Perry repeated to the Committee that he believed the head wound "was located in the occipital-parietal region of the skull and the right posterior aspect of the skull was missing."[53] Dr. Carrico told the Assassinations Committee, "The head wound was a much larger wound than the neck wound. It is 5 by 7 cm., two and a half by three inches, ragged, had blood and hair all around it, located in the part of the parietal-occipital region... above and posterior to the ear, almost from the crown of the head."[54]

How can another set of photographs and X-rays exist, neither of which agrees with the reports of the doctors in Dallas or the autopsists in Bethesda?

In Harold Weisberg's *Postmortem* and Josiah Thompson's *Six Seconds In Dallas*, we find Dr. Humes' Warren Commission testimony that the X-rays and photographs that were taken were exposed and destroyed.[55] We have other testimony that the Secret Service did this.[56] Then where did the pictures we do have come from? Certainly, these pictures do not remotely resemble the wounds we know about, which are supported with overwhelming evidence.

It is safe to conclude that the photos are forgeries or have otherwise been altered. The doctors at Parkland clearly identified the rear head wound to the Warren Commission. More recently, these same doctors denounced the official autopsy photos when shown them by co-author Livingstone. Co-author Robert Groden also found evidence of forgeries in his work for the House Assassinations Committee. The overwhelming weight of evidence indicates the photos are forged.

Dr. Charles Wilber, a forensic scientist, wrote that, "In fact, there is really no evidence from the autopsy that the pathologists did a thorough search of the President's head to see whether more than one bullet hit him in the head. As far as is known, the hair was not combed carefully to identify other entrance wounds. Usually, when there is a question of bullet wounds to the head that might be hidden, the hair is combed and even parts of this hair are shaved off to get a clearer picture of what occurred."

REPORT ALTERED

It now appears, as stated by Dr. Wilber, that "The complete autopsy report as written by the pathologists was altered during its route through military channels. Certain sections were removed. Admiral George Burkley, who was President Kennedy's personal physician, admitted that he doctored the autopsy report. What happened to the first report that went to Admiral Burkley? Two months passed before he released portions of the autopsy. Probably the other parts were destroyed or altered in some way. This is not a frivolous suggestion because the first report that was written, the original draft that indicated where the bullets went into the body and came out of the body; the report that indicated where the wounds were, how many bullets were there, and the paths of these bullets; the report that indicated whether any bullets were still in Kennedy's body, was burned by Doctor Humes. It is very difficult to understand how the original draft of such an important autopsy could be burned..."

Dr. Wilber writes, "A lie begets further lies... awareness of the devastating results of lying as official policy... No lie can be justified in terms of the end result. For, in the long run, an official lie begins a chain of further lies, so that when the truth finally surfaces, there is revealed a stinking morass of interlocking lies that cause long-term, if not permanent, damage to the government."[57]

WHERE IS THE DEATH CERTIFICATE?

Stanley Keeton, another researcher, writes, "One can look in vain through the Warren Report and Exhibits and never find a basic evidentiary document. This document is the death certificate of President Kennedy. Until 1975, it had been suppressed from public examination. The death certificate was drafted on November 23, 1963, by Dr. George Burkley. According to Burkley, the non-fatal posterior wound was located in the back, at about the third thoracic vertebra."[58] This is exactly where the holes in the clothes are, and where the wound appears on Dr. Boswell's drawing. "It is pertinent that the death certificate was drafted on November 23, the day before Burkley verified the autopsy face sheet (Boswell's drawings). This proves Burkley was not verifying a 'mistake' when he signed the autopsy face sheet, for he knew Boswell correctly located the wound on the back. The significance of the face sheet and the death certificate matching in regard to the wound on the back cannot be overemphasized. It cannot be argued that Burkley drafted the death certificate based on inaccurate information, for he too was present at the autopsy."[59]

The Top Secret transcript of the January 27, 1964 executive session of the Warren Commission made this an incontrovertible fact. The non-fatal posterior wound was located in the President's back, at a point *lower* than the anterior neck wound. J. Lee Rankin (General Counsel to the Warren Commission) commented: "Then there is a great range of material in regard to the wounds, and the autopsy and this point of exit or entrance of the bullet in the front of the neck, and that all has to be developed much more than we have at the present time."

He goes on to say, "We have an explanation here in the autopsy that probably a fragment came out the front of the neck, but with the elevation the shot must have come from, and the angle, it seems quite apparent now, since we have the picture of where the bullet entered in the back, that the bullet entered below the shoulder blades* to the right of the backbone, which is below the place where the picture shows the bullet came out in (above) the neckband of the shirt in front, and the bullet according to the autopsy didn't strike any bone at all. That particular bullet, and go through. So that is how it could turn and – "

Representative Boggs: "I thought I read that the bullet just went in a finger's length."

Mr. Rankin: "That is what they first said. They reached in and they could feel where it came; it didn't go any further than that, about part of the finger or something, and then they proceeded to reconstruct where they thought the bullet went... So the basic problem, what kind of wound it was in the front of the neck is of great importance to the investigation. We believe it must be related in some way to the three shots from the rear."

Senator Cooper: "You mean in the back?"

Mr. Rankin: "One, or something from a shot at the top of the head."[60] Obviously, the Commission did not have the same autopsy report we now have. Stanley Keeton writes that "The only logical explanation for this discrepancy is that the final autopsy report delivered to the Commission in late December 1963 was changed by March 1964, when the lone assassin theory necessitated the transformation of a back wound into a neck wound."[61] Rankin did in fact have an autopsy picture which showed a back wound rather than a neck wound, although it was later denied that the Warren Commissioners had ever seen the pictures.

Beneath all the scientific jargon about authentication is ultimately only one method by which experts test photos: Observation in stereo. That method depends upon only one factor: *Eyeballing*. It is a matter of judgement, and there is nothing whatsoever scientific about it. It can depend upon the eyesight, attitude, momentary fitness or political persuasion of the observer. This method is also heavily dependent upon whether the observer knows what he is looking for.

Keeton goes on to say, "The truth is that the alleged autopsy

---

*We know that the FBI report written by two agents – Sibert and O'Neill – who were present for the autopsy, made clear that the wound was far down on the back, but this is not the report referred to by Rankin.

photographs and X-rays have never been and cannot be authenticated. They are totally at variance with the autopsy report itself, and with all the other evidence... We must conclude that the autopsy photographs in the National Archives which show a wound in the back of the President's neck cannot be authentic... it is apparent that some of the autopsy materials have been *fabricated*."[62]

PART III   The Conspiracy

"It's the quality and not the length of a man's life that counts. If a man is assassinated while he is fighting to save the soul of the Nation, his death contributes more than anything else to its redemption..."

"It really doesn't matter with me now, because I've been to the mountaintop. Like anybody I would like to *live* a long life. Longevity has its place. But I'm not *concerned* about that now, I just want to do God's *will*. And he's allowed me to go up to the mountain, and I've looked over and I've seen the Promised Land."

– Martin Luther King, on April 3, 1968, the evening before he was murdered, upon learning of an assassination threat.

"We were operating an intensive vendetta against Dr. King in an effort to destroy him."

–Testimony of an Atlanta FBI agent to the House Select Committee on Assassinations.

All of this was in a class with what J. Edgar Hoover did "not long after Martin Luther King was gunned down on the balcony of his Memphis motel on April 4, 1968," Jack Anderson wrote in December 17, 1975. "Hoover sent word to me that the motive behind the murder was not racism but cuckoldry, that the assassin apparently had been hired by a jealous husband.

"The FBI vendetta against Dr. King didn't end with his murder.

The old FBI bulldog J. Edgar Hoover, who had tried to blacken King's name while he was alive, also tried to tarnish his death.

"I have held back this story for more than seven years... But Hoover's incredible attempt to panic King into committing suicide, it seems to me, abrogates any right he may have to confidentiality.

"Yet I was reluctant to believe ill of Hoover. But in late 1970 I happened to be on an airplane with the late Hale Boggs, then the House Democratic leader. He told me how members of Congress were being intimidated, if not blackmailed, by Hoover. He said that the FBI would come upon a skeleton – a woman, a vice, a shady business associate – and then get word to him that an accusation against him had reached the FBI and they wanted to alert him so he could be on his guard. From then on, the Congressman was likely to be a captive of Hoover's."

"Dr. Martin Luther King's widow said yesterday that his assassination apparently was caused by a government conspiracy and that investigations into his slaying should be reopened... 'The way he was documented and followed around by Hoover and the CIA... it would have to have been attached to the forces of our government that felt he was a threat to the system.'"

"The FBI has acknowledged that it undertook a harassment campaign to discredit King but has concluded that Ray acted alone in King's assassination."

–From newspaper reports.

"If both the past and the external world exist only in the mind, and if the mind itself is controllable – what then?"

– 1984, George Orwell

CHAPTER 6

TAMPERING WITH THE EVIDENCE

There has been considerable tampering with the evidence in this case. The pattern of tampering points clearly to a conspiracy by elements within the government to cover up the origins of the assassination. It would appear that there are powerful forces at work in this case who are able – even today – to influence events.

The Zapruder film of the assassination was at first withheld from the public and the original film was torn and spliced twice.[1] Two crucial frames were reversed in publication by the Warren Commission and by the FBI to give the illusion that the President's head was going forward with an apparent shot from behind him.[2] Dan Rather, then an obscure Texas journalist, later gave a play-by-play narration of this film on TV, though the public was not allowed to see the actual Zapruder film. Rather stated that the head was going forward with the shot.[3] Many years later, Rather retracted his statement. *Life* magazine added to the confusion by printing three different versions of the film stills within a matter of hours.

There was an apparent bullet mark found on the sidewalk in Dealey Plaza which pointed precisely at one of the manholes on the triple overpass –the most natural sniper's nest.[4] Earl Golz, a reporter from the *Dallas Morning News*, had this portion of sidewalk removed, after

101

writing to co-author Livingstone that "Those shots probably came from those manholes." The manhole the bullet mark pointed to was then paved over. It is no longer possible to find the south manhole, but the north manhole is still there.

From these manholes, all a sniper had to do was cover his head with some cardboard, have the rear end of a car parked over his head, and fire through the balustrade down on the President's car about to travel beneath the underpass where he was concealed.

Numerous bullet fragments recovered after the assassination have disappeared,[5] and Dr. Vincent Guinn, who was charged with examining the fragments purported to be evidence in the case, found that *none* of the fragments corresponded to anything listed by weight as evidence in the case in 1963-64.[6]

DID RUBY PLANT THE BULLET?

The "pristine" or "magic" bullet could have been planted on the stretcher, perhaps even by Jack Ruby. It has been definitely established that Ruby was present at Parkland Hospital when the President died.[7] It is not known if Ruby planted the bullet, but he was certainly there. The bullet does not show evidence of ever having gone through bodies. It appears to have been carefully fired into cotton or water so that it would preserve the lands and grooves which would link it to the rifle allegedly belonging to Lee Oswald: it was not in fact the bullet that was found on a stretcher at Parkland, but was switched for the original later on. Darrell Tomlinson, the man who found the original bullet, said it looked entirely different than the present "official" bullet CE 399. "This (switching) could have been done only by some federal officer, since it was in government possession from that time on. If this is true, then the assassination conspiracy would have to have involved members of the federal government and was an 'inside' job," writes assassination critic Josiah Thompson.[8]

The President's brain is missing, and that is the primary source of evidence indicating how many and what kind of bullets struck him in the head.[9] The pathological slides from the autopsy are also missing.[10]

Additional missing evidence in this case are "color photographs taken of the interior of the President's chest. These photos are crucial to a determination of the path of the bullet that purportedly entered the President's upper back."[11]

Governor Connally's clothing, which would have shown the trajectories and other data, was laundered.[12] His clothes were taken from Congressman Henry Gonzalez, later chairman of the Assassinations Committee for a brief time.

Many witnesses were intimidated, killed, or died mysteriously.

There is no conceivable way that mobsters Carlos Marcello, Santos Trafficante or Jimmy Hoffa (whom the former chief counsel of the Committee, G. Robert Blakey, would like to implicate in these crimes) could have done all this alone or covered any of it up. Neither these Mafia bosses nor the men who work for them had this kind of access to the evidence.

A FORGED DIARY

Perhaps the most important evidence of tampering comes from the documents and photographs surrounding the investigation. It is clear many of these were forged or altered. The autopsy photographs and X-rays are clearly fabricated. The "backyard" photographs of Lee Oswald are also forgeries.

Even Oswald's diary was forged. "Handwriting experts told the House Assassinations Committee in 1978 that the diary was written by Oswald but on the same paper and in a continuous pattern in one or two sittings... The Committee also noted the dates and events described in the diary on occasion occurred *after* the time Oswald purportedly wrote about them... making it a forgery done in Russia."[13]

Gore Vidal, a prominent author, implies that Arthur Bremer's diaries might have been written by Howard Hunt, although he hedges on this by saying that, "although H.H. is a self-admitted forger of state papers, I do not think that he actually had a hand in writing Bremer's diary on the ground that the journal is a brilliant if flawed job of work, and beyond H.H.'s known literary competence."[14] Interestingly, we find many stylistic similarities between Oswald's diary and that of Arthur Bremer (whose apartment some of Nixon's men either planned to break into or were present in[15]) shortly after Bremer's attempt to shoot George Wallace in 1972.* There are also similarities with the notebooks of Sirhan Sirhan (Robert Kennedy's alleged assassin). Oswald's hand-printed "diaries" hardly seem compatible with his hand-written letters.[16] They are clearly not written by the same man.

The Oswald signatures on so many documents could have been easily forged and in fact, to any amateur, do not all appear to be by the same man. There is an interesting series of articles on this subject by Professor Jerry Rose in his magazine, *The Third Decade.*[16]

Further tampering is found in an HSCA Report: "The Committee also attempted to have its handwriting experts analyze other documents such as the order for the rifle and the envelope in which it was mailed. The original had, however, been destroyed, and microfilm copies that existed were not suitable for conclusive tests."[17]

Military intelligence had a file on Oswald,[18] just as the CIA had a 201 (personnel) file on him,[19] which they have finally produced, greatly incomplete. But the military file "has been destroyed."[20] How and why? It happened because Oswald was in all probability an agent of the Office of Naval Intelligence.

At least 37 documents are missing from Oswald's CIA 201 file, and hundreds more are still being withheld from the public.[21]

In 1967, the National Archives disclosed that a "letter from Capt. Fritz to the (Warren) Commission, June 9, 1964, on spent shells found in the Texas School Book Depository" was among the items missing from the Archives' collection of Commission records.[22]

The National Archives disclosed the same year that two records of the Warren Commission pertaining to the arrest of assassination suspect Jim Braden are missing.[23] These are "Records of the Dallas Police and County Sheriff's Office concerning arrests on November 22, 1963" and a "photograph... showing a man being arrested or under arrest near the Dal Tex Building," in Dealey Plaza, on November 22, 1963. Other photographs of the Braden arrest do exist, however.

The CIA had destroyed alleged secret tape recordings of Oswald

---

*Governor George Wallace of Alabama was shot by Arthur Bremer during the Presidential campaign of 1972, but survived. It is doubtful that Richard Nixon would have been re-elected President, since Wallace had split the vote, until the shooting forced him to withdraw. See "Bremer, Wallace and Hunt" by Gore Vidal in *The Assassinations, Dallas and Beyond*, edited by Peter Dale Scott, Paul Hoch, and Russell Stetler, pp. 386-392.

at the Cuban and Russian Embassies in Mexico City in 1963. They also destroyed the transcripts,[24] and were never able to produce photographs of Oswald there, which seems strange, since everyone going in or out of the Cuban and Russian Embassies was photographed.

Following the assassination, the traffic sign in Dealey Plaza was removed. Witness James Hicks remembers seeing a bullet hole in it. No record of who ordered the sign removed, or why, can be found. The night before Hicks was scheduled to testify to the New Orleans Grand Jury in this case, he was severely beaten and pushed through a plate glass window. He survived.[25]

An 8mm. film was seized from a witness known as the "Babushka Lady" (Beverly Oliver), she thinks by FBI agent Regis Kennedy. This film then disappeared. It was probably much better than the Zapruder film. It was shot with a good camera and lens, very close to the President during the shooting, just across the street from Zapruder, and with no road signs in the way. Interestingly, Oliver was married to George McGann, a mobster and known killer who was later murdered. She claims that they met secretly for two hours with Richard Nixon in a Miami hotel in 1968.[26]

Miss Oliver was an employee of the Colony Club, which was next door to Jack Ruby's Carousel. She knew Jack Ruby well, and it seems more than strange that she was filming the motorcade and the assassination. She was one of several witnesses who said that Ruby and Oswald knew each other well.[27] She said that she saw CIA contract agent David Ferrie at Ruby's club so often, she thought he was one of the managers.

In 1976, the National Archives disclosed that two letters written to Warren Commission General Counsel Rankin were missing from the National Archives collection: a "Letter of David Belin to J. Lee Rankin, January 23, 1964, on interrogation of Oswald by Dallas Police Department" and also a "Memorandum of Griffin to Rankin in August 1964" dealing with a number of inquiries to be made of various agencies, including unidentified prints found on the cartons in the Texas School Book Depository.[28]

Also in 1976, the National Archives informed the House Subcommittee on Government Information that two documents of Joseph Ball were missing from the Warren Commission records stored at the

Archives: "Memorandum (60 pages) of Ball and Belin Concerning Identity of the Assassin" and a "Draft Chapter Submitted by Ball and Belin in early June 1964."[29]

MORE MISSING DOCUMENTS

In 1976, the National Archives disclosed that two of Leon Jaworski's* letters to the Warren Commission were missing from the records of the Commission: a "Letter of December 18, 1963" expressing a continuous "willingness to assist in any way" and a "Letter of Leon Jaworski to J. Lee Rankin, May 8, 1964."[30]

In 1976, yet another letter was found missing from the Archives: "A Letter of Gerald Ford, April 7, 1964, concerning expediting the FBI investigation" was among the Warren Commission documents missing from the Archives building in Washington.[31]

Also missing from the Archives building in Washington are "FBI Laboratory technical records concerning spectrographic analysis of ballistics evidence," as well as "FBI Laboratory report concerning examination of Presidential limousine."[32]

Other evidence of crucial importance has gone missing.

A photograph of the assassination taken by Mary Moorman was taken from her by Deputy Sheriff John Wiseman, who gave it to Chief Criminal Deputy Sheriff Allen Sweatt. It supposedly went to the Secret Service, where it disappeared. A second photograph taken by Moorman is well-known and has been studied extensively; but this picture too, showing the motorcycle policemen in front of the Presidential limousine, has disappeared from the evidence.[33]

The official copy of the Dallas Police Dictabelt of the police radio transmissions made during the assassination, and the shots on it, are missing from the National Archives.[34]

"Tape recordings of Dallas Police Department radio broadcasts" were missing.[35] Two sets of reports dealing with "operation security

---

*Leon Jaworski was a special counsel to the Warren Commission, as well as to the Attorney General of Texas in 1963. He was given the assignment of investigating charges that Oswald was a government agent with the CIA or the FBI or both. Jaworski quickly reported that there was nothing to the story. In 1973, when President Nixon fired Attorney General Eliot Richardson and the Special Prosecutor investigating Nixon, Archibald Cox, Nixon appointed Jaworski to replace Cox.

involving the transfer of Lee Harvey Oswald" were found missing in 1976.[36]

A "Letter from Capt. Fritz to the Warren Commission, June 9, 1964, on spent shells found in the Texas School Book Depository" is missing.[37]

A letter from the Commission to Lt. Jack Revill, asking for "records relating to a possible pro-Castro demonstration by Oswald in Dallas," is missing.[38]

A letter pertaining to the "interrogation of Oswald by DPD written by David Belin to J. Lee Rankin" is missing.[39]

Perhaps the most important piece of missing evidence is indicated in this statement by George O'Toole, former Chief of the CIA's Problems Analysis Branch: "Wecht and Smith (Dr. Cyril Wecht and Robert Smith of the Committee to Investigate Assassinations – a private research group) report that an unidentified army general claimed to have been in overall charge of the autopsy, that orders were given not to dissect the President's back-throat wound, and that a roll of film taken during the autopsy was seized from a medical corpsman by a Secret Service agent, who then deliberately destroyed it."[40] Was this the film taken by Lt. William Pitzer, who was later apparently executed?

A man who appeared to be a government agent was seen picking up a bullet and photographed doing so, just after the assassination, in Dealey Plaza. This bullet was never recovered.[41]

Regis Blahut, an employee of the CIA, was arrested for breaking into the safe of the Assassinations Committee and tampering with the autopsy photographs.[42] This incident was never adequately investigated.

Testimony in this case was often changed or reversed to get the desired "right result." Witnesses were intimidated or threatened by federal officials; and many have died under mysterious circumstances. So many witnesses died in connection with Jim Garrison's prosecution of Clay Shaw, a CIA operative implicated in the conspiracy, that Garrison's case eventually collapsed.

Testimony was often ignored or buried if it did not conform to official conclusions or versions.

"The committee firearms panel determined that the evidence stored in the National Archives ballistically matched the bullets fired by the FBI in 1964 tests from the Mannlicher-Carcano found by Deputy

Boone. Since the rifle had been test-fired numerous times since 1963, its barrel had been altered by wear, and bullets the panel fired from the rifle did not match either the FBI test cartridges or those found on the sixth floor of the depository or that found on the stretcher."[43] In many of these cases, the alleged murder weapon disappears or changes. The first police to reach the sixth floor of the Texas School Book Depository reported finding a German Mauser, not an Italian Mannlicher-Carcano rifle.

A note Oswald wrote to FBI agent Hosty in Dallas was destroyed by Hosty on orders of FBI office chief J. Gordon Shanklin. It was flushed down a toilet.[44]

A MISSING CAMERA

Oswald's Minox camera disappeared from the evidence. "Dallas police detective Gus Rose said the camera, loaded with exposed film, was found by police during a search of Oswald's seabag on either the day of the assassination or the next day. An inventory of Oswald's property taken from the Irving residence was made in the Dallas FBI office four days after the assassination and listed 'one Minox camera' under item number 375. The day after the property was delivered to the FBI Laboratory in Washington, a second published inventory showed no listing for a Minox camera. The word *lightmeter* was substituted for *camera* under item 375.

"The FBI tried unsuccessfully to persuade Rose to change the police property list to report a Minox lightmeter rather than a Minox camera with film, Rose said. Two months after the assassination, the FBI finally placed into its records a Minox camera which admittedly was not Oswald's. A bureau report said the Minox camera was obtained January 31, 1964 from Mrs. Ruth Paine, at the Irving home and that it belonged to her husband."[45]

Minox cameras are occasionally used for espionage. Photos Oswald had in his possession, taken in Russia and the Far East, appear to be of interest only for intelligence purposes.

This pattern of tampering with the evidence is consistent throughout the case and shows a massive effort to cover up the truth. One or two pieces of missing or misinterpreted evidence could be written off to chance, but not on the scale we see here.

It is just a "coincidence," Sheriff Jim Bowles of Dallas told co-author Livingstone, that seconds after the last shot was fired, the Morse code signal "V" for "victory" happened to be heard over the Dallas Police radio.[46]

"It's just a heterodyning." Bowles said. "Just a coincidence."

*"When I used to read fairy tales I fancied
that kind of thing never happened, and
now here I am in the middle of one."*

– *Alice in Wonderland*, Lewis Carroll

CHAPTER 7

STRANGE DEATHS

The original Committee staff of the 1976 House Assassinations Committee and some of the Congressional leadership (though not all of the Committee members themselves) believed strongly there was a conspiracy in the deaths of both President Kennedy and Dr. Martin Luther King, Jr. Other staff members were determined not even to consider the possibility of conspiracy. They were not interested in the evidence but set out from the beginning to denounce all conspiracy theories. A study of the work undertaken by the Committee shows that they first made a list of all the charges made by the critics of the Warren Report. This new Committee seemed for most of its life determined to find no conspiracy, and to confirm the original findings of the Warren Report. Each issue and piece of evidence was examined by comparing it to the massive body of the generally disbelieved Warren Report. After each piece was made not to fit, it was discarded and not allowed to be used to back up or reinforce each additional challenge to the official fiction.

By the time the Committee was actually able to start its investigations some months after it began, a new leadership was empowered, which was far more skeptical and far too conservative to allow itself to believe that either murder was the result of a conspiracy.

This was the *modus operandi* of the Committee and its panels, until the development of the acoustical evidence very late in the Committee's life. There was not going to be any conspiracy, until the last days of the Committee, when they were forced to admit the validity of the acoustical evidence.

Nowhere is the Committee determination not to face the facts more evident than in the deaths of key witnesses. The Committee's publications numbered in the tens of thousands of pages, but only two pages covered their entire "investigation" of the deaths of witnesses in John Kennedy's murder. We quote here: "A widely held belief that has been fostered by some of the critics is that the death rate of individuals connected in some way to the assassination has been improbably high,"[1] Chief Counsel G. Robert Blakey began. "The editor of a weekly newspaper in Midlothian, Texas, Penn Jones Jr., started it all by publishing his mysterious death theory in a book *Forgive My Grief*, in 1966. Jones assembled details of the deaths and of the connections of the deceased to the assassination – " Blakey then called Jacqueline Hess of Baltimore. "Mr. Chairman, Jacqueline Hess, the Committee's chief of research for the Kennedy assassination investigation, has been in charge of the mysterious deaths project."

100,000 TRILLION TO ONE

Ms. Hess, who took over from Donovan Gay, swore to tell the truth, and launched into a denunciation of a *London Sunday Times* article that said the odds were 100,000 trillion to one that so many witnesses would die so soon after the assassination, no matter what the cause. The punch line of her learned presentation is that "We had thus established the impossibility of attempting to establish, through the application of actuarial principles, any meaningful implications about the existence or absence of a conspiracy."[2] She then goes on to say that they nonetheless decided to look into the deaths of 21 witnesses, some of whom they themselves added to the list because "they had died too recently to be included in most of the critics' literature."[3] We are not informed as to the rest of her methods of evaluation, except that they tried to get some of the records in the cases. How, we don't know. "Our final conclusion on the issue is that the available evidence does not establish anything about the nature of these deaths which would indicate that the deaths were in some manner, either direct or peripheral, caused by the assassination of President Kennedy or by any aspect of the subsequent investigation."[4]

THE NAMES ON THE LIST

The alphabetical list begins with Edward Benairdes (sic). There was no Edward Benairdes anywhere in this case. This name was made up.

The list goes on: Albert Guy Bogard, Hale Boggs, Lee Bowers Jr, Bill Chesher, Nicholas Chetta, David Goldstein, Thomas Hale Howard, William Hunter, Clyde Johnson, Dorothy Kilgallen, Thomas Henry Killam, Jim Koethe, FNU Levens, Nancy Jane Mooney, Teresa Norton, Earlene Roberts, Harold Russell, Marilyn April Walle, a.k.a. Betty McDonald, William Whaley, James R. Worrell, Sam Giancana, and John Roselli.[5]

The Congressional list includes only a small number of those who died mysteriously in the case. If the "investigator" had checked the Congressional Record, she would have found that many Congressmen and Senators, including the first two chairmen of the Committee, were deeply disturbed by the murders of Sam Giancana and Johnny Roselli.[6] The disappearance of Jimmy Hoffa was no accident, either. But Giancana and Roselli were on the lists of witnesses being called before the Senate Intelligence Committee. One talked too much and the other may have, so apparently they were bumped off.[7]

After the list was read, Congressman Bob Edgar said, "Thank you. I think it very helpful for the record that those names be included. Can you indicate why Mr. DeMohrenschildt's name was not included?"[8] (DeMohrenschildt, a close friend of Oswald, had long established intelligence ties.)

Hess: "His was one of those which deemed further investigation and became part of a great investigative effort."[9] DeMohrenschildt died of a gunshot wound the day a committee investigator located him.[10] Critic and assassination researcher Edward Jay Epstein had an interview scheduled with him that day, too.[11] Edgar: "That was not part of the exact study?" Hess: "It was in terms of the compilation of data. I compiled the data on his death and any police reports, et cetera, as part of this project. But then in terms of subsequent investigation that was done by the investigators."[12]

"The widow of George DeMohrenschildt, who was a friend of both Lee Harvey Oswald and Jacqueline Kennedy, has told the *Star-Telegram* (Fort Worth) she does not believe her husband committed suicide the day he was scheduled to meet with a representative of the House Assassinations Committee." She thought they would kill her too. "They may get me too but I'm not afraid... It's about time somebody looked into this thing." She admitted that her husband worked in intelligence, that he was friendly with H.L. Hunt and Bob Kerr, the oil men, and that his closest friend at the time of the assassination was Dallas' top CIA man (J. Walter Moore) and another Fort Worth man "connected with a military-oriented security organization." "Her belief is that Lee Harvey Oswald was an agent of the United States, possibly of the CIA, and that he did not shoot Kennedy.

"We always said the Cubans did it (the Kennedy assassination). The Cuban refugees did it. Everything points to it... George didn't think Oswald did it and I don't either. Oswald was a very kind, very meek person... I have the suspicion that he (Oswald) was our agent and that he was drilled in the Russian language. I think he was drilled because he knew too much Russian and knew it too well in too short a time. You know, Russian is a hard language. I think maybe he was a CIA agent.

"Something is being covered up, somewhere by somebody. There was a definite proof that he (Kennedy) was not killed from the back (the Warren Commission's conclusion) but from the front... It's about time that somebody speaks up while they can still talk." She said that they would set up an accident and kill her.[13]

NAMES MISSING FROM THE LIST

The first name missing from the list of dead witnesses is Lee Harvey Oswald. Former Dallas Chief of Police Jesse Curry ended his book: "Witnesses to the shooting wondered if there wasn't a gleam of recognition in Oswald's eye when Ruby stepped out from the newsmen. Police investigation was never able to turn up a definite link between the two men."[14]

Oswald was a dead man from the moment Kennedy was murdered. It has been suggested that the intent was to kill Oswald in the alley outside the theater where he was arrested, expecting him to run out, so that he could be shot while "escaping." But he stood up and shouted, "I am not resisting arrest!"[15] and otherwise made an effort to save himself.

This is hardly the behavior of a fanatical killer. Still others believe he was never supposed to leave the Texas School Book Depository alive. Clearly, Oswald was the first witness to die.

Deputy Sheriff Buddy Walthers found a bullet in the grass beside Elm Street shortly after the assassination, and turned it over to someone identifying himself as an FBI agent. Walthers knew too much, and he talked too much. He was shot through the heart during a police shootout in 1969. It was admitted that he "could" have been shot by a fellow officer.[16]

Deputy Sheriff Roger Craig saw a man run down from the Depository and get into a Rambler station wagon. He later saw that man in Captain Will Fritz' office. It was Oswald, and Oswald told him the Rambler belonged to Ruth Paine, and to leave her out of it. Craig was interviewed by Assistant Counsel David Belin. He was shot at, threatened, driven from job to job, and finally died of a gunshot wound. Craig marked 14 alterations of his testimony to Belin when he got a copy of it after the Warren Report was published. Craig was not allowed to see his testimony before it was printed nor make changes. The Rambler station wagon was photographed in Dealey Plaza just after the shooting.[17]

Penn Jones Jr., one of the first critics of the Warren Report (who "started it all") wrote, "On May 15, 1975, Roger D. Craig died in Dallas. The treatment Craig received after John F. Kennedy was assassinated, we think, caused his death. Reluctantly, we do admit that Craig pulled the trigger to end his life... Roger Craig was a great American."[18] He had been shot at before, received many threats, lost jobs, and been reduced to poverty.

The first legitimate name on the Assassinations Committee's "mysterious death project" list is Albert Guy Bogard, an employee at the Downtown Dallas Lincoln-Mercury dealership. Before the assassination, the alleged Oswald went to Downtown Lincoln-Mercury, where Bogard worked, and test-drove a car.

Gary Shaw and Larry Harris write, "With Bogard as his passenger, 'Oswald' test drove a car on Stemmons Freeway, hitting speeds over 75 miles per hour. Upon returning to the showroom 'Oswald' told Bogard he did not have enough money for a down payment but said he would be coming into 'a lot of money in the next two or three weeks.' He told the credit manager that if financing could not be arranged he might 'go back to Russia where they treat workers like men.'

"Again the Warren Commission tells us that this was not the real Oswald. As stated earlier, the real Oswald did not drive, and on this date the Commission placed him in Irving writing a letter... Yet Bogard passed a lie detector test about the incident, and his co-workers corroborated his story... Bogard, 41, was found dead in his car in a Hallsville, Louisiana cemetery on February 14, 1966. A hose had been connected to the exhaust and the other end inside the car with windows up; the ruling was suicide." [19]

THE DOWNTOWN LINCOLN-MERCURY CONNECTION

Downtown Lincoln-Mercury had supplied some of the cars for the Presidential motorcade. In addition to Bogard, there was another employee at the dealership who is connected to the case. He is Jack Lawrence, who had been with Downtown Lincoln-Mercury for only a month at the time of the assassination. It was "recalled that 30 minutes after the assassination Lawrence, muddy and sweating profusely, came running into the dealership and was overcome by nausea. His abandoned vehicle was later found parked behind the wooden fence on the grassy knoll." [20]

"Jack Lawrence was arrested later that afternoon and held in jail for 24 hours. Judging from his peculiar behavior on November 22, one cannot help but garner the idea that he was somehow involved in the assassination." [21]

Independent researchers have since discovered that the cover story Lawrence used to get hired was completely phony. He quit this job the day after the assassination. According to the "Babushka Lady," Lawrence "was frequently seen in Jack Ruby's Carousel Club and was a close friend of Ruby's roommate, George Senator." He was known as an ardent Right-Wing speaker, and had been living in Los Angeles before coming to Dallas. [22]

Lawrence had borrowed the car from the dealer the night before the assassination and did not bother to report to work with it the following morning; he only showed up shortly after the murder. He had mud on his clothes and was pale and sweating; he ran to the restroom and threw up. [23]

Lawrence was an expert marksman in the service. He had left this car behind the stockade fence, where some other employees went to get it. His fellow workers called the police.[24]

His phony references, from a car dealership in New Orleans, had not been checked by his new employer.[25] New Orleans was where much of this plot was hatched. Bogard also died in Louisiana.

Congressman Hale Boggs of Louisiana, who was one of the seven Warren Commissioners, is next on the list. He disappeared without a trace on a flight in Alaska. Speaking of the "magic bullet" theory just before his mysterious death, he said, "I had strong doubts about it." The fact that Boggs' plane simply disappeared makes it a little strange. Especially since Boggs had been the recipient of damaging material on the lives of critics of the Warren Report and the FBI investigation of the President's death, given to him by J. Edgar Hoover just prior to his death, leading Boggs to mount an attack on the FBI and accuse them of "Gestapo tactics." Ron Kessler wrote in the *Washington Post* that Congressman Boggs' son, a Washington lawyer, said that "the experience played a large role in his father's decision to publicly charge the FBI with "Gestapo tactics" in a 1971 speech alleging the Bureau had wiretapped his telephone and that of other Congressmen."[26]

MORE WITNESSES, MORE SUDDEN DEATHS

Lee Bowers Jr. is next on the Congressional list. He was in the railroad control tower behind the Grassy Knoll and saw two men behind the fence, a puff of smoke during the shooting, and a lot of activity. Just before the assassination, he saw a car driving behind the fence, with a man speaking on the radio. He said three unauthorized cars drove back there a half hour before the assassination, although the area was supposed to have been closed off by police. He said the first car was a 1959 Oldsmobile station wagon with out-of-state plates and a Goldwater sticker. The next car was a 1957 black Ford, with the driver appearing to use a radio. Both cars left after cruising around. The third was a 1961 Chevrolet Impala with out-of-state tags and a Goldwater sticker, which came and left ten minutes before the shooting started.

"More important than these observations is the fact that Bowers saw two 'strangers' standing near the wooden fence prior to and at the time of the shooting. One of these men was middle-aged and fairly heavy-set. The other was in his mid-twenties and wearing a plaid shirt or jacket; this fits the description of the man carrying the rifle case seen by Miss Mercer."*

When Bowers began to describe the "commotion" behind the fence during the shooting, he was cut off by Joseph Ball of the Warren Commission. He was going to say, as he told others later, "There was some unusual occurrence – a flash of light or smoke or something which caused me to feel like something out of the ordinary had occurred there."[27]

Bowers died at age 41 in a one-car crash near Midlothian, Texas, on August 9, 1966. The Medical Examiner said that Bowers was in some kind of a "strange shock" at the time of the accident.[28] There are drugs and other substances which intelligence agents use that can be administered to people in various ways which will cause them to have fatal heart attacks, drive them to suicide, or go into "strange shocks."

Next on the list is Bill Chesher, who was said to have information linking Ruby to Oswald. He died of a sudden heart attack in March, 1964.[29]

Then we find Nicholas Chetta. He supposedly died of a heart attack on May 25, 1968, during the time of District Attorney Jim Garrison's investigation of the assassination. He was the Coroner of New Orleans and a key witness in Garrison's case against Clay Shaw, accused of conspiracy to murder President Kennedy. He served at the death of David Ferrie, and performed autopsies on Ferrie, Dr. Mary Sherman, Robert Perrin, all witnesses connected to Garrison's case.[30] His brother-in-law and sometime assistant, Dr. (Professor) Henry Delaune was murdered on January 26, 1969.[31] Note that none of these witnesses – David Ferrie, Dr. Mary Sherman, or Robert Perrin – is on the list investigated by Hess for the Assassinations Committee. Obviously, a clear pattern would have emerged that Garrison's key witnesses were exterminated, thus causing the case to collapse.

Why isn't David Ferrie on the Congressional list? *The Washington Post's* George Lardner Jr. was with him right up to the time he died of a strange "brain hemorrhage" on February 22, 1967, [32] and Lardner covered the Assassinations Committee for the *Post*. Ferrie was one of

---

*Julia Mercer made an affidavit that she saw a man carrying a rifle case up the Grassy Knoll before the assassination. Sylvia Meagher and others cite Mercer as an example of many witnesses ignored by the Warren Commission, the FBI, and the Secret Service. (WC Vol. 7, 352, Vol. 19, p. 483; Meagher, *Accessories After the Fact* p. 9, 21.)

the most important characters in the whole case, and had originally been arrested as a suspect a few days after the assassination. He was Garrison's most important witness.[33] He was a CIA contract agent who knew both Ruby and Oswald,[34] and also worked for another suspect, Carlos Marcello, the Godfather of New Orleans.[35]

The next name missing from the list is Dr. Mary Sherman, who was connected to Ferrie. She was shot in bed and set on fire.[36] Clyde Johnson, who is on the official list, was beaten the day before he was to testify in Garrison's trial, and murdered in a shotgun attack not long afterwards.[37] He knew of the personal relationship between Clay Shaw, David Ferrie, Oswald, and Ruby.[38]

Aladio del Valle, David Ferrie's close friend, was killed in Miami *the same hour* that Ferrie died in New Orleans on February 22, 1967. He had been shot in the heart and his skull split open with a machete.[39] He was an anti-Castro exile and was being looked for by Garrison as a witness.[40]

Dr. Chetta was a key witness against Clay Shaw.[41] Chetta performed the autopsy on Robert Perrin, who died of arsenic poisoning,[42] and who was the husband of Nancy Perrin Rich, a key witness in this case. She testified that her former boss Jack Ruby was involved in Cuban arms smuggling deals.[43] Perrin is not on the list, but ought to be.

David Goldstein is next on the official list. He helped the FBI trace the revolver used in the murder of Officer Tippit, and died of "natural causes" in 1965.[44] FNU Levens, who is on the list, died of "natural causes" on November 5, 1966. Levens operated a burlesque theater in Fort Worth that employed some of Jack Ruby's girls.[45]

RUBY'S CRONIES

Thomas Hale Howard, who appears on the official list, had been at Ruby's apartment the night Ruby shot Oswald, with Ruby's roommate George Senator, and Bill Hunter and Jim Koethe, all of whom, except for Senator, shortly died.[46] Hunter was shot to death in a police station.[47] Jim Koethe was killed with a karate chop to the throat as he came out of a shower in his Dallas apartment on September 21, 1964.[48] Howard died of a supposed heart attack in Dallas.[49] He was observed acting strangely for a couple of days before.[50] There was no autopsy. Tom Howard was Ruby's lawyer.[51] Hunter, a newsman, had written a story about him: "Within minutes of Ruby's execution of Oswald before the eyes of millions watching television at least two Dallas attorneys appeared to talk with him." One of these lawyers was Tom Howard. Hunter was killed in a police station in Long Beach, California, on April 24, 1964, shot through the heart a few months before Howard died.

We know that at one time a CIA man lived underneath Jack Ruby's apartment.[52] Was Ruby's place bugged that night, and did these men pay with their lives for meeting there?

Page 363 of the Warren Report says, "One conceivable association (between Ruby and Oswald) was through John Carter, a boarder at 1026 North Beckley Avenue while Oswald lived there, Carter was friendly with Wanda Joyce Killam, who had known Jack Ruby since shortly after he moved to Dallas in 1947 and worked for him from July 1963 to early November, 1963."

Wanda Joyce worked for Ruby, and her husband Thomas Henry (Hank) Killam is on the official "strange deaths project" list. His throat was cut in March of 1964. He had told his brother, "I am a dead man, but I have run as far as I am going to run."[53]

"SUICIDES"

Next we find the name of Dorothy Kilgallen. We do not find the name of Mrs. Earl T. Smith, her close friend and confidante, who died of "indeterminate causes" two days after Kilgallen died.[54] Dorothy Kilgallen was a nationally known columnist and TV personality who attended Jack Ruby's trial. In November, 1965, she told a friend that she was going to break the assassination mystery "wide open." Five days later, she was dead of unexplained causes, and she, too, was ruled a "suicide."[55]

Hess nexts lists Marilyn April Walle, also known as Betty Mooney McDonald (sic), on her official list of those "investigated" by the Select Committee on Assassinations. Marylyn April Walle is someone else entirely, although she also died violently. Both worked as strippers for Jack Ruby. Betty MacDonald was once at a private party with the Oswalds and the DeMohrenschildts.[56] Betty Mooney MacDonald (correct spelling) was the alibi for Darrell Wayne Garner, the man accused of shooting Warren Reynolds.[57] Her testimony freed him. A week later, in February, 1964, she was arrested and an hour later was found hung to death in her jail cell.[58]

Marilyn Moone Walle, also known as "Delilah," Marilyn April Walle, or Marilyn Magyar Moon – a dancer employed by Ruby on the day Kennedy was killed – was planning a book on the assassination. She was shot to death on September 1, 1966. Her husband was convicted of the crime, but there is reason to suspect that her death was in fact related to her involvement with Ruby and what she might have known about the assassination.[59]

Ms. Hess also lists Nancy Jane Mooney, in her confusion, as a separate person, when this was another name used by Betty MacDonald.

Teresa Norton was another of Ruby's strippers and a police informant. She was shot to death in Houston in August, 1964. Her real name was Karen Bennett Carlin, or "Little Lynn."[60]

Earline Roberts is on the list.[61] Roberts, Oswald's last landlady, said that a police car drove by after the assassination, honked its horn and then moved on while Oswald was in the house.[62] She said that an Officer Alexander was sometimes there.[63] Could this be the violent Right Wing Assistant District Attorney Bill Alexander, who knew Ruby well and who later prosecuted him for Oswald's murder? Ruby went to see Alexander the day before he killed Oswald.[64] Mrs. Roberts died of heart failure on January 9, 1966.

Harold Russell is also on the list. He was a witness to the escape of Tippit's killer. He went berserk at a party and told his friends he was going to be killed. Someone called the police to calm him. He was hit by a policeman and died shortly afterward, in February of 1967.[65]

William Whaley was the cab driver who supposedly helped Oswald get away from the assassination site. He died in a strange freak car accident in December, 1965. He was the first cab driver to be killed in Dallas while on duty since 1937. He would have been a witness to whatever Oswald might have said just after the assassination, if Oswald was in fact in his cab.[66]

James R. Worrell, who said he saw the assassin run from the School Book Depository,[67] died in a car-motorcycle accident.[68] "I heard the fourth shot,"[69] he said to Warren Commission Counsel Arlen Specter, saying he saw a man in a dark sport coat run out of the back door of the Depository, and walk up Houston Street going south. Worrell died on November 9, 1966, at the age of 23.

This testimony was corroborated by Richard Randolph Carr, who saw a heavy-set man wearing a hat, tan sportscoat and horn-rimmed glasses on the sixth floor of the Depository. Just after the shooting, Carr saw two men run from either inside or behind the building and get into a Rambler station wagon and speed off north on Houston. Carr then got down to the ground from his perch on the girders of the new courthouse building and saw the same man in a tan jacket hurrying away. Carr was not called to testify. He was intimidated by the FBI, who told him that he had better keep his "mouth shut." "They told me 'If you didn't see Lee Harvey Oswald in the School Book Depository with a rifle, you didn't witness it.'" Then his real trouble began. One night, 12 night-riding Dallas policemen and detectives searched his house, tearing it up. They took his sons off to jail, held one overnight, and tried to make them confess that there were "stolen articles" in their father's house. Threatening phone calls came telling him to "get out of Texas," so he finally moved to Montana. One day, he found three sticks of dynamite wired to the ignition of his car. He was going to testify in the Clay Shaw trial in New Orleans. He too was almost shot, but was able to catch the gunman with the help of a policeman next door. He testified in New Orleans, and then was stabbed in Atlanta. Carr shot and killed one of the men who attacked him. He was left alone after that for several years, having nailed two of his would-be killers. In 1975, as talk of the new investigation began, he started getting threatening phone calls again.[70]

Fletcher Prouty tells us that this is "The Hand." He says that the conspiracy is very much alive, and this kind of intimidation and violence is clear evidence.

Carolyn Walther was another witness who saw two men in the area of the "Oswald window" at the time of the shooting. She said that the man with the rifle was wearing a white shirt and had light hair. To his left, she saw another man in the same window wearing a brown suit-coat. She was not called to testify before the Commission. Her testimony and Carr's are corroborated by Roger Craig, and Mr. and Mrs. Arnold Rowland.[71]

THE GIANCANA-ROSELLI CONNECTION

Last on Hess' list are the names of Sam Giancana and John Roselli. The man who hired her, Congressman Downing, asked questions about their deaths, as did nearly everyone in Congress, since they were involved in the assassination plots against Castro, and the word was that those plots may have back-fired in some way and resulted in the assassination of President Kennedy. At least, this is what Roselli was feeding Jack Anderson of *The Washington Post*.[72]

Both Roselli and Giancana were doing a lot of talking, or at least threatening to. Roselli was talking about JFK's murder to Jack Anderson,[73] and Sam Giancana was talking to the Senate Intelligence Committee.[74] Giancana was killed with a .22 pistol; this is not the favored piece of the Mob, but it is preferred by intelligence agencies, whose own hit men like small, quiet pistols with no kick.[75] They just take more bullets to kill a man. No self-respecting killer would ever do a job for the Mob with a .22 pistol, at least not in those days. They prefer hand-held 45-caliber cannons and sawed-off shotguns.

The fact that there was a massive wipe-out at about that time of other mobsters of note, as well as much of the top command of the FBI, was not considered by the Committee. Top former intelligence people tell us that there is a spook war going on in the United States. Jim Hougan writes about it in his book *Spooks*.

Another name not on the Committee's list is that of Karyn Kupcinet, daughter of a childhood friend of Ruby. She was murdered two days after Kennedy.[76] She had foreknowledge of the assassination and was overheard by a telephone operator talking about it.[77]

Rose Cherami was thrown out of a moving car by two other Ruby employees. At the hospital after the "accident," she gave advance notice of the Kennedy assassination. She later stated that Oswald and Ruby were "bedmates." She was killed in a hit and run accident in 1965.[78]

Captain Frank Martin of the Dallas Police told the Warren Commission that he "had better not talk," and then died of "cancer" under "suspicious circumstances, in June of 1966."[79]

RUBY'S DEATH: CANCER?

Jack Ruby developed cancer and died rather quickly – on January 3, 1967, shortly after he was granted a new trial. Before he died, Ruby insisted they had injected him with the cancer.[80]

Officer Tippit died even faster, and there is extensive evidence that he and Ruby knew each other,[81] but the Warren Commission said that this was another Tippit on the Dallas police force and that people were confused.[82]

Hiram Ingram, a Dallas Sheriff, stated that he had knowledge of a conspiracy. He fell and broke his hip and died of "cancer" three days later,[83] on April 4, 1968. He was a close friend of Deputy Sheriff Roger Craig, before his death.

The husband of Beverly Oliver, the "Babushka Lady," George McGann, was murdered. The killing was never solved. It took place in the house of Ronny Weeden. Weeden knew Charles Harrelson in prison. Harrelson, who was convicted of murdering U.S. District Judge John H. Wood Jr., says Weeden did it. He also says that Weeden has disappeared, and that he "had a reputation as a hit man." Weeden's name is in McGann's personal notebooks, and Beverly remembers him. Best man at the McGann wedding was Russell D. Mathews, Jack Ruby's longtime friend and Harrelson's admitted idol.

Interestingly, Harrelson has also claimed that he participated in the assassination plot to kill Kennedy. Some observers believe he is among the "tramps" photographed after their arrest in the railyards behind the Grassy Knoll. Incredibly, no records were kept of the men who were arrested.

Missing from the official death list – only because he survived a gunshot wound in the head in January, 1964 – is Warren Reynolds.[84] Reynolds was a witness to the Tippit shooting. He followed the killer for a block, and swore that it was not Oswald. Two days after he was interviewed by the FBI, he was shot in the place where he worked.[85] The prime suspect was Darrell Wayne Garner, who was released on the alibi given by Betty Mooney MacDonald, who was shortly found hanging in a jail cell.[86]

MANY MORE DEATHS

Before the Final Report of the Warren Commission was issued, eight persons directly or indirectly connected with the assassination died. Seven of the eight deaths were violent. There were many more deaths in the next three years or so.

Edward Benevides is presumed to have been killed by mistake in

February, 1964, in place of his brother, Domingo, who had witnessed the murder of officer Tippit. Domingo's life had been threatened before Edward's murder.[87]

Lt. Cmdr. William Bruce Pitzer was found shot to death in his office at Bethesda Naval Hospital on October 29, 1966. The government ruled that his death was a suicide, and Maryland authorities were unable to investigate properly. An autopsy was performed at Bethesda, but it was kept secret and neither researchers nor even his widow have been able to obtain the autopsy report. All reports indicate it was murder. Pitzer may have taken extensive films at the autopsy. Dennis David, a medical corpsman present at the autopsy, was a friend of Lt. Cmdr. Bruce Pitzer, who he said "filmed in detail the Kennedy autopsy." Pitzer "was shot with a 45-caliber pistol... I've always believed he was murdered," David said. All records of this tragedy have been covered up. In 1988, co-author Livingstone interviewed the family of Bruce Pitzer, who remain convinced that he was killed and did not commit suicide.[88] Pitzer, trained as an X-ray technician, may have had something to do with the X-rays which we find to be fake. He was deeply troubled by Kennedy's death.

Gary Underhill was a former CIA agent, and the former military affairs editor of *Life Magazine*. He was very well known in Washington and at the Pentagon. He fled Washington shortly after the assassination and told his friends that the Far Eastern group in the CIA was involved in the President's murder. He was shot, execution style, on the left side of the head. Though he was right-handed, his death on May 8, 1964, was ruled a suicide.[89]

Antonio Veciana, a star witness before the House Committee, was shot at and narrowly escaped death.[90]

Before former Deputy Sheriff Roger Craig shot himself, he was seriously injured when his car engine mysteriously exploded.[91] Craig was with Boone and Weitzman when they found the rifle in the Book Depository. Craig wrote, "Deputy Eugene Boone and I found the rifle which I might add was a 7.65 Mauser, so stamped on the barrel."[92] Weitzman signed an affidavit to this effect.[93]

When Craig was pushed to the point of suicide by joblessness, ostracism, poverty and fear, he left a suicide note that said, "I am tired of this pain."

Guy Banister, a major figure in this case, and a former FBI man well connected with the Office of Naval Intelligence, died, along with his partner Hugh Ward, within a few days of the Warren Commission's completion of its hearings.[94] Some say Banister had a bullet hole in his body. Strange that these two men, who figure so prominently in this story, should die at that precise moment in 1964.

Hugh Ward did not die alone. He was the pilot of a plane which crashed in Mexico, killing Mayor DeLesseps Chep Morrison of New Orleans.[95] Connections with the State of Louisiana seem to have spelled death for many people in this case.

In addition, Clay Shaw himself seems to have died in very mysterious circumstances, in New Orleans.[96] Shaw had been indicted and tried by New Orleans District Attorney Jim Garrison for conspiracy in the murder of President Kennedy. He denied at the time that he was intimately connected to the CIA, but this was later confirmed.*

"Before Shaw was reported dead, a neighbor observed an ambulance pulling up in front of the Shaw home. Then two ambulance attendants carried a stretcher with a figure on it covered by a sheet into the house. The two men then quickly left with an empty stretcher and a few hours later Shaw was reported 'found dead in his home alone'." The body was embalmed before the coroner could examine the body and determine the cause of death.

Maurice Brooks Gatlin, Sr., was an associate of Guy Banister, involved with the CIA, and was a legal counsel to the Anti-Communist League of the Caribbean. He either fell or was pushed from a window in Panama in 1964. He said once that he had $100,000 of CIA money for a Right Wing group in France that was going to kill President de Gaulle.[97]

The following also died in shootings: Carlos Prio, the former President of Cuba, was shot to death one week after George DeMohrenschildt died of a gunshot wound. The Assassinations Committee wanted to talk to him as well.[98]

Regis Kennedy, an FBI agent who seems deeply involved in this case, died in 1978 shortly after talking to the Assassinations Committee. William Sullivan, a top assistant to J. Edgar Hoover, whom the Committee wanted to speak to, was shot to death in 1977 during what

---

*It was confirmed by Victor Marchetti, former executive of the CIA and the author of *The CIA and the Cult of Intelligence*.

He reported that Director Richard Helms was very concerned about the case and Shaw's cover.

appeared to be a liquidation of the entire high command of the FBI. Six top men died in six months in 1977.[99]

Also dead by gunshot is William Pawley, who worked with John Martino. Pawley figured most prominently in the Cuban aspect of these affairs, and persuaded Clare Booth Luce to finance anti-Castro Cubans.[100]

Martino had begun to talk about these things, but then died of a "heart attack." He claimed personal knowledge of the plot to kill the President. He said, "The anti-Castro people put Oswald together. Oswald didn't know who he was working for – he was just ignorant of who was really putting him together. Oswald was to meet his contact at the Texas Theatre," (the movie house where Oswald was arrested)[101] in what appears to have been a setup to kill him while he would try to escape. "There was no way we could get to him. They had Ruby kill him."

But all of these bodies did not convince Ms. Hess or the Committee, which said that, "our final conclusion on the issue is that the available evidence does not establish anything about the nature of these deaths which would indicate that the deaths were in some manner, either direct or peripheral, caused by the assassination of President Kennedy or by any aspect of the subsequent investigation."[102] Really?

President and Mrs. Kennedy arrive in Dallas November 22, 1963.

The Warren Commission's version of the assassination.

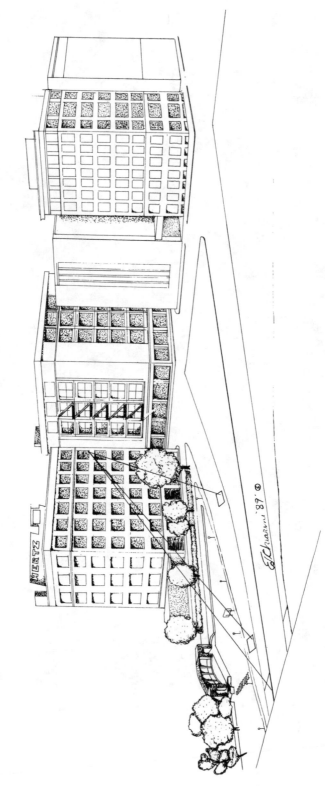

A–Only three shots were fired.
B–One missed entirely, striking the south curb of Main St.
C–The 1st or 2nd caused 7 separate non-fatal wounds in 2 grown men.
D–The 2nd or 3rd struck the President in the head, killing him.
E–All three shots were fired from the sixth floor of the Texas School Book
    Depository, easternmost window.
F–Lee Harvey Oswald fired all of the shots.

Dealey Plaza showing known and suspected firing points.

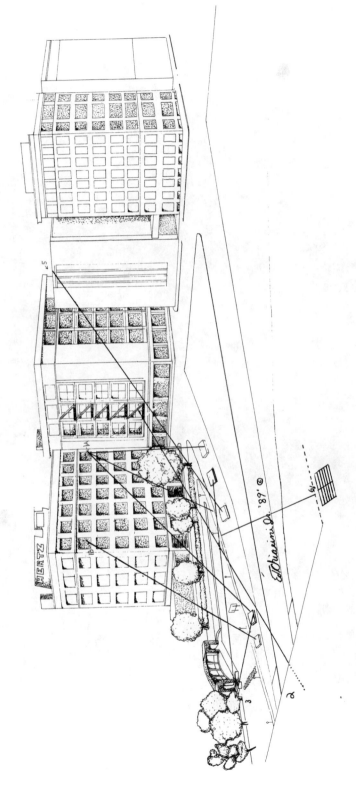

① TEXAS SCHOOL BOOK DEPOSITORY
② TRIPLE UNDERPASS
③ GRASSY KNOLL & STOCKADE FENCE
④ THE DAL-TEX BUILDING
⑤ THE DALLAS COUNTY RECORDS BUILDING
⑥ MANHOLE ON SOUTH KNOLL

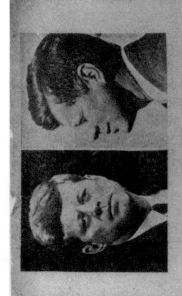

Anti JFK newspaper ad November 22, 1963.

Anti JFK handbill in Dallas, November 22, 1963.

The Motorcade before the last fatal turn.

Cropped version of the Altgens photo published by the Warren Commission. Through the windshield we can see that the President has been shot. JFK is behind the inside mirror, & Governor Connally is just to the left of the mirror.

President Kennedy sat on the rear seat with Governor Connally on the jump seat directly in front of him.

View through a rifle scope from the TSBD window, with the car at the same position it would have been at Zapruder film frame #210. This is the moment of the first possible shot from the "sniper's nest" as the car emerged from under a large oak tree which had obscured the view from the window until that point. However, both the Zapruder film and a slide taken by Phillip Willis show that the President was struck while the view from the sixth floor was obstructed.

Uncropped version of a photo taken by A.P. photographer James Altgens. Through the windshield, note that the President has been hit and is clutching his throat, with his wife's hand on his wrist, and that the Secret Service men in the follow-up car do not react. This photo proves that the car was beneath the tree during the first shots and that they came from other than the assassin's window. In a good copy of the photo, one can count the center stripes in the street back to the corner to determine exactly where the car was.

Mrs. Kennedy and Secret Service agent Clint Hill on the trunk of the Lincoln Limousine.

The motorcade on Stemmons Freeway on the way to Parkland Hospital.

"Get men on top of that over/underpass. See what happened up there. Go up to the overpass."
— Police Chief Jesse Curry, seconds after the shots.

This arrow points to a policeman running up the grassy knoll immediately after the shooting.

The police and crowd run up the Grassy Knoll, chasing the sniper they heard firing there. A policeman and others were turned back by men showing SECRET SERVICE badges. Later it was determined that there were no SECRET SERVICE agents there.

Crowd and police at the top of the knoll next to the triple overpass.

The beginnings of the crowd chasing "...a man up there running, or getting away...at the top of the slope (knoll)." He was of "average height and of heavy build" and "wearing a brown raincoat and hat." He ran "in the direction of the railroad tracks."

The police and witnesses behind the stockade fence. They found several muddy footprints and there are unconfirmed reports of an empty bullet shell. This was where eyewitness Lee Bowers saw two men just before the shooting and it's the exact spot from where the acoustics experts found that the frontal head shot originated.

A policeman examines a spot where a bullet struck during the assassination.

Deputy Sheriff Buddy Walthers and Officer Foster allow an unidentified man to pick up what witnesses and the Fort Worth "Star-Telegram" said was a bullet…, He put it in his pocket but it has never been seen again.

Walthers and unidentified man examine bullet in the grass.

The angle of the mark traces back to the Dallas County Records Building NOT the Book Depository!

James Tague was hit on the chin by a concrete fragment caused by a bullet striking the south curb of Main Street, near the end of the shooting. (Inset) Tague a moment after the shooting.

The curb where a bullet struck.

The sidewalk alongside the President's car, where a bullet struck.

Two different views of the "sniper's window" estimated to have been taken at 15 and 30 seconds after the shooting. Note the movement of the boxes between the two pictures and the additional shape in the right side area in the extreme blow-up on the right. Note too that the window was only open about half as far as it could go. Lee Oswald was encountered in the second floor lunchroom 72 to 90 seconds after the assassination by TSBD superintendent Roy S. Truly and Officer Marion L. Baker. He was calmly drinking a Coke. He was not out of breath and was calm. It was not possible for Oswald to have descended five floors in that time, particularly if he stopped to rearrange boxes.

One representation of the book cartons in the sniper's nest. There were about a half dozen different versions in all. Each labelled as if it was the true representation of the box positions.

Another version of the sixth floor "Sniper's Nest." Note the change in the boxes.

(Left and below) Showing where a bullet fragment cracked the limousine's windshield.

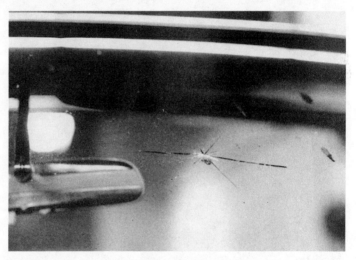

Bullet strike in the chrome just above the windshield of the President's limousine.

A rifle found in the Texas School Book Depository.

One of several? There were reports of three or four rifles being found in and around the Texas School Book Depository besides the Italian Mannlicher-Carcano 6.5 (which when found was reported as being a German Mauser 7.65).

"Henry, the Secret Service told me that they had taken care of everything – there's nothing to worry about."

– John Kennedy to Henry Gonzalez
on November 21, 1963

CHAPTER 8

THE SECRET SERVICE PROTECTION

Why was a man 54 years old, whose reflexes were slow, allowed to drive the Presidential limousine? The time between the first *admitted* shot and the last shot was not just six seconds. It was actually 8.3 seconds. (From the first to the last of the six actually recorded shots, 10.5 seconds elapsed.) What did Secret Service driver Bill Greer do during that time? Did he speed off at the first shot as Secret Service procedure required?

No! In fact, Greer all but stopped the car and let the shooting go on. We are told that there was a lapse of 7.4 seconds between the second and third shots, although there is evidence of additional shots during that time. What did any of the Presidential guards do? We can see them in the photos on the follow-up car, standing impassively on the running boards – doing nothing at all, while the President is clearly being hit. LBJ's guards seem to be reacting several cars back, though, and protecting him.[1] "These men had traveled 200,000 miles with the President. Somewhere along the line, they had neglected the first rule of security: They had lost their reflexes."[2]

Clint Hill was the first to react, when he ran up to the car after everything was over, and it took him about 12 seconds. The cars crept along at 10 or 12 miles per hour.

127

"Ten hours after the assassination, Secret Service Chief James Rowley knew that there had been three gunmen, and perhaps four, firing in Dallas that day, and later on the telephone Jerry Behn remarked to Forrest Sorrels (head of the Dallas Secret Service) 'It's a plot.' 'Of course,' was Sorrel's reply. Robert Kennedy, who had already interrogated Kellerman, learned that evening from Rowley that the Secret Service believed the President had been the victim of a powerful organization," Hepburn writes.[3] Secret Service guard Roy Kellerman sat in the front seat of JFK's car, along with the driver.

Former Colonel Fletcher Prouty, who has not been afraid to describe the true nature of this assassination as a coup by what he calls the *Secret Team*, handled Secret Service details for President Eisenhower. Prouty says that Kennedy was deliberately stripped of his security, and the plotters were aware that he would have no protection that day in Dallas.

STRIPPED OF SECURITY

The bubble, even if it had been on the car, would not have protected the President, for it was *not* bullet-proof. That was just a dodge. What was wrong was everything else: No-one was watching the windows of the buildings, there were no Secret Service men in Dealey Plaza, and the manholes and the parade route were not checked. Senator Yarborough, who was just a few cars behind JFK's, said that "...All of the Secret Service men seemed to me to respond very slowly, with no more than a puzzled look. Knowing something of the training that combat infantrymen and Marines receive, I am amazed at the lack of instantaneous response by the Secret Service when the rifle fire began."[4] The President could easily have been saved. The wound in the throat was only minor. Seven or eight seconds were to pass before he was hit fatally, and the car all but stopped. No-one moved.

"Whenever DeGaulle travels by car, he is protected by forty-seven motorcycle policemen spread out in rows. Several police cars precede and follow the Presidential vehicle, and the car immediately following the President contains a sharpshooter and a photographer equipped with an automatic Japanese camera...

"There were only four motorcycle policemen at Dallas and all were following President Kennedy's car, making them totally ineffective. The role of a motorcycle policeman in this case is 1) to make it difficult to fire at the President from a crowd, and 2) to stop anyone who tries approaching the car."[5]

The Assassinations Committee found that "The Secret Service was deficient in the performance of its duties."[6] "The fact was, however, that two threats to assassinate President Kennedy with high-powered rifles, both of which occurred in early November, 1963, were not relayed to the Dallas region."[7]

THE PARTY THE NIGHT BEFORE

The House Assassinations Committee "reexamined the allegation that several had been out drinking the evening before and the morning of the assassination. Four of the nine agents alleged to have been involved were assigned to the motorcade and had key responsibilities as members of the President's follow-up car. The supervisor of the agents involved advised that each agent reported for duty on time, with full possession of his mental and physical capabilities and was entirely ready to perform his assigned duties. Inspector Thomas Kelly, who was in charge of an evaluation of Secret Service performance in the assassination, testified before the Committee that an investigation of the drinking incident led to a conclusion that no agent violated any Secret Service rule."[8]

Secret Service regulations state that "all members of the White House detail and special agents cooperating with them on Presidential and similar protective assignments are considered to be subject to call for official duty at any time while in travel status... Therefore, the use of intoxicating liquor of any kind, including beer and wine, by members of the White House detail and special agents cooperating with them or by special agents on similar assignments, while they are in travel status, is prohibited... Violation or slight disregard... will be cause for removal from the service." None of those men were fired or even reprimanded.

"In an effort to reach its own conclusion about the drinking incident, the Committee reviewed film coverage of the agents' movements at the time of the shooting. The Committee found nothing in the reactions of the agents that would contradict the testimony of the Secret Service officials."[9]

The owner of the bar where they were drinking (the Cellar), Pat

Kirkwood, said, "After midnight the night before, some reporters called me from the Press Club, which didn't have a license to sell drinks after midnight. Said they had about 17 members of the Secret Service and asked if they could bring them to my place. I said sure. About 3:30 in the morning, these Secret Service men were sitting around giggling about how the firemen were guarding the president over at the Hotel Texas. That night got the Cellar mentioned in the Warren Report. But we were involved in the Kennedy thing in other ways. Jack Ruby used to come over Friday nights and steal my girls. Lee Harvey Oswald washed glasses for two nights at the San Antonio Cellar.... We didn't say anything, but those guys were bombed. They were drinking pure Everclear (alcohol)."[10]

Two of the Kirkwoods' closest friends were Lewis McWillie and Bennie Binion, both former Dallas-Fort Worth area gamblers. McWillie was one of Jack Ruby's closest friends, and had visited him in Cuba. "McWillie consolidated his Syndicate connections through his association in Havana with Santos Trafficante, well-known Syndicate member, of Tampa, Florida; Meyer Lansky; Dino Cellini and others who were members of, or associates of, The Syndicate." Here is an important connection between the underworld, as Jim Marrs writes, Pat Kirkwood – the owner of the bar where the Secret Service men had been drinking, and his father – and "Some of the wealthiest and most powerful men in Texas... Sam Rayburn (Speaker of the House of Representatives at the time), H.L. Hunt, John Connally, Clint Murchison, and L.B.J."[11]

THE DIRECT ROUTE

The Committee tells us, "As the Dallas SAIC Forrest Sorrels told the Warren Commission, he selected the Main-Houston-Elm turn through Dealey Plaza because it was the 'most direct' route to the Trade Mart." We are told that rather than go straight down Main Street, which would have forced the motorcade to make a difficult reverse turn to get on the Freeway, the detour was decided upon.[12] "However, this... failed to make clear that the Trade Mart was accessible from beyond the triple overpass in such a way that it was not necessary to enter the Elm Street ramp to the expressway. The motorcade could have progressed westward through Dealey Plaza on Main Street, passed under the underpass, and then proceeded on Industrial Boulevard to the Trade Mart." Assistant Dallas Police Chief George Lumpkin told the Secret Service that the Industrial Boulevard route was not good because it was "filled with winos and broken pavement." "Advance agent Lawson informed Committee investigators that he had nothing to do with the selection of the Main-Houston-Elm turn before November 14... Sorrel's Warren Commission exhibit no. 4 suggested that both men drove the entire route on November 18. It is not certain that both men knew about the turn earlier than this date."[13]

As for the dispute about the car's bubble, we are told that Bill Moyers, the President's press assistant, had been on the phone to Mrs. Harris, informing her that the President did not want the bubble. He told Harris to "get that Goddammed bubble off unless it's pouring rain."[14]

Captain Lawrence of the Dallas Police talked about the meeting with the Secret Service concerning the distribution of the motorcycle police in the motorcade. He said that the Secret Service changed the order. "Lawrence said there would be four motorcycles on either side of the motorcade immediately to the rear of the President's vehicle. Mr. Lawson stated that this was too many, that he thought two motorcycles on either side would be sufficient, about even with the rear fender of the President's car. Lawrence was instructed to disperse the other two along each side of the motorcade to the rear."[15]

"There are several instances of failure by motorcycle officers to adhere to Lawrence's final plan involving two cycles on each side and to the rear of the Presidential limousine."[16]

"The Secret Service's alteration of the original Dallas Police Department motorcycle deployment plan prevented the use of maximum possible security precautions. The straggling of Haygood and Baker, on the right rear area of the limousine, weakened security that was already reduced due to the rearward deployment of the motorcycles and to the reduction of the number of motorcycles originally intended for use.

"Surprisingly, the security measures used in the prior motorcade during the same Texas visit show that the deployment of motorcycles in Dallas by the Secret Service may have been uniquely insecure.

"...It may well be that by altering Dallas Police Department Captain Lawrence's original motorcycle plan, the Secret Service deprived Kennedy of security in Dallas that it had provided a mere day before in Houston."

"Besides limiting motorcycle protection, Lawson prevented the Dallas Police Department from inserting into the motorcade, behind the Vice-Presidential car, a Dallas Police Department squad car..."[17]

"Lawson was asked by the Committee why... he made no mention ... of the Dallas Police Department homicide car that Curry believed on November 14, to have been included and whose absence Curry protested at the meeting of November 21. He answered that 'the Dallas Police Department could have put it (a Dallas Police Department car) in on their own;' that 'he could not recall who took it out;' that he was 'not sure it was scheduled to be there;' and that 'he didn't know who canceled the Dallas Police Department car because he didn't know who decided to include it.' "[18]

After the President was allowed to be killed, "An exasperating aspect of the entire affair was the strange manner in which the Secret Service conducted itself before, during, and after the event... the evidence received by the FBI was given to the Warren Commission... crucial evidence in the hands of the Secret Service was kept from the Warren Commission..." wrote Charles Wilber, M.D.

THE JAMMED MICROPHONE

A motorcycle microphone was stuck open for eight straight minutes beginning 30 seconds before the firing started, preventing communications on that channel. "Is something the matter with channel 1?" " '1' seems to be... have his mike stuck... there is a motorcycle officer up on Stemmons with his mike open on Channel 1. Could you send someone up there to tell him to shut it off?" (Dispatcher) (190:) "I'm up on Stemmons. I'll check all these motorcycle radios."

There was no way to know who had jammed radio communications this way, or where the officer was; least of all could they have known he was on Stemmons.

Why did one of three lead motorcycle policemen riding abreast (apparently H.D. Freeman) separate himself from the motorcade in front of the Texas School Book Depository? This is clearly seen in the Zapruder film of the assassination. No-one to this day knows for sure who it was or why it happened.

MORE CONNECTIONS

It is worthwhile to remember that the Mayor of Dallas was Earle Cabell, and his brother was General Charles Cabell, who had been the Deputy Director of the CIA, in charge of clandestine operations. Clandestine Operations people run the CIA, rather than intelligence analysts. General Cabell was fired by President Kennedy along with the other top men in the CIA after the Bay of Pigs disaster.[19] There is reason to believe that Cabell worked to undermine President Kennedy's Secret Service protection.[20] New Orleans District Attorney Jim Garrison certainly believed this to be true. The father and grandfather of the Cabell brothers had been sheriffs of Dallas, and so they had considerable influence within the CIA and the city of Dallas. Cabell later went to work for Howard Hughes, and "reportedly worked closely with Robert Maheu." He also worked closely at times with E. Howard Hunt of CIA and Watergate fame.[21] Significantly, William Guy Banister, a former FBI agent who worked closely with the CIA and ONI (Office of Naval Intelligence) and who appears to be implicated in the conspiracy in some way (he last lived in New Orleans, where he died in a suspicious manner) also worked closely with Maheu. Maheu figured prominently in Watergate and the fall of Richard Nixon, and CIA assassination plots against Castro. Maheu was closely intertwined with important Mafia and criminal figures, such as Johnny Roselli and Jimmy Hoffa, who are implicated in the assassination of the President.

LETTING IT HAPPEN

Colonel Fletcher Prouty, who has considerable knowledge of the CIA, says, "No one has to direct an assassination – it happens. The active role is played secretly by *permitting* it to happen. Kennedy was killed by the break-down of the protective system that should have made an assassination impossible. Once insiders knew that he would not be protected, it was easy to pick the day and the place... those responsible for luring Kennedy to Dallas were not even in on the plan itself." They didn't have to be: "All the conspirators had to do was to let the right 'mechanics' know."[22]

Former Chief of Police Jesse Curry writes, "The next day, Thursday (November 14, 1963), the planning for the President's motorcade security began to take shape. At that time, Assistant Chief Charles Batchelor and I met with Mr. Winston G. Lawson, the Washington representative of the Secret Service, and Mr. Forrest Sorrels, the Dallas Agent in charge of Secret Service activities. In this meeting it became very clear that Mr. Lawson would emerge as the central figure and primary planner of all security arrangements..."[23]

"In what could be a coincidence, Secret Service Agent Winston Lawson, who was responsible for selecting the route of the motorcade in Dallas... had been an Army counterintelligence agent."[24] The Assassinations Committee found that on November 22, 1963, security precautions were "uniquely insecure," and Lawson was responsible for many of those precautions. Chapter 9 discusses several other Army intelligence connections in this case. It would appear the early information given to the police about Oswald came from local Army Intelligence.[25]

WHO CALLED OFF THE SECURITY?

Colonel Fletcher Prouty told the authors, "This is the greatest single clue to that assassination. Who had the power to call off or drastically reduce the usual security precautions that always are in effect whenever a President travels?... The power source that arranged that murder was on the inside... They had the means to reduce normal security and permit the choice of a hazardous route. It also has had the continuing power to cover up that crime."*

Penn Jones Jr., editor of the journal of assassination research, *The Continuing Inquiry*, wrote: "It was Jack Puterbaugh who made the decision to hold the luncheon in the Trade Mart 'because of the proximity to Love Field', and it was Puterbaugh who made the decision to take the un-authorized and unnecessary detour in Dealey Plaza."[26] Originally, the limousine would have proceeded straight down Main Street when it came to the end of the business district, and then gone directly onto Stemmons Freeway. Ordinarily, Secret Service regulations provide that the Presidential limousine is to proceed at a good speed and not take unnecessary or hazardous routes which would slow it down. The procedural manual requires the car to move at 44 miles an hour.[27]

*See also *The Anatomy of Assassination*, by Fletcher Prouty, p. 208-9.

But the route was changed so that the car made a right turn at Houston Street, at the end of the business district, and after a short block, made a left turn onto Elm Street, which led it towards and past the School Book Depository and down a small hill beneath the triple underpass. This was a perfect ambush site.

Although a number of Secret Service men were assigned to the Trade Mart, none were placed in Dealey Plaza.[28] A few good guards would have prevented the assassination.[29]

But what actually happened in the motorcade was that one of the motorcycles, seen in the Zapruder film, ahead of the limousine, leaves the motorcade entirely when it is beginning the final turn down Elm Street. This man is in the lead and simply disappears, going straight. He has left the motorcade. This evidently confuses one of the other cyclists with him. The motorcade has slowed to eight miles an hour in making the final turn – the fatal turn.[30]

Just before this turn, a killer in the alleged "assassin's window" had a clear shot at the President, unobstructed, as the car came *towards* him for one whole block, very slowly.[31] The cars had only moved at 12 miles an hour that day. J. Edgar Hoover, when asked why the assassin did not fire at this time, but waited until the cars were going away from him, said that there was a tree in the way. Hoover told the Warren Commission, "The reason for that is, I think, the fact there are some trees between his window on the sixth floor and the cars as they turned and went through the park." There was no tree remotely near this field of view.[32]

"Assistant Chief Batchelor would coordinate the security pre-operation between various elements and agencies,"[33] Dallas Police Chief Curry says. Batchelor and Secret Service Agents Sorrels and Lawson drove along the parade route in advance. "As Lawson suggested the speeds and timed the route, Assistant Chief Batchelor wrote down the number of men to be assigned at each intersection."[34] But there was no-one in Dealey Plaza – no-one looking at the windows, checking the manholes, the rooftops.[35]

The limousine was supposed to be seventh in line, but somehow ended up behind the lead car.[36] It could not go faster than the lead car, with Police Chief Curry in it.

The press bus usually goes just ahead of the President, and it was supposed to in this motorcade. But it ended up at the very end of the motorcade, the fourteenth vehicle.[37] This of course prevented the press from filming the assassination.

Who was responsible?

Prouty writes, "And when those rifles crackled over Dealey Plaza in Dallas, Texas on November 22, 1963 and John F. Kennedy's brain was splattered across the road, they had made their move into the big time. They took over control of the President and of the Presidency. The man they killed was no longer a problem and they had made certain that his successor, Lyndon Johnson, heard and remembered the sound of those guns. It is the sound of those guns in Dallas, and their ever-present threat, which is the real mechanism of control over the American government."[38]

ABRAHAM BOLDEN

Finally, there is the sad story of the first black man to work for the United States Secret Service, Abraham Bolden. He was appointed by President Kennedy, and was stationed at the White House. He said that White House Secret Service operations were terribly lax, and that he was transferred to the Chicago office for trying to blow the whistle.

In Chicago, Bolden stated that he received an FBI teletype shortly before November 1, 1963 detailing a plot by four men to shoot the President in Chicago with high-powered rifles. The FBI denies that there ever was such a teletype, and there seems to be no record of it. Bolden says that two of the subjects were arrested and detained in the Secret Service office in Chicago on November 1. Bolden was shortly indicted, tried, and imprisoned for a long time on trumped-up charges of accepting a bribe.

Bolden said that word had reached the Secret Service that Kennedy was to be assassinated by four Cuban gunmen. All of the agents in the Chicago office were involved in the investigation, but no records remain, and no-one seems to remember anything about it. Bolden claims that he was framed because he tried to tell the story of the plot he knew about to Warren Commission Counsel Lee Rankin.[39] He made the call from a White House telephone, which he says was a fatal error. He was immediately detained, taken to Chicago within 24 hours, and criminal charges were placed against him at once.

It has been difficult to confirm from Chicago Secret Service officials the threat about which Bolden tried to inform the Warren Commission, and they have refused to comment.

The influence of the Secret Service over Marina Oswald began shortly *before* her husband was murdered, when they arranged for her to be hidden from other government agencies,[40] putting her up in a motel owned by the Great Southwest Corporation, which was controlled by the Wynne family of Dallas, and by the Rockefellers.[41] The Secret Service then helped arrange for the motel's manager, a Wynne family employee (James Herbert Martin), to resign and become Marina's manager.[42] "Wynne was under Federal investigation concerning government funds he was receiving through a Murchison family corporation, some of which ended up as payoffs to the law firm of Bobby Baker."[43] Martin and his lawyer found $25,000 for Marina. It then appeared that former CIA employee Isaac Don Levine was coaching her before her testimony to the Warren Commission.[44] Norman Redlich's Warren Commission memo of February 28, 1964, stated that, "Marina has repeatedly lied... on matters which are of vital concern." And "Martin had his own contacts with men on the fringes of the underworld, including Jack Ruby."[45]

Men were seen seconds after the assassination on the Grassy Knoll showing Secret Service identification, and the Secret Service denied that any of their men were there.

It is significant that the Secret Service and other agencies failed to act on information concerning both the plot alleged by Bolden and that of the Milteer plot known to the Miami Police. Both leads provided information that a group of conspirators planned to shoot the President, yet no action was taken. Given the behavior of the Secret Service the night before, during the early morning hours prior to the assassination, during the assassination itself, and after the assassination in taking the body at gunpoint from the Texas authorities, the Secret Service is open to suspicion. This suspicion is heightened by their involvement with Marina Oswald, their destruction of film during the autopsy, and their refusal to give up any of the evidence which ultimately fell into their hands.

e means of defense against foreign danger historically have become the instruments of tyranny at home."

– James Madison

CHAPTER 9

LEE HARVEY OSWALD

"These people have given me a hearing without legal representation or anything," Oswald said.

"Did you shoot the President?"

"I didn't shoot anybody, no sir... I'm just a patsy."[1]

Another newsman again asked Oswald if he had shot the President. "I don't know what you're talking about. My wife and I like the Presidential family... They are interesting people... I am not a malcontent. Nothing irritated me about the President." Marina Oswald and George DeMohrenschildt, who were closest to Oswald, insist that he very much liked President Kennedy, right up to his death.

Police Chief Jesse Curry wrote: "Oswald's response was typical: 'I don't know what you're talking about, what's the idea of this? What are you doing this for?' " Ordinarily, assassins are proud of their crimes and admit them at once.

Then they began the transfer of Oswald to another jail, and in the middle of this, as Jack Ruby was coming down the ramp, Jesse Curry writes: "I was called to take a phone call from Dallas Mayor Cabell in my office... I stayed in my office to give the report to Mayor Cabell," while Oswald was being killed.

"Witnesses to the shooting wondered if there wasn't a gleam of recognition in Oswald's eye when Ruby stepped out from the newsmen..." Curry wrote.[2]

The Assassinations Committee found that "Lee Harvey Oswald fired three shots at President John F. Kennedy. The second and third shots he fired struck the President. The third shot he fired killed the President."[3] Note carefully the manner in which this is written. The repetition of "he" as in the "shots he fired... the third shot he fired..." This assertiveness in itself must be mistrusted, and especially the repetition of the word "he" is abnormal and suspicious.

There has never been any hard evidence either placing Oswald in the "assassin's window" or demonstrating that he fired the rifle. In fact, extensive evidence indicates that he did not shoot anyone that day.

"According to a former FBI agent and a current intelligence insider, only half the CIA's documents on Oswald were surrendered... Why? What was Oswald's connection with the U.S. Intelligence community?" Steve Parks asked in *The Baltimore Sunday Sun* on November 21, 1976.

"The Office of Naval Intelligence contacted Oswald while at Atsugi sometime during 1958. Oswald then taught himself fluent Russian in his first year as a Marine. No ordinary Marine could possibly have the time to do that without going to a high-powered military language School. He was stationed at the Top Secret U-2 Spy base at Atsugi, Japan, and preached that 'Marxist morality is the most rational' in history and that Communism is 'the best system in the world today.' " His buddies called him "Oswaldkovitch."

The Marines did nothing about removing this "com-symp" from the intelligence base. Instead, he received further training in Taiwan in 1958 for six weeks. He was given a new pay status, and his pay records show that he was sent to Taiwan, but the rest of his service records conceal that he was ever there.

District Attorney Jim Garrison said, "The Warren Commission indicated to you and to the American people that Oswald must have learned Russian on his bunk at night, studying, because he was such a Marxist, such a Communist, he wanted to get over to Russia, and yet a slip of the tongue occurred during the testimony of Commander Folsom – if you look at the Folsom testimony you'll find him referring to Oswald's grade in an Armed Forces Russian examination. P.R.T. 21, Practical Russian Test 21, United States Army Examination. He was taught Russian by the United States government.

"You will recall that Oswald is supposed to have been a defector to the Soviet Union when he was discharged from the U.S. Marines, and yet one of his first jobs on his return from Russia was at Jagger, Stover, Childs, a company which did high level, high security work for the United States government, including photography and special kinds of mapwork. In 1963, when this communist defector sought a passport, he got one in 24 hours."[4]

The facts suggest that Oswald was trained as an agent. The House Assassinations Committee found that many of Oswald's military records had disappeared.

Oswald had requested a discharge several months before it was due, and to everyone's amazement, got it in eleven days.[5] A top secret Warren Commission memo says "He undoubtedly obtained the discharge fraudulently."

OSWALD IN RUSSIA

As soon as Oswald was discharged, he very quickly left the country for London on September 21, 1959. He claimed he was going to the Albert Schweitzer College in Switzerland. Oswald arrived in Southampton on October 9. He lied to customs, saying he would stay in London one week, then go to Switzerland. The next day, he flew to Helsinki, Finland, on a private or military flight, which could have only been arranged by government agents. There were no commercial flights to Helsinki that day.

On October 14, he obtained a visa to the Soviet Union, arriving in Moscow by train on October 16. He told his tourist guide that he wished to defect to the Soviet Union. There were a total of seven U.S. defectors that year to Russia and the Russians were wary of them, considering them potential spies.

Oswald had special knowledge of the latest in U.S. radar, and the U2 spy planes flying missions over the U.S.S.R. and China. Nevertheless, the Russians denied him entry. Oswald slashed his wrists, and after release from the hospital, went to the U.S. Embassy, told them he wished to renounce his citizenship, and threatened to reveal the military secrets he had. Oswald was evidently speaking for the Russian microphones surely planted in the embassy, for he seemed to be "following a pattern of behavior in which he had been tutored by person or persons unknown... that he had been in contact with others before or during his Marine Corps tour who had guided him and encouraged him in his action," according to John A. McVickar, the U.S. Embassy Vice Consul.

The trick worked. Oswald was admitted to the Soviet Union as a stateless person and sent to Minsk, where he got a "free apartment, a job in a radio plant, and a higher salary than the plant manager."

HOME AGAIN

Oswald was quiet for a couple of years. He then wrote the U.S. Embassy asking for his passport back and stating that he wished to go home. He had met Marina Prusakova, 19, a lovely young girl, at a dance. She lived with her uncle Ilya, a colonel, it is believed, with the KGB. They were married on April 30, 1961.

The State Department loaned them $435.71 and overlooked Oswald's previous letter renouncing his citizenship, exempted Marina from U.S. immigration laws, and in direct contradiction of orders from the FBI and the State Department, returned his passport to him some months before Oswald was to travel West. J. Edgar Hoover didn't want the passport given to Oswald for fear the Russians would substitute their own "Oswald." Intelligence agencies in those days, the CIA included, could or would attempt to convince even a substituted agent's mother that he was in fact her own son when he wasn't. Sometimes it worked.

Marguerite Oswald insisted that her son was a government agent even then and right up to the time he died.

Oswald's passport doesn't indicate that he ever crossed the border, after leaving Moscow by train, June 1, 1962. "They crossed the border at Brest on June 2. Two days later, they departed from Holland on the *SS Maasdam*," according to the Warren Report. Marina's passport shows she crossed into West Berlin legally, but "It must be assumed he (Oswald) slipped across the border undetected," Parks writes. "The Berlin checkpoint (Helmstedt) was no place to be caught trying to come in from the cold." Any Germans who tried to get over the wall there were being shot, and it would appear that Oswald was afraid to cross, separated from Marina for fear he would be exposed as an agent, and was picked up by secret military means, possibly by helicopter.

It is generally felt among researchers that Oswald was being debriefed in Amsterdam; nothing of that kind seems to have happened when they arrived in the U.S., at a time when any traveler from behind the Iron Curtain was questioned. "It's hard to believe" that the government would not want to talk to a former Marine who had defected to the Soviet Union, threatened to give away military secrets, and who had brought back a Russian wife.

The Embassy in Moscow had sent a cable to the CIA, FBI, ONI, and INS about Oswald; the first 42 spaces are blanked out, so something important is certainly being hidden.

Oswald applied for and got his passport back a year later, almost at once. He had paid back all of the money he owed the government quite soon after returning from the Soviet Union, although an examination of his income at the time makes it difficult to imagine how he was able to do so. In addition, with Oswald's track record as a defector, it seems preposterous that he would be given his passport, unless he was on government business.

It must be assumed that Oswald had been an agent who was "sheep-dipped" in his defection*. He applied for his discharge to be upgraded to Honorable, and for re-enlistment recommendations, claiming "the special knowledge I have accumulated through my experience since release from active duty in the Naval Reserve." (He was in the Soviet Union at the time, threatening to give away U.S. military secrets and renouncing his citizenship!)

Back in the United States, Oswald associated with persons in the CIA. His associates, in an obvious attempt to discredit the FPCC (Fair Play for Cuba Committee) were from the Cuban Revolutionary Council (CRC), which was created by the CIA's Howard Hunt. Elements of this group were referred to by some, including President Johnson, as a "Murder, Incorporated."

Frank Sturgis, another CIA agent and Howard Hunt's long-time friend (both of them were later arrested in the Watergate burglary), was at the Cuban exile training camp Oswald visited near New Orleans at Lake Pontchartrain in 1963.

---

*Sheep-dipped is an intelligence term which refers to a formalized covert personnel system to conceal agents. An agent is given another name and the credentials and background to make him appear to be something he is not. Three separate parallel files are maintained: 1) A regular life file; 2) Active duty file; 3) A phony file. A CIA or a U.S. Army agent might be put through Marine Corps training without the Marines knowing that he is their agent, or an agent might be made to appear to be a defector to obtain the confidence of radical groups in the United States, as with Oswald.

Oswald's contacts with numerous agents of the government, along with his trail of post-office boxes, conflicting documents and aliases, "mark him as some kind of Intelligence operative." In the months leading up to the assassination, "Oswald look-alikes, apparently planted evidence, would incriminate him as a violent personality with leftist sympathies."[6]*

Upon studying Oswald's Russian diary, we and others believe that it could not possibly have been written by Oswald, or in fact anyone other than a forger. There are simply too many literary allusions, a vocabulary far too complex, using such words as *splendid, abound, unobtainable, especially enthusiastic* and so on, all spelled quite correctly, to have been written by someone with such bad grammar and spelling as the diary attempts to portray. Alongside numerous known letters and handwriting samples of Oswald's, the hand-printed diary is clearly fake.[8]

OSWALD'S RIFLE

No-one ever found a box of 6.5 mm bullets for Oswald's gun among his possessions after the assassination. It seems highly unlikely that he had only the four bullets that were in the clip allegedly used in the assassination. (It was alleged that only three shots were fired and the fourth shell remaining in the gun was not used.)

According to the House Committee the evidence against Oswald is as follows: "Lee Harvey Oswald owned the rifle that was used to fire the shots from the sixth floor window..."[9]

No matter how much study one does of a rifle in a picture taken from a considerable distance, as were the photos of the rifle on the way out of the Depository in the hands of police, it is very difficult to make a positive identification.

"The Warren Commission concluded that Lee Harvey Oswald owned the rifle found on the sixth floor of the Texas School Book

*Jack Ruby, who was intimately involved with big time mobsters and Cubans running guns to Cuba before the assassination, told Werner Tuteur (his prison psychiatrist) just before he died of suddenly discovered "cancer" shortly after he was granted a new trial that he knew "who had President Kennedy killed" and that he was "framed into killing Oswald."[7] Ruby had connections to the most powerful criminals in the country, starting with Al Capone, Jimmy Hoffa and Santos Trafficante and many others, some of whom were involved in the CIA plots against Castro which may have resulted in Kennedy's death.

Depository. Since the Commission further concluded that Oswald was the assassin of the President, his background is relevant." [10]

THE COMMITTEE'S CASE AGAINST OSWALD

(a) **"Biography of Lee Harvey Oswald"** To tell us that he owned the rifle, they begin with where he was born, where his family moved to, the fact that he came from a broken home, and that he was a chronic truant and emotionally disturbed. Oswald then went into the Marines, and afterwards "he traveled to the Soviet Union where he tried to become a Soviet citizen." Not that he **defected,** just traveled.

Then he married a 19-year-old Russian woman and returned to the U.S., "and soon became acquainted with a number of people in the Dallas-Fort Worth Russian-speaking community... Marina followed in November, but their marriage was plagued by intermittent feuding.

"In March," according to the Warren Commission, Oswald purchased a Mannlicher-Carcano rifle and telescopic sight from a Chicago mail order house. He also ordered a .38 caliber Smith & Wesson pistol from a Los Angeles firm..."

"According to Marina Oswald, he probably used the rifle in an attempt in April to kill Edwin A. Walker, a retired Army General who had been relieved from his post in West Germany for distributing right-wing literature to his troops..." General Walker was relieved from duty by President Kennedy. Despite Marina's testimony, Oswald's link to the Walker shooting has never been proven.

The Committee wrote in Note 11, p. 55: "Marina Oswald, because of her testimony, played a central but troubling role in the investigation of the Warren Commission. A great deal of what the Commission sought to show about Oswald rested on her testimony, yet she gave incomplete and inconsistent statements at various times to the Secret Service, FBI and the Commission. Marina's role in the Committee's investigation was less central..." [11]

The Committee's Report goes on to say, "In April 1963, Oswald went to New Orleans. Meanwhile, Marina and the baby moved to the home of a friend..." Oswald had numerous adventures, "expressed an interest in the Fair Play for Cuba Committee... went to Mexico City in the later part of September. He visited the Russian Embassy and Consulate and the Cuban Consulate there..." and after being thus established as a leftist or a Communist, has more adventures and "Shortly after the assassination of President Kennedy on November 22, 1963, Dallas Patrolman J.D. Tippit was shot and killed. At approximately 2 p.m., Lee Harvey Oswald was arrested in the Texas Theatre. He was subsequently charged in the murder of Tippit and named as a suspect in the Kennedy assassination." [12]

It might be proposed that this method of presentation, along with the long introduction in the beginning of the Report lasting twenty pages and titled **FINDINGS OF THE SELECT COMMITTEE ON ASSASSINATIONS IN THE ASSASSINATION OF PRESIDENT JOHN F. KENNEDY IN DALLAS, TEXAS, NOVEMBER 22, 1963. INTRODUCTION: THE KENNEDY PRESIDENCY IN PERSPECTIVE**, of not altogether accurate history, is intended to soften the reader up. This introductory history at the beginning of the Report tells of the many problems that occurred in the world during Kennedy's Presidency and implies how many enemies the President might have made. After first telling us what happened to Lincoln, McKinley, and Garfield, the Report goes on to say on page 28: "Southeast Asia... In November 1962, Secretary of Defense Robert McNamara announced that the United States was winning the war in South Vietnam." We were not told that three weeks before the President was shot, he had ordered the withdrawal from Vietnam to begin, with all troops to be out by 1965. [13] This is a basic reason why John F. Kennedy was murdered, and the fact that the House Assassinations Committee overlooked this in its narration of the history of that period, and instead cast doubt on the rationality of the Kennedy administration by quoting one of its members who said that the U.S. was winning there, is political.

The whole narration of Oswald's past consists of similar innuendo meant to set him up as the patsy.

"As noted, the Warren Commission had traced the chain of possession of the alleged assassination rifle and determined that the name on the money order and purchase form used to buy the rifle was 'A. Hidell,' which it determined to be an alias used by Oswald. It also determined that the rifle was sent to a Dallas Post office box rented on October 9, 1962 by Oswald. Through handwriting analysis, the Commission determined that Oswald had filled out and signed the documents relative to the purchase and receipt of the rifle. Moreover, the Commission received testimony that Oswald owned a rifle and that it was not in its usual storage place at the residence of Michael and Ruth Paine in Irving, Texas, when police searched the residence on the afternoon of November 22, 1963."

THE PALMPRINT

"Photographs of Oswald holding a rifle were also recovered from among his personal possessions, and the Commission concluded that the rifle in the photograph was the one found on the sixth floor of the book depository. A palmprint taken from the barrel of the rifle was identified as a latent palmprint of Oswald. Finally, the Commission treated as significant evidence a brown paper sack on which was identified a latent palmprint of Oswald. It contained fibers that were determined to be identical to certain fibers of a blanket in which Oswald had allegedly wrapped the rifle."

"The Committee concluded that the rifle found on the sixth floor of the book depository was the murder weapon. This determination, coupled with the Warren Commission evidence on Oswald's ownership of the rifle, if accepted, proved conclusively that Oswald was the owner of the murder weapon."[14]

It is questionable whether the rifle had ever been fired that day, let alone by Oswald. Further, Oswald may have owned or had the gun at one time, but none of this means that he fired it during the assassination. There remains powerful evidence that Oswald was not on the sixth floor at the time of the firing, nor for the preceding half hour, and there is not one shred of evidence to place him there.[15]

"Nevertheless, doubt has been cast on the evidence that Oswald owned the rifle in question. Critics of the Warren Commission have asserted that the chain of possession is meaningless, because more than one Mannlicher-Carcano was issued with the serial number 'C2766'. They have also argued that the photograph of Oswald holding the rifle is a fake and that his palmprint was planted on the barrel."[16]

There wasn't any palm print on the barrel or anywhere on the gun when the FBI got it. A few days later the Dallas police department told them they *lifted* a palm print from the rifle, and to make the case a bit stronger, said that it was beneath the barrel, between it and the stock, indicating that Oswald handled the gun only when it was disassembled,[17] if at all. Actually, we wonder if the very small part of a palm that might leave a print on a narrow rifle barrel would leave enough of a print to identify a human being, let alone a specific person. Certainly Oswald did not have time to wipe his prints from the gun after the shooting and be found in the second floor lunchroom, as he was, less than two minutes after the firing ended.[18] As well, there were no prints on the revolver they claim he had when he was arrested.

In fact, the Warren Commission doubted that the palm print allegedly lifted from the alleged murder weapon was legitimate. An August 28, 1964 memorandum from Rosen to Belmont at the FBI referred to a conversation with Rankin and said, "Rankin advised because of the circumstances that now exist there was a serious question in the minds of the Commission as to whether or not the palm print impression that has been obtained from the Dallas Police Department is a legitimate latent palm impression removed from the rifle barrel or whether it was obtained from some other source and that for this reason this matter needs to be resolved." (TCI March 1978, p. 2) Lt. Day of the Dallas Police testified before the Warren Commission: "No, Sir, I could not make a positive identification of these prints."

"The Committee decided that one way to determine whether Oswald did, in fact, own the murder weapon was to test the reliability of the evidence used by the Warren Commission to establish ownership and to subject the available evidence to further scientific analysis. The Committee posed these questions:

"Could the handwriting on the money order used to purchase the rifle and the application for the post office box be established with confidence as that of Lee Harvey Oswald? Are the photographs of Oswald holding the rifle authentic, and is that rifle the one that was found in the book depository after the assassination?"

The Committee went to its questioned documents panel. "The panel was asked to determine whether all of the documents were written by the same person...The questioned documents panel determined that the money order and the post office box application were filled out and signed by the same person and that the handwriting on them was identical to the handwriting on the two fingerprint cards..." They were the fingerprint cards he allegedly signed in New Orleans, when he was clearly acting as an agent of Guy Banister, former SAC of the FBI in Chicago. "Although Oswald was fingerprinted when he was arrested in Dallas on November 22, 1963, he refused to sign the card..." "On the basis of this analysis, the Committee determined that Oswald bought the weapon in question..."[19]

This is still shaky, since the signatures could have been forged on all the documents. As well, there is strong evidence that Oswald was acting as a government agent throughout this period, or as an agent working with Guy Banister and others with intelligence connections who used Oswald in their operations, and who probably put him up to purchasing the gun, if indeed he purchased it all.

The Committee then rushes on without any further evidence, and in the next sentence refers to "The backyard photographs... of Oswald holding the rifle, with a pistol strapped to his waist and also holding copies of *The Militant* and *The Worker* were taken by his wife in the backyard of Oswald's home... according to the testimony of Oswald's widow, Marina... There has been considerable controversy about the photographs. While in the custody of the Dallas police from November 22 to November 24, 1963, Oswald claimed that he did not own a rifle and that the photographs were composites, with his head superimposed over someone else's body. The Warren Commission, however, concluded that the photographs were authentic. Critics of the Commission have questioned the authenticity of the photos for reasons generally based on shadow inconsistencies, an indication of a grafting line between the mouth and chin, inconsistent body proportions and a disparate square-shaped chin."[20]

What the Committee refers to above is the fact that the prominent shadows on the face, beneath the nose, eyebrows, and the cleft of the chin, show that the sun is directly overhead, but that the shadows from the body standing up, along the ground, and the shadows on the ground from other objects show that part of the photo was taken at a late hour, when the shadows were long. These pictures are clearly forged, as Oswald himself said.

"To determine if evidence of fakery was present in these photographs, the photographic evidence panel first sought to determine if they could be established as having been taken with Oswald's Imperial Reflex camera."[21] There follows information on how the test was done, and "In contrast" to the panel's method, "some of the critics who claimed the photographs were faked relied on poor quality copies for their analysis. Copies tend to lose detail and include defects that impair accurate representation of the photographic image... After subjecting these original photographic materials and the camera alleged to have taken the pictures to sophisticated analytical techniques, the photographic evidence panel concluded that it could find no evidence of fakery." Nothing that this panel did resolved the clear evidence of forgery. The issues were simply ignored.

"The photographic panel found no evidence of fakery in the backyard photographs." "Thus, after submitting the backyard photographs to the photographic and handwriting panels, the Committee concluded that there was no evidence of fakery in the photographs and that the rifle in the photographs was identical to the rifle found on the sixth floor of the depository on November 22, 1963." Having pretended to resolve these issues, the Committee concluded that "Lee Harvey Oswald owned the rifle from which the shots that killed President Kennedy were fired."[22]

"4. LEE HARVEY OSWALD, SHORTLY BEFORE THE ASSASSINATION, HAD ACCESS TO AND WAS PRESENT ON THE SIXTH FLOOR OF THE TEXAS SCHOOL BOOK DEPOSITORY BUILDING."

"The Warren Commission found that Lee Harvey Oswald worked principally on the first and sixth floors of the Texas School Book Depository... He had, therefore, ready access to the sixth floor... a number of them (employees) said that they saw and heard Oswald in the vicinity of the sixth floor throughout the morning of November 22, 1963." The key words here are "vicinity" of the sixth floor, and through the "morning." The assassination occurred at 12:30 P.M. and no witness placed Oswald above the second floor after noon. In fact, he was placed consistently on the first and second floors.

PHYSICAL EVIDENCE OF OSWALD'S PRESENCE

"... Materials were examined for fingerprints, including a long, rectangular paper sack that was discovered near the southeast corner window and cartons that were found stacked adjacent to the window. The paper sack, which was suitable for containing a rifle, showed a latent palmprint and fingerprint of Oswald; one of the cartons showed both a palmprint and fingerprint identified as belonging to Oswald, and the other showed just his palmprint.

"The Committee was aware that Oswald's access to the sixth floor during the normal course of his duties would have provided the opportunity to handle these items at any time before the assassination. Nevertheless, the Committee believed that the way the boxes were stacked at the window and the proximity of the paper sack to the window from which the shots were fired must be considered as evidence indicating that he handled the boxes in the process of preparing the so-called sniper's nest and that he had used the paper sack to carry the rifle into the depository."[23]

Oswald's fingerprints were probably on nearly every box on the floor, and the above proves nothing as far as his prints on specific boxes is concerned. Anybody could have stacked the boxes in the specified manner. The trouble with the paper sack story is that there were no oil stains on the sack from the rifle, which was oily, according to the FBI.[24] Again, Oswald could have handled that and left fingerprints on it as he performed his work.

The source of the story that Oswald carried "curtain rods" to work the morning of the assassination, Buell Frazier, insisted that the package was eight inches shorter than the disassembled murder weapon.[25] His sister agreed. Frazier showed that Oswald could not have carried the rifle under his armpit, with the base in his hand, which is the way he said Oswald carried the package that morning. The disassembled rifle was 35 inches long. The fact is that the rifle, disassembled, was about one foot longer than it was humanly possible to carry in the manner described by Frazier, who drove Oswald to work.

OSWALD'S WHEREABOUTS

"He could have still been on the sixth floor at 12:30. There was no witness who said he saw Oswald anywhere at the time of the assassination, and there was no witness who claimed to have been on the sixth floor and therefore in a position to have seen Oswald, had he been there."[26] In fact, Oswald was not known to have been on the sixth floor anytime after noon.

Oswald was placed at the second floor lunchroom at 12:15. Carolyn Arnold, a co-worker, claimed that "about a quarter of an hour before the assassination, I went into the lunchroom on the second floor for a moment... Oswald was sitting in one of the booth seats on the right-hand side of the room as you go in. He was alone as usual and appeared to be having lunch. I did not speak to him but I recognized him clearly."[27] She is certain that it was at 12:15 or a little later. She told the FBI it was 12:20-12:25 (see Weisberg *Photographic Whitewash* p. 210-211 and *Dallas Morning News* 11/26/78, p. 13a, story by Earl Golz).

The motorcade was due at 12:25. If Oswald planned to kill the President, he would have been in the sniper's nest long before then. As it happened, the motorcade was five minutes late, and came by at 12:30.

It has been established that at exactly 12:15, Arnold Rowland (as well as Carolyn Walther, and Ruby Henderson) saw two men with a rifle in the sixth floor window, and this is backed up by Rowland's wife, who saw them too. They thought they were Secret Service agents.[28]

The weight of the evidence, therefore, would now indicate that Oswald was *not* the sniper.

Further evidence supports this conclusion. Nitrate tests were given to Oswald to see if he had fired a gun. They were negative for his cheeks, which indicated that he had *not* fired a rifle. His hands showed some nitrate evidence, but he could have got these deposits from handling a newspaper or many other items present in the depository. The positive results on Oswald's hands indicated he had not washed, making his cheek results all the more conclusive.[29]

Within two minutes of the last shot, Oswald was seen by three witnesses on the second floor: "Since all were outside the depository when the shots were fired, their statements that it took them about two minutes to get to the second floor were reasonable. It appeared equally reasonable that in those same two minutes Oswald could have walked from the sixth floor window to the rear stairway and down four flights of stairs to the second floor."[30] *Could* have, but it is not *likely*.

The Warren Report said Officer Baker and Roy Truly saw Oswald on the second floor 1.25 - 1.5 minutes after the shooting.[31] Re-enactments of this feat found that it was very difficult, if not impossible, to get down all that distance at a dead run in two minutes, and Oswald was not breathing hard.

Oswald was a poor shot in the Marines, and marksmanship rarely improves after leaving full time military service.[32] The finest marksmen tried to duplicate his feat and were unable to do so.[33]

In fact, the bolt of the alleged murder weapon was very difficult to work,[34] and as the evidence now stands, no-one in the world could have got off two shots in 1.6 seconds and hit anything, let alone a moving target, and certainly not with Oswald doing the shooting.

LEE HARVEY OSWALD'S OTHER ACTIONS TEND TO SUPPORT THE CONCLUSION THAT HE ASSASSINATED PRESIDENT KENNEDY

The case starts to get even thinner at this point. It seems strange that Oswald, if he was about to kill the President, would be sitting having lunch quite some distance and four floors from the "sniper's window." (and that he had no known animosity whatsoever toward the President, and in fact liked him, as has been established[35]).

We are told on page 59 of the Report that Oswald went home, changed clothes, and walked nearly a mile before allegedly shooting Tippit. "The Committee investigated the murder of Officer Tippit primarily for its implications concerning the assassination of the President. The Committee relied primarily on scientific evidence. The Committee's firearms panel determined positively that all four cartridge cases found at the scene of the Tippit murder were fired from the pistol that was found in Lee Harvey Oswald's possession when he was apprehended in the Texas Theatre thirty-five minutes after the murder."[36] There is an important note here: "Since Oswald's revolver had been partially modified to shoot different ammunition than the type it was manufactured to shoot, it was not possible for the panel to determine whether the bullets that killed Tippit were fired from it."[37] This raises once again the question as to what gun did the shooting. Do they mean an automatic pistol?

On the afternoon of the assassination, Sgt. Gerry Hill was interviewed by CBS: "What kind of weapon did he use to kill the officer with, Gerry?"[38]

"A thirty-eight snub nose that was fired twice, and both shots hit the officer in the head. PSE* tests show that Hill was lying, when he said 'fired twice,'" George O'Toole writes in *The Assassination Tapes*.

---

*PSE, or Psychological Stress Evaluator, is a type of lie detector test which is conducted from voice recordings. See O'Toole's book for an extensive discussion.

"The revolver alleged to have been found in Oswald's possession was never linked to the Tippit murder with complete certainty."[39] And Tippit was hit four times, not twice.

No evidence was ever presented that the handgun attributed to Oswald was ever fired, and there were no fingerprints on it whatsoever, indicating that it was wiped clean, and had likely been planted on Oswald.

Once again, we do not know *when* the cartridge cases were fired, since they also appeared to have been planted at the scene, and in fact were not all the same company's ammunition.[40]

"In addition, the Committee's investigators interviewed witnesses present at the scene of the Tippit murder. Based on Oswald's possession of the murder weapon a short time after the murder and the eyewitness identifications of Oswald as the gunman, the Committee concluded that Oswald shot and killed Officer Tippit. The Committee further concluded that this crime, committed while fleeing the scene of the assassination, was consistent with a finding that Oswald assassinated the President."[41] Thus, in half a page, the Committee tells us that Oswald killed Tippit. In fact, several witnesses tended to establish the opposite, that two men did the shooting, and that neither one of them was Oswald.[42]

The above section of the Report says that he was fleeing the scene of the assassination. Employees were told to go home, but "The Committee found that while most of the depository employees were outside of the building at the time of the assassination and returned inside afterwards, Oswald did the reverse; he was inside before the assassination, and afterwards he went outside. That Oswald left the building within minutes of the assassination was significant. Every other depository employee either had an alibi for the time of the assassination or returned to the building immediately thereafter. Oswald alone neither remained nor had an alibi."[43]

It does seem possible that immediately after the shooting Oswald had some idea what had really happened. He knew he had been set up as the patsy, and so went home, changed his shirt, and perhaps got his gun. The witnesses who saw two men in the upper windows of the Book Depository described their clothing, and it did not at all resemble what Oswald wore.

The FBI originally said that fibers which were found on the rifle butt *could* have come from the shirt that Oswald was wearing when he was arrested. This shirt was entirely different from the one he had on during the time of the assassination. This only means that he may have handled the rifle once when he had that shirt on, but proves nothing else.[44]

The first report the police sent out said that Tippit had been killed with an *automatic pistol*. Gerald Hill, the policeman who said it, knew the difference, and it is impossible to confuse an automatic pistol shell with that of Oswald's alleged revolver, a different type of gun.[45] In frame-ups the guns are more often than not switched. The patsy has to be linked to some weapon, and that is clearly what happened in the Tippit case. Again, there is not one shred of solid evidence linking Oswald to this crime.

Witnesses say that the killers were walking in the direction of Oswald's house.[46] It hardly seems likely that in the few minutes from the time Oswald left his house at about 1 P.M., he could have walked a mile and then doubled back. What might be more important is that Jack Ruby lived nearby, and perhaps Oswald was going to meet him or his contact in the movie theater.

The Committee presents no real evidence to say that Oswald killed Tippit. No-one ever did. We do know that a police car stopped at Oswald's house at about the time he was there, honked its horn several times, and then went on. We don't know what police car that was, but it seems likely that it was Tippit.[47]

Oswald left his house about four minutes after 1 P.M. Tippit was shot at 1:12 or thereabouts. Oswald would have to have covered 9/10 of a mile in that time on foot: There is simply no real evidence to indicate that he was there and perpetrated the murder.[48] The plotters needed to create a side issue, a flanking movement, to buttress their case against Oswald.

OSWALD: A CAPACITY FOR VIOLENCE?

On this page of the Report we learn that Oswald had a capacity for violence because he "shot Tippit," "took a shot at General Walker," and allegedly resisted arrest in the Texas Theatre. "Such evidence is supportive of the Committee's conclusion that Oswald assassinated President Kennedy."[49]

THE MOTIVE

"Finding a possible motive for Oswald's having assassinated President Kennedy was one of the most difficult issues that the Warren Commission addressed. The Commission stated that 'many factors were undoubtedly involved in Oswald's motivation for the assassination, and the Commission does not believe that it can ascribe to him any one motive or group of motives...'"[50] and this section of the report then ends after two more pages of speculation as to his possible motives.

The Warren Report tells us that shortly before the assassination, "Two Australian girls who saw Oswald on the bus to Mexico City relate that he occupied a seat next to a man who has been identified as Albert Osborne, an elderly itinerant preacher. Osborne denies that Oswald was beside him on the bus. To the other passengers on the bus it appeared that Osborne and Oswald had not previously met, and extensive investigation of Osborne has revealed no further contact between him and Oswald. Osborne's responses to Federal investigators on matters unrelated to Oswald have proved inconsistent and unreliable, and, therefore, based on the contrary evidence and Osborne's lack of reliability, the Commission has attached no credence to his denial that Oswald was beside him on the bus."[51]

Albert Osborne was really John ("Jack") Bowen, as he finally admitted to the FBI.[52] When Oswald was captured, we are told that he had a library card in his wallet with Jack L. Bowen's name on it. (This card later disappeared from the evidence.) Bowen was employed at Jaggers-Chiles-Stoval, where, of course, Oswald had worked when 602 Elsbeth Street was Oswald's claimed address.[53] Moments after the assassination, police arrested three "tramps" behind the Grassy Knoll – whom they shortly released. "Of the three so-called bums escorted by the police after the assassination of President Kennedy, one of the names used by the old man in the middle was 'Albert Alexander Osborne.' He also used 'Howard Bowen,'* and he had a son. The old man was thought to be the "House Mother" of a group of American assassins stabled in Mexico at that time."[54]

---

*Penn Jones wonders whether the CIA's Howard Osborne, whom Richard Helms named during the Watergate hearings, is the same man.

The John Bowen placed with Oswald in Mexico may well have been John Grosse, an ex-con, who was also working at Jaggers-Chiles-Stoval, a defense contractor.[55] It would certainly appear that this evidence provides a clue to the assassination, as John Bowen was not the only American linked to Oswald's trip to Mexico. CIA operative, William George Gaudet got a visa to go to Mexico along with an alleged Oswald on September 17, 1963.[56] Bowen and Gaudet provide early evidence to the careful positioning of Oswald as a "patsy."

Oswald used the name Osborne* when he ordered Fair Play For Cuba Committee pamphlets in New Orleans.[57] Gaudet went to Mexico at the same time as an alleged Oswald[58], and later admitted he knew Oswald in New Orleans.[59] The Warren Commission did not want to reveal Gaudet's link to Oswald's Mexico trip and his name was concealed from the public until an official blundered in 1975, accidently releasing his name in documents. The official reply to inquiries regarding the deleted name next to Oswald's on his visa application was, "No record of PM824084 located."[60] Gaudet later said that he had once seen Ruby in New Orleans, and that he saw Oswald with Guy Banister.[61]

"The first member of the Warren Commission to publicly voice doubt as to the Commission's conclusions cited this bus trip (that of Oswald and Osborne-Bowen to Mexico City) as a key reason for his suspicion.[62] In mid-January of 1970, the *Washington Post* reported that Senator Richard Russell indicated that he now believed that there had in fact been a secret conspiracy behind the Kennedy assassination. Senator Russell, who had also served in the important position of Chairman of the Senate CIA Oversight Committee, said of Oswald: 'I think someone else worked with him.' Russell further stated: 'There were too many things... some of the trips he made to Mexico City and a number of discrepancies in the evidence, or as to his means of transportation, the luggage he had and whether or not anyone was with him... caused me to doubt that he planned it all by himself.'"[63]

It would appear that Bowen-Osborne,* who worked with Oswald in Dallas, and who traveled constantly and extensively throughout the world, was a tail. He followed people. No-one has ever been able to

---

*Bowen-Osborne was a fanatical Nazi during the Second World War. (Summers, p. 370)

figure out his source of funds, and his cover of "itinerant preacher" was just that, a cover. It is likely that he was an intelligence agent.

The man in the photos whom the CIA first claimed was Oswald going to the Cuban and Soviet Embassies in Mexico City, which the CIA later had to admit was not Oswald, looks a lot like Jim Hicks, who was in Dealey Plaza at the time of the assassination. Some say he was the radio communications man for the snipers.[64] No-one has been able to identify the man in the CIA's pictures, but it is clearly not, as the CIA claimed, Lee Harvey Oswald.

The Oswald who went to the Cuban Consulate in Mexico City made just as much trouble as possible, so he would be sure to be remembered. The man was remembered, and the Consul, two others present, and Fidel Castro gave extensive interviews to the Assassinations Committee about that visit.[65]

The Consul, Senor Azcue, when shown a photograph of Oswald on the application form, said: "This gentleman was not, is not, the person or the individual who went to the consulate... the man who went to the consulate was a man over 30 years of age and very, very thin faced... He was blond, dark blond.

"The individual who visited the consulate is one whose physiognomy or whose face I recall very clearly. He had a hard face. He had very straight eyebrows, cold, hard, and straight eyes. His cheeks were thin. His nose was very straight and pointed."[66]

The later third Chairman of the Assassinations Committee, Louis Stokes, interviewed Premier Castro. Castro told Stokes, when he and Representative Preyer and others were in Havana: "There is something that I can guarantee. The Cuban government believes that Azcue is a serious and honest man; and that he has never said something differently from what he said the first time. I mean, he is a person you can trust."[67]

A CIA spokesman denied that the agency had a report of a meeting between Oswald and Cuban agents: "The agency is aware of only one such specific allegation, and that was debunked,"[68] he said. But David Atlee Phillips, the former CIA Station Chief in Mexico City, persisted in his allegation before the Assassinations Committee.[69]

Attorney Edwin J. Lopez, who conducted the Mexico City investigation for the House Assassinations Committee concerning the alleged Oswald visit, personally concluded that Oswald was in some way associated with the CIA, and was just a patsy. He found that an imposter had made all the "Oswald" visits to the Soviet and Cuban Embassies--partly on the basis of the CIA photos taken from three sites. He specified that the surveillance was around the clock,[70] contrary to what was claimed by David Atlee Phillips.[71]

THE FRAME

"If Oswald was framed for the murder of President Kennedy, then someone would have to have selected him for the role some time before November 22. Many skeptics have speculated that Oswald was selected from the Dallas police subversive files. But all the Dallas police authorities stoutly denied that they had a file on Oswald or had even heard of him... Yet on the afternoon of November 22, Lieutenant Revill... wrote a memorandum to Captain Gannaway about a conversation he had just had with an FBI agent concerning Oswald. Revill headed the memo, 'Subject: Lee Harvey Oswald, 605 Elsbeth Street.' Oswald never lived at that address, but he had lived at 602 Elsbeth. However, he had not lived at the Elsbeth Street address since March, 1963... If the police did not have a file on Oswald, where did Revill get the Elsbeth Street address?

"That question was asked of Lieutenant Revill by Allen Dulles when the policeman appeared before the Commission."[72] There is no answer regarding his source. Also, that afternoon a list of employees of the Texas School Book Depository was made up, and submitted by Lt. Revill. Oswald's name was at the top, with the address at 605 Elsbeth. "The Revill memorandum and the Westphal and Parks memorandum both contain an eight-month-old address, and both have the same error in the street number. Both had to come from the same source, but what was it?... If the state intelligence agency had been keeping a dossier on Oswald, they might have had an out-of-date and slightly erroneous address which they gave the Dallas police..."[73] But writer and former CIA agent George O'Toole established that there was no file other than newspaper clippings in Austin. He goes on to try to track this down, and finds that if officer Bentley "really found the Hidell identification when he examined Oswald's wallet, then he should have reported this fact in his official account of the arrest," and that Gerald

Hill and Bentley appear to be lying about calling in the information on the Hidell card when they captured Oswald. There is no record of such a call in the transcripts of the police tapes. Hill was the technical advisor for the famous CBS "documentary" on the assassination, and a former TV newsman. It seems likely that Hill and Bentley would have said something that day during their radio interviews about the false Alek Hidell alias allegedly in Oswald's wallet, which became the link with the order for the weapons (including the Mannlicher-Carcano) from the mail order houses in the name of Hidell. Interestingly enough, the Post Office threw away all records of the Hidell name used to rent the Post Office box, and they did it right after the assassination. Bentley wrote: "On the way to the City Hall I removed the suspect's wallet and obtained his name."[74]

O'Toole says, "That's it. There is nothing (on that transcript) about Alek Hidell or any other alias identification; there is nothing about calling any alias information in to the dispatcher. Bentley's report seems to imply very clearly that he found only one name on the cards in the wallet, and that name was Lee Harvey Oswald."[75]

"If Oswald was not, in fact, carrying false identification when he was arrested, did he ever use the Alek Hidell alias at any other time?"[76] O'Toole says that Oswald did, and very likely while acting as a government agent, and "he must have been framed; and either the Mannlicher-Carcano rifle was not his and had been planted on him, or else the rifle was his but had been brought to the Book Depository that day by someone else. I am inclined to believe the latter."[77] The former CIA man then concludes that the ID was planted after the assassination, which means that the authorities set it up.

CURIOUS ROLE OF ARMY INTELLIGENCE

Military intelligence would have known what the security precautions were for the President's trip to Dallas, because of their close relationship with the Secret Service. The 112th Army Intelligence Unit at Fort Sam Houston, Texas was preparing for duty in Dallas in anticipation of the President's visit, when it received orders not to report to that city.[78]

Nevertheless, Lt. Colonel George Whitmeyer, the commander of the local Army Intelligence reserve, was in the police pilot car which preceded the motorcade, and an Army Intelligence officer was with James Hosty 45 minutes before the parade, on Main Street.[79] Hosty was the FBI agent who had been to see Marina Oswald; his name and car plate number were in Oswald's notebook, and he destroyed a note allegedly written to him by Oswald. Hosty was the bridge-playing companion of General Edwin Walker's aide, Robert Surrey,[80] who printed and distributed the "Wanted for Treason" leaflets against the President the day of his visit and assassination.[81]

An Army Intelligence officer, James Powell, was trapped in the Dal Tex building after it was sealed off following the assassination. By coincidence, this is also where another suspect, Jim Braden* was arrested.[82]

"Still another Army intelligence officer turned up that afternoon, this time riding from the assassination site with Dallas Police Lieutenant Jack Revill of the criminal intelligence division.[83] Where, then, did Revill obtain the Oswald information? Most likely from the unidentified Army intelligence officer who rode with him from Dealey Plaza. For, the 112th Military Intelligence Group, which had a field office in Dallas, carried in its files information on a "Harvey Lee Oswald" residing at 605 Elsbeth Street in Dallas.[84] Army intelligence lists Oswald's address as 605 and the list submitted by Revill says 605. This helps explain why the police began searching so quickly for Oswald when no less than eleven other depository employees were missing from the building after the assassination. It suggests that Army Intelligence was responsible for alerting the Dallas Police about the designated patsy, Lee Harvey Oswald."[85]

Is it possible the men on the Grassy Knoll flashing Secret Service credentials were instead "Army intelligence agents ostensibly detailed to Presidential security for the day? Were they the assassins spotted by eyewitnesses on the scene? Why did a local Army intelligence unit claim falsely on November 22 that Oswald was a Cuban defector? We can only speculate, because the Army destroyed its files on Oswald, a fact The House Assassinations Committee called 'extremely troublesome.'"[86]

*Braden's real name was Eugene Hale Brading, a.k.a. Edgar Eugene Bradley, of Los Angeles, an ex-convict allegedly connected to the Mob in Southern California. (Dallas Sheriff's Office Nov. 22, 1963; Peter Noyes *Legacy of Doubt,* New York, Pinnacle Books 1976, p. 30, 21-22, 33-6, 96; Robert Sam Anson *They've Killed the President,* New York, Bantam 1975, P. 329-30).

OTHER CONNECTIONS

On the day of the assassination, an employee of Guy Banister told the New Orleans police and the FBI that Banister and David Ferrie were involved in the assassination. Jack Martin also said that Ferrie and Oswald were involved with each other. The National Archives reported that an "original statement of David W. Ferrie transcribed in (Warren) Commission document 205" was missing.[87]

Former CIA agent Victor Marchetti later revealed that Clay Shaw—the primary target of New Orleans District Attorney Jim Garrison's investigation – David Ferrie, and one of Garrison's Cuban suspects were in fact CIA people, and that Richard Helms had ordered others in the CIA to help them and stymie Garrison. Marchetti said that Helms was very worried about Garrison's probe.[88]

We know that Helms did all he could when he was the CIA's liaison with the Warren Commission to stymie that probe.[89] He was, of course, Howard Hunt's good friend and idol.[90]

Following the assassination, Captain Will Fritz had Oswald brought in for interrogation. Just after Oswald was arrested, Fritz was called over by Sheriff Bill Decker, and Fritz had to leave and travel nearly a mile to have a private talk with Decker because they did not want to talk on the phone. They had parted only a little while before, but in the meantime Oswald had been taken into custody. Fritz came back to his office in the City Jail Building where Oswald was being held, and met Deputy Sheriff Roger Craig outside his office. Craig looked through the glass and told Fritz that the suspect was the man he had seen escape the area of the killing. The two men entered the room where Oswald was and Fritz said: "This man saw you leave."[91] (The Warren Commission said Oswald left the Depository area by bus and cab.)

Oswald replied with agitation, "I told you people I did." Fritz said, "Calm down, son, we are just trying to find out what happened. What about the CAR?" Oswald answered, "That STATION WAGON belongs to Mrs. Paine, don't try to get her involved in this." (Emphasis ours.) Craig distinctly remembers that Fritz said "car" and Oswald replied "station wagon." "Just about this time Captain Fritz got a telephone call from Sheriff Decker requesting Fritz to come talk with him... Apparently... it was something which could not be said over the telephone or police radio. Fritz later denied to Joseph Ball of the Warren Commission that Craig was ever there."[92]

According to Craig the driver of the car was a Latin-looking man. This must be added to numerous other reports linking Latin or Cuban men to the assassination. Craig said that the driver had been arrested a moment before, and was immediately released by someone posing as a Secret Service agent. Several years later, Craig saw a picture of Edgar Eugene Bradley and thought that was the man posing as a Secret Service agent.[93] But Craig's identification of Oswald going to a car that may have belonged to Ruth Paine was printed in the *Dallas Morning News* the day after the assassination. Instead of confirming or even recording Craig's account of events, the Warren Commission accepted Captain Fritz's denial that Craig had been to his office that night. Yet newspaper photographs showed Craig in the office with Oswald.[94] David Belin of the Warren Commission came to talk to Craig in Dallas, and changed or altered Craig's testimony in 14 places.[95]

On the morning of the assassination, Craig's boss, Sheriff Bill Decker, ordered his deputies to "take no part whatsoever in the security of the Presidential motorcade."[96] Decker had a crackshot rifleman – Harry Weatherford – on top of the Dallas County Jail Building during the motorcade, close by Oswald's alleged sniper's nest. A young researcher tried to talk to Weatherford once and asked if he had shot at Kennedy. Weatherford's response was: "You little son-of-a-bitch, I kill lots of people."[97]

Mary Ferrell, another researcher in this case, reports "a mid-70's luncheon in which Fritz said, to a friend, that Lyndon B. Johnson called him the day after the assassination and said 'You've got your man, the investigation is over.' Also unresolved is the fate of Fritz' notes of his Oswald interrogations. He told the Warren Commission he kept no notes, but was not asked why. According to writer Gary Mack, the wife of one of Fritz' best friends recently told researchers that Fritz had secretly recorded his Oswald interrogations... The tapes are supposedly safe. She added that Fritz was afraid for the safety of his family and relatives, and that Oswald had admitted being a member of the Intelligence community."[98]

It appears that the Assistant Chief of Police, Charles Batchelor, who was in charge of security precautions for the motorcade and Oswald's transfer to another jail, lost both his charges. His reward was to be promoted to Chief of Police. There are indications that he brought Ruby into the police station basement to kill Oswald. But it was Lt. George Butler, an extreme Right Winger, who was in immediate charge of Oswald's transfer and who gave the "all clear" to bring the prisoner into the basement. He frequently escorted oilman H.L. Hunt to various public engagements, as former FBI agent William Turner points out in *Ramparts*.

There is speculation that Oswald might have survived Ruby's bullet, but the police took him into an office, laid him on a desk, and gave him artificial respiration. This procedure was sure to kill anyone with an abdominal wound, by aggravating the bleeding.[99]

The disputed photograph of a man whom the CIA claimed was Oswald supposedly leaving the Soviet Embassy on October 4, 1963, was described in a secret affidavit to the Warren Commission by Richard Helms. It was Helms, the liaison between the CIA and the Warren Commission (he later became the CIA's Director) who prevented Yuri Nosenko, the Russian "defector," from testifying before the Warren Commission on what he knew about Oswald in Russia. Nosenko had handled Oswald's KGB file in Russia. Nosenko, a friend of John Paisley, a CIA executive who was later murdered, was then locked in a vault and starved for three years.[100] The Assassinations Committee took extensive evidence from the CIA about the treatment of Nosenko and the value of his information.

George DeMohrenschildt, who was about to be murdered or die of a "suicide" within an hour or so of being located by both the Committee's ace investigator, Gaeton Fonzi, and Edward J. Epstein, knew Oswald quite well. DeMohrenschildt knew Oswald better perhaps than anyone in Dallas, and he had an intelligence background himself. He was a White Russian Count, and he liked and respected Oswald. DeMohrenschildt wrote a manuscript describing Oswald and their relationship, which the House Assassinations Committee published in full, and said: "Lee is innocent of Kennedy's assassination... and we proved that he was rather an admirer of Kennedy's."[101]

He goes on to say that the Warren Commission was to "distract attention of the American people from the people involved in the assassination of President Kennedy." He tells us that Oswald spoke almost flawless Russian, and other Russians "were amazed by Lee's almost perfect command of the language..." "Lee's English was perfect, refined, rather literary, deprived of any Southern accent. He sounded like a very educated American. But to know Russian as he did was remarkable – to appreciate serious literature – was something out of the ordinary." Can this be the same man who wrote Oswald's alleged diaries?[102]

The Report of the House Committee tells us on page 251 that "The Oswald who contacted the Russian and Cuban diplomatic compounds reportedly spoke broken, hardly recognizable Russian, yet there is considerable evidence that Lee Harvey Oswald was relatively fluent in this language." The Report also tells us that Silvia Duran, a secretary at the Cuban Consulate – who made what she thought was a positive identification of Oswald – described an Oswald who looked nothing like the one who died in Dallas. In spite of this, the House Committee found that it was probably Oswald who visited there.

Clearly, Oswald was no ordinary lone nut assassin.

Oswald had to have been trained in the Russian language by the military. He was stationed at Atsugi Air Base in Japan, the famous U-2 base, and eventually spent a couple of years in Russia as a "defector." He returned with a Russian wife of noble background, who had an uncle high up in the secret police.

Robert Sam Anson describes the following strange events: On November 7, 1963, a man who identified himself as Oswald on a ticket for a rifle he left to be repaired, visited a gun and furniture shop in Dallas.[103] Two days later, a man walked into a car dealership in Dallas, identified himself as Lee Oswald, said he was soon expecting a lot of money and wanted a new car, and took a demonstration ride. The man looked just like Oswald, according to the salesman, Albert Guy Bogard, but Bogard's co-workers said that Oswald was only five feet tall, 9-11 inches too short. Also, this Oswald drove the car at high speeds on the freeway, but the real Oswald could not drive. Bogard later "committed suicide."

On September 25, someone later identified as Oswald from his picture being shown on TV, went to the Veterans Administration office in Austin, Texas, a restaurant, and a print shop. But on that day Oswald was placed in New Orleans by the Warren Commission.

On November 8, a man cashed a check with a grocer, and identified himself as Oswald.[104] He was also seen by a barber, who heard Oswald make "Leftist" remarks. But the real Oswald was at work that day at the Book Depository.[105]

On November 9, a man who looked like Oswald went to a rifle range and made himself very conspicuous, firing at other people's targets, firing rapidly, and making a lot of noise. The real Oswald was at work that day, too.[106]

"When the incredible shrinking Oswald arrived in the United States (from Russia), he was met by Spas Raikin, who saw him standing alongside Marina. 'There was no significant difference between his (Oswald's) height and that of his wife,' Raikin later recalled. 'He was my height. I am certain of that.' Spas Raikin stands 5'6", about the same as the photograph of the man in Minsk, and three inches shorter than the Oswald who was killed in Dallas," Anson writes.[107]

Someone introduced as Oswald visited Sylvia Odio, a Cuban exile, on the night of September 26, but "Oswald" was in New Orleans on that day, whoever he was.[108]

A few hours after the assassination on the same day, anti-Castro Cubans went to Clare Booth Luce with intelligence information on Oswald they could only have obtained through CIA or intelligence sources.[109] Mrs. Luce's husband, Henry, was very tight with Allen Dulles, the former Director of the CIA whom Kennedy had fired along with General Charles Cabell and Richard Bissel for their role in the Bay of Pigs operation.* Howard Hunt was a close friend of Allen Dulles; Dulles was one of the Warren Commissioners, after being fired by President Kennedy. Hunt ghost-wrote *The Craft of Intelligence* for Dulles. Hunt was the Political Officer for the Bay of Pigs invasion, and handled the Cubans; Richard Nixon, for whom Hunt had worked, had been the White House operations officer for the invasion when he was Vice President under President Eisenhower. Hunt had helped run operations for Nixon against Aristotle Onassis in the late '50s [110] and later carried out the Watergate break-in as part of the Campaign To Reelect the President (CREEP), when Nixon was the President years later.

*The plan was to try to trap the President into using American Armed Forces to back up the invasion, and in order to do this, there were extensive misrepresentations made to the President about the plans and the invasion. For instance, they didn't tell him that the invaders were landing in an isolated swamp so far from the mountains they were to retreat to, that there was no hope of getting there. The President was also told that the population would rise up spontaneously and support the invaders.

The anti-Castro Cubans who went to Mrs. Luce hoped that she could be used to plant information on Oswald with her husband and *Time* and *Life* magazines. They told her that Oswald had made several trips to Mexico City and talked with Castro Cubans there. But only the CIA and the FBI knew of the alleged Mexico trip.

The Cubans also told Mrs. Luce that Oswald had tried to infiltrate their anti-Castro group in New Orleans. Mrs. Luce told them to take their story to the FBI, which they say they did. They were told by the FBI in no uncertain terms to shut up or risk deportation. One was then murdered, and another was deported. These Cubans knew Mrs. Luce because she financed a boat they had used to attack Cuba, in violation of President Kennedy's orders.*

This incident was similar to others aimed at linking Oswald to Castro. Those responsible obviously had intelligence connections.

On November 24, a Nicaraguan, Gilberto Ugarte Alvarado, went to the American Embassy in Mexico City and told them that he was in the Cuban Consulate on September 17 and saw Oswald paid $6,500 by Cubans who discussed the assassination with him. This story was later demolished. [111]

A week later, a letter was sent to Oswald (AFTER he was dead) from Havana saying that Oswald had been paid by Pedro Charles to do some killing. A second letter said he was paid $7,000 by Charles. [112] The Warren Commission called these a hoax, but obviously did not see that they were misinformation planted by intelligence sources.

Clearly, someone was laying a trail leading to Oswald, the designated patsy.

Antonio Veciana, an anti-Castro Cuban leader and CIA agent, testified to the Assassinations Committee that an intelligence agent, "Maurice Bishop," asked him just after the assassination to ask his cousin in the Cuban Embassy in Mexico City "to see if he, for money," would say that he saw Oswald in Mexico City in the Cuban Embassy. [113]

Veciana told the Committee that Bishop was deeply involved in the attempts by Alpha 66, a violent Cuban exile group, to murder Castro. [114]

---

*Mrs. Luce told the Schweiker Committee that Dulles called her himself and asked her to get out of the boat business.

Jack Anderson quotes Bishop as having said: "You have a cousin working for Cuban intelligence in Mexico. Why don't you just ask him, saying we'll bribe him, if he said it was really him that Oswald met." [115]

Anderson wrote: "Perhaps the CIA could have sought to tie Kennedy's killer to the Castro government." "The agent, who used the name Maurice Bishop, recruited Mr. X to plan an attempt on Castro's life." Mr. X continued to work for "Bishop" for 12 more years.

"A mystery witness has sworn to congressional investigators that a Central Intelligence Agency agent introduced him to Lee Harvey Oswald in Dallas three months before Oswald gunned down President John F. Kennedy." [116]

Two months after the House Assassinations Committee was established, a storm of newspaper articles began to swirl around it. Among them was a major story in *The Washington Post*, November 26, 1976, headlined "CIA Withheld Details on Oswald Call." The source for Ron Kessler's story was David Atlee Phillips, who had worked at the CIA's station in Mexico City during the alleged visit by Lee Harvey Oswald to the Soviet and Cuban embassies. For the first time, Phillips claimed that the CIA had monitored and tape-recorded the alleged Oswald's conversation with both the Russian and Cuban embassies.

"But it was not then turned over to the FBI, which has responsibility for investigating possible spies, and it was not later turned over to the Warren Commission during its investigation of the assassination. The unanswered question is why not?"

It is highly doubtful that the real Oswald ever went to Mexico City. The question is, why did Phillips, a propaganda specialist, come out into the open with this story at the time when the Assassinations Committee was just beginning to investigate John Kennedy's murder? The *Post* said that Phillips saw the transcripts of Oswald's conversation, and heard the tapes. Shortly afterwards, the CIA destroyed both the tapes and the transcript. It seems very peculiar that a week after someone is alleged to have gone to those embassies the evidence of the visit would be destroyed, especially since the translator said that the transcript was so important that they wanted it made on the spot.

Destruction of that evidence would fit with the fact that the photograph of the man the CIA claimed was Oswald entering the embassy was not of him, but this fact did not establish itself for years, until the photograph was released.

Phillips went out of his way to champion this story of Oswald in Mexico. Why was he so intent on implicating Oswald in some sort of connection with Cuba or Russia, and then had nothing to back it up? Phillips was quick to go to *The Washington Post* with this story in 1976, but why did he not go to the FBI and the Warren Commission in 1963? The *Post* said that a partial transcript was given to the Warren Commission but that "For unexplained reasons they failed to include Oswald's offer of information and his suggestion that the Russians would want to pay his way to the Soviet Union." The FBI was told only that a Lee Oswald had made contact with the Russians. The reason was that the rest of this was fabricated to bolster the case against Oswald, making him out as a leftist. The CIA had told the Warren Commission that it had only learned of most of Oswald's activities in Mexico City *after* the assassination.

Senator Richard Schweiker identified Phillips as being "Maurice Bishop," a CIA operator who was accused of trying to get a Cuban to implicate Oswald in Kennedy's murder. We believe that this was part of laying the false trail which helped frame Oswald as the patsy in the assassination. Other evidence implicates "Bishop" in the assassination of the President, and it may very well have been that Phillips was involved.

Unfortunately, the House Committee refuses to release any information about its long interviews with Phillips, or the report on its trip to Mexico City to investigate all of this. Why not?

It would seem that David Atlee Phillips of Fort Worth, the head of his own CIA as he ran the Association of Retired Intelligence Officers before his recent death, held a key to the assassination.

PART IV   The Case

"We have the forms of institutions, rather than the reality. Form masquerades as substance. Our Congress is not a congress, the unions not unions, and the newspapers are not newspapers. It is impossible to organize and it cannot be efficient. In such conditions it is impossible to be just."

– Scherer Garcia

"We have sacrificed reality to words and delivered up our people to the ravenous appetites of the strong. Liberal, democratic ideology, far from expressing our concrete historical situation, disguised it, and the political lie established itself Constitutionally. The moral damage it has caused is incalculable: It has affected profound areas of our existence. We move about in this lie with complete naturalness."

– Octavio Paz

"The American attitude is that of the economically rational man: If these people are willing to be shafted, then I will shaft them. If I can bribe or force or manipulate them to my advantage, I will. Since we in the United States have a stronger culture, then we will shaft them."

– Samuel del Villar

"I can't believe that!" said Alice.
"Can't you?" The Queen said in a pitying tone.
"Try again: draw a long breath, and shut your eyes."
Alice laughed. "There's no use trying." She said:
"One can't believe impossible things."
"I daresay you haven't had much practice," said the
Queen. "When I was your age, I always did it for half-
an-hour a day. Why, sometimes I've believed as many
as six impossible things before breakfast."

Through the Looking-Glass, Lewis Carroll

CHAPTER 10

FAKE PHOTOS

"That is not a picture of me; it is my face, but my face has been superimposed – the rest of the picture is not me at all, I've never seen it before... That small picture is a reduction of the large picture that someone I don't know has made... someone took a picture of my face and faked that photograph," Oswald said.[1]

Concerning the famous pictures of Oswald armed with guns and leftist newspapers, the Committee arrived at the following conclusion before they were going to admit to any conspiracies in this case: "Despite the Warren Commission's efforts to show that the backyard photographs were genuine, critics have persisted in doubting their authenticity. In general, the critics base their allegations of fakery on their observations of shadow inconsistencies, an indication of a grafting line between the mouth and chin, inconsistent head and body proportions, or a disparate square-shaped chin.

"This position has received support from scientists who had not previously been associated with Warren Commission critics. For example, Malcolm Thompson, a British forensic photography expert... at the request of the BBC, had examined copies of the backyard photographs and concluded they were fakes. Similarly, a photographic analyst with the Canadian Department of Defense reached the conclusion that these photographs were composites."[2]

But the 1976 House Select Committee on Assassinations reached a different conclusion. "The panel detects no evidence of fakery in any of the backyard photographs."[3] Of course, the panel would not: "Initially, an effort was made to limit membership on the photographic evidence panel to individuals who had never done any work for the U.S. Intelligence community. Nevertheless, after spending weeks contacting various photographic specialists, it became apparent that most of the leading photographic scientists in this country have done some intelligence-related work. Accordingly, a previous affiliation with an intelligence agency was not considered to be an automatic basis for precluding someone from membership on the panel."[4]

If you could hold these photos in your hands, you would see with your own eyes what Detective Superintendent Malcolm Thompson of England, who ran the Police Forensic Science Laboratory Identification Bureau at Scotland Yard for 25 years, observed. He is also the former president of the Evidence Photographers International Council and a fellow of the Institute of Incorporated Photographers, the Royal Photographic Society and the Institute of Professional Investigators. "...the retouching is very obvious in certain parts of the picture... Without doubt that shows this area between the head and the pillar has been retouched and the retoucher has just not been careful enough."[5]

"So you think that those shadows have actually been touched in?" "They have been touched in," Thompson said.[6]

The House Committee Report states: "The 133-B negative (CE749) was digitally processed at the Aerospace Corp. and the University of California Image Processing Institute using several different image processing techniques. This process confirmed that the grain distribution was uniform."[7] But, and this is a big but, because the dispute is whether a picture of Oswald's face was, as he claimed, pasted onto someone else's body: "Under very carefully adjusted display conditions, the scanned image of the Oswald backyard negative did exhibit irregular, very fine lines in the chin area. Although the cause of these lines has not been definitely established, there is no evidence to indicate that they are the result of an attempt to fake the photograph."

THE TRUE ISSUE

"...the probability of the lines being caused by very faint water stains is heightened by the observation of very noticeable stains in the neck and ear area, and discussed below. These marks are found in the work of photographers who pay inadequate attention to the washing and drying steps in the processing of film..."[8] Why are these marks just around the area that has been retouched? Co-author Robert Groden, a photographic consultant to the Committee, says, "The visual areas of retouching cannot be easily dismissed."[9] So they are ignored. The issue, the true issue, is, as Thompson says, "...there has been retouching done in the chin area which is what one would expect if my conclusion is correct, that this face has been added on to the chin... The head itself, I have seen photographs of Oswald and his chin is not square. He has a rounded chin. Having said that, the subject in this picture has a square chin but again it doesn't take any stretch of the imagination to appreciate that from the upper lip to the top of the head is Oswald and one can only conclude that Oswald's head has been stuck on to a chin, not being Oswald's chin,"[10] said Thompson.

"Allegations of fakery...(a) Unnatural lines in the vicinity of Oswald's chin... It has been alleged that there is a line that runs directly across Oswald's chin and is evidence of compositing. No unnatural line indicative of fakery could be discerned by the panel on either the original negative or first-generation prints when these materials were visually inspected using magnifying and microscopic equipment, varying density exposures, and digital image processing."[11] The line across the chin will not be seen when magnified by the above methods. The line is something you can see with your eyes. "As noted earlier, photographic images such as the backyard pictures are composed of very small, irregular shaped grains of silver suspended in a gelatin layer. On a given photograph, a uniformly exposed area has a generally uniform distribution of such grains. In contrast, on composited photographs, the grain distribution may be noticeably different."[12]

"When the panel microscopically examined the area above and

below the horizontal chin cleft in the backyard pictures, no difference in grain structure could be found."[13]

"While subsequent generation prints of the backyard pictures appear to show a line running across Oswald's chin, this phenomenon is not surprising because copy prints often have higher contrasts than originals."[14] However, in a composite photograph, a fake, successive generations bring out the contrast line.

We will get to more important matters, but for now, this case hinges on numerous fake photographs. "The backyard pictures were also visually inspected with stereoscopic techniques that permitted the prints to be viewed in three dimensions. This was possible because the camera's movement between exposures 133-B and 133-A resulted in two views, only a short distance apart, of a single scene. When these two pictures are viewed together in a stereo viewer, they give rise to a three-dimensional image. This analytic technique is useful in the detection of fakery because photographs of prints, when viewed in stereo, will not project a three-dimensional image unless made from different viewpoints along one axis. (NOTE: Identical photographs or photographs made from the same camera position will not generally exhibit stereoscopic characteristics. Nevertheless, if a camera is stationary and photographs of a subject that moves are viewed stereoscopically, the subject may exhibit three-dimensional properties, which the background will not.) Further, any retouching of an original photograph of a scene can be detected because when two photographs of that scene are viewed in stereo, the retouched item will appear to lie either in front of, or behind the plane in which it should be lying. It is virtually impossible to retouch one or both images of a stereo pair with enough skill to escape detection when viewed stereoscopically."[15]

It is "virtually impossible," but not entirely impossible, when done by a professional forger, a specialist in faked documents.

"Finally, in addition to these methods of visual inspection, the materials were studied photogrammetically. Photogrammetry is the science of ascertaining the positions and dimensions of objects from measurements of photographs of these objects. In the Oswald backyard pictures, photogrammetry was given particular emphasis in studying critical shadow areas. Conclusion: The panel detects no evidence of fakery in any of the backyard picture materials."[16]

JACK WHITE

When Jack White, a longtime assassination researcher, got up to testify about the photograph, the Committee tried to make a fool of someone who has worked on this case for many years. He demonstrated with an entirely different method that the pictures were fake. They asked him, "To what extent, if any, did you compute photogrammetically the effect of an object's tilt on its apparent length in the photograph?"[17]

"As I said, I am not a scientist, I don't indulge in that sort of thing." Jack White examined different photographs of the various rifles we are told were the murder weapon. "I found that most of the reference points through which I extended vertical lines could not be made to line up." Genzman, his questioner, asked: "Did you line up the metal parts?" "Yes. I made prints where the metal parts of the rifle, that is, from the muzzle to the trigger guard, were all identical lengths." Genzman: "After lining up the metal parts, what did you determine about the stocks?" "I determined that the butts were different lengths after lining up the metal parts."[18]

Frazier, who drove Oswald to work the morning of the assassination, demonstrated that Oswald could not have carried a rifle, even disassembled, in the cup of his hand, beneath his armpit, as he did carry the "curtain rods" that morning. Did someone substitute a shorter gun in the Archives? "Yes. Here we have the Archive rifle, the Warren Report rifle, all the way from the muzzle through all the metal parts, in fact all the way to the comb, which is this little notch in the stock of the rifle. All of that matches exactly. Only from here back, less than one-fifth length of the rifle, does not match… It is my opinion that we have been shown by the authorities more than one gun as being the assassination weapon."

Goldsmith: "When you did this study, did you compute photogrammetically the effect of tilt on the way that the length of an object appears in a photograph?"[19]

"I conducted a study by photographing a yardstick from three different –"

"Mr. White, answer my question. Did you compute photogrammetically –"

"What is photogrammetically? Describe to me what photogrammetically is."

"I just have one more question, Mr. White. Do you know what photogrammetically is?"

"No."

"I have no further questions, thank you."

Jack White got in a parting shot: "Thank you. I appreciate the opportunity to present this as a private citizen who has no large budget to work with. I am just an ordinary person who has observed a lot of things and I am really here to present questions rather than answers."[20]

Rather than deal with real issues such as the fake photographs or the different rifles alleged to be the murder weapon, the Committee preferred to grapple with side issues such as whether or not the backyard photos were taken with Oswald's Reflex camera. Co-author and photographic expert Robert Groden was having none of this. He told the Committee, "You were all aware that some of the arguments presented were no longer issues and that some of them never really were. The true issues were not accurately dealt with in the hearings. These were the discrepancies of the head to body size as well as the height-to-rifle length ratio and the visual retouching of the skin and surrounding area."[21]

The panel of experts alleged that the minute indentations along the film plane aperture matched those of the pictures. Jack White said in his final minute, "There was one area of questioning which I had hoped to get into, which because of the shortness of time before lunch I was not permitted to go into. That is the question of the DeMohrenschildt picture. The DeMohrenschildt picture shows a much larger amount of background around the edges than any of the photographs, 133-A, B or C. To me, this indicates that the DeMohrenschildt picture is printed full negative. In fact, we can verify this because it is printed with a black border around the edge, the black border being the clear area around the edge of the negative.

"According to the FBI, the picture, CE-133-B, was identified as being taken with Oswald's camera because it could be matched to the film plane aperture. Yet, if the DeMohrenschildt picture shows a larger background area and it is taken from the same camera viewpoint, then 133-A, B and C have all been cropped and, therefore, if there is more background area in the picture, then it could not possibly be matched to the film plane aperture."[22]

The Committee had no answer for this.

"Have you ever had occasion to take the original negative from 133-B and analyze it with a computer by a technique called 'digital image processing'?" "No, obviously not."

"Have you had any training in analytical photogrammetry?" Goldsmith asked. "No."

"Have you had any formal training in forensic photography?" "No."

"Have you had any formal training in the study of shadows in photographs?" "No."[23]

STRANGE SHADOWS

Now we are getting to the nitty-gritty. The shadows on Oswald's face, cast by his nose and eyebrows, clearly show that the sun is directly overhead, but the long shadows on the ground show that the sun is in the late afternoon. "Did you notice any peculiarities on the shadows of these pictures?" "Yes. If you consider each photograph as if you are looking at the face of a clock, it is quite obvious that in 133-A the ground shadow of the figure is pointing to ten o'clock, in 133-B the ground shadow of the figure is pointing to twelve o'clock. In 133-C, the shadow is again pointing to ten o'clock, but even though the figure is shorter, it is casting a longer shadow; in fact, the shadow goes six or seven inches up the fence."[24]

Detective Superintendent Thompson says, "The body shadows don't relate to the other shadows in the picture and one can only come to the conclusion that this body has been placed in the background and photographed but all the shadows here are swinging to the left where as this shadow is slightly to the left but also behind the body is common to both pictures, but when one examines the shadow content, one sees the gun at an angle to the body, which does not relate to the angle of the shadow. The gun is reaching far more out to the right, more in a horizontal position here in relation to the body shadow than the gun is actually being held by the person."[25]

"When one measures the pictures, photograph A is enlarged slightly greater than photograph B but even allowing for that, the shadow detail in the static areas of the picture, that is in particular on the staircase here, the shadows are so exact that there is no doubt in my mind, it is either a common negative used to produce the two prints or two successive negatives with the camera on a tripod and neither camera nor tripod moved in any way between the two exposures."[26]

"Again we have a shadow underneath the nose. In photographs A and B you see Oswald's face in a different posture and yet the shadow under the nose hasn't moved or if it has moved, it is only fractional compared with the actual movement we see in the face and one comes to the conclusion that it is the same picture used for both faces, possibly in this face here he has got a scowl on his face and there has been retouching done in the chin area which is what one would expect, that this face has been added on to the chin..."[27]

"Does it strike you as strange that the police did not find those photographs, despite an intensive search on the day of the assassination and only found them the next day?" "It does, it does seem unusual. One would think that the officers involved would be highly experienced officers, would know and have been trained to carry out the search of the premises."[28] It is not so strange when you consider that there are no transcripts of the many hours of interrogation the same police force, the FBI and the Secret Service subjected Oswald to.

"Is there any possibility in your mind that those two photographs are genuine?"

"I don't think there is any possibility, having examined them for a considerable time it is my considered opinion that they are not genuine."

Jack White speaks next: "By the way, at the time that these pictures were made, there is no grass on the ground in Dallas, and there are no leaves on the trees. The date of these pictures supposedly is March 29. I live in Texas, and I see the trees come out. It is usually late April before you have this amount of foliage on the grass, the bushes, and the trees. So I think shadows were added by transparent retouching, just as the British photo expert said."

"Some of the shadows were added improperly. For instance, the shadow of the post by the head of the figure on B is much wider than the same shadow on A. And also as he pointed out, when they cut their airbrush frisket, the knife must have slipped because the post becomes crooked in B and it is not crooked in A."[29] Thompson says: "...the area we see in shadow is far in excess of what it should be and of course that is the area to which I referred earlier on where the pillar coming down does not continue in a straight line but has this bulge in it."[30]

Co-author Robert Groden and Peter Model wrote, "In the bottom photo (CE 133-B), Oswald's head is cocked slightly to his left, yet the shadow directly under his nose (see top close-up of CE 133-A) moves not in relation to the light source but to the angle of his head."[31]

Their answer to this is that either Oswald or the camera moved slightly between the two photographs, and so the nose shadow would remain the same.

"Does the apparent bulge in the left edge of the post to the right of Oswald's head appear to be due to retouching or other alteration of the image in photograph number CE 133-B?"

"What could be perceived as an indentation in the post in CE 133-B is believed by the undersigned to be an illusion resulting from the location of a shadow of a branch or a leaf along the left edge of the post."[32] They then present some newly invented evidence to try to corroborate this. Nonetheless, there is clearly visible to the naked eye a large area of gray retouching between the head and the post in CE 133-B.

The Committee tries to denounce it: "Aside from the obvious question of whether Oswald would place his signature on a fake picture," (there is only the opinion of some handwriting "experts" that he signed it) "for the photograph to have been faked would have required access, within just a ten-day period, to Oswald's backyard, his camera, rifle (knowing that this would be the assassination weapon), and newspapers."[33] David Belin, still defending the Warren Report to former CBS newsman Daniel Schorr, said, "I don't happen to believe that Oswald was part of any conspiracy, and as a matter of fact, the very fact that twelve years have passed and there really is no concrete evidence of conspiracy is in itself evidence of the fact there was no conspiracy." "Or," Schorr answered, "that it was a very good one."

If Oswald was living with or surrounded by people who were connected with intelligence operations, and who were setting him up as the patsy, they would have been able to get into that backyard. They would have had his camera, and they would have had his rifle. It may never have been his rifle, and he may never have even seen it. And they would have had his newspapers, which could have been bought in the usual fashion. Also, it is unlikely that anyone would be reading both the *Worker* and the *Militant*, since the two papers are of opposing ideologies – unless that person was involved in an intelligence operation.

We have only the testimony of Marina Oswald to say that she took the pictures. She would say anything to avoid deportation, and she has given different stories each time. She did not recall how many pictures she took. First she said one, but they found two; then years later, they found a third, interestingly enough, among the possessions of George DeMohrenschildt, who was in all probability working closely with Oswald. Even he wrote in his book that Oswald was innocent.

Marina first told the FBI that she took the photos in late February or early March, but of course there were no leaves then, or grass. She told the Warren Commission that the first time she ever saw the rifle was toward the end of March. She then said that she took the photos within seven or ten days of that. Blakey now tells us that "A rifle and a *revolver* were shipped to Oswald from different mail order houses on March 20. So they decided that the picture was taken on a Sunday, March 31, 1963."[34] But there are no leaves on the trees then, and no grass.

Jack White looked at these pictures for years. "Mr. White, what was your method of analysis?"

"I utilized various methods. First of all was just scrutiny, you might say – just looking at the photos to see how things in one photo compared with things in the other photos. I also made measurements. I made photocopies and printed them in various sizes. I made transparencies which I overlaid one over the other to make certain comparisons, and things of that sort."[35]

White outlines his evidence for the faking of the photos, and says, "It is fairly obvious after the fact that they were made to implicate Oswald in the assassination by tying him to the alleged assassination weapon."[36] Fake photographs were used to implicate Oswald and fake photographs were used to alter the findings of the autopsy – the pattern is consistent.

(Far left) Lee Harvey Oswald as a teenager in the Civil Air Patrol.

(Left) David Ferrie, Oswald's superior in the CAP.

(Below right) Hidell ID allegedly found on Oswald.

The "Oswald" and "Hidell" I.D. cards. Alek James Hidell was alleged to be Oswald's alias.

(Left) Oswald Library ID. Note the name Jack L. Bowen. Jagger-Chiles Stoval did secret map work for the military.

Lee Harvey Oswald in New Orleans handing out Hands Off Cuba leaflets.

(Left) Between 72 and 90 seconds following the assassination, Oswald was seen calmly drinking a Coca-Cola in the second floor lunchroom of the School Book Depository.

(Right) Oswald left the Depository for his rooming house.

(Below) The Tippit murder scene.

Aquella Clemmons witnessed two men murder Officer Tippit. The man who pulled the trigger was heavy set and had close cropped curly hair. It was NOT Lee Harvey Oswald!

Officer Jefferson Davis Tippit.

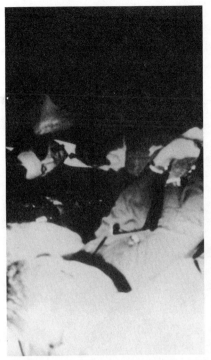

Oswald at the moment of his arrest at the Texas Theatre.

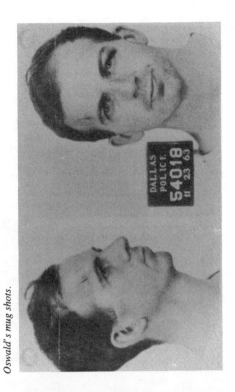

Oswald's mug shots.

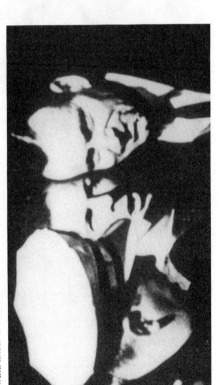

The Texas Theatre where Oswald was arrested.

Oswald under arrest.

The press conference Oswald called ''short and sweet.''

Jack Leon Ruby.

Jack Ruby at the midnight press conference.

Jack Ruby steps up to silence Lee Harvey Oswald.

The murder of Lee Harvey Oswald.

CE-133-A

CE-133-B

"CE-133-C"

These pictures were forged in advance of the assassination to make Oswald appear violent, and show him with weapons allegedly used in the murders of President Kennedy and Police Officer J. D. Tippit. When shown the photo on the top left, Oswald stated that it was his head pasted on someone else's body. Note that the shadows on the face come from a noon sun directly overhead, but the body shadows on the ground are from sunlight low on the horizon, at least six o'clock in the evening.

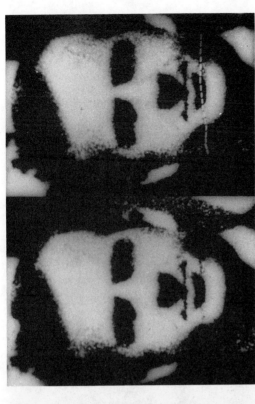

The crop line in the chin becomes more evident in successive generations of the photos. The crop line is shown (right). (CE-133-A)

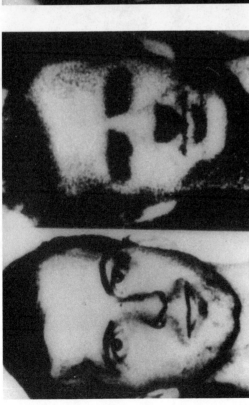

Chin transplant. Oswald's chin was pointed and had a cleft. In the picture on the right, the man has a square chin. (CE-133-A)

URGENT   1:45 AM EST 11-17-63 HLF   1PAGE

TO   ALL SACS

FROM   DIRECTOR

THREAT TO ASSISINATE PRESIDENT KENNEDY IN DALLAS TEXAS

NOVEMBER TWENTYTWO DASH TWENTYTHREE NINETEEN SIXTYTHREE.

MISC INFORMATION CONCERNING.

INFO HAS BEEN RECEIVED BY THE BUREAU
BUREAU HAS ~~DISCOMERIDXINFORMATION~~ DETERMINED THAT A MILITANT

REVOLUTIONARY GROUP MAY ATTEMPT TO ASSINATED PRESIDENT

KENNEDY ON HIS PROPOSED TRIP TO DALLAS TEXAS ~~DURINGXTHEX~~

~~XWEEKXOFX~~ NOVEMBER TWENTYTWO DASH TWENTYTHREE NINETEEN

SICTYTHREE.

ALL RECEIVING OFFICE SHOULS IMMIDIATELY CONTACT ALL CIS;

PCIS LOGICAL RACIAL AND HATE GROPUP INFORMANTS AND DETERMINE IF

ANY BASIS FOR THREAT. BHRGEU SHOULS BE KEPT ADVISED OF ALL

DEVELOPEMENTS BY TELETYPE .

   SUBMI Y FD THREE ZERO TWOS AND LHM

OTHER HOFFICE HAVE BEEN ADVISED

   END AND ACK PLS

   MO....
   DL.....

   NO.....

KT TI TU CLR..@

A photograph (above) of General Edwin A. Walker's house was claimed to be found among Oswald's possessions. It was mutilated to eliminate the license plate of the car by the time the Warren Commission published it (below). It was claimed by the Warren Commission that it was Oswald who fired a shot at Walker on April 10, 1963. At that time the bullet was a 30.06 but the Warren Commission claimed that it was a 6.5 Carcano bullet. All of this was an attempt to show Oswald as having a violent nature.

(Far left) New Orleans District Attorney Jim Garrison was the only public law enforcement official to ever attempt to get a conviction against anyone linked to the conspiracy.

CIA Operative Guy Banister. Ferrie worked for him. He also ran Oswald as an agent in anti-Castro activities.

(Far right) CIA Operative David Ferrie, also worked for mafia chieftan Carlos Marcello.

Clay Shaw.

At his trial Shaw claimed he had never met David Ferrie. Here is proof that he did. These two pictures of them both at a gay party were taken before the assassination.

(Far left) Joseph Adams Milteer. Right wing fanatic, who had advance knowledge of the assassination.

Willie Somersett. Informant.

Milteer traveled to Dallas and witnessed the assassination.

(Far left) In Dealey Plaza.

At home.

Beverly Oliver, the "Babushka Lady," in Dealey Plaza during the shooting. She filmed the assassination, but FBI agent Regis Kennedy (above right) took her film, and it was never seen again. She apparently knew Ruby well.

Oswald's friend, Count George DeMohrenschildt had strong ties to the intelligence community. He died under mysterious circumstances.

Eugene Hale Brading, alias Jim Braden was a mafia operative who knew David Ferrie. He was arrested in Dealey Plaza.

Three "tramps" taken for questioning soon after the shooting. They were found in railroad boxcars. The police kept no records as to their identities, nor did they photograph them. The tall tramp resembles Charles Harrelson, a professional hit man who claims he participated in the assassination of President Kennedy. Harrelson is currently in prison for murdering a Federal Judge.

It seems unlikely that they were truly "tramps." They were all clean shaven and had new haircuts. They had good shoe leather, and there is not a single frayed collar or cuff among them.

Man with what appears to be a radio transmitter in his back pocket just after the assassination. Jim Hicks claimed in court documents that the picture was of himself, and that he was the radio coordinator in the murder.

Jim Hicks after the assassination. Hicks told District Attorney Jim Garrison that the communications center for the assassination was at the Adolphus Hotel, across the street from Jack Ruby's Carousel Club on Commerce Street.

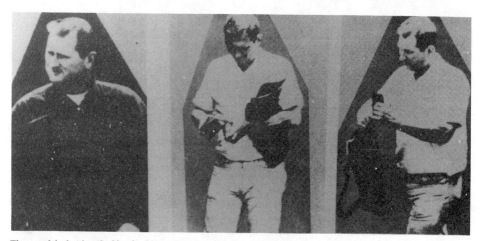

The man falsely identified by the CIA as Oswald in Mexico City. Note the resemblance with Jim Hicks.

David Atlee Phillips

Sam Giancana

Howard Hunt

Frank Sturgis

John Roselli

Richard Nixon   Jack Ruby

Carlos Marcello

Gerald Ford

Santos Trafficante

(Below) The paper rifle case: Not a single drop of gun oil or matching crease.

FD-302 (Rev. 3-3-59)

FEDERAL BUREAU OF INVESTIGATION

Date _____ 11/30/63

1

found the brown paper bag shaped like a gun case near the scene of the shooting on the sixth floor of the Texas School Book Depository Building. He stated the manager, Mr. TRULY, saw this bag at the time it was taken into possession by Lt. DAY, according to DAY, had not seen this bag before. No one else viewed it. TRULY furnished similar brown paper from the roll that was used in packing books by the Texas School Book Depository. This paper was examined by the FBI Laboratory and found to have the same observable characteristics as the brown paper bag shaped like a gun case which was found near the scene of the shooting on the sixth floor of the Texas School Book Depository Building. The Dallas police have not exhibited this to anyone else. It was immediately locked up by DAY, kept in his possession until it was turned over to FBI Agent DRAIN for transmittal to the Laboratory. It was examined by the Laboratory, returned to the Crime Laboratory. This bag was examined November 24, 1963, locked up in the Crime Laboratory. This bag was returned to Agent DRAIN on November 26, 1963, and taken back to the FBI Laboratory.

Lt. DAY stated no one has identified this bag to the Dallas Police Department.

on _11/29/63_ at _Dallas, Texas_ File # _DL 89-43_

by Special Agent _VINCENT E. DRAIN/cs_ Date dictated _11/29/63_

129

False document. The FBI altered their document (Dallas 89-43: 11-29-63 pg 1) To say that Lee Harvey Oswald created the paper rifle bag from materials obtained from the Texas School Book Depository. This proves that he did not, so the FBI rewrote the report, but someone forgot to destroy the original.

The frontier is wherever a man faces a fact.

– Adlai Stevenson

CHAPTER 11

EVIDENCE

The Committee has told us they found that Oswald had a violent background and therefore was the killer of President Kennedy.[1] The Committee based this conclusion on very slender evidence of violence, one example being that he had allegedly taken a shot at General Walker.

When a patsy is set up, he generally does not have the gun that the real hit man will use. We often find in these cases that the gun changes by the following day, or later on, if need be. In the Walker shooting, the police reported at the time that a 30.06 caliber bullet, steel-jacketed, had been fired at him.[2] Of course, such a bullet could not be fired from Oswald's gun, so the bullet eventually became a 6.5 mm suitable for a Mannlicher-Carcano.[3]

General Walker had a very good look at the bullet that had come into his house, and saw that it was mangled. He then examined the bullet that was used by the Assassinations Committee as an exhibit, and said that it was not the same bullet.[4] The exhibit was clearly a bullet, but the one he found in his house was so mangled that it no longer resembled a bullet.[5]

There is no evidence to link Oswald to the Walker shooting, and

181

in fact the whole thing may have been staged. Walker has no reason to protect Oswald, at least publicly, but he has said that the bullet they have as evidence is clearly not the one that was fired at him. This means that the evidence has been deliberately tampered with, probably because the caliber wasn't right.

A MYSTERIOUS HOLE

The photograph of Walker's house that the Dallas police first found was tampered with by the time the Warren Commission exhibited it. A hole was cut in the photo that removed the license plate number of the car parked in the driveway. Jesse Curry published a photo of Oswald's possessions, and in this picture is the photo of Walker's house with the license plate intact.[6] The car is a 1957 Chevrolet. Interestingly enough, one of the General's men reported a few days before the shooting that a Cuban or Latin drove around the house in a 1957 Chevrolet.[7] It would be pretty hard to miss a 1957 Chevrolet in *1963*.

Furthermore, Marina Oswald, whose testimony much of the time is very questionable,[8] insists that there was no hole in the picture when she first saw it.[9] When and how did the license plate number get cut out before the Warren Commission published it? And why?

THE TIPPIT SLAYING

As for the pistol-revolver-automatic which Oswald was supposed to have had at the time of his arrest, Officer Gerald Hill examined the cartridges at the scene of the Tippit murder and found they had the clear marks of an automatic weapon, not a revolver.[10]

Three bullets were apparently removed from Officer Tippit, although we are told that four shots were fired. The FBI Laboratory report tells us that two of the bullets they were given were made by Winchester-Western, and the third by Remington-Peters, and that two of them are .38 Specials.[11] Oswald at this point had a .38 Special Smith and Wesson revolver, Serial Number V510210, Assembly No.6524.[12] Test bullets were fired from the gun for comparison, and "no conclusion could be reached as to whether or not C251 through C253 were fired from the same weapon or whether or not they were fired from C15. In addition, it was found that even consecutive

.38 Special bullets test fired from the C15 revolver could not be identified with each other. In this connection, it should be noted that the barrel of C15 was designed for .38 S&W bullets and, therefore, it is slightly
larger in diameter than barrels designed for .38 Special bullets. Firing
of undersized bullets could cause erratic passage of the bullets down
the barrel, resulting in individual microscopic characteristics which are
not consistent." [13]

Is it rational that someone would put ammunition into a gun that
did not fit it properly? It is rational if they did not want it to be provable
that the bullets did not come from Oswald's gun. We have just seen that
the bullets recovered from Tippit could not be connected to the gun that
belonged to Oswald.

"The barrel of the weapon could also be changing due to the ac-
cumulation of lead in the barrel or to wear. That one or both of the above
conditions existed is apparent from the fact that consecutive .38 Special
test bullets obtained from the C15 revolver could not be identified with
each other." [14]

How could this have been a new revolver that Oswald had just
bought a short time before? There is no evidence or even opportunity
for him to have fired the gun often enough for it to be worn out.

Without exception, witnesses at Dealey Plaza, and the doctors who
commented on it, said that the President had been shot with a high-
powered rifle. The Mannlicher-Carcano is not a high-powered rifle, but
a medium to low-powered rifle. [15] Yet, it is inconceivable that a hard
(military) jacketed bullet, [16] specifically designed to pierce a body,
would or could have been fired from a distance of 100 to 250 feet or
so and stopped in President Kennedy's back after an inch or two, which
is in fact what the evidence says.

MISSING SHOTS

There is evidence of at least three missing shots having been fired
in Dealey Plaza. Jesse Curry published a photo of the spot where one
slug hit the curb and another picture of an FBI agent picking up
something from the grass. Deputy Sheriff Buddy Walthers found a
.45 caliber slug there. A man came up and identified himself as being
from the FBI, and in the presence of Walthers and a policeman, as well

as a photographer who took several pictures of the event, picked up the bullet and put it in his pocket. This bullet landed on the left side of the limousine, in the grass just off the curb.[17]

The shot that hit the curb had no copper jacket, and caused bystander James Tague to be slightly wounded by concrete fragments.[18] The shot which hit the cement just by the manhole on the south side of Elm St. appears to have come from the Records building.[19] A long bullet mark mentioned previously was on the sidewalk near the lamp post on the north side of Elm, in front of where Zapruder was standing.[20] This mark points directly at a manhole which existed on the south end of the triple underpass. Numerous witnesses thought a bullet hit the sidewalk there. The police, immediately after the shooting, drove a car up on the sidewalk and parked it over the mark, and no-one could see it.[21] The mark was later removed and the manhole it pointed to was paved over.

Nothing further has been heard of the .45 slug which the FBI man picked up. It is another one of those crucial pieces of evidence that have simply been obliterated.

Revolver shots, or shots from a pistol or automatic, from anything but a high-powered pistol, would not show up on the tape made by the police during the shooting.[22] We have testimony from Secret Service men present that they thought they heard a revolver being fired.[23] Some researchers believe that a shot was fired from the sewer next to the car, over which the police car shortly parked (also covering up the bullet mark on the sidewalk), and that this shot was from a revolver.[24] In addition, Ralph Repphert wrote in the *Baltimore Sun* that one of the gun experts used by the Warren Commission believed that one of the Secret Service men "accidentally" shot the President during the course of the assassination.[25] Although this seems to be a fantastic idea, it is not beyond the realm of possibility. They are certainly covering up a lot of things in this case, and that might account for some of the cover-up, unless the Secret Service was part of the plot, as Colonel Fletcher Prouty suggests. Dr. Charles Wilber wrote: "Interpretation of the fatal head wound by several attending surgeons suggested a high velocity hand gun bullet fired at close range."[26]

It is also important to note here that the lengths of the various rifles alleged to be the murder weapon have varied. Men cut off portions of their rifle stocks to fit the length of their arms, and as Jack White testified, many have noted that there are considerable differences in the various guns alleged to have been Oswald's.[27] The fact that they now claim to have fired the alleged murder weapon so many times that bullets can no longer be traced to it[28] seems to fit very well the pattern of destruction of evidence in this case.

Pistols with silencers would be difficult to detect during the shooting, when loud rifles were used.

FILM TAMPERED WITH

The only available print of the Zapruder film at the time was extensively tampered with. Frames 155 and 156 do not exist.[29] This was where the film was spliced the first time, although both the government and Time Inc., the owner of the film, denied that this happened. The Warren Commission only began to print the frames with Z 171. What was on those earlier frames? The Warren Commission told us that the first shot that could have possibly been fired was at frame 210 of the Zapruder film, because a tree was obstructing the line of fire from the "assassin's" window until then.[30] For unexplained reasons, the Assassinations Committee has implied that shots were fired prior to that time, and the acoustical study of the tape made during the shooting places the first shot at precisely frames 155 and 156.[31]

It should become clear how the pattern of lies, tampering, and missing evidence fits. The acoustical panel states that the first bullet reached the area of the limousine at frames 157 to 161. What has been called "jiggle analysis" of the film shows that people have startle reactions to gunfire, and each time there was a shot Zapruder jiggled his camera.[32] But we do not have the two crucial frames to test this reaction.

In fact, the President is aware of the shot in frame 157. Where did that shot come from, if not from the window because the tree was in the way? It may very well have come from just behind the Book Depository, from the Dallas Textile building where the unidentified figure of a man appears in a window on the second floor behind a fire escape.

The Committee says a second bullet was fired and hit at frames 188-191,[33] which is supported by both the acoustical analysis and the Zapruder film, which shows the President's reaction to a hit in those frames. The Zapruder film blurs at *this point.*

THE MOST IMPORTANT PIECE OF EVIDENCE

The film has again been tampered with at frame 207 and it is spliced,[34] with four frames removed to frame 212[35] where the Warren Commission placed the first shot. Why? We now know that frames 208-211 have all been removed.[36]

The original film was bought by Time Inc. It was the single most important piece of evidence in the case, and they put a junior employee to work on it, who, while enlarging the movie, is said to have damaged all those frames.[37] Is it credible that after paying hundreds of thousands of dollars for the film, they would have treated it this way? William Bader of the Senate Intelligence Committee said: "You don't have to manipulate *Time Magazine*, because there are Agency (CIA) people at the management level."[38]

Everybody – the FBI, the Secret Service, the Dallas Police, and the Warren Commission – said that no shot could have been fired through the tree before frame 210. The reason for this splice and removal of the frames is that in the original, the film photographed retired Major Philip Willis just at the moment that he was taking a picture of the motorcade, across the street from Zapruder; and he took that picture as a startle reaction to the shot that hit the President.[39] If Willis was putting down his camera after snapping the picture, that would have been in the deleted frames. This had to be deleted because it would have proven that the first shot took place where the Commission and the authorities said Oswald could not have fired. The shot at 189-191 hit the President in the throat,[40] from the front.

Was this the reason for mutilating the film?

The sprocket area might also have shown the reactions of bystanders on the sidewalk to a bullet which struck there, over which a police car later drove and parked, covering it up for most of the afternoon.

By frame 220, Kennedy's hand is up to his throat, where he has been hit. At frame 226, he is struck in the back and propelled forward.[41] This is the shot that would later be converted by Arlen Specter and Gerald Ford into the magic bullet, which supposedly struck both Kennedy and John Connally. Interestingly enough, we have a "heterodyning" effect on the police recording at this point, caused by a microphone being turned on at the same instant, perhaps, and no shot is heard on the tape, or so they say.[42]

Certainly John Connally is not in fact hit at this time. He is hit at frame 237, when he is obviously struck by a high-powered bullet.[43] His cheeks puff up, the wind is knocked out of him. He has repeatedly testified, as has his wife, that he could not have been hit with the same bullet that hit the President, and certainly no-one could take such a near mortal wound and not be battered by it, moved by it at that instant, like a rag doll.

The Assassinations Committee admits to no shots whatsoever between frames 188 and 295, a period of six seconds.

The second immense anomaly left by the new investigation is the fact that there was no way the first two shots could have been fired by the gunman with just 1.6 seconds between them. The gun could not be loaded, aimed and fired in under 2.5 seconds or so, and even then it would take the best marksman in the world to hit such a target. Tests have shown this to be all but impossible.[44]

THE ALTGENS PHOTOGRAPH

At frame 255, AP photographer Ike Altgens took the most famous photograph of the assassination. The Warren Commission severely cropped this picture[45] so that we cannot see the cars farther back in the motorcade and the reaction of the Secret Service four cars back, while Kennedy's guards are doing nothing. And we cannot pinpoint precisely how far the car is from the corner, which shows in the original picture. This would show that the first hit occurred while the President was still shielded from the assassin's window by a large tree.

Altgens is one of the best witnesses to what happened. He was standing near the President when Kennedy was hit in the head. "There was flesh particles that flew out of the side of his head in my direction where I was standing, so much so that it indicated to me that the shot came out of the left side of his head."[46]

EYEWITNESS AND EXPERT TESTIMONY

Dr. Wecht, former President of the American Academy of Forensic Science, told the Assassinations Committee, "I have raised some questions concerning the head wound and the possibility ... of a second shot fired in synchronized fashion from the right side or the lower right rear, synchronized with the head shot that struck the President in the back of the head."[47] Wecht has long studied this case, and was one of the first to see the alleged autopsy evidence. He is an acknowledged expert in his field.

It is interesting that Senator Christopher Dodd also thought that another shot had to have been fired from the right side or right rear *by another gunman* along with those the Warren Commission admitted to, in addition to the shot from the Grassy Knoll.

"The Committee considered whether proper synchronization of the tape to the film should assume that the shot from the Grassy Knoll hit the President at Zapruder frame 312. It did so because Dr. Michael Baden, Chairman of the Committee's Forensic Pathology Panel, acknowledged there was a possibility, although highly remote, that the head wound depicted in Zapruder frame 312 could have been caused by a shot from the Grassy Knoll, and that medical evidence of it had been destroyed by a shot from the rear a fraction of a second later."[48]

The Committee answered this question with an easy out: "It was determined by medical, ballistics and neutron activation evidence that the President was struck in the head by a bullet fired from a rifle found on the sixth floor of the TSBD. For that bullet to have destroyed the medical evidence of the President being hit at Zapruder frame 312, it would have had to have struck at Zapruder frames 328-29. But a preliminary trajectory analysis, based on the President's location and body position at frame 328-29 failed to track to a shooter in the sixth floor southeast corner window of the Depository..."[49] Another gunman could have fired from elsewhere.

The Committee conducted a preliminary "blur analysis" of the Zapruder film. It appeared that Zapruder was startled by the shots and jiggled the camera. In a microscopic footnote to the above, the Committee wrote "The blur analysis conducted by the photographic evidence panel appeared to be more consistent with the Grassy Knoll shot striking the President."[50] This means that a shot could also have come from the manhole on the bridge ahead, facing the car and above it.

There is a postscript discussing the blur analysis that was done on the Zapruder film. "This analysis indicated that the blurs occurring at frames 189-197 and 312-334 may reasonably be attributed to Zapruder's startle reactions to gun shots... The possibility that other blurs on the film might be attributable to Zapruder's reactions to gunshots could not be confirmed or dismissed without additional data."

A more serious problem arose, but was again sidestepped: "The acoustical analysis had indicated both the first and second impulse patterns were shots from the vicinity of Texas School Book Depository, but that there were only 1.66 seconds between the onset of each of these impulse patterns. The Committee recognized that 1.66 seconds is too brief a period for both shots to have been fired from Oswald's rifle, given the results of tests performed for the Warren Commission that found that the average minimum firing time between shots was 2.3 seconds."[51] Again, there was an easy answer: "The tests for the Warren Commission, however, were based on the assumption that Oswald used the telescopic sight on the rifle."[52]

So the Chief Counsel of the Committee, G. Robert Blakey, got out there in the weeds and fired off some rounds with a similar weapon and without the scope. "It found that it was possible for two shots to be fired within 1.66 seconds. One gunman, therefore, could have fired the shots that caused both impulse pattern 1 and impulse pattern 2 on the dispatch tape."[53] But to say that he could have fired the two shots and that he did fire the two shots are two different matters. Neither the Chief Counsel, his assistant, or any of their marksmen were able to hit anything within that time span. Certainly, Oswald, a poor shot, could not have done so. Imagine trying to load, aim and fire a bolt action rifle within one and a half seconds at a moving target.

The most serious problem of all was not dealt with. The Warren Commission found that no shots could have been fired before frame 210 of the Zapruder film because a tree was in the way between the window and the limousine, as Dallas Police Chief Jesse Curry wrote.[54] The acoustics tests show that if the tape is synchronized with the fourth impulse to frame 312 of the Zapruder film as the head shot and final shot or impulse on the tape, the first shot came at frame 157-161, and the second at frame 188-191;[55] both shots came before it was possible to shoot from the "assassin's window." This is why HSCA Report author Richard Billings wrote that "The acoustical analysis had indicated both the first and the second impulse patterns were shots from the vicinity of the Texas School Book Depository..."[56] *Vicinity.*

The evidence shows that another sniper, perhaps the real sniper, was in fact firing from behind and below the corner window of the TSBD, as Senator Dodd believed. "The strongest evidence that one gunman did, in fact, fire the shots that caused both impulse patterns was that all three cartridge cases found on the sixth floor of the Texas School Book Depository came from Oswald's rifle."[57]

If this is strong evidence, then we are in trouble, because they have nothing to back up this fantasy. They are trying to back it up with the following: "In addition, the fragments from two bullets that were found were identified as having been fired from Oswald's rifle."[58] As we have seen, there is no way that this has in fact been done or can really be done. The cartridge cases could have been planted there, and – from the way in which they were laid out – probably were, and they could have been fired at some other time. What evidence was there that the so-called Oswald rifle had been fired that day? It did not have the characteristic odor of a recently fired gun.

Certainly if the first shot missed, as the Committee says, and the second bullet hit both men at frame 188 to 191, then the fragments from the so-called pristine "nearly whole bullet" are the above-mentioned fragments linking these two shots to the Oswald window. However, if the fragments weigh more than was lost from the bullet recovered, which they do, then something is drastically wrong with the official version. The missed shot did not hit the car, but more likely was the one that struck James Tague after hitting a curb farther down the street.

There had to be two gunmen firing the first two shots within that 1.6 seconds.

Assuming that there was a shot at frames 157 to 161, which co-author Robert Groden and the Committee found to be the first shot, "This would be consistent with the testimony of Governor Connally who stated that he heard the first shot and began to turn in response to it. His reactions, as shown in Zapruder frames 162-167, reflect the start of a rapid head movement from left to right."[59] This is the first time Connally's testimony has been considered, since he also said that he was not hit with the same shot that later hit the President. That was disregarded.

"...the second shot hit the limousine's occupants at about Zapruder frame 188-191. The (photographic) panel noted that at approximately Zapruder frame 200 the President's movements suddenly freeze, as his right hand seemed to stop abruptly in the midst of a waving motion. Then during frames 200-202, his head moves rapidly from right to left. The sudden interruption of the President's hand-waving motion, coupled with his rapid head movements, was considered by the photographic panel as evidence of President Kennedy's reaction to some 'severe external stimulus.'"[60]

"Finally, the panel observed that Governor Connally's actions during frames 222-226, as he is seen emerging from behind the sign that obstructed Zapruder's view, indicated he was also reacting to some 'severe external stimulus.'"[61] According to this, the Governor is not reacting to the bullet that nearly killed him for a period of two seconds, which is highly unlikely. Independent analysis of the film by the person who has done the most work on it over the years, co-author Robert Groden, photographic consultant to the Committee, finds that Connally is not struck by a bullet until frame 236, and Connally agrees.

Dr. Cyril Wecht, a member of the medical panel, testified as a minority of one that "it is my opinion that no bullet could have caused all these wounds, not only 399, but no other bullet that we know about or any fragment of any bullet that we know about in the case."[62]

NO EVIDENCE

This is what Governor Connally and his wife said as well.[63] In fact, few believe that the President and the Governor could have been hit by the same bullet. But the medical panel found that they were, just as the Warren Commission did, without a shred of evidence to back it up. Dr. Wecht, former President of the American Academy of Forensic Science, outlined his reasons at length. He has been consistently misquoted and his testimony changed[64] by former Vice President Rockefeller and David Belin*.

"Since the medical, ballistics and neutron activation analysis evidence, taken together, established that the President was struck by two bullets fired from Oswald's rifle found on the sixth floor of the Texas

---

*In 1973 President Ford (one of the seven Warren Commissioners) established a commission to investigate illegal U.S. intelligence organization excesses and operations within the United States, and as a side issue to hear a few questions about President Kennedy's murder, since the intelligence agencies were accused of having killed him. The Commission was headed by Vice President Nelson Rockefeller and became known as the Rockefeller Commission. It was generally considered to be a whitewash.

The Chief Counsel was David Belin, who had been an Assistant Counsel for the Warren Commission and to this day is its chief defender. Numerous witnesses accused him of changing their testimony in 1963-4, and all of the primary critics of the Warren Report who were asked to testify before the Rockefeller Commission concerning new evidence in John Kennedy's murder stated that their testimony had been changed or distorted.

School Book Depository, the committee sought to determine if such shots could have struck the President, given the known position of his body, even if the grassy knoll shot struck him at Zapruder frame 312."[65] The result of this was that the fourth shot came at frame 328 of the Zapruder film, after the head shot. They rejected what logic told them, since "it was determined by medical, ballistics and neutron activation analysis evidence that the President was struck in the head by a bullet fired from a rifle found on the sixth floor of the TSBD."[66] Missing is the photographic evidence of the Zapruder film, which clearly shows the President being struck from in front. Yet, the shot more likely came from the manhole on the overpass ahead to the left of the car. Only a split second separated the two shots. Witnesses and Secret Service men reported more than four shots at the time, and a fusillade, or "bursts."

"Accordingly, if the shot from the grassy knoll occurred at frame 312, no shot fired from the TSBD would have struck the President in the head at any time. Such a finding is contrary to the weight of the scientific evidence. The committee concluded, therefore, that the shot fired from the grassy knoll was not the shot visually represented at Zapruder frame 312; that the shot from the grassy knoll missed President Kennedy..."[67]

The Committee failed to question many matters with due deliberation. If the medical evidence was forged, then their trajectory analysis was wrong and their ballistic evidence was invalid.

THE NIX FILM

A film was taken by Orville Nix at the moment of impact on the head, but the public never heard about this film. For many years after the murder, most Americans had the impression that there was only one film, the Zapruder film. In fact, there were a number of films taken, and many photographs. Much of the rest of the evidence was seized by the authorities and suppressed.[68] The Nix film was taken across the street from Zapruder. This film also makes very clear that the President has been hit from the front and is being driven – rocketed – backwards. But the important thing about this film is that you can see what appears to be one of the gunmen aiming a rifle at Kennedy. He is on the Grassy Knoll, just where many witnesses placed him, and where they saw a puff of smoke.[69]

In fact, 42 witnesses told the Warren Commission that there were guns in front of John Kennedy.[70]

In the 18 frames surrounding frames 412 and 413 of the Zapruder film, we see what appears to be a man with a rifle in the place behind the bushes to Kennedy's right front.[71]

The Warren Commission decided, against all the medical evidence, that one bullet had done the job of hitting Kennedy and Connally, because more than one gunman would have represented a conspiracy. So the Committee went along with most of the rest of the conclusions of the Warren Commission, such as the magic bullet theory, because they are not ready to reveal the whole story.

HOW MANY SHOTS?

A more rational exposition of the evidence of gunshots, from the theories presented by the Warren Commission and the Assassinations Committee, is that the President was shot four times, Connally once or perhaps twice, and James Tague was hit with debris from another stray shot that missed. The firm knowledge among researchers is that the President was struck in the throat from in front, then struck in the back. Governor Connally was then hit with a separate shot, and then the President was struck twice in the head, first from behind and then from in front, at nearly the same instant.

Our research indicates that Governor Connally was struck in the wrist and thigh by a separate bullet, after the President was hit in the head, at about frame 328, when the audio tapes indicate another shot. James Tague was hit by a stray miss somewhere near the end of this time frame.

This gives a total of six or seven shots, which is the number of shots on the tape, counting a heterodyning effect.

There are six shots definitely recorded on the tape. There may have been additional simultaneous shots which would record as one. The three shots that the Warren Commission created were never more than an attempt to limit the number of shots to the number of empty bullet shells found in the Depository and to fit the available time.

"...It was possible to plot the path of the bullets out to their source... All three trajectories intercepted the southeast face of the Texas School Book Depository building. While the trajectories could not be plotted with sufficient precision to determine the exact point from which the

shots were fired, they each were calculated with a margin of error reflecting the precision of the underlying data. The margins of error were indicated as circles within which the shots originated. The southeast corner window of the Depository was inside each of the circles."[72]
"...The Committee conducted a trajectory analysis for the shot that it ultimately concluded struck both the Governor and the President. It was based on the location of the limousine and the body positions of President Kennedy and Governor Connally at Zapruder frame 190 and the bullet's course as it could be determined from their wounds. When President Kennedy's entry and exit wounds were used as reference points for the trajectory line, it intersected the Texas School Book Depository within a 13-foot radius of a point approximately fourteen feet West of the building's southeast corner and approximately two feet below the sixth floor window-sills. When President Kennedy's exit wound and Governor Connally's entrance wound were used as the reference points for the trajectory line, it intersected the Texas School Book Depository within a 7-foot radius of a point approximately two feet West of the southeast corner and nine feet *above* (emphasis added) the sixth floor window sills."[73]

It has often been postulated that one of the real assassins was on the roof of the building, just above the window, separated by the seventh floor, or about nine feet above the window. But there is a fundamental inconsistency on page 47 of the Report, which says: "The panel concluded that the two bullets that struck the President came from behind and that the fatal shot was moving in a downward direction when it struck the President."[74] "The panel did not attempt to determine the slope of the bullet that struck the President's back because the moment of impact was not thought to be visible in the film. This decision by the forensic pathology panel was made well before the photographic panel reached its conclusion regarding the President's and Governor Connally's reactions as shown in the Zapruder film."[75]

We can't put too much store on any trajectory analysis in this case. The main problem is that there is no clear way to determine when the President was first struck, since both he and Governor Connally are hidden behind a sign during crucial seconds of the Zapruder film, and since it is more than likely that the President was struck with a different bullet from that which hit Connally. As with the Warren Commission's guess finding that only three shots were fired based on the three cartridge cases found, any trajectory is mere guesswork.

"The photographic evidence panel studied evidence possibly relevant to the question of the origin of the shots, as follows:

"The panel examined a motion picture of the southeast corner window of the depository taken a short time prior to the shots. While there is an impression of motion in the film, the panel could not attribute it to the movement of a person or an object and instead attributed the motion to photographic artifacts.

"The panel studied two photographs taken within minutes of the assassination. While no human face or form could be detected in the sixth floor southeast window, the panel was able to conclude that a stack of boxes in the window had been rearranged during the interval of the taking of the two photographs.

MORE FILMS AND WITNESSES

"There is evidence, a motion picture film made by Charles L. Bronson, that some independent researchers believe shows a figure or figures in the sixth floor depository window several minutes before the shooting... because of its high quality, it was recommended that the Bronson film be analyzed further."[76] This study is still being conducted.

John Powell, a prisoner at the Dallas County Jail just across the street from the "assassin's window," also on the sixth floor, said that he and many inmates very clearly saw two men in the "assassin's window," who were adjusting the telescopic sight of the rifle one of them had. One of them appeared to be a Latin.[77]

The most important point in this, and the Bronson and Hughes films, is the evidence of movement in two windows eight feet apart – including "Oswald's window," tending to prove that there had to be two men there.[78] This is backed up by Carolyn Walther, who noticed two men with a gun in a corner window of the building.[79] She said one of the men was kneeling and pointing the gun downward, and he was resting his arms on the windowsill. Another man was standing beside the kneeling man with the rifle.

Ruby Henderson saw two men in an upper window less than five minutes before the shooting, and she thought one of them was a Latin.[80] Arnold Rowland also spotted a Latin-looking man in the "Oswald window" fifteen minutes before the shooting, but he saw a man with a rifle in a window at the other end of the floor.[81] Evidently, the sniper either shot from another window, or moved across the building to find a better spot.

The point is that there may have been two men in the window or adjacent windows. This conforms to the use of two men in each sniper team in a military-style ambush, where one man fires and the next man retrieves shells and acts as a lookout. Congressman (now Senator) Dodd, a former member of the Committee, believes that it was probable that only two shots were fired from the window, and the third cartridge case had been in the chamber of the rifle and was ejected before the firing began. One of the members of the photographic panel, Robert Selzer, believes that there was certainly movement in the Hughes film and that it was probably human, and in more than one window.[82]

THE SAME RIFLE?

"While the Committee relied primarily on scientific analysis of physical evidence as to the origin of the shots, it also considered the testimony of witnesses..."[83] The Report then goes on to tell us that Deputy Sheriff Luke Mooney found the three rifle shells and "the rifle Boone found, a 6.5 millimeter Mannlicher-Carcano..."[84] Affidavits sworn at the time of the assassination by Deputy Sheriff Seymour Weitzman state that the gun was a German Mauser: "Over the years, skepticism has arisen as to whether the rifle found in the Depository by Deputy Boone is the same rifle that was delivered to the Warren Commission and is presently in the National Archives. The suspicion has been based to some extent on allegations that police officers who first discovered the rifle identified it as a 7.5 millimeter German Mauser. The controversy was intensified by the allegation that various photographs of the rifle, taken at different times, portray inconsistencies with respect to the proportions of the various component parts.

"To resolve the controversy, the Committee assembled a wide range of photographs of the rifle... The examination by Committee photographic consultants determined that all photographs were of the same rifle."[85]

This totally ignores a sworn affidavit by Deputy Sheriff Weitzman – a man with extensive experience in guns, who owned gun shops, who had a graduate degree in Engineering – that the gun was a Mauser, a favored weapon of snipers. It is highly improbable that he could have confused a German Mauser with the alleged assassin's rifle,[86] since the Mannlicher-Carcano clearly has inscribed on it: "Made in Italy."[87]

The other problem the Committee sidesteps here is that the rifle in the Archives may not be the same one the Warren Commission had, and a close reading of the above quotes makes it clear that the Committee has a problem with that too, when they say: "Since the rifle had been test-fired numerous times since 1963, its barrel had been altered by wear, and bullets the panel fired from the rifle did not match either the FBI test cartridges or those found on the sixth floor of the depository or that found on the stretcher."[88]

The Report goes on to say, without elaboration: "There is no medical evidence that the President was struck by a bullet entering the front of the head. The possibility that a bullet entered the front of the head, and the possibility that a bullet could have struck the President and yet left no evidence is extremely remote."[89] It is only "remote" if the evidence has been destroyed: The brain stolen, the autopsy pictures forged, the X-rays fabricated and the testimony of many doctors disregarded. Dr. Charles Wilber states that the frontal wound was in fact drawn on the autopsy face sheet.[90]

FRONTAL WOUND ON THE HEAD'S LEFT SIDE

The Zapruder, Nix, Muchmore, and Bronson films corroborate evidence of a frontal shot. The Dallas death certificate read: "The cause of death was due to massive head and brain injury from a gunshot wound of the left temple."[91]

The President's wife climbed far out on the rear of the car to retrieve the back of the President's head, which went rearward.

Dr. Marion Jenkins, of Parkland Hospital, said, "I thought there was a wound on the left temple area: I thought there was a wound in the hairline and right above the zygomatic process."[92] Dr. Jenkins said that he was feeling for a pulse and felt the wound at the left temple. The priest, Father Oscar Huber, said that there was a "terrible wound" over his left eye.[93] A bystander, Norman Similas of Toronto, Canada, said that as President Kennedy passed him, "I could see a hole in the President's left temple and his head and hair were bathed in blood."[94] Dr. Adolphe Giesecke also thought he had seen a wound in the left temple.[95]

Motorcycle policemen Hargis and Martin riding at the left rear of the President's limousine were splattered with the President's blood and brains. Hargis testified to the Warren Commission,[96] "I was splattered with blood and brain, and kind of bloody water." He parked his motorcycle and ran up on the Grassy Knoll where he felt the shot came from, as Dallas Police Chief Jesse Curry wrote.[97] There was no doubt in Hargis' mind where the shot came from. A piece of bone found by Billy Harper, given to the Chief Pathologist at Methodist Hospital and identified as occipital bone, was found 25 feet behind and to the left of the car's position when the President was hit in the head, according to the Secret Service.[98] Occipital bone comes only from the back of the head, indicating a frontal shot. Deputy Constable Seymour Weitzman also found pieces of bone at the curb and on the grass to the left of the car, indicating that a shot from the front hit.[99]

Bystander Charles Brehm saw "That which appeared to be a portion of the President's skull went flying slightly to the rear of the President's car and directly to its left. It did fly over toward the curb to the left and to the rear."[100] The motorcycle policemen to the right rear of the President's limousine were not struck with any debris; neither were the people in the front seat of the limousine. The debris went in *only* one direction: backwards and to the left! The limousine was moving so slowly during the ambush that after the President was hit in the head, Clint Hill ran up to the limousine from the follow-up car and climbed onto the trunk. Only then did the driver of the limousine accelerate and leave the scene.

The President's head moves rearward from the moment of impact of the bullet at 100 feet per second per second in the films. Why did *Life Magazine* publish more than one version of the stills from the film in their October 2, 1964, issue? They withdrew the first version, substituting frame 313 of the Zapruder film which showed Kennedy's head exploding "forward," as the picture was captioned, for frame 323 which showed him pushed back in the seat by the force of the shot an instant later. The Warren Commission reversed other frames for the same purpose as well.[101]

Over 40 witnesses stated that a gun was fired from ahead of the car on the Grassy Knoll.[102]

An AP dispatch that day from Dallas stated that Dr. Malcolm Perry "Said the entrance wound was in the front of the head." Officer James

Chaney said the President was "Struck in the face."[103] He was so badly damaged, apparently, that the coffin had to remain closed. S.M. Holland, a bystander, said the bullet hit "part of his face."[104] NBC News reported that day "that a bullet struck him in front as he faced the assailant." And many doctors and nurses described his throat wound, in addition to the head wound being a frontal shot, as also having been caused by a shot from the front.

Dr. Boswell's drawing of the head wounds, still stained with the President's blood, show a three centimeter wound in the left eye-temple area. Charles Wilber writes that the President's face "was significantly disfigured at the time of autopsy to an extent that the mortician would not cover over the injury in such a way as to permit an 'open coffin.'"[105]

The trajectories of the brain, skull, and flesh matter from the President's head at the time of the fatal head shot demonstrated that he was hit by a powerful shot from in front of him, which blew his head and body along with it in the direction that the debris was thrown – along the original path of the bullet.

BALLISTICS AND THE TESTS

Deputy Constable Seymour Weitzman was the man who first found the rifle in the Book Depository,* and he identified it as a German Mauser.[106] One of the three cartridges could not have come out of the rifle because of the dent* on it.[107] The Dallas Police turned over only two of the shells to the FBI,[108] and one expended cartridge has a dented lip and shows marks indicating that it had been loaded and extracted from a weapon at least three times.[109]

*The House Committee says "The Rifle Boone Found." The panel says that a Mannlicher could be mistaken for a Mauser and that the caliber cannot be determined merely by looking at it, ignoring the information that was in fact stamped on the guns as to make and caliber for both guns. We are talking about several rifles here; the Warren Commission gun is not the same size as that ordered by Oswald from Kliens, and the gun Weitzman and Craig found is not the same as that which Boone found. "The rifle which Boone found" is the same kind of double talk that allows an intelligence agency to deny they have a file on Lee Harvey Oswald when it is filed under Harvey Lee Oswald. See O'Toole 17, 18 on Mauser.

*"It is the opinion of the panel that the dent on the mouth of the CE543 cartridge case was produced when the cartrige case was ejected from the rifle. This condition was duplicated during test firing..." but/and "There was no evidence in the form of multiple extractor or ejector marks on the cartridge case to indicate that it was chambered in the rifle more than once." What happened to them? The Findings and Conclusions of the Fire-arms Panel; 7HSCA 365 to end.

Commission Exhibit 2003 states the evidence listed by the police, which they collected: "1. Italian make 6.5 rifle... Found by Dept. Sheriff Weitzman..." We have noted how the Assassinations Committee clearly changed this evidence to say something else: that someone else found the rifle.[110] The police have already changed what Weitzman found from a Mauser to an Italian rifle. It is only one more step before he disappears altogether in the latest retelling.

Appeals Judge Jim Garrison wrote: "The neck wound, with the indications of a bullet entry but no exit, was to be the last real hurdle for the planners of the assassination. Afterwards, the federal government would seize control of the investigation despite its complete lack of legal authority..."[111]

Anthony Summers wrote in *Conspiracy*, "The Committee was further convinced by sophisticated modern tests which had not been made sixteen years ago. Dr. Vincent Guinn, a chemist and forensic scientist, broke new ground with his "neutron activation" tests—a process in which the bullet specimens were bombarded with neutrons in a nuclear reactor. The results were impressive, and appear to resolve fundamental areas of controversy."[112] Neutron activation tests had been conducted years ago in the case, but the results were kept secret.

"...concluded that these represented only two bullets and that it was 'highly probable' that both were of Mannlicher-Carcano manufacture – the ammunition designed for the rifle found in the Book Depository. The phrase 'highly probable' is the cautious formal language of the scientist going on the record, but a personal interview with Guinn confirms that he is highly confident of his conclusion."

Gary Shaw writes, "While it is not mentioned in the report or the 26 volumes (of the Warren Report), CE 399 and other bullet fragments were also subjected to Neutron Activation Analysis (NAA), a test even more definitive than spectrographic analysis. In simple terms, NAA is a highly sophisticated technique in which differences in the composition of objects is measured by bombarding the objects with radiation down to parts per billion."[113] Summers does not tell us any of this, let alone that the test was run 16 years before. Harold Weisberg battled in court for years to get those results, as the dead President's brother, Senator Edward Kennedy, well knows.

"In another letter from Hoover to Rankin (not released from the Archives until 1973), the FBI Director reports: 'While minor variations in composition were found by this method, these were not considered to be sufficient to permit positively differentiating among the larger bullet fragments and thus positively determining from which of the larger bullet fragments any given small lead fragment may have come.'"[114] This means that the tests were inconclusive. Gary Shaw goes on to say that "this letter emerges as one of the most damaging pieces of evidence against the single-bullet theory, for what Hoover does not mention is that with NAA the amount of difference between particles is virtually meaningless; *any* difference, no matter how small, is both sufficient and irrefutable. The tests *were* conclusive, and they prove that JFK and the Governor were indeed struck by separate bullets."[115]

Spectrographic analysis tests were also run by the FBI, and the government has made every effort to suppress the results. Had the results stated conclusively, as Shaw points out, that the fragments in Connally were the same as those taken from the magic bullet, and from Kennedy's head and from the floor of the limousine, the government would have had those results in the first chapter of its Report.[116] Harold Weisberg finally got the actual test results after another long suit, and they were again inconclusive.[117] Hoover again wrote Rankin about the tests, and said that the composition of the fragments was "similar" and that "no significant differences were found."[118] We have already seen that there were different bullets involved. Who was Hoover covering up for?

It is not the practice of FBI agents and the Secret Service to confuse fragments with missiles. We have the following evidence that a bullet was in fact recovered from the body of President Kennedy. There is a receipt from the Treasury Department, Protective Research Section, signed by Robert Bouck for "the following items from Dr. George G. Burkley:... One receipt from FBI for a missile removed during the examination of the body."[119] We have the receipt from two FBI men present in the autopsy room, Francis X. O'Neill, Jr. and James Sibert: "We hereby acknowledge receipt of a missle (sic) removed by Commander James J. Humes, MC, USN, on this date."[120] These men were from Baltimore. What were they doing in Bethesda in the autopsy room? Why weren't high-ranking men sent from Washington?

Admiral (then Captain) David Osborne thought he saw an intact bullet roll out from the wrappings of President Kennedy and onto the autopsy table. When again contacted by the Committee, the Admiral said that he was not sure that he actually did see a missile.[121]

THE FRAME-UP

George O'Toole, former chief of the Problems Analysis Branch at the CIA, thinks that the Dallas Police, that is, certain key personnel among them, helped blame Oswald for the murders of Kennedy and Tippit. "The frame-up formula is much simpler than might be imagined... recruit some police, not the entire department, just a few key officers who are in a position to fabricate a chain of evidence linking the scapegoat to the crime, officers in the crime scene search unit, the crime lab, and perhaps a polygraph examiner to confirm the truthfulness of witnesses against the fall guy and impugn the word of those who might exonerate him."[122]

The Dallas Police ran off numerous copies of the backyard photograph allegedly of Oswald, and distributed it among themselves, obviously firming up the idea that Oswald was the killer. They never bothered to tell the Warren Commission about these pictures.

But most important, as Gary Shaw writes in *Cover-up* "...no less than the Assistant Chief of Police was recruited to personally escort Jack Ruby into the Dallas Police Station basement to kill Oswald."[123] Co-author Harrison Livingstone went to Dallas and talked to the attorney for Roy Vaughn, the policeman on duty guarding the ramp at the time Jack Ruby was supposed to have passed Vaughn and shot Oswald. The attorney, James Niell, claims that Ruby never did pass Vaughn, but entered the police station with Assistant Chief of Police Charles Batchelor, who later became the Chief of Police.

Batchelor was in charge of security precautions for both the motorcade of November 22, and the transfer of Oswald on November 24.[124] He lost both his charges, and was promoted to Chief when Curry retired.

The original source of the Batchelor story was apparently Red Davis of the Dallas Police, who stated to Officer Vaughn, after Vaughn took and passed a lie detector test: "God, you shouldn't even have to do that," and told him that Batchelor took Ruby inside via the elevator.[125]

Vaughn says he took three lie detector tests that show he told the truth. Niell says that another lie detector test given to Daniels, who was standing with Vaughn at the ramp, shows that he did not tell the truth.

Vaughn was told by Chief Byrd to see City Attorney Alex Bickley, who told him not to file a suit because "the truth might come out about how Ruby got into the basement." Vaughn filed the suit anyway. He resented having taken the heat all these years, and being depicted as part of a criminal conspiracy.

The Assassinations Committee admitted that Ruby had help getting into the basement,[126] probably because of the strength of this evidence, but they would not admit what really happened. Niell says that someone started to search the basement of the Dallas P.D. before the transfer of Oswald, and Batchelor told him not to. Daniels, the witness who said he saw Ruby's entrance down the ramp, told Roy Vaughn right after the shooting that he did not see Ruby, but later changed his story. Niell says someone pressured Daniels to lie.

Ruby told Tom Johnson, a journalist and close friend of Earl Golz, and a former aide to Lyndon Johnson: "It is the most bizarre conspiracy in the history of the world. It'll come out at a future date." "I walked into a trap when I walked down there. I wasn't clean enough. It was my destiny. I'd taken 30 antibiotic and dexidrene pills. They stimulate you."[127]

Ruby told reporter Tom Johnson that he got his .38 Colt Cobra from Roy Brantly. "I became panicky when I saw Brantly's name on the witness list. 'Steve, I sent guns to Cuba in 1959,' but all I did was relay a call. Brantly denies he ever got the call."

Former Chief of Police Jesse Curry told Tom Johnson that he did not think Oswald acted alone. "We don't have any proof that Oswald fired the rifle, and never did. Nobody's yet been able to put him in that building with a gun in his hand."[128]

Later on, we will consider oilmen Clint Murchison's and H.L. Hunt's interest in this case. Clint Murchison owned Holt, Rhinehart and Winston, which was J. Edgar Hoover's publisher. Both Hoover and Richard Nixon were at a meeting at Murchison's house the night before the assassination.[129] H.L. Hunt financed the writing of the book *Khrushchev Killed Kennedy* by Michael Eddowes, through Hunt's American Volunteer Group, according to Earl Golz of the *Dallas Morning News* .[130]

There were many Right Wing extremists in Dallas who hated Kennedy and all liberals. Some of them were policemen in Dallas, and Assistant D.A. William Alexander was one of these extremists. It has been suggested that Alexander was in the police car that stopped in front of Oswald's house around 30 minutes after the assassination. He was in on the arrest of Oswald at the Texas Theatre shortly after, and was "waiting with a group of policemen in the alley behind the theater." [131] It is believed that someone intended to murder Oswald there, but was foiled when Oswald didn't run out of the theater.

The man who was in command of the search that found the cartridge cases on the sixth floor was Officer Gerald Hill, [132] a friend of Jack Ruby and a Right Wing activist. [133] But the discovery of the spent shells was attributed in the official report to Deputy Sheriff Luke Mooney. [134] Hill was in the second police car to arrive at the scene where Tippit was murdered, and he was at the Texas Theatre when Oswald was apprehended. Riding with Hill was William Alexander. [135] Why would an assistant D.A. be playing cop? Alexander was known to be a crazy hot-head who said on the day of the assassination, after the arrest of Oswald, "Yes, he is a Goddamn Communist." Later that day, he was ready to charge the prisoner with killing the President "as part of an international Communist conspiracy." Later, he advocated that Earl Warren be hanged because of his liberal views and Supreme Court decisions. "He is alleged to have threatened to kill a man in the courthouse by jamming a pistol to the man's head and saying 'You son of a bitch, I will kill you right here!'" [136]

His friend Officer Hill testified that he had custody of the .38 revolver supposedly found on Oswald. He was questioned before the Warren Commission by David Belin, who would be one of our first suspects at the top of the list for the cover-up of this conspiracy. [137]

Belin: "Now, you said as the driver of the car, Bob Carroll, got in the car, he handed this gun to you?"

Hill: "Right, sir."

"All right, then, would you tell us what happened? What was said and what was done?"

"Then I broke the gun open to see how many shells it contained and how many live rounds it had in it."

"How many did you find?"

"There were six in the chambers of the gun..." He is speaking of a revolver.

IMPOSSIBLE CLAIMS

How in the world could Oswald have shot Tippit four times if his gun was still fully loaded? Had he had time to reload it? Wouldn't he have had extra shells left on him if he had reloaded it? Was the gun ever fired?

In the murder of Tippit, it should be noted that revolvers do not eject shells. If the shells found at the scene came from a revolver, they were deliberately planted.

In Hill's arrest report for Oswald, he wrote, "When the pistol was given to me, it was fully loaded and one of the shells had a hammer-mark on the primer."[138]

The Assassinations Committee and the Warren Commission have told us that Oswald shot Officer Tippit. This seems extremely unlikely, because there simply wasn't enough time for him to get from his house to the murder scene and then to the movie theater. He did not fit the description of the killers given by witnesses, and there was no evidence that the hand weapon attributed to him was fired that day. The first thing the police would do is establish that a gun had been fired or not fired. There were no fingerprints on the weapon either.

George DeMohrenschildt wrote in his manuscript that Oswald owned a Beretta,[139] which certainly is not the above hand-gun.

Oswald was the patsy for this one, too. It may be that it was merely a coincidence that a police officer was killed a short time after the assassination, or that there was some sort of love triangle at the root of it. The clear truth is that framing Oswald for the murder nailed the lid on Oswald's coffin.

Witnesses said six or seven shots were fired.

– Dallas Times Herald, afternoon edition
November 22, 1963

CHAPTER 12

ACOUSTICS

Just as the House Committee was about to finish its work without finding a conspiracy, members were forced to admit that "Scientific acoustical evidence establishes a high probability that two gunmen fired at President John F. Kennedy; other scientific evidence does not preclude the possibility of two gunmen firing at the President..."[1]

The Dallas Police recorded their radio transmissions, and a Dicta-belt was long known to exist that was made during the moments of the assassination. "The Commission recognized that acoustics might be used to resolve some questions about the shots fired at the President. It had obtained a tape recording, an alleged on-the-scene account of the assassination made by Sam Pate, a Dallas radio newsman, but an FBI examination of the tape 'failed to indicate the presence of any sounds which could be interpreted as gunshots.'

"The Commission independently submitted the tape for analysis to Dr. Lawrence Kersta of Bell Telephone Acoustics & Speech Research Laboratory... The spectrograms indicated there were six nonvoiced noises..."[2] That is as far as it went, and the results of Dr. Kersta's tests were not mentioned in the Warren Report.

The original tape of the Dallas Police Department recordings has disappeared from the National Archives.

It has long been believed by researchers that at least six or seven shots were fired during the assassination. The Warren Commission admitted to only three. The Commission had no hard evidence to back up a limit of no more than three shots, except that they had found three shell casings in the "sniper's window," and they would not admit to more snipers elsewhere, in spite of strong and compelling testimony to the contrary – powerful scientific evidence. They would not or could not admit to more than two bullets causing wounds, saying the third bullet missed the target and hit James Tague, a bystander.

Gary Mack and other researchers in Texas pressed for an examination of the Dallas Police Dictabelt. The Committee, of course, did not want anything to contradict "the desired result," and did not submit the recordings for tests until May of 1978, a few months before the Committee would wind up its work. This did not allow enough time for adequate examination and reporting of the results. In fact, the initial report from Dr. James Barger of Bolt, Beranek and Newman in Cambridge, Mass. was nearly suppressed. "The firm was also selected by Judge John J. Sirica to serve on a panel of technical experts that examined the Watergate tapes in 1973."[3] The Report went on to say that "it did not appear that an acoustical analysis of these tapes or Dictabelts was performed for the Warren Commission by the FBI or any other agency or private organization."[4] We were told only that the Bell Labs did test the tape.

"BBN (Bolt, Beranek and Newman) converted the sounds on the tape into digitized waveforms and produced a visual representation of the waveforms. By employing sophisticated electronic filters, BBN filtered out repetitive noise," such as repeated firings of the pistons of a motorcycle engine. It then examined the tape for "sequences of impulses" that might be significant. (A "sequence of impulses" might be caused by a loud noise – such as gunfire – followed by the echoes from that loud noise.) Six sequences of impulses that could have been caused by a noise such as gunfire were initially identified as having been transmitted..."[5]

HOW MANY SHOTS?

Keep in mind that they are talking about six such noises that might be gunfire. The Committee eventually admitted to at least four shots, one more than the Warren Commission, but, as Robert Blakey, who for a time was the Chief Counsel of the Assassinations Committee, has often said, "There are six or seven shots on the tape." (Two of the shots are nearly simultaneous, which causes some confusion regarding the number of shots fired.) They weren't ready to reveal all this, so the Committee simply ignored two or three shots.

"These six sequences of impulses, or impulse patterns, were subjected to preliminary screening tests to determine if any could be conclusively determined not to have been caused by gunfire during the assassination. The screening tests were designed to answer the following questions: (1) Do the impulse patterns, in fact, occur during the period of the assassination?"[6]

According to this, any shot which occurred just before or after what was previously conceived as the first and last shot was not counted. This caused great difficulty when the acoustics test found that one of the impulses came from the Grassy Knoll, and that it was followed by another impulse less than a second later. This was known as "Blakey's Problem."

"Are the impulse patterns unique to the period of the assassination?"[7] Yes.

"Does the span of time of the impulse patterns approximate the duration of the assassination as indicated by a preliminary analysis of the Zapruder film? (Are there at least 5.6 seconds between the first and last impulse?)"[8] The 5.6 second standard was based on a preliminary examination of the Zapruder film that showed Kennedy and Connally reacting to their wounds. This 5.6 second standard was derived before the photographic evidence panel had reported the results of its observations of the Zapruder film.

"Does the shape of the impulse patterns resemble the shape of impulse patterns produced when the sound of gunfire is recorded through a radio transmission system comparable to the one used for the Dallas police dispatch network?[9]

"Are the amplitudes of the impulse patterns similar to those produced when the sound of gunfire is recorded through a transmission system comparable to the one used for the Dallas police dispatch network?"[10]

All six impulse patterns passed the preliminary screening tests. (Emphasis added.)[11] All *six*.

THE BEGINNING OF THE END

Here was a moment of great historical significance. It marked the beginning of the Warren Commission's demise as a legitimate investigation.

"BBN next recommended that the committee conduct an acoustical reconstruction of the assassination in Dealey Plaza to determine if any of the six impulse patterns on the dispatch tape were caused by shots and, if so, if the shots were fired from the Texas School Book Depository or Grassy Knoll. The reconstruction would entail firing from two locations in Dealey Plaza – the depository and the knoll – at particular target locations, and recording the sounds through numerous microphones."[12]

"The theoretical rationale for the reconstruction was as follows: The sequence of impulses from a gunshot is caused by the noise of the shot, followed by several echoes. Each combination of shooter location, target location and microphone location produces a sequence of uniquely spaced impulses. At a given microphone location, there would be a unique sequence of impulses, depending on the location of the noise source (gunfire) and the target, and the urban environment of the surrounding area"..."The time of arrival of the echoes would be the significant aspect of the sequence of impulses that would be used to compare the 1963 dispatch tape with the sounds recorded during the 1978 reconstruction."[13]

"The echo patterns in a complex environment such as Dealey Plaza are unique, so by conducting the reconstruction, the committee could obtain unique 'acoustical fingerprints' of various combinations of shooter, target and microphone locations. The fingerprint's identifying characteristic would be the unique time-spacing between the echoes. If any of the acoustical fingerprints produced in the 1978 reconstruction matched those on the 1963 Dallas police tape, it would be a strong indication that the sounds on the 1963 Dallas police dispatch tape were caused by gunfire recorded by a police microphone in Dealey Plaza."[14]

"At the time of the reconstruction in August 1978, the committee was extremely conscious of the significance of Barger's preliminary work, realizing, as it did, that his analysis indicated that there possibly were too many shots, spaced too closely together, for Lee Harvey

Oswald to have fired all of them, and that one of the shots came from the grassy knoll, not the Texas School Book Depository." [15]

The problem with this, it was later discovered, was that the police recording was made from a moving motorcycle. Stationary microphones used in the test would make the calculations more difficult.

The second problem was that only two sniper locations were assumed, rather than more, to account for the six or possibly seven shots. [16] There is an interruption in the recording, a heterodyning caused by another microphone being turned on. There are reasons to believe that there was a seventh shot at that point, and co-author Robert Groden believes that the possible shot at that point struck President Kennedy in the back and did not exit, because of his reactions recorded on film.

There are strong reasons to believe that snipers were facing the car, located in a manhole at the northwest juncture of the triple overpass and the stockade fence, and in a manhole at the southwest corner of the overpass – both looking down on the car from each side as it approached – and another sniper on the second floor of the Dal-Tex Building behind the limousine, near the building where Oswald was supposed to be. This is important because the tests that were conducted only admit to four of the six shots for which there is evidence. There is no question but that there are at least two more gunshots on the tape, but the tests were not complete enough to determine where these shots came from. That is, they couldn't get a precise match between the sounds of the test shots and those on the tape, which were probably fired from other locations with different echoes and configurations.

"Accordingly, impulses one and six on the dispatch tape did not pass the most rigorous acoustical test and were deemed not to have been caused by gunfire from the Texas School Book Depository or grassy knoll." [17] What were they, if not shots? When Richard Billings wrote this, he was very careful to name the two locations so that everyone would understand that there were other possible firing locations. The most likely places were the manholes and the Dal-Tex Building. The first impulse is 1/2 second before the second, and the sixth is 7/10 of a second after the fifth. [18] These demonstrate the existence of a third, and possibly a fourth, gunman.

As for the Grassy Knoll, the testers placed a shooter at a point on the stockade fence near where witnesses and the Mooreman photograph had indicated another sniper was located. Given the echo patterns obtained, the noise had to have originated at the very spot behind the picket fence on the Grassy Knoll that had been identified, indicating that it could not have been a backfire from a motorcycle in the motorcade.[19]

NOT JUST IMPULSES, BUT GUNSHOTS

All six impulses are ten decibels above every other noise on the tape,[20] and can only be gunshots.

A serious problem now arose for the Committee, because the Grassy Knoll shot was the third and not the final shot in the sequence of four shots they were going to admit to. As Chairman Stokes said privately, "We all know that the fatal head shot came from in front."[21] The whole Committee and staff knew this, as the Zapruder film makes clear beyond question. But no-one is willing to publicly acknowledge the evidence.

The head shot occurs at frame 312 of the Zapruder film, and so the sequence of shots had to be moved around that benchmark, making the Grassy Knoll shot appear to miss the President, and the final shot of the admitted four strike the President in the head from behind. The Report put it like this: "Nevertheless the possibility of frame 312 representing the shot fired from the grassy knoll, with the fourth shot consequently occurring at frame 328, was also considered. The problem with this possibility is that it appeared to be inconsistent with other scientific evidence that established that all the shots that struck the President and the Governor came from the Texas School Book Depository."[22]

Gary Mack writes: "Billings and others had difficulty writing about the acoustics evidence. Once corrected for the tape speed, the time between shots 3 and 4 was only a half second, or 9 Z frames. Therefore, if Z 312 was the head shot, shot #4 was fired at Z 321 not 328."

ACOUSTICAL EVIDENCE QUESTIONED

There have been a number of assaults on the acoustical evidence in this case. That was to be expected. First, some tried to say that there was no microphone open in Dealey Plaza at all, but it was possible to predict precisely where a microphone had to be at the instant of each shot by the length of the echoes and the time it took the sound to travel. A motorcycle policeman, H. B. McLain, had been photographed in that precise spot in the motorcade.

The FBI then tried to denounce the evidence and flatly repudiated it, without conducting any tests of their own, without even knowing how to analyze the scientific data presented in the evidence. They simply denounced it, and then had to sheepishly retract their denunciation and admit to Robert Blakey and others that the FBI did not know how to analyze the data.

Desperate defenders of the Warren Report mounted still another assault on this evidence. The National Science Foundation was asked to set up a Committee under Dr. Norman Ramsey to study the recordings alleged to be the originals. They found a voice on the Dictabelt beginning to speak just as the shooting apparently ended. The new theory was that if the voice (Sheriff Bill Decker) began speaking at that point on Channel 1, the acoustical findings were invalid because the same voice says the same thing a minute after the shooting on the Channel 2 recording. Dr. Barger told us on January 23, 1981, "I don't agree with them and I'm sure lots of others won't either." Barger found that one voice was dubbed over another, and there was a timing discrepancy which he says you can prove by timing it with a stop watch. On any recording, there is a hum tone; each successive copy will have an additional hum tone. Dr. Barger found that there are two 60-cycle hum tones on the Dictabelt, clearly showing that it is a copy, and therefore that it did not re-record properly, or has been tampered with.

Gary Mack then says that this must not be the original Dictabelt; a second Dictabelt was made from the first, and there is a timing discrepancy on Channel 1. It can't be the original Dictabelt. You can hear some of Channel 2 on Channel 1. Some of Channel 1 is missing. "It's not a complete copy," Mack says, and he says that he can't imagine that it was accidental. In other words, it's deliberate tampering with the evidence. Gary Mack writes: "There is strong evidence of substitution with the police recordings."[23]

Nevertheless, it would seem that the tape even as it is now, contains irrefutably evidence of a number of shots. The echoes display the particular signature of a supersonic high-powered rifle bullet, preceded by a shock wave. These scientific effects were precisely duplicated by the

Assassinations Committee in Dealey Plaza, and were not or could not be motorcycle back-fires or anything else.

A policeman, Jim Bowles – now the Sheriff of Dallas – who knew Sheriff Decker for many years says that the voice is not Decker's at all. The fact that the Ramsey report was not issued for three years shows how much trouble they had with it.

The microphone was open for six minutes, which cut off communications from other officers. A dispatcher shouted on Channel 2 at about 12:34 P.M. "There is a motorcycle officer up on Stemmons with his mike stuck open on Channel 1. Could you send someone up there to tell him to shut it off?" Chief Curry shouted instructions on this channel (2) just beforehand. The interference on Channel 1 stopped then. *But first there is an electronic beeping in precisely the Morse code signal for "victory."* [24]

Anthony Pellicano, a critic of the Barger study who, interestingly enough, had criticized Bolt, Beranek and Newman's (Barger's employer) previous findings that the famous 18-minute gap on the Nixon tapes was a deliberate erasure, said, "I'm sure there was a conspiracy." He thinks that "the assassin wanted to try to jam the communications, but he didn't really know too much about it. He thought if he would get a radio transmitter and get a crystal for the same frequency and held that button open and generate some noise over that thing he could be able to mask a lot of the communications. It all depends on how close he was to the receiver." Earl Golz writes in the *Dallas Morning News,* "On the other hand, the open microphone didn't have to be a policeman's and could have been held open intentionally, according to Pellicano." [25]

Photographs appear to show Jim Hicks in Dealey Plaza just after the assassination with a radio at the time of the assassination, and his affidavit given to Jim Garrison appears to substantiate this. [26] "Shortly after admitting his role to Garrison, Hicks was locked up in a military hospital for the insane." (Shaw) It would appear that either a policeman who was privy to the plot kept his mike open to disrupt communications, or someone was in fact jamming them. As many as four mikes may have been open.

The Motorola radios used by the police had Automatic Gain Control (AGC), which changes the volume when loud noises appear, such as shots. But the Dallas engineers who designed and installed the radio system deny that the Channel 1 receiver had AGC, contrary to the crucial assumption of the Ramsey Panel. Dr. Barger assumes the system did not have AGC. Gunshots have certain characteristics when recorded. The acoustical scientists who studied this Dictabelt used 26 echoes measured in Dealey Plaza to an accuracy of within one foot. With three variables (two shooters and one microphone), they measured by a form of triangulation the precise locations of each at specific fractions of a second. Those test results, when compared to the original DPD recording, yielded either a match or a degree of non-match. Only one set of data matched, and with a certainty of better than 95%. This data pointed clearly at H.B. McLain as the officer whose radio was on during the shooting.

At the time these results first became known, the motorcycle policeman, H.B. McLain, was interviewed. He admitted to Jerry Cohen that he was "about 150 feet" behind the President when he was killed. The acoustical analysis found that the open mike was 154 feet behind the limousine at the instant of the third shot. Photographs show McLain's numbered motorcycle in exactly this spot. Professor Mark Weiss and Ernest Aschkenasy, the experts employed by the Committee to study the acoustic evidence, learned from their audio data that the open mike was mounted on the left side of the bike and pointed down toward the street. McLain confirmed this to the HSAC. He admitted that he had had many open mike problems in the past.

Earl Brown, a former Dallas Police officer, told Earl Golz that the motorcade stopped shortly after the shooting for 30 seconds to talk on the entrance ramp to Stemmons Freeway, and McLain probably would have had to stop, too. When the motorcade started moving again to go to the hospital, McLain probably started off too, turning on his siren then and thereby freeing his stuck mike. About 30 seconds after the last shot, the motorcycle is heard to quickly accelerate, then a few seconds later, decelerate, idle, and then disappear. This seems to be when he could have stopped with the motorcade.[27]

THE CARILLON BELL

Sheriff Jim Bowles thinks that the mike was on at the Trade Mart, and therefore could not have been in the motorcade. He doesn't believe the shots were recorded at all. He failed to explain where the shots on the tape could have come from, or what else they might be. A carillon can be heard in the background of the tape. It appears that several mikes were on during the shooting. At the Trade Mart, police were monitoring the two channels on the radios of two police cars. They knew immediately of the shooting from Channel 2.

The FBI was quoted in the newspapers on December 2, 1980 as saying the experts "did not scientifically prove that a gunshot was fired by a second gunman from the Grassy Knoll area of Dealey Plaza during the assassination of President Kennedy." The FBI then flatly said that the sounds on the Dictabelt did not necessarily come from Dealey Plaza, and there was no proof the sounds heard on the recording were gunshots rather than some other sounds or electrical impulses produced internally by the Dallas Police Department radio system. Then the FBI admits that they have no intention of conducting the study it would take to properly resolve the question.

"There were three ways to show whether the Dallas Police recording picked up the sounds in Dealey Plaza during the assassination," the FBI said, according to the article in the Warrenfeller III Report: "If it can be shown acoustically that the other information on the recording just before, during, and just after the pertinent time period was exclusively from Dealey Plaza, then there is a very high probability that the four impulse patterns (thought to be gunshots) also represent sounds produced in Dealey Plaza.

"But a carillon bell is heard on the recording about seven seconds after the last gunshot sound.

"No known carillon bells have been located in the vicinity of Dealey Plaza," the FBI said. The carillon was again recorded in 1964, during a news broadcast on the first anniversary of the assassination.

"The recording also picked up brief voice signals from other transmitters and lacked sounds such as cheering crowds or recognizable voices that would indicate the sounds were produced in Dealey Plaza." What they evidently overlooked was that the Automatic Gain Control (AGC) would reduce all lower volume sounds such as the noise of crowds and/or other voices to far below audible levels.

"Another way of showing that the gun sounds in the recording came from Dealey Plaza would be to show a uniqueness in the echo patterns," observed the FBI. Of course the patterns *were* unique, but the FBI didn't take the time to study them. Had they done so, the uniqueness of the patterns would have been apparent. They are like audio fingerprints.

The FBI originally tried to say that they tested the recording, but later had to quietly retract the statement and pass the matter on to the National Academy of Sciences.

In spite of its highly independent-sounding name, the NAS study was fully funded by the Justice Department and staffed with "reliable" panel members.

Having referred the matter to the NAS, the FBI tried to apply the *coup de grâce.*

In an effort to determine whether or not the tape could have recorded sounds coming from somewhere other than Dealey Plaza, the FBI's signal analysis unit compared the recorded sound impulses from the Dallas tape to impulses found on recordings of shootings of five Communists in Greensboro, N.C. and found the impulses were similar. That proved, the FBI said, that the sounds on the 1963 tape were not unique to Dealey Plaza.[28]

Note this bizarre reasoning. They say that the sounds on the tape sound like just any old shots, therefore, they could have come from anywhere. Needless to say, this doesn't explain how shots got on a police tape. But the FBI anticipated this objection and concluded, "the sounds on the tapes in Dallas could have been shots or electrical impulses generated by the radio."

What the FBI report does not answer is how come the shots only appear during those 10 1/2 seconds? How come they have certain echo patterns and shock waves that only bullets would produce?

Even Robert Blakey said the FBI report was "superficial, shoddy, and shot full of holes." He noted that the FBI failed to perform any field tests of its own.

The Assassinations Committee had recommended that the Justice Department investigate the evidence of conspiracy it found in the assassinations. Instead, we got a dishonest attempt to refute specific findings, rather than an investigation of the evidence pointing to conspiracy.

On November 7, 1981, Earl Golz wrote in the *Dallas Morning News* regarding the NAS results: "Harvard University physics Professor Norman S. Ramsey, chairman of NAS panel, refused to comment on the Decker voice discovery, which was made by Steve Barber, he was favorably impressed with Barber's discovery and had voice prints made to confirm it was the same Decker statement recorded on both police Dictabelt machines.

"Barber said his experience as a percussionist had trained him to hear sounds that most other people don't. He said he acquired a copy of the police tapes and played them over and over trying to hear the sound of gun shots.

"Decker can be heard over the police radio instructing the sheriff's office to 'move all men available out of my department back into the railroad yards there (to the west of the book depository) to try to determine just what and where it happened down there. And hold everything secure until the homicide and other investigators can get there.'

"The sheriff's radio command clearly was made after police chief Curry is heard over the same Channel Two radio stating the motorcade is 'on our way to Parkland Hospital. Have them stand by. Get men on top of that over – underpass. See what happened up there. Go up to the overpass.' (The underpass and the overpass are the same thing. It and the railroad yards were behind the Grassy Knoll, and in front of the President's car.)

"Decker then takes the microphone from Curry and directs attention to 'up on the railroad, the right of way there. I'm sure it's going to take some time for you to get your men in. Throw every one of my men in there.' Decker then repeats his order to throw all available deputies into the yards."

THE SHOTS REMAIN

In the end, the shots are still there, no matter what is happening with the voices. It is thought, as Robert Blakey, the former Chief Counsel of the Assassinations Committee, states in the same article, that the stylus on the Dictabelt simply jumped, jolted back "and recorded over the same place that it originally recorded."

The other channel shows that Decker did not appear to be speaking while the shooting was going on, but one minute later. The panel of experts convened by the government therefore appears to base its repudiation of the findings of the Committee on this contradictory evidence. It might be assumed that Decker first tried to talk, but had to wait until Curry was done.

Bowles says that officers with call numbers 100 and 91 tried to use their radios at that time, and 91 thinks it is Bowles trying to speak, not Decker.

Bowles also thinks that the first Curry transmission was about

15 seconds after the last shot.[29] Curry did not know if anyone had been hit until a motorcycle policeman talked to him. All agree that 20 to 40 seconds may have elapsed.

Dr. Barger's spectrograms show (in his testimony of September 11, 1978 before the Assassinations Committee) that there were at least four other microphones on, or attempting to get on, the channel. Another possibility is that Decker tried to grab the microphone and alert his office after the first two shots on Channel 1. Perhaps Curry switched to Channel 1, but was cut off by Decker. Decker's voice could have been picked up speaking in the background in the police car; that does not necessarily prove a timing discrepancy.

"As I see the situation," Gary Mack wrote to Dr. Ramsey, the physicist, "the panel is far from making a definitive conclusion; the 'Decker' message is, at best, a small, unsupported indication of a possible error. Of all the known evidence, only the 'Decker' message does not support the BBN analysis. But it does not disprove that there are shots from Dealey Plaza on the tape."

Congressman (now Senator) Christopher Dodd dissented from the findings of the Committee because he was troubled by the finding that Oswald fired the other three shots, when the tapes showed that only 1.66 seconds separated two of them.[30] The three shots came from the vicinity of the School Book Depository, but not necessarily directly from it. Evidence indicated that the shots came from just behind the building. Dodd felt that there was a third gunman, this one behind the President's car.

GAPS IN THE RECORDING

The Channel 2 recording was made on a Gray Audograph which was voice-actuated. This means that there were many gaps in the recording process. Bolt, Beranek and Newman found that there were no gaps originally in the Channel 1 recording at the time of the assassination. They analyzed what they were told by the HSCA was the original Dictabelt, compared it with a multi-generation tape copy and found them essentially identical.[31] Vaughn and Barber felt that there was a one-minute gap in Channel 1. A great deal of the problem has to do with the time the shooting is thought to have begun. BBN found that it began at 12:30:47, whereas Barber found that it began 65 or more seconds earlier.

During the broadcasts, the Dallas dispatcher notes the time every so often, but this is subject to some error by the angle at which he had to look at his clock, and the FBI and Dallas Police found in a test with stop watches in 1964 that the time was often out by as much as one minute. There were three different dispatchers working at the time of the assassination, and they used three different clocks. The clocks got out of synchronization by as much as one minute over the course of a month before they were reset. During the assassination, there was a great deal of confusion and pressure, and the time checks could not be expected to be perfectly accurate. And the Channel 2 recording had stopped twice at Curry's two transmissions: his "at the underpass" report and his "Parkland Hospital" transmission. The BBN report states clearly that there is no way of knowing how long the machine was off during the two recordings. Vaughn and Barber equated the two tape times to each other nevertheless, using the simultaneous transmissions by Decker on Channel 2 and both faint and incomplete on Channel 1, a few seconds after the last shot. The "gap" is not on Channel 1.

In the case of the FBI review of the BBN findings, "there appears to be a deliberate attempt to mislead by comparing irrelevant information with scientific facts."[32]

RECORDINGS IGNORED

The FBI, in fact, did not examine or listen to the original Dictabelt, the original tape copy or any other recorded version of Channel 1, or at least has not publicly admitted doing so. They ignored all recordings altogether in their review of the Assassinations Committee findings. They conducted "a review of the written findings and oral testimony" only, in their own words. There were no laboratory tests. They did not use the test firing recordings made in Dealey Plaza for comparison. In fact, they could not understand the data produced by the tests at all. They did not study the actual wave form of the Grassy Knoll shot, but instead relied on the fuzzy reproduction in 8 HSAC and decided it was of poor quality, "Probably due to the recording process."

The FBI used the public testimony of the scientists before the hearings of the Committee, when in each case the data was incomplete and later modified. The secret FBI report which they would not release but we have obtained, said that a microscopic analysis of the grooves of the recordings should have been performed to determine whether there were bubbles or scratches. The FBI was clearly unaware that such a scratch or defect would produce no echo-like pattern, which is what was in fact recorded. The FBI and the Warren Commission admitted long ago that the Dictabelt was badly worn from many playings. BBN used the "original" taped copy of a Dictabelt, and there was no way to study that because tapes have no grooves that can scratch.

The FBI at no time speculates as to what else the impulses on the tape might be, if they were not shots. The FBI merely tried to deduce their result, and it is a faulty exercise in deductive reasoning, Mack writes. The FBI "is trying to give us the appearance of a solid product of investigative research but the conclusions are not supported by the facts. The media then reported it as fact. The same thing happened with the NSF study."

As for the carillon bell heard on the recording seven seconds after the last shot, BBN found this was roughly in the key of A, closer to A-flat; with the final tape speed correction of 4.3%, the bell was subjected to spectrum analysis and the apparent pitch was found to be 438 cycles per second.

The bell is not very faint on the DPD recording, and appears for only 1/3 of a second.[33] In 1964, KXAS-TV News filmed with sound from Dealey Plaza, and recorded a similar bell. This bell had disappeared by 1978, so this provided an easy out for the simple-minded to say that if there is no bell in 1978, there was no bell 15 years earlier, in 1963. This argument is then used to say that the impulses (shots) on the tape did not come from Dealey Plaza.

Twelve blocks from Dealey Plaza, a bank used to operate a carillon bell which could be heard all over Dallas. When Kennedy's motorcade passed, they played "Hail to the Chief." That tape still exists.[34]

Warren Commission Exhibit 705 includes a transcript of the radio communications but does not contain the two known Decker statements heard on Channel 2. It does, however, begin with a 12:30:40 time notation that could only come from a continuous recording.

The Secret Service had three separate channels that were monitored at a Dallas hotel as well as from Air Force One and from the first five cars in the motorcade (including Curry's).

Jack White suggests that Decker in the rear seat of Curry's car, which was in front of the fatal car, told Curry while Curry's mike was open to "Call head-quarters and tell them to get some men up on the overpass and (hold everything secure) and Curry responded ("I got it") and then closed his mike till his later transmission. Decker later took the mike from Curry and made his own call.[35]

THE EVIDENCE STANDS

In the end, the evidence of quite a number of shots on the tapes will stand, and nothing the critics have said changes that fact.

The FBI chiefs preordained – within hours after the assassination – that Oswald alone killed President Kennedy. With the House Assassinations Committee Report, the Government would have to abandon the lone assassin theory. Once committed, it was difficult for the government to extricate itself. The tape with the shots absolutely refutes this finding, so the tape has to be discredited. The Government knew that in 1963. A memorandum for Bill Moyers from Deputy Attorney General Katzenbach dated November 25, 1963, said, "It is important that all of the facts surrounding President Kennedy's Assassination be made public in a way which will satisfy people in the United States and abroad that all the facts have been told and that a statement to this effect be made now.

1. The public must be satisfied that Oswald was the assassin; that he did not have confederates who are still at large; and that the evidence was such that he would have been convicted at trial.

2. Speculation about Oswald's motivation ought to be cut off, and we should have some basis for rebutting thought that this was a Communist conspiracy or (as the Iron Curtain press is saying) a right-wing conspiracy to blame it on the communists. Unfortunately the facts on Oswald seem too pat – too obvious (Marxist, Cuba, Russian wife, etc.). The Dallas police have put out statements on the Communist conspiracy theory, and it was they who were in charge when he was shot and thus silenced.

3. The matter has been handled thus far with neither dignity nor conviction. Facts have been mixed with rumor and speculation. We can scarcely let the world see us totally in the image of the Dallas police when our President is murdered.

"I think this objective may be satisfied by making public as soon as possible a complete and thorough FBI report on Oswald and the assassination. This may run into the difficulty of pointing to inconsistencies between this report and statements by Dallas police officials. But the reputation of the Bureau is such that it may do the whole job."[36]

YET ANOTHER "REPORT"

On May 14, 1982, the National Academy of Sciences issued their "Report" of the Committee on Ballistics Acoustics after a three-year wait. This can be added to the long trail of "reports" or cover-ups which do not address the evidence. The NSA admits that they did not conduct the tests of the tape that they themselves recommend, and that "because its charge was only to examine the acoustical evidence, the Committee has not reached a conclusion as to whether or not there was a shot from the grassy knoll, nor has it examined or reported on the question of whether or not a single individual was involved in the assassination..." "The Committee has concluded that the acoustical analyses do not demonstrate that there was a grassy knoll shot."

Assassination researcher Gary Mack writes, "The *methodology* was never questioned, and rightfully so, since the physics and geometry of the approach had been accepted scientific fact for over 50 years; the specific *application* of those principles to the problem was questioned, though, because an error had to have been made somewhere..." The "original" Dictabelt *must be a copy* of another Dictabelt or tape recording. "This is where the evidence of editing becomes apparent," according to Mack. He says that there is scientific evidence of dubbing and deletion on Channel 1 in the BBN report to the HSCA and in the Warren Commission books. Mack says that the Dictabelt must be a copy of the real original, probably edited: "Somewhere along the line someone played the real original on one machine and copied it on another running about 5% too fast. The gunshot impulses were not tampered with, but something was added and/or deleted."[37] Probably it had to do with more than one gunman.

"So the focus of the NAS Panel has shifted significantly from questioning the conclusions of the HSCA scientists to questioning the authenticity of the Dictabelt itself." This is a valid criticism.

The scientific committee rejects the conclusions of the previous scientists only on the basis that "Sound spectrograms... show conclusively that a segment of Channel II is recorded on the Channel I Dictabelt at the same location as the relevant acoustic impulses. From the Channel II recording it is clear that the message of concern was broadcast one minute after the assassination... this identification between the two channels shows that the sounds analyzed by BRSW/WA occurred one minute after the President had been shot and the motorcade had left Dealey Plaza, admitting that 'The Committee was greatly helped in its studies by the suggestion volunteered by Steve Barber...'"

There are simple explanations for this, but the Committee never bothered to investigate them: That other microphones were open, and that we don't know which tape they were listening to, but it certainly was not the original. It is known that a number of copies were made under less than scientific circumstances, and voices may have been recorded at the wrong place on the tape. The Committee simply does not address the problem of the shots themselves and the fact that they cannot be anything else but shots on the tape. Instead, the Committee tries to dismiss the fact that there are shots on the tape because someone starts talking just as the shooting finishes on one tape, and a minute afterwards on another channel. This is another in a long line of nonreports. As Chairman Stokes of the Assassinations Committee said, "The tapes were not the primary reason for our finding of a conspiracy, but only confirmed what we already knew."

Jim Bowles, now the Sheriff of Dallas, was in 1963 a supervisor of the radio division. He prepared the first transcript of the Dictabelt for the Warren Commission. He says that within a very short time of Kennedy's death, the original recordings were borrowed by government agents and returned to him afterwards.[38]

WERE THE TAPES COPIED?

It is quite probable that the Dictabelts were copied, the original kept by the Government and the copy returned to the Dallas Police with forged signatures on them. It is also possible that the recordings were edited to remove any talk of a second or third gunman, although the agents probably did not realize the tapes had the shots on them.

Every time a recording is copied, the copy will record an additional 60 Hz hum tone. The recordings studied by the House Committee scientists have that extra hum tone, indicating they are copies, not the originals.

If the tape is indeed made from a copy of the original Dictabelt, this would explain the voice-overs and other anomalies on the tape, especially if it was edited. The fact remains that the impulses can only be shots, and they can be heard after other noises are screened out. But we can add the recordings to other materials in this case which show evidence of tampering and forgery.

GUNFIRE MATCHED TO
Z FRAMES

Perhaps the best proof of the validity of the sound recordings was presented in 1976 to the House Assassinations Committee by co-author Robert Groden, Dr. Mark Weiss and Dr. Ernest Aschkenasy. They worked for hours in the basement of the Library of Congress on the day the evidence had to be presented to the Committee. Repeatedly, they synchronized the sounds of gunfire to the Zapruder film, using both of the last two shots as the sync point for the "head shot(s)." They all came to the same conclusion. The audiotape revealed at least four shots that were scientifically provable, and at least two more impulses with an extremely high probability of being additional shots.

Only the sixth floor window of the Texas School Book Depository and the stockade fence on the Grassy Knoll were tested as suspected firing points, while 16 other suspected possible locations were ignored. Had these other points been tested and the results recorded, it is probable that the result would have been "six or more shots fired from at least three firing points."

Using only the four definite shots on the tape, they found that the synchronization –using the fourth shot –did not match action on the film nearly as well as the synchronization of the third shot. Utilizing the most advanced computer techniques, the scientists were able to isolate the echo patterns of the shots on November 22, 1963, to test firings the Committee had performed fifteen years later. The results were:

Shot #1 – From behind.
Shot #2 – From behind.
Shot #3 – From the right/front, from the Grassy Knoll.
Shot #4 – From behind.

In addition, both the first two shots and the last two shots were fired too close together to have come from the "Oswald rifle."

In all likelihood, the fatal shot did not come from the Book

Depository (from behind), but rather from the Knoll; whether or not Lee Oswald was firing, someone else had actually killed the President.

When the fourth shot matched the head shot, no other shots aligned to a verifiable action on the film. But when the third shot was matched up, *every other impulse matched an action on the film exactly.*

"We (Groden, Weiss, Aschkenasy) met with Robert Blakey and told him what the results were, showing him the two versions of the film, one with the third shot matched to the head shot, and the other with the fourth shot matched," Groden says.

Professor Blakey took co-author Robert Groden aside and ordered him not to express to the Committee any conclusions that he had drawn from his study of the film and tapes. The Congressmen (and the world) were to be told that the fatal shot came only from the rear, and the fourth shot was to be the only one to be considered the head shot.

Because of this, some members of the Committee did not accept the frontal head shot hit correlation with the film. Several Congressmen commented that the third shot seemed to fit better. Blakey told them that they were wrong, and that the third shot definitely missed. This, of course, isn't credible.

SOME BASIC CONCLUSIONS REGARDING THE EVIDENCE

Every description of the back and neck wounds of the President shows that the back wound was larger (4 to 7 mm in diameter) than the anterior throat wound (3 to 5 mm), and so the same bullet could not have entered in the back and exited from the throat, as an entry wound is smaller than an exit wound. Every doctor in Dallas originally described the throat wound as an entry wound – a shot from the front.

This means that John Connally, as all the evidence and testimony shows, was hit with a separate bullet from behind. Connally's wounds, as well as the President's, were caused by at least three different gunmen – not one: two from behind and one from in front. The acoustical tapes corroborate this.

It is significant that of all the evidence that was turned over to the Secret Service, much of which they failed to turn over to the FBI or the Warren Commission, none was ever released to the public. Crucial evidence was retained by the Secret Service and never shared with the Warren Commission. Much of that evidence has simply disappeared.

All the autopsists testified strongly that the pristine bullet alleged to have wounded both victims could not have done so. Yet, Arlen Specter bullied and pushed the doctors when they testified, and finally ignored all their testimony when it did not suit his magic bullet theory.

The Warren Commission wasn't interested in the known evidence, but only in finding no conspiracy. Lawyers totally unqualified to deal with this type of case, without the benefit of expert advice, determined the facts without proper cross-examination of witnesses, and changed or distorted testimony to suit their construct. Nevertheless, the adversary system is not designed to find the truth, but for winning a case. The facts are often kept out of the record in order to make one's case. That is what the Warren Commission did, and the fact is that the Chief Justice of the Supreme Court, Earl Warren, was not competent or did not have the time to run the proceedings. Neither were the lawyers involved. That's why they were picked. The "investigation" was intended to self destruct.

It appears the Report of the Warren Commission was politically motivated by those who knew that there was evidence of a conspiracy coming from their own ranks. Government agencies had to cover up because they were implicated. John J. McCloy said in the secret Commission meeting of December 5, 1963, "I have a feeling that we have another obligation than the mere evaluation of the reports of agencies, many of which as you suggested, or some of them at least, may be interested, may be involved. There is a potential culpability here on the part of the Secret Service and even the FBI, and these reports, after all, human nature being what it is, may have some self-serving aspects in them... we were simply posed before the world as something that is evaluating government agencies' reports, who themselves may be culpable."

We now know that many witnesses were never interviewed, including numerous Dallas police and eyewitnesses.

In addition, strong evidence that the President was shot in the face from in front was ignored.

An apparent bullet or tumor seen in the brain was also ignored. FBI agents reported that surgery had been performed on the head before the autopsy. The autopsy was grossly incomplete and deliberately sabotaged. The military or others prevented the autopsy from following proper procedure.

Expert evidence shows that John Connally had a lot more metal in him than was lost from the nearly whole bullet found at Parkland. Evidence also shows that no such bullet could have struck bone, as this bullet was alleged to have done, and survived undeformed. The evidence shows that no bullet could have followed the trajectory to strike both men.

It is also clear from the acoustical evidence and from the Zapruder film that the President was struck by the first bullet long before it was possible to fire from the alleged sniper's window.

Eyewitnesses and acoustical analysis point to a fusillade of shots in Dealey Plaza. These shots came from at least three general directions and perhaps more, and the medical evidence corroborates the number of shots on the recordings, as well as other evidence of the number of shots.

The type of head wound suffered by the President was caused by either a hunting style bullet – rather than a military jacketed bullet such as that found on the stretcher – or a hand gun. This bullet fragmented, and skull bone is considerably softer than rib and other bones. It is unusual, if not impossible, for a military jacketed bullet like those found in the "sniper's window" and at Parkland to fragment – as did the bullet which struck the President in the head. The brain was macerated.

At least two bullets came from in front, one hitting the President in the throat and another hitting him in the head.

The autopsy report states that Kennedy's brain weighed 1500 grams, or 53 ounces, more than the weight of an average adult brain (50 ounces). Dr. John Lattimer, who denounces all conspiracy possibilities in this case, and who is therefore a hostile witness, states that 70% of the brain was missing. The maximum weight of an adult brain is 65 ounces. All medical reports indicate that most or a very large amount of the brain was gone. Therefore it appears unlikely that the brain cited in the autopsy was Kennedy's.

The evidence indicates that the pristine bullet was not found on either the President's or John Connally's stretcher, but on another stretcher, where it had been planted, perhaps by Jack Ruby who was in the hospital at the time.

The bullet entered John Connally at a downward angle of 25 degrees, at the extreme right edge of his torso, just at the armpit in back, and the bullet which struck the President hit him at a downward angle of 45 to 60 degrees, six inches down on his back. It did not exit, in fact, it did not penetrate farther than two inches, and was below the anterior neck wound.

The doctors chosen to perform the autopsy had no experience with gunshot wounds and limited knowledge of forensic science. They were not even experienced at performing autopsies. Despite the inexperience of the autopsists, no additional outside medical support was sought. Rolls of film made during the autopsy were destroyed. The victims' clothes were not properly examined. There was no consultation with the attending physicians in Dallas prior to the autopsy. Wounds were not probed or dissected, and one wound was not even discovered, although the autopsy report was falsified to say that this was done. The autopsy report was not dated, and the original notes and drafts were burned. At best, the autopsy was bungled. At worst, there was a wholesale cover-up. Lacassagne, one of the founders of forensic science, said, "A bungled autopsy cannot be revised."

The Warren Report conflicted strongly with the testimony and reports of those who were present at the autopsy. The doctors were not allowed to see the surviving pictures and X-rays, and neither was the naval corpsman who was asked to draw pictures of the wounds for the Commission. Competent medical artists were not called. When the pictures were finally seen years later, the wounds were not in the positions noted in the autopsy report or by the doctors who allegedly wrote it.

The autopsy photographs are of such poor quality that the President cannot in fact be identified as the subject in some of them, nor can individual photographs be related to the autopsy at all. The photographs are unverified and probably inadmissible in a court of law. These photographs have been questioned by virtually all the medical witnesses.

The autopsists' testimony that the large hole in the back of the head was an exit wound was also ignored, as was the evidence of other witnesses in Dallas who claimed it was an exit wound, and that it was in the back of the head.

The President's body was taken illegally by force from the proper Texas state authorities by Secret Service agents. Technically, the Federal Government never had any jurisdiction in the case, and did not have the authority to take the body or to perform the autopsy. The State of Maryland has jurisdiction over whatever crimes may have been subsequently committed at Bethesda Naval Hospital.

Admiral Burkley, the President's physician, admitted that he doctored the autopsy report, but he was never called to testify before the Commission, and never asked why he did so.

Even though Dr. Burkley described the rear wound in his death certificate as being well down on the back, the Warren Commission moved it up to the back of the neck.

Burkley's death certificate was dated the day after the President's autopsy, when the doctors had been told about the wound in the throat from in front and after they had finished with the body. Surprisingly, the certificate still does not mention any wound in the throat.

In addition, the autopsy pictures and X-rays were not attached to the autopsy report as regulations required.

The autopsists and others were silenced with the threat of courts martial, and witnesses in Dallas were tampered with, visited by "government" agents and told what to say or silenced. Dennis David, a witness at the autopsy, said a Secret Service agent had him type a memo just afterwards, which was not shown to the Warren Commission. The memo "stated that four large pieces of lead were removed from

Kennedy. They were not separate bullets but had jagged edges like shrapnel. There was more material than would come from one bullet, but maybe not enough for two," he said.

David, who saw many wounded men while serving in Vietnam, said he saw slides of Kennedy's wounds. "It looked like they came from in front," he said. He said there was so much fear that a conspiracy was involved that no-one was taking any chances. The unlawful orders not to perform certain procedures during the autopsy were against even military regulations.

Microscopic slides made from the wounds, the brain, and various photos and X-rays from the autopsy have disappeared, along with many other important pieces of evidence.

Dr. Boswell drew a picture of a wound over the left eye-temple area during the autopsy, but this was omitted from the report: he also indicated that the back of the head was missing. Other evidence of additional damage to the skull and brain is also not mentioned.

The drawing made by the corpsman for the Warren Commission of the bullet entering and exiting the head falsifies the extreme flexion of the head. The neck and head are bent downward, which was clearly not the case in the films of the head shot. This falsification was the only way to illustrate a downward trajectory of the alleged rear entry into the head near the external occipital protuberance, shown in the proper place in the drawing. When the films became known, the autopsy pictures of the back of the head, when finally seen years later, had moved the rear head entry more than four inches to nearly the top of the head to maintain a downward trajectory from the rear with the head straight up and down.

The position of the back wound was falsified in this same illustration to show it in the back of the neck, six inches above its actual location. The drawings of the wounds by the enlisted man were based on mere speculation, yet the Commission's lawyers made no objection.

The Parkland doctors saw evidence of a wound in the chest, and inserted chest tubes to drain the resulting fluid. The autopsy did not report the entry of the tubes, since the official report would deny that a bullet had entered the chest (from behind). The interior chest photographs which would show these wounds are missing.

The large defect described as an exit wound in the back of the head does not show in any of the autopsy pictures, and is nowhere remotely near where all the witnesses described it. The autopsists strongly questioned the autopsy pictures and insisted they were inaccurate, as have many other Dallas witnesses.

There are many examples of testimony being changed, distorted, or ignored, and of the transcripts themselves being changed to reflect the "official" scenario. There is an unquestionable pattern of fabricated, forged, and falsified evidence.

For instance, when the FBI and Dallas police examined the alleged murder weapon, there were no fingerprints or palm prints on it. Sometime later, a palm print was presented as having been lifted from the gun by the Dallas police.

The Commission carefully phrased certain of its conclusions in language that indicated they were not certain how many shots were fired, and allowed the press and the public to draw certainties from it, while the Commissioners maintained plausible deniability.

Gerald Ford, a member of the Commission, said, "I think you'd have to read very carefully what the Warren Commission said, and I as a member of the Warren Commission helped to participate in the drafting of the language... We said that the commission had found no evidence of a conspiracy, foreign or domestic. Those words were very carefully drafted." Ford went on to say, "But the Commission was right when it made its determinations and it was accurate at least to this point and I want to reemphasize that as to the evidence that we saw."

Charles Wilber points out that "the rejection of autopsy evidence and other data was planned so that the carefully worded 'no conspiracy' conclusion was on the surface true, but only because of culpable ignorance on the part of the Commission. Did the Commission see only what it wanted to see or what the staff wanted it to see?"

The FBI report of the autopsy said that there appeared to have been surgery to the head, but there is no other supporting evidence to indicate the body was tampered with. This was probably a layman's interpretation of the destructive damage caused by the bullets.

The newspapers reported that a bullet had lodged in the President's back, and the *Washington Post* said that the FBI claimed that the bullet was found deep in his shoulder. We have a receipt from the FBI men present at the autopsy for a "missile." This is, of course, one bullet too many. We have evidence of still other bullets not mentioned in the official evidence. The FBI certainly didn't confuse a fragment with a missile.

"Again the pathologists cannot be faulted in this deception. They were caught in a maelstrom created by ruthless men who had the power and lack of morals that permitted them to manipulate history."(Wilber p. 103)

"The quality of the selection process in admitting 'screened' individuals to see the autopsy materials was best illustrated by the first medical man approved to look at some of the material in custody of the National Archives. He was not a forensic scientist; he was not a pathologist; he was not an expert in crime detection. He was a urologist, an expert in diseases of the kidney, bladder, and associated organs of the human body." (Wilber p. 133)

The FBI report after the autopsy insisted that Governor Connally had been hit with a separate shot, which meant two snipers from the rear, since the rifle could not be reloaded quickly enough to hit both men with different bullets.

The secret autopsy photographs and X-rays are fabricated. They wouldn't be secret if no-one had any doubts about their authenticity and they supported the government's case.

The pattern of conflicting testimony, the autopsists' and other medical witnesses' refutation of the autopsy photographs, the evidence of forgery and tampering in the backyard photos, the indications of per-jury and subornation of perjury and the long list of missing or destroyed evidence make it clear that far more is involved in the assassination of President Kennedy than a mere second gunman on the Grassy Knoll. The above evidence points clearly to conspiracy and high treason.

PART V   Political Affairs

"The general thrust of the Kennedy military policy was to assert a political domination of the military leadership which is hostile to the traditions and practices of American government..." John F. Kennedy was telling the Joint Chiefs that they must accept his judgement of military matters."..."The Presidential dictum was of course contrary to law and should have been disregarded by the Joint Chiefs of Staff... If the military leader is then willing to submit the professional integrity, morale, and effectiveness of his service or services to the adverse judgments of inexperienced politicians, he is not fit to hold office."

– Major General Thomas Lane:
The Leadership of President Kennedy

"There is little in education, training or experience of most military officers to equip them with the balance or judgement necessary to put their own ultimate solutions... into proper perspective in the President's total strategy for the nuclear age."

– Senator William Fullbright

The President shall be the Commander-In-Chief of the Armed Forces...

– *The Constitution of the United States*

"Mr. Ryan said Washington was only now getting around to prosecuting Nazi collaborators because of the anti-Communist mood that long prevailed in the United States.
" 'Back in the early 50's and mid-50's, when this work really should have been done rather than in 1980, McCarthyism was at its height, anti-Communism was at its height, and most of these people were anti-Communists,' " he said.
" 'There was a tendency to measure their worth as citizens on the basis of their anti-Communism rather than on what they had done during the Holocaust.' "

– *The New York Times*, February 6, 1980.

CHAPTER 13

PEOPLE AND SINISTER CONNECTIONS

The House Assassinations Committee continued to get itself trapped in areas that it wanted to avoid. Private citizens volunteering information were a particular source of embarrassment. Take for example the wife of Larry Huff, a former Marine navigator, who wrote the Committee saying her husband had participated in a military investigation of the assassination run out of Camp Smith, Hawaii. Her husband willingly cooperated with the Committee, but supporting information was extremely hard to get. No reports of the investigation survived. However, it is clear Lt. Gen. Carson A. Roberts was the man in charge.[1] "The teams were dispatched to Japan and Dallas and the report of the investigation was classified 'Secret – For Marine Corps Eyes Only.' " Larry Huff read it.[2]

Huff had written down the serial number of the plane that flew to Japan; its commander was Chief Warrant Officer Morgan. A friend of

235

his knew about the plane going to Dallas. "On April 19, 1978, the Department of Defense responded that the Air Force had no records on Roberts or Morgan and that it had no flight records concerning either military plane identified in the Committee's request. Regarding the records of the alleged military investigation, the Department of Defense responded that it had no record that the Air Force Office of Special Investigations had conducted an investigation into the assassination of President Kennedy in Japan or California in 1963. The Department explained that it believed the alleged investigation was being confused with an investigation that was conducted on Oswald's half-brother, John Edward Pic."

"According to the Department, the Pic investigation records were destroyed because no 'derogatory information' (which presumably means information which would have been relevant to the assassination investigation) was developed."[3]

This is a classic example of "plausible deniability." If they can stall long enough, the Special Commissions and Committees close up and go home. So, we find that the DOD "had no record that the Air Force Office of Special Investigations had conducted an investigation into the assassination of President Kennedy." Both they and the Committee are pulling another fast one. The Office of Naval Intelligence, the Defense Intelligence Agency, etc., might have conducted the investigation. They can file these things anywhere, and the way intelligence operations are conducted, someone in an Air Force uniform might really be in the Navy. The Committee had asked, beside flight records, for "Any and all records, including classified material, concerning or referring to an investigation by the Marine Corps or the Air Force Office of Special Investigations into the J.F.K. assassination."[4] Yet even these precise questions left room for evasion.

"Huff stated under oath that on December 14, 1963, he departed Kaneohe Base in Hawaii in a C-54-T aircraft, serial number 50855, for Wake Island, with Chief Warrant Officer Morgan as pilot... Huff stated that there were ten to twelve CID military investigators on that flight." (They went to Atsugi.) "Huff said he learned the purpose of the trip by the CID investigators through conversations on the plane during the flight."[5] Huff was the navigator. They dropped the men in Japan, and he later went back to pick them up. "On the return flight, he had spoken with the investigators about their work in Japan and was told they had spent the entire stay investigating Oswald. Huff said that during that flight he was allowed to read the report prepared by the investigators. He described the report as being typewritten, about twenty pages, and classified 'Secret, for Marine Corps Eyes Only.' Huff recollected that the substance of the report dealt with interviews of individuals and that it contained psychological evaluation of Oswald. Huff remembered the conclusion being that Oswald was incapable of committing the assassination alone. Huff said he read the report for about thirty minutes."[6] This report disappeared from the evidence.

Huff had Secret Security clearance, and so was able to read the report. "He surmised that the report would be kept in intelligence files either at the Intelligence Division of Camp Smith or with the Commandant of the Marine Corps in Washington, D.C. Huff also stated that soon after the assassination in November, 1963, he had received word of another investigative team which was to travel to Dallas to investigate the assassination."[7] Huff then outlined his evidence for this. The man Huff named "stated that he did not believe he had participated in a flight to Dallas. Moffitt stated he is certain that he never told Huff that he participated in either the planning or execution of a trip to Dallas in connection with the assassination investigation."[8] But then, on the next page, we learn that "Moffitt said he did not know for sure if he traveled to or from Dallas in November 1963..."[9] Moffitt provided his log books, and his notations for that period carry only the type of plane and not the destinations or origins of the flights, "such as are made for all of the other months in the book."[10]

"The Committee was unable to locate retired gunnery sergeant H.E. Aubrey, who was identified as the chief CID investigator at Camp Smith in November-December 1963."[11]

This report ends with a letter from the pilot, former CWO Roger C. Morgan, who writes, "My personal log books do reflect the fact that I was the commander of a flight from Kaneohe Bay, Hawaii to Tachikawa AFB in Japan and return on the dates in question. The aircraft type was a C-54, assigned to Marine Aircraft Group 13, Kaneohe Bay, Hawaii. The aircraft bureau number was 50855. The names of the other crew members or passengers is not contained in these personal records, but could be found in official records."[12] Except that it appears that they no longer exist.

OSWALD AND TIPPIT

The Oswald-Tippit connection was another troubling area for the House Assassinations Committee. "Questions have persisted about why Officer Tippit would have been in the (Oswald's) neighborhood, including, had Tippit received enough information on the suspected assassin of President Kennedy to have been able to identify Oswald as the possible suspect, and was there anything suspicious about Tippit's location in that part of Dallas after the assassination, when other police officers had been ordered to the Dealey Plaza area or Parkland Hospital immediately after the assassination?"[13]

The Warren Commission did not ask questions about what Tippit was doing in Oak Cliff, so close to the homes of Jack Ruby and Oswald, nor did they call any relatives of Tippit to testify about his associations or activities. The Committee learned that Officer Murray James Jackson had known Tippit well for some 20 years, and he was the dispatcher who sent Tippit to Oak Cliff at the time that *all* other policemen went downtown.[14]

As private researchers had previously found, there was a restaurant called the Dobbs House on North Beckely Street, where Oswald lived. "Tippit had a habit of coming into the Dobbs House each morning. An employee in the restaurant, Ada Dowling, indicated that on one occasion when Tippit was in the restaurant, Lee Harvey Oswald came in to be served. She did not know if they knew each other."[15]

But the heart of the dispute comes from "Wes Wise, a reporter with KRLD-TV in Dallas at the time of the assassination and later mayor of Dallas, who said that he had received information about a car near the scene of the Tippit shooting that was traced to Carl Mather, a close friend of Tippit's. A man named Pate told Wise that a mechanic who worked for him 'had observed a car in the parking lot of the El Chico restaurant on the afternoon of November 22 after radio reports were being broadcast about the shooting in Dealey Plaza.' "[16] They took the license plate off the car: Texas PP 4537, described as a 1957 Plymouth four-door. The mechanic described the car as red, and Wise told this to the FBI on December 4, 1963. That plate number was issued for a 1957 Plymouth owned by Carl Mather of Garland, Texas. The FBI went to look at the car, but found that it was light blue over medium blue. Mrs. Mather was interviewed by the FBI, and said that her husband was at work on November 22, 1963 until about 2 P.M. "when he came by their home to take the family to the Tippit home to offer their condolences. Mrs. Mather said the two families were friends. Mrs. Mather did not state in the interview which car her husband was driving that day at the time of the assassination or the Tippit shooting. No FBI report of an interview or contact with Carl Mather was located."[17]

The mechanic, T.F. White, was interviewed by the FBI and said the car was red. He certainly had the license plate right. He said the car was in the parking lot at about 2 P.M. White insisted that the man sitting in the car looked like Lee Harvey Oswald. Oswald was apprehended in the Texas Theatre about 2 P.M. "White said that after he saw the man sit in the car for a short time, the man left in the car at a high rate of speed, going west on Davis street... White reiterated that he had correctly copied the number of the car and that after seeing the news reports of Oswald, he thought Oswald was possibly identical with the man White had seen in the car."[18]

MORE CONNECTIONS

When Carl Mather was interviewed by the Assassinations Committee, he stated that "on November 22, 1963, he had worked all day at the Collins Radio Co., in Richardson. Mather said his boss at the time at Collins was J.A. Pickford."[19] The Mathers said the FBI never interviewed Carl, but talked to his wife twice. She said that they never owned any kind of red car. "Mather described his background as including security clearance for electronics work. He has been employed with Collins Radio Co. for twenty-one years. One assignment involved work in Brandywine, Md., at Andrews Air Force Base, where he did electronics work on then Vice President Lyndon Johnson's airplane Air Force Two."[20]

"...Wise recalled having dinner with the Mathers and described Carl Mather as 'too nervous to eat,' but his wife was 'cool, very cool.' "

"There was an additional allegation of a red car near the scene of the Tippit shooting. A witness to the Tippit murder, Domingo Benavidas, testified that at 'about 1:00 o'clock,' on November 22, 1963,... Benavidas said in his testimony that a car which he believed to be a red Ford was parked in front of him on Tenth Street. He described the driver of the red car as about 25 or 30 years old. Benavidas said the man pulled over in his car 'when he heard the scare' but did not get out of the car. He was located about six cars from the police car" (Tippit's). White had said "he believed the car to be a red 1961 Falcon..." (Ford)[21]

From this evidence, it would appear that someone borrowed the license plates from Mather's Plymouth and then returned them.

"The Committee did locate and interview a man who said he was at the scene of the Tippit shooting but never came forward with information."[22]

"Committee investigators interviewed Jack Ray Tatum... he saw a young white male walking on the sidewalk near the squad car. Both the police car and the young man were heading *east* on Tenth Street. As Tatum approached the squad car, he saw the young male leaning over the passenger side of the police car, with both hands in his zippered jacket. Tatum said that as he drove through the intersection of Tenth and Patton Streets he heard three shots in rapid succession... At that point he saw the police officer lying on the ground near the front of the police car, with the young male standing near him. Tatum said the man ran toward the back of the police car with a gun in his hand. The man then stepped back into the street and shot the police officer as he was lying on the ground. The man then started to run in Tatum's direction. Tatum said he then sped off in his car and last saw the man running south on Patton toward Jefferson."[23]

The Committee ends this report with what researchers had previously noted: that Tippit worked part-time at Austin's Barbecue, and that the owner, Austin Cook, was a member of the John Birch Society. "Cook was asked if he had known Jack Ruby, Cook replied that he may have met Ruby, but he could not recall." We learn that Cook sold a business which was later bought by Ralph Paul, a close friend of Ruby. Ralph Paul lived at the time of the assassination in the lower level of the home of the Bowmans, who were partners with Cook, and who sold the Bull Pen to Ralph Paul. "According to Mrs. Bowman, Ralph Paul expressed great concern for his friend Jack Ruby after the shooting of Oswald."[24]

The Committee talked to the former wife of Austin Cook; she said that "Ralph Paul was a mutual friend of the Cooks and Jack Ruby."[25]

Ruby went out to dinner with Paul the night before President Kennedy's murder. The owner of the restaurant where they ate – Joseph Campisi – was well connected with the Mafia, and came to see Ruby later in jail. Ruby stayed in touch with Paul throughout the fateful weekend.[26]

SUDDEN WEALTH

Oswald's friend, George DeMohrenschildt, who had strong ties to the intelligence community, seems to have had a large amount of money come his way at the time of the assassination. This also happened to Ruby. Ruby was broke until the day of the assassination. He was in deep trouble with the Internal Revenue Service, owing them nearly $40,000. He was chronically broke, but in the week of the assassination, he gave the impression of new-found wealth, and on the day of the murder, he went to the bank after the President was killed. He had $7,000 in cash, half of which was still on him when he shot Oswald.[27] Other reports say the trunk of his car was full of money.

We might explore how others appear to have benefited from the assassination. The stock and commodity exchanges were in a panic at the time of the assassination due to the collapse of the financial empire of Tino DeAngelis, who was sued the day before by the Bunge Corporation, a concern in Argentina with apparent Nazi connections. The market began to plunge, and large brokers were threatened with bankruptcy. November 22 was a crucial day on the stock exchange *before* news of the assassination hit the floor. When that news came, the market fell 24 points in half an hour and trading had to be closed at 2:07 P.M. It was rumored all over New York and half way around the world that someone had inside knowledge of the assassination, because certain individuals made over $500 million, selling short.

Oswald also seemed to have money at times when he should not have. When he "defected" to the Soviet Union, he had only $203 in his bank account, and yet spent about $1,500. The Warren Commission said that this money came from "savings."[28] Upon his return to the U.S., Oswald seemed to be spending beyond his income, and to this day we are not permitted to see his tax returns, although we are allowed to see Ruby's.

SOME WIN, SOME LOSE

These facts point clearly in the direction of the true nature of events.

For instance, we can observe the rise of some men to power after the assassination, and the fall of others.

Arlen Specter, who invented the magic bullet theory along with Gerald Ford, became the District Attorney of Philadelphia, and later a U.S. Senator. Gerald Ford went on to become President following Nixon's resignation. Specter was rejected by the voters when he ran for Mayor of Philadelphia, as Ford was rejected when he ran for President.

Warren Commission Assistant Counsel David Belin headed the Lawyers for Nixon-Agnew, and later became the head of the Rockefeller Commission investigation of intelligence activities and the possible involvement of intelligence agents in John Kennedy's murder. When Nixon resigned, Ford became President and appointed Rockefeller Vice President.

Burt Griffin, a Commission lawyer, tried to get Police Sergant Patrick Dean to change his story about how Ruby got into the basement to shoot Oswald, and Griffin threatened him.[29] Griffin became a judge.

Marina Oswald suddenly became rich upon the murder of her husband and the President. The Secret Service first hid her away in a motel owned by the Great Southwest Corporation, which was controlled by the Wynne family of Dallas, partners of Clint Murchison. Murchison was the recipient of large loans from the Teamsters' pension funds. Bedford Wynne was "probably Murchison's top political fixer in Washington."[30] The Rockefellers, of course, were deeply involved in the oil business, and Kennedy's threatened retraction of the oil depletion allowance would have hurt them badly. President Nixon was long backed by major oil interests, and it was the "major multinational oil companies which in 1963 lobbied successfully for U.S. intervention in Vietnam," Peter Dale Scott writes.

Because of a storm of controversy, President Ford, Nixon's appointed successor, had Vice President Nelson Rockefeller investigate intelligence activites, and Rockefeller appointed David Belin (formerly of the Warren Commission) Chief Counsel. The investigation was a whitewash, but in the middle of it more controversy arose with the revelation that there may have been a link between Watergate and the assassination of President Kennedy. David Belin conducted a brief "investigation" of that issue, and absolved Howard Hunt of complicity.[31] George DeMohrenschildt, Oswald's mentor and Intelligence babysitter, once worked for a Murchison oil company, Three States Oil and Gas.[32]

"Murchison's lawyers Bedford Wynne and Thomas Webb had just, in the November 22, 1963 issue of *Life* magazine, been named as members of the 'Bobby Baker Set.'" Wynne was already under federal investigation concerning government funds he was receiving through a Murchison family corporation, some of which ended up as payoffs (via Thomas Webb) to the law firm of Bobby Baker. "Bobby Baker was, of course, Lyndon Johnson's right hand man. The Texas Murchison family... were close to both Lyndon Johnson and above all J. Edgar Hoover."[33] Murchison's empire overlapped with that of Mafia financial wizard Meyer Lansky and Teamster leader Jimmy Hoffa.[34] Penn Jones, Jr. claims that Hoover and Nixon were at Murchison's house the night before the assassination.[35]

RUBY'S CONNECTIONS

"Ruby also knew at least one member (E.E. Fogelson, 23H346) and probably others (e.g. Billy Byars, 23H363), of the influential Murchison-Wynne set of Texas gambling millionaires, the so-called 'Del Charro Set,' who among other activities bankrolled the Gettysburg farm of President Eisenhower and paid for the annual Del Mar racetrack holidays of their good friend J. Edgar Hoover. Ruby alluded circumspectly to this high-level connection in one of the most mysterious and garbled sections of his testimony before the Warren Commission, when he mentioned some Cuban gambling business linking himself to an 'attorney in Dallas' called Alfred McLane (transcribed in the Warren Commission Hearings as 'Mark Lane,' 'Lane,' and 'McClain' (5H205). Justice Warren recognized the allusion – 'Alfred was killed in a taxi in New York' (5H206). This was apparently the late Alfred E. McLane, who had represented the oil-gas interests of the Murchisons, Wofford Cain of the Del Charro set, and Lyndon Johnson's business representative Franklin Denius."[36]

"With political connections as high as these, one can understand why the Warren Commission declined to investigate Ruby's series of nationwide phone calls and visits in late 1963 to Teamster connections such as his Cuban host Lewis McWillie (14H459)...,"[37] and a long list of names follows.

"Richard Nixon should still be asked whether his trip to Dallas involved him with representatives of the Great Southwest Corporation, or of Wynne, Jaffe, and Tinsley (the Wynne family law firm), since there are anomalies in his 1964 deposition to the FBI about this trip which exactly parallel anomalies in William McKenzie's testimony to the Warren Commission. It seems legitimate to ask the question... whether this brief trip had anything to do with the CIA 'Bay of Pigs thing' which so troubled President Nixon after the Watergate break-in."[38]

William McKenzie was Marina Oswald's attorney, and he was the office-mate of Pete White, whose name was in Ruby's notebook. "One possible reason why the Warren Commission would avoid studying the Wynne-McKenzie-White relationship is the powerful political connections which the Wynne-McKenzie law firm enjoyed with both political parties." "The Wynnes' real estate deals involved powerful national and local Republican figures like the Rockefellers. A $453,000 real estate sale which they concluded with Pepsico in September 1964 is the apparent explanation for Richard Nixon's 'law business' in Dallas for Pepsico from November 20 to 22, 1963, a visit which terminated just three hours before the assassination."[39] Nixon, at the time, was a Wall Street lawyer. He was quoted in the business pages of the *New York Times* on November 22 as saying, "I am going to work as hard as I can to get the Kennedys out of there. We can't afford four more years of that kind of administration."

"...Secret Service agents helped arrange for Marina to sign a contract making a Wynne employee, James Herbert Martin, her business manager (CD470.24). Martin and his lawyer then arranged for a $25,000 payment to Marina, Robert Oswald, and themselves; this payment, ostensibly from Meredith Press for a book that would never be written, was actually arranged by two top officials of *Time-Life*, C.D. Jackson and Edward K. Thomson, through their Dallas representative Isaac Don Levine."[40] These men were known as Cold-Warriors. "This was the period in which it quickly became clear that (as a Warren Commission counsel wrote in a memo of February 28, 1964) 'Marina has repeatedly lied... on matters which are of vital concern.' There are signs that Marina was being coached as to what to say by those selected to be present at her private testimony. Among them was former CIA employee Isaac Don Levine, who spent an intensive week with Marina just prior to her first testimony before the Warren Commission on February 3, 1964.

UNDERWORLD CONTACTS

"Martin (Marina's manager) had his own contacts with men on the fringes of the underworld, including Jack Ruby. Shortly after Marina's testimony, Martin was fired: he was replaced by a lawyer, William A. McKenzie, who appeared to have no connections with Martin. In fact, however, McKenzie had been only a short time before a law partner of Bedford Wynne, resigning from the Wynne law firm (which also represented George DeMohrenschildt, as well as Great Southwest Corporation) to become Marina's attorney." There must have been big money in representing Marina. "The Warren Commission failed to pursue unsolicited sworn testimony that McKenzie had improperly coached Marina on what to tell the FBI (2H321, cf. 336-37), even though an FBI memo corroborated that Marina had in fact said just what McKenzie was supposed to have told her to say."(22H785)[41]

OSWALD AND THE POLICE

Captain Will Fritz of the Dallas Police Department told his friends that "when the President of the United States called me and *ordered* the investigation stopped, what could I do?"[42] Fritz was the interrogator of Oswald who "officially" made no tapes or transcripts of the questioning. President Johnson pre-empted the investigations which were to get under way by appointing the Warren Commission to do the job. Fritz persisted in his inquiry until this alleged call from Johnson, the new President, who was so closely tied to the Wynnes and Murchisons.

Jesse Curry, the Chief of Police, was about to go down to the basement of the police station to supervise the transfer of Oswald to the County Jail when his phone rang, and the Mayor, Earle Cabell, kept him on the line until Oswald had been shot by Ruby. Curry says in his book, *JFK Assassination File*, "The physical evidence and eyewitness accounts do not clearly indicate what took place on the sixth floor of the Texas School Depository at the time John F. Kennedy was assassinated."[43]

As for the alias, A. Hidell, attributed to Oswald, which appeared on a card alleged to be in his wallet when he was captured, the police called in on the radio that they had one Lee Harvey Oswald, and apparently did not see a card later saying that he might have been Hidell.

Sergeant Gerald Hill, who helped capture Oswald, also failed to mention the Hidell card during radio interviews that day, and it seems highly unlikely that he would not have mentioned such a card if he had seen it, or that he would have been able to know whether he had Hidell or Oswald when he opened the wallet, *if* the false ID were in it. Clearly, the card must have been planted later in order to link the rifle ordered by A. Hidell to Oswald.[44]

CUBAN CONNECTIONS

One important link in this case is David Atlee Phillips, who has been accused by government employees and investigators (with inconclusive results) of using the name "Maurice Bishop" during his activities with the CIA in connection with the secret war against Cuba.[45] Phillips was not a supporter of John Kennedy and his policies. His home was in the Dallas-Fort Worth area, and he was very close to Howard Hunt.

The CIA used a Cuban, Antonio Veciana, who was directed and advised by an American he knew as Maurice Bishop. "Veciana revealed further that at one meeting with Bishop in Dallas in late August or September 1963, he saw with him a young man he later recognized as Lee Harvey Oswald."[46]

Veciana and Bishop discussed the assassination shortly after it occurred. "I was afraid... we both understood. I could guess that he knew that I was knowledgeable of that and I learned that the best way is not to know, not to get to know things that don't concern you, so I respected the rules and I didn't mention that ever."[47]

"Bishop told Veciana that if he could get in touch with Ruiz, he would pay Ruiz a large amount of money to say publicly that it was him and his wife who had met with Oswald." Ruiz, Veciana's cousin, worked in Castro's intelligence service in the Cuban Embassy in Mexico City. Frank (Fiorini) Sturgis, caught along with Howard Hunt in the Watergate, had worked for Castro, too. Sturgis had also helped to try to plant a false trail leading to Oswald at the time of the President's murder.

We know that Watergater Frank Sturgis is purported to have driven to Dallas with "Oswald." Phillips, a propaganda specialist, was the Chief of the Western Hemisphere Division of the CIA, and was stationed in Mexico City at the time of the alleged Oswald visit before the assassination. Previously, he had been stationed in Havana with Howard Hunt.

Other persons who worked for the CIA told the Committee that Phillips used the name Maurice Bishop.[48] Phillips denies this. Phillips was part of the hotbed of Kennedy haters, and disobeyed the President's orders by continuing to motivate Alpha 66 and other violent anti-Castro groups to raid Cuba at a time when the United States was seeking a *détente*. Antonio Veciana said that Bishop felt the best thing for the country was to overthrow the President. Bishop tried to pay people to say that Oswald had been paid by the Cubans and Russians to kill Kennedy,[49] and Phillips has spent a great deal of time trying to link Oswald to the Cuban and Russian Embassies in Mexico City, where he, Phillips, was stationed. These visits are highly doubtful, if not clearly fabricated by somebody wanting to frame Oswald.

Senator Schweiker has identified Dave Phillips as possibly being the same man in the CIA who used the *nom-de-guerre* "Maurice Bishop."

It has not been established that Phillips was Bishop. The Committee felt that Veciana was lying when he was confronted with Phillips and said that wasn't Bishop.[50] It seems highly unlikely that Phillips would fail to recognize Veciana, since Veciana was one of his top operatives.

On June 16, 1980, Anthony Summers confronted Phillips on the ABC Today Show with the accusation that Phillips had used the name Bishop. The results were inconclusive. Phillips has waged a powerful legal battle against anyone implying that he might have been involved in the assassination of President Kennedy. This information remains insufficient to make any firm judgement as to whether Phillips was indeed "Maurice Bishop." Nor is there conclusive evidence tying Hunt and Sturgis to the assassination of President Kennedy.

Whatever their motives, it is clear that Howard Hunt and Frank Sturgis played fast and loose with the truth. For example, Sturgis said he met Hunt around 1961, but Hunt says he did not meet Sturgis until 1972.[51] Sturgis does not remember where he was on November 22, 1963. He must be one of the few adults in America over 35 who does not recall where he was on the day President Kennedy was killed.

The Assassinations Committee found that Sturgis was involved in operation "Cellula Fantasma," an anti-Castro operation. Veciana says that "Maurice Bishop" was also involved.[52]

We know that the teenaged Oswald was in David Ferrie's Civil Air Patrol unit in New Orleans.[53] This is an important connection, since Ferrie was so deeply involved with Guy Banister,[54] the former FBI man and CIA operative in New Orleans, and with Mafia chieftain Carlos Marcello.[55] They were all involved in the anti-Castro operations, which President Kennedy tried to control. Attacks by Cuban exile groups on Soviet ships in Havana from American bases caused serious difficulties for the government. (Banister and his partner, Hugh Ward, died within ten days of the conclusion of the Warren Commission's hearings.)

Some of these Cubans trained near Lacombe, close to New Orleans. In April, 1963, Kennedy tried to stop the raids and attacked them publicly. Hordes of FBI men and other government agents arrested the Cubans and CIA men.

David Ferrie was reportedly one of the instructors at Lacombe. On July 31, 1963, the government captured this camp and munitions dump, which contained a large quantity of explosives. The property was controlled by William McLeney, a former Havana casino operator.[56]

The Cuban raids continued illegally, and the government raids to close them also went on.[57] Frank Sturgis was one of those rounded up.[58] Some of these men and their friends had underworld connections. Many of those who complained the most about Castro were dispossessed Havana mobsters. Havana had been the Mafia's world capital.

Veciana says that in March of 1963, when his men attacked a Soviet ship, it was under the direction of the CIA's "Maurice Bishop," and "Bishop" was doing all he could to make trouble between Russia and Kennedy.[59] This fits closely with what we know was the policy of many CIA officers, who were conducting their own foreign policy. Desmond Fitzgerald, a CIA agent, was handing assassination instruments to Rolando Cubela to kill Castro, saying that he represented Robert Kennedy and was a U.S. Senator.[60] It would seem, though, that only David Atlee Phillips would have had the authority to move Alpha 66 to attack Russian ships.

Strong evidence was developed by the Assassinations Committee that Oswald, David Ferrie, and Clay Shaw went to Clinton, Louisiana together,[61] and that Oswald had been at the anti-Castro training camp with Ferrie. The Assassinations Committee found the witnesses "credible."

Victor Marchetti, former assistant to the Director of the CIA, says he was told by Richard Helms that David Ferrie and Clay Shaw were contract agents in the CIA.[62] Ferrie was frequently seen in Guy Banister's office by Banister's secretary, Delphine Roberts. Roberts says that Oswald went there too,[63] and he used that address on his Fair Play for Cuba Committee leaflets. Banister was clearly running Oswald as an *agent provocateur.*

AN ONI CONNECTION

Guy Banister, who had been in charge of the Chicago FBI office, "became associated with the Office of Naval Intelligence through the recommendation of Guy Johnson, an ONI reserve officer and the first attorney for Clay Shaw when he was arrested by Garrison."[64] Such an association with the ONI would have reinforced the set-up of Oswald as the patsy for the assassination, as Ferrie had known Oswald since he was a teenager, and Oswald probably went to Russia for the ONI (see Steve Parks in the *Baltimore Sunday Sun,* November 21, 1976).

During the Shaw trial, Sergio Archacha Smith, a primary actor in this drama, removed himself from New Orleans to Dallas, where he was protected by Assistant D.A. Bill Alexander and the Dallas Police Department. Governor John Connally would not sign the extradition papers during the Shaw trial.

Another witness, David L. Lewis, saw Oswald with Ferrie and Carlos Quiroga, a friend of Archacha Smith, with Banister.[65] Banister's secretary's daughter also saw Banister and Oswald together.[66] There are other witnesses as well to these meetings.

Following testimony before the House Committee, Veciana was shot at and hit in the head, but he survived.[67] He had a spotless reputation, but was put into prison on a narcotics charge as a result, he says, of a frame-up by the CIA.

FRIENDS AND NEIGHBORS

Certain crucial evidence for the Warren Commission hung on the testimony of a 19-year-old boy, Buell Wesley Frazier. He had driven Oswald to Irving after work the night before the assassination, and back to the Texas School Book Depository where they were both employed. This boy was picked up for questioning, arrested, and apparently told what to say. He said that Oswald picked up a package he said contained "curtain rods" and took it to work. The Warren Commission said that the rifle was in the package, although Frazier indicated that the package was far too small to contain the disassembled rifle.[68]

The boy was very frightened, and would have said anything he was told to say. The FBI red-flagged his file and made sure that even former intelligence people did not know his whereabouts. Those who apparently gave him a lie detector test falsified the results.[69]

The first broadcasts about the assassination said that the police had found a British .303 rifle.[70] This was the type of weapon owned by Buell Wesley Frazier.[71] The rifle rapidly changed to a Mauser, then to the Mannlicher-Carcano. Frazier was briefly arrested that night and the police took his British .303 from him. Researcher George O'Toole asks, "Could Frazier have been a conspirator, given the job of implicating Oswald in the assassination?" It may be that Frazier, young and easily influenced, or frightened, was used, like many others in this affair.[72]

Again, the answer may be found in the great lengths J. Edgar Hoover and Attorneys General Ramsey Clark and John Mitchell went to to prevent the spectrographic evidence from coming out. The original neutron activation analysis tests conducted by the Atomic Energy Commission for the Warren Commission were also buried.

What is perhaps most interesting here are the relationships of the people involved. When Oswald needed a job, Ruth Paine, the Oswalds' landlady in Irving, Texas, had a friend, Linnie Randle, her neighbor, who suggested that Oswald apply for work at the Texas School Book Depository. Mrs. Randle's brother was Buell Wesley Frazier.[73]

We have previously indicated the connection between Ruth's father and George DeMohrenschildt, a former employee of Clint Murchison, well connected in intelligence circles. Young Frazier's lifelong friend was John M. Crawford, a close friend of Jack Ruby.[74]

Crawford died in a weird plane crash in 1969. He was the pilot on the flight, which left late at night. *The Dallas Morning News* of April 18, 1969 reported, "A stereo set was still playing in Clark's trailer home at the airport when investigators checked Wednesday morning, indicating he may have left in a hurry.

"An airport attendant said the position of the wheel blocks where the plane had been stored in its hangar indicated the departure had been carried out in a rush." Six people died in the crash, including the airport manager, another couple and their two children. The ignition keys were still in the cars of all three men, and the woman left her purse on the seat of one of the cars.[75]

We don't know what the rush was about, but Crawford, living at an airport, was certainly prepared for a fast get-away.

THE WEB

Peter Dale Scott wrote, "There is now sufficient evidence of an intricate web of interlocking gambling and law-enforcement interests in which Ruby had enmeshed himself since leaving Chicago for Dallas in 1947, to suggest that the full story of Ruby's associates would have been embarrassing. Not only to the Syndicate but also to various Dallas law-enforcement authorities *and* J. Edgar Hoover and the FBI."[76]

Don't embarrass the Bureau.

Robert Oswald, Lee's brother, insists that Lee and Ruby knew each other, as did other people at the Carousel Club.[77] We are even told that David Ferrie managed the Carousel for a time, and that he and Oswald were always together.[78] The Babushka Lady (Beverly Oliver) said that Ruby introduced "Lee Oswald from the CIA" to her. She says that she saw Oswald in the Carousel many times, as well as Ferrie, and Jack Lawrence who worked at Downtown Lincoln-Mercury.[79] But the Assassinations Committee would only go so far as to tell us that yes, Oswald was in fact in Ferrie's Civil Air Force Patrol Unit as a teenager.[80] Ferrie and Ruby were reputed homosexuals, and Ferrie's notorious penchant for young boys finally got him fired from his job as a pilot with Eastern Air Lines.[81] This must have been the source of his power over Oswald, and he must have been the person who took Oswald over at an early age and put him together, turning him into an agent, pointing him in whatever direction Ferrie wanted Oswald to go. Like a guided missile, he became a double agent, an *agent provocateur,* and finally the victim of the double-cross.

Victor Marchetti tells us that Clay Shaw – who was a contract agent of the CIA – David Ferrie, E. Howard Hunt of the CIA, Frank Sturgis and Bernard Barker, as well as General Charles Cabell and Richard Nixon, were all working together in the CIA's Bay of Pigs planning operation.[82]

And who was Richard Nixon's military liaison when "the covert training of Cuban exiles by the CIA was due, in substantial part, at least, to my efforts"? (*My Six Crises*) None other than Maj. Gen. Robert Cushman, USMC, whom Nixon later made Deputy Director of the CIA, and who played a large role in the Watergate case.[83]

NIXON, HOFFA AND THE MOB

Late one night not long after President Kennedy was killed, co-author Harrison Livingstone was driving with the widow of Senator Millard Tydings. Tydings was a grand old man of the Senate, known as "the Judge," and he was there for a generation. Mrs. Tydings talked at length about the Roosevelt years, Senator Joe McCarthy, the Cold War, and Richard Nixon, during the Second Great Red Scare. She described Nixon, and said that he made her skin crawl. Mrs. Tydings made the point that Nixon was always backed by Big Oil, ran the CIA when he was Vice President, and seemed to be connected with a number of unsavory characters. His longtime association with Murry Chotiner, who defended many Mafiosi, his friendship with Bebe Rebozo while he was in the White House – and their Cuban friends – appeared to be a symbol of these unsavory connections. While he was in the White House, both Nixon's brother Donald and his nephew worked for the biggest swindler in history, Charles Vesco, and after Nixon's fall, Donald Jr. was still living with Vesco. The mother of former Senator Joseph Tydings of Maryland, who was the youngest United States Attorney in American history (appointed by President Kennedy), said with disgust, "There's Mafia around the White House!"

Washington attorney Bernard Fensterwald writes, "Speculation about Richard Nixon centers upon his close ties to various men who have been associated in some way with Organized Crime operatives of the Mafia – ties that included some of the men who were closest to him: Murry Chotiner; Charles Colson; and Bebe Rebozo...[84] Drew Pearson and Jack Anderson reported that Richard Nixon had earlier received substantial support for his first campaign (for the House of Representatives in 1946) from the powerful and notoriously brutal leader of the Los Angeles Mafia, Mickie Cohen..."[85]

The Mob had always threatened to put their man in the White House. In this sense, the government was Organized Crime, and Organized Crime did kill President Kennedy.

The *Los Angeles Times* article, "The White House, the Teamsters and the Mafia," included a quote from an FBI man who stated that, "This whole thing of the Teamsters and the mob and the White House is one of the scariest things I've ever seen... We don't know what to expect out of the Justice Department."[86]

When the Watergate tapes were released in 1974, we heard the President of the United States, Richard Nixon, discussing with his staff how to launder money to pay off the Watergate burglars by using the Mafia. "Maybe it takes a gang to do that," Nixon suggested to his listeners.[87]

The head of the Justice Department during the Nixon years was Attorney General John Mitchell. He had a wife who became famous during the Watergate scandal. She was so disturbed by what she felt was the secret nature of the Administration, that she would drink too much and call up reporters, whereupon she was spirited away and soon died, another one of those mysterious deaths in the Watergate, of which there appear to be more than a few. She had called UPI reporter Helen Thomas and told her, "Nixon is involved with the Mafia. The Mafia was involved in his re-election."[88]

After being the first President in American history forced to resign, Nixon's first public appearance was "at the notorious La Costa Country Club for a golf tournament run by the Teamster boss Frank Fitzsimmons." The *New York Times, Newsweek,* and other publications have stated that "La Costa is widely reported to be a prime gathering place for well-known Syndicate figures. Among those playing in the early October, 1975, golf tournament – along with Nixon and Fitzsimmons – were Anthony Provenzano, Allen Dorfman, and Jack Presser."[89]

Jimmy Hoffa and the Teamsters contributed heavily to Nixon's losing campaign against John Kennedy in 1960, and, of course, hated the Kennedys.[90] Earl Warren highly praised Hoffa and the Teamsters, saying that he had "admiration" for them, and called the union "not only something great of itself, but splendidly representative of the entire labor movement."[91] This was at a time when Senator John Kennedy was on the McClellan Committee and his brother was chief counsel of the crime-busting committee that was in hot pursuit of the Teamsters for criminal activities and Mob connections. Later, Nixon pardoned Jimmy Hoffa from a Federal penitentiary. Kennedy had threatened to break Hoffa, to which Hoffa responded, "He should live so long."[92]

Jack Ruby had strong ties to people connected to the Teamsters, especially known Teamsters hit-men Dave Yaras and Lenny Patrick.[93] Ruby's sister told this to the Warren Commission, but because they had Yaras' name spelled as Yeres, they did not make the connection.

We know that in 1947 "Nixon intervened on behalf of a Chicago gangster who was about to be called as a witness before a congressional committee." The memo, written by an FBI staff assistant, states, "It is my sworn statement that one Jack Rubenstein of Chicago, noted as a potential witness for hearings of the House Committee on Un-American Activities, is performing information functions for the staff of Congressman Richard Nixon, Republican of California. It is requested Rubenstein not be called for open testimony in the aforementioned hearings." "That same year, Rubenstein moved to Dallas, Texas, and changed his name to Jack Ruby..."[94]

"...IT CAN BE SAID..."

We will recall that Earl Warren was a Republican Governor of California, later became the Chief Justice of the U.S. Supreme Court, and then headed the Warren Commission. Earl Warren and Gerald Ford, who later succeeded Nixon and pardoned him, came to Dallas after the assassination to see Jack Ruby in jail. Ruby was closely watched during the interview by the Dallas authorities and begged, "I may not live tomorrow to give any further testimony... I can't say it here... it can't be said here. It can be said, it's got to be said amongst people of the highest authority... and following that, immediately give me the lie detector test after I do make that statement... Gentlemen, if you want to hear any further testimony, you will have to get me to Washington soon, because it has something to do with you, Chief Warren... I want to tell the truth, and I can't tell it here."[95] Of course Sheriff Bill Decker was right there. Ruby begged many times during the interview, "Gentlemen, unless you get me to Washington, you can't get a fair shake out of me."

Warren told him that they couldn't take him to Washington: "Well, the public attention that it would attract, and the people who would be around. We have no place there for you to be safe when we take you out, and we are not law enforcement officers, and it isn't our responsibility to go into anything of that kind."

Picture this conversation between a gangster/murderer and the

Chief Justice of the Supreme Court: "Chief Warren, your life is in danger in this city, do you know that?" After Warren told Ruby that Ruby wouldn't be safe in Washington, Ruby said, "...they made certain precautions for you coming here, but you got here."

They argued about this at length. Ruby said, "you said you have the power to do what you want to do, is that correct?... But you don't have a right to take a prisoner back with you when you want to?"

"No; we have the power to subpoena witnesses to Washington if we want to do it..."

"Yes; but these people aren't Jack Ruby."

"No; they weren't."

"They weren't."

"...so we are not treating you differently from any other witness."

"I tell you, gentlemen, my whole family is in jeopardy. My sisters, as to their lives." "Well, it is too tragic to talk about," Ruby added. "At this moment, Lee Harvey Oswald isn't guilty of committing the crime of assassinating President Kennedy. Jack Ruby is." And then, "There is an organization here, Chief Justice Warren, if it takes my life at this moment to say it, and Bill Decker said be a man and say it, there is a John Birch Society right now in activity, and Edwin Walker is one of the top men of this organization – take it for what it is worth, Chief Justice Warren. Unfortunately for me, for me giving the people the opportunity to get in power, because of the act I committed, has put a lot of people in jeopardy with their lives... Don't register with you, does it?" Ruby asked.

"No; I don't understand that." Warren replied. Ruby read it on Warren's face.

"Would you rather I just delete what I said and just pretend that nothing is going on?"

"...Mr. Ruby, I know what you feel about the John Birch Society."

"Very powerful."

"I think it is powerful, yes I do."

Ruby said, "Maybe something can be saved, something can be done. What have you got to answer to that, Chief Justice Warren?" For nearly three hours, Ruby had been pleading to be taken to Washington. "Well, I don't know what can be done, Mr. Ruby, because I don't know what you anticipate we will encounter," said the Chief Justice of the United States.

Representative Ford asked: "Is there anything more you can tell us if you went back to Washington?"

"Yes; are you sincere in wanting to take me back?"

"We are most interested in all the information you have."

"...I am used as a scapegoat... But if I am eliminated, there won't be any way of knowing. Right now... I am the only one that can bring out the truth to our President... I know that your hands are tied; you are helpless," Ruby said with resignation. How did he know this? Warren's interview with Ruby was just for show. If he had wanted to let Ruby talk, he certainly had the power to take him to Washington.

Joe Tonahill spoke up. "Who did you think is going to eliminate you, Jack?" It was Tonahill who talked Ruby into using the cover-story that Ruby had shot Oswald to spare Mrs. Kennedy the strain of coming to testify against Oswald.

"I have been used for a purpose, and there will be a certain tragic occurrence happening if you don't take my testimony and somehow vindicate me..." he answered. "But we have taken your testimony," the Chief Justice told him. "We have it here. It will be in permanent form for the President of the United States and for the Congress of the United States, and for the people of the entire world. It is there. It will be recorded for all to see. That is the purpose of our coming here today. We feel that you are entitled to have your story told."

"YOU HAVE LOST ME..."

"You have lost me though. You have lost me, Chief Justice Warren."

"Lost you in what sense?"

"I won't be around for you to come and question me again." And he wasn't. He developed a fast case of cancer in a couple of years, and died. Ruby himself believed he contracted cancer by injection.[96]

"Well, it is very hard for me to believe that. I am sure that everybody would want to protect you to the very limit."

A couple of times, Ruby asked "Chief Warren" if he knew a man named Storey, and Gordon McClendon. Why did he ask Warren this? Had he heard that Warren might know them? At another point, Ruby could not recall the details about someone he knew, Alfred McLane. Warren *did* know: "Alfred was killed in a taxi in New York," Warren said.[97]

"The most dangerous activities are those that are usually the least visible. U.S. intelligence officers working for the CIA and other agencies have fattened their wallets by moonlighting for the private apparatus."

– *Spooks,* by Jim Hougan

CHAPTER 14

DEADLY POLITICS

Consider the strange case of the Russian exile count, living in Dallas, deeply involved in the oil business, "with right wing connections,"[1] ties to H.L. Hunt, and who was also linked to the CIA Bay of Pigs Operation.[2] The count's name is George DeMohrenschildt, and he befriended the Oswalds. DeMohrenschildt paid many visits to their home, took them to parties, and spent long hours with Oswald.[3] DeMohrenschildt was an educated man, a member of the foreign nobility, with ties to intelligence circles,[4] a man who was once suspected of being a spy. What was he doing so close to Oswald? Oswald had been made out to be a red-neck, uneducated, lone-nut assassin.

DeMohrenschildt was quite close to President Duvalier ("Papa Doc") of Haiti, and "according to Dryer, Jacqueline Lancelot related to him that President Duvalier had once implied that the American President might not remain in office... during a speech to Haitian troops in a port city, Duvalier allegedly said that 'the big man in the White House wasn't going to be there much longer.' "[5]

"The possible association between George DeMohrenschildt and William Avery Hyde may have some significance because Hyde is the father of Ruth Paine, the woman with whom Marina Oswald was living at the time of the assassination. The connection is intriguing because there was never any intimation by the Warren Commission that DeMohrenschildt had more than a brief acquaintance with Ruth Paine."[6]

The Assassinations Committee was deeply concerned about "the apparent suicide of DeMohrenschildt in 1977 on the day he was contacted by both an investigator from the committee and a writer* about Oswald."[7]

DeMohrenschildt, who had a connection to the Bouviers, Jacqueline Kennedy's family,[8] "claimed that the last time he and his wife saw the Oswalds was in January, 1963...."[9] In a manuscript about Oswald, he "wrote that he and his wife had stumbled upon the gun photo in February 1967 in boxes of their belongings that they had placed in storage in early 1963 before their departure for Haiti in May, 1963... He explained that the photo was among English practice records that he and his wife had loaned to Marina Oswald, and that somehow the Oswalds had managed to return those records, including the photograph, to the DeMohrenschildts' possessions.

"In the manuscript (reproduced in Vol. XII) DeMohrenschildt identified the handwritten date of the photograph, '5/IV/63' as April 5, 1963 – and stated that at that time he and his wife 'were thousands of miles away in Haiti.' " That statement contradicts the statements DeMohrenschildt made to Warren Commission and State Department officials about the dates of his travel to Haiti.

"The circumstances of the DeMohrenschildts' learning that Oswald owned a rifle, DeMohrenschildt's comment to Oswald about the Walker shooting, and the circumstances of the 'discovery' of the gun photograph in the DeMohrenschildts' possessions may indicate knowledge the DeMohrenschildts had about the violent turn Oswald's political inclinations had taken that have not been fully explored."[10]

ALLEGATIONS OF DEMOHRENSCHILDT INTELLIGENCE CONNECTIONS

"In his Warren Commission testimony DeMohrenschildt stated that he believed he had discussed Lee Harvey Oswald with J. Walton Moore, whom DeMohrenschildt described as a government man – either FBI

*Edward Jay Epstein.

or Central Intelligence."[11]... "In 1963 J. Walton Moore was employed by the Central Intelligence Agency in Dallas... In an Agency memorandum dated April 13, 1977, Moore set forth facts to counter a claim... that Lee Harvey Oswald was employed by the CIA and that Moore knew Oswald. In that memo, Moore is quoted as saying that according to his records the last time he talked to George DeMohrenschildt was in the fall of 1961. Moore said that he had no recollection of any conversation with DeMohrenschildt concerning Lee Harvey Oswald...

"Other documents in the DeMohrenschildt's CIA file indicated more contact between Moore and DeMohrenschildt than was stated in the 1977 memo by Moore. In a memorandum dated May 1, 1964, from Moore to the Acting Chief of the Contacts Division of the CIA, Moore stated that he had known George DeMohrenschildt and his wife since 1957... Moore said also in that 1964 memo that he saw DeMohrenschildt several times in 1958 and 1959." DeMohrenschildt was also making regular reports to the CIA: His CIA file "contained several reports submitted by DeMohrenschildt to the CIA on topics concerning Yugoslavia." Moore told the Committee that "he had 'periodic' contact with DeMohrenschildt for 'debriefing' purposes over the years after that..." "Moore then denied that any of this had to do with Oswald. But DeMohrenschildt was not sure in his Warren Commission testimony to whom in the CIA he had talked to about Oswald."[12]

MORE THAN CASUAL ACQUAINTANCES

When DeMohrenschildt was moving from Dallas to Haiti, he had a secret meeting with a Pentagon intelligence person, Dorothy Matlack, in Washington. She was the Assistant Director of the Office of Intelligence of the Army, liaison with the CIA. She only admitted to this one meeting with DeMohrenschildt, but when Joseph Dryer, a stockbroker with Loeb & Rhodes in Palm Beach, was questioned by the Committee and asked if he recognized any of a list of names read to him, he recognized Dorothy Matlack's name right off, and that of William Avery Hyde, Ruth Paine's father. These do not appear to have been casual acquaintances.[13]

"Dryer said in the interview that Lancelot told him shortly after the Kennedy assassination that a 'substantial' sum of money, $200,000 or $250,000, had been deposited in De Mohrenschildt's account in a bank in Port-au-Prince... Lancelot said her source of information was the person who handed out the funds at the bank. The money in the account was subsequently paid out, although she did not know to whom, and DeMohrenschildt left Haiti soon after." [14]

The meeting between Matlack and DeMohrenschildt occurred on May 7, 1963. Matlack said that she thought she was just seeing Joseph Clemard Charles, a close associate of President Duvalier of Haiti, and a banker. DeMohrenschildt's CIA file has a memo of this call: "the purpose of the call was to arrange a meeting between Charles and an Agency representative for noon of that day... Mrs. Matlack said George and Jean DeMohrenschildt accompanied Charles to this meeting and that their presence was a 'surprise' to her. She did not know what role DeMohrenschildt was serving, but felt he 'dominated' Charles in some way...! 'I knew the Texan wasn't there to sell hemp.' "

"Mrs. Matlack said she was so disturbed by DeMohrenschildt at the meeting that she discussed it with the FBI liaison. [15]

"Because of the potential political information Charles could give about the current situation in Haiti, the CIA became the primary contact with Charles." And of course DeMohrenschildt was right there with him in Haiti. "Dryer stated that he was told by Charles that a large amount of money had been placed in DeMohrenschildt's account in Charles' bank just before De Mohrenschildt left Haiti." [16] And, as we have seen, Dryer told the Committee that other monies, "$200,000 or $250,000," had been put into his account in still another bank.

"Mrs. Matlack said she was first informed about the visit of Clemard Joseph Charles to the United States in 1963 by Col. Sam Kail, an Army Intelligence officer who was working in Miami at that time." [17]

We wonder, along with Joanne Braun – an independent researcher – whether Kail is Col. Robert Castorr, or perhaps Col. FNU Caster, who researchers think met with Cuban exiles in Dallas, or the colonel Nancy Perrin Rich says received money from Ruby at a meeting. Kail was one of those at the Havana Embassy whom "Maurice Bishop" advised Antonio Veciana to contact. [18] Why didn't the Committee investigate this?

It would appear from the information that we now have on De Mohrenschildt that he had hidden far more extensive intelligence connections than was previously realized, as well as connections to the power structure in Dallas and across the country. His trip to Haiti removed him from immediate suspicion in the assassination. In June, 1976, DeMohrenschildt completed a manuscript which he claimed named names. "That's when disaster struck. You see, in that book I played the devil's advocate. Without directly implicating myself as an accomplice in the JFK assassination I still mentioned a number of names, particularly of FBI and CIA officials who apparently may not be exposed under any circumstances. I was drugged surreptitiously. As a result I was committed to a mental hospital..." [19] and, it would appear, they either killed him or drove him to suicide.

DeMohrenschildt's wife told Jim Marrs, a Dallas reporter, "He must have still harbored guilt feelings about his work for the Germans during World War II, because he told me 'It's the Jews. They have caught up with me!'..." During the War, DeMohrenschildt had been briefly detained on suspicion of being a German spy. Nothing further was heard on this until his wife spoke with Marrs.

DeMohrenschildt's wife believes that her husband was programmed to take his life on command. She says her husband was sent to a new doctor in Dallas, Charles Mendoza. Jim Marrs writes in *Cover-Ups* (May, 1985) that a check was made with the Dallas County Medical Society, and Mendoza had registered with the association just two months before he began treating DeMohrenschildt. Mendoza left Dallas in December, 1976, shortly after George entered Parkland for mental problems. The forwarding address the doctor gave proved false.

"With the information now available about CIA mind-control experimentation and behavior-modification, and the known connections between George and that agency (A CIA memo from former Director Richard Helms made public in 1978 showed he filed numerous reports as an informant for the spy agency), it is more than a little suspicious that his mental problems didn't begin until his 'treatment' at the hands of this shadowy doctor," Jim Marrs writes.

"George underwent two to three hours of 'therapy' at a time with Dr. Mendoza, which involved intravenous injections. George did not know exactly what the injections were." Jeanne DeMohrenschildt says, "Mendoza also insisted that we buy all of George's medicine from the pharmacy near his office. He explained that he was a part owner and the medicine would cost less that way. But I checked with my usual pharmacy and learned that the medicine prices were the same, if not lower, than the doctor's pharmacy. I confronted Mendoza with this information and demanded to know exactly what kind of medicine and treatments he was giving George. Mendoza became very angry and upset. But I learned nothing useful."

DeMohrenschildt quickly deteriorated emotionally, tried to take his life, became paranoid, and finally appears to have shot himself. His wife says she believed that he received a phone call on the day he died, or a command of some kind which triggered his death, the day the Assassinations Committee located him.

THE DALLAS POWER STRUCTURE

In 1963, the Mayor of Dallas was Earl Cabell, whose brother Charles had been the Deputy Director of the CIA until Kennedy fired him. These men leaned politically to the far right, and the most powerful men among them in Dallas were the oilmen H.L. Hunt, Syd Richardson, and Clint Murchison. They were all adamantly opposed to John Kennedy's policies, and were convinced he was leading the country to ruin. We know that H.L. Hunt, perhaps the richest man in America, was spirited out of Dallas an hour after the assassination by the FBI and flown to Mexico, where he remained for one month.[20]

He was the top bankroller of many Right Wing causes, and he hated the Kennedys.[21] Hunt's son's name was found in Jack Ruby's notebook,[22] and Ruby went to the Hunts' offices the day before the assassination, at the same time Jim Braden visited them.[23] Braden was arrested shortly after the assassination, in the Dal-Tex building.[24] He was a well-known Mafia courier and founder of LaCosta.[25] A famous note apparently written by Oswald and addressed to "Mr. Hunt" asked about his position. We might imagine that this note was directed either to one of the Hunts or to E. Howard Hunt.[26]

H.L. Hunt was a longtime backer of Richard Nixon,[27] and Nixon was known to be supported by "an untold amount of oil money..."[28] (*Drew Pearson Diaries*). In 1968, Hunt had tried to get Gerald Ford made Vice Presidential candidate with Nixon.[29]

The same CIA Domestic Contacts man in Dallas, J. Walton Moore, who had numerous contacts with DeMohrenschildt, wrote from Houston on February 14, 1969 that "Mr. H.L. Hunt has been very concerned that District Attorney Garrison will try to involve him in the Kennedy Assassination..."[30] An investigator Garrison had fired was later found looking for work with Hunt.[31]

General Charles Cabell briefed Kennedy on the Bay of Pigs invasion preparations just before the election in which Kennedy defeated Nixon.[32] He did not tell the candidate that he and others were planning to kill Castro. In fact, they never told him, and this is where we begin to understand the Dallas-Hughes-CIA-Mafia-anti-Castro-Cuban connection, which resulted in the President's murder. The Senate Intelligence Committee, Jack Anderson, former Warren Commission staffers and others have often stated that if the Warren Commission had been told about the assassination plots against Castro, it might have changed their whole view of Kennedy's assassination. But does this mean that Castro retaliated by killing the President? No. It means that some of the men who were involved in that plot, which the President tried to control,[33] later played central roles in his assassination. The apparatus set up to destroy Castro ended up destroying John Kennedy.

"The oilmen have little difficulty in getting their candidates elected to office – they control the press, radio and television. Their influence over the police and judicial authorities is such that only the most insignificant criminal and civil cases, and those in which they have interests at stake, are ever brought to court."[34]

OIL DEPLETION AND THE HUNTS

"It was the oil depletion allowance that made Hunt rich. He did in a few years what it took John D. Rockefeller a lifetime to accomplish. When Kennedy threatened to retract the depletion allowance, the right wing-John Birch hate machine was cranked up against him." "Hunt's letterhead describes him as an 'operator'... His personal bodyguard is made up of former FBI agents. Years ago he acquired the habit of acting through intermediaries. He has his own intelligence network, and his decisions are carried out by a powerful general staff. His business interests are so extensive that he subsidizes (along with other important oilmen) most of the influential men in Congress, men like Lyndon Johnson. Hunt was one of the financial backers of Senator Joseph McCarthy, whose deputy Roy Cohn attracted his attention and has since worked for him on several occasions.[35]

"Hunt is the most powerful American propagandist of the Far

Right. In 1951 he financed 'Facts Forum,' a series of radio and television programs which was later replaced by 'Life Line,' a one-sided series of 15-minute radio broadcasts carried daily on 409 stations throughout the country. His propaganda campaign costs him $2 million a year... He once declared 'We should do whatever our generals advise us to do.' " He was close friends with a number of famous generals: General George C. Kenney, former Commanding General of the Strategic Air Command, who wanted to knock out Russia in a preemptive strike with nuclear weapons; General Albert Wedemeyer, an active John Bircher; and Admiral James Van Fleet. Leader of this warrior clan was General Edwin A. Walker, a Texan who returned to Dallas after leaving the Army and contacted H.L. Hunt. Then, with the support of the John Birchers, the Minutemen, and several of his former subordinates in the U.S. Forces in Germany, he launched an extremist and militarist campaign. Robert A. Surrey, Walker's "associate," had the financial backing of Hunt's companies... By the winter of 1962-3, plans were being made for a preemptive strike.

"Hunt is the Big Man in Texas, the Giant, the richest and the stingiest, the most powerful and the most solitary of the oilmen..."[36]

"The opinions and the aversions of obstinate old men often lead to excesses. Embittered Puritan potentates frightened to see their lives drawing to an end are an even greater danger... In the streets of Texas, 'Knock Out the Kennedys' stickers were already appearing on bumpers and windshields."[37]

The book from which these quotes are taken, *Farewell America,* was supposedly written by a "James Hepburn" or "pseudonym, actual author or authors unknown," published in Europe and traced to the Presidential Palace and French Intelligence by Bill Turner, a former FBI man who has worked hard in this investigation.[38] In it, we find that "At 12:23 on November 22, from his office on the 7th floor of the Mercantile Building, Haroldson Lafayette Hunt watched John Kennedy ride towards Dealey Plaza, where fate awaited him at 12:30. A few minutes later, escorted by six men in two cars, Hunt left the center of Dallas without even stopping by his house.

"At that very moment, General Walker was in a plane between New Orleans and Shreveport. He joined Mr. Hunt in one of his secret hide-aways across the Mexican border. There they remained for a month, protected by personal guards, under the impassive eyes of the FBI. It was not until Christmas that Hunt, Walker and their party returned to Dallas."[39]

General Walker's aide, Robert Surrey, told the *Midlothian Mirror* that he played bridge regularly with James Hosty, [40] the FBI man who had been to see the Oswalds, and who destroyed a note written to him by Oswald.[41] At the same time, Oswald was seen attending meetings at which General Walker was present or spoke, after he was alleged to have shot at Walker. One meeting was held to raise money for the DRE, a Cuban anti-Castro group. Walker's address and phone number were in Oswald's notebook. "General Walker and Colonel FNU Caster, a close acquaintance of Walker, have been trying to arouse the feelings of the Cuban refugees in Dallas against the Kennedy administration," said Mrs.C.L.Connel, a witness.[42]

There is extensive evidence that Jack Ruby was involved in supplying arms to the Cubans and knew Walker. William McEwan Duff, who worked for Walker, says he saw Ruby go to Walker's house. Nancy Perrin Rich, who worked for Ruby, testified that Ruby came to a meeting also attended by an Army colonel, who ran a discussion of arms deals, and that he received money from Ruby.[43]

HOOVER AND THE FBI

What about J. Edgar Hoover and the FBI? What role did they play in the events leading up to the assassination? According to James Hepburn, "In 30 years on the job, J. Edgar Hoover has developed an intelligence system which nothing – no racket, and certainly no conspiracy – can escape. Through its extensive network of informers, the FBI knows everything worth knowing that goes on in the United States even in areas that lie outside its legal jurisdiction. The Dallas conspiracy was born and took root in places where the FBI was well represented... By mid-October, Hoover had been informed of the existence of a plot and was familiar with many of the details... The week before the President's departure for Texas, Hoover knew exactly what was going to happen. Why did the FBI fail to intervene?"[44]

When Oswald went to New Orleans, he went to see Carlos Bringuier, a leader of the anti-Castro movement in New Orleans,[45] who was deeply involved in the illegal arms and training camps Kennedy had closed.[46] Oswald evidently tried to infiltrate Bringuier's group, but

Carlos was suspicious and put him off.[47] Oswald immediately began handing out Fair Play For Cuba Committee leaflets, which were pro-Castro, and stamped on some of them was the same address on Camp Street where Guy Banister had his offices.[48] Banister was the former head of the Chicago FBI office who was intimately connected with the CIA's Cuban activities in New Orleans, which Kennedy opposed.[49] Bringuier found Oswald on the street and there was an argument, and Oswald told Carlos to hit him.[50] He was obviously a *provocateur.* Oswald was arrested, asked to see an FBI man, and was promptly released.[51] Oswald then appeared on a broadcast interview as a representative of the FPCC in New Orleans, of which he was the only member.[52]

Senator Richard Schweiker said: "I think that by playing a pro-Castro role on the one hand and associating with anti-Castro Cubans on the other, Oswald was playing out an intelligence role. This gets back to him being an agent or double agent... I personally believe that he had a special relationship with one of the intelligence agencies, which one I'm not certain. But all the fingerprints I found during my eighteen months on the Senate Select Committee on Intelligence Activities point to Oswald as being a product of, and interacting with the intelligence community."[53]

"A MYSTERIOUS FELLOW"

President Johnson said of Oswald, "He was quite a mysterious fellow, and he did have a connection that bore examination, and the extent of the influence of those connections on him I think history will deal with more than we're able to now."[54] For his part, Senator Richard Russell, one of the members of the Warren Commission, said he never believed Oswald planned the assassination alone.

We recall that at the evening press conference when Oswald was brought before reporters and introduced as a member of one of the Right Wing Cuban groups, Jack Ruby was there and shouted out a correction that Oswald was a member of the FPCC.[55] How did Ruby know this? How was the mistake made in the first place? Ruby was clearly involved in Cuban affairs from the beginning.[56]

"The right-wing Cuban *émigrés* were bitter and infuriated by the humiliating defeat at the Bay of Pigs, blaming President Kennedy for refusing to permit direct American military participation in the invasion. The CIA, whose conduct of the whole affair brought the agency into disgrace and jeopardy, had made arrangements to overrule President Kennedy if he cancelled the invasion at the last minute, so that the landing at the Bay of Pigs would go ahead regardless of Presidential orders. The revelation that the CIA had contemplated countermanding the White House, on top of its incredible bungling of the invasion from beginning to end, suggested an early end to what has been called 'the invisible government,' and a threat to their Cuban *protégés.*"[57]

"In August, 1960, The CIA took steps to enlist members of the criminal underworld with gambling syndicate contacts to aid in assassinating Castro[58] (*Senate Intelligence Committee Report on Foreign Assassinations.*)" The Kennedys were deadly enemies of the Mob, and the CIA and the Mob worked "hand in glove," as Chairman Gonzalez of the Assassinations Committee told the authors.

The Senate Intelligence Committee Report goes on to say that Allen Dulles personally approved the plots, the two top planners for which were Richard Bissell and Sheffield Edwards. It says that "Bissell recalled that 'in the later part of September' there was a 'meeting in which Colonel Edwards and I briefed Mr. Dulles and General Cabell,' about the plan to assassinate Castro. Bissell testified that 'Colonel Edwards outlined in somewhat circumlocutious terms the plan that they had discussed with syndicate representatives.' He stated that Edwards had said: 'That contact had been made with (the underworld), that a plan had been prepared for their use... that the plan would be put into effect unless at that time or subsequently he was told by Mr. Dulles that it should not be.' "[59]

BUCK-PASSING

From here on, all of this gets very murky, with everyone passing the buck. The Senate Intelligence Committee tried to find out who authorized the plan in the first place. Both Bissell and Edwards testified that they were authorized to plan the murder by Dulles and his Deputy Director General Charles Cabell.[60]

"It is clear, then, that even if Dulles was informed about the use of underworld figures to assassinate Castro, subordinate Agency officials had previously decided to take steps toward arranging for the killing of Castro, including discussing it with organized crime leaders."[61]

Robert Maheu, the top aide to Howard Hughes, later the employer of Gen. Cabell, was the initial intermediary who went to Mafia leader John Roselli to begin setting up the murder plots.[62] Howard Hunt proposed some of these plots, and worked with his close friend Manuel Artime on them.[63] Artime later handled the first "hush money" payments to the Watergate burglars for Hunt.[64]

Of crucial importance is the fact that both the CIA and the Senate Committee concluded after their investigations that the CIA had tried to conceal the assassination plots from President Kennedy and his brother.[65] On May 7, 1962, CIA officials told Robert Kennedy that there had been assassination plots, but they had now ended. In fact, they were being stepped up, using the Mafia as the instrument of Executive Action.[66]

The CIA prepared to go ahead and invade the Bay of Pigs on their own without Presidential approval, and hatched illegal assassination plots with the Mafia. All of this points to affairs spinning dangerously out of control. This spiral of lawlessness resulted in the germination of the plot against the President himself.

When Richard Helms replaced Richard Bissell, who was fired by the President, he activated new contacts with John Roselli in April 1962 to begin planning another murder attempt. At this time, William Harvey was coordinating the plots with the Mafia, and he and Helms dropped Sam Giancana and Robert Maheu from the plots. They also concealed the plots from the new Kennedy-appointed Director of the CIA, John McCone. Helms later testified, "I was enormously busy with a lot of other things.... I guess I must have thought to myself, well this is going to look peculiar to him and I doubt very much this is going to go any place, but if it does, then that is time enough to bring him in the picture. It was a Mafia connection and Mr. McCone was new to the organization and this was, you know, not a very savory effort."[67]

For his part, General Cabell of Dallas was quite familiar with the use of the Mob for Executive Action.

The Senate Intelligence Committee Report said, "The Attorney General was not told that the gambling syndicate (assassination) operation had already been reactivated, nor, as far as we know, was he ever told that the CIA had a continuing involvement with U.S. gangster elements."[68]

The Senate Committee and the CIA established that Edwards (a CIA operative) had prepared a fraudulent internal memorandum for the files a week later, which also deceptively stated that the CIA had terminated the conspiracies. In his Senate testimony, the CIA's William Harvey admitted that the internal CIA memorandum (May 14, 1962) "was not true, and Colonel Edwards knew it was not true."[69]

THE BAY OF PIGS

Kennedy replaced General Cabell, because he believed Cabell did a poor job during the planning and execution of the Bay of Pigs Operation, which Cabell ran in the absence of Dulles.[70] As a result of poor logistics planning, the men on the beach ran out of ammunition. All their ammunition was in one ship, which was blown up by a jet trainer. The President had been given the impression that the invaders would make their way inland and become guerrillas, but that was not the plan at all. "The proximate cause of their defeat, according to the full-scale investigation later conducted under the chairmanship of Gen. Maxwell Taylor, was a shortage of ammunition, and the reasons for the shortage illustrate all the shortcomings of the operation."[71]

Theodore Sorenson, Kennedy's closest policy aide, tells us that the CIA then cancelled a convoy bringing more ammunition. The CIA coordinators "called off the convoy without consulting the President."[72] And "The CIA's stated plan was to destroy Castro's air force on the ground before the battle began... That plan failed."[73]

Kennedy allowed a limited air cover by unmarked Navy jets in the last hours to escort the Cuban exile B-26s to Cuba. But this was bungled by bad planning, as they got "their directions from the CIA, they (the Cuban exile B-26s) arrived on the scene an hour before the (American) jets, who received their directions from the Navy; and whether this tragic error was due to a difference in time zones or instructions, the B-26s were soon downed or gone, the jet mission was invalidated before it started, and without ammunition the exiles were quickly rounded up."[74] And "the immediate invasion area was not suitable for guerrilla warfare, as the President had been assured, the vast majority of brigade members had not been given guerrilla training, as had been assured; and the eight mile route to the Escambray Mountains to which he had been assured they could escape was so long, so swampy, and so covered by Castro's troops that this was never a realistic alternative."[75]

"The CIA's close control of the operation, however, kept the President and the Cuban exile force largely uninformed of each other's thinking; and its enthusiasm caused it to reject the clear evidence of Castro's political and military strength which was available from British and State Department Intelligence and even from newspaper stories."[76]

The Bay of Pigs operation was a fiasco, and someone had to take responsibility. As the senior military representative, Cabell took the fall. His firing by Kennedy must have come as a terrible blow. He clearly had a strong reason to hate Kennedy.

On September 16, 1973, the *Washington Post* reported that "New Orleans District Attorney Jim Garrison as late as March 1971, was preparing to accuse another person of conspiring to assassinate President John F. Kennedy. Garrison's intended defendant this time was the late Air Force General Charles Cabell, former deputy director of the Central Intelligence Agency."[77] The basis for Garrison's charge was never revealed and tested in court. We know from Garrison that Cabell had been in New Orleans in November of 1963. We also know that Cabell went to work for Howard Hughes, whose man Robert Maheu was, as a consultant when Kennedy fired him.[78] Maheu and Cabell had worked together in the plots to kill Castro. After he was fired, Cabell served on the board of Air America, a CIA operation, and lawyer-researcher Bernard Fensterwald tells us that Cabell and Maheu continued to work closely together.[79]

Howard Hunt also knew Cabell, and worked closely with him in 1954, when they overthrew Arbenz in Guatemala. Cabell was Hunt's coordinating superior during the operation. Frank Wisner, whose suicide in 1966 raised many questions, also worked closely with them.[80] Again, Hunt worked closely with Cabell during the Bay of Pigs operation.[81] Cabell tried twice during the night before the invasion, even having Rusk awaken Kennedy at 4 A.M., to get new air cover, but was told no.[82] Criticism of the U.S. intervention was rapidly mounting around the world. He never forgave Kennedy, nor did the anti-Castro Cubans.

When the Senate began investigating the CIA-Mafia plots, they could find out almost nothing about Cabell's role. When President Johnson discovered that we were "running a damn murder incorporated" in the Caribbean, he had the CIA prepare a report on the assassination plots because he was suspicious that they might have led to Kennedy's death. During the investigation, Richard Helms protected Cabell. General Cabell was never interviewed by the investigators, although he was deeply involved. "There just wasn't much information around on Cabell... very, very little," an attorney for the Senate Committee said.[83] Interestingly, Helms was also the CIA's liaison with the Warren Commission. He did not give them anything they did not ask for.[84]

Cabell wasn't the only person associated with this case who was involved in murder plots. According to Frank Sturgis, CIA operative and Watergate burglar, Cabell's subordinate "Howard (Hunt) was in charge of a couple of other CIA operations involving 'disposal' and I can tell you, *some of them worked.*"[85]

"The more I have learned, the more concerned I have become that the government was involved in the assassination of President Kennedy."

– Victor Marchetti, former executive
at the Central Intelligence Agency,
and author of *The CIA and the Cult of Intelligence*

CHAPTER 15

FROM DALLAS TO WATERGATE

President Eisenhower was not a well man during his final years in the White House. This was ideal for those who wished to manipulate and control events. His Vice President, Richard Nixon, was not particularly liked by Eisenhower. Nevertheless, the President's waning energy placed considerable power in Nixon's hands. One of his functions as Vice President was to chair a committee then known as Special Group 54-12. The Special Group coordinated actions of the CIA and Military Intelligence. This is where the first plots against the life of Castro – some of which employed the Mafia – were sanctioned, and the outline for the Bay of Pigs invasion was approved. Nixon was the White House action officer for these plans.[1]

A member of the 54-12 group was longtime Nixon associate Alexander Haig, who underwent an almost instant advancement from Colonel to four-star General when Nixon was later elected President. His later advancement to Secretary of State under President Reagan has been cited as a demonstration of America's lack of faith in diplomacy as a tool of foreign policy.[2] E. Howard Hunt, the compulsive spy, and Frank Sturgis, both of whom were long involved in assassination plots, were also connected to 54-12.[3]

The CIA, Hunt's and Sturgis' employer, became diverted from its

272

main course at this time, which was countering the perceived threat of the Soviet Union and China. Increasingly, the CIA became focused on controlling events in Third World countries. No Third World country received more attention in those days than Cuba.

Hunt wrote in his memoirs, *Give Us This Day,* that he had strongly recommended the assassination of Castro, and he was deeply involved in the coordination of those plots. Robert Cushman, a Marine Corps Officer, shared an office at the CIA with Hunt in the 1950s, and they remained friends right up through Watergate, when Cushman rose to be Deputy Director of the CIA under Nixon.[4]

Marion Cooper, who worked for the CIA, said that he attended a meeting on January 1, 1955, in Honduras, at which the planning for the assassination of the President of Panama, Jose Antonio Remon, was discussed in detail. Present were the team of killers hired to do the killing, and the Vice President of the United States, Richard Nixon.[5] "The following day Remon was machine-gunned to death."[6]

Former CIA man Cooper has been tested with a polygraph examination and passed with the highest rating. This story was given to Senator Church, and was mostly verified by Chicago journalist Joe Pennington. Commission Document 279 – "Assassination of Jose Remon, Panama" – remains classified in the National Archives.

Drew Pearson and Jack Anderson detailed in 1959 the connections of Murry Chotiner, Nixon's longtime political manager. Chotiner and his brother handled the legal defense of 221 mobsters prosecuted during the three years of Nixon's rise from Congressman to Senator to Vice Presidential nominee.[7] In addition, Chotiner, who knew where all the bodies were buried, died in somewhat mysterious circumstances. On January 23, 1974, Chotiner's car was struck by a government truck, and he suffered a broken leg. He died from this injury a week later.

In 1976, Howard Kohn wrote "The Hughes-Nixon-Lansky Connection,"[8] which extensively documented the connections between Nixon and Organized Crime. This especially included Meyer Lansky, the Godfather of Godfathers.

THE RUBY CONNECTION

Jack Ruby made several visits to Cuba after Castro came into power. He visited certain mobsters Castro had imprisoned, and it is believed that he saw Lansky himself, whom Ruby referred to as Mr. Fox.[9]

When Nixon was thrown out of office by an exhausted nation, he retreated to San Clemente for several months and did not poke his head out. When he did, the first place he went was La Costa, the magnificent nearby retreat of the Mafia and Earl Warren, built by Mo Dalitz. Nixon was there with Teamsters President Frank Fitzsimmons, Tony Provenzano, Jack Presser and Allen Dorfman, the latter two also of the Teamsters.[10] Who was one of the founders of La Costa? Jim Braden, who was arrested at the Dal-Tex building minutes after the assassination in Dallas under an alias, then released.[11] He said he was in Dallas on "oil business," and it was found that he had been at the office of H.L. Hunt, as had Jack Ruby, the day before the assassination, at nearly the same time.[12]

Richard Nixon tells us in *My Six Crises* that he was behind the attempt to overthrow Castro. Castro, remember, was not against the United States when he first came to power; after all, he received considerable help from the CIA in his campaign to defeat Batista. CIA operative Frank Fiorini (later Sturgis) helped Castro with guns and advice, and served as an intelligence officer for him. After Batista's fall, Sturgis ran the casinos for a while, until Castro closed them down and arrested Mafia people there, such as Jack Ruby's close friend Lewis McWillie, who managed the Tropicana Casino.[13]

The night before the assassination, Jim Braden, whose real name is Eugene Hale Brading, stayed at the Cabana Motel in Dallas, and Jack Ruby went there around midnight. Ruby went to the Cabana to see Lawrence Meyers, whose companion was Jean West. She usually lived in Chicago, and interestingly enough, David Ferrie had called her, according to his phone records, two months before.[14]

Braden had an office in New Orleans in the fall of 1963, according to author Peter Noyes: Room 1701 in the Pere Marquette Building. "During this same period in late 1963, Davie Ferrie was working for Carlos Marcello on the same floor... in the same building... just down the hall from Braden – in Room 1707," writes Bernard Fensterwald.[15]

THE KISS OF DEATH

Joe Civello, a friend of Jack Ruby in Dallas, reported to Marcello, who hated Kennedy. Bobby Kennedy had summarily deported Marcello, who is reported to have been flown back into the country by CIA pilot David Ferrie. "Take the stone out of my shoe," Marcello is alleged to have said of the Kennedys.[16]

The Assassinations Committee tells us that Brading used the name James Bradley Lee in 1951 and knew one James Dolan, who knew Jack Ruby well. The Report tells us that Dolan knew both Marcello and Florida Mafia chieftain Santos Trafficante. It is suspected that Trafficante had John Roselli killed in Miami. Trafficante especially wanted to see Kennedy dead, though he denies it. "Mark my words: He's going to be hit!" Trafficante is reputed to have said.[17]

Now we come full circle, because the CIA's Frank Sturgis of Watergate, Castro's "Superintendent of Games of Chance" in 1959, was "heavily involved with the Mafia, particularly the Santos Trafficante-Meyer Lansky syndicate in Florida."[18] We find, too, that Bernard Barker, the leader of the Watergate burglars, "had once been associated with the Mafia. Like Frank Sturgis, the reported Barker involvement with the Mob had centered around the Miami area controlled by syndicate boss Santos Trafficante and Meyer Lansky." Barker had also been Howard Hunt's top deputy during the Bay of Pigs.[19]

Howard Hunt tells us in *Give Us This Day,* "But for Castro and the Bay of Pigs disaster there would have been no such 'Committee' (Fair Play for Cuba Committee) and perhaps no assassin named Lee Harvey Oswald." What does he mean? Robert Morrow, a former CIA operative, implies in his book *Betrayal,* that they killed President Kennedy for failing to back the Bay of Pigs operation.

Hunt, who was deeply involved in many assassination plots, "spent August and September 1963 in Mexico City in charge of the CIA station there. Through an extraordinary coincidence, Lee Harvey Oswald also visited Mexico City during September, 1963, although no-one has been able to prove that this was true."[20]

The Report of the House Assassinations Committee says, "The Secret Service, FBI and CIA were not involved in the assassination of President Kennedy."[21] This originally read "as agencies," indicating that "renegade" agents *might* have committed the crime. In fact, Chairman Stokes said that they "did not find any *official* involvement of government in the assassination." References to the military were conspicuous by their absence, and the emphasis on "official" was more than significant.

Nevertheless, there is powerful evidence that people at or near the top in these organizations participated in the conspiracy. "There was a suggestion of complicity by agencies of the U.S. Government. This was one of the principal reasons for the Warren Commission's creation."[22] What is left unsaid is that this is also one of the principal reasons for the creation of the Assassinations Committee in 1976.

JOHNSON, BAKER, SMATHERS

It has been suggested that President Kennedy was planning to drop Lyndon Johnson as Vice President in his reelection campaign. Johnson was a close friend of Governor Connally, who is a Director of Syd Richardson's oil empire, and who cried, "My God, they are going to kill us all!" when the shooting started. Kennedy was probably going to replace Lyndon Johnson of Texas with Senator George Smathers of Florida. One of Smathers' secretaries was Mary Jo Kopechne, who later went to work for Ted Kennedy.

Bobby Baker, Lyndon Johnson's longtime henchman, knew that Johnson was going to be dumped because his secretary, Carole Tyler, roomed with Mary Jo Kopechne, Smathers' secretary. Miss Tyler was killed in a strange plane crash in the sea just off Ocean City, Maryland, close to Bobby Baker's Carousel Hotel (which had been a scandal itself), along with her pilot. Mary Jo Kopechne was killed in Senator Edward Kennedy's car in 1969. Kopechne was no ordinary secretary.[23]

Smathers was a close friend of the President.[24] As Kennedy became increasingly disturbed by the activities of the CIA, he confided in Smathers, who recalled, "I remember him saying that the CIA frequently did things he didn't know about... He complained that the CIA was almost autonomous."[25]

MAKING ITS OWN RULES

Evidence of the CIA operating on its own outside the law was not difficult to find. Not only was the CIA making its own rules, it was even making its own foreign policy.

Take for example the case of Desmond Fitzgerald, chief of the CIA's Cuba division, who masqueraded as a U.S. Senator, and told AM/LASH (the code name for CIA assassin Rolando Cubela – later arrested and imprisoned by Castro) that Castro's overthrow would be fully supported by the U.S. This was shortly after Jack and Robert Kennedy had been working secretly through Ambassador Attwood to reestablish diplomatic relations and normalize affairs with Cuba. At the same time, Fitzgerald* was telling Cubela that he was Robert Kennedy's personal representative. This came at the same time when the CIA was still trying to kill Castro.[26]

It has been established that Kennedy and Smathers were close friends, and yet we find that Smathers also had ties to Nixon. "Although some have tried to put Nixon in Florida in the Forties, the accepted meeting between Nixon and Rebozo is said to have occurred in 1951 when George Smathers, then Florida Senator, suggested that Nixon, tired from a hard campaign, recuperate in the Florida sun. He put him in touch with Rebozo, who took him deep-sea fishing."[27] "It was Rebozo, along with Smathers, who was instrumental in helping to form the presidential compound at Key Biscayne. Smathers had bought a ranch house there in 1967, leased it to Nixon during and following the 1968 campaign, and sold it to the President-elect in December of that year."

THE CUBA LOBBY

There was in the early 1960s a strong Cuba lobby. These people cared more about Cuba than anything else in the world, and they would, as Nixon said about Charles Colson, *do anything*. This lobby was made up of more than just Cuban exiles and CIA renegades; it also contained many members of the underworld. Havana had been the international capital of the Mafia, and they desperately wanted it back.

Howard Hunt was heavily involved with the Cuban exiles, and worked intensely to overthrow Castro. It is a matter of history that these men, both the Cuban exiles and their CIA handlers, could not be controlled, and they proceeded with plots and attacks on their own, often without authorization. In fact, this "rogue elephant" behavior became a problem for the entire CIA. Once the wheels of the bureaucracy that controlled assassination plots and military activities were set in motion, there seemed to be no way to control it. Kennedy's attempt to control

*His daughter Frankie Fitzgerald is the author of *Fire in The Lake,* a book about Vietnam.

these activities was considered one more betrayal by the Cuba lobby, as was his attempt to control the CIA.[28] In a similar example of renegade government, J. Edgar Hoover, the head of the FBI, was also out of control, and maintained his power through blackmail.[29]

Hunt quit the CIA and went to work for President Nixon. He continued to use CIA facilities, and to involve them in his schemes and operations for the White House. He prevailed upon them for disguises and other help, and asked "for car-rental credit cards in his assumed name of Edward J. Hamilton (sometimes he used a set of documents in which his name appeared as Edward Warren.)"[30]

We pick up the story again in *The Curious Intrigues of Cuban Miami* by Horace Sutton: "By now Hunt had moved over to work for the Committee to Re-Elect the President (better known as CREEP), and, soon, so did his Miami-Cuban connections. Shortly after the famed Key Biscayne strategy meeting in March, 1972, at which, according to Jeb Stuart Magruder's testimony to the Watergate Committee, John Mitchell, then Attorney General, approved plans to maintain a surveillance on the Democrats, reservations for a suite of rooms were made in the Fontainebleau Hotel in Miami Beach, which was to be headquarters for the Democrats during their convention." Strangely enough, the reservations booked to coincide with the Democratic convention were made by an executive at the Miami Beach First National Bank, who said he needed them for a friend named Edward Hamilton. The head of Miami Beach First National is Frank Smathers, Jr., the brother of former Senator George Smathers, who first introduced Richard Nixon to Key Biscayne and sold him his house there.

"Edward Hamilton is an alias that was used by Frank Sturgis (as well as by Hunt)...It was through Senator Smathers' efforts that Fiorini got his citizenship back. At that point he assumed the name of Frank Sturgis."[31]

Jack Anderson wrote an article about his friend Sturgis-Fiorini in *Parade Magazine*, a Sunday supplement, which featured Sturgis on the cover in May 1961 after the disaster at the Bay of Pigs, entitled "We Will Finish the Job." The account told of Fiorini's daring exploits harassing Castro by boat and plane.

President Kennedy and his brother were strongly opposed to *any* assassination plots, and did all in their power to stop them when and if they found out what was going on. Kennedy shut down, or tried to shut down, the CIA and Cuban exile bases in the U.S. The President had the FBI raid these camps throughout the U.S. and wherever he could find them. The Cubans never forgave him, and the book *Betrayal* by Robert Morrow, a CIA agent, makes clear the depth of hatred they had for the President.

ASSASSINATION TARGETS

Lately, we have learned that Jack Anderson himself and others were assassination targets of the Hunt crew.[32] A column in *The New York Times* is headed "Assassination Plots Described By Liddy." Gordon Liddy says in his book, *Will*, written after a long silence, that Hunt himself was a target.

"...During their sworn Senate testimony in 1973, John Dean, and Jeb Magruder admitted that 'the Liddy Plan,' first unveiled in Attorney General Mitchell's office on January 27, 1972, had originally involved not only break-ins and buggings, but also kidnappings – a capital offense – and muggings. Magruder has written of the proposed kidnappings: "As noted previously, the Senate Intelligence Committee established that Liddy accompanied E. Howard Hunt to a secret meeting with a former CIA physician, during Hunt's alleged plot to drug and/or murder columnist Jack Anderson..."[33] And somebody probably killed one of America's great drunken heroines, Martha Mitchell, after beating her up and kidnapping her. Howard Hunt's wife, too, was apparently murdered along with nearly everyone else in the airliner with her. The survivors of the plane crash in the middle of Chicago told quite a tale.

Fortunately for the country, these men were captured in the Watergate, probably set up by one of their own number, James McCord. McCord wrote two books, *A Piece of Tape*, and another book, perhaps far more important, which was contracted for but never published. The most important chapter of that book was called "Nazi Germany and How Close We Came."

We learn that "the capture of the Watergate burglars in the capital that night, Sturgis-Fiorini included, created a flurry at the Fontainebleau in Miami Beach. The man from the Smathers bank arrived at the hotel and asked that the reservations that had been made in the name of Edward Hamilton, the Sturgis-Fiorini alias, be changed..."[34] But this might have been Hunt, too: "When captured in Washington, Sturgis was found to be carrying a full set of fake identification papers, including a Mexican visa made out to Edward Hamilton, the name in which the Committee to Re-Elect the President originally had engaged rooms at the Fontainebleau. Jack Anderson arrived at the bail hearing and asked that Sturgis be released in his custody."[35]

A TRIPLE CROSS

Smathers, we find, was a great hater of Fidel Castro.[36] President Kennedy, who had befriended Smathers, the good friend of Nixon and Rebozo,[37] may have been set up for the triple cross. The fact that his secretary was still involved with Edward Kennedy years later may have enabled opposing spooks and political foes to use her at a crucial moment to try to destroy Edward Kennedy and kill her in the process.

Kennedy himself was no fan of the Cuban leader, but Smathers found President Kennedy "horrified" at the idea of assassination; he refused to be pushed around.[38] Smathers stated that he heard Kennedy say that "the CIA had arranged to have Diem and Trujillo bumped off."[39] Various CIA officials and others have tried to claim that Kennedy approved the assassination plots, and that his brother Bobby knew about them. This is absolutely untrue. Bobby Kennedy did find out about some of it, and he did all he could to put a stop to it. RFK said, "I stopped it... I found out that some people were going to try an attempt on Castro's life and I turned it off." To believe otherwise is to negate the entire moral focus of the Kennedy brothers.[40]

Tad Szulc told the Senate Intelligence Committee that when Kennedy asked him, "What would you think if I ordered Castro assassinated?" Szulc replied that he did not think it a good idea and that the idea of political assassination was wrong. "Kennedy said he had been testing me because he was under great pressure from advisors in the intelligence community (whom he did not name) to have Castro killed, but that he himself violently opposed it on the grounds that for moral reasons the United States should never be a party to political assassinations. 'I'm glad you feel the same way,' he said."[41]

Not only were the Kennedys opposed to the CIA's assassination plans, but Robert Kennedy was involved in a major effort to put the CIA's partner in this affair, the Mafia, out of business. Mafia leaders like Chicago's Giancana and New Orleans' Marcello were feeling the heat. Robert Kennedy's Justice Department had prosecuted Sam Giancana, and found that the CIA was protecting him, because Giancana was being used in the plots to kill Castro. RFK was incensed. The CIA sent their lawyer, Lawrence Houston, to see him. Kennedy told him, "If you ever try to do business with organized crime again – with gangsters – you will let the Attorney General know."[42] Nevertheless, the CIA went ahead with their attempts to kill Castro without telling the President's brother, as the Report of the Assassinations Committee tells us.

OSWALD'S CUBA CONNECTION

Dan Rather, who knows far more about this case than anyone realizes, intimated some of this when he asked in August of 1973: "Lee Harvey Oswald, the man who shot President Kennedy. Did he ever know or have contact with E. Howard Hunt or Gordon Liddy or any of the others in that mysterious and dangerous crew convicted in the Watergate crime?"[43]

It is clear from much of Oswald's history that he was closely involved in Cuban activities and with people who knew Howard Hunt. Furthermore, we have statements and testimony from Marita Lorenz that Frank Sturgis and Oswald drove west together. This was probably an Oswald double (New York Daily News, November 3, 1977). "…Ms. Lorenz, in her testimony… adds that Sturgis had also fired at the President." A report in the December 4, 1963 Sun Sentinel in Florida by a reporter who knew Sturgis stated that Sturgis claimed to have been in contact with Oswald at one time, and that Oswald had tried to infiltrate his International Anti-Communist Brigade.[44]

CONNECTION BETWEEN 1963 AND 1973

In March of 1973, it had become apparent that Nixon's men, and perhaps Nixon, would be prosecuted, so Nixon had to consider the appointment of a Special Prosecutor. What follows is an account of those connected with the Warren Commission and President Kennedy's case, and those connected to Watergate: Nixon, Howard Hunt and Frank Sturgis, who was suspected of involvement in assassinations. Charles Colson, known in Washington as the assassin-master, who was Howard

Hunt's boss, tried to recruit J. Lee Rankin as the first Special Prosecutor days after James McCord began to expose the Watergate cover-up.[45] Rankin was the General Counsel to the Warren Commission, "And thus held the single highest-ranking staff position on the Commission. Rankin was the man in overall charge of the Commission investigation and served as the Commission's chief liaison to both the CIA and FBI...'It was, very simply, a Rankin operation.' "[46] It was Rankin who prevented any further investigation of the single bullet theory at the Warren Commission, though others believed the theory was impossible.[47]

Rankin systematically buried criticism from his own staff of the evidence and of the official Report: "No more memorandums. The Report has to be published." At another point, he became angry when Wesley Liebeler and William Coleman found information supporting the evidence given by Sylvia Odio (that Oswald had visited her at the time he was supposed to be in Mexico): "At this stage, we are supposed to be closing doors, not opening them."[48]

In late 1973, Nixon and Colson recommended to the prosecutors that Rankin be used to edit out "national security matters" on the White House tapes.[49]

On March 21, 1973, the day Nixon instructed John Dean and H.R. Haldeman to pay "hush money," Colson discussed with Nixon hiring Rankin, who was good at closing doors. Colson told Nixon that he thought if Nixon asked Rankin to take the job as Special Prosecutor, Rankin would take it after Colson spoke to Rankin. But Nixon put off hiring a Special Prosecutor at that time.[50]

"John Dean selected as his defense attorney another man intimately familiar with the assassination of President Kennedy. In April of 1973, Dean retained Charles Shaffer shortly before he went to the Federal prosecutors and turned state's evidence against the Nixon circle. Charles Shaffer had served as Administrative Aide on the Commission and unlike other top Commission aides, had been recommended for the position by Robert Kennedy."

John Dean was in fear for his life, and was later protected by U.S. Marshals. "Deep Throat" told Bob Woodward of the *Washington Post* that Nixon had threatened Dean personally. "Dean has publicly stated... that there are still 'very big' revelations yet to emerge from the Watergate mystery."[51] What revelations?

"In April, 1975, John Ehrlichman also selected as his first defense attorney another man connected to the Warren Commission: Joseph A. Ball. Ehrlichman was then facing initial charges relating to his key role in the Ellsberg burglary. Joseph Ball had served as Senior Counsel to the Warren Commission and had been in charge of 'Area II' of the Commission's investigation: the 'Identity of the Assassin'."[52]

Bernard Fensterwald, who was later the lawyer for James McCord, and founder of the Committee To Investigate Assassinations, points out that John Ehrlichman's novel *The Company* is about "a President and his CIA Director who are black-mailing each other over a past assassination plot that had involved CIA elements."[53] Many feel that the plot actually referred to the murder of President Kennedy, and that the CIA Director in the novel was a thinly disguised portrait of Richard Helms.

Fensterwald, who also represented James Earl Ray at one time, was the lawyer for Marianne Paisley, whose husband, John Arthur Paisley, an executive in the CIA, was apparently murdered while sailing his boat, the *Brilig*, on Chesapeake Bay. The Medical Examiner of Maryland, Russell Fisher, denied that he was murdered, in spite of testimony given by the Calvert County Coroner, Dr. Weems, in the presence of co-author Harrison Livingstone. Fisher was incensed when he heard that the Coroner had gone against Fisher's suicide verdict. Fisher angrily told us, "Where the hell did he (Weems) get to be such an expert, anyhow? I don't think my subordinates should be spouting off about things they don't know about." Fisher said he was "mad as hell" at his "subordinate."[54]

In 1968, Fisher headed up the Clark Panel, which backed the magic bullet theory. Paisley was a friend of Yuri Nosenko, the "defector" who came here with information from the U.S.S.R. on Oswald, and there was far more to Paisley than the papers first revealed. But the point is that Dr. Weems is a physician, not a "subordinate." Fisher had organized Maryland, with all of its military bases (including Bethesda Naval Hospital) into a military province for medical purposes. He was trying to control things, as shown by his close association with the Armed Forces Institute of Pathology. It is said that if you can control the Medical Examiner, you control the evidence.

Fensterwald was Paisley's next-door neighbor, and Paisley knew plenty. Victor Marchetti told co-author Livingstone and Steve Parks of the *Baltimore Sun* that Paisley was murdered because he was "about to blow the whistle."

"If you wanted to commit a murder and get away with it, Maryland is the place to do it," Doctor Cyril Wecht told Livingstone.

Woodward and Bernstein point out in *The Final Days* that Nixon wanted to appoint Leon Jaworski as Special Prosecutor five months before he actually did, after firing Archibald Cox. "Jaworski had served as Special Counsel to the Attorney General of Texas. The Warren Commission had given Jaworski the assignment of investigating various allegations in Texas that Lee Oswald had been a government agent of either the FBI or CIA. Jaworski, after a brief investigation, reported back to the Commission that there was absolutely nothing to the story."[55] Jaworski was present when Earl Warren and Gerald Ford questioned Jack Ruby in jail.

Then Nixon tried to hire John J. McCloy as Special Prosecutor for Watergate. McCloy was a member of the Warren Commission, and a leading proponent of the magic bullet theory. "McCloy still remains an ardent defender of the Warren Commission findings, claiming that no evidence of a conspiracy was ever found."[56]

Richard Nixon certainly knew who to run to for help when he had to cover up and bury the charges against him and his gang. He appointed former Warren Commission member Gerald Ford as Vice President on October 12, 1973, but not until a close examination all but proved that Ford had violated national security by illegally publishing top secret transcripts, which he appropriated from the Warren Commission files in his ghost-written *Portrait of the Assassin*. In this book, Ford went out of his way to make Oswald appear to be the assassin and to bury criticism of the Warren Report.[57]

On November 5, 1973, after the Saturday Night Massacre in which Nixon fired Attorney General Eliot Richardson, who had replaced John Mitchell, and Archibald Cox, Nixon hired Leon Jaworski as Special Prosecutor.

On November 22, 1973, the tenth anniversary of the assassination, Nixon's secretary, Rose Mary Woods, who took the rap for the 18-minute gap with her famous stretch, faced another kind of stretch: possible prosecution for erasing the critical portion of the tape dealing with the assassination of President Kennedy. She hired Charles Rhyne, a personal friend of Nixon, who was an official observer in monitoring the Warren investigation and advising on the individual rights of various witnesses.[58]

On December 5, 1973, Nixon asked Arlen Specter, former Democrat and Warren Commission Counsel, to head his legal defense. Specter met with Haig but finally turned the job down; it was then taken by James St. Clair. Specter was the author of the magic bullet theory when he was Counsel to the Warren Commission. There, he was working on "Area I" of the investigation: "The Basic Facts of the Assassination."[59] Specter was the protégé of John Mitchell, and served as Co-Chairman of the Pennsylvania CREEP in 1972.[60]

Albert Jenner, one of the key authors of the Warren Report and head of "Area III: Oswald's Background History, Acquaintances and Motives," was approved by Nixon to be the GOP'S minority counsel on the Impeachment Investigation of the House Judiciary Committee under Peter Rodino.[61]

APPROVING HIS OWN INVESTIGATOR

Think about that: Nixon *approved* one of the men who was going to investigate *him*. Jenner was going to be Nixon's Chief Legal Counsel on the Committee, but gave up when the evidence against Nixon began to mount.

Attorney General John Mitchell, under Nixon, "ordered the Justice Department to block the release of crucial ballistics evidence from the Kennedy assassination on grounds of national security, in November, 1970."[62] This was the FBI's secret spectrographic analysis of the bullet and bullet fragments recovered following the fatal shooting of JFK and near killing of Connally.

This evidence is one of the keys to the assassination. As we have said earlier, what is known about that evidence shows that the fragments recovered from Connally did not match those from Kennedy and from the "magic bullet." The very fact that Mitchell and Nixon were trying to cover this up is frightening and disturbing. Mitchell tried to fight assassination researcher Harold Weisberg's suit to get this report, and he had the Justice Department file "an unusual supplemental motion to dismiss the spectrographic suit on the grounds that the release of the FBI analysis 'would seriously interfere with the efficient operation of the FBI' and would also 'create a highly dangerous precedent in this regard.'" The U.S. Attorney then disclosed during the hearing in November, 1970 that "... the Attorney General of the United States (Mitchell) has determined that it is not in the national interest to divulge the spectrographic analysis." The suit was dismissed, and the Report of the analysis disappeared from the National Archives.[63]

Bernard Fensterwald was Harold Weisberg's Attorney in that suit, which was partly responsible for the passage in 1974 of a crucial amendment to the Freedom of Information Act. Edward Kennedy, the surviving Kennedy brother, asked during the floor debate, "As I understand it... the impact and effect of your amendment would be to override (the above decision). Is that correct?" "The Senator from Massachusetts is correct," replied Senator Hart, whose amendment it was.

Kennedy: "Then I support it and urge my brother Senators to do so too."

A CRUCIAL TAPE

One of the most important White House tapes was the tape dated June 23, 1972, just after the break-in at the Watergate was discovered. When this tape was disclosed in August of 1974, Nixon resigned within a few days. On the tape, Nixon says, "... this Hunt, that will uncover a lot of things. You open that scab, there's a hell of a lot of things... This involves these Cubans, Hunt and a lot of hanky-panky...

"... just say (unintelligible) very bad to have this fellow Hunt, ah, he knows too damned much, if he was involved – you happen to know that? If it gets out that this is all involved, the Cuba thing, it would be a fiasco. It would make the CIA look bad, it's going to make Hunt look bad, and it is likely to blow the whole Bay of Pigs thing which we think would be very unfortunate – both for the CIA and for the country..."[64]

H.R. Haldeman tells us in *The Ends of Power,* "In all of those Nixon references to the Bay of Pigs (in the White House tapes) he (Nixon) was actually referring to the Kennedy assassination... After Kennedy was killed, the CIA launched a fantastic cover-up... The CIA literally erased any connection between Kennedy's assassination and the CIA... in fact, Counter Intelligence Chief James Angleton of the CIA called Bill Sullivan of the FBI (Number Three man under J. Edgar Hoover, who later died of a gunshot wound) and rehearsed the questions and answers they would give to the Warren Commission investigators."[65]

Haldeman was the President's Chief of Staff. Haldeman's statement is just one more clue pointing to *high treason*.

PART VI   The House Assassinations Committee

"The Press twisted, distorted, and lied, and has made every effort to wreck this investigation. There are certain vested interests in this country that don't want the truth to come out."

> –Judge Charles Sweet in 1976, speaking
> about the Assassinations Committee.

"Ideas have been the most dangerous forces in the history of mankind."

> –Justice William O. Douglas

"We always have stories killed or buried for various political reasons. Somebody makes a call to the managing director or the head of a station, and that's it: The story will be squelched – it's just too hot. They're afraid of an injunction coming down on the station…"

> –Michael Douglas

It is far pleasanter to sit comfortably in the shade rubbing red pepper in a poor devil's eyes than to go about in the sun hunting up evidence.

> –Sir James Stevens, 1883

"How does the CIA co-opt a Congressional Committee?"
"They've got guys on all those committees. That's part of their business. It's simple to put people on."

– Colonel Fletcher Prouty, author of
The Secret Team

CHAPTER 16

THE INVESTIGATION BEGINS

The story hit the papers not long before the Assassinations Committee was set up in 1976 – Congress established a special committee to investigate intelligence matters. Senator Richard Schweiker, on the sub-committee investigating foreign assassinations, was corresponding with co-author Harrison Livingstone. He and Senator Hart were looking into some aspects of the assassination of President Kennedy. "The American people were denied the truth about the Vietnam war, the Cambodian bombing, and Watergate. I do not think we yet know the whole truth about the Kennedy assassination," Senator Schweiker said on June 23, 1976.[1] Some of the correspondence between Livingstone and Senator Schweiker disappeared in the mail.

HILL PANEL TO HEAR COLBY,
REPORTERS ON CIA – MEDIA TIES

"The House Intelligence Committee announced yesterday that former Central Intelligence Agency Director William E. Colby, plus several ambassadors and reporters will testify on ways the CIA uses the media. The testimony will be taken beginning December 27 by the panel's intelligence oversight subcommittee chaired by Rep. Les Aspin (D-Wis.).

"We don't intend to make exposés of the names of newsmen who

291

might have had a close relationship with the CIA in another era when a different ethical and professional standard prevailed," Aspin said.

"We want experienced intelligence officers to tell us what kinds of relations with the press they consider useful and ethical and why. And we want the media to tell us what kinds of relations they consider harmful or unethical and why.

"In addition to Colby, other witnesses in five days of hearings are to include: former CIA officials Ray Cline, David Phillips and John Maury; Joseph Fromm, U.S. News & World Report; Herman Nikel, Fortune Magazine; free lancers Tad Szulc and Ward Just; Former Ambassadors William Porter, L. Dean Brown and William Truehart."[2]

Then came the stunning news. Banner headlines in the Oakland Tribune on September 17, 1976, shouted: **NEW PROBE OF JFK, KING KILLINGS SET.**[3] This was followed by an Associated Press bulletin.

"WASHINGTON (AP) – The House today voted to launch an investigation into the assassinations of President John F. Kennedy and civil rights leader Martin Luther King.

"On a 280-65 vote, the House adopted a resolution to establish a special 12-member investigating committee specifically charged with inquiring into the circumstances of the assassinations of Kennedy and King. The panel would have discretion to look into other cases as well.

"...Downing* told the House before the vote that 'in the case of President Kennedy, I am convinced there was a conspiracy involved. I do not know the identity of the conspirators or their motives. That should be investigated in depth. The Warren Commission which investigated Kennedy's death concluded that Lee Harvey Oswald was the sole assassin of the President.

" 'The investigation of King's death is based on information that includes allegations involving the removal of a black policeman and two firemen from their posts in Memphis shortly before the assassination of the civil rights leader...'

"Downing was quoted as saying that it was a push by Black Caucus members because of 'new information' they say they have received which persuaded the powerful Rules Committee to clear the resolution for floor action.

---

*Thomas Downing, the first Chairman of the House Select Committee on Assassinations.

"Although this information has been in the public domain since 1969, it appeared that at least some of it had never been investigated by the FBI...

"Downing said 'Much vital information was withheld from the Warren Commission.'"

But Downing's motion was not accepted without protest. "There was little opposition expressed in debate on the resolution, but Representative B.F. Sisk (Dem-Calif) argued it could accomplish little. 'For God's sake, if you have any respect for the dollars of the taxpayers, let's vote this resolution down,' Sisk said."

THE REAL POWER

Sisk's rear guard action against the investigation, whatever his motive, indicated a belief that events in Washington were important – that Washington was the center of power. But the future Chairman of the Assassinations Committee, Henry Gonzalez, saw things differently. "We're just little people here," he told Livingstone. "We haven't got any power." The real power rests with the shadow government, a far Right Wing apparatus based along the San Diego-Vegas-Dallas-New Orleans-Miami axis, which had a death grip on the heart of Washington, through Langley, Virginia, where the headquarters of the CIA is located.

"Some people think that the CIA took over, that they are the real government," Livingstone said. "There's a lot of folks here who would agree with that," Gonzalez replied. He had been with President Kennedy when he died, and he knew the truth.

By a vote of five to one, Congress established the Select Committee on Assassinations. It was a risky decision which moved the country one small step closer to the truth. Hundreds of interested people hurried from across the nation to be there, to make certain that the investigation was honest and stayed on course. Others, however, were bent on sabotaging and destroying the investigation. There had previously been a number of secret investigations of the assassinations in Congress. None had produced any concrete results. Forces which had thwarted earlier efforts set out to block the House investigation.

In addition to the pressure brought by Coretta King (the widow of Martin Luther King) for a new investigation, co-author Robert Groden played a major role in the establishment of the House Select Committee on Assassinations. Groden, his wife Christine, and social activist

Dick Gregory brought Groden's optically enhanced version of the Zapruder film to the ABC-TV show "Goodnight America," hosted by Geraldo Rivera. This was the very first public airing of the film, and it had a major impact on the nation. Among the viewers of the nationally aired program on March 6, 1975, were a handful of students from the University of Virginia, including Andy Purdy and Mike Holm. They got in touch with the Virginia Congressional Delegation, and at 9:15 A.M., April 15, 1975, the Grodens showed the film and other evidence at the Capitol to the Virginia Congressional Delegation. This was the first time any Congressional group had ever seen the Zapruder film, or any of the other assassination film footage or slides.

Christine Groden says, "We were asked many intelligent and probing questions in all areas of the investigation, and asked for our conclusions. They really cared, especially Congressman Downing." Two days later, Representative Thomas Downing introduced a resolution to reopen the case. This resolution was then coupled with that of Congressman Gonzalez, and led to the creation of the Committee.

As soon as the Committee was appointed, the CIA managed to have a man planted in the office of the Committee in House Annex No. 2, as "liaison," in their MH/CHILD project, as a sort of "babysitting." The Chief Counsel agreed that the Report would be turned over to the CIA for study before it was published.

The CIA had planted Richard Helms on the Warren Commission as "liaison," and he did not volunteer any help or information. "I've worked with the CIA for years," Chief Counsel Robert Blakey said. "Would they lie to me?"[4] Blakey was with Robert Kennedy the morning his brother was murdered.[5]

The original Resolution 204 put in by Congressman Gonzalez asked that three murders be investigated: those of John and Robert Kennedy and Martin Luther King, as well as the attempted murder of George Wallace, which appears to have been a conspiracy linked to the others. This resolution never got anywhere.

Yet the evidence was there to be seen and it was all too familiar: Sirhan's shots missed Robert Kennedy, while a second gunman executed RFK from behind. Sirhan was the designated patsy. In the summer of 1976, King's widow, Coretta, journeyed to Washington with powerful evidence indicating that her husband had been killed with the aid of an intricate plot which stripped him of his security. Black police and firemen stationed nearby had been removed from the area at the last moment, according to a careful plan.[6]

The pattern of security stripping made it quite clear to Mrs. King that the murder was well planned, and that government employees were involved. The FBI and J. Edgar Hoover, of course, had been King's deadly enemy. The evidence was presented to the Speaker of the House, Carl Albert, who was about to retire, and he put forward the dormant proposal for an investigation. But the power brokers in Washington were frightened at the prospect of any investigation that would find conspiracies linking all these terrible crimes, plus the shooting of George Wallace. Consequently, a new resolution was introduced, which asked that only the murders of King and President Kennedy be investigated.[7]

The "investigation," established in September, promptly expired in December with the end of that Congress, allowing plenty of time for those opposed to the investigation to block the effort. There was a bitter fight in January and March of the following year to keep the Committee alive.[8]

Richard A. Sprague, a Philadelphia prosecutor, was named Chief Counsel and Staff Director.[9]

The Establishment had given a few selected "critics" access to interviews with Warren Commission people, in order to control criticism of the Warren Report. The goal was to minimize damage, and if possible, to prevent the truth from coming out. It was not necessary for them to claim the Report was a lie, because when the time came, they would pop up like jack-in-the-boxes and say the Russians or Castro or the Mafia did it.

One such insider seemed to be David Belin. Belin had been a member of the Warren Commission and Chairman of the Lawyers for Nixon-Agnew. President Ford later appointed him to head up the Nelson Rockefeller Commission to investigate charges against the intelligence agencies, specifically, charges that Nixon's henchman Howard Hunt helped murder President Kennedy.

EXHUMING OSWALD

Later on, as these terrible crimes came close to exposure, Michael Eddowes, the author of *Khrushchev Killed Kennedy* (later republished and retitled as *The Oswald File*), brought a suit in Texas to exhume

Oswald's body, since he and Epstein, the author of *Legend* and *Inquest,* were propounding the theory that Oswald had been captured in Russia and the KGB substituted a Russian agent for him, who later murdered the President. They wanted to exhume the body in the grave because they thought they wouldn't find Oswald.

"Somebody has raised the question as to who is in that grave. The easiest way to find out is to... run some tests," said the Medical Examiner of Dallas, Dr. Charles Petty. This was after the Committee issued its Report in 1979.

So they dug him up in 1981,[10] and it "was Oswald," apparently, nipping in the bud the real exhumation needed: that of President Kennedy. Somebody had been standing up a lot of straw men to be knocked down.

On December 10, 1975, the United Press reported: "Representative Thomas Downing, calling for a congressional investigation, said Monday he believes a 'foreign conspiracy supported by a domestic cover-up' led to the 1963 assassination of President Kennedy...'"[11] Cuba was to be the new patsy. If that didn't work, Khrushchev killed Kennedy, and if that wouldn't wash, then the Mob did it. If the Mob didn't do it, then maybe there were two lone nuts, including the one they would find on the Grassy Knoll. The storm was about to break.

MORE ALLEGATIONS

The August 3, 1976 United Press dispatch said that Chairman Thomas Downing had "distributed a 79-page packet compiled by author Robert Morrow, entitled *Motivation Behind the Assassination of John F. Kennedy,* suggesting right-wing Cuban exiles sought Kennedy's assassination in retaliation for his withdrawal of air support for the Bay of Pigs invasion.

"The material also alleged then Vice President Richard Nixon was 'the CIA action man in the White House' in earlier stages of planning for the Bay of Pigs attack and that Mr. Nixon had promised a right-wing Cuban exile leader he could eliminate left-wing anti-Castro exiles after the invasion.

---

*The exhumed body showed no trace of the craniotomy, which was performed at Oswald's autopsy in 1963. If this was Lee Harvey Oswald, who had the craniotomy performed and what happened to that body?

"Morrow alleged that a recognized right-wing leader of Cuban exiles, Mario Garcia Kohly Sr., told him a year ago he had an understanding with the CIA that top left-wing Cuban exiles "would be eliminated after a successful invasion at the Bay of Pigs.""

"...Nixon, while a lawyer in the 1960s, served Kohly, apparently without fee.

"Downing would not vouch for its authenticity, but he said the material 'does raise a number of questions which I believe need to be answered. I would like to know what was behind the intense interest shown by President Nixon and his staff in the Bay of Pigs.' "[12]

SMOKING GUN

A lot of people got on the side of the winners when the bullets started flying. "Senator Schweiker said he believed the key to Kennedy's slaying lay in Oswald's relationships with both pro- and anti-Castro factions," *The San Francisco Examiner* reported.[13] "Senator Richard S. Schweiker (Republican-Pa) suggested yesterday that the 1963 murder of President John F. Kennedy may have been in retaliation for repeated American attempts on the life of Cuban Premier Fidel Castro."

The article went on to say, "Reopening of the investigation recalled a belief of President Lyndon Johnson that Oswald did not act alone. Johnson told interviewers he believed that Kennedy was killed in retaliation for a thwarted assassination attempt by a CIA-backed team of killers in Havana." This clever statement gives the impression that President Johnson actually said that Castro killed JFK, when in fact he had said he thought the CIA-backed team of killers killed his predecessor after failing in their attempts to kill Castro.

President Nixon's right hand – H.R. Haldeman – wrote in *The Ends of Power:* "And when Nixon said, 'It's likely to blow the whole Bay of Pigs,' he might have been reminding (CIA Director) Helms, not so gently, of the cover-up of the assassination attempts on Fidel Castro – a CIA operation that may have triggered the Kennedy tragedy and which Helms desperately wanted to hide."

Haldeman wrote in his memoirs that Nixon was clearly concerned that Hunt knew a great deal and might talk. On the White House tapes, Nixon is recorded as saying, "It would be very bad to have this fellow Hunt (talk), he knows too much...". Nixon earlier told Erlichman, "This fellow Hunt... will uncover a lot of things... you open that scab... this involves the Cubans, Hunt and a lot of hanky panky." [14]

"I went back to see the President and told him his strategy had worked. I had told Helms that the Watergate investigation 'tracks back to the Bay of Pigs.' So at that point... he said, 'We'll be very happy to be helpful.'

"And so the 'smoking gun' conversations were created – to rest, stored on a reel of tape in a closet, gathering dust until August 1974."

They had to keep everybody's mouth shut about why they broke into the Watergate for CREEP, President Nixon's reelection committee, and raided and bugged the Democratic Party headquarters. Watergate was no accident, it began as a cover-up of another cover-up.

THE HUNT CONNECTION

According to an internal CIA memorandum allegedly written in 1966 by Tom Karamessines, an assistant to Richard Helms, E. Howard Hunt, the Watergate burglar and longtime helper of Richard Nixon, while working for the CIA, was in Dallas on the day President John F. Kennedy was murdered. [15] Hunt has vehemently denied this, and sued the authors of *Coup d'État in America (CIA),* a book by A. J. Weberman and Michael Canfield which maintains that Hunt was one of the tramps photographed in Dealey Plaza just after the murder. Nixon later admitted that he, too, was in Dallas on the same day, after denying it for some time. [16]

The memo, allegedly read and initialed by Richard Helms and Sammy Helperan, discusses a concern among the CIA bosses that the presence of Hunt at Dealey Plaza might be uncovered.

Victor Marchetti, the author of *The CIA and the Cult of Intelligence,* suggests that the CIA had thought about taking a "limited hang-out," and was willing to concede that CIA agents may have been involved in an assassination plot against the late President. CIA executives were admitting that a "renegade" band of agents acting on their own may have made the hit. [17]

Later, after Arlen Specter's colleague Richard Sprague was fired as Chief Counsel of the Assassinations Committee and replaced by Robert Blakey, co-author Harrison Livingstone asked Blakey about the memo. "This memo does not exist!" he said. "It never happened. It is a lie. This story has done terrible damage to Howard Hunt!" Interestingly enough, Blakey defended Hunt repeatedly.

It was Hunt who forged cables falsely accusing President Kennedy of ordering the murder of Diem in Vietnam.[18] He was also accused of plotting the murder of columnist Jack Anderson and many others.[19] Hunt was involved in the plots to kill Castro, and knew some of the hit-men. His Cuban Watergate burglars were not all choirboys, either.

The Rockefeller Commission had also stumbled on alleged CIA implication in the Kennedy assassination. The former Counsel to the Warren Commission, David Belin, had been dusted off by President Ford – also formerly of the Warren Commission – and made to run the Rockefeller Commission. Professor Peter Dale Scott, a former Canadian diplomat, relates the following story about the Rockefeller Commission and President Ford: "Daniel Schorr, then the CBS reporter on CIA activities, said that Ford told a White House luncheon with editors of *The New York Times* that he had to choose the Rockefeller Commission members very carefully, because 'There was the danger that the commission would trip over matters a lot more sensitive than domestic surveillance.' "

"Which matters?" the *Times* editors asked President Ford.

"Off the record, like assassinations."

"Schorr surmised later that the whole panoply of the Rockefeller investigation was to keep attention focused on the CIA's domestic surveillance, which had apparently leaked from a 1973 internal report of the CIA, hoping to keep under wraps other more dangerous parts of the same report.

"But when unanswered questions about a CIA aspect to the Kennedy assassination were raised before the Rockefeller panel, Belin – rather than investigating them – referred them to the CIA itself for a possible reply. That reply was never made. Instead, the Rockefeller Commission chose to ignore nearly all the work of the long-time Warren Commission critics – including the charge – since proven correct, that the CIA withheld relevant material from the Warren Commission – responding only to charges that Howard Hunt and Frank Sturgis (also captured in the Watergate) had both been present in Dallas on November 22, 1963...

"Watergate established as a fact that cover-ups, 'in the interests of national security,' could be ordered by the White House and carried out by the CIA and FBI."

Like his colleague Howard Hunt, "Frank Sturgis, one of the six Watergate burglars, had been named in Warren Commission documents as the author of false stories about Lee Harvey Oswald," wrote Professor Scott in the *News-Herald*.[20] Later, a storm of newspaper articles and controversy enveloped the Assassinations Committee, and bits and pieces of the truth began to emerge. *The New York Daily News* told the most chilling tale of all: "A former spy says that she accompanied Lee Harvey Oswald and an 'assassin squad' to Dallas a few days before President Kennedy was murdered there Nov. 22, 1963." The House Assassinations Committee is investigating the story.

"Marita Lorenz, former undercover operative for the CIA and FBI, told the News that her companions on the car trip from Miami to Dallas were Oswald, CIA contract agent Frank Sturgis, Cuban exile leaders Orlando Bosch and Pedro Diaz Lanz, and two Cuban brothers whose names she does not know.

"She said they were all members of Operation 40, a secret guerilla group originally formed by the CIA in 1960 in preparation for the Bay of Pigs invasion...

"Ms. Lorenz described Operation 40 as an 'assassination squad' consisting of about 30 anti-Castro Cubans and their American advisers. She claimed the group conspired to kill Cuban Premier Fidel Castro and President Kennedy, whom it blamed for the Bay of Pigs fiasco...

"She said Oswald later visited an Operation 40 training camp in the Florida Everglades. The next time she saw him, Ms. Lorenz said, was at midnight in the Miami home of Orlando Bosch, who is now in a Venezuelan prison on murder charges in connection with the explosion and crash of a Cuban jetliner that killed 73 persons last year.

"Ms. Lorenz claimed that this meeting was attended by Sturgis, Oswald, Bosch and Diaz Lanz, former Chief of the Cuban Air Force. She said the men spread Dallas street maps on a table and studied them...

"She said they left for Dallas in two cars soon after the meeting. They took turns driving, she said, and the 1,300 miles trip took about two days. She added that they carried weapons – 'rifles and scopes' – in the cars...

"Sturgis said he had been questioned already about the assassination by the Senate Watergate Committee, the Senate Intelligence Committee, the House Assassinations Committee, and by former Vice President Nelson Rockefeller's commission that investigated the CIA.

" 'I told them all that I had nothing to do with a conspiracy to kill Kennedy'... and added that he had given the committees evidence that there was a conspiracy to kill Kennedy and that 'Castro, the Russians and certain Americans' were behind it.

"Sturgis reportedly recruited Ms. Lorenz for the CIA in 1959 while she was living with Castro in Havana. She later fled Cuba but returned on two secret missions. The first was to steal papers from Castro's suite in the Havana Hilton; the second mission was to kill him with a poison capsule, but it dissolved while concealed in a jar of cold cream.

"Informed of her story, Sturgis told *The News* yesterday: 'To the best of my knowledge, I never met Oswald.' "[21]

A few days after this story came out, Sturgis was arrested in Lorenz' apartment, where he had gone to discuss matters with her. Then she testified before the Asssassinations Committee. What happened to this testimony? "Documentary and photographic evidence alleging Sturgis' involvement in the assassination of President Kennedy was turned over to a special House Assassinations Committee in Washington." *The New York Daily News* reported.[22] "...Ms. Lorenz, in her testimony... adds that Sturgis had also fired at the President."

Despite the evidence given by Lorenz, the House Committee remained unimpressed. "The Committee found no evidence to support Lorenz' allegations."[23]

Just after the assassination, Frank Sturgis was quoted in the Pompano Beach *Sun-Sentinel* as saying that Oswald had been in touch with Cuban Intelligence the previous year, as well as pro-Castroites in Miami, Mexico City, and New Orleans.[24]

For his part, Oswald had stated clearly, "I didn't shoot anybody." Tapes examined with Psychological Stress Evaluators by former CIA man George O'Toole show that Oswald was telling the truth.[25]

THE FALSE TRAIL

A very careful false trail had been laid to Oswald, setting him up as the patsy, and forcing the CIA and the FBI to cover up the assassination. Who laid that false trail? The evidence is clear and strong that Oswald had in fact worked for intelligence agencies, and that elements of the CIA had killed the President, in concert with other elements of the power structure of the country, in a coup which placed a frightened President under the conspirators' control.

On September 22, 1975, *The New York Times* reported that "the Central Intelligence Agency secretly tape-recorded two telephone conversations between Lee Harvey Oswald and the Cuban and Soviet embassies in Mexico City eight weeks before President Kennedy was shot to death Nov. 22, 1963, government sources familiar with the events said Saturday... The call to the Cuban Embassy, the sources said, was not associated with Oswald until after Kennedy's death..."[26]

This story again surfaced one year later when the Committee was established. Its champion was CIA executive David Atlee Phillips, a close friend and colleague of E. Howard Hunt.

"This conversation," Ronald Kessler wrote in *The Washington Post*,[27] "was intercepted and recorded by the Central Intelligence Agency at the time. But it was not then turned over to the FBI, which has responsibility for investigating possible spies, and it was not later turned over to the Warren Commission during its investigation of the assassination.

"The unanswered question is why not?...

"*The Post* has also determined that the CIA, for unexplained reasons told the Warren Commission that it learned of most of Oswald's activities in Mexico City only after the assassination. The fact is, however, that the CIA monitored and tape-recorded his conversations with both the Russian and Cuban embassies in Mexico City in the fall of 1963, before Kennedy's death...

"Thus, when Oswald showed up in Mexico City in late September and telephoned the Russian embassy, his conversation was picked up from the wiretap. A transcript was made and circulated in the CIA offices in the American Embassy in Mexico City...

"The Oswald transcript, according to a CIA translator who worked with Scott, aroused a lot of interest. 'They usually picked up the transcripts the next day,' he said. 'This they wanted right away.'

"What the transcript contained is a matter of some dispute, and the CIA says it routinely destroyed the tape before the assassination. But some people who saw the transcript or heard the tape before the assassination recall that Oswald was trying to make a deal.

"One of them is David A. Phillips, a former CIA officer, who now heads the Association of Retired Intelligence Officers and is a leading defender of CIA activities. Phillips was stationed in Mexico City at the time.

"The transcript revealed, Phillips recalled, that Oswald told the Soviet Embassy: "I have information you would be interested in, and I know you can pay my way (to Russia).'"

"The Warren Commission later concluded that the Russians and Cubans were not much impressed by Oswald. This view is supported by Silvia Duran, a Mexican citizen who worked in the Cuban embassy at the time of Oswald's visit. She talked to Oswald on September 27, 1963, and recalls the meeting in some detail... Duran said she called the Soviet Embassy and was told Oswald's application for a visa would take three to four months to process. Informed of this, Oswald 'got really angry and red. He was gesticulating.' Duran said she had to call for help from the Cuban Consul who got into a shouting match with Oswald and told him to get out...

"Even after Kennedy's assassination, the CIA failed to turn over to the Warren Commission the full transcript of the telephone intercept it had made in Mexico City. Oswald's offer of information to the Russians in exchange for passage was omitted from the transcript, and the CIA claimed it did not know of most of Oswald's activities in Mexico City until after the assassination...

"When asked if they could explain the agency's actions, some CIA officers stationed at the time in Mexico City said the CIA may have had a relationship with Oswald that it sought to conceal. The CIA has denied this."

The article ends with mention of both David Belin's and Senator Schweiker's opinion, intimating foreign involvement. "David Belin, who was an assistant counsel to the Warren Commission and later executive director of the Rockefeller Commission's probe of the CIA, said that if the Warren Commission had known of Oswald's conversations and other new information, it would have been less sure that the assassination was not part of a foreign conspiracy."

Two years later, the Assassinations Committee found that there were at least two gunmen firing at the President, and that there "probably" was a conspiracy. Things were getting too close for comfort for those who wittingly or unwittingly helped in the cover-up. David Belin began writing violent denunciations of the Final Report of the Committee in *The New York Times Magazine*[28] and in the *National Review.* His article in the *National Review*[29] entitled "The Second Gun Syndrome," states flatly "There was no second gunman." He also claimed that "the first Chairman of the House Select Committee on Assassinations – Congressman Henry Gonzalez – fell victim to the misrepresentations of assassination sensationalists, asserting, at the outset, that a second gunman had fired at President Kennedy..." Gonzalez, of course, had seen the shooting. Belin had not.

TWO OSWALDS?

The *real* first Chairman of the Assassinations Committee, Thomas Downing, said on the floor of the house on September 17, 1976: "When Oswald visited Mexico City in September 1963, someone made several visits and phone calls to the Soviet and Cuban Embassies using the Oswald identity. That there is some doubt that the person visiting and phoning the embassies was in fact Lee Harvey Oswald is evidenced by the fact that many photographs of 'Oswald' were taken by CIA cameras outside both embassies. Each and every photograph which has been pried loose from the government – and they are still withholding some – are of a man who is about 6 feet 2 inches, 175 pounds, 35 years old, and burly. 'Our' Oswald was 5 feet 9 inches, 135 pounds, 24 years old, and slim. The pictures are obviously not of Oswald, though so identified by the CIA.

"At the same time, the CIA – through some unknown means – tapped and taped the telephone calls of 'Oswald' to the Soviet and/or Cuban Embassies. These recorded conversations were withheld from the Warren Commission. Had they been made available today, voice prints of them could be made and compared with voice prints of known conversations of Lee Oswald. Then we would know for sure if there was someone else using Oswald's identity in Mexico City. And, if there are two Oswalds, for sure, we can wager great odds that there was a conspiracy involved in the death of our President."

One problem with the alleged Oswald being in Mexico City at that time was that on September 25 another Lee Harvey Oswald, went to the Austin, Texas, Veterans Administration office, a restaurant and a print shop.[30]

DISINFORMATION

On November 13, 1976, a new story broke. The Associated Press reported: "The Justice Department reportedly has uncovered a 1964 memo by J.Edgar Hoover in which the late FBI director said he was told Lee Harvey Oswald discussed in advance with Cuban officials his plan to kill President John F. Kennedy... quoted informed sources as saying that Hoover said in the memo that he was told of the discussions between Oswald and the Cubans by a highly reliable informant who learned about them personally from Prime Minister Fidel Castro of Cuba." This planted story was a classic example of disinformation. The story goes on to say, "It has previously been disclosed in documents recently released by the CIA under the Freedom of Information Act that Oswald visited the Cuban Embassy in Mexico City less than two months before Kennedy was killed in Dallas November 22, 1963.

CUBA, THE NEW PATSY

"There has been speculation that if Cuba was involved in the Kennedy assassination, it was to retaliate for CIA attempts on Castro's life. Castro has denied that Cuba played any part in Kennedy's death.

"*The Washington Post* quoted sources as saying the Hoover memo was addressed to the Warren Commission, which investigated the assassination. But the sources were not certain if the memo ever reached the commission.

"John McCone, CIA director at that time, told the Post the memo was 'unknown to me.'

"David Belin, a legal counsel to the Warren Commission, said 'I have absolutely no recollection of such a memo. If such a document did exist, I'm sure that we never saw it...'"

For days, this story dominated the press. Cuba was going to be the new patsy.

On November 14, the AP reported, "The informant said his information came directly from Fidel Castro, was based on a report Mr.

Castro had received from officials of the Cuban Embassy in Mexico City, which Oswald visited September 27, 1963, according to this source's account of the memo... The source said he had personally read the memo but discounted its significance... and discounted a report that the memo had been discovered only recently in Justice Department files, saying it had been provided to a Senate intelligence subcommittee headed by Senator Richard Schweiker..."

The New York Times reported on November 14: "The memorandum... is part of a packet of new material found in Government files that will be turned over to a special Congressional investigating committee, reliable government sources said today...

"The newly discovered memorandum was prepared in 1964..."

The memorandum did not exist. This was just disinformation – but from which source? Who was behind it?

The next day, the Chairman of the Committee said that they would subpoena the memorandum. The Committee had not yet held a formal meeting, but it was already being pushed around by a sophisticated disinformation campaign. "Representative Thomas Downing (Dem. Va) said he is aware of the memo only through news reports. *The Washington Post* reported Saturday that the 1964 memo had been discovered recently by the Justice Department. But he said 'I feel sure it was' a request from his committee, established to prove the assassinations of Kennedy and civil rights leader Dr. Martin Luther King, Jr., that led to discovery of the memo.

"His comment, made at a meeting of the panel, appeared to conflict with statements made to the Associated Press by an informed source who said the memo had been provided to a Senate intelligence subcommittee earlier this year..."

On November 17, the UPI reported, "Central Intelligence Agency Director George Bush said Tuesday he does not believe newspaper reports that FBI Director J. Edgar Hoover wrote a memo claiming Lee Harvey Oswald had contacted Cuba prior to President Kennedy's assassination. 'It's my information that such a memo does not exist.' Bush said. Bush predicted the memo would be proven fake or nonexistent. He said other allegations against his own agency have turned out to be false on investigation.

"Bush admitted the CIA had been guilty of abuse of power, but defended the need for an intelligence gathering agency, covert operations and spying in other countries."

THE MISSING MEMO

On November 16, the Associated Press reported, "A Justice Department source disputed that account, saying 'I don't think anybody (outside the Justice Department) has seen that memo.' " Perhaps the informed source meant that nobody anywhere, even in the Justice Department, had seen the memo.

But Jack Anderson had beat them all. On the comics page of *The Washington Post,* where they carry his articles, he wrote: "Within hours after President Kennedy's death, the U.S. Embassy cabled information from Mexico City suggesting that the Cubans may have been behind the assassination. Our sources say that the CIA developed similar information in Washington."[31] Who was speaking to the AP and to Anderson in those crucial weeks of the Committee's formation? Anderson also had a different patsy to sell.

The Committee later went and talked with Premier Castro in Havana, and with the former Cuban consul in Mexico City, and an employee there, Sylvia Duran, but unfortunately they did not get to Duran before the Mexican police scared the daylights out of her. She, like Ruby, wanted to be taken to Washington, where she thought she could speak freely.

On November 27, 1976, they flew down to Mexico City to interview the translator for the CIA, and a typist who prepared a transcript of a telephone call allegedly made by Lee Harvey Oswald to the Soviet Embassy.[32] "The action followed four hours of closed-door session testimony given yesterday to the committee by David Atlee Phillips, a retired CIA officer, who saw a transcript of the conversation before the assassination. (The Committee refused to release its 280-page report on these matters, and on Oswald in Mexico City. Yet this is some of the most crucial evidence in the case.)

"The Washington Post reported Friday that Phillips, the translator, and a typist each said Oswald was offering to give the Soviets information and requesting free passage to Russia. A transcript of this conversation given to the CIA contained no such exchange or intimations.

"The Post also reported that Phillips, the translator, and the typist said Oswald identified himself. The CIA has claimed agency officials were not aware of the Oswald call in question or other calls at the time because they did not know who had made them."[33]

"However, John McCone, who was CIA director at the time, said in a telephone interview yesterday that the information reportedly in the Hoover memo was 'unknown to me. Its hard for me to believe that such a memorandum existed without it being known to me and to the staff of the Warren Commission.' " McCone was on the Warren Commission. Jack Anderson went on to write, "The first person to reach Robert Kennedy's side after the shooting was CIA director John McCone who remained alone with Robert at his McLean, Virginia home for nearly three hours. McCone swore to us that Castro's name was never mentioned during that three hours. But CIA records show that the next day McCone not only mentioned Castro to the next President, Lyndon Johnson, but briefed him on the information from Mexico City.

"Yet, incredibly, no-one brought the Cuban connection to the attention of the Warren Commission. We were the first to get word of the anti-Castro plot to Chief Justice Earl Warren, the commission Chairman, four years later."[34]

Who was talking to Jack Anderson? It appears Frank Sturgis of Watergate and Mafioso John Roselli were the sources of this false trail. Both were familiar with assassinations, as they had been involved in assassination plots against foreign leaders.

A Gallup survey found that 80% of Americans believed that others besides Lee Harvey Oswald were involved in the assassination of President Kennedy.[35] The cover-up was coming unstuck.

At this point, even Tass got into the act, saying that the attempted appointment of Theodore Sorensen as Director of the CIA by President-elect Carter might have been blocked to prevent the Agency's "complicity" in the assassinations of President Kennedy and Martin Luther King from being made public. "Mr. Zorin said that Mr. Sorensen was one of the closest associates of Mr. Kennedy. It is not difficult to imagine what some people in the CIA felt when thinking about the prospect of having Theodore Sorensen at the head of the agency. It appears that to this day some influential people in the CIA are ready to go to any lengths to prevent the truth about the CIA's role in those crimes from surfacing."[36]

This was the type of confusion and conflict the Committee was faced with from the beginning. They were descending into a hall of mirrors, with a thousand false leads and trails leading nowhere. But each false lead consumed great amounts of money, time, and good-will. In this labyrinth, the Committee's energies were drained away and much of its work lost. The valid evidence the Committee had before beginning its work was almost forever buried, and with it the public's right to know. With the Committee's demise, the public's Constitutional right to a government safe-guarded from control by secret influences and secret government would be all but destroyed. It was Operation Chaos, and they were lost in the thicket, in the labyrinth.*

*Operation Chaos was the CIA's counterpart of the FBI's COINTEL program. It was run by James Angleton, and included surreptitious (and illegal) mail openings and other forms of surveillance against private citizens in the United States during President Nixon's tenure. Operation Chaos corresponded somewhat to the Administration's proposed Huston Plan.

*"'You don't have to manipulate Time Magazine,'
William Bader of the Senate Intelligence Committee said,
'because there are Agency people at the management
level.' (Central Intelligence Agency people.) 'The press
has a responsibility not to pervert the truth for profit or
partisanship and not to knuckle under to the pressure of
any of those forces that want the facts suppressed. Men
and women who have no other interest than to report the
truth as they see it can affect the fate of us all.'"*

– *Morality in America,* J. Robert Moskin

CHAPTER 17

HOW THE INVESTIGATION FOUNDERED

"I've worked with the CIA for twenty years," Chief Counsel
G. Robert Blakey said. "Would they lie to me?"[1]

After it was first established – almost at the end of a Congressional
session – the Committee on Assassinations had only three and one-half
months of life before it expired. After this first deadline, a fight ensued
to restart the Committee. Despite this valiant effort, the investigation
was doomed, even though the Committee was reconstituted.

The process was flawed from the beginning. If, as many suspect,
elements connected with the CIA had murdered the President, and if
the Committee had to use the CIA to investigate various matters, as did
the Warren Commission, then the CIA would be investigating itself.
It is not hard to guess where such an investigation would lead – nowhere.

The first Chief Counsel, before he was forced out, was prosecutor
Richard Sprague. Sprague attracted other prosecutors, and soon, large
numbers of them appeared in the waiting rooms of Congress. Despite

their numbers, many of those hired were the wrong type of people for an investigation of this nature.

They were tough and aggressive, but lacked any detailed knowledge of the case. Time did not permit them to become familiar with the evidence. Among those who thoroughly understood the facts were many critics of the Warren Commission. But with very few exceptions, these so-called "critics" were excluded from staff positions on the Committee.

"What have you read about the assassination of President Kennedy? What book?" co-author Livingstone asked Sprague at a news conference.

"Not too much."

"What did you read?"

"Nothing."

"Nothing?"

"I believe in keeping an open mind, in gathering and sifting the evidence. We don't want biased people connected with the investigation."

There were more difficult hearings before the Rules Committee when the new year 1977 came and the Committee was ordered to get its house in better order or expire in March.

Observers were drawn to the investigation like moths to a candle. Some were ordinary citizens, and others were dedicated to breaking open the case. These outsiders were just barely tolerated by the guards, by the staff, by receptionists, by the press corps and other functionaries within the "government."

Congressmen Sam Devine and John Anderson were dead set against the establishment of the Committee, then got themselves appointed to it. In addition to Devine, a former FBI agent, Representative Preyer, a former federal Judge, got on the Committee.

The hearings were held in secret, just like the Warren Commission's secret "investigations," and there were "executive sessions" and witnesses "in camera." The Committee got to see co-author Robert Groden's optically enhanced version of the Zapruder film of the assassination, but the media weren't allowed to see it.

"What did you see?" co-author Harrison Livingstone asked as the Congresspersons and staffers emerged from looking at the Zapruder film. "What was in the film?"

"Well, you can see the President's head plainly moving backward."

"Backward?"

"Yes, backward, as though he was shot from in front."

"From the Grassy Knoll?"

"No. It was more like the shot came from the Triple Underpass."

"Oh."

He wasn't supposed to have been shot from in front.

"But didn't the shots come from behind?"

"Well, yes, that's what they said at the Warren Commission." How could he be shot from in front from behind? That was the front-page question of 1963.

The media were allowed in to see the stills of the body of Martin Luther King. There was no dispute about how many shots had struck him. There was just one shot. The photos were clear, indisputable.

They showed King's body and the wound in vivid color. Those pictures were safe to show. Yvonne Burke, Democratic Congresswoman from California, had tears in her eyes. "What did you feel when you saw the body of Martin Luther King with the bullet wound in it?"

What was she supposed to feel? "You know I knew him. We all knew him," she said. There was great pain in her face, and her eyes were filled with tears. "I knew him very well."

"Did you know him, Congressman Stokes?"

"Yes, we all knew him," Stokes said. His eyes, too, were wet with tears. There were tears and pain in all their eyes. "It made you feel sick inside to see the way in which a great man like this had been destroyed," Stokes said.

THE FIGHT FOR RENEWAL

As 1976 turned into a new year, the Committee expired and a stiff fight for its renewal ensued. At this crucial juncture, David Burnham of *The New York Times* unearthed reams of scandal against the Chief Counsel, publishing a full page of material damning to Richard Sprague. Burnham and George Lardner Jr. of *The Washington Post* nearly brought the Committee down. Burnham was the reporter Karen Silkwood* was going to meet the night she was murdered.

---

*Karen Silkwood was a nuclear materials worker at the Kerr-McGhee plant in Oklahoma. She was attempting to blow the whistle on unsafe working conditions by meeting with Burnham. It is believed that her car was run off the road on the way to see him, and she was killed. It also appeared that radioactive materials had been placed in her apartment.

George Lardner* was with Jim Garrison's principal witness, David Ferrie, the night he mysteriously died. Ferrie's death ruined Garrison's case against Clay Shaw.

Both the Chairman of the Committee, Thomas Downing, and the Speaker of the House retired, and Henry Gonzalez took over as Chairman of the Assassinations Committee, with Tip O'Neill as Speaker. O'Neill was hostile to the Committee and the investigation.†

O'Neill laid down the law, and the Committee was given a few weeks to get straightened out, prepare a budget, and secretly drive out Gonzalez. He soon became trapped in a death struggle with his Chief Counsel, who was determined to force him out.

It was soon clear that the staff intended to run the investigation, not the Congressmen. Sprague forbade staff persons to speak to any of the Congressmen on the Committee, answer any of their questions or speak to reporters.[2]

Sprague had made it clear that he would tape every witness and subject the tape to voice stress analysis to test them for lying.[3]

Finally, Gonzalez fired Sprague, but Sprague, confident of support from others who wanted Gonzalez out, all but barricaded himself in his office, and refused to leave. The eleven other Representatives on the Committee voted against Gonzalez' attempt to fire Sprague, and for probably the first time in the history of the United States Congress, a Chairman of a Committee found that he could not fire a staff member.

So Gonzalez quit. In his place, Louis Stokes was appointed Chairman and Sprague stayed on, but his battle with Gonzalez and the scandals unearthed in Philadelphia, had shattered his credibility – he could not long survive. Despite growing pressure for his resignation, Sprague refused to quit. He had done the hatchet job they had asked of him. Why couldn't he stay? The "critics" shucked and jived and said they were for Sprague because he was a tough prosecutor and had convicted Tony Boyle in the murder of Jock Yablonski. (The conviction was later overturned.) They saw that he was hiring a great many prosecutors, and they all thought this was going to be a tough, honest investigation.

But it was all a sham. Sprague was a good friend of Arlen Specter. Sprague was on camera or being interviewed every day. He was just

---

*George Lardner, Jr., is the son of the famous author Ring Lardner.
†Gonzalez was not yet formally the Chairman. See note at end of the chapter.

another media personality to be exploited for all he was worth.[4]

The Committee was rigged with some of the weakest and youngest Congressmen in the House, and those who could be counted upon for support in continuing the Warren Commission fiction. Each member only maintained contact through a member of his staff who acted as liaison with the Committee.

Although no longer Chairman, Gonzalez did not retreat quietly. He claimed the investigation was being sabotaged "because vast and powerful forces including the country's most sophisticated criminal element won't stand for it..." He said on March 6, 1977, that the murders would never be investigated in a meaningful way, and that the Committee was "a put-up job and a hideous farce that was never intended to work... There's something very strange going on in this country – strange and frightening."[5]

TRYING TO SNUFF OUT THE INVESTIGATION

The origins of the dispute between Gonzalez and Sprague were interesting. According to a December 2, 1976 article in the *Washington Post* by George Lardner Jr., Bernard Fensterwald and Mark Lane had sought out Richard Sprague, and had Chairman Downing hire him. The Committee had only three to four months of life left when they set it up. Clearly some people thought they could snuff out the investigation before it had a chance of being extended with the next Congress. They certainly tried.

Bernard Fensterwald, who had been a lawyer for James McCord and James Earl Ray, the accused assassin of Martin Luther King, was one of Downing's chief advisers, and Fensterwald had set up the Committee to Investigate Assassinations (CtoIA). Gerald Alch, a former lawyer for James McCord, testified before the Senate Watergate Committee that the CtoIA had received money from McCord Associates. The checks were cashed daily by Lew Russell, who gave them to Fensterwald. *The Washington Star* carried an article entitled "Assassination Inquiry Stumbling: Is Fensterwald a CIA Plant?"[6] "In a telephone interview," wrote Bill Choyke, "Fensterwald first acknowledged that he had connections with the CIA and then scoffed at the suggestion. 'I am on the payroll,' he said... Downing, who called

Fensterwald 'a good source of information... extremely knowledgeable,' said he was aware of vague accusations of the link between Fensterwald and others having CIA connections. But the congressman has discounted these claims.

"The controversy has focused on Washington Attorney Bernard Fensterwald, who for more than a year has closely advised probe chairman Rep. Thomas Downing, D-Va., on the political assassinations. Fensterwald, said one source, has been 'fairly close to him (Downing) every step of the way.' Gonzalez was totally opposed to Fensterwald, even as an adviser.

"Fensterwald is currently a law partner with Robert McCandless, whose former law firm even Fensterwald concedes represented several CIA proprietary firms. However, McCandless has claimed he did not know of CIA involvement with the firms." Mark Lane went to interview Richard Sprague in Philadelphia for the job as Chief Counsel and Staff Director. Lardner wrote on December 2, 1976, "Lane said he made clear that he was 'calling without portfolio' but asked Sprague, then in private practice, if he would be interested in the job.

"He said the first thing you should know is that I worked for Arlen Specter (former Philadelphia District Attorney and ex-Warren Commission Lawyer, who authored the 'single bullet' theory). I said 'I don't see that as a problem at all. In one week, you're going to be up to your hips in evidence of conspiracy.'"[7]

They were hiring a man who said, "I have not, as of this date, read the Warren Commission report or testimony. But I never read any books by the (Commission's) critics, either."[8]

"Sprague has even avoided talking about his job, particularly as it relates to the Kennedy assassination, with his friend and onetime boss, Arlen Specter. 'I did not talk to Arlen before I took this thing,' Sprague says," with plausible deniability.

On January 2, 1977, Sprague came under full assault from David Burnham of the *New York Times*, who detailed some of the many scandals Sprague had been involved in while in Philadelphia. At that point Gonzalez attempted to take over the Committee, and from then on, he was at war with Sprague, a war that would eventually remove both of them from the Committee.

THE COMMITTEE SELF DESTRUCTS

The Los Angeles Times wrote that "Some of the proposed investigative techniques have stirred objections. One is the use of hidden electronic transmitters to secretly record the remarks of potential witnesses; this is a thoroughly bad proposal that, if implemented, would invade the constitutional rights of the subject of the inquiry. The committee also wants authorization to buy lie detector machines and stress evaluators, which ascertain the amount of tenseness in a recorded voice. This latter smacks of mere gimmickry, unless a need for these devices is shown."[9]

The critics failed to mention that the staff justified using these devises not to create evidence to be used against anyone, but rather to more effectivly sift through testimony of witnesses to separate the truth from false leads and disinformation. No-one's rights were going to be violated, in their minds, even those who presented false testimony. These were the good intentions behind that mess, in any event.

Jumping the gun not long afterwards, *The Baltimore Sun* wrote an editorial about the Committee entitled **"Kill It."**[10]

OBJECTIONS TO SPRAGUE'S IDEAS

Lardner wrote on January 11: "Sharp objections have been raised to a number of the Assassinations Committee's proposed purchases and investigating techniques. With Downing still chairman, the committee staff recently sought approval to buy five suction-cup devices that are used to tape-record telephone conversations. In another letter submitted under Downing's name, the committee sought authority to install 'transmitter cutoff arrangements for listening-in purposes on two of the committee's telephones.'"[11]

"House Administration Committee Chairman Frank Thompson Jr rejected both of those requests, which apparently originated with the Assassinations Committee's office manager, former Downing aide Rick Feeney.

"For his part, Edwards said he was satisfied that Gonzalez wants to conduct a 'low-key, responsible investigation.'

"Emphasizing that he was speaking for just himself at this point, Gonzalez not only disavowed the telephone gadgetry that Thompson disapproved, but he also expressed distaste for some of the equipment chief counsel Sprague wants to purchase, such as two 'mini-phone recording devices.'

"The $2,200 kits feature tiny transmitters that can be hidden in the clothing of committee investigators. Sprague has denied that they would be used to make secret tape-recordings. But he insisted that the equipment would be needed for 'certain surveillance activities.'"

Sprague, when he came to Washington, promptly rented an apartment in the plush Watergate, then went off to Acapulco on vacation without telling anyone. Gonzalez, who was working like a madman to repair the damage and get things moving, could not find Sprague. Finally an aide told Gonzalez that Sprague was in Acapulco.[12]

Sprague had originally proposed a budget of $6.5 million for the first year of operation, and this money and the other issues raised created a fire storm around the Committee and almost killed it. Gonzalez labored mightily to correct the situation, testifying for long periods before the Rules Committee. He wrote out strict guidelines for the Committee to follow.

"Sprague, back from a vacation in Acapulco, saw Gonzalez alone. 'Do you have confidence in me?' Sprague asked. 'I do not,' Gonzalez replied. 'If I had known in September what I know now, I would never have affirmed your appointment.'" *Newsweek* carried this very public fight into February.[13]

Gonzalez met with Attorney General Griffin Bell and got him to suspend the staff's access to FBI files. "This man is berserk," claimed Gonzalez. Sprague refused to give a statement of his outside income and other background information. He seemed determined to embarrass the investigation and drive out Gonzalez. Sprague finally usurped the power of the Congressman, and determined that he alone would run the investigation. He took no orders from Gonzalez. Earlier, in an unheard-of gesture, he entered a caucus to speak for the continuation of the investigation. Many Congressmen were deeply offended by this action.

Lardner wrote, "He quickly asserted himself in an opening blitz of public statements, television and newspaper interviews, and even policy pronouncements about what the committee would and would not do. Critics, such as Rep. Robert E. Bauman of Maryland, charged angrily that Sprague 'virtually assumed the role of chairman of the committee.'

"...Sprague insisted upon, and was granted complete authority over hiring and firing of personnel on the assassinations committee."[14]

He spent money without regard to budget constraints and the Committee soon ran out of funds, causing the staff to go for some time without being paid.

Gonzalez said, "I am like a guy who's been slugged before he's got a chance to fight."

Representative "Bauman charged later that Sprague was turning the investigation into a 'circus' and suggested that the controversy 'might be' resolved if Sprague quit."[15]

"It is obvious that Sprague has been running the Committee," House Speaker Thomas P. O'Neill told a reporter. "It shouldn't have been that way. Gonzalez is running it now."

Frustrated and angry, Gonzalez called Sprague a rattlesnake and an unconscionable scoundrel, and then quit. He saw no alternative "under the circumstances that now exist." He said Sprague was unscrupulous. Gonzalez never had any support from the leadership of the House in the dispute. "Rep. Gonzalez Trying to Fire Sprague" the *Post* headlines screamed.[16] It was at this point that Gonzalez fired Sprague. The other members of the Committee were rounded up by Sprague. If it wasn't a circus at the beginning, it certainly was now.

"It was an exercise in futility. The fix was in," Gonzalez said, and called the investigation a farce. "Henry is a free man now in a way few members have ever been," concludes one Washington friend. "It's the kind of freedom that comes from not being afraid. Most guys up here are governed by fear," Kemper Diehl wrote. Gonzalez had a spotless reputation for his integrity and his Spartan way of life.

"When the committee finally did meet on Feb 7, a bloc of four black congressmen, led by Rep. Walter Fauntroy quickly made it clear that they were totally under the influence of Chief Counsel Sprague, according to Gonzalez. He said this bloc was bolstered by Rep. Richardson Preyer of North Carolina and by Republican Rep. Sam Devine of Ohio.

"To show you how the committee was programmed to self-destruct, Devine was put on it even though he had voted twice in Congress against creation of the committee... the remaining five members were a bunch of wafflers or 'showboats.'"[17]

Meanwhile, witnesses were getting *killed*, and the Committee's second time extension was about to expire. On March 29, 1977, the day before Sprague himself was finally forced out. George DeMohrenschildt died of "suicide" and Charles Nicoletti joined the long death list of witnesses. House Assassinations investigators "started making telephone calls trying to track down Nicoletti on March 28, the day before he was executed." And just to make sure, they firebombed his car after pumping three bullets into the back of his head.

"Nicoletti, Giancana, and Roselli were all executed while targets of questioning about a possible link between the Castro plot and Kennedy assassination... saying there appeared to be some sort of mysterious purge of potential witnesses in the Kennedy case..." *The Star* wrote, reporting on a *Rolling Stone* article. [18]

Meanwhile, *The Washington Post* editorialized, "The final answer may turn out to be that there can be no final answers. The committee ought to reconcile itself right now to the possibility that this could be its maximum contribution to public understanding of these tragedies." [19]

NEW STAFF

Everything changed in April, 1977. The Committee got a new Chairman, Louis Stokes, and hired a new Chief Counsel, a professor of law, G. Robert Blakey, from that bastion of the Establishment, Cornell University. He was a veteran of the Organized Crime and Racketeering section of the Department of Justice. There was some hope that he would do the job right, but he intended to find no conspiracy. Indeed, almost two years later, up to the last minute, they were still not going to find a conspiracy in either murder, but they finally had to admit "there probably was a conspiracy" in each of the deaths.

Even under its new Chairman and Chief Counsel, the bad press continued: "the most self-destructive stratagem," wrote Jerry Policoff and Scott Malone in *New Times*, "allegedly involved subornation of perjury, receipt of stolen property and the monitoring and tape-recording of phone calls by an undercover agent, reportedly in the employ of the committee. The agent's name was Oliver Patterson, a self-identified former informer for the FBI." [20]

And so the criticism of the Committee continued. It was justified. Perhaps six months of investigation actually took place in the 2 1/2 years of the Committee's life. In the end, Blakey was still determined not to find any conspiracies, but he was trapped by two of the members of the Committee, who insisted on a different result due to the acoustical and other evidence.

THE VOTE TO CONTINUE THE INVESTIGATION

Following his resignation, Henry Gonzalez of San Antonio was an object of general ridicule. But had he remained Chairman, it is likely he would have gotten at the truth. Louis Stokes of Ohio took over and did his best. But he was not the man for the job. After the departure of Gonzalez and Sprague, the man who really ran things in concert with Blakey was Richardson Preyer on the Kennedy subcommittee, a former Federal Judge from North Carolina and a staunch member of the Establishment.

Congress was overrun with former FBI people, on the staffs, on loan from the FBI and retired. The most powerful Republican on the Committee, Sam Devine, was a former FBI man. He and Judge Preyer kept things under control. Stokes was easy to manipulate (he later became Chairman of the House Intelligence Committee). "They had their chance and they blew it," said Dr. Humes, one of President Kennedy's autopsists.

The crucial final vote came determining the fate of the investigation. Lindy Boggs, widow of the disappeared Hale Boggs of the Warren Commission, helped tip the balance during the debate on the Floor, saying that her husband would have wanted it to go on.

Late the night before that debate, they finally got rid of Sprague. The investigation would be ended if he did not quit. So they got rid of him, but by then terrible damage had been done.

Blakey's first act on taking over was to hold a press conference to say that there would be no more press conferences. A tight lid of secrecy was clamped on the Committee and soon everyone interested in the investigation began to drift away. The reporters went away, and the public soon lost interest. Even the "critics" who had argued so long for the investigation drifted away.

Everyone packed up and went home. There were no interviews, and no word on what the Committee was doing for 18 months or more. But whatever else they were doing, the Committee was clearly spending lots of money. The Committee did publish a huge volume on Organized

Crime, which had little or nothing to do with the assassination. Organized Crime was Blakey's area of expertise. Blakey implied that Organized Crime murdered the President, hoping this would satisfy Congress and the public. Meanwhile, the limited resources of the Committee were being drained away.

In the end, the Committee consumed millions of dollars and accomplished little. The Select Committee never did the simple things required to get at the truth. Reluctantly, the Committee identified the existence of a "conspiracy" in the Kennedy and King assassinations. But the admission of "conspiracy" was a small breakthrough – the public had suspected it for years. The real truth about who was behind the conspiracies was left undisturbed.

† Note from page 313. Select Committees are dead at the end of each Congress and must be reconstituted. The Assassinations Committee remained in limbo for some weeks at the beginning of the new year. Gonzalez took up the job of trying to reinstate it, as he was ostensibly suppossed to be named Chairman by the new Speaker, Thomas O'Neill. Gonzalez was left holding the bag, put in a position of having to defend the past record of the Committee, which was under heavy attack by his colleagues for steps taken by the Committee's retired Chairman, and the Chief Counsel dumped on Gonzalez. It was a very unfair situation for anyone to be in, and in the end, Gonzalez – caught in the middle – lost.

CHAPTER 18

THE END OF THE INVESTIGATION

The Assassinations Committee burst into the news again in the summer of 1978 after a long somnolence, with a series of quick, short, staged public hearings, all very carefully planned. It was clear from these events that they weren't seriously looking to find any evidence of a conspiracy.[1]

They let John Connally speak first, and he repeated what he had told the Warren Commission: that he wasn't hit by the same bullet that hit President Kennedy, so there had to be two assassins. "I must say to you," Connally testified,[2] "as I said to the Warren Commission, I do not believe, nor will I ever believe, that I was hit with the first bullet. I don't believe that. I heard the shot, I heard the first shot. I reacted to the first shot and I was not hit with that bullet. Now, there's a great deal of speculation that the President and I were hit with the same bullet, that might well be, but it surely wasn't the first bullet and Nellie (his wife) doesn't think it's the second bullet. I don't know. I didn't hear the second bullet. I felt the second bullet." And his wife said, "I know it was the second shot that hit the governor."[3] This testimony is very hard to circumvent, but the Committee did it. According to this testimony, there had to be two snipers firing from *behind* them.

When Connally was hit, he said "No, no, no, no." "Then I said

322

right after I was hit, I said, 'My God, they are going to kill us all!' – It was as if someone had come up behind me with a doubled up fist and just hit me in the back right between the shoulder blades."[4]

That afternoon, September 6, 1978, co-author Robert Groden, a photographic consultant to the Committee who had made the famous optical enhancement of the Zapruder film, testified. He was very carefully restricted by the Committee. Groden was able to say a few things, but the major news he had was silenced altogether. He was not allowed to mention his findings of forgery in the autopsy photographs, or to state that the Committee's synchronization of the recorded shots to the Zapruder film was greatly incorrect.

Congressman Richardson Preyer asked him, "From the Zapruder film and your analysis of that, is it your opinion that the first shot that hit President Kennedy also hit Governor Connally? I wasn't quite clear on your description of that."[5]

"It would appear photographically that analysis of the film would show that the two men were struck by at least two if not more separate nonfatal shots prior to the head shot."

"Would you say that again, each man was hit by at least two shots?" Preyer asked.

"No, more than the single bullet was involved in the actual non-fatal wounding of both men."

"But you are not giving your opinion as to whether the shot which hit President Kennedy in the throat, the first shot, whether that was the shot that hit Governor Connally or not?"

"I do not believe that they are the same bullet. I severely question that particular conclusion."

"Have any questions been raised about the Kennedy autopsy photographs?" Preyer asked Groden.[6]

"The autopsy photographs also came into a great deal of challenge by the Warren Commission critics in that the reports dealing with the autopsy photographs from different groups going into the Archives to view them gave such markedly different results, at least verbal results, as described in relationship to each other and to the medical personnel at Parkland Hospital who seem to describe totally different wounds than those seen in the photographs described."

"Fine." That was as far as Groden was allowed to go on the subject of the autopsy photographs. Most significantly, however, the Committee did publish Groden's statement that the photos were forged. Some people on the Committee knew very well that the autopsy evidence was fake, but they could not go so far as to say it. So they allowed Groden to say it for them. Groden went on to say that the famous "backyard" photographs of Oswald holding a rifle and radical publications were fake too, with a face pasted onto someone else's body.[7]

Then the great cover-up began. The following day the medical panel of experts testified and buried the evidence, the truth.[8] The whole panel were friends either of the autopsists, or of the Medical Examiner of Maryland, who had been on the Clark Panel of 1968. One member was later indicted, and another was fired by the Mayor of New York for saying that Vice President Nelson Rockefeller died while having intercourse with his girlfriend.[9]

"Eight medical experts backed the Warren Commission conclusion that there was no conspiracy behind John F. Kennedy's assassination, asserting Thursday it was possible a single bullet passed through the President and struck John Connally," the AP crowed.[10] Only three months later, the Committee was trapped into admitting there was indeed a conspiracy to kill the President.

"Baden, New York City's chief medical examiner, said the experts also agreed that the first bullet, which passed through the President's neck, came from behind, but could not tell whether it came from above or below.

"The expert's testimony disputes theories that some shots came from the side of the Presidential motorcade or in front of Kennedy, particularly from the Grassy Knoll to his right. It supports the commission's conclusion that Oswald killed Kennedy alone, firing three shots – one of which missed – from a sixth-floor window behind Kennedy.

"Baden, raising a new controversy, said all nine experts agree the second bullet entered Kennedy's scalp four inches higher than reported by a trio of doctors who conducted the original autopsy...

"Baden also said the original autopsy also had the entry wound of the first bullet, through Kennedy's neck, two inches too low."

By this time, even Dr. Humes, one of the autopsists, was confused and saying that he could have been wrong.[11] If there had ever been a truly public examination and trial of these matters, we might have a far different result, as the testimony of autopsist Dr. Pierre Finck before Jim Garrison had shown.

Then they staged a panel of "22 experts" to agree that "Gunshot lines computed from a film taken during John F. Kennedy's assassination support the Warren Commission's conclusion that a single bullet struck both the president and John Connally. Calvin McCamy, speaking for a 22-person panel of experts, said virtually all the experts agreed that the now famous roll of film taken by amateur photographer Abraham Zapruder might show Kennedy and Connally reacting to being hit by a single shot."[12]

Richard Helms of the CIA got up to talk about AM/LASH* and Soviet defector Yuri Nosenko. And they got Marina Oswald, Gerald Ford and James Earl Ray to testify, and nobody would believe any of them. It was a great show and a lousy investigation, as Jerry Policoff and William Scott Malone wrote in *New Times*.

Time Magazine tried a pre-emptive strike, and headed up the October 2, 1978 issue's report: **"Dousing a Popular Theory."** *Time* said that the popular theory being doused was that Castro might have arranged Kennedy's murder. The Committee played portions of a tape of Castro talking to the Committee. "There have been reports that Oswald, when seeking his visa to Cuba, told Cuba's Mexican Consul, Eusebio Azcue, of his plans to kill Kennedy and that the information was relayed to Castro, who did not take it seriously... Azcue recalled Oswald as having been 'discourteous' when his visa application was rejected, but said that he never talked about Kennedy."

Time neglected to tell the reader that Azcue and Castro insisted that Oswald never talked to them, but that Azcue met someone posing as Oswald. Meanwhile, *Time* repeated the government line: "In September 1963 Oswald sought a visa to enter Cuba at the country's consulate in Mexico City."

Former President Ford "acknowledged that the CIA had never told the Warren Commission about its attempts to assassinate Castro. 'Why we weren't given it, I frankly don't understand.'"[13]

Richard Helms, former Director of the CIA, grew very angry and red in the face during seven hours of the third-degree from the Committee. "Why single me out as the guy who should have told the Warren Commission?"[14] He got angrier and angrier. "I should have backed up a truck and taken all the documents down to the Commission."[15]

Florida Mafia chieftain Santos Trafficante testified before the Committee: "Mr. Trafficante," Chairman Stokes said, "Will you tell us when and where were you born?"[16]

"At this time, I want to exercise my privilege and my constitutional right to take the Fifth Amendment."

They then gave him immunity from prosecution.

"Mr. Trafficante," the Chairman began, "I believe at the point you interjected your motion, I had asked you to tell us when and where you were born."

"Tampa, Florida. November 15, 1914."

"What is your current occupation?"

"I am retired."

Several pages passed in the questioning.

"Mr. Trafficante," said the Chairman – the fact that the Chairman was questioning him meant that he was a pretty important witness – "When was the first time you were ever approached by any individual who was affiliated with or working for the Central Intelligence Agency?"

"It was around either the latter part of 1960, or first part of 1961."

" And can you tell us who was the person who first contacted you?"

"Mr. John Roselli."

"Can you tell us the substance of the conversation you had with him?"

"Well, he told me that CIA and the United States Government was involved in eliminating Castro... and if Mr. Gener, if Mr. Macho Gener, if I knew about him, knew what kind of man he was. I told him I think he was a good man, he was against Castro anyhow, and that is about it. Then he introduced me to Mr. Maheu and then Mr. Giancana came into the picture..."

"Mr. Trafficante, I want to ask you a question that is very important to this committee, and that is, did you have any foreknowledge of the assassination of President Kennedy?"

"Absolutely not; no way." Notwithstanding his testimony, Trafficante had been quoted as saying of Kennedy prior to the assassination: "Have you seen how his brother is hitting Hoffa? He doesn't know that kind of encounter is very delicate. Mark my words, this man Kennedy is in trouble, and he will get what is coming to him. He is going to be hit."

Trafficante vehemently denied having predicted the President's murder. "I never made the statement that Kennedy was going to get hit..." Trafficante told the Committee.

MORE MOB CONNECTIONS

"Mr. Trafficante, do you know Carlos Marcello?"

"Yes, sir."

"What was your personal relationship with him?"

"Just friendship. No business, never had no business dealings with him; no way, shape or form. I see him once in a while when I go to New Orleans. He's come to Miami, I think, once to appear before a grand jury. I seen him there."

Marcello was someone else who was quoted as threatening Kennedy. "Take this stone out of my shoe," he said, following his return to America after being deported by Robert Kennedy.

The public was about to get a new patsy: the Mob.

Jack Anderson wrote: "perhaps the most feared mobster in the under-world is Florida's Mafia chieftain, Santos Trafficante. House investigators approached his Miami hideaway, therefore, with some apprehension.

"He appeared at the screendoor to accept their subpoena. Shove it under the door he said softly. They peered through the screen. The sinister Trafficante was pale, and his hands were shaking.

"He may have reason to shake. The House Assassinations Committee had taken a sudden interest in the murder last July of mobster John Roselli. Before he died, the flamboyant Roselli hinted that he knew who had arranged President John F. Kennedy's assassination. Carefully hedging, he told an incredible story that implicated Trafficante.[17]

The New York Times reported on the front page that Roselli was murdered as a "direct result" of his Senate testimony about the Kennedy assassination.[18]

Anderson continued, "Twelve days before his death, Roselli dined with Trafficante at the fashionable Landings Restaurant in Fort Lauderdale, Fla. It is the custom of the Mafia to wine and dine a wayward member before he is executed..."

Anderson went on: "We furnished the committee with a more likely motive for the murder. We got the story from Roselli" himself bit by bit, over the past six years. The CIA had figured that the Havana underworld must have killers who could eliminate Castro. The CIA, therefore, spoke secretly to Howard Hughes' chief honcho in Las Vegas, Robert Maheu, about the project. Maheu recruited Roselli, then the Chicago Mob's debonair representative in Las Vegas.

"Roselli looked upon the assassination mission as an opportunity to gain favor with the U.S. Government. But he lacked the stature to deal with Santos Trafficante who controlled the Havana underworld. Roselli enlisted his own superior, Chicago godfather Sam Giancana to approach Trafficante –

"So they tried to kill Castro and failed. Castro, according to Roselli, had tortured the would be assassins and had learned about the plot on his life. It would be the sort of irony that Latin-Americans appreciate, Roselli suggested, for Castro to use the same plotters to retaliate against the U.S. President.

"According to Roselli's speculation, Castro may have used these underworld elements, most of them Cubans from the old Trafficante organization, to arrange the assassination of Kennedy.

"They may have lined up Lee Harvey Oswald as the assassin or may have used him as a decoy while others ambushed Kennedy from closer range. Once Oswald was captured, the Mob couldn't afford to let him reveal his connection with the underworld. So Roselli speculated that Jack Ruby, a small-time hoodlum with ties to the Havana underworld, was ordered to eliminate Oswald."

Roselli's old boss Sam Giancana also met an untimely end before he could testify to the House Committee. He was murdered in his basement –shot in the head with a silencer-equipped .22 caliber weapon. His daughter claimed he was "killed by the same people who killed Kennedy."[19] The .22 caliber is a favorite weapon of intelligence agencies. The Mob, certainly, doesn't use anything as understated as a .22 pistol.

This chilling connection between Organized Crime and U.S. government intelligence agencies greatly disturbed Committee Chairman Gonzalez. During a four-hour interview with the author, Gonzalez said, "We have nothing, we have no law, no government, no justice, no nothing as long as you have that intimate tie-in between the governmental law enforcement agencies at the highest level and the criminal element of our country. They're cheek by jowl and they continue to be."

"They're the same outfit now, the CIA and the Mafia."

"Oh, I'm telling you that we have nothing – forget about liberty, government, law – as long as we allow that to exist."

MORE EXPERT TESTIMONY

There was some testimony from Dr. James Barger, a sound expert, who had been examining a Dictabelt or sound recording made by the Dallas police during the shooting. "Barger startled the Congressmen by saying there could have been four shots and thus a second gunman..."

Completely ignoring the growing weight of evidence, *Time Magazine* wrote on September 25, 1978, "There will undoubtedly be some people who will always believe a fourth shot was fired. But at the halfway point of the month-long hearings on the Kennedy Assassination, the overwhelming weight of the evidence heard by the committee points to the same conclusion reached by the Warren Commission: Oswald, acting alone, killed Kennedy."

Another magazine reported at the same time: "Several members of the committee, including Stokes himself, are convinced that Oswald was not alone. One Stokes staffer even claims his boss believes in the 'three assassin theory.'

"We have a tape which shows that there were four shots, not the three the Warren Commission said. The Committee's experts are certain that one man could never shoot four times in such a short space of time..."[20]

If John Connally is right and he was hit by a separate bullet, not the Warren Commission's "pristine bullet," and if, as the Committee was about to find, there was another gunman on the Grassy Knoll who fired; then there were at least five shots fired, counting the miss that wounded bystander James Tague and the two bullets which hit President Kennedy. But President Kennedy may have been struck three times – twice in the head and once in the back – if not four times, with still another bullet hitting him in the throat from in front. That would be six shots. There is evidence of more.

Dr. Cyril Wecht, the Coroner of Pittsburgh and former President of the American Academy of Forensic Sciences, testified before the Committee. He had previously testified before the Rockefeller Commission on the assassination, accusing that Commission of "deliberately distorting and suppressing" part of his testimony.[21] Wecht is regarded by many as the nation's leading expert on forensic pathology.

"Dr. Wecht, is it your opinion that no bullet could have caused all of the wounds to President Kennedy and Governor Connally or that

Commission Exhibit 399 (the pristine bullet) could not have caused all of the wounds to both men?[22]

"...it is my opinion that no bullet could have caused all these wounds, not only 399, but no other bullet that we know about or any fragment of any bullet that we know about in this case."

"I have raised some questions concerning the head wound and the possibility... of a second shot fired in synchronized fashion from the right side or the lower right rear, synchronized with the head shot that struck the President in the back of the head."[23] Dr. Wecht then went on to complain that they needed the brain to properly examine the evidence, but that long ago he had discovered it was missing from the National Archives.[24]

He then said that certain tests should have been performed, and that a doctor acting on his own had done them. "Why our panel of distinguished experts with all our expertise and this staff representing a very prominent committee which, in turn, represents the House of Representatives of the United States Congress, why such tests could not be performed is beyond me. I feel constrained to say that they were not performed because people knew full well what the results would be... we are talking about what the condition of the bullet would be if it went through these bones."[25]

"Dr. Wecht, is it your opinion, then, that not only is the conclusion of the forensic panel that Commission Exhibit 399 (the pristine bullet which went through all those bones and made all those wounds in President Kennedy and John Connally) is consistent with the wounds, incorrect, you feel it is demonstrably false, is that correct?"[26]

"It is absolutely false... I have repeatedly, limited to the context of the forensic pathologist, numerous times implored, beseeched, urged, in writing, orally, privately, collectively, my colleagues; to come up with one bullet, that has done this. I am not talking about 50 percent of the time plus one, 5 percent or 1 percent – just one bullet that have done this... At no time did any of my colleagues ever bring in a bullet from a documented case... it broke two bones in some human being, and look at it, its condition, it is pristine."

"I stand here today and I wonder where that bullet is? Maybe it will be presented by the next member of the majority who has conveniently been sandwiched on the other side of me sometime tomorrow."

It is important to note that in the end, the Committee stayed with the "magic bullet theory," saying that only one bullet hit both men at the same time, but found that there was indeed a fourth shot, which they said missed, as did the first or second shot. The new shot was, they admitted, fired from the Grassy Knoll. They left the door open this way because they knew that there were more than four shots on the sound recording of the assassination.

The Committee had even more intricate "expert testimony," including the results of neutron activation analysis of the bullet fragments found in Kennedy's head, in the car, and in John Connally, compared with the "pristine" bullet. The results of the original tests performed for the Warren Commission were suppressed.

Dr. Vincent Guinn testified before the Committee, giving the results of the tests he made of the fragments given him.[27] But immediately afterward, he said that *none* of the fragments he tested weighed the same (and therefore could not have been from the same bullet) as those tested by the Warren Commission.[28] The evidence was once again distorted.

The AP carried an article saying that "House Assassinations Committee investigators say they have a lead indicating there may be too many bullet fragments to support the Warren Commission's conclusion that Lee Harvey Oswald acted alone in assassinating President John F. Kennedy.

"The head nurse in the operating room the day President Kennedy was killed told them four or five fragments – not one clean bullet – were removed from former Gov. John Connally.

"If the fragments weigh more than a missing piece of bullet, the Warren Commission's conclusion that a single bullet went through Kennedy's body and wounded Mr. Connally would be destroyed..."[29]

The fragments did in fact weigh more than anything lost from the "pristine" bullet – a lot more.

Dick Lester, a Dallas night watchman, found a bullet down by the railroad tracks near Dealey Plaza, and the Committee got into a struggle with the FBI over it.[30] The FBI wanted to get the bullets out of the National Archives without telling the Committee, to "test" them to see if they compared with the bullet Lester found. The Committee asked the Archives to retain custody of the bullets.

A former employee of the CIA testified that Oswald was in fact an agent of the CIA when he was sent to Russia. "The witness, James B. Wilcott... contended in an interview that conversations with colleagues in the agency's Tokyo station after President Kennedy's assassination convinced him that Oswald, who had served as a Marine in the Far East had been recruited by the agency to infiltrate the Soviet Union."[31]

A note was then presented to the Committee,[32] written by Oswald, according to the FBI: "Dear Mr. Hunt, I would like information concerning my position. I am asking only for information. I am suggesting that we discuss the matter fully before any steps are taken by me or anyone else. Thank you, Lee Harvey Oswald"

It was generally thought that this might be to H.L. Hunt, the oil baron, but it could be to CIA agent and Watergate burglar E. Howard Hunt.

Why Hunt had been dispatched by Charles Colson to break into the apartment of Arthur Bremer within hours of Bremer's attempt to kill George Wallace is a question that has never been answered. These orders were later cancelled after Hunt objected. President Nixon then ordered Colson to have the FBI seal off Bremer's apartment, according to a classified Secret Service report. Why did Nixon do this?

Not long after this, the whole top command of the FBI was wiped out, and the number three man, William Sullivan, author of *The Bureau*, a book critical of Hoover, was killed in a "hunting accident."

"The House Assassinations Committee issued a subpoena for former FBI official William C. Sullivan's papers shortly after he was killed to keep them from being destroyed..."

Meanwhile, the safe of the Assassinations Committee was broken into by one Regis Blahut, the CIA's liaison with the Committee.[33] The break-in was kept secret for a year.

Blahut removed the autopsy photographs of the President from their sleeves and put them in a drawer, leaving his fingerprints on everything. As for Professor Blakey, sources said, he had always been concerned about the possibility that some of the gruesome Kennedy autopsy photos might get out and destroy the Committee's reputation. "No one who has seen those photos would have any doubt that they should not be made public," one source said. "The one thing that would have done us (The House Assassinations Committee) in, would have been for those photos to be publicly released." It's the other way around: it is imperative that all the autopsy photographs be published. Publishing the pictures is the most effective means of establishing historical truth and exposing this great crime.

DOUBLESPEAK

"We were never satisfied that someone else wasn't involved in the break-in."[34] Now *there* is doublespeak. Blahut worked for James McCord in the Office of Security at the CIA. Perhaps McCord was the double agent who entrapped Howard Hunt in the Watergate, and thus destroyed Richard Nixon. Both operations may have been "forced disclosure." Maybe Blahut was trying to draw attention to the forged autopsy photos, which should have been published so that everyone, including the witnesses, could see that they were fake.

Since Blahut's viewing of the autopsy materials occurred only one week after co-author Robert Groden – Committee staff photo consultant – wrote a memo to Professor Blakey questioning the authenticity of the photographs, Groden believes that the break-in was ordered to determine the basis of his report. Someone wanted to know more about the "crop lines" (indicating forgery) on the photos, which Groden found.

HOW MANY SHOTS?

Months later, on December 21, 1978, just as the Committee was about to expire, full-page headlines in the *Baltimore Sun* read, "**2 shot at Kennedy probers think**." The *Sun* went on: "Audio test cited by legislators.

"Grand Rapids, Mich. (AP) – New evidence shows 'beyond a reasonable doubt' that four shots were fired, from two directions, at President John F. Kennedy when he was murdered in Dallas 15 years ago, two members of the House assassinations committee said yesterday..."

They finally found one of the other gunmen, the one on the Grassy Knoll. All this came only five weeks after the *New York Times* wrote "**On Laying Murders To Rest**": "If the United States keeps reopening investigations of the assassination of President Kennedy... well then let Italy reopen an inquiry into the assassination of Julius Caesar... if the committee continues on its present course, the committee will make two important contributions after all. The first concerns the billow of conspiracy theories generated by the Dallas assassination... In airing such theories it first appeared that the House Committee was putting the

Warren Commission on trial. Instead, the committee has put the conspiracy theories on trial – and found them invalid."[35]

In fact, right up to the end, the papers did their best to prepare the
public for a finding of no conspiracies. And that's how it might have
ended had they not became trapped by the evidence. There was no
escape this time.

On December 31, 1978, the Committee made it official: "Conspiracy charged in JFK death, House unit believes King was also victim of plot.

"(AP) – The House Select Committee on Assassinations said
yesterday it has concluded that President John F. Kennedy 'was probably assassinated as a result of a conspiracy.'

"The committee also said it 'believes, on the basis of the cir-
cumstantial evidence available to it, that there is a likelihood that James
Earl Ray assassinated Dr. Martin Luther King as a result of a conspiracy.'" But what kind of conspiracies?

"The Committee recommended that the Justice Department review
its findings and 'analyze whether further official investigation is war-
ranted in either case.'

"The Committee's findings were issued only one day after its final
public hearing, at which a pair of acoustics experts presented evidence
which they said indicated a virtual certainty that a second gunman may
have fired at the Kennedy motorcade. They said the second gunman
likely was stationed near the so-called grassy knoll in Dealey Plaza.

"The new acoustical evidence, involving scientific tests on a tape
recording made from a Dallas police officer's motorcycle radio during
the time of the assassination, seemed to contradict the Warren Commission's conclusion that Oswald alone was responsible for the President's slaying... The new evidence, however, asserted that a fourth shot
was fired, and that the shot missed the Kennedy limousine... 'The Committee is unable to identify the other gunman or the extent of the conspiracy' the panel's report added.

"The committee said it believed that neither the Soviet nor Cuban
government was involved in Mr. Kennedy's assassination. It also said
that it did not believe Cuban groups opposed to the government of Fidel
Castro were involved in the assassination, but the available evidence
does not preclude the possibility that individual members may have been
involved.

"Similarly, the committee said it did not believe that 'the national syndicate of organized crime' was involved as a group although individual syndicate members might have been.*

"And the panel stated flatly that the Secret Service, FBI and Central Intelligence Agency were not involved in the assassination, although it said the Secret Service 'was deficient in the performance of its duties...'"

Another six months would pass before the actual Report was issued, while it and the supporting 27 volumes of evidence and legislative proposals were sanitized.

The preliminary Report said, "The Department of Justice failed to supervise adequately the Domestic Intelligence Division of the Federal Bureau of Investigation. In addition, the FBI, in the Domestic Intelligence Division's COINTELPRO campaign against Dr. King, grossly abused and exceeded its legal authority and failed to consider the possibility that actions threatening bodily harm might be encouraged by the program."

Chairman Stokes said that they "did not find any official involvement in the assassinations." References to actions by the military are conspicuously absent.

Although the Summary of Findings and Recommendations says that intelligence agencies had nothing to do with these assassinations, the recommendations are interesting. The House was asked to prepare "Charter legislation for the Central Intelligence Agency and Federal Bureau of Investigation, addressing the following issues: the proper foreign and domestic intelligence functions of the intelligence and investigation agencies of the United States," and so on.

There were many such recommendations. One of the more interesting was that legislation should be considered that would "make the assassination of a Chief of State of any country, or his political equivalent, a Federal offense if the offender is an American citizen or

*The Committee at no time ever said or implied the later. (Pages 147-180 of the Report) Although the "available evidence does not preclude the possibility that individual members may have been involved," the Report then carefully refutes any such possibility. Nevertheless, Robert Blakey and Richard Billings wrote, "How sound was our conclusion that organized crime was responsible for the assassination of the President?" (*Parade*, November 16, 1980). Both are an example of the way in which the Committee's findings were distorted, and Blakey's theorys were attributed to the Committee itself.

acts on behalf of an American citizen, or if the offender can be located in the United States."

Congressman Stokes, the Chairman of the Committee, said on national television that Sunday morning that there was no dissent among Committee members concerning the finding of a conspiracy in the assassination of President Kennedy. He added, "It is important to realize that the acoustical evidence is not the reason why we found that there was a conspiracy in the murder of the President. The acoustical evidence merely corroborated much other evidence proving a conspiracy, including scientific and eye-witness testimony."

With this unexpected finding, the CIA became desperate. On January 6, 1979, *The Washington Post* crowed in a famous editorial headed "**The Evidence of 'Conspiracy'**":.... The committee's finding that President Kennedy 'was probably assassinated as a result of a conspiracy' appears to be based solely on scientific, acoustical evidence... If the committee is right about a fourth shot from the Grassy Knoll, could it have been some other malcontent whom Mr. Oswald met casually? Could not as many as three or four societal outcasts, with no ties to any one organization, have developed in some spontaneous way a common determination to express their alienation in the killing of President Kennedy?... it is possible that two persons, acting independently, attempted to shoot the President at the same time."

TWO LONE NUTS?

Former Federal Judge Richardson Preyer, the Congressman in charge of the subcommittee investigating Kennedy's murder, said then that the evidence of a conspiracy was "incontrovertible," and he indicated that there was strong evidence that individual members of Organized Crime were involved, but by July he changed his tune. In his statement, which he read to the final press conference of the Committee when its Report was issued, he stopped reading for a moment and said that we have to consider the possibility that there were two lone nuts.

The *Baltimore Afro-American* carried an article on January 9: "However, a former chief counsel of the House Assassinations Committee, also cited evidence that a fourth bullet was fired. Kenneth Brooten said an unexplained wound in President Kennedy's upper back could prove his assassination resulted from a conspiracy. Brooten said that the wound, still unexplained, was found during an autopsy on the President's body at the Naval Medical Center in Bethesda, Md.

"Two Navy enlisted men who were in the autopsy room at the time of the discovery, according to Brooten, were ordered to leave and 'we don't know if a bullet fragment was found after those men left,' Brooten declared."

The Committee admitted that the back wound was lower than the neck wound, and as Dr. Wecht testified, "The panel... was in unanimous agreement that there was a slight upward trajectory of the bullet through President John F. Kennedy..."[36] This is extremely important: How in the world can a bullet be fired from the sixth floor window, strike the President in the back, and yet have a slightly upward direction? There was nothing to cause it to change course, and then with a slightly upward direction, exit the President's neck and embark upon a roller-coaster ride with a major dip, because it then proceeded – under the single bullet theory – through John Connally at a 25-degree angle of declination.

VINDICATION?

Slowly, painfully, the truth was emerging. Eventually even the *The Washington Post* had to admit the obvious on December 30, 1978. "**For Conspiracists Vindication Day: Government is Beginning to Acknowledge What Really Happened**'"

"The old guard, the zealots who have been preaching into the wind about cover-ups and conspiracies these many years, had a rare day of vindication yesterday."

"Outwardly, they sat in the front row of the circus tent-like hearing room with their overstuffed briefcases, complaining about how the House Assassinations Committee had stolen their research, and fiddled away its millions.

"'There's nothing of any substance that has come out of these hearings that wasn't already in the public domain,' declared Harold Weisberg, the patriarch of them all, who had boycotted most of the previous months of hearings.

"But beneath the crusty exterior of the critics was a quiet sense of inward pride, a feeling of vindication, that slowly and reluctantly their theories and research were getting an official stamp of approval...

"In the world of lawyers and congressional hearings, scientists with big bucks to spend always have more credibility than freelance investigators who operate on a shoestring.

"But there was a certain beleaguered resentment among the researchers and theorists, many of whom have devoted years of their lives to investigating the assassination. Many of them hold little truck with their fellow critics, even less with the House Assassinations Committee. 'It's a miracle that so much evidence in the case has been turned up by a group of freelancers working on a shoestring. We couldn't be in this room if it hadn't been for the freelance investigators.'

"The assassination community, as the researchers and theorists have come to be called, was an odd lot as it gathered yesterday. Each member carried a briefcase, stuffed with newsletters and documents to use as 'proof' that his work was the first and the best on the subject."

Just before Christmas 1978, George Lardner wrote in the *Washington Post*, normally very hostile to any evidence in the case, "New scientific tests for the House Assassinations Committee reportedly show that a shot fired at President Kennedy's motorcade from the grassy knoll in Dallas 15 years ago landed in or near the presidential limousine. 'It seemed to have stopped in the presidential limousine,' one source said. Another source said 'it would be more accurate to say that it apparently landed in the area of the presidential limousine, plus or minus 10 feet.'

"With little more than a week to go... The Warren Commission concluded that only three shots, all from behind, all fired by Lee Harvey Oswald from the sixth floor window of the Texas School Book Depository, were fired in Dealey Plaza as the motorcade passed through.

"The House Assassinations Committee was on the verge of reaching a similar conclusion in a 600 page final report... 'Kennedy was not hit from the front, but he was shot at from the front,' one committee source said. 'I think we've proved the 'single bullet theory' (that one bullet struck both Kennedy and Connally). Ironically, we have also established that there were two gunmen.'

"Critics of the Warren Commission have contended for years that at least one of the bullets that hit the President came from the front. The only bullets and bullet fragments analyzed in the House inquiry came from Oswald's rifle, but the critics remain suspicious, pointing out that a number of bullet fragments are inexplicably missing."[37]

"The experts can tell within two feet of where the shot came from' a committee source said, 'beyond a reasonable doubt that there was a gunman on the grassy knoll,'" Lardner wrote.

The test is simple. The echo patterns are plotted mathematically, and traced to every building and other object that they bounce off. The work is precise. A rifle shot has a supersonic wave, a shock wave preceding the speed of sound. In other words, a rifle shot has a signature.

For a time, controversy erupted over the acoustical evidence. **"Dallas Police Dispute Evidence of 2nd. JFK Gunman on Tape,"** Lardner wrote in the *Post* on January 6, 1979. But in the end, the evidence held up and shattered forever the Warren Commission conclusion that Oswald acted alone.

Soon the scientists and the lawyers refuted the claims of the Dallas Police and the conservative element that was trying desperately to bury the "new" evidence.

On January 3, co-author Harrison Livingstone went to Washington to get the "Summary" of the Final Report, and talk to people on the Committee. There, he saw a copy of the *Atlanta Constitution* with a full-page article headlined: **"Probers Hint Mob Involved In JFK Death"** by Seth Kantor. Kantor is the author of a book about Jack Ruby, and the man who first reported that Jack Ruby was at Parkland Hospital when the President lay dying.

The *Atlanta Constitution* article read, "...in a startling series of conclusions, the committee report is expected to say that Ruby: Did not enter the police station without help, as he claimed, and did not enter from the Main Street ramp as he claimed."

Ruby "Lied about not stalking Oswald in the police station through the weekend and planned the killing for at least one day."

The *Atlanta Constitution* did not tell the whole story. Later, evidence would indicate that Ruby was escorted into the station with the Assistant Chief of Police, later Chief of Police, Charles Batchelor.[38]

A FORMAL ANNOUNCEMENT

The day after the report of the Committee was released, the full Committee met before the American and international media in the Cannon Caucus Room, a large, high-ceilinged, somewhat ornate room. Network film crews were lined up on a stage in the center of the room. Some tourists were allowed in the back of the room to see U.S. history being rewritten. It wasn't the whole truth, but it was a beginning.

Chairman Louis Stokes read a short prepared statement, followed by prepared statements read by Congressmen Fauntroy and Preyer.

They were announcing formally that *there was a conspiracy in the murders of both Martin Luther King Jr. and President Kennedy*. The date was July 18, 1979.

Then the questions began. "How many books are there in the set, Chairman Stokes?" The room was packed with reporters. George Lardner of the *Washington Post* wanted to know: "Professor Blakey, I understand a copy of the report was rushed to Bantam and given to them for reprint last week. Can you tell us how that publisher was chosen, why they got the book in advance of anyone else, and how much you were paid to do this?"

"I was paid $3,000 to write the introduction to the report. We got the book to them as quickly as we could so that the public would be able to see it right away." The Report actually sold few copies.

Another reporter asked, "There has been a feeling that the CIA co-opted this investigation. What do you think about that?"

"No, it didn't happen," was the reply.

Livingstone's courage nearly failed him. He had kept silent, watched by the managers of the Press Galleries. He was afraid to speak. The room was crowded with most of the Washington Press Corps. Before the press conference began, he had handed out copies of his articles and of Steve Parks' *Baltimore Sun* front-page story about the forged autopsy photos. As soon as it was printed, it was forgotten. Now Livingstone gave this material to Steve Long and others. Long had the courage to begin the first real questioning, because this was the last time anyone would ever get to question the Committee.

Preyer was talking about the visit of the "alleged" Oswald to the Embassy in Mexico City, but he did not question that it really was Oswald. "...that Oswald said at the Mexican Embassy that Kennedy ought to be assassinated... We decided that Oswald did not make those statements."

"Was that report wrong or manipulated, could you tell me?" someone asked.

"Pardon me?"

"It was a deliberate falsehood?"

"It was wrong. Not a deliberate falsehood."

Livingstone stood up, terrified. "Who would have laid the false trail, when they went to the Cuban Embassy and made those statements, if it wasn't Oswald? The statements were made but it wasn't Oswald. The CIA said it was Oswald."

"Well, *we don't think Oswald made those statements at the Mexican Embassy.* We have very substantial testimony to that effect," Preyer said. This was news to us, because it is not in their final Report.

"So then someone was laying a false trail..."

"No, I don't think it was a false trail. Something like this happens when you have a lot of rumors... There are rumors that he had been at the University of Mexico. Those don't necessarily mean someone is laying a false trail. They mean that after an assassination sometimes people like to feel they are part of the action."

"But that evidence was reported prior to the assassination, someone was posing as Oswald."

"Well, the 'Two Oswalds Theory' is something that got a lot of attention from the Committee and, of course, in Mexico at the Embassy there, that's the theory which we deduced from Mr. Azque who was the Ambassador from Cuba there who indicated that he didn't think the man who appeared at the Embassy was the man in the photograph (Oswald)."

Then Steve Long began to speak. "Mr. Preyer and Mr. Stokes, former high-ranking CIA officer and author, Mr. Victor Marchetti, believes the CIA ran an operation against your committee. In view of the activities of Mr. Blahut in his handling of the autopsy photos and also in view of an article in the July 9, *Baltimore Sun,* a front page article which quoted a consultant to your committee, Mr. Robert Groden, who said that he believed that four autopsy photographs of Kennedy are forgeries, what is your response to these allegations?!"

"Well, I don't know of any evidence that the CIA ran an operation against the committee. As for Dr. Groden, it is his judgment against all of the judgment of our panel of scientific experts that there could have been some matting applied to some of the photographs that covered up a head wound – entrance wound. We went to great trouble and great care to authenticate both the X-rays – and identified them, absolutely being the X-rays of President Kennedy, by dental work and dental X-rays. We authenticated the photos. They were reviewed in detail by a panel of photographic experts which used all sorts of depth perception analysis. I don't recall the name for it, but the kind of analysis which – if there was a matting – would indicate immediately that there was a matting done on the photographs. Nothing of that sort was shown. The photographs are authentic and they show, I think very clearly, just what they intend to show. I don't know how Dr. Groden would know what was under these – the matting – which he says obscures a head wound. I think if you would study the report of our photographic panel you will be convinced that the autopsy photographs and the X-rays have been very thoroughly authenticated." Of course, the Committee's Report actually said that the photos and X-rays could not be authenticated.

"Judge Preyer," Livingstone asked, "two questions: Why are the X-rays that you've reproduced in Volume I severely cropped; and a number of bones – namely the mandible, the odontid process, the globe and so on, are missing from those X-rays so that they cannot be identified, as though the head was severed from the body? Secondly, I believe Mr. Groden's position on the matted photograph is that the center of the picture was cut out, because all of the doctors testified that the back of the head was blown off. And the picture on page 234 does not coincide with the testimony of the doctors who saw the body in Dallas."

Preyer replied: "Mr. Blakey may want to enlarge further on this. One of the problems we have had in presenting the photographs and X-rays as public documents was the feelings of the Kennedy family. I think it would be outrageous to the country as a whole if we laid out just baldly those X-rays and those photographs all in gory detail. What we did was have a panel of experts review those and testify in detail about it and then we produced illustrative diagrams and we cleared those diagrams with the counsel for the Kennedy family. But we had to authenticate the autopsy in view of the controversy. As for those diagrams there are some minor changes made in the descriptive diagram from that point of view. But there is nothing that falsifies any information," Preyer said. This was almost completely untrue. The Committee published the X-rays and precise tracings of some of the photos. Remember, the autopsists had questioned the alleged photos and X-rays.

"But the drawing on page..." Livingstone was cut off by the Chairman: "Mr. Lardner?"

"When will the eight final volumes be out?"

FURTHER INVESTIGATIVE EFFORTS

Not satisfied that the Committee had revealed the whole story, Steve Parks of the *Baltimore Sun* sent co-author Livingstone to Dallas to follow up the investigation a few days later. Four months later, the *Sun* printed (obscured in a long story) the first results of this investigative effort. Steve Parks wrote, "Why for instance, did the chief counsel for the committee, Robert Blakey, fail to disclose the surreptitious tampering with autopsy photos by an employee of the Central Intelligence Agency? Mr. Blakey himself was formerly associated with the CIA. And we are expected to regard this as coincidence...

"Why were the doctors at Parkland Hospital who tried to save the president's life and who declared him dead never consulted about the autopsy (conducted by military authorities), and why have the autopsy photos never been shown to these doctors? Earlier this year, during an investigation by the *Sun*, one doctor who had been given access to copies of the photos said the president's head wounds in the picture were not consistent with what he recalled seeing that day 16 years ago. Another doctor who viewed an artist's reproduction of another photo published in the House committee's report voiced similar doubts.

"Why did the House Committee conclude that all of the bullets which struck the President were fired from behind when there is conclusive evidence that it could not have happened that way?...

"Which leads us to the most troubling question of all. Why would so many otherwise reputable people participate in an apparently willful obstruction of justice? Perhaps it is not altogether willful. Perhaps the truth is so large that they, like many Americans, simply can't accept its enormity..."[39]

Later, Ben Bradlee, Jr. and the *Boston Globe* would corroborate Livingstone and *The Sun* story.

CONCLUSION: HOUSE COMMITTEE FINDINGS

One way or another, someone was going to blunt the House Select Committee findings. In the end, it was done by putting off the release of the findings concerning the acoustical evidence until the last day of the Committee's life, just as they had put off for years inquiring into it in the first place. That hot potato was then handed to the Justice Department to "investigate;" of course it would remain there and be ignored. In this way, the Committee never conducted complete acoustical tests, never called all the witnesses to the wounds together with the autopsy evidence, never asked the hard questions about the missing evidence or the anomalies in the evidence.

"Blakey is certain his investigation zeroed in on the only suspects. He is sure he uncovered enough evidence to satisfy history, if not a court, that organized crime killed JFK," Jeff Goldberg wrote. Yet Blakey never presented one iota of evidence to prove this, and the Committee certainly never intimated that Organized Crime did it, although it allowed that individual elements might have been involved. "Originally Blakey set out to prove there were no shots recorded on the tape." But when the experts found additional shots on the tape, this became "Blakey's problem." Since they did not conduct a proper investigation, they were then stuck with a conspiracy at the last moment, and had to pin it on someone. "The Mob killed the President of the United States and got away with it..." Blakey says.

Why wasn't everything possible done during the life of the Committee – during this "last investigation" – to ensure that all possible tests were completed with the tapes? The National Science Foundation presented a paper on just what else needed to be done. But they were eager to get it behind them, just as the Warren Commission and the Dallas Police had been eager to find a quick solution. "Homicide was that way," a former Dallas policeman said. "Here they were solving this case, here they arrested a suspect (Oswald) in one day and cleared up the murder of a president in one day. Man, that was really a super-duper police department. They didn't want to have to look for anybody else, and they didn't even want to know about it, really. They wanted to clear up the case."[40]

But others were not so easily satisfied. "This report has serious shortcomings," Carl Oglesby wrote in *Clandestine America,* "It pulls its punches. It insinuates much about the Mob and JFK's death which it then says it doesn't really mean. It is alternately confused and dogmatic on the subject of Oswald's motive. It tells us it could not see all the way into the heart of the CIA or FBI darkness. Its treatment of the technical evidence in the crucial areas of shot sequencing and the medical evidence is shallow and unconvincing."

A former investigator for the House Committee, Gaeton Fonzi, wrote, "There is not one investigator – *not one* – who served on the Kennedy task force of the Assassinations Committee who honestly feels he took part in an adequate investigation, let alone a 'full and complete' one.

"So after all these years and all those spent resources – after the last investigation – what the Kennedy assassination still needs is an investigation guided simply, unswervingly by the priority of truth. Is it unrealistic to desire, for something as important as the assassination of a President, an investigation unbound by political, financial or time restrictions?

"Yet this was the last investigation. Chief Counsel Bob Blakey himself said it at his first staff meeting. Again and again, he emphasized the restraints inherent in a Congressional probe. He never considered a higher mandate. He never considered the Kennedy assassination an extraordinary event or a possible manifestation of internal corruption within the institutions he was so bent on protecting. He never considered using his position to demonstrate a loyalty to principles higher than those institutions. He never considered a mandate to conduct a 'Full and complete' investigation as coming from the American people."[41]

Silvia Odio, among the strongest witnesses to conspiracy in the case, said after it was over, "I feel outraged that after so many years we have not discovered the truth for history's sake, for all of us. I think it is because I'm very angry about it all – the forces I cannot understand and the fact that there is nothing I can do against them. That is why I am here to testify."[42]

"Bob Blakey never felt what Silvia Odio feels. He never felt the frustration and anger that lives within her, the outrage that the truth has not been discovered after so many years. I'll always remember what she told me when the Committee had changed its mind about permitting her to tell her story to the American people. Her words echo in my mind: 'We lost,' she said. 'We all lost.'"[43]

PART VII   The Bay of Pigs and National Security

"Edward Hunter... a CIA propaganda operator who worked under cover as a journalist... saw that there were techniques 'to put a man's mind into a fog so that he will mistake what is true for what is untrue, what is right for what is wrong, and come to believe what did not actually happen actually had happened, until he ultimately becomes a robot.' Creating such a state in which a man who knew too much could be made to forget had long been a prime objective of the ARTICHOKE and MKULTRA programs."

John Marks, *The Search for the Manchurian Candidate*

"The administration is reported to be seeking repeal of legislation that now requires the CIA to report covert operation plans to eight separate House and Senate committees. The new plan would require reports only to the Intelligence Committees of both houses. Proponents say this would reduce the chances of a leak to the press; but what they really mean is that it is harder for the CIA to co-opt eight committees than two. History clearly shows that once the agency need only report to the Intelligence Committees, which inevitably see themselves as protectors of their client agency, it need hardly report at all, since no real overseeing will result."

– Tom Wicker, *The New York Times,* January 1980.

"America is the very incarnation of doom. She will drag the whole world down to the bottomless pit."

– Henry Miller

You must wonder when it is all going to end
And when we can come back home.
We have to stay at it.
We must not be fatigued.

– John Fitzgerald Kennedy, November, 1963

CHAPTER 19

WHY KENNEDY WAS KILLED:
THE WAR PARTY IN POWER

The murder of John F. Kennedy was not an abstraction. A real human being was killed that day in Dallas, and with that death was born the greatest unsolved murder of this century. As with all homicides, there are suspects. The first among them are those persons who had a great deal to gain from the murder of the President, both financially and politically. Who were these enemies of John F. Kennedy with the motive, opportunity and means to commit the murder, and the capacity to engineer a massive cover-up for a quarter-century? Who had the means to control the outcome of four separate government investigations into the crime?

Let us remember Watergate and what it taught us about government lies and the men around President Richard Nixon. Let's not forget the violence the men in Watergate admitted to, the plots of Gordon Liddy, Howard Hunt, and Charles Colson – the murderous violence that was in these men, for Watergate was no accident. Watergate was not just a political dirty trick, the mere bugging of opponents; it was intimately connected to the assassinations.[1]

America has not been the same since the several major political murders and other crimes struck at the U.S. Great turmoil and disaster

349

befell the United States, and its star has sunk low on the horizon in its own Time of Troubles. America is in danger of losing its allies, as its behavior alienates most of the rest of the world.

At the time of the assassination, the Secret Team – or The Club, as others call it – manipulated the affairs of state. This group is not a formal organization. It is composed of some of the most powerful and wealthiest men in the United States, and Richard Nixon was a member of it. The Secret Team runs the United States, and to a large extent, they have circumvented the Constitution. They are highly suspicious of the democratic process, and they have consistently tried to control and manipulate elections. John Kennedy was a great threat to this group because he was his own man. He had his own money, and he owed few favors. President Dwight David Eisenhower warned the nation in his last address as President: "Beware of the Military-Industrial Complex!" Even he saw the growing threat presented by this group, which put him in power. Richard Nixon, who was Eisenhower's Vice President, displayed no similar concern. He went on to lose a bitterly contested election to Kennedy.

Eisenhower was perhaps the first to voice his concern with the power of the hidden government, but he wasn't the last to grapple with the issue. Kennedy confronted the problem with classic Irish stubbornness, and was assassinated. Each President since then has had to face the same difficulty and some were more successful than others. The Secret Team did things to each President to make him understand that the power did not lie with the Presidency. His mandate may come from the people, but the power – and policy making – came from outside, from this shadow government. They did things to each President to make him understand that his life and administration depended upon the Secret Team and The Club's control. John Kennedy's murder was an example to all who followed, telling them to toe the line, and to do as they were told. He, like Roosevelt, was considered a traitor to his class. Let others handle policy and foreign affairs. In the process, the nation's treasury was looted, its military defeated and all but destroyed, and its economy badly damaged and mortgaged to foreign countries as America became a debtor nation. Flag waving, super-patriotism, defense and "national security" was the cover for these men to enrich themselves and entrench themselves in power. Democracy was their front, not their means. They wanted little wars here and there to grind up military equipment. They wanted and needed the Vietnam War, and Kennedy was preparing to remove the United States of America from Vietnam. Ultimately, the Vietnam War was worth 220 billion dollars in business to the War Party. They never intended to win the war, but just keep it going, consuming material at a great rate, and incidently, American soldiers and Vietnamese civilians.

The Club, or *Power Control Group*, wanted to bring America into Vietnam, and as Fletcher Prouty explains in the article on the origins of the Vietnam War appended to this book, they are able to force the course of events in the direction they desire through the use of covert operations and the Secret Team. The whole purpose and function of the CIA and other intelligence operations had to be subverted in order to gain control of their covert action capabilities, and that of the Defense Intelligence Agency, the Office of Naval Intelligence, and other agencies, and most recently, the National Security Council, which under the climate President Reagan created became just one more instrument of covert operations.

This Club, a loosely knit, informal organization, has gradually established a shadow government with a secret, institutionalized covert action capability outside the official government. Their covert action capability is in deep cover and based in other nations, as well as having its roots in the United States. Recent revelations during the Iran-Contra hearings concerning the desire of former CIA Director Casey to establish such a capability outside Congressional scrutiny were just a red herring to misdirect public attention from the fact that such an operation has existed for a long time. An analogy may be drawn with the method by which the CIA created a cover by having some men take a very calculated fall. Some of its operatives "defected" and wrote or publicized information that appeared to expose operations and agents of the CIA, when these operations were already long known abroad, and when the real covert capability was being transferred to the Defense Intelligence Agency. In fact, the capability is moved every few years so as to maintain a safe cover.

Anti-Communism is only the cover story of this operational capability. It is there to achieve short-term policy objectives or to serve the needs of a specific corporation or industry at any given moment. The problem is that the world is trying to knit together, and America's continued reliance on covert actions and interference in the domestic affairs of foreign nations, often in blatant disregard for national sovereignty, has destroyed the credibility of the United States. In the process, America has wasted vast resources in what history will show were mostly counterproductive efforts, greatly delaying whatever change America was trying to bring about, and often causing the exact opposite of what the United States was secretly trying to do. Most people know when they are being manipulated, don't like it, start to hate, and fight back. Perhaps dealing up front is a better policy. The fall of the Shah and the Iranian revolution is a good example of such counterproductive activity on the CIA's part. We might mention, also, that Fidel Castro is *still* in power 28 years after America threw everything it had at him.

HOW IT COULD HAPPEN

How did the Secret Team bring about the death of President Kennedy? The plotters had only to let the right mechanics know that the President would not be well protected and they would take care of the rest, covering it up as accessories after the fact. It is unlikely that any such conspiracy would not have involved more shooters than the two snipers suggested by the House Committee. A proper ambush requires more than two snipers; a proper crossfire would certainly involve at least three or four sniper teams,[2] and the murder had all the earmarks of a carefully planned military style ambush. Unravelling the cover-up indicates its origin.

We can begin to understand how this assassination could have happened, how so many witnesses could have died, if we try to look at some hard and ugly facts. One of them is that in certain cities in the world there is a lot of violence and sometimes police violence. Dallas, Philadelphia, Detroit, and Rio de Janeiro are examples of cities where violence is a major factor in the culture and social fabric. The American Friends Service Committee, a Quaker organization, conducted a long study of what they felt were "hundreds of illegal police murders" in Philadelphia. They concluded that it is sometimes the practice of the police to summarily execute persons caught in the commission of a crime. This sort of thing does not happen in most cities, but it does happen. It can only happen if it is officially condoned.

If you murder the cut-outs, the middle men between those who hired the assassins or put them up to it, the middle men between the operations director of the assassination and the hit men, the middle men between the men who put someone up to forging evidence, to fabricating evidence, to destroying evidence, and if you kill the witnesses who know far too much, then there won't be much of a trail to follow. The pattern of things in this case clearly proves that all of this has happened. There is a pattern of drawing a fog over the evidence, of deliberate misinformation, and sowing deliberate confusion.

Ask yourself, how did Martin Luther King die? And how did his brother die in his swimming pool? And what kind of shots or attack were made on other members of his family? What about the shooting of George Wallace in 1972, without which Richard Nixon most probably never would have been re-elected? The murder of Robert Kennedy? The murder of Allard Lowenstein who found a conspiracy in the murder of his friend, Robert Kennedy? The near murder of Edward Kennedy? The murder of black children by bombings and other means, the death of civil rights workers and numerous others? America has a bloody history right up to today. The long history of the radical Right-Wing white supremacist Black Legion* in the North and the Ku Klux Klan in the South, the assassination of President Lincoln, the massacres of hundreds of thousands of Indians over two centuries, the massacres of townspeople by John D. Rockefeller's men, the deaths of countless labor organizers and union men over the years. These are part of our history whether we like it or not. If nations are to rise above the jungle, they must at all times face their past and deal with it. Witnesses died in the Watergate affair, in the shooting of Wallace, in the assassinations of Martin Luther King, Robert Kennedy and John Kennedy. It really happened.

Prolonged study of this case over the years teaches many lessons. For a complete product of our culture, only gradually liberating ourselves from the brainwashing of our upbringing, the case leads one into the deeper mysteries of our culture. There is something very wrong with our whole system of law when assassins go free and honest men are persecuted. The *way* we take evidence, the *way* we weigh evidence, what we choose to believe, whom we choose to accuse, calls into question the fundamental underpinnings of our society.

Are we a nation of laws, truth, and justice, or is all that a sham?

---

* The Black Legion was a secret terrorist organization of White supremacists which operated in Michigan, Illinois, Ohio and Indiana during the mid-1930s. Arson, bombing, torture and murder were among the Legion's anti-labor techniques.

Archibald MacLeish, in his famous 1949 article in the *Atlantic*, "The Conquest of America" – recently reprinted there – wrote, "...we lost our way as a people, and wandered into the Russian looking-glass, primarily because we were unable to think."

We have been conditioned to believe that everything is all right, but it isn't. We long ago lost the American dream of the Jeffersonian State. We let ourselves be had.

Death Squads and the White Hand[3] may be functioning even now in America. People said that what happened in Nazi Germany or Latin America could never happen in America, but it has happened and is happening. The Neo-Nazis, the KKK and the mentality that goes with them is living proof.[4]

"I'm afraid for America. Afraid even now as I speak to you about this assassination," Dick Gregory says, speaking before thousands of students on college campuses. They tried to kill him, and murdered his driver.

It has been said that all the political assassinations of the 1963-73 period are connected, and that the liberal/centrist leadership of the country is being exterminated, as in banana republics. The result is that the majority no longer vote, having no-one to vote for. This violence, which intimidates everyone else, is destroying the democratic political process in this country, leaving America with all of its power to be run by straw men.

Clearly, the Kennedy, King, and Wallace shootings were conspiracies, each supported by a cover-up. We are no different from other nations experiencing a *coup d'état* where the victors suppress the losers and their defenders, and suppress as much information as they can. We now know of extensive government involvement with the media,[5] but the whole truth has not been revealed. Certainly the media is unwilling to admit that they were wrong in accepting without question the Warren Report. Their failure to investigate, points to the gullibility of the press, and deliberate control and manipulation of the news.

How could it have all happened without someone finding out the truth? To begin with, the circle of conspirators was relatively small, but they had at their disposal all the apparatus of government and the underworld. A government is compartmentalized, like an intelligence agency, a bee hive of independent but related activity, so that the people in Dallas didn't know what was going on in Washington at the CIA or the Warren

Commission, and the local police were ignorant of what was happening in the autopsy room in Bethesda, Maryland. A story can be published somewhere with new evidence, but it does not get carried by the wire service, so vital information is suppressed, controlled, and limited in distribution. In fact, we have to ask why certain things are published in the case at all, when it is full of disinformation. This book, on the other hand, could not be published in the U.S. for many years.

WHY PRESIDENT KENNEDY WAS KILLED

"The CIA will have to be dealt with," Kennedy had said following the Bay of Pigs fiasco. Instead it was Kennedy who was "dealt with."

Kennedy accepted the blame for the aborted Bay of Pigs invasion, but the CIA was really responsible. The CIA had made a mess of the whole operation, particularly the air and logistical support for the landing forces. Immediately after the Bay of Pigs, the Agency began to plan a second invasion, training Cuban exiles and soldiers of fortune in Guatemala, on No-Name Key in Florida, and on the north shore of Lake Pontchartrain in Louisiana. During the Cuban missile crisis, President Kennedy reached an agreement with Nikita Khrushchev that the United States would stop the "secret war" against Cuba, which included assassination attempts on President Castro and the planned second invasion.

The President ordered the CIA to cease its invasion plans, but the training continued. Angered and outraged by the Agency's rogue elephant behavior and arrogant attitude, Kennedy sent in the FBI and the police to break up the paramilitary training camps. Arrests were made, and arms and ammunition were confiscated or blown up. High-level CIA personnel were fired by the President, including Director Allen Dulles, Deputy Director General Charles Cabell, and Deputy Director of Planning Richard M. Bissell. (Later, in an astonishing and inexcusable move, Dulles would be named one of the seven Warren Commissioners investigating the assassination.) It was at this time in 1961 that President Kennedy told Senator Mike Mansfield that he would tear the CIA "into a thousand pieces and scatter it to the winds."

The President underestimated the power of the CIA and its radical rightist backers. A decade later, Richard Nixon would make the same mistake.

Kennedy had made powerful enemies. Some he had fired, but many remained in positions of power.

After the Bay of Pigs, when the remaining Cuban exiles and the CIA began planning for the second invasion of Cuba, CIA contract employees and agents were training the exiles. Spirits were high with the prospect of successfully overthrowing Castro at last. Training and planning went well until October, 1962, when Kennedy sent FBI and other agents to Florida and Louisiana to break up the training camps.

In the exiles' eyes, Kennedy had now betrayed them for the second time in two years. They hated Kennedy now as much as they hated Fidel Castro.

The exiles were involved with a group of CIA contract agents known as "the No-Name Key group." This group figured prominently in the assassination-conspiracy investigation conducted in the late 1960s by New Orleans District Attorney Jim Garrison.

Witnesses and supporting evidence points to CIA/anti-Castro involvement in the assassination. Victor Marchetti, an author and former CIA executive, claims the CIA considered at one point taking "a limited hangout" and admitting some of its members were involved in the assassination.[6]

ORGANIZED CRIME

During the Church Committee investigation and hearings in the mid-1970s, it was revealed that the CIA had contracted with important Organized Crime figures to plot the assassination of Fidel Castro.[7] Over a dozen attempts had failed. The working relationship between the Mob and the government may have played a role in the President's murder.

Under the Batista regime in Cuba, Organized Crime made millions of dollars every day through gambling and prostitution. When Castro took over, he shut down the casinos, threw out the Mob, and imprisoned some Mafia figures. Naturally, this did not sit well with Organized Crime figures in America who wanted Castro out and the casinos reopened. They desperately wanted the second CIA sponsored invasion to take place, and did everything they could to support this effort. But the Cuban missile crisis agreement ended any chance of a military invasion to overthrow Castro. Unknown to the President and his brother (as the Senate Intelligence Committee investigation later found), the Mob contracted with the CIA to assassinate Castro.

While this was happening, Robert Kennedy was engaged in the most serious crackdown on Organized Crime in U.S. history. The Kennedy brothers' open war against Organized Crime provided a strong motive in the plot against the President.

It is almost certain that Mob elements were used in part of the plot. The final report of the House Select Committee on Assassinations states that "The Committee believes... that the national syndicate of organized crime, as a group, was not involved in the assassination of President Kennedy."[8] The Committee's Report goes on to demonstrate that FBI surveillance would have turned up evidence of any such plot. This does not preclude the use of low-level Mob elements by their intelligence agency controls.

Santos Trafficante, Carlos Marcello, Johnny Roselli, Sam Giancana and Jimmy Hoffa, among others, had a motive and possible means to kill the President. Mob watchers feel, however, that none of them would have made such a daring move alone for fear that exposure would bring a far costlier attack on Organized Crime as a whole. The "Commission," which is the committee of all the crime family leaders in the Mafia in the United States, would have had to make such a decision together, and since they did not do so, it would have been impossible for any individual to break discipline and put everyone else into jeopardy, unless they were given the green light from outside powers.

In 1959, Roselli and Giancana met with Howard Hughes' right-hand man, CIA operative and ex-FBI man Robert A. Maheu, to put together a team to assassinate Fidel Castro.[9] This plot dovetailed with the CIA's planned invasion of Cuba, forging an alliance between the groups with the common goal of wresting Cuba away from Castro. This alliance later turned on the President and killed him.

Jack Ruby had strong lifelong connections with Organized Crime,[10] dating back to his childhood in Chicago, where he ran numbers for Frank Nitti, who was Al Capone's "enforcer." Ruby, born Jacob Rubinstein, was involved in the December 1939 murder of Leon Cooke, secretary-treasurer of the Waste Handlers' Union in Chicago.

Ruby appears to have been hand-picked to silence Oswald after the supposed assassin survived November 22. Although the FBI reported to the Warren Commission that they could find no link between Jack

Ruby and Organized Crime, Ruby's telephone bills for the weeks and hours just prior to the assassination showed a clear connection with the Mob.

The Mob clearly had reason to hate the Kennedys, both because of their Cuban policies and their war on Organized Crime. It is interesting to note that after John Kennedy's death, prosecutions of Organized Crime figures declined by 83%,[11] as Robert Sam Anson tells us. He writes, "Organized Crime had considerable cause for relief; for with Kennedy's murder... the statistics added up to a quiet, largely unnoticed surrender in the war Robert Kennedy had declared. It had cost only one casualty: the life of his brother."

But – and this is a big "but," no-one in Organized Crime had the means to forge and plant the medical evidence in this case, not to speak of much other incriminating planted and forged evidence against Oswald. Nor could the Mob engineer the disappearance of evidence from the National Archives. The Mob could not have covered up the crime. Only government agencies had people capable of planning and covering up such a murder.

MILITANT HATE GROUPS AND THE ULTRA RIGHT WING

Although there is no formal link between these factions, there is a very strong likelihood that personnel involved in the assassination also had ties to one or more of these groups: the National States Rights Party, the Minutemen, the Ku Klux Klan, the White Citizens' Council, the American Constitution Party, and various other groups with a similar philosophy. We know that Joseph Milteer, a Right Wing extremist, appeared to have advance knowledge of the plot to kill Kennedy. He described the planned assassination to a police informant in amazing detail. He was later photographed in Dealey Plaza.

There has always been a radical right in the United States and they have always functioned through violence and intimidation. Conservative opinion often served them well, permitting the long history of lynching, repression, racism, the general climate of violence, anti-intellectualism, political terror and assassination. The Mafia served their purpose as well, as have the military and their backers. They *need* the Cold War and widespread fear to do all this. They *create* crime to feed that fear.

There were at least two central reasons why militant hate groups wanted to get rid of President Kennedy: his civil rights policies, and Cuba.

Kennedy's record on civil rights incensed the racist Right Wing, who bitterly hated him for helping Blacks. More than a quarter century later, it is perhaps difficult for us to understand the depth of resentment and fear which Kennedy's civil rights policies elicited.

As for Cuba, the groups felt that Kennedy was a traitor for allowing a Communist government to exist in the western hemisphere. They hated him and thought him a coward for not taking further military action against Castro and Cuba – even if it led to World War III. "Better dead than red" was their favorite slogan, and they clearly thought Kennedy was selling out the country.

A number of Right Wing organizations talked about murdering Kennedy. These Right Wing extremist organizations had large followings in the South. In Texas they had the active financial support of rich oil barons, who also cozied up to numerous prominent retired high ranking military officers.

THE KENNEDY PRESIDENCY AND HATRED

President Kennedy had increased greatly in his popularity throughout the country and the world during his 1000 days in the White House. The whole world looked to him for leadership and inspiration, and his wit, charm, and intelligence gave the entire planet the first real lift it had had since the ashes and smoke cleared from the battles of World War II. It appeared that Kennedy would have been easily re-elected, and as Eisenhower said, he would have been a great President. And he was taking us to the moon.

For this popularity, the young President was hated by that part of the Establishment which despised the democratic tradition in America. They considered Kennedy a demagogue, as certain leading intellectual journals made him out to be a few years ago, during a brief period of revisionist history. [12] Kennedy was mistrusted because he was so popular, because he spoke to the poor and downtrodden, the disadvantaged, minorities, intellectuals and artists.

Kennedy reached out to Martin Luther King, and extended hope to black people, Chicanos, and Latin America. He placed his brother in charge as Attorney-General, and J. Edgar Hoover and the Mafia were soon feeling the heat. The greatest bust of Organized Crime in our history began.

Kennedy signed a nuclear test ban treaty with the Soviet Union, and the military and the Right Wing hated him for it. He was also reorganizing the Pentagon and trying to get the CIA under control.

Kennedy sat down with Chairman Khrushchev and hammered out a *détente* with the Soviet Union which lasted for years until the leadership of Leonid Brezhnev and President Jimmy Carter. Kennedy was hated for making peace with Russia, and the Ultra Cold Warrior Sect wanted tension with the Soviet Union. They couldn't control the President, so they killed him.

Kennedy made up his mind to tolerate Castro. He refused to invade and conquer Cuba, and was preparing to normalize relations. Kennedy knew that if the U.S. invaded Cuba, Castro had armed every man, woman and child, and the whole population would fight us. Many innocent people would die. It is noteworthy that the two nations have managed to co-exist ever since, with no blood shed. Throughout all of the many years that followed, the United States retained its large Naval Base at Guantanamo Bay in Cuba in peace.

Kennedy forced the steel companies to rescind a price rise that was made in violation of the antitrust laws, and in doing so, he added to his list of enemies.

He threatened to remove the oil depletion allowance for the oilmen and oil companies, the most powerful lobby of all, the primary supporters of Richard Nixon.

President Kennedy listened to General Douglas MacArthur, the architect of Japan's defeat in World War II. MacArthur warned him "not to get involved in a land war in Asia. Get out of Vietnam." General MacArthur had learned his lessons in Korea.

The French had suffered a terrible defeat in Indochina by Ho Chi Minh, and had been thrown out. Why did the CIA and their powerful backers seek to fill their shoes? Why? Because there was money in it: $220 billion, when it was finally over.

Bobby Kennedy was a double threat because of his attack on organized crime. J. Edgar Hoover insisted that there was no Organized Crime problem in the United States.[13] It was a fiction. Hoover was the man who indirectly helped to kill Martin Luther King and others. In his way, he condoned Organized Crime, masked behind the cover of clean-cut young G Men. He was ruthless and did not hesitate to blackmail anybody in politics.

Johnson was a captive of the War Party, and he could do nothing after the assassination of Kennedy. When President Carter unexpectedly tried to talk about the assassination on national television, he was instantly cut off. There was no sound for nearly half an hour, but viewers all over America could see Carter sitting there like a fool. In fact, each President upon entering office was destabilized by this Secret Team, shots taken at them, and things done to them. Presidents were mistranslated, intimidated, controlled, and actually terrorized in some cases, so that they got the message that the power lay beyond the White House gates.

After so many years of propaganda, the reader and members of the public who still care must begin to view Kennedy's murder as a turning point, a *coup d'état* or *coup de maître* that altered the course of American and world history.

It is strange that so little of the real history of America ever gets communicated. "Why don't they just tell us the truth? Just once, I would like to be told the truth," a young school teacher in Coalstrip, Montana said. "Why do they cover it up? Why do they cover it up?" Dr. Bashour asked, in Dallas. He had treated President Kennedy at Parkland Hospital as he lay dying.

TERRIFYING LINK

Who in American history has been implicated in this type of massive destruction of evidence, subornation of perjury, documented assassination plots, and so on, in the Alger Hiss case, the Watergate case, the forging of State Department cables? There was only one bunch.

Nixon surrounded himself with what was known as the Berlin Wall, a long succession of advisors with Germanic names: We recall at the top of his "German General Staff" as it was also known, Haldeman, Erlichman, Krogh, Klindienst, Kissinger (the Rockefellers' emissary) and many others.

The selection of German names was no accident. Many of the brighter staff people close to Nixon came to him from the University of Southern California, and the University of California at Los Angeles, where there were fraternities that kept alive the vision of a new Reich. America has for a long time harbored this dark side of its character, one of violence and the Valhalla of Wagner and Hitler.

But Gordon Liddy was the one in whose mind "Triumph of the Will" was the most alive. Some of these men would watch the great Nazi propaganda films in the basement of the White House until all hours of the night, and drink, in fact get drunk with their power, with blind ambition, as one of them wrote. Exposure of the crimes caused some of these men to face what they had done, recover their sense of self and change for the better. Charles Colson even got religion, he claims. Liddy was known to have shot off his gun at a urinal and made numerous threats. Bernard Fensterwald writes, "G. Gordon Liddy has been reliably linked to two separate alleged murder plans during his work for Nixon's top aides, and one other actual completed murder, during his previous FBI service." [14] One of Nixon's top aides, Jeb Magruder writes of the Liddy Plan, "It was mind-boggling. It included mugging squads, kidnapping, sabotage, the use of prostitutes for political blackmail (which Liddy described as "high-class girls, only the best") break-ins to obtain and photograph documents, and various forms of electronic surveillance and wiretapping... Liddy explained that the proposed kidnap squads would seize radicals, and inject them with some drug that would render them unconscious." [15]

Fensterwald writes, "Liddy was apparently in a position to obtain the various drugs and/or poisons that were envisioned in his original Watergate plans." [16] Frank Sturgis was quoted as saying that Liddy "was always talking about 'disposal' – about killing people" and that he had a "hit man" complex. [17] Dan Rather suggested on CBS that there might be some kind of connection between John Kennedy's assassination and Watergate. Joseph Califano, a top aide to President Johnson, told Rather in a November 1975 interview that "when all the activities of the CIA were flushed out – then maybe the whole story of the Kennedy assassination would be known." [18]

One of Nixon's top assistants took a dislike to a reporter, and had him invited to a private showing of a movie. The reporter sat down, and soon was seized by the hair from behind and his head cruelly jerked back and cracked against the back of the seat. The man's head was held there for some time, and then he was let go. He turned to see the Presidential assistant, who said, "Oh, I thought you were someone else." Egil Krogh attempted to gain the cooperation of a physician in a drug enforcement program to be directed out of the White House, but the doctor would not agree. Krogh said, "That's all right, doc. We'll destroy you. And we'll destroy anyone who gets in our way." This "out of control" behavior explains many of the real reasons why Nixon was set up and overthrown. But there were many others. Among them was a ruthless shakedown of American businesses for 50 to 100 million dollars by the Committee to Re-elect the President (CREEP). Individual corporations were tapped for a million bucks a shot. Or else they were prosecuted for anti-trust violations.

Sensitive and reliable sources tell us that there is a copy of the 18-minute gap in the Nixon tapes. The Secret Service always makes back-up tapes. Why did they keep quiet about this one?

When there is a fundamental schism within the body politic, as there is in the U.S., between ways and means, between violence and peaceful solutions, Kennedy's death has particular significance. With his death, the forces of violence took control.

With a few exceptions, Nixon must be the only person old enough to remember who did not recall where he was the day the President died. Immediately after the murder he denied that he had been in Dallas on November 22.[19] William Manchester has documented that Nixon was there, and Nixon was quoted in the *New York Times* the following day, in a business story datelined *Dallas* November 22, as saying that he would do everything in his power to ensure that Kennedy was not reelected.

The so-called "Babushka Lady," a young woman employed at the Colony Club at the time, took what is probably the best film of the assassination, standing close to the President during the shooting. She told author Gary Shaw that FBI man Regis Kennedy took her film from her, and no-one has ever seen it since. She knew Jack Ruby and was married to a mobster in the area. Interestingly, she and her husband met with Nixon for two hours in Miami during the Presidential campaign of 1968.[20]

Now we can understand why Nixon's men would want to kill *Washington Post* columnist Jack Anderson, when Anderson claims the Mob killed Kennedy, or that the plots to kill Castro backfired and resulted in Kennedy's death. It all becomes terrifyingly clear.

In 1975, a Senate Intelligence Committee spokesman said that Jack Anderson had been marked for assassination by Nixon's men. The *Washington Post* quoted reliable sources as saying "E. Howard Hunt, the former CIA agent who helped engineer the Ellsberg and Watergate burglaries, told associates that he was ordered to kill Anderson with an untraceable poison obtained from a former CIA doctor, but that the scheme was dropped at the last minute."[21]

Hunt was deeply involved in the plots to assassinate Fidel Castro, and he tried to frame President Kennedy for the murder of Premier Diem in Vietnam by forging cables.

It is interesting that J. Edgar Hoover died suddenly at a crucial moment in his struggle with Nixon and the CIA, two weeks before the shooting of George Wallace – a shooting which ensured the re-election of Nixon. Hunt and Gordon Liddy were among the chief henchmen of the CIA and Richard Nixon. A report in the *Harvard Crimson* stated that evidence given to the Senate's Ervin Committee said break-ins of Hoover's apartment were led by Gordon Liddy and Cubans, and that "a poison of the thyon-phosphate genre was placed on Hoover's personal toilet articles." This induces fatal heart attacks.

WHO KILLED PRESIDENT KENNEDY?

Who killed President Kennedy? It took a combination of the CIA controlled Cuban exiles, Organized Crime, and the Ultra Right Wing, with the support of some politically well connected wealthy men to pull it off. They carried out the assassination through a complex series of overt and covert actions – and through failure of the President's protection at the critical moment.

All of these seemingly disparate groups had much in common. The CIA and Organized Crime used some of the same operatives; this was certainly the case in Southern Florida and Louisiana. Santos Trafficante employed many of the same Cubans the CIA was hoping to use to overthrow Castro. Jack Ruby ran guns to Cuba during the Revolution on behalf of the CIA and the Mob. CIA operatives like David Ferrie and Guy Banister, who were closely linked to Oswald and Ruby, also had close ties to New Orleans Mafia boss Carlos Marcello. As for far Right Wing organizations, these were filled with a strange assortment of

Cuban exiles, police officers, intelligence operatives, oil barons and retired military officers.

The following narration is based on intense discussions between the authors and various former high ranking (and dissident) intelligence officials, military officers, political figures, and other powerful persons in a position to know the facts. In some cases, names were given with great certainty of individuals formerly connected to the intelligence agencies, whom the informants believe were involved in the assassination.

In particular, a faction employed by the intelligence agencies during the Bay of Pigs operation (for which then Vice President Richard Nixon was the White House action officer) was responsible for the assassination of the President. Some of these men had worked for or been associated with one agency or another, so it is difficult to determine exactly their true connections. Civilians with powerful backing operating in the intelligence agencies at the time, some with a military background, planned and covered up the murder of the President, with the help of allies in the Secret Service, the Dallas authorities and at Bethesda Naval Hospital.

To carry out the assassination, the President was lured into a trap in Dallas, and his Secret Service protection was compromised. The entire government was manipulated, both before the murder and directly afterwards. President Johnson saw the murder and could guess exactly what happened. "I never believed that Oswald acted alone..." President Lyndon Johnson said. And he believed that the CIA was somehow connected to the plot that killed his predecessor.

The gunmen were Cubans and Cuban Mafia, and professional hit men brought in from elsewhere in the world. They operated in teams of two, with perhaps additional killers stationed along the way. They had walkie-talkies and escape routes. Some of them were in manholes around the car, one in front to the left, one in front to the right. Another may have been in the sewer directly beside the car with a clear shot at point-blank range, still another was behind the stockade fence on the Grassy Knoll. Other gunmen were behind the car once it was in the center of the field of fire. The recorded shots were simply too close together to have come from less than three or four guns.

The Warren Commission identified only one gunman. Fourteen

years later in 1978, the House Select Committee on Assassinations admitted to at least two assassins. The next investigation, when it comes, will likely acknowledge that there were several gunmen and that there was a far deeper plot than anyone officially dared admit in the past.

KENNEDY, VIETNAM AND THE WAR PARTY

The CIA and the American ambassador ran the Vietnam War. They had persuaded President Kennedy that it was necessary to send military advisors to Southeast Asia to support the South Vietnamese; by mid-1963, however, Kennedy realized that this policy was failing, and would ultimately lead to wider U.S. involvement. Just before President Kennedy died, he had the Secretary of Defense, Robert McNamara, and the Chief of the General Staff, General Maxwell Taylor, announce a schedule for *total withdrawal from Vietnam*, and he had started to withdraw the troops.

On September 2, 1963, President Kennedy had said, "I don't think that unless a greater effort is made by the Government (of South Vietnam) to win popular support that the war can be won out there. In the final analysis it is their war. They are the ones who have to win it or lose it. We can help them, we can give them equipment, we can send our men out there as advisors, but they have to win it, the people of Vietnam against the Communists. We are prepared to continue to assist them, but I don't think that the war can be won unless the people support the effort and, in my opinion, in the last two months, the government has gotten out of touch with the people."

The coup followed and on November 14, 1963, one week before his death, President Kennedy began to withdraw the first 1000 of the 16,000 men stationed in Vietnam. He said that they would be home by Christmas, and that all the troops would be out in another year.

"The President's order to reduce the American military personnel in Vietnam by one thousand before the end of 1963 was still in effect the day he went to Texas. A few days after his death, during the morning, the order was quietly rescinded," wrote Kenneth O'Donnell and Dave Powers in *Johnny, Johnny, We Hardly Knew Ye*. Both close friends of Kennedy, they told Tip O'Neill that they heard two shots from the Grassy Knoll.

Immediately after the assassination, the Pentagon and President Johnson "re-evaluated the situation" and escalated the war. Johnson had sworn never to send American boys to Vietnam, but the murder of his boss rapidly led to a reversal of this policy. Escalation of the war in Vietnam began literally hours after Kennedy's assassination.

"The significance of the Dealey Plaza assassination was that the warfare sector of the government seized power from the President," Jim Garrison wrote.[22]

Fletcher Prouty wrote that "It was less than one month after that tragic date that the same two travelers, McNamara and Taylor, returned again from Saigon and reported to a new President that conditions were bad in South Vietnam and we would have to make a major effort, including American combat troops and a vast 'sophisticated' clandestine program, against the North Vietnamese.

"The Secret Team struck quickly. While the echo of those shots in Dallas were still ringing, the ST moved to take over the whole direction of the war and to dominate the activity of the United States of America.

"In the face of these shocking and terrifying events, who could have expected a man who had been in the range of gunfire that ended the life of his predecessor, to make any moves in those critical days that would indicate he was not going to go along with the pressures which had surfaced so violently in Dallas? He knew exactly what had happened there. He did not need to wait for the findings of the Warren Commission. He already knew that the death of Lee Harvey Oswald would never bring any relief to him or to his successors."[23]

Are the assassins who pulled the triggers in Dealey Plaza November 22, 1963, still alive? More importantly, are the power brokers who ordered the assassination and the on-site "handlers" who organized it still among us? The answer is yes, they still move among us and in some cases still influence events. At the cocktail parties of retired intelligence officers and others "in the know," their names are mentioned in hushed tones.

Can they be brought to justice? With the necessary resources and political will, they can be brought to trial. Many of the prosecutors associated with the 1976 House investigation believed that with more money and a little more time, indictments would have been forthcoming.

We have put off this question for an entire generation. Are we ready now to face the truth?

"I believe the murder of the President was provoked, primarily by fear of the domestic and international consequences of the Moscow Pact: the danger of disarmament which would disrupt the industries on which the plotters depended and of an international détente which would, in their view, have threatened the eventual nationalization of their oil investments overseas."

– Who Killed Kennedy,
Thomas G. Buchanan, 1964

CHAPTER 20

SPECIAL OPERATIONS
AND THE SECRET TEAM

The Deputy Director of the CIA during the Bay of Pigs Invasion was General Charles Cabell, whose brother Earle was the Mayor of Dallas at the time of the assassination. The discussion that follows takes us into the fundamental policy conflicts that arose from the time of the failure of the invasion, which contributed to the murder of the President.

Cabell was in charge of clandestine operations. This, not intelligence gathering, was the main thrust of the CIA and this area controlled the direction and leadership of the CIA. "The paramount condition underlying any approval for clandestine operations is absolute control at the top," writes Fletcher Prouty in *The Secret Team*. "The ST will come up with operational schemes all the time and will seek approval for as many as it believes it can get away with. The only way to cope with this is for the President to make it clear that there will be no covert operations without proper approval and that he will always be in a position to cancel or disapprove of any and all operations as he sees fit. Truman and Eisenhower knew this and practiced it. Kennedy learned it at the Bay of Pigs. Eisenhower had terminated major operations in Tibet, Laos, and Indonesia without escalating them into open war. Until his death Kennedy had held the line at the limited level of covert activities in Indochina, and American participation there was theoretically restricted to an advisory capacity. (Of course, we all recognize that this advisory role is, in many cases, pure combat.)

"...Clandestine operations that become large, that are permitted to continue and to be repeated, that become known or compromised – and that still continue, as in Laos – are very dangerous and can lead to open hostilities and even war. Thus when the ST proposed a vastly escalated covert campaign against North Vietnam in December 1963, they were laying positive plans for the major military action that followed in 1965."[1]

How many Americans know that we were making war on North Vietnam as early as 1963?

Within 30 days of Kennedy's death, all this had changed drastically. In his report of December 21, 1963, Robert McNamara, Secretary of Defense, stated: "Viet Cong progress had been great during the period since the *coup*. We also need to have major increases in both military and USOM staffs."

Within hours, really, of the murder of the President, America went to war. This whole nightmare tracks back to the Bay of Pigs disaster. Howard Hunt wrote in *Give Us This Day*, "Castro's beachhead triumph opened a bottomless Pandora's box of difficulties that affected not only the United States but most of its allies in the Free World." This line of reasoning reflects not only Hunt's point of view but the thinking of others, such as General Thomas Lane, author of *The Leadership of President Kennedy*. Lane writes in his chapter on the Bay of Pigs: "This false concept of his own role and obligation led President Kennedy to attempt detailed control of matters beyond his own comprehension. In doing so he failed to use properly lieutenants who were masters of the operations in progress." ... "Planning and preparation for the assault on Cuba had been initiated by the United States Central Intelligence Agency with the approval of President Eisenhower... This was a CIA Operation."[2]

Prouty writes, "As the Kennedy Administration settled into their official chairs, some of them were selected to hear about the Cuban in-

vasion plans, and some were not. The first big move was ready to come
on stage. The ST was ready to show the Kennedy Administration how
things would be done from that time on for the future."[3] (See also *Of
Kennedys and Kings*, by Harris Wofford.)

"As these plans were revealed to the inner circle of policy advisors
in the Kennedy administration, objections were raised. At a special
White House staff meeting on April 5, 1961, called by the President to
weigh the final decision to launch or halt the invasion, Senator Fulbright
objected to the proposed use of force to topple Castro. He argued that
such unilateral use of force would seriously damage United States
prestige and foreign policy objectives in the hemisphere and in the
world."[4]

"Present at the meeting were Rusk, McNamara, Dillon, Mann,
Nitze, Berle, Dulles, Bissell, Bundy, and Schlessinger, Fulbright, and
General Lemnitzer. In other words, this meeting was heavily weighted
with Cold Warriors."

"There was provision for United States carrier-based air support
to be used if necessary."[5] In other words, America was going to be
drawn into an attack on another nation. "After the discussion, the President approved the planned invasion (Prouty says approval came on April
16) but with the proviso that there should be no direct participation of
the United States Armed Forces... Mr. Bissell, Mr. Dulles, and General
Lemnitzer should have protested the presidential change of plans. There
has been no evidence that they did so."[6]

The CIA planes that were used had Cuban Air Force insignia
painted on them, and they were flown by American pilots. "The pre-
invasion bombardment designed to destroy the Castro Air Force began
on April 15, 1961. Pilots of the attack bombers who landed in the United
States used cover stories that they had fled from Cuba. United States
government spokesmen denied knowledge of any attack on Cuba.[7]

"In the United Nations, however, pressures on the United States
increased rapidly. Delegates were becoming skeptical about Ambassador Stevenson's denials, impressed by Cuban and Soviet charges.

"... The President then gave instructions that the D-day morning
strikes in support of the invasion" should not take place at that time
unless those having the responsibility felt that it was so important it had
to take place "in which case they should call him (the President) and

discuss it further."[8] "Allen Dulles, who should have been at the President's side in that critical hour, was absent in Puerto Rico."[9]

Lane says that the cancellation of the air strikes was ordered by Secretary of State Dean Rusk, but Prouty told us it was Bundy.[10] "General Cabell, Deputy Director of the CIA and Acting Director in the absence of Allen Dulles, made vigorous protest to Secretary Rusk... but was rebuffed. Secretary Rusk seemed to have taken charge of the operation in the absence of Allen Dulles."[11]

The exiles landed, but Castro had four jet trainers which survived the pre-invasion attacks, and the men on the beach had no air cover. *The whole world watched this invasion.* "When these aircraft appeared over the beachhead, they were unhampered in attacking troops and equipment ashore and the supply ships and forces afloat off the beachhead. Destruction of the ships carrying ammunition and supplies for the landing forces placed the whole operation in immediate jeopardy."[12] And the troops were defeated and captured.

THE PRESIDENT UNDER PRESSURE

Lane tells us that when President Kennedy "weakened his resolve under pressure from the United Nations... he betrayed an uncertainty about his original decision. It seemed that an inbred political instinct to move with the pressure caused him to hedge by modifying the invasion plan... If the President had given his decision to General Cabell he would have received a prompt estimate of its implications... He and Secretary Rusk clearly had no personal competence to judge the issue. They had expert advice at their call but they did not use it.

"President Kennedy's refusal to use United States aircraft to protect the beachhead and destroy the Castro planes reveals the confusion of his thinking. He was incapable of weighing the relative importance of criticism in the U.N. and disaster to an invasion which he personally had launched...[13]

"That he became involved in such tactical details of a military operation betrays the fundamental error of the Kennedy leadership. He had a staff well qualified to handle such details."[14] And four pages back: "Would the leader surrounded by pygmies be capable of living up to the image he had created?... Great organizations are made with building blocks. The leader does not direct every detail of activity. He places in each block of the organization a lieutenant who can direct its work..." [15] Lane goes on at length on his own idea of leadership, which boils down to wishing Kennedy had left the small matter of the use of American forces to back up the Cuban exile brigade to his lieutenants.

"The inescapable conclusion is that President Kennedy failed to grasp the critical values of United States interest in the Bay of Pigs invasion... In this event the good leader would have approved the recommended plan with a single admonition, 'You cannot fail in this undertaking!' Then he would have settled back to observe the performance of his staff. When the U.N. criticism arrived, he would have remained serene in the knowledge that the ouster of Castro would win the approval and admiration of the free world... The President and his coterie of neophytes in government could not be shaken out of their dreams even by the reality of disaster." [16] Here we see the military mind at work in full dudgeon.

Lane goes on to claim that, "The toppling of Castro would have raised United States prestige in the world to new heights." [17]

In fact, the invasion was poorly planned. The CIA is not basically a military outfit, and was not competent to run an operation of this scope. The Pentagon has its own large military capability and may think that it can run its own wars, but they can't, as we learned catastrophically in Vietnam. Kennedy was given false briefings by the military and the CIA. In essence, they lied to him. Kennedy understood that the brigade would go ashore, head for the mountains, and fight a guerilla campaign. They wanted to go home, so let them. It was their war, as he was later to say about Vietnam just before his death. [18]

"Few men in the new Government had any idea of what was being put into shape for the Cuban invasion. Those who did, knew only bits and pieces of the whole plan. These men were not accustomed to the double-talk and undercover language and actions of the Agency. They heard briefings, but they did not know what they really meant. On the other hand, a large number of the new Kennedy team were old CIA hands. They did know exactly what was going on, and they used their special knowledge and experience to further isolate those who did not." [19]

Supreme Court Justice William O. Douglas, recalling a discussion he and Kennedy had about the Bay of Pigs, said, "This episode seared him. He had experienced the extreme power that these groups had, these various insidious influences of the CIA and the Pentagon on civilian policy, and I think it raised in his own mind the specter: Can Jack Kennedy, President of the United States ever be strong enough to really rule these two powerful agencies? I think it had a profound effect... it shook him up!"[20]

Prouty goes on to write, "Can any President learn about, comprehend, and then believe what he had learned about this whole covert and complex subject? Can any President see in this vast mechanism, in which there is so much that is untrue and hidden, the heart and core of the real problem? Will any President be prepared to confront this staggering realization when and if he does uncover it? Is this perhaps the great discovery which President Kennedy made, or was about to make? It is not just the CIA and the DOD that are involved. It is also the FBI, the AEC, the DIA, elements of State and of the Executive Office Building, NSA and the hidden pulse of secret power coursing through almost every area of the body politic. It extends beyond into governmental business, the academic world, and certain very influential sectors of the press, radio, TV, papers, magazines, and the publishing business. Before any President can rule this covert automatic control system, he must find out it is there – he must be aware of the fact it exists – and he must devise some means to discover its concealed activity.

"President Kennedy made a valiant attempt to affect control over this system with his directives NSAM 55 and 57, as a start. If he had more actively utilized the NSC system, and if he had structured a really strong and effective Operations Coordinating Board or its equivalent, he might have had a chance to grasp control of some segments of this intragovernmental cybernetic machine... But, as a result of the Bay of Pigs, the inquiry, and the realization by 1963 of how, despite his great efforts, he was still unable to wrest control from and to rule the ST machine, he was beginning to develop an NSC/OCB technique of his own, which by 1965 might have accomplished this task had he lived to perfect it.

"Kennedy's battle was not all with the ST. He was going through the same pressures with other groups – not the least of which was his quixotic contest with the immensely powerful and ruthless professional education establishment and the equally powerful parochial Catholic school hierarchy... there is in evidence more than enough pressure from any one of several of these groups, or their more radical subgroups, to support the germ of the idea that a sinister conspiracy may have arisen from these pressures. For these groups realized that Kennedy was gaining real knowledge, experience, and political power and that he had to be removed from office before winning the inevitable mandate from the U.S. public which was certain to be his in 1964."[21]

When Virgilio Gonzalez got caught in the Watergate, he made a long affidavit, which Jim Hougan discusses in his book *Spooks*. "If the Gonzalez affidavit is to be believed, the United States is a police state run by a dangerous consortium of CIA officers, private intelligence agencies and White House entrepreneurs."[22]

THE SECRET TEAM

Fletcher Prouty describes how "the Bay of Pigs operation went off pretty much by itself and foundered"..."But President Kennedy was also not the type to permit such a thing to hit him twice. He was smart, tough, and politically alert."[23] A long secret investigation was conducted by the Kennedys, at which time they were sold a bill of goods on another approach of the Secret Team: Flexible response, counterinsurgency, and pacification. "No one should underestimate the role played by Bobby Kennedy. Nothing in his strenuous career had prepared him to become a military strategist or battlefield tactician; but few men in this country were more experienced in the ways of the Government, and few men were tougher than Bobby Kennedy... The evidence is that Bobby Kennedy was not misled in his appraisal of the real problems underlying the serious and tragic failure of the Bay of Pigs operation. He came very close to seeing how terribly significant the real meaning of clandestine operations is and how gross an impact the failure of such operations can have upon national prestige and credibility. It is entirely possible that had John Kennedy lived to serve until re-elected, sometime during his Administration the genie of clandestine operations would have been put back into the bottle and the CIA might have been returned to its legally authorized role of an intelligence agency and no more."[24] Robert Kennedy headed the secret group investigating the Bay of Pigs disaster.

"The committee hearings ended in May of 1961... Out of these meetings came three most interesting and remarkable documents... The

White House issued three National Security Action Memorandums of a most unusual and revolutionary nature... They prescribed vastly limited stipulations upon the conduct of clandestine operations. NSAM #55 was addressed to the chairman of the JCS, and its principal theme was to instruct the chairman that the President of the United States held him responsible for all 'military-type' operations in peacetime as he would be responsible for them in time of war... there was no misunderstanding the full intent and weight of this document. Peacetime operations, as used in that context, were always clandestine operations... It did not say that the chairman should develop such operations. In fact, accompanying directives clarified that issue to mean that clandestine operations were to cease, or at least to be much restricted... This NSAM therefore put into the chairman's hands the authority to demand full and comprehensive briefings and an inside role during the development of any clandestine operation in which the U.S. Government might become involved.

"The usual NSAM was signed by one of the senior members of the White House staff... NSAM #55 was most singular in that it was addressed only to the chairman of the JCS with an information address notation for the DCI, the Secretary of State, and the Secretary of Defense; and the order was signed personally by President John F. Kennedy. There was to be no doubt in the minds of any of the inner group of the Kennedy Administration concerning the President's meaning and intentions. The fact that the DCI received his copy as 'information' was alone sufficient to heavily underscore the President's message."[25]

Men like CIA chief Allen Dulles did not like being told how to run his agency. J. Edgar Hoover didn't like it, either. Following the Bay of Pigs fiasco, Dulles was eased out. He was clearly no admirer of Kennedy. Why then did Dulles end up on the Warren Commission investigating John Kennedy's murder?

"It had become clear to the Kennedys and to their inner 'family' that CIA lack of leadership in the Bay of Pigs had been the cause of its failure. The total lack of on-the-spot tactical leadership was the first element Kennedy attacked once the hearings had concluded. This document more than anything else sealed the fate of Dick Bissell, and Allen Dulles. When the chips were down, they had not been there, nor had they made their presence felt."[26]

Prouty has told us that, in fact, they weren't there because the invasion was deliberately sabotaged in order to embarrass Kennedy.[27] As General Lane wrote, "There could be no greater contribution to Castro power and prestige than an invasion failure. Castro could not have done better if he had planned the operation himself."[28]

It was General Cabell, whose brother was the Mayor of Dallas and one of the motorcade organizers, who controlled the air strikes by the CIA planes, which were launched days ahead of time so that there was no surprise and plenty of time to hide Castro's jets. There were many other problems with the planning, and the whole invasion force became sitting ducks. "NSAM #56 was not a significant document and was more intended to fill a small chink in the leaking dam than to reroute the whole stream of events. But what it lacked in thunder was more than made up by NSAM #57. We have been saying much about clandestine operations and of the very peculiar nature of this type of business. When it has all been reviewed one of the principal conclusions must be that the United States Government is inherently and operationally incapable of developing and successfully carrying out clandestine operations, primarily because they run at total opposites to our basic way of life. America should be an open society, and clandestine operations are the desperate efforts of a closed society.

"When the Pentagon Papers series was published by *The New York Times*, it was noticeable for its omission. It is this sort of 'educated' omission that makes the Pentagon Papers suspect in the eyes of those who have been most intimately connected with that type of work. NSAM #57 is a controversial document that has not been released to date.

"The principle behind NSAM #57 is absolutely fundamental to the whole concept of clandestine operations. It not only restates the idea that clandestine operations should be secret and deniable, but it goes beyond that to state that they should be small. It plays on the meaning of 'small,' in two areas of interest: First, unless they are very small they should not be assigned to the CIA; and second, if they are not as small as possible they have no chance of remaining secret and therefore have no chance, by definition, of being successful clandestine operations."[29]

"This later issue flies right in the face of the CIA..."[30] Prouty's book should be read by everyone concerned with matters of national interest. He explains how the CIA had defined countless operations over the years so that they could get control of them and expanded their empire. Now Kennedy was cutting them down to size.

"Thus by the very size of its activities in so many areas, the CIA had exceeded all reasonable definitions of clandestine. This new Kennedy directive hit right at the most vulnerable point in the ST game at that time."[31] Naturally, the fighting began over what was "large" and what was "small." This kind of fight could only be resolved with a gun, and there was far too much money at stake. Half of Health, Education and Welfare's budget was concealed CIA funds, as well as every other agency in the government, such as the Forest Service, and secret operations were big money for the military industrial complex. Howard Hughes, for instance, had a huge empire which largely lived on CIA money. He was their chief cover in many operations. Take Operation Desktop, the illegal planting of missiles on the floor of the oceans. In addition, the *Glomar Explorer*, owned by Howard Hughes (or was it the CIA? The DIA?) had a good cover salvaging sunken Gulf Class Russian submarines from 16,000 feet.

"Opposing Allen Dulles was like fighting your adversary on the brink of a cliff. He was willing to go over as long as he brought his opponents with him. He believed the handwriting on the wall, and he had sounded out the Kennedys. He knew that they learned a lot from the Bay of Pigs; and he knew where the Kennedys' Achilles tendon was and he had hold of that vital spot."[32]

Prouty says it would be worth a chapter or even another book to tell us what happened to those NSAMs in the end.

"It used to be that anti-Communist activity was carried out against Communist countries, governments, and territory. There had been a gradual drift away from that. The new counterinsurgency philosophy and doctrine meant that anti-Communism would now be waged in non-Communist countries."[33]

"In the hands of Lemnitzer, NSAM #55 meant no more clandestine operations, or at least no more unless there were most compelling reasons. In the hands of Maxwell Taylor (who replaced Lemnitzer), this meant that he was most willing to take full advantage of the situation and to be the President's key adviser..." Lemnitzer had been sent to Paris to head up NATO and "One further factor played into this situation. It is quite apparent that Kennedy did not fully realize the situation he had unintentionally created. To him and to his brother, Maxwell

Taylor was the model of the down-to-earth soldier... He was their man. They did not realize that even in his recent book *The Uncertain Trumpet* he had turned his back on the conventional military doctrine and had become a leader of the new military force of response, of reaction, and of undercover activity – all summed up in the newly coined word 'counterinsurgency.' Kennedy was not getting an old soldier in the Pentagon. He was getting one of the new breed. Taylor's tenure would mark the end of the day of the old soldier and the beginning of the Special Forces, the peacetime operator, the response-motivated counterinsurgency warrior who has been so abundantly uncovered in the conflict of the past ten years in Vietnam.

"This was the climax of a long bit of maneuvering within the Government by the ST and its supporters. To accomplish their ends they did not have to shoot down the Kennedy directives, NSAM #55 and #57... they simply took these memoranda over for their own ends, and ignored them when they were in conflict with whatever it was they wanted. They buried any opposition in security and need-to-know and in highly classified "eyes-only" rules. Then, with all the top positions covered, they were in charge, they were ready to move out to wherever secret intelligence input would find a soft or intriguing spot... So very few people have ever seen the real documents, and fewer have acted on them."[34]

"More real control can be put on the Government from the inside by not doing and not permitting to be done those things which had been instructed and directed to be done than by other more conventional means. One of the best examples of this is what happened to this most important document, NSAM #55. Nowhere else was Kennedy's strong desire for control more in evidence than in that paper and the ones that followed it, like NSAM #57. Thus it was that events marched relentlessly on towards Vietnam. The only ones who stood in the way were the President and his closest intimates – and they had been neatly outmaneuvered,"[35] Prouty writes.

WRONG DECISIONS?

While Kennedy was trying to assert control over the military and intelligence community with NSAM 55 and 57, others were preparing to resist. To gain insight into the mind of those who were determined to stop the President, we need only read Admiral Ben Moreell's foreword to Lane's book on Kennedy. He says, "The major tragedy of his regime is not that President Kennedy made so many wrong decisions; it lies in the fact that he had been permitted to seize power which enabled him to make those decisions without regard to constitutional limitations on his authority. That is the way of dictatorship!"[36] It seems to have escaped Moreell that Kennedy didn't seize power. He was elected.

Later in his book Lane says, "The presidential command failure was strikingly illustrated in the removal of Major General Edwin A. Walker from command of the Twenty-Fourth Infantry Division in Germany. The shocking injustice of that action was obscured by unrelated political charges and counter-charges launched in the United States after General Walker resigned from the Army."[37] Walker was distributing Right Wing literature to his troops. He went home to Dallas and agitated as a civilian.

This book by Lane talks constantly of the Constitution and a soldier's duty, as does Moreell. "... the failure of leadership depicted by General Lane flows from a pernicious subversion of constitutional government by virtue of powers voluntarily ceded by or wrested from the Congress, the actions of the Supreme Court in supporting socialist and egalitarian doctrine; and the usurpation of rights which, under the Constitution, reside in the States or the people." "The President has exercised authority the effect of which is to accelerate many drastic changes in the concepts of the legitimate functions of government, as these were conceived by the Founding Fathers."[38]

Lane then goes on to say, "The general thrust of the Kennedy military leadership was to assert a political domination of the military leadership which is hostile to the traditions and practices of American government."[39] "If the military leader is then willing to submit the professional integrity, morale, and effectiveness of his service or services to the adverse judgments of inexperienced politicians, he is not fit to hold office."[40]

"Its tenor was disclosed in the Joint Chiefs of Staff approval of the Moscow Test Ban Treaty of 1963 for political reasons. General Taylor informed the Senate that the agreement was, on military analysis, against the interests of the United States but that political advantages outweighed the military advantages... John F. Kennedy was telling the Joint Chiefs that they must accept his judgement of military matters. The Presidential dictum was of course contrary to law and should have been disregarded by the Joint Chiefs of Staff."[41]

Kennedy said shortly before they killed him, "You must wonder when it is all going to end. And when we can come back home. Well, it isn't going to end... We have to stay at it. We must not be fatigued." (November, 1963).

Lane speaks for the long-suffering military: "When the Soviet Union closed the autobahn access to Berlin in 1948, General Clay wanted permission to open the way with his own forces. He did not ask for more troops for the operation. His request was denied and the expensive air lift was undertaken. Secretary of State Marshall informed Ambassador Murphay that the Joint Chiefs of Staff considered the United States army too weak to undertake the autobahn reopening against possible Soviet resistance! Such a military appraisal is beyond comprehension. At the time the United States had in its atomic weapons such superiority over the Soviet Union as no power in history has ever had over a potential opponent..."[42]

THE BISSELL PHILOSOPHY

When you finish this book, you might want to go and read or re-read Victor Marchetti and John Marks' *The CIA and the Cult of Intelligence*. The Appendix to their book contains just one article, "The Bissell Philosophy," as expressed in a meeting in 1968 at the Council on Foreign Relations.

Richard Bissell had been fired by Kennedy following the Bay of Pigs, along with General Cabell and Allen Dulles, the high command of the CIA. He was one of the Bay of Pigs planners. In 1968, he was still preaching the secret interventionism that has got this country into such terrible trouble throughout the world.

America, and Kennedy, was being driven inexorably towards war from the day after the failure of the Bay of Pigs. Prouty tells us in *The Secret Team* that almost immediately following the failure, significant numbers of men who were involved in the Cuba project began moving to the Far East.[43] Prouty himself believed that this "War Party" favored intervening in Southeast Asia, and killed the President.

Prouty says the dimensions of the conspiracy which killed the President can be ascertained by observing who got what jobs afterwards: Who took what power and who did what.

Nixon, who was in Dallas the day of the assassination, prosecuted the Vietnam War with all the power he could muster. He was always supported by money from the big oil companies, and it was those companies that wanted American military involvement in Southeast Asia. Later he tried to hire many of the people involved in the cover-up on the Warren Commission when he met his Watergate.

Our history is one of conflict between the hard-liners and the "soft-liners," that is, those who would try to find some other way than war, short of appeasement or selling out. War is meant here to include clandestine operations in Third World countries, for we long ago gave that up in "Communist countries."

"The most remarkable development in the management of America's relations with other countries during the quarter-century since the end of World War II has been the assumption of more and more control over military and diplomatic operations at home and abroad by men whose activities are secret, whose budget is secret, whose very identities are secret – in short by a Secret Team whose actions only those implicated in them are in a position to monitor and to understand.

"The Secret Team (ST) consists of security-cleared individuals in and out of government who receive secret intelligence data gathered by the CIA and the National Security Agency (NSA) and who react to those data, when it seems appropriate to them, with paramilitary plans and activities..." "At the heart of the Team, of course, are a handful of top executives of the CIA and of the National Security Counsel (NSC) most notably the chief White House adviser to the President on foreign policy affairs. Around them revolves a sort of inner ring of Presidential officials, civilians, and military men from the Pentagon, and career professionals in the intelligence community. It is often quite difficult to tell exactly who these men really are, because some may wear a uniform and the rank of general and really be with the CIA and others may be as inconspicuous as the executive assistant to some Cabinet officer's chief deputy..." "All true members of the Team remain in the power center whether in office with the incumbent administration or out of office with the hard-core set. They simply rotate to and from official jobs and the business world or the pleasant haven of academe."[44]

"The New York Times shocked the World on Sunday, June 13, 1971, with the publication of the first elements of the Pentagon Papers." (This is a gross and crafty misnomer, since all too few of those papers actually were *bona fide* military papers. They may have been written under Pentagon headings; they may have been signed by "military" officers or "military department civilians," but for the most part, they were not actually military papers. They represent the papers of a small group of civilians, some of whom worked in the Pentagon, and their military (real and cover) counterparts.) The first document the *Times* selected to print was a trip report on the situation in Saigon, credited to the Secretary of Defense, Robert S. McNamara, and dated December 21, 1963. This was the first such report on the situation in Indochina to be submitted to President Lyndon B. Johnson. It came less than 30 days after the assassination of President John F. Kennedy, and less than 60 days after the assassination of President Ngo Dinh Diem of South Vietnam and his brother and counselor Ngo Dinh Nhu."[45]

"Reports such as the October 2, 1963, document were not written in Saigon and they were not written by the men whose names appeared on them. This pivotal report was written in Washington by members of the ST."[46]

This is the crux of why the President was killed. He had tried to stop the war in Vietnam and just before he died, began to wind it down*.

"... that report which may stand out in history as one of the key documents affecting national policy in the past quarter-century – not so much for what it said as for what it signified."[47]

"Thus, what was considered to be a first prerequisite for a more favorable climate in Vietnam was fulfilled. With the Ngo family out of the way, President Kennedy felt that he had the option to bring the war to a close on his own terms..."[48] This is not to say that he wanted them dead, but he certainly wanted them out of the way. And as Fletcher Prouty tells us, this happened often enough to bring down a Third World government. "... whenever United States support of the government in power is withdrawn and a possible *coup d'état* or assassination is not adamantly opposed, it will happen..."[49]

There had been murderous unrest in Vietnam under the Diems. There had been rioting and Buddhist monks were immolating themselves regularly. "The Kennedy Administration gave its support

---

*Facts on File Nov. 1963, p.339, 418, Larry Newman's quote *Baltimore Sun* August 8, 1983; Ralph Martin: *A Hero For Our Time*.

to a cabal of Vietnamese generals who were determined to remove the Ngos from power..."[50] "Then Kennedy sent McNamara and General Taylor to Saigon in late September to find out what was happening. Kennedy was trying hard to set the stage for a withdrawal, but he was being out-manoeuvered.

"The CIA's clandestine operation in Vietnam was growing into a full scale war which could not help but draw in ever greater U.S. military forces. This was precisely the sort of situation NSAM 55-57 had sought to avoid. John Kennedy wasn't the only President to have anticipated this sort of problem developing from uncontrolled clandestine operations. "... As soon as World War II was over, President Truman dissolved the OSS to assure that clandestine operations would cease immediately. Six months later, when he founded the Central Intelligence Group, he expressly denied a covert role for that authority and restricted the DCI to a coordinating function."[51] Just after the assassination of President Kennedy, former President Truman said: "For some time I have been disturbed by the way the CIA has been diverted from its original assignment. It has become an operational arm and at times a policy-making arm of the government. I never had any thought... when I set up the CIA, that it would be injected into peacetime cloak-and-dagger operations. Some of the complications and embarrassment that I think we experienced are in part attributable to the fact that this quiet intelligence arm of the President has been so removed from its intended role."[52]

Senator Fulbright, whom the ST hated, said, "But this secrecy... has become a god in this country, and those people who have secrets travel in a kind of fraternity... and they will not speak to anyone else." He was Chairman of the Senate Foreign Relations Committee. In his book, *The Arrogance of Power*, he wrote, "In the world family of nations, sovereignty is one of the key conditions of existence, and sovereignty is inviolate. Even if we talk about some small country such as Monaco or Luxembourg, the code of nations regards their sovereignty to be as precious as that of the United States or the USSR. The day this code breaks down will be the beginning of the end of world order and of a return to the rule of brute force. Liberty begins as the aspiration of the individual, and sovereignty is the measure of the absolute power of a state. As we look around us today, we see an erosion of this fundamental of international society. It is for this reason that we must look into this situation and consider how important it is to the world community to uphold principles that we hold to be essential and priceless assets of our civilization... Since sovereignty is priceless and must be inviolate, it is fundamental that no nation has the right to do that which if every other nation did likewise, would destroy this fragile fabric of civilization..."[53]

What has been the cost of not heeding Fulbright's words? "The cost to the United States was very great, much greater than most people realize because so much of what actually took place was concealed quite effectively from the American people, although it was not unknown to the Indonesians, the Chinese, and the Russians, and for that matter, to any other country that chose to know. As a result of that costly Cold War battle, again the attrition of the United States was considerable and that of the USSR was negligible."[54]

"The Bay of Pigs was another such major battle. We made a great investment in resources and in our world prestige. Russia's contribution was again little more than words..." "This has been the scoring for the Cold War almost all the way along."[55]

"There was almost no way in which anyone in the United States Government could unravel the whole clandestine business. But at least a beginning was made as a result of a most unexpected series of events and as a result of some very shrewd and clever work by Bobby Kennedy and his closest associates."[56] Prouty goes on to talk about NSAM #55 again: "No more Bay of Pigs." "This was a powerful memorandum, which set forth Kennedy's views without equivocation. It was in fact more positive as an action against the nonaddressees than it was for the addressee, the JCS (Joint Chiefs of Staff).

"I was the officer responsible for briefing this paper to General Lemnitzer and to the other Chiefs of Staff, and that NSAM rested in my files. There need be no misunderstanding about what the memo meant, what the President meant, what Lemnitzer understood and did, and what the other Chiefs of Staff understood.

"... and if Kennedy had lived to assure that it was followed as he intended it to be, there is a very good chance that United States involvement in Indochina would never have been escalated beyond the military-adviser level. He had learned his grim lesson at the Bay of Pigs, and as his directive made clear, he was not going to become involved in that type of operation again. If evidence of this is needed, consider how he handled the missile crisis in Cuba a year later. Once he had been convinced of the gravity of the situation, he directed the mobilization of sufficient troops, overtly, and challenged the Cubans and the Soviets to comply with his demands. He respected the proper employment of military power and had seen how undercover military power fails."[57]

But "Kennedy's directive had been turned into an encouragement to CIA to go out and start small fires and count on the military to bail them out. This may seem an odd conclusion – almost funny – but it is exactly how we got into Vietnam in spite of the directives from the White House. The ST is perfectly capable of turning a No into a Yes by its gift of irrepressible argument."[58]

"Even as late as the attacks on the villages in the My Lai complex (a village massacred by U.S. troops), it was the Agency intelligence functionary who told the military to attack."[59] "Then, after President Kennedy died, the ST retained control of most of the Vietnam war from its earliest birth pangs to the peak of escalation. Even to this day (written in 1972) the combat phase of the Vietnamese war, which is called 'pacification' and which in fiscal year 1972 cost more then $1 billion, is totally under the direction and control of the CIA."[60]

We will let the devil have his due. In January 1971, President Nixon was interviewed by reporters, and Nancy Dickerson pinned him down about his promise to end the war, which, of course, did not end for a long time afterwards – not for years. "Mr. President, speaking of your campaigns, you made the kickoff address in New Hampshire in 1968... You made a speech how the next President had to give this country the lift of a driving dream... Well, as yet, many people have failed to perceive the lift of a driving dream. I wondered if you could articulate that dream for us briefly and tell us how you plan to specifically get it across to the people in the next two years."

"Miss Dickerson, before we can really get a lift of a driving dream, we have to get rid of some of the nightmares we inherited. One of these nightmares is a war without end. We are ending that war... But it takes some time to get rid of the nightmares. You can't be having a driving dream when you are in the midst of a nightmare."[61] Nixon may have been just as much a victim of the Secret Team as the others – a willing victim, perhaps, at first, but in the end still a victim.

Co-author Harrison Livingstone has read many of Nixon's campaign speeches, and has found that Nixon repeats two words over and over: peace, dream, peace, dream, peace, dream. He was lulling us to sleep as a nation. These words appeared with such repetitiveness as to make clear that a top propagandist was writing those speeches. The war did not end when Nixon was elected. It got worse. Huge secret wars were conducted with some of the most massive bombing raids in history. We fought in Laos, Cambodia and elsewhere, and the nation never even knew about it. The Vietnam War went on throughout Nixon's first four years, and in order to get reelected, Henry Kissinger and Nixon told us "Peace is at hand." They said they were about to sign a peace treaty. But as soon as the votes were counted in Nixon's reelection, the most massive bombing raids in the entire history of the world began.

Will we learn anything from this lesson? There are many lessons to be drawn from those years, but those lessons won't be taught in American schools.

Whenever one powerful group thinks that the end justifies the means, and flagrantly breaks the law, when we turn our backs on the very democratic institutions and traditions we most value, when violence and murder become political tools, then we enter a nightmare world in which we are all at risk. Once descended into the underworld of darkness, it is impossible to emerge unscathed. That is the true significance of what took place in Dealey Plaza on the 22nd of November, 1963.

A nightmare, yes. And they killed him.

Afterword

AFTERWORD

After this book was typeset in 1988, several witnesses at President Kennedy's autopsy at Bethesda Naval Hospital came forward and spoke publicly on KRON-TV, in San Francisco, to the central issue of the authenticity of the autopsy photographs and X-rays which is raised in this book. What they said was as startling as their testimony to David Lifton, and the House Select Committee on Assassinations investigators some years ago that the body did not arrive at Bethesda in the same condition, casket, and wrappings as it had left Dallas.

Jerrol Custer, the man who took the X-rays at Bethesda, was shown copies of them by Sylvia Chase of KRON, who asked, "Is this the X-ray picture that you took and is this the wound that you saw on the President?" "No. This area here was *gone*. (demonstrating the back of the head) There was no scalp there. Not this area," he said emphatically, pointing out the very large missing area on the right in front of the ear in the alleged X-rays. "I don't believe this is the autopsy X-ray." He demonstrated from the front top of the head all the way back to the back of the neck: "This part of the head was gone." Custer very strongly disputed the photographs and X-rays, as did the others.

Custer said, "from the top of the head to the base of the skull. That part was gone." Demonstrating the back of the head to the top. Clint Hill, the Secret Service man who had run after the President's limousine during the shooting and climbed on the trunk, as Jackie Kennedy was retrieving part of the President's head from it, wrote: "I noticed a portion of the President's head on the right rear side was missing and he was bleeding profusely. Part of his brain was gone. I saw a part of his skull with hair on it lying in the seat."

Hill told the Warren Commission "The right rear portion of his head was missing. It was lying in the rear seat of the car. His brain was exposed."

There was a deliberate cover-up by investigators of the medical evidence by the House Assassinations Committee because the X-rays are clearly incompatible with the photographs. That is, the X-rays show a large portion of the head missing which is not missing in the photographs, and show the scalp and skull intact in places where every single witness testified that there was no scalp or skull.

Paul O'Connor at Bethesda states he found the body in a body bag, and that he could not have confused that with the rubber sheet Kennedy left Dallas in. O'Connor insisted that the body arrived fifteen to twenty minutes before Jacqueline Kennedy and the ambulance carrying the bronze coffin from Andrews Air Force base, and that it was in a simple cheap shipping casket. Dennis David said that the body arrived in a black ambulance, "like a hearse." The body was in "just a gray casket....a metal shipping casket...not the bronze casket."

In addition, O'Connor reiterated what he told David Lifton years ago, "My job was to remove the brain. There was no brain to remove. The brain wasn't there."

Dennis David said that they did not talk about what they had seen for years because they had all been told to "keep their mouths shut," were threatened with courts-martial, and "we were afraid....we knew about the deaths of witnesses."

He said, "the end of the hole in the back could be felt with the finger. There was no point of exit and the bullet was not in the body."

KRON also interviewed Aubrey Rike, an ambulance attendant in Dallas at the time, and he insisted that he and Dennis McGuire had wrapped the body in a rubber sheet before closing the coffin, saying that it was not in a body bag when it left Dallas. He also insisted that it was in the bronze coffin and no other.

Each of the Bethesda Hospital personnel present at the autopsy described on KRON a large wound in the back of the head, exactly where the Dallas doctors and nurses described it, each demonstrating with their hands, but extending forward along the top of the head. This is the area where the FBI men present at the autopsy wrote that there had been surgery. In addition, each of the hospital technicians said that the brain was missing from the head when they received the body, and they all said that the body was not in the same casket and wrapping it was in when it left Dallas. In view of the anomalies in the time the plane landed in Washington and the time the body was supposed to have been received at Bethesda and the start of the autopsy, the suspicion arises that someone did in fact steal the body in order to examine it and remove evidence that would prove there was more than one gunman.

Floyd Riebe, a photographic technician who took the pictures of the body at Bethesda, said that the President had "a big gaping hole in the back of the head. It was like somebody put a piece of dynamite in a tin can and light it off. There was nothing there." This is far more damage than could have been done by a military jacketed bullet, but instead by an explosive or frangible bullet, as appears when the head is struck in the Zapruder film. Riebe was shown the autopsy photographs, and strongly disagreed with them, saying, "The two pictures you showed me are not what I saw that night." "What did it look like?" (Demonstrating the back of the head) "It had a big hole in it. This whole area was gone." With regard to the pictures and X-rays, Riebe said "Its being phonied someplace. Its make-believe."

Paul O'Connor, also present at the autopsy, described an "open area all the way across into the rear of the brain." He demonstrated that the whole top of the head was gone clear to the back. These men—when asked about the small, neat bullet entry wound in the cowlick in the otherwise intact scalp on the rear of the head —said that they didn't know what that was or how it got there.

O'Connor was shown the autopsy photographs and he said "No, that doesn't look like what I saw...A lot worse wound extended way back here," and he demonstrated with his hand to the back of the head.

The recent publication of a set of alleged autopsy photos show no part of the rear of the head missing. The only defect showing on the skull is a large hole on the top of the head extending far over to the left side, equally on the left and right sides, with a small flap of scalp and bone reflected back on the right, or open. There has never been any testimony or evidence that the large defect ever was on any part of the left side of the head.

The Zapruder film shows the flap of scalp and bone opening up on the right around the ear during the shooting, and brain pressing outward. Evidently, the President's wife—as she held her dying husband's head in her lap—pressed this back into place, closing the wound, as it was not generally noticed in Dallas, except for a couple of doctors that noticed a fracture there, and a ridge of over-lapping bone. The only thing that the witnesses in Dallas saw was the large hole in the back of the head, with no scalp left. Nobody saw any large wound on the left, top, or front of the head. There was no large missing area across the top of the head at that time. The X-rays show a quite different wound *entirely* on the right front of the head and face with nothing on the left, or past the back half of the head.

A Central Independent TV program made in England and shown around the world (but not in the United States) also had Dr. McClelland demonstrate the wounds. He drew a picture of a big hole in the back of the head. "It would be a jagged wound that involved the half of the right side of the back of the head. My initial impression was that it was probably an exit wound. So it was a very large wound. Twenty to twenty-five percent of the entire brain was missing. My most vivid impression of the entire agitated scene was that his head had been almost destroyed. His face was intact but very swollen. It was obvious he had a massive wound to his head. A fifth to a quarter of the right back part of the head had been blasted out along with most of the brain tissue in that area."

Dr. Paul Peters also was interviewed. He said, "We decided that the President was dead, and Dr. Clark, the Chairman of the Department of Neurosurgery, had come in the meantime and he had walked up to the head of the patient and looked inside at the wound and shook his head. He had a large—about 7 cm—opening in the right occipital-parietal area. A considerable portion of the brain was missing there, and the occipital cortex—the back portion of the brain—was lying down near the opening of the wound. Blood was trickling out."

First, the testimony on KRON strongly restated that there was a large hole in the back of the President's head. Dr. Charles Carrico said on television, "There was a large—quite a large defect about here (and he demonstrated a large hole in the very back of the head)

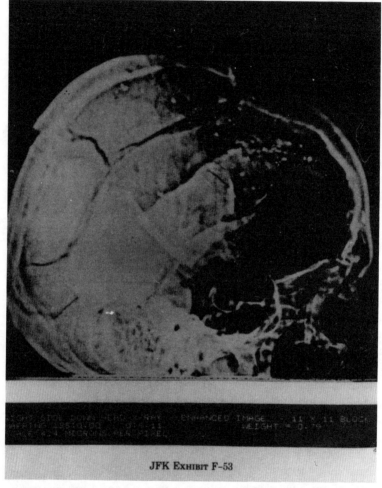

JFK Exhibit F-53

Lateral head X-ray. There is no exit defect in the rear of the head. There is massive damage to the right front face, none of which shows in the photographs. No damage to the right side of the face was ever described by any witness, Jerrol Custer, the X-ray technician who took the X-rays, says this is false. Some witnesses described damage to the left front of the face, but, again, such damage does not appear in the photos. Dr. Robert McClelland stated on television in the summer of 1989 that the X-rays show a large wound to the right face, with an eye missing. "There was no damage there," he said, "and the X-rays are not compatible with what we saw. I don't understand that, unless there has been some attempt to cover up the nature of the wounds."

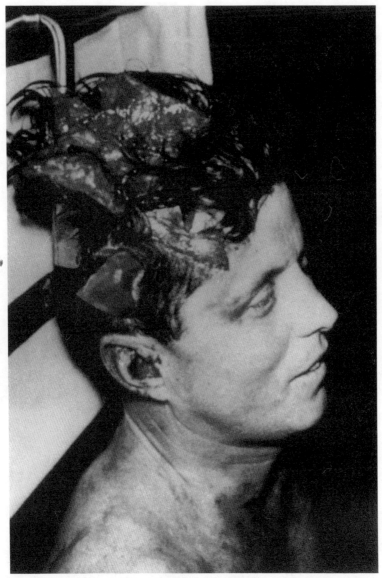

Right side of the head—there is no damage to the face as shown in the X-ray, and no damage to the back of the head. This picture is completely incompatible with the X-ray of the side of the head.

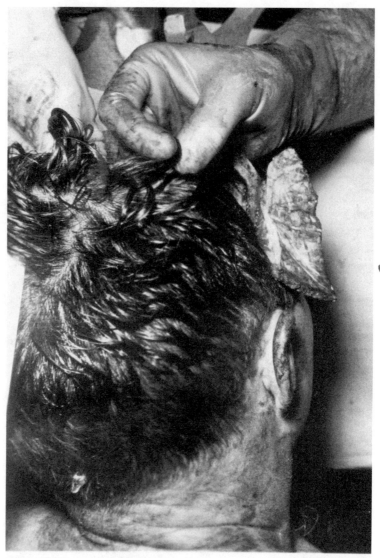

Rear of the head. This is a composite (forged) photograph which masks the large defect in the very back of the head described by all witnesses in Dallas, and at Bethesda Naval Hospital. Floyde Riebe, the photographer who helped take the autopsy photos, says this picture is forged. This picture and some of the others were shown to Chief Justice Earl Warren, who was so horrified that no questions were asked. It supposedly showed an entry wound in the cowlick, and no evidence of the large exit wound there from a shot in front. Thus an investigation of the medical evidence was never undertaken by the Warren Commission.

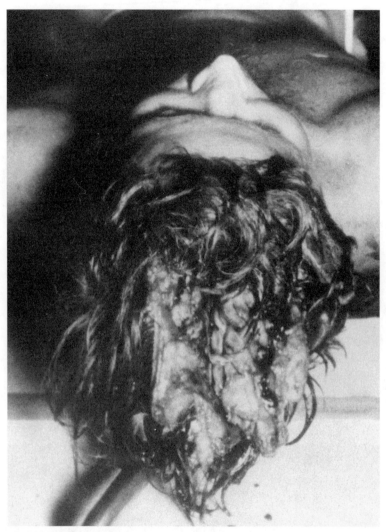

Top of the head. Note large missing area corresponding to the FBI report: Surgery to the top of the head. There was no damage to the top of the head seen in Dallas. The conspirators sawed off the top of the head and removed the brain and bullets before the autopsy.

on his skull." Dr. Ronald Coy Jones said, "My impression was there was a wound in this area of the head" (demonstrating a large hole in the back of the head.) On viewing the alleged autopsy X-ray, he said, "Certainly I can tell you that the wound was not here (demonstrating the forehead from over the right eye back to the temple and to the top of the front part of the head where the wound shows on the X-ray). There was no damage to the face that was visible." The alleged x-rays clearly show massive damage to the right front of the head extending into the temple, forehead and face down to the eye, but no hole in the back of the head. The X-rays are incompatible with the photographs, which show no injury to the face.

Nurse Audrey Bell said "There was a massive wound at the back of his head." Dr. Robert McClelland carefully demonstrated a large hole in the back of the head and said "It was in the right back part of the head—very large." All of these witnesses were filmed independently, and each demonstrated the wound in exactly the same place. Dr. McClelland said, "a portion of the cerebellum fell out on the table as we were doing the tracheostomy." He was asked "So the wound was very far back here?" (interviewer demonstrates the back of the head). "Right." "So the wound was in the back of the head?" "Right." Six doctors in Dallas had described seeing cerebellum on the table.

Then the show began to point out the conflicts that have developed in the evidence. Dr. Michael Baden (who never saw the body) said on the same broadcast that the cerebellum was intact in the photographs of the wounds. Dr. McClelland addressed this problem directly: "That was one of my more vivid memories of the whole thing. That was particularly grim to see that portion of the brain ooze out of the wound as I stood there looking at it. That stays with you pretty much." Dr. Jenkins had described as late as 1977 the cerebellum protruding, but he changed his opinion after seeing the photographs, some made from the angle looking down at the top of the head. "It did look like cerebellum. It still looks like it, but its obviously not—" he said, looking at the alleged photographs of the head wound. Fake photographs will cause witnesses to change their perceptions of what they saw.

Paul O'Connor, the autopsy technician from Bethesda, again

strongly denounced the photographs on another show. "The whole side of his head was gone. I don't know where those things came from but they are wrong. Totally wrong," he said of the autopsy photographs and x-rays.

The four autopsy doctors insisted years ago that the rear head entry was five inches from where it shows in the photographs and X-rays. This, together with the other questions about these films raised by the others at the autopsy demonstrates forgery.

Major Phil Willis was interviewed, along with his family who all saw the shooting at close range. They were most emphatic that the back part of his head was blown out right in front of them. They described a frontal head shot and were sure it came from the Grassy Knoll. Willis said, "I'm very dead certain at least one shot came from the front." His daughter said the "back of his head blew off." In addition, Willis took slides which have been closely studied by researchers over the years.

Perhaps the best witnesses to the wounds in Dallas were the nurses who washed and prepared the body for the coffin. Diana Bowron and Patricia Hutton, supervised by Doris Nelson, performed this task, but others including Margaret Henchliffe, helped out, and an orderly, David Sanders. Doris Nelson, the supervising Emergency Room nurse, carefully inspected the body. Ben Bradlee, Jr., asked her, "Did you get a good look at his head injuries?" "A very good look," she replied. "Oh, I did see it. When we wrapped him up and put him in the coffin. I saw his whole head." She was then asked if the alleged autopsy photos were accurate. "No. Its not true. Because there was no hair back there. There wasn't even hair back there. It was blown away. Some of his head was blown away and his brains were fallen down on the stretcher."

Could there have been a flap of scalp hanging down from the back of the neck that could have been pulled up to cover such a large hole, at least as big as a fist, and as big as two fists by the time the body arrived at Bethesda? No flap of scalp shows in any of the alleged autopsy photographs, except for the small, unrelated hinged flap of scalp with attached bone in the right parietal area. The top of the head shows some long locks of hair hanging down as the head lies on the autopsy table, but they clearly could not cover a hole in the back of the head.

Four of the men who worked with the President's body at Bethesda, told Sylvia Chase at KRON that the body did not arrive in the same coffin that it was alleged to have left Dallas in, and that it was in a body bag. We believe that these men are credible. The authors have questioned whether it was possible for the body to have been removed on the plane as it was being flown back to Washington, but we now believe that that must have happened as David Lifton has said, or that the body was removed from its coffin in Dallas after it was closed, and taken back to Washington on the spot.

It is clear that the body did not arrive in the same condition. The men from Bethesda insist that the brain was entirely gone from the head, and that the top of the head was missing, as the FBI report of the autopsy had said. We believe that the conspirators stole the body, which may be why the Secret Service took the coffin at gunpoint away from the Dallas authorities. The coffin may have been empty at that point and they didn't dare let it be stopped. The conspirators then removed the bullets from the body so that the true nature of the conspiracy could not be revealed ballistically, and took it to Bethesda, where it was put back into its coffin.

Although David Lifton may be wrong on some points, he should be commended for having persuaded so many witnesses to talk who were intimidated for all of these years, and for his pioneering work on these points. His theory that the body was altered and the head reconstructed in order to make the autopsy photos may or may not be correct, for our studies indicate that the pictures are forgeries. The one certain thing that emerges is that none of the official stories add up, and that the evidence was tampered with.

In particular we are troubled by the "missile" that the FBI report said was recovered at the autopsy. But not from the body. A whole bullet in almost perfect shape rolled out from the President's wrappings onto the floor. Admiral Osborne picked it up, and they all examined it. Since the bullet was not in the body, it would appear that it had been planted. This bullet was given to the Secret Service and later disappeared from the evidence. Admiral Osborne told Lifton—after the House Committee discounted his story— "There was a bullet there, and it was totally intact. What happened to it, I don't know, but the Secret Service took it...I know that it was there because I saw it...it fell out on the table, and I think everybody spotted it. All of us were right there. We spotted it at the same time, essentially.'' The investigator from the House Committee covered over the whole issue.

As he has said before, Darrell Tomlinson said on the KRON show that the pristine or magic bullet found on a stretcher at Parkland could not have come from Connally's stretcher.

Nurse Audrey Bell repeated on this show that the throat wound did not look like an exit wound and that it was an entrance wound, as so many other witnesses have stated. A previously unknown witness, Donna Willie, who was working at Parkland Hospital at the time, said, ''the President had a wound in his throat that the Commission said was an exit wound or was made from a tracheotomy...the entry wound is always small, and the exit wound is much larger. I saw the entry wound in the front of the President's neck. I know he was shot from the front, and I couldn't understand why that wasn't released,'' she told Nicole Levicoff of the Jenkintown *Times Chronicle*.

As for the only show that dealt with the medical evidence which was broadcast nationally during the 25th anniversary observance of the President's death, Dr. Robert McClelland, one of the Dallas doctors, commented on it extensively, afterwards, calling it a cover-up. McClelland was on the show that he later denounced. He believes that there was a conspiracy and cover-up in the case, and that the President was shot in the head from the Grassy Knoll. ''Somebody is concealing the whole plot. There was somebody on the Grassy Knoll who shot at the President and blew his head off...I'm sure that whoever was concerned about a conspiracy coming out in this country was concerned that some of these 25th anniversary shows like the ones in England and in France where they couldn't control the content like they could here, was going to stir up a lot of concern again, which—whoever these people were —at high levels or wherever, felt like that could not be allowed to occur, and if it could be prevented, they would do that. One of the ways to do that would be to make this immanently reasonable sounding film that Walter Cronkite—sort of America's father figure—narrated, and to say, well, granted, this could have happened, that could have happened, but nobody can really prove anything. Therefore, I guess we're left with a Warren Report again. And that is an absurdity, I think.''

Much of the case revolves around whether the Dallas doctors and nurses could have been mistaken about the location of the large defect in the head. To back up their medical knowledge and descriptions are the common sense observations of many other people who saw that the back of the head was gone, and that there was no scalp there. If there was a flap of scalp there, as Walter Cronkite had Doctor McClelland "speculate," then why does it have a different skin color than the surrounding head, and why is the hair color different?

The authors consulted two coroners and several doctors, including Dr. McClelland, and all say that when a rifle bullet exits the skull, taking with it large pieces of bone, it badly damages the scalp, blowing away some of it. A nice, neat flap cannot result. Dr. Charles Wilber, a former Colorado coroner, said that "with a rifle bullet, you always have a significant piece of scalp missing over the exit defect. You always have a defect in the scalp." Dr. Cyril Wecht, the Coroner of Pittsburgh, agrees. "You would get a loss of some scalp. The scalp would be lacerated by the explosive effect and the fracture of the underlying calvarium. The photographs of the back of the President's head don't show any lacerations of the scalp in the back. The lacerations certainly should show on the photographs." They don't. The scalp is completely intact, except for what is alleged to be a very small entry wound. "The X-rays that I saw do not show any large defect in the posterior," Wecht said.

Dr. Wecht went on to speak to the issue of alleged altering of the body in order to explain the appearance of the wounds in the photographs and X-rays. "Its such incredible nonsense. It can't be done physically. You can't doctor wounds. You don't know what you're dealing with—you can't restructure a skull if you have fractures. If you bring the fractured pieces together and pull the scalp over it, you might be able to mask the fractures for someone who is looking at it and taking photographs of the overlapping scalp. But an X-ray will reveal the fracture lines. By putting the fractured pieces in apposition, you in no way obscure the fracture lines.''

The X-rays alleged to be of Kennedy are not his and are substituted. The man who took the X-rays at Bethesda, Jerrol Custer, told the authors exactly what he told Sylvia Chase on KRON-TV in San Francisco. He took a lot of time to observe the wounds: "There was a large hole in the back of the head, and there was a big hole in the scalp there." The authors asked Custer, "in other words, that photo of the back of the head—which is in some dispute—would have shown that, if the scalp was shredded and macerated as you describe, it would have shown that in the photographs?" "Absolutely!" "But what you saw was an actual hole in the scalp itself in the very back of the head, in the occipital area where the large defect was?" "Right."

The authors asked him if he had seen the Walter Cronkite show on the assassination. "That was very superficial." "But was a flap of scalp there that could have been pulled up to cover the hole in the very back of the head?" Custer replied, "there was a king size hole in the back of the head, and that area was torn." From their observations at the autopsy at the time, Custer and the other Navy enlisted men all thought that the President had been shot from in front, and that the large hole in the back of the head was an exit.

"Do you feel that the X-rays—you're absolutely sure in your own mind that they don't show what you saw that night?"

"Lets put it this way—in the lateral skull films it looks like part of the front of his face is gone. But if you look at the autopsy photographs, there's nothing gone there. His eye should have been completely gone on that film, which it never should."

The key to the case is the fact that the X-rays and photographs are completely incompatible with each other. This proves that they are forgeries. In addition, if the X-rays and photos do not show the wounds as Custer and the other Bethesda and Dallas witnesses saw them, then the body was not altered to fake its' appearance, but the pictures were—so as not to show a shot from the front.

Another major discrepancy is the fact that the photographs of the top of the head show a large hole extending clear across from right to left, (corresponding to the hole that was marked "missing" on the autopsy face sheet drawing) equally on both sides of the head. This is completely incompatible with the X-rays which show the large defect on the right extending only as far as the midline from the front to the back of the head. In addition, there are no photos showing the brain inside the head, which they say was missing when the body arrived.

The rear head wound that Custer and the other men from the Bethesda autopsy describe who spoke out in 1988, is the same wound that was seen in Dallas, and which is in fact described in the autopsy report. Like the autopsy doctors themselves in their interview with a panel for the House Committee, they state that there was no entry wound in the cowlick area where it appears on the photographs of the back of the head. The large hole would have been there.

Dr. Paul Peters told the authors on December 28, 1988, that he did not remember any flap of scalp in the back, but he remembered the scalp there as "being badly torn....I'm sure part of it was missing."

Dr. Charles Baxter quoted Dr. Kemp Clark to Ben Bradlee, Jr., at the head of the operating table, as saying "My God, the whole back of his head is shot off." Clark picked up the back of the head to show it to Dr. Grossman, who also saw the second fractured area in the right parietal area. Baxter said that he could not see the large hole because it was in the very back of the head and it could not be seen without picking up the head. Baxter said that he saw the wound in the right parietal area. "It was such a benign wound that we thought it was an entry wound."

Nurse Patricia Hutton said that the only reason she could see the large head wound before they prepared the body for transport was because his head was somewhat off the cart and she could see the back of the head. She tried to put a pressure bandage on the large defect, but it was useless. She said the wound was low on the head, and about the size of a fist.

Dr. Richard Dulaney told Bradlee, "I didn't really examine it. Somebody lifted up his head and showed me the back of his head. We couldn't see much until they picked up his head. I was standing beside him. The wound was on the back of his head. On the back side." They lifted up the head and "the whole back-side was gone." "It was a big gaping wound."

Clearly, something is drastically wrong with the autopsy photographs, because there is no large defect at all in the back of the

head, other than two very small possible wounds the diameter of a
bullet or fragment that could not be confused with an exit wound.
We may be looking at President Kennedy's face in these tragic
composites, but not his head.

Dr. Ronald Jones told co-author Livingstone that the large hole
was directly in the back of the head. "He had a lot of damage to the
scalp. It was blown away."

We note that the X-rays show the right side of the face and
forehead gone, along with the top of his head in that area. This does
not show on the photographs. Even with the small flap of scalp and
attached bone opened which shows in the photographs, the X-rays,
if authentic, would not show the present huge area of bone missing.
Nobody can discount the reaction of the X-ray technician who took
these pictures. He was incredulous and astonished. In a criminal
investigation such as this, one must observe and weigh the de-
meanour and bearing of the witness, as Senator Ervin of the Watergate Committee used to say. In this case, these witnesses are credible, fantastic as their story is. The only people who are truly not
credible are the government investigators. If the large hole in the
back of the head was simply covered over with a flap of scalp, then
where is a photograph or X-ray which shows the back of the head
with the large defect, with the scalp reflected back, described by
everyone? There is none.

The first doctor to see what he said was a bullet entry wound
near the left temple was Dr. Leto Porto. This was described by Dr.
Robert McClelland in his report.

Important testimony appeared on the British show with regard
to the Grassy Knoll gunman, and concerning Jack Ruby's shooting
of Oswald. Beverly Oliver, a singer employed at the Colony Club
at the time of the assassination, knew Ruby well. For many years
she did not talk about the case because she was aware of the many
deaths of people who knew too much. Oliver was also known as the
"Babushka Lady" because she was standing beside the limousine
filming the motorcade when the President was shot. An FBI agent
took her film away from her, and it was never seen again.

Oliver saw "the back of his head come off" and saw a figure
firing on the Grassy Knoll and a flash and gunsmoke there, as did

former U.S. Senator Ralph Yarborough (interviewed extensively on this broadcast, along with former Governor John Connally) and many others. She believes her film may reveal much more. "I had the best shot of the assassination...and probably the only one with a good shot of the Grassy Knoll."

Perhaps more importantly, she stated that two weeks before the assassination, she went over to the Carousel Club during a break in her performance, and sat down at a table to have a drink with Jack Ruby, "Jada," and someone Ruby introduced to her, saying "Beverly, this is my friend Lee." She later realized the man was Lee Harvey Oswald.

Jada (Janet Adams Conforto) had told reporters the day after the assassination that Ruby knew Oswald, and Oliver related that Jada joined the ranks of mysterious deaths, so she kept her mouth shut.

Former Dallas police officer Billy Grammer was answering telephones the night after the assassination when he received a call he later recognized was from Jack Ruby. The caller asked that they change the means of transferring Oswald to the county jail. "If you move Oswald the way you are planning, we are going to kill him," the caller said. Grammer said, "This was the man I was talking to last night...He knew me, and I knew him. He knew my name." Ruby was evidently trying to get out of his assignment to kill Oswald. The route was not changed, and Ruby shot Oswald the next day. "It was not a spontaneous event," the policeman said, saying that the murder was planned, and that Ruby was made to do it.

Don Archer, a policeman, went to see Ruby in his jail cell to tell him that Oswald had died, and that Ruby would get the electric chair for it. Archer said that Ruby was greatly relieved at the news, as though his (or someone else's) life depended upon it.

Gordon Arnold, a service man, tried to film the motorcade from the carpark behind the picket fence on the Grassy Knoll, and was chased away by a man in a suit showing CIA credentials. Arnold moved away and filmed from an area close to the stairs, and he seems to appear in enhanced versions of the Moorman photograph shown on the broadcast, standing close to a rifleman firing. He said that a shot whistled close by his left ear and he hit the dirt as he had been trained to do. A second shot was fired close "over my head," and then he was confronted by a gunman in a blue policeman's uniform, without a hat, and with dirty hands, who kicked him and asked Arnold if he was filming, and then took his film away from him.

Arnold's testimony concerning a man in a policeman's uniform dovetails with an image in the Moorman photograph of a gunman in what appears to be a policeman's uniform ("Badgeman"). Next to him there appears to be a man in a railroad worker's shirt, and perhaps a hard hat. Shortly after the shooting some tramps were taken into custody from the railroad yards, and marched through the Plaza by some policemen. The manner of this "arrest" is far from any known police procedure. The policemen do not have the men in handcuffs, and are walking at some distance in front and behind the men in a casual manner, their shotguns held in anything but the prescribed manner.

An important witness was presented on the British show who was not allowed to give his testimony at the time of the assassination, perhaps because he was a deaf-mute, and they couldn't understand him. Ed Hoffman says that the FBI tried to pay him not to say anything more about what he saw. He was on the freeway with a good view into the area behind the picket fence and saw two men there, one of whom, wearing a black hat and a blue jacket, fired at the motorcade. The gunman passed his rifle to the other man and walked away. The second man disassembled it and put it in a tool box, and walked towards the railroad tracks.

Walter Cronkite claimed on the Nova show that the acoustical evidence was not proven due to the research of Steve Barber, a drummer, which was confirmed by the NAS panel showing that crosstalk with Sheriff Decker's voice can be heard during the shooting, Ergo: The tape cannot be authentic. Cronkite and these "experts" totally ignore the fact that the tape appears to be a copy and not the original, which would account for crosstalk, and the acoustical fingerprints of the forth shot on the recording completely match the acoustical fingerprints of the test shot from the Grassy Knoll made for the House Assassinations Committee. The fingerprint, or graph, does not match the other shots from the Depository. These fingerprints are according to incontrovertible laws of physics.

Twenty-five years ago the worst tragedy since Pearl Harbor

struck at the United States. It was a stunning blow that effected nearly everyone in America, and a large part of the world. The night of the tragedy, the big bell of Westminster Abbey in London tolled for one hour, as though the King or Queen had died. 300,000 people marched by torchlight in Berlin, and all radio programming was cancelled in Ireland. Every store in Paris closed up and the Champs Elysees was almost deserted on a Friday night. New York City came to a total stop, and churches in Baltimore and all across the nation filled up with people in mourning. The opera was canceled in Vienna. Thousands of people gathered on the lawn in front of Bethesda Naval Hospital in utter silence for hours. At the moment President Kennedy was pronounced dead, 68 % of all the people in the United States knew of the shooting, and shortly almost every single person in America knew of it and no-one would ever forget what they were doing at the moment they heard of his death. Nine out of ten people, according to studies, suffered deep grief. Four out of five people felt "the loss of someone very close and dear." As William Manchester wrote, it "was the most spectacular single American disaster since Pearl Harbor. An entire nation had been savaged, and the nation realized it." Half the people in America wept, and when the news penetrated the far flung corners of the Earth where Kennedy's humanity had been felt, an anguish spread that was not much dissipated by time. Even today one finds in the most remote places and countries portraits of President Kennedy. He was everyone's President. This is what that man meant to America and the world. Sean O'Casey wrote, "Peace, who was becoming bright-eyed, now sits in the shadow of death; her handsome champion has been killed. Her gallant boy is dead. We mourn here with you—poor sad American people." It was as though the entire nation of Ireland was destroyed that day.

Twenty-five years after President Kennedy was so brutally murdered, his passing was marked with many radio and television shows, magazine and newspaper articles, and books. Very many hundreds of people went to his grave in Washington and remembered his life and death, and a large group gathered at the spot where he was killed in Dallas, as happens there every year when a memorial service is conducted by Penn Jones, Jr. Many millions of people from all over the world have gone to his grave at Arlington National Cemetery over the past quarter of a century. It is therefore clear the great impact his life and death had on this country and the world, and how the man's memory lives, how stunned are the living and those who were not even alive then—even now by what they have lost.

Shortly after the murder, people began placing bouquets of flowers on the grass in the Plaza where he was shot. Soon so many flowers were there that the hillside was covered. Films of that poignant scene shown in the Fall of 1988 twenty-five years after he died still bring tears to the eyes, and we know just how much that man meant to us.

That is why we remember him and try to uncover the truth of his death, because the loss was so very great. As each year passes we know that loss is the greater and does not diminish with time. We lost a part of our hearts, and even the children who were not alive then know it and study his life and his death. Life goes on, but with regard to this obscene and brutal murder, the man we all know to have been very human, caring, flawed, and very funny, is forever gone in flesh, but not in our hearts, thoughts and minds. The fact that he was the nation's leader clearly is not what touched us the most. No other President's death since Lincoln so deeply effected the country. He had become a part of us all, and we loved him. The few that hated him killed him, but it is our love and the rapport he established with everyone that survives in our soul.

We close with the comments of two important people in this tragedy. On the Central TV program Dr. Cyril Wecht commented on the reason why the brain was not sectioned and studied as is supposed to have been done in an autopsy, and disappeared: "I am very suspicious and I think it's the height of a sinister activity in the post-assassination cover-up in this case, to make sure the brain was not examined. There could be no visualization of its interior. Its as if it never existed."

There is a certain symbolism in the taking of that man's brain. His brain is what they were afraid of. Cannibals ate the brains of their enemies to get some of their cunning. They forgot to take Kennedy's heart. That resides in all of us.

Paul O'Connor, one of the autopsy technicians at Bethesda Naval Hospital, said at the beginning of the broadcast that "There was a monstrous cover-up of everything. I know it, and so do the people who covered it up." We all know it.

STUNNING NEW EVIDENCE
IN THE JFK CASE

By Harrison E. Livingstone © 1998

On July 31, 1998, the Assassination Records Review Board (ARRB), a federal agency, released hundreds of pages of new interviews it had conducted with the doctors and other medically related personnel connected with the autopsy of President John F. Kennedy. After thirty-five years, we have more pieces of the puzzle. The statements of the witnesses corroborate the theory of alteration of the autopsy evidence put forward in my books. A sinister picture of tampering with the evidence lurks just beneath the surface as each witness describes missing photographs, missing X rays, the brain gone, and numerous photographs and X rays in the official record that are not what they saw during the autopsy. Someone or some agency played a massive shell game with the evidence, switching or destroying materials. Until I published four books arguing the alteration or destruction of the visual autopsy evidence, no one ever dared to suggest that the case had been faked. It was assumed that the official evidence was authentic. The JFK case was rather simple, once one understood that almost everything in it was fake.

The autopsy doctors could not recognize certain aspects of the photographs and X rays. They insisted that a number of photos and X rays are missing, and they maintained that the entrance wound in the back of the head is not shown in the photographs or X rays. The inventories do not add up.

After many years of thinking about those involved in the autopsy, it seems to me that the most credible witnesses are the FBI agents who were present. These men were trained and experienced criminal investigators and, like good cops, are able to see through people and ascertain the truth rather quickly. It was their job to make an outside record of the events that night, in spite of the possibility that J. Edgar Hoover, longtime director of the FBI, was involved in the plot to kill Kennedy and overthrow his administration. The recent testimony of the former FBI men is not in the interests of the deceased Hoover or the official story.

Former FBI men James W. Sibert and Francis X. O'Neill were qualified to make a record of what happened at the autopsy and have now commented at this late date on the conflicts that have arisen. Sibert was a bomber pilot and base operations commander in World War II[1] and had great experience with men and life. O'Neill has had vast executive experience in the FBI.

I wish to start with their testimony to the ARRB because it is so startling that they insist that something is radically wrong with the photos that show the back of the president's head. (Note that there was an entirely new focus in the 1996–8 investigation: the focus was on the question of authenticity of the autopsy materials because the task of the ARRB was to gather all available materials in the case and provide them to the National Archives, which was to open those materials for public inspection, except for the vital autopsy photos and X-rays that were excluded by the JFK Act. In the process, the chief investigator, Jeremy Gunn, attempted to determine the authenticity of the materials.

"If we could now look at the sixth view, which is described as the 'wound of entrance in right posterior occipital region.' Photograph No. 42. Mr. Sibert, does that photograph correspond to your recollection of the back of President Kennedy's head?"

"Well, I don't have a recollection of it being that intact, as compared with these other pictures. I don't remember seeing anything that was like this photo . . . That's why his head is raised here. It's been elevated, hasn't it? But still, that—that wound was back here. The hair looks like it's been straightened out and cleaned up more than what it was when we left the autopsy." The picture was taken before the autopsy began.

"Do you remember earlier in the deposition when I asked you if— when you observed the body immediately after the photography—photographs had been taken, if the hair had been cleaned or combed in any way? And as I recall, you said, no; that it still seemed pretty messy."

"During the rest of the autopsy, it did."

"So, does that photograph correspond to what you recall from the autopsy of President Kennedy?"

"From what I can recall, I didn't really see anything that was this 'neat'—I guess, is the best word to use—as compared with what I observed that night."

"I'm going to show you again the drawing that you made, No. 188—where you have drawn a wound, which just a moment ago you said was even larger than here."

"That's true, I'd like to redraw that. That's not large enough."

"But do you see anything that corresponds in Photograph No. 42 to what you observed during the night of the autopsy?"

"No. I don't recall anything like this at all during the autopsy. There was much—Well, the wound was more pronounced. And it looks like it could have been reconstructed or something, as compared with what my recollection was and those other photographs."

"Steve (Tilley), if we could look at No. 43, which is a very similar view. Again, this is a somewhat different exposure but a view of the same thing."

"I'd make the same statements relative to this photograph as I did for the other."

" . . . So, in conclusion, would it be fair to say that the photographs that we have been looking at from the sixth view do not correspond with what you observed on the night of the autopsy?"

"Right. These four. Again, I say, I was in error there. That was a much larger wound than that."

"Now you're referring to your exhibit No. 188."

"Right."

"And you think that the wound should have been much larger than the one that you drew."

"Yes."[2]

FRANCIS X. O'NEILL

Congressman Francis X. O'Neill, Jr., the former FBI man present with Sibert at the autopsy of President Kennedy, was equally emphatic about the photos showing the back of someone's head. (The reader is referred to my 1995 book, *Killing Kennedy and the Hoax of the Century*, Carroll & Graf, to study Dr. Pierre Finck's, the chief forensic specialist at the autopsy, powerful denunciation of the same photos to the HSCA investigators in 1977, which starts on page 36. This evidence was kept secret until I published it.) Interestingly, both former FBI men criticize Senator Arlen Specter of Pennsylvania, a counsel with the Warren Commission, who, along with then Congressman Gerald Ford, invented the "magic bullet theory," which both FBI men ridicule.[3]

O'Neill is shown the sixth view, or "wound of entrance in right posterior occipital region," Color Photograph No. 42. "I'd like to ask you whether that photograph resembles what you saw from the back of the head at the time of the autopsy?"

"This looks like it's been doctored in some way. Let me rephrase that, when I say 'doctored.' Like the stuff has been pushed back in, and it looks like more towards the end than at the beginning. All you have to do was put the flap back over here, and the rest of the stuff is all covered on up."

"Prior to the time the first incision was made, did you ever see that the hair had been cleaned, or combed, or pressed back in any way?"

"No, I don't recall if it did. No, I don't recall that." Then O'Neill is asked if the markings he made showing the placement of the wounds of entry and a large defect, on a drawing for the HSCA, were accurate. "Do you see the wounds that you identified in the drawings that you made in 1978 (Author's note: See page 348 of *Killing Kennedy*) on the autopsy Photograph 42, which is—again, we're looking at the wound of entrance."

"No, I don't see the wounds . . ." The fourth view, No. 38, which shows the posterior view of the wound, is shown to him. "Yeah, I can see it's the same way. It's very similar to it, yeah."

"Does the back of the head in Photograph No. 38—the one that's on your left now—does the head wound look like what you saw on the night of the autopsy?"

" . . . Quite frankly, I thought that there was a larger opening . . . in the back of the head."

" . . . But the views that you're seeing do not correspond exactly with what you recall?"

"I specifically do not recall those—I mean, being that clean or that fixed up. To me, it looks like these pictures have been . . . It would appear to me that there was a—more massive wound, such as the other photographs depicted. I'm not saying that these have been doctored or phonied up in any particular way at all. It just would appear to me—and I don't recall anybody going ahead and cleaning up that section, just for the sake of having the photographs taken."[4]

O'Neill is asked about the brain photographs and is shown the eighth view, or "basilar view of brain."

Gunn: "Can you identify that in any reasonable way as appearing to be the—what the brain looked like of President Kennedy?"

"No," O'Neill responds.

"In what regard does it appear to be different?"

"It appears to be too much."

"If you could elaborate a little bit on what you mean by 'it appears to be too much'?"

"Well, from this particular photograph here, it would seem that the only section of the brain which is missing is this small section over here. To me, that's not consistent with the way I recall seeing it. I do recall a large amount of what was identified to me as brain matter being on the back of Kellerman's jacket and Greer's jacket. And, to me, that was a larger portion than that section there. This looks almost like a complete brain."

He is shown another photograph of the brain, No. 50, "superior view of the brain."

"Does that look approximately the size of what you recall President Kennedy's brain being when it was removed from the cranium?"

"In all honesty, I can't say that it looks like the brain that I saw, quite frankly. As I described before, I did not recall it being that large. . . I don't recall it being that large. It could have been, but I can't swear on a stack of Bibles that it was."[5] For a picture of the superior surface of this brain, see the drawing on page 130 of 7 HSCA on the medical evidence. There is clearly very little brain missing.

O'Neill finds it odd that Kennedy's eyes are wide open in some pictures and nearly closed in others, a problem that was pointed out by numerous other observers. "In some, the eyes are open all the way. And in some of them, they're almost closed . . . It just seems a bit odd to me that this picture, they're—looks 100 percent wide open. Yet on some of the others, they don't look nearly that open at all." "Do you recall from the night of the autopsy whether the eyes were ever opened?" "Yes, I do. Yes, very much so. As I mentioned, I think, originally, and also in my notes that the eyes were open. This is the way it would look to me."[6]

JOHN T. STRINGER

John Stringer, the photographer at the autopsy, also commented on this: "Do you have any recollection as to whether the eyes of President Kennedy were open at any point during the autopsy?" "Yes." "Were they open at all points during the autopsy?" "Well, they kept trying to close them, and they'd open again."[7]

John T. Stringer, from Baltimore, is known in the official evidence as being the principal photographer (except for an assistant from the Navy Medical School). He insists that he was the only one taking photographs during the autopsy. He told the ARRB that some of his photographs were missing, a fact long established by doctors and other witnesses at the autopsy.

Stringer made clear that there were views of the brain that were not taken at the autopsy, and others were missing. Dr. James J. Humes, the principal pathologist who conducted the autopsy, stated most emphatically that at least three crucial photographs and some X-rays were missing.

Humes complained bitterly in the 1997 interview that no one knows what happened to the president's brain after he gave it to the president's personal physician, Admiral George G. Burkley. This was first discovered by Dr. Cyril Wecht, medical examiner of Pittsburgh, and later confirmed by the House Select Committee on Assassinations (HSCA).

It would seem that Stringer took the photographs we have in the official record today. "And did you take a basilar view of the brain?" "No."[8] "Mr. Stringer, if I remembered correctly from earlier testimony, you said that you had not recalled that there were any basilar photographs of the brain of President Kennedy. Can you identify whether the photographs that are in front of you now are basilar or superior views of a brain." "They're basilar." "If I recall correctly, earlier in your testimony, you said that there were identification cards that were used for identification of the brain when photographs were taken. Was that correct?" "Well, there's a ruler there, but there's no identification on there." "Based upon these being basilar views of a brain and based upon there being no identification cards, are you able to identify with certainly whether these photographs before you now are photographs of the brain of President Kennedy?"

"No, I couldn't say that they were President Kennedy's. I mean, there's no identification. All I know is, I gave everything to Jim Humes, and he gave them to Admiral Burkley." . . . "Mr. Stringer, during the course of the deposition you identified three different factors relating to photography of the brain that would suggest that you would have had an identification number in it; you would not have used a film pack; and you did not take a basilar view of the brain. Is that correct?" "Think so, yeah. Whether I took that, I don't know. But, see, this is from a film pack, because they are numbered. This is film number two, film number one, and three. And that's from a film pack . . . Because when it comes out of a holder, it is identified by the notch, because you have to load it in the holder with a notch." "So, the first three black and white negatives would, presumably, have been taken sequentially by a black and white film pack; is that correct?"

"Right. That's the way it was done."[9]

Are the major conflicts that are being brought out here a memory problem? Memory problems often come up in this material over many years, now thirty-five years after the tragedy, but one can put the recollections of the witnesses in order and collate them with all that is known and certain conclusions can safely be drawn by weighing this evidence. When numerous witnesses say the same things in conflict with the official story, we can bet on the witnesses, even though they may contradict themselves on some other points.

Stringer identifies the entry hole into the back of the head in one of the photos: "Are you able to identify the hole that the doctors identified on the night of the autopsy as being the entrance wound in the skull?" "I think this was a piece of bone, but it was down near there—right about there." "You're referring to what appears to be a piece of matter or something." "Yes." "That is near the hairline?" "Mm-hmm. But it was near there." "And you're certain that that's where the doctors identified the entrance wound as being; is that correct?" "Yeah, yeah, I would think so. That's what I remember."

"I'd like to point out the spot that appears somewhat red that is near the end of the ruler, and ask you whether that was an entrance wound, or whether the doctors during the night of the autopsy identified that as an entrance wound?"

"I don't think so, no."

"Do you know what that red spot is that appears to be, in layman's terms, near the cowlick?" "It looks like blood. I would say it was. There was blood all over the place. But I don't think it was anything out of the ordinary. I don't think there was a hole there for the bullet wound. You would have seen the hole." "Well, can you see the hole in any of the photographs that you're looking at?" "I haven't so far, no. But it was down, right about in here."[10]

Stringer can't explain why there are no identification tags in the autopsy photos. He is asked, "Mr. Stringer, I'd like you to look particularly closely at occipital area of President Kennedy's head in the color transparencies, and tell me whether you are able to ascertain whether there has been any change at all in the photograph from the time that you took the exposures on November 22—" "That's the way I saw it. I don't see any hole there." "Are you able to determine whether the color transparencies that are in front of you now are camera originals versus duplicates made from the camera original?" "I'd say they're camera original."[11]

"And do you have any recollection as to whether the hair was cleaned, cut, or wiped off in any way?" "I don't think it was ever cleaned, or cut, or wiped off." The discussion of the back of the head and apparent matting continues for several pages. "That's where they're trying to say it's been retouched."[12]

Stringer recalls that a picture of the body cavity is missing.[13] Discussing the 1966–7 inventories they did, he is asked, "Do you remember whether you had an opportunity to question the accuracy of anything in the documents?"

"We talked about there being missing photographs." Stringer mentions that the inventory is wrong. "That there were other photographs taken?" "Yes." "Another one that you had mentioned previously in your deposition was a full view of the body from above." "Yes." "And you don't see that photograph—" "No, I haven't seen it at all." "Would it be fair to say, then, that in the first inventory that we have record of, that was signed by you, a document dated November 22nd—that that inventory was incorrect? There were more photographs than were recorded on that inventory?" He agrees that both that list and the 1966 list of pictures taken at the autopsy are wrong. "I think Dr. Humes, also, says there were some taken up by the top of the lung area . . ." "Can you explain to me any reason why Drs. Humes, Boswell, and yourself would have signed this statement in 1966, saying that it's a complete inventory, if you had reason to believe it was not a complete inventory?" "No." "Did anyone tell you to sign it?" "I don't know. I know we did talk about all of the pictures that were exposed were not there, because I brought up a thing about Captain Stover and his receipt of that."[14] Unless much of the autopsy was invented. The family provided a good cover, since they didn't want a complete butchering.

It is pretty frightening to hear this comment throughout these new transcripts: "The photographs that you've looked at so far are all of the photographs that we have at the Archives that are purported camera originals taken during the night of the autopsy."[15] He is then asked if he can remember other views that aren't present and he describes some. So what happened to the missing pictures? If this stuff is merely falling through the cracks, if the case could be explained in terms of the fallibility of man, that is one thing, but the real reason is far more sinister than clerks sitting over at the Archives playing cards with this material. The transcript of Stringer's deposition is 228 pages in length and undoubtedly holds more valuable information than I can provide in a paper less lengthy than a book. The work product of the Board with several depositions of this length does not make for a quick study.

Stringer was asked by Douglas Horne if he "could tell us what President Kennedy's head looked like when it was unwrapped." "It was covered with matted blood. There was a fist-sized hole in the right side of his head above his ear." "Please describe which happened first, X rays or photography, and describe how you went about doing the photography." "X rays were taken first. They were then developed, and read right there in the morgue before I did anything. About one hour elapsed between the time the X rays were taken and the time the first photos were taken."[16] That is a crucial hour, with the room cleared of witnesses. Some doctor might have searched for bullets without anyone knowing what was happening, and it appears that much more of the head was damaged than had been observed in Dallas. Was this the "Ball peen hammer incident"?

"Was the hair washed or combed or rearranged in any way?"

"Nothing was done to clean the body or comb the hair before I started taking photographs. Some of the hair might have been slightly moved while X rays were taken, but nothing was washed or combed . . . I first took a full-body photo from above the body after the wrappings were removed. I did this standing on a ladder, still using the tripod mount. The tripod is just raised higher than usual in this case. Then I moved in and started taking close-up photos as directed by Dr. Humes."[17] Stringer confirms that a wound was probed: "The probe was inserted in the throat wound in the front of the neck." This is the first time we hear this. Is he merely trying to help out the doctors, or did he actually see it?

"Please describe the photography of the brain, including who was

present." "Well, Drs. Humes and Boswell were there, as well as a corpsman. The brain was sectioned, like a piece of meat, and the sections
showed all of the damage. Each section was laid out on a light box,
which provided a white background in the photos, with an autopsy tag
or card next to it with the autopsy number on it."[18] We have the words of
the supplementary autopsy report: "In the interest of preserving the
specimen coronal sections are not made."[19] And we have the quotes in
this paper describing a slice of the brain on view at the Armed Forces
Institute of Pathology.

"When you helped conduct the Inventory at the National Archives in
1966, were you of the belief then that some photos were missing (and how
many)?" "Yes, we all did, and I know we discussed that with each other.
I think about six to eight photos were missing, something like that." And
he tells us that there were no empty film holders, so that wasn't the reason. There is no photograph of the body taken from a ladder, either.

"The photographs we have viewed from the present collection at
the National Archives do not show autopsy tags in the field of view. Did
you use autopsy tags when you took the whole set of photographs?" "It
would have been standard practice to do this; I think we did. I don't
specifically recall for sure but I think we did, particularly on the close-
ups. They might have been cropped out of the prints. I do remember laying autopsy tags next to the sections of the brain when I photographed
those." "Were photos taken throughout the autopsy, and what time did
you finish? Did you stay for the embalming?" "Yes, throughout the
autopsy. We stayed for almost the entire embalming. I don't think I got
home until 4 A.M. We took no photos during or after the embalming."
"Did anyone else take pictures during the autopsy?" "No. And I can't
see how anyone could have shot any other photos."

DR. PIERRE FINCK

Dr. Finck, after trying to blow the whistle on the fake photos,[20] still had
something of substance to add, evidently exhausted by age, interrogations, committees, commissions, boards, "buffs," and colleagues: "At
the time that you completed the autopsy of President Kennedy, did you
believe that the standards as set forth in the autopsy manual had been
satisfied for the autopsy of President Kennedy?"

"You mean at the time the autopsy was completed?"

"Yes."

"I didn't—I did not ask myself the question. We examined the wounds and there were questions answered following the autopsy. It was clear that there was a wound of entry in the upper back, but it is, thanks to Dr. Humes, that next morning he found out there was a wound in the front of the neck. At the time of the autopsy, we did not see the exit in the front of the neck. For the head it was clear, but for the neck it was not, so this was clarified the next day. So to answer your question, at the time the autopsy was completed, there was still no answer. It shows once more that you have to wait for certain things to be put together." Notice how the wound in the neck, described by the surgeons in Dallas as a wound of entrance (and they are the only witnesses) is converted to a wound of exit?! "Do you believe that everything that was done, everything that should have been done during the time of the autopsy on President Kennedy, was in fact done during the autopsy? Was there any procedure, for example, that should have been performed that was not performed?"

"The removal of the organs of the neck. In my training we were trained to remove the organs of the neck. And in this particular case, they were not removed." "Isn't that particularly important in the autopsy of President Kennedy in the sense that there is believed to have been a wound that went through the neck?" "Yes." "And isn't it important in a medical/legal autopsy to be able to track the course of a bullet through the body?" "Yes." He then explains that they tried to probe the wound in the upper back but failed, as is well known. "From what I recall, we stated the probing was unsuccessful. That's all I can remember." "My question is did you find any evidence during the course of the autopsy that would link the wound in the upper back to the exit wound in the throat?" "I don't recall." "Do you recall anyone during the course of the autopsy suggesting that the bullet wound in the upper back might have exited from the throat?" "I don't remember." There immediately follows a discussion about moving body landmarks used in the autopsy report when fixed body landmarks should have been used. "So that the mastoid process would not be a standard fixed body landmark for the purposes of identifying the location of a wound in the thoracic region, is that fair to say?" "Yes."[21]

They look at the death certificate signed by the president's personal physician, Dr. George Burkley, and Gunn asks about what Burkley wrote: "Do you see the reference there to the third thoracic vertebra?" "Yes." "For the purpose of locating a wound in the back, would the third thoracic vertebra be considered to be a fixed body landmark?" "Yes." "Was Dr. Burkley correct in identifying the posterior back wound as being at the level of the third thoracic vertebra?" "I don't know." "Did you make any attempt during the night of the autopsy to locate the upper back entry wound with any vertebra?" "I don't recall." "Is there any reason that you would not have attempted to locate the back wound in connection with a vertebra?" "No."[22]

The discussion turned to the measurements and weights that should have been recorded during the autopsy, and were not. "Should the brain have been weighed before it was put in formalin? . . . Is it standard autopsy practice when the brain is removed in an autopsy to weigh a brain—" "Yes." "Before it is put in formalin?" "Yes." "Is there a reason that that was not—the brain weight was not recorded for President Kennedy?" "I don't know." "Do you recall whether the brain was weighed before it was put in formalin?" "No, I don't." . . .

"Are there any weights of any organs of the neck that appear on the autopsy face sheet?" "I don't see organs of the neck on that autopsy face sheet . . . So you mean we removed organs of the neck?" "You removed organs—" "Oh, they were not removed, the organs of the neck. I know so."[23]

The point is that the brain ended up weighing more than an average male brain, and the liver weighed 1,000 grams less than a normal male liver, which is 1,650 grams. Either a "1" was dropped when they fudged the weights and intended to write in 1,650 grams, or he had a very small liver, which is possible. Jaundice can cause the liver to shrink, and certainly Kennedy appeared at times to have an abnormal color. He might also have contracted malaria in the South Pacific during World War II.

Another issue is discussed when it appears that the brain was not examined extensively enough to surmise the path of bullets in its fresh state, just after removal from the body.[24] Finck does argue that the X-rays of the brain, taken before his arrival, might have given more information about bullet pathways.[25]

Dr. Finck is very firm that the entry into the back of the head was precisely where they placed it at the time of the autopsy, 2.5 cm to the right and slightly above the external occipital protuberance.[26]

They examined the X-rays at the 1996 deposition and looked at the anterior/posterior view and began discussing the 6.5 mm object that the Clark Panel found to be on the outer table of the skull at the back (see discussion in this book and those of Dr. Mantik in my last book): "Are you able to determine yourself right now whether this X ray is an X ray of President Kennedy?" "No." "I would like to draw your attention to a portion, to an object that is on the right hemisphere that is circular in shape, reasonably prominent there (indicating) . . . Do you know what that object is?" "I don't. It's a radiopaque object, opaque to X rays." "Do you recall at the time of President Kennedy's autopsy being made aware of an object, radiopaque object in his head that would be commensurate with the dimensions of that object as it appears in the X ray?" . . . "If I remember an object being of approximately that size?" "Yes." "I don't." "Does that object as it appears seem to you to be larger or no different from the types of bullet fragments that were removed from President Kennedy?" . . . "I don't. But that doesn't mean I didn't see it. It means I don't recall." They look at the right lateral view of the skull X ray (No. 2): "Do you recall this X ray as having been an X ray taken at the autopsy of President Kennedy?" "I don't." "Do you recall in any X rays of President Kennedy there being a radiopaque show trail that crossed from the X ray left to right?" "No, I don't recall." "From this X ray of President Kennedy, are you able to identify the approximate location of an entrance wound in the skull?" "I don't." "Is it surprising to you at all that you would not be able to identify an entrance wound in the skull?" "No, because it is a different type of evidence. I have looked at wounds. I was able to identify entry and exit when looking at wounds." "So it wouldn't be unusual not to be able to identify an entrance wound from an X-ray of the skull? Is that a fair statement?" "Yes."[27]

About this linear "snow" trail of dustlike tiny fragments commented upon in the 1963 autopsy report as leading from the small hole of entry in the back of the head low down to the hairline to the forward part of the head, it now is across the very top of the head, quite some distance above the four-inches-higher position of the new hole of entry discovered by the Clark Panel in 1968. Both the 1968 higher entry and the higher "snow" trail did not exist in 1963.

It is interesting that Dr. Finck does not recognize the linear, very directional (as Dr. David Mantik calls it) "snow" trail of tiny fragments at all—that it has apparently moved several inches higher to the top of the head, and may never have been present in the first place. How could a military jacketed bullet break up in this fashion? It must have been some other type of missile such as a soft-nosed bullet.

Mantik explained to me that the largest of the tiny fragments is at the back of the head, indicating a shot from in front. Mantik is not only a radiation oncologist, but also a professor of physics, and his training tells us that the larger bullet fragments contain the most energy and therefore travel the farthest in the head. He also feels that this is not just an "explosion" in the head, as the doctors call it, but delineates a bullet track across the top of the brain because it is so "directional" and linear.

The autopsy report put it this way: "Roentgenograms of the skull reveal multiple minute metallic fragments along a line corresponding with a line joining the above-described small occipital wound and the right supra-orbital ridge." This, obviously, cannot be the line we now see starting from the front of the head and moving backward. So, it becomes an "explosion" and not the linear path of a bullet in the new interviews because the doctors know damn well that it doesn't begin at the entry hole they identified low down in the head.

THE ORIGIN OF THE AUTOPSY PHOTOGRAPHS

In a major surprise in the case, Saundra K. Spencer, a trained autopsy photographer,[28] who was the Navy technician who processed the color autopsy film at Anacostia brought by Secret Service agent James K. Fox and Robert Knudsen, states that none of the official autopsy photographs presently in the National Archives corresponds to anything she developed and printed a few days after the autopsy. After being shown each autopsy photograph, she insisted that she had never seen any of them.[29] Knudsen was in reality her direct supervisor.[30]

This means that there is no chain of evidence for the present set of pictures in the Archives and that their origin is unknown. In other words, James K. Fox brought undeveloped films (the Secret Service lab in the EOB could not process color photographs) to the Navy photo center on November 27, returned with the color positives on December 9, and left with prints, while someone played an elaborate shell game with the pictures, which breaks the chain of evidence. All the official records state that the film he brought, had processed, and left with on those dates were the present official photographs. *They are not according to the woman who printed them.* In addition, as described below, the film from the autopsy was actually brought to Anacostia the day after the autopsy, on November 23rd,[31] and the memo described in item No. 9 of the April 26, 1965, transfer from Evelyn Lincoln's (JFK's secretary) inventory from Lt. V. Madonia to SS Agent Fox, dated 29 November 1963, are missing from the National Archives.[32]

SAUNDRA SPENCER

"She said that on November 23, 1963, the day after the assassination, probably in the afternoon, a Federal agent whom she believes was named 'Fox' arrived at the NPC Quarterdeck and she went down to escort him up to the still photography lab. Fox delivered to her 3 or 4 duplex film holders which contained 6 to 8 sheets of film; she said this film was color negatives. She was positive this film was color negatives, not color positive transparencies." Normally, only Knudsen tasked her, taking film to her and directing her work. "She said that Vince Madonia did not help with this processing job, and that as far as she knew, Chief Knudsen did not accompany agent Fox during Fox's visit; she also said that this one visit on November 23 was the only photographic event related to autopsy photography in which she participated."[33] She described the images she saw: "Views were 'body shots,' and not like the normal autopsy photographs she had experience with from her previous duty at Pensacola, in that there was no one in the background, and she does not remember any instruments in the photographs; the views were also unlike other autopsy photographs she had seen, in that the body of the President was 'very clean,' explaining that there was 'no blood and no gore' visible; she remembered no measuring devices visible either; no identification tags or cards visible in any of the photos; a wound at the base of the front of the President's neck which was circular, and about the size of the round end of a person's thumb; she remembers a wound in the back of the President's head which she described as a 'blown out chunk' about 2 to 2.5 inches wide located in about the center of the back of the President's head, about 3 or 4 inches above the hairline at the back of his head; the top of the head was not visible in the photos, so she said she could therefore not tell us whether there was any damage to the top of the head; she remembered no damage to the right side of the President's head; she said that the people helping her were junior to her in rank, and remembered the name of one" (Carol Ann Bonito) as helping her develop the autopsy photos.[34]

Spencer also said that one test print was made of each image, and then one print, "So would it be fair to say that, at maximum, there were two prints made of each negative?" "That is correct."[35] Filters were used, and 8" × 10" prints were made of each image. Fox stuck to her "like glue" while she worked (presumably, then, he was in the lab), and took everything when he left. She said that in her division, color positive transparencies were never developed. She did not see any color transparencies on November 23, 1963, nor did she subsequently hear of any autopsy photography on color transparency film.[36]

Why, on November 27, would the Secret Service have only negatives and color positives made from the film and no prints until a few days later (black and white prints in their own labs, and color prints made at Anacostia December 9)? If they wanted to leave a false trail leading to Anacostia for a different set of pictures—different from the ones we now have, which we know to have among them some that were altered, it may be that the two weeks in the official record between processing undeveloped film and making color prints was the period in which the alterations were made. It makes no sense that they would merely develop the unprocessed film and not make prints on November 27, 1963, unless, perhaps, they were going to be altered.

Even though the official record shows no record of processing the autopsy films prior to November 27, the films were processed at both Anacostia and in the Secret Service photo lab in the Executive Office Building the day after the assassination. An elaborate shell game is being played with the photos, and the purpose becomes evident when the various versions of the pictures were soon seen—all over Washington. A sophisticated propaganda and disinformation game was at work. One person saw one thing; another was shown contradictory pictures. In one of my books I describe how I repeatedly spoke to people who knew of others who privately possessed sets of the autopsy photos.

JOE O'DONNELL

One of the White House photographers in 1963, Joe O'Donnell, worked with Robert Knudsen, the chief White House photographer. Knudsen showed O'Donnell two different versions of the same photograph: one showed a photograph of the president's head with a hole evident, and another showed a photograph of the president's head without a hole evident.[37] Knudsen, who worked for five presidents, accompanied Secret Service agent Fox to Anacostia at least twice to process films and prints. According to his own testimony to the HSCA, he was sent to Bethesda the day after the assassination.[38]

O'Donnell was interviewed by the Board and he confirmed that Knudsen showed him autopsy photographs of President Kennedy. "Mr. O'Donnell was a government photographer, employed by USIA in 1963, who was frequently detailed to the White House to perform various photographic tasks during the Kennedy Administration . . . Within the week after President Kennedy's assassination, on two occasions Robert Knudsen showed him autopsy photographs of President Kennedy. On the first occasion, he was shown approximately 12 ea 5" × 7" B & W photos. The views included the President lying on his back, on his stomach, and clasps of the back of the head. He said that the back-of-the-head photograph(s) showed a hole in the back of the head, about 2" above the hairline, about the size of a grapefruit; the hole clearly penetrated the skull and was very deep. Another one of the photographs showed a hole in the forehead above the right eye which was a round wound about ⅜" in diameter which he interpreted as a gunshot wound.

"The second occasion occurred a few days later, when Knudsen showed him a second set of photographs, once again about 12 ea 5" × 7" B & W prints. On this second occasion, the back-of-the-head photograph(s) was intact, and showed no hole in the back of the head. Instead of a hole, he remembers seeing neatly combed hair which looked slightly wet, or damp in appearance. Another photograph he remembers showed President Kennedy lying on his back, with an aluminum probe emerging from his stomach or right side.

"He said it was his impression that Knudsen had taken the photographs himself, but that he had never specifically asked him that question. He said he never discussed with Knudsen the apparent discrepancy between the two back-of-the-head photos.

"He said Jacqueline Kennedy told him, in response to his questions about her apparent attempt to 'escape' from the limousine in Dallas during the assassination, that she was not trying to escape, but rather was trying to retrieve a part of President Kennedy's head from the back of the limousine (i.e., the trunk lid)."[39] This man, O'Donnell, had attended MIT, was a Marine combat photographer in World War II, and photographed wounded men and observed gunshot wounds. He was sent to Hiroshima and Nagasaki to take pictures on the ground, and as a result was so affected by radiation that he had to walk with two canes and a damaged spine and could not stand up straight. All of his WW II photos were "lost" by the government, and he well knew that power.

During a second interview with the Board, "O'Donnell said he remembers a photograph of a gaping wound in the back of the head which was big enough to put a fist through, in which the image clearly showed a total absence of hair and bone, and a cavity which was the result of a lot of interior matter missing from inside the cranium. He said that another image showed a small round hole above the President's right eye, which he interpreted as an entry wound made by the same bullet which exited from the large wound in the back of the head."

It was O'Donnell who showed the Zapruder film to Jacqueline Kennedy at a private screening at the USIA building a few weeks after the assassination. No one else was present. "He said that following her viewing of the head shot sequence in the film, Jacqueline Kennedy told him in a very forceful way, 'I don't ever want to see that again,' which he said that he interpreted as an order to alter the film so as to remove the offending images of the head shot—namely, a halo of debris around the President's head. He told us he knows it was wrong, but that he removed about ten feet of film from the Zapruder film." O'Donnell was under the impression that he had the original film.[40]

He feels it was his suggestion to Jackie Kennedy that resulted in her decision to bury John Kennedy on the hill by the Lee mansion at Arlington. O'Donnell told her that Jack said that he could "live up here forever" and she said, when O'Donnell told her this, "then that is where we will put him."

THE SECRET SERVICE

When questions began to be asked about the sequence of events and the chain of evidence, the Secret Service chief, James J. Rowley, whose agency had custody of the autopsy materials from November 22, 1963, to April 26, 1965, prepared a statement that was given to Barefoot Sanders, Assistant Attorney General at the Department of Justice, on 23

February 1967. "On or about November 27, Bouck handed the photographic film to James J. Fox, U.S. Secret Service, and instructed Fox to take the photographic film to the U.S. Navy Photographic Laboratory. Fox took the photographic film to the U.S. Navy Photographic Laboratory on or about November 27, 1963. The black and white film was processed, black and white negatives were developed, and color positives were made from the colored film. The processing and development was done by Lt. V. Madonia, U.S. Navy . . . A few days later, black and white prints were made by Fox in the Secret Service photographic laboratory. On or about December 9, 1963, at the direction of Mr. Bouck, Fox took the colored positives back to the U.S. Navy Photographic Laboratory and observed while enlarged color prints were made."[41] Saundra Spencer was the woman who processed the color prints at Anacostia for Madonia.

The Secret Service did not want to admit that the black and white films were developed the day after the autopsy in the Secret Service's own lab in the Executive Office Building.[42] It seems to me that copies of the initial photographs were retouched and doctored to show different things to different people. There have been other examples in the JFK case of conflicting affidavits and reports with the same signature on both. I, along with Steve Barber and others, saw two completely different autopsy photographs of the right side of the head.

Although Fox recalled only one or two sets of prints being made,[43] Knudsen told Andrew Purdy at the HSCA that seven sets was more likely.[44]

If the record compiled by Mark Crouch—a friend of Fox—is correct, Fox was the originator of one set of black and white photographs corresponding to what we now have in the National Archives, but which were secretly produced somewhere else, perhaps in the Secret Service lab at the Executive Office Building. These black and white prints were later colorized and rephotographed. These are the photographs whose authenticity I brought into question in 1976. The Fox set of pictures spread rapidly throughout the JFK research community after 1988 and were widely published. They are apparently identical to those in the National Archives.

SPENCER AGAIN

Spencer said that the photos she processed showed no blood or "opening cavities" and that the wounds were small. "It was quite reverent in how they handled it."[45] It would appear that this set of pictures was merely a false trail and was rapidly faked in the intervening days and brought to her for printing so that the real photo lab work would remain secret.

"Did you ever see any other photographic material related to the autopsy in addition to what you have already described?" "Just, you know, when they came out with some books and stuff later that showed autopsy pictures and stuff, and I assumed that they were done in—you know, down in Dallas or something, because they were not the ones that I had worked on." "Can you describe for me what you saw as best you can recollect?" "Briefly, they were very what I consider pristine for an autopsy. There was no blood or opening cavities, or anything of that nature. It was quite reverent in how they handled it." "If I can just ask for some clarification. Do you mean that the body appeared to be clean, had been washed? Is that what you are suggesting?" "Yes." "And that was different from what you had seen in other autopsy photographs, is that right?" "Yes. In other autopsies, they have the opening of the cavity and the removing of vital organs for weighing and stuff of this nature. The only organ that I had seen was a brain that was laid beside the body." "And that was in the photograph of President Kennedy?" "Yes." "So there was a brain in the photograph beside the body, is that correct?" "Well, yes, by the side of the body, but it didn't appear that the skull had been cut, peeled back and the brain removed. None of that was shown. As to whose brain it was, I cannot say." . . . "Did you see any photographs that focused principally on the head of President Kennedy?" "Right. They had one showing the back of the head with the wound at the back of the head." "Could you describe what you mean by the back of the head?" "It appeared to be a hole, inch, two inches in diameter at the back of the skull here." "You pointed to the back of your head. When you point back there, let's suppose that you were lying down on a pillow, where would the hole in the back of the head be in relationship to the part of the head that would be on the pillow if the body is lying flat?" "The top part of the head." "When you say the 'top of the head,' now is that the part that would be covered by a hat that would be covering the top of the head?" "Just about where the rim would hit." She described a wound at the base of the front of the neck. "Do you remember approximately how large that injury was?" "Just about the size of like your thumb pressed in." "What is your best recollection of the approximate size of the wound on the throat that you identified before?" "Just about like that, just like a finger, half-inch . . . It appeared clean, pristine, it wasn't an immediate wound, it had some cleaning done to it or something."[46]

"Tell me whether you can identify the color transparency of View No. 1 and Image No. 29, as having seen that before."

"No." "In what respect is the image No. 29 different from what you previously saw?" "Like I said, there was none of the blood and matted hair."[47] The reader is referred to the transcript at the end of this book for the rest of her responses for all of the autopsy photos, which is one of the most startling revelation in the history of this nation. She did not identify a single one of the pictures she was shown as being those she processed on November 23, 1963, and in fact described entirely different pictures.

But one question, which has come up with other witnesses, is, "Do you recall whether there was a metal holder for the head on the images that you developed?" "I don't remember a metal holder."[48]

"Could you look at the back of the print and see whether that paper corresponds to the image that you brought with you today, please." "No." "It doesn't correspond. So, the paper that these prints are printed on is not the paper that you were using at NPC in November, 1963, is that correct?" "Correct."[49]

"Could you look at the place on the back of President Kennedy's head that corresponds to where you identified a wound in the back of the head. Do you see that wound present in these photographs?"

"No, I do not."

"Would this view have shown the wound that you previously saw in the photographs of President Kennedy's head?"

"Yes. The wound that I saw would have been approximately in this area."

"If we described that as very roughly the cowlick area, would that be fair to say?"

"Yes."[50]

"In terms of the locations of the wound, do you see any differences or similarities with those that you developed in November 1963?" "No, there is no similarity."[51]

One of the pictures she described was a view of the body with the brain lying alongside it on the table.[52] Nothing like this is in the official evidence, and the brain was removed and placed in a can with formalin soon after the autopsy began. It is doubtful that such a picture would have been posed, and it is irrational that the Kennedy family or widow would have such pictures made. Other cameras were not allowed into the room, but statements previously published suggest that Lt. Commander William Bruce Pitzer, chief of the audiovisual department at the hospital, was in fact filming the autopsy from the gallery.[53]

"Ms. Spencer, you have now had an opportunity to view all of the colored images, both transparencies and prints, that are in the possession of the National Archives related to the autopsy of President Kennedy. Based upon your knowledge, are there any images of the autopsy of President Kennedy that are not included in those views that we saw?"

"The views that we produced at the Photographic Center are not included."(author's italics)

"Let's start with a conjecture as to whether the photographs that you developed, and the photographs that you observed today, could have been taken at different times."

"I would definitely say they were taken at different times."[54]

She says that the pictures she developed must have been taken later, and " . . . there had to be some massive cosmetic things done to the President's body." When were they taken, before or after the present official set? "I would say probably afterwards." "So you would think that the photographs that you developed were taken after reconstruction of the body?" "Yes."

"In the photograph that you saw in November of 1963, with the brain lying next to the body, were you able to observe whether there had been any damage to the brain?"

"No, it was not damaged as this brain, as the brain on these photographs were."[55] She was viewing the official set that everyone, by now, has seen. Her theory was that a second set of pictures was shot for public release, if necessary. Yet, there is not a scrap of evidence for such pictures having been taken after the autopsy. There was, however, a rumor of a fresh brain having been taken to the autopsy.

Another major discrepancy turns up at the end of her deposition: "This is in reference to a document that is labeled Exhibit MD 121, that appears on its face to be a cover sheet and a memorandum signed by James Fox dated February 16, 1967 . . . Can you tell me anything that you perceive in the document either to be accurate . . . or inaccurate and different from what your own recollection is?"

"During the time that I saw Agent Fox, he did not have any black and white film with him. The only thing he had in his possession was color film, and he remained with us while we processed it and printed it. It was not printed on different days."

"Mr. Fox says that this happened on November 27th, 1963, which would be approximately five days after the assassination. Does that correspond with your recollection as to when he came to—or when an agent came to the NPC [Naval Photographic Center]?" "No. My recollection was before the burial of President Kennedy." "And in the statement by Agent Fox, he refers to color positives. From what you have said before, that would not be—" "No." "—correspond with what you yourself observed, is that correct?" "Right. The only thing that we processed was color negative material." "Mr. Fox also refers to going with Chief Robert Knudsen. You knew Mr. Knudsen, is that correct?" "Yes. Chief Knudsen was our liaison boss between the White House and the Photographic Center, he was not with the agent when the agent came, and if he was in the building, he would have come up." "So to the extent that Mr. Fox is correct in what he makes on the statement, this is not the event that you yourself witnessed, would that be fair to say?" "That is correct."[56]

MRS. ROBERT KNUDSEN

The widow of former White House photographer Robert Knudsen stated that her husband told her he had "photographed the autopsy of President Kennedy." This new information seems not only incredible but also impossible. He also told her that the Secret Service had destroyed the film. Mark Crouch has said that Fox told him that a Secret Service executive burned many of the autopsy photos and X-rays.

Gloria Knudsen told ARRB investigator Douglas Horne that "one of the former Navy people she called said that he did recall one particular photo which showed the back of the President's head 'blown out.' I asked her to recall as precisely as she could whether this person said 'back of the head' or 'top of the head,' and she said the person to whom she spoke last week definitely said the 'back' of the head was blown out in the photograph he sighted. She told me that her husband told her on

one occasion that he knew who had had custody of the autopsy photographs, and that he therefore could deduce who had been responsible
for some of them disappearing, but that he was not going to stick his
neck out, because he had a family to protect. She also reiterated her husband's firm belief that the photographs of the back of the head which
show it to be intact were forgeries."

Mrs. Knudsen had more to say, describing a burglary of her house
shortly after her husband testified to the HSCA, and she wondered if
there was a connection between the two events. "She somewhat cryptically reminded me that her husband was a man who did not talk much,
and who very reliably could keep secrets, and told me that sometimes
people in the military are required to 'take secrets to the grave' with
them, when ordered to do so by competent authority, regardless of what
attempts are later made to get them to talk."

The paragraph following the above tells us how some people interfere with witnesses: "I asked Gloria Knudsen if she knew how Dr.
Randy Robertson found her, and she said that he told her he got the
information from the Review Board. I told her that this was patently
untrue—that we were forbidden from violating privacy in this manner
and that we had not shared her address or telephone number with anyone, nor had we shared the contents of her ARRB interview with anyone. She said Dr. Robertson also represented himself as the only person
with access to the JFK autopsy materials in the Archives, but that she did
not believe that."[57] At this point she was too scared to give to the Board
the names of her Navy friends who could verify the story of her husband
and the autopsy photographs.

Knudsen told the Board that her husband worked for five presidents
from Truman to Nixon as White House photographer; said her husband
felt extremely close to President Kennedy, and was emotionally broken
by the assassination; said her husband would never lie, was a deep
thinker, and was an extremely intelligent person who always carefully
measured his words.

She also told the Board that her husband " . . . had participated in
another investigation into the assassination which she thought the public knew nothing about, and said she would bring the letter which invited
him to appear in this forum with her to ARRB . . . All family members
agreed that he had met Air Force One at Andrews, accompanied the official motorcade to Bethesda, and had photographed the autopsy of Pres-

ident Kennedy. He had told them it was the hardest thing he had ever had to do in his life, in the emotional sense, since he reportedly had a brotherly relationship with President Kennedy. All 3 family members said that they did not see their father for 3 days after he left the house (i.e., until after the funeral on November 25, 1963), with the exception of Saturday, November 23, 1963 when they were allowed to view the casket lying in state in the East Room of the White House, where Mr. Knudsen was working that day."

Family members said that Knudsen witnessed and photographed probes inserted in the president's body that left no doubt of the number and direction of bullet trajectories; his father testified to the HSCA that there was more than one probe inserted into the body at once;[58] son Bob thought that his father had described three probes in the body (two in the thorax/neck, and one in the head).

" . . . They all claimed their father told them that he was the only one in the morgue with a camera, and believed he was the only person to photograph the autopsy.

"The Secret Service took his film from him as soon as he had exposed the various pieces of film, which he thought strange, since he was personally acquainted with the agent and thought that the agent trusted him;

"After he appeared before the HSCA in 1978, he told his family (at different times) that 4 or 5 of the pictures he was shown by the HSCA did not represent what he saw or took that night, and that one of the photographs he viewed had been altered. His son Bob said that his father told him that 'hair had been drawn in' on one photo to conceal a missing portion of the top-back of President Kennedy's head;

"All three family members agreed that Mr. Knudsen appeared before an official government body again sometime in 1988, about 6 months before he died in January, 1989. They all had the impression that it was 'on Capitol Hill,' and that it may have been a congressional inquiry of some kind. They were unanimous that Mr. Knudsen came away from this experience very disturbed, saying that 4 photographs were 'missing,' and that one was 'badly altered.' Mrs. Gloria Knudsen used the phrase 'severely altered' regarding the one altered photograph when recounting her husband's statements afterwards. She further elaborated that the wounds he saw in the photos shown him in 1988 did not represent what he saw or took. He also told them that some of the details in the room in the background of the photos were wrong. He had recounted that this experience was a waste of time for him because as soon as he would answer a question consistent with what he remembered, he would immediately be challenged and contradicted by people whom he felt already had their minds made up.

"Mr. Knudsen expressed skepticism with his daughter Terri over the years about the conclusions of the Warren Report in regard to the President's wounds and the manner in which he was shot, because of the observations he had made the night of the autopsy."[59]

ROBERT KNUDSEN

Much of this is credible. The problem is the official record that cites Stringer as the medical photographer, and that there are no photographs showing the probes in the body. But the room was cleared at various times for X rays to be taken. It has always seemed to me plausible that the autopsy was worked in shifts, and perhaps Knudsen was brought in to take pictures when material witnesses were gone, thus some sort of charade was acted out with other "doctors" probing the body, when he was taking pictures.

Knudsen was clear in his HSCA testimony recollecting long probes stuck in the body, which were photographed. Indeed, such photos or X-rays showing these probes were described in the Bob Richter memorandum connected to the CBS investigation.[60] Knudsen was dead soon after the secret "investigation" where he evidently talked too much. When testifying to HSCA investigators, Knudsen said, "If the prints were examined, and then I would not be in the spot that I am, that I am sworn not to disclose it. It would give a very definitive answer to you as to the number of probes."[61]

Later, Knudsen is asked, "Are you confident now that you saw metal probes in the photographs?" "Yes." "Are you confident that the metal probes were actually through the wounds when you saw them?" "Yes, I am certain of that, because it showed the point of entry and exit with the probe." . . . "I am certain on the Kennedy there were the probes showing the point of entry and exit." "How many probes were there that you saw in a given picture at one time?" "I know there were two." "Two metal probes that were through wounds when you saw them?" "Yes."[62] "I said the minimum was two." "What was the most?" "Over this period of time, I am not certain. It seems to me that there were three in one picture, but this I will not state for sure."[63] Three would be too many shots for the rifle and assassin, as one of the shots he fired was a miss.

"Where did they enter and where did they exit?" "One was right near the neck and out the back." "The front of the neck and out the back of the neck?" "The point of entry-exit." "The metal probe extended from the front of the neck to the back of the neck?" "One was through the chest cavity." "Did it go all the way through?" "Yes. It seems to me that the entry point was a little bit lower in the back—well, the point in the back was a little bit lower than the point in the front. So the probe was going diagonally from top to bottom, front to back . . . Right about where the neck-tie is."

"Approximately how much lower than that would you say the other probe, which went through the chest cavity?" "I would put it six, seven inches." "From the side view, you saw both probes?" "Right." "You just indicated where the probe came out, on the lower—" "It seemed to me that it was right around mid chest." "The probe that you said you could see coming out of the neck, the front of the neck, where was it out of the back of the neck? How high up would you say that one was?" "About the base of the neck."[64] Knudsen is shown the photos, which he recognizes are not originals, and points to the tracheotomy incision as the place where the probe exited.[65]

The reader should keep in mind that Diana Bowron, the British nurse who washed Kennedy's body at Parkland, told me that the photograph of Kennedy's back that I published in *Killing the Truth* was not his back, and she captioned the photo, "This is not the back I saw."[66] She circled a place indicating a bullet entry, well down on the back, farther down than the official story is willing to admit.

Purdy asked Knudsen if there were any photos showing a probe through the head.[67] He cannot recall a photo of the chest being opened, and the "negative"[68] upon which he noted the probes through the body including the torso did not have the chest opened up. He says in this interview that he did not see the probes through the body on a print.[69] It seems to me that this means that that photo was already excised from the collection, and was not among those that Knudsen may have actually possessed—a fact that he hid from the HSCA interrogator. He didn't want them to know he had the pictures, which were all over Washington. One man who had them was author and book publishing editor Eugene ("Tom") Gervasi. His house was raided, according to his brother who told me this, just after he died and the pictures taken—a pattern that holds up throughout the case when people die who might have documents federal agencies don't want to let out. Gervasi was a retired officer in counterintelligence and died in 1988.

"I took the black and white in one darkroom and gave the color—I believe it was Vince Madonia who took the color into the adjoining color darkroom so we could process simultaneously. So, while Jim Fox stood outside to see that we were not disturbed—" "You processed the black and whites?" "Yes." "You processed it at the Naval Photographic Center." "Naval Photographic Center." No one helped him and he was in the darkroom alone. "I was in the black and white darkroom processing and the color was in the next room being processed."[70] It was Admiral Burkley who told them to process the film.[71]

"You personally developed the black and white film?" "Right." No one else was in the room when you did it?" "That is right." "It is James Fox's recollection that he did the black and white developing at the Secret Service lab. That is inconsistent with your recollection." "He may have printed black and whites at his lab. The black and whites were developed at the photographic center at the same time that the color was." "You personally have a specific recollection of having developed the black and white negatives?" "Right. Jim stood outside the darkroom door." "It is also Mr. Fox's recollection that some of the black and white sides of the film holders either had no film in them or they were not exposed." "The black and white was film pack. The film holders were color. To the best of my knowledge, there were no black and whites in the holders. I know there was a pack." "It is also your recollection that all of the exposures came up well, of the black and whites?" "Right." "You said maybe one of the colors either was underexposed or overexposed?" "It could not have been overexposed. There is no exposure." "If there was one like that—" "There is something shady about the third piece of film we took with us."[72] Purdy does not ask him what he meant by this, so we can only imagine.

There follows in the transcript a discussion of how they were to make prints from the processed films, and Knudsen describes a meeting with Admiral Burkley, possibly Jim Fox, and Taz Shepherd.[73] Shepherd was a White House naval aide married to Senator John Sparkman's daughter.[74] Sparkman was an ardent Kennedy hater.

"Do you have any personal knowledge about when and where the black and white prints were made?" "No." "Do you know that they were not made at the Naval Photographic Center?" "I do not know for a fact. I assumed that Jim Fox made the black and white prints. He had black and white capabilities within the Secret Service. The reason we got involved was the color capability which he did not have."[75] Later he says, "I am certain that there is the one shot of the body erect, two probes through it."[76] Knudsen indicates that he processed the black and white, meaning developing the film, and "I assume that Jim is the one who made the prints."[77] He says that "Sandy" (Saundra) Spencer worked on color at the naval lab.[78]

He is questioned again about the probe, for which we have no photo: "The only reason I say I thought it was a metal probe, in my recollection, it was a rod. Twenty-four inches long, probably; three-eighths of an inch in diameter. It appeared to be aluminum, stainless steel."[79] Sounds like he was at the autopsy, doesn't it? "Jim is the one who apparently printed the black and white. I know the black and white did not go into the Photo Center for printing, so I would assume that Jim did it. Why this sticks in my mind, that there was one with these two probes through the body that nobody else recalls, it puts a question in my mind, and yet—but I could not imagine where I could get the idea from, if I had not seen it. And yet it is starting to bother me now that there is nothing in the autopsy report about it. Certainly that would be in the autopsy, if it were true . . . At this point, I am confused why it sticks in my mind so strongly that there was this photograph, yet nobody else recalls it, and it is apparently not in any report. If it is not in any report—I cannot conceive why it would not be in—the report. If it were there—it is really bothering me as to why it does stick in my mind so much . . . I am trying to rack my mind on why this should stick in my mind so strongly that there was this photograph, and yet no other signs of it. It bothers me, but I cannot think of any reason that it would stick in my mind if I hadn't see it."[80] Purdy had impressed upon Knudsen, earlier, that he was the only witness saying that there had been a photograph of probes through the body. Indeed, no one ever testified to it. Did it happen? I think so. Knudsen was an honest man. He is now dead, but he has left us this legacy, this hint of the real truth of too many bullets through the body.

Speculation that Knudsen took a set of pictures at the autopsy or during the embalming remains speculation and there is no testimony or documentation that he ever did so. Either Mrs. Knudsen misunderstood her husband, or there was a semantic problem in interpretation of what he said. It is claimed that he said he took the pictures, but what he might actually have said was that he took them to Anacostia to be processed.[81] Knudsen told the House that seven sets of color prints were made on December 9, 1963.[82]

The body was prepared for burial at the Navy Hospital by employees of Gawler's funeral home. The work was concluded at 3:30 A.M. Fifteen minutes later, according to the report written by the Marine Sergeant in charge of the guards in the halls, the casket was removed from the morgue. At 0350 Mrs. Kennedy departed with the casket for the White House.[83] It is unlikely that the photos described by Saundra Spencer as developed at Anacostia were taken at the White House where the coffin lay in state, under heavy guard, nor were they taken at Bethesda by Knudsen, who is not on the list of those present in the morgue.

THE SECRET SERVICE

"When shown the HSCA summary of its interview with Miami SAIC John Marshall (specifically, Marshall's twice expressed opinion that there may have been a Secret Service conspiracy), Mr. Boring expressed surprise at those sentiments and said he had never heard that opinion expressed by SAIC Marshall, a personal friend of his. When shown the HSCA interview summary of its interview with Miami field office SA Ernest Aragon (specifically, Aragon's allegations of Secret Service security lapses), he said he would not agree with that statement, and expressed the opinion that SA Aragon may not have known what he was talking about . . . Mr. Boring was asked to read and comment on several pages of the HSCA 6/1/77 interview transcript[84] of its interview with former graduate student James Gochenaur, in which Gochenaur recounted a very long conversation he reportedly had with SA Elmer Moore in 1970. Mr. Boring examined the portions of the transcript in which Gochenaur quoted Moore as saying that Kennedy was a traitor for giving things away to the Russians; that it was a shame people had to die, but maybe it was a good thing; that the Secret Service personnel had to go along with the way the assassination was being investigated ("I did everything I was told, we all did everything we were told, or we'd get our heads cut off"); and that he felt remorse for the way he (Moore) had badgered Dr. Perry into changing his testimony to the effect that there was not, after all, an entrance wound in the front of the president's neck . . . Mr. Boring made clear during the interview that he felt Lee Harvey Oswald had shot President Kennedy acting alone, and that there was no shot from the grassy knoll."[85] Boring also founded the Retired Secret Service Agent's Association. It's a good way to keep track of people and maintain control and propaganda.

As for Dr. Finck's missing notes,[86] Robert I. Bouck, former chief of the Protective Research Section of the Secret Service, who played such a big role in the history of this case, said that he stayed in his office on the evening of the assassination until two in the morning before going home. "Prior to going home, he said he received documents, doctor's notes and other records, and undeveloped photos following the end of the autopsy. He said the doctor's notes were handwritten, and were written on prepared forms; in response to detailed follow-up questions, he said these notes were much more than 2 or 3 pages, and constituted a 'sheaf of papers.' He stated items of President Kennedy's clothing, such as the shirt, etc. were received at the same time as the autopsy materials. He said that the autopsy materials were received all at the same time, and included several little cans containing the brain and other biological materials. He said some of these cans or 'round canisters' had material which 'sloshed' inside; two of the canisters were about 4" × 5" or so in size, and that one might have been labeled as brain matter. He said that he had a four-drawer lock-file safe which was fireproof and had a combination lock on each drawer . . ." [87]

Well, if he had the brain (and probably the heart), then it wasn't in the Admiral's closet, as the official story tells us. Was it returned to Bethesda for the supplemental brain exam? Hardly likely; so they stole a substitute from someone who could not protest and whose family would never know. In fact, it would seem that if Humes did not have his notes (certainly Finck was missing his), then he had to make up quite a bit, if he could not remember the facts. This adds credence to my theory that the measurements and weights were fudged—made up because they never had Kennedy's brain. Certainly the one they had weighed far too much to be his. Certainly Humes would never admit that he wrote the autopsy report without his notes.

Toward the end of the above interview, "Mr. Bouck stated that his personal opinion was that although Lee Harvey Oswald was the assassin, he did feel that there was a conspiracy."

"Who asked SA Fox to make the black and white prints at the Secret Service lab?" "I did—that would have been me. Fox would never have done anything like that on his own without my permission. I gave him his instructions on all the autopsy photography. I remember that they said they wanted them done, and I then gave him his orders." "Do you know why Fox went to the Navy Photographic Center at Anacostia to develop the pictures instead of taking them back to Bethesda where autopsy photography was normally done by the photographer who took the pictures?" "I'm pretty sure Dr. Burkley was the one who asked for the photos and that he suggested Anacostia, and may even have made the preliminary arrangements, and then I may have called to confirm the arrangements. Yes, it was Burkley, I believe. We didn't use Bethesda because Burkley would have suggested the Navy lab at Anacostia."[88] Bouck remembered showing the pictures to Warren Commission staffers, probably Specter and Rankin, but we know that Chief Justice Warren and probably other commissioners saw them as well.

"Jeremy Gunn recounted a story involving the opinion of a former CIA employee who had stated that President Kennedy was not very popular with many Secret Service agents, and asked Mr. Bouck to comment on that allegation. Mr. Bouck stated that he did not feel that was true . . . "[89]

The House Assassinations Committee found that the Secret Service protection on the day of the murder was "uniquely insecure." I went into this in some detail in *High Treason*. The HSCA said, "The Secret Service was deficient in the performance of its duties on the day John Kennedy was killed."[90]

PIECES OF THE PUZZLE

Knudsen told the HSCA that there were "approximately ten color negatives" made in seven sets, and, "There was one total film pack. There would have been twelve negatives, black and white."[91]

Dr. Robert Frederick Karnei, whom I first interviewed in 1991 and who was not known to have been at the autopsy table until then, was interviewed by the ARRB.[92] He said that he " . . . remembered repeated instances, during the numerous attempts to probe the back wound, when photographs were taken of a probe in the President's body (at approximately 9:00 P.M.), and seemed more certain of this recollection than of any other during his ARRB interview. He remembers that John Stringer was photographing the autopsy, and that Stringer used both a camera that required the use of film-holders for individual sheets of film, and also a 35 mm camera. He said that there was a second person taking photographs, whom he initially described to ARRB staff as a FBI or S.S. agent . . . " because the man was in civilian clothes and Karnei thought that all civilians in the room were federal agents. This could have been Knudsen.

"When asked how autopsy photographs were normally identified, he said that it was standard procedure for the autopsy number to be placed on some measuring device (showing scale), and then to be photographed somewhere in the field of view in each autopsy photograph. However, he also said that he could not remember whether this procedure was used the night of the autopsy, or not.

"When asked whether John Stringer had used a ladder at the autopsy to take pictures, Dr. Karnei was of the impression that Stringer (who was short, only about 5'2" in height) had 'stood on something' to take some photographs, but could not remember what he had stood on." He did not recall any photographs being made during the later stages of the embalming and burial preparations, which he attended.[93]

One should not be quick to ridicule staged investigations and staged medical examinations. Politics is open warfare, and slander and dirty tricks are standard. Some people will do anything to destroy an enemy, and the truth in the JFK case threatens many interests. Congress has had secret investigations before. It's a good way to intimidate witnesses. The military, in particular, would do anything when confronted with "security risks." Whistle blowers for fraud and kickbacks in military procurement contracts might be killed. Sure enough, Knudsen, the much-praised White House photographer for five presidents, was shortly dead. The control and destiny of a great nation was at stake in getting John Kennedy out of the way.

Another conflict in what the autopsy photos show is the metal brace or stirrup that we see holding up the president's head. Corpsmen at the autopsy insisted to me years ago that they used a wooden block,[94] and sure enough, several other witnesses whom the Board interviewed said the same thing.

The morticians were also clear that the only scalp missing was in the back. It was about the size of an orange, just about what everyone at the autopsy drew. I first published this in *High Treason 2* (pages

100, 199, 579-581. Tom Robinson described to the Board, as he had to me years ago and to the HSCA,[95] that there was a hole in Kennedy's right forehead[96] that he filled with wax. He also told the Board that there were three small holes in his cheek,[97] which he also plugged to prevent leakage of the embalming fluid. Robinson described for the Board a hole in the back of the head where there was no scalp, " . . . centrally located right between the ears," and a " . . . blow-out" which consisted of a flap of skin in the right temple of the President's head, which he believed to be an exit wound based on conversations he heard in the morgue amongst the pathologists.[98] The description of the hole in the back of the head was repeated by John Van Hoesen, another of the undertakers, who said the hole was the size of an orange in " . . . the centerline of the back of the head, and its location was inthe upper posterior of the skull." This was demonstrated to be " . . . at or just below the cowlick area."[99]

Tom Robinson said that he had a recollection of a very long, malleable probe being used during the autopsy, and his " . . . most vivid recollection of the probe is seeing it inserted near the base of the brain in the back of the head (after removal of the brain), and seeing the tip of the probe come out of the tracheotomy incision in the anterior neck. He was adamant about this recollection. He also recalls seeing the wound high in the back probed unsuccessfully, meaning that the probe did not exit anywhere."[100] This means that the doctors did know that there was a bullet in the throat where the tracheotomy was. They had to shut up about it because such a shot could not explain the damage to the head and the wounds to John Connally. Some of the original reports from Dallas the day of the murder said that a fragment or bullet had exited the throat after striking the head.

Robinson was shown the autopsy photos and did not see the small "shrapnel" holes in the right cheek in the pictures, he thinks because of the poor quality of the photos. He was asked to point out the large hole in the back of the head and again demonstrated where it should have been, saying, " . . . it just doesn't show up in this photo."

When shown the Top of Head/Superior View of Cranium (corresponds to B & W Nos. 7–10): "Robinson frowned, and said with apparent disagreement, 'This makes it look like the wound was in the top of the head.' He explained that the damage in this photograph was 'what the doctors did,' and explained that they cut the scalp open and reflected it back in order to remove bullet fragments (the fragments he had observed in a glass vial). ARRB staff members asked Robinson whether there was damage to the top of the head when he arrived at the morgue and before the brain was removed; he replied by saying that this area was 'all broken,' but that it was not open like the wound in the back of the head.

"Robinson said that he saw the brain removed from President Kennedy's body, and that a large percentage of it was gone 'in the back,' from the 'medulla,' and that the portion of the brain that was missing was about the size of a closed fist. He described the condition of the brain in this area as the consistency of 'soup.' He said that the brain was 'not cut up' at the autopsy."[101]

Earl McDonald, a medical photographer trained by John Stringer, offered some " . . . general observations of discrepancies between the official collection of autopsy photos at NARA and what he would expect to see if he had shot the autopsy photos himself." (It was stated here that the publicly available reproductions were ascertained by ARRB staff to be faithful (if degraded) representations of authentic autopsy photos at the National Archives): There are no autopsy tags visible in any photos; no whole body photos in the collection; no photograph of the brain (at autopsy) immediately following removal from the cranium; no photograph of the inside of the skull (following removal of the brain); no photograph of the reassembled skull; no photograph of the chest cavity; no close-up of the back wound; no wide-angle view and/or medium-field view of the cranium to go with the close-up in the collection). "When asked by ARRB staff what grade he would assign if he were asked to grade the present collection of autopsy photos, he said he would grade them 'quite low' because, among other reasons, the collection was not comprehensive (that is, did not represent the range of views that should have been depicted from either a normal autopsy, or especially one involving gunshot wounds). He also said that " . . . he never saw the stirrup used (for the head of the deceased) as it is in the autopsy photographs of President Kennedy, but instead saw a wooden chock or block, and said that there was no wooden furniture in the autopsy room as appears in the photos, and no telephone where it appears in the photos, observations pointed out to me by Paul O'Connor and the other corpsmen (which I previously published). James Sib-

ert also told the ARRB that he did not recall the stirrup or metal support being used that we see in some of the pictures.[102]

McDonald further told the Board that " . . . the photographer who
shot the autopsy would always develop his own film (both B & W and
color) in the lab at Bethesda, that this was virtually mandatory. He could
not recall one instance of autopsy or medical film being taken to the
Navy Lab at Anacostia for developing; he thought that would be very
strange, since he said that facility was surrounded by barbed wire, had
the reputation of doing 'secret' photo-intelligence work of some kind,
and everyone knew no one was supposed to talk about the kind of work
that went on at Anacostia."

Finally, McDonald makes the point that all autopsy photos normally include full body shots, which none of the extant pictures show.
These are taken from left and right lateral views, plus obliques from
both sides, plus from above on a ladder, including sequential full body
shots as clothing or wrappings were removed, piece by piece; and all
photos at an autopsy should display a card with a prominent case number; and when photographing trauma such as a wound, he said there
would usually be a series of three views such as a wide-angle first, then
a medium field-of-view shot, and then an extreme close-up, for authentication and identification when viewing the photos later. "He said the
regimen for use of autopsy tags, and for taking full body photos and
varying series of increasing close-ups of the same wound are things that
would not have changed between 1963 and the 1970s, because they
were standard practice; and that furthermore, it was John Stringer who
had taught him these procedures."[103]

The HSCA also found major fault with the photos from the technical standpoint, as I outlined in *High Treason*.[104]

In view of information that much of the material was burned by
Bouck,[105] it would seem likely that photographs and X-rays were also
switched. The disappearance of the brain and all other tissue specimens
from the autopsy, although speculated to have been obtained by Robert
Kennedy but never proven, would destroy any DNA samples that could
have later been used to prove that the brain was not Kennedy's—if, as
the evidence strongly indicates, it wasn't.

The brain might or might not be at the Smithsonian. "At this point
he volunteered that he had seen President Kennedy's brain during the

1964–65 period, which he stated had been kept in a locked room at the AFIP (Armed Forces Institute of Pathology) National Museum of Health and Medicine." When questioned more closely about whether he meant it was the entire brain or just part of it, Ken Vrtacnik " . . . responded that the item on display was one long section, tan in color, immersed in liquid, laying in a stainless steel tray inside a glass case. He repeatedly stated that it had wooden pegs (or arrows) through it which were routinely used in gunshot wound cases to show the trajectory of bullets." How many pegs, he was asked? At least two was his answer. When asked how he knew it was the President's brain, he was positive for two reasons: It was labeled "president Kennedy's Brain" or words to that effect; " . . . and it made a big impression on him at the time because of his interest in the assassination, and because of the tight control placed on viewing of the specimen."[106]

Let's depart from the photos and X rays for a moment, the major focus of this paper, and try to put the larger picture into perspective. Paul O'Connor, who assisted at the X ray, thought that the president's skull had been disrupted by someone beating on it with a "ball peen hammer."[107] Certainly that would be a good way to mess up the evidence before the autopsy. "Israel told her the orderlies saw one doctor in the autopsy room at the Medical Center who was waiting for some time prior to the arrival of the body. When the body arrived, many people were forced out of the room and the doctor performed some type of mutilation of three bullet punctures to the head area. The doctor was working at a very 'hurried' pace and was done within a few minutes, at which point he left the autopsy room." This was a story told to a biologist at the National Institute of Health across the street from Bethesda Naval Medical Center.[108]

We must consider the medical community who would requisition for themselves a slice of the president's brain for a specimen jar at the Armed Forces Institute of Pathology. The daughter of Admiral Burkley, Nancy Denlea, told Douglas Horne of the ARRB that her father told her that he was very upset that the Warren Commission never called him to testify. She said that her father had once shown her photographs of the president's brain, and proudly said that it was her father who had ensured that the brain was saved.[109] An attorney for the family (William F. Illig) claimed that Admiral Burkley had information indicating that others beside Oswald might have participated in the assassination.[110] Burkley, who had been with Kennedy in Dallas and who controlled events at the autopsy, was in a key position in the White House. He retained a set of autopsy photographs from the first round of seven sets of prints described by Robert Knudsen as having been distributed to the Secret Service, Robert Kennedy, Ted Kennedy, and the National Archives.[111]

Above, we learned that the brain might not have been "saved." What did that mean? Did it mean that someone would have discarded or destroyed it? It was not put into the coffin for burial, according to the HSCA findings.[112]

Robert Knudsen evidently showed the autopsy photographs to a number of people. Was he one of those with his own set, along with Burkley? We know that Fox had a set for many years. I personally know of a general who had a set. Yet Knudsen tells Andy Purdy of the HSCA that "I never saw the prints after we brought them back." "Did you have a chance at any time to examine the prints closely enough that you now have a recollection of what they showed?" "Oh, yes." "When did you examine them that closely?" "At the time that I was examining for technical quality, a lot of things were apparent."[113] Then how was he able to show the picture to Joe O'Donnell, another White House photographer? Why didn't Purdy ask him if he had copies of the pictures?

The following is a constant problem in this case: Dr. Boswell stated that he thought Dr. Richard L. Davis, a neuropathologist, was present at the supplemental examination of the brain,[114] but Davis told the ARRB: "I never saw President Kennedy's brain."[115] Davis knew the procedure for brain exams at Bethesda well, and the brain would be weighed *twice:* first, immediately after removal, and second, at the supplemental examination (after fixation), before any procedures were performed. He said that at Bethesda in 1963, brains were being fixed by a process called perfusion, which was a variation of arterial embalming. He said that perfusion involved injecting formalin solution by gravity into the major arteries of the brain, at the same time that the brain was immersed in a bucket of formalin solution. He said that perfusion speeded up the fixation process so that a brain could be cut at supplemental exam "in less than a week," and that you might be able to cut a brain in only 2 or 3 days as opposed to 10 to 14 days for immersion fixation only.

Previously, there had been no evidence that there had been any sectioning of the brain, which normally is done whenever there is a gun shot wound, but in the ARRB reports, there appears to be evidence that at least some sections were sliced off.

Throughout the evidence it appears that the government and military personnel routinely lie and contradict each other. This can make getting at the truth difficult when the credibility of each witness is thus compromised. For example, if they forgot to weigh the brain when it was removed from the body, this can lead to a dozen more lies, unless they didn't dare record it because the brain was switched.

There was desperation more than three years later to cover-up facts about the autopsy evidence. A document headed "President Johnson's notes on conversation with acting Attorney General Ramsey Clark—January 26, 1967," says, "On the other matter, I think we have the three pathologists and the photographer signed up now on the autopsy review and their conclusion is that the autopsy photos and X rays conclusively support the autopsy report rendered by them to the Warren Commission though we were not able to tie down the question of the missing photo entirely but we feel much better about it and we have three of the four sign to an affidavit that says these are all the photos that they took and they do not believe anybody else took any others. There is this unfortunate reference in the Warren Commission report by Dr. Humes to a picture that just does not exist as far as we know. I am checking further to see where the pictures were at all times."[116]

Where did the materials go? Velma Reumann (née Vogler) "has a strong, independent recollection of Navy Photographic Center personnel boxing up all photographic materials (everything we—the film department—had) related to the assassination on the orders of Robert Kennedy and sending them to the Smithsonian Museum for permanent storage sometime within 6 months or so after the assassination . . . In order to test the strength of her Smithsonian recollection, I asked her whether she may have been confusing the Smithsonian with the National Archives or some other government body; she replied emphatically that she knew the difference between the National Archives and the Smithsonian, and reiterated that the boxed material went to the Smithsonian. She said she was certain of this because she, herself, was required to call an official at the Smithsonian to discuss the imminent transfer, and recalls the individual to whom she spoke was as surprised by the selection of the Smithsonian as she was."[117] So how do we square this with being told that NPC handed back all copies of prints that were made to the Secret Service? We don't know that they had any prints at NPC after Fox left. According to others, they kept nothing. Clearly, everybody made copies of whatever came into their hands and kept them. But has anyone thought to check the Smithsonian for this load of forensic and historical materials?

All through the record are listings for color positive photo "transparencies," yet Vincent Madonia, the officer in charge of the color photo lab responsible for what Fox and Knudsen brought to him, told the ARRB that " . . . he did not recall any transparencies being developed, only prints. He said there was no good system for making prints from color positive transparencies. NPC had the capability to develop transparencies and make internegatives, but he did not remember this happening following the JFK assassination."

He also said that he knew Robert L. Knudsen, and " . . . he may have been there that weekend (right after the assassination)." As soon as he had said this, however, he said, " . . . take that out of your notes, I shouldn't have said that, I'm not sure."[118] "When asked if he remembered any JFK autopsy photography done the weekend following the assassination, he said that there was 'a lot of traffic, a lot of pictures' done that weekend following the assassination. At one point he also used the phrase 'a lot of documents' done that weekend. He said there were a lot of Secret Service and FBI agents at NPC Anacostia all weekend, and that the developing activity at NPC went on for the whole weekend, for 3 full days. He said that the federal agents were overseeing the processing of film."[119] Well, the Navy was there to serve. The question is, with a fully capable photo lab at Bethesda, how come the pictures were not developed there if they were going to do it right away, as they apparently did, but somewhere else? How come they lied in the official record about when this work was done?

Madonia said that the White House lab, which worked behind locked doors at Anacostia, kept their own records and the ARRB should look for their files. Apparently, the ARRB struck out.[120]

THE X RAYS

Some of the X rays were burned by being held too closely to the light by the radiologist, Dr. John H. Ebersol.[121] Here are the credible statements made by Jerrol Custer to the ARRB in 1997. In this instance, it was evidence of additional shots, X-ray No. 14 (anterior-posterior view of lower pelvis, hips, and upper femurs):

"Are you able to identify that as having been taken on the night of November 22nd?" "Yes, sir. More fixer burns." "Those are the brown patches again?" " . . . No metal fragments . . . " "Now, you had raised, previously in the deposition . . . the possibility of some metal fragments in the C3/C4 range." "I noticed I didn't see that." "You didn't see any X rays that would be in—that would include the C3/C4 area?" "No, sir." "Are you certain that you took X rays that included C3/C4?" "Yes, sir. Absolutely." "How many X rays did you take that would have included that?" "Just one. And that was all that was necessary, because it showed—right there." "And what, as best you recall, did it show?" "A fragmentation of a shell in and around that . . . that area . . . There were bullet fragmentations around that area—that opening." "Around C3/C4?" "Right." "And do you recall how many fragments there were?" "Not really. There was enough. It was very prevalent." "Did anyone make any observations about metal fragments in the C3/C4 area?" "I did. And I was told to mind my own business. That's where I was shut down again." "You have, during the course of this deposition, identified three X rays that you are quite certain that you took, but don't appear in this collection. Are there any others that you can identify as not being included?" "That's the only three that come to my mind right now; the two tangential views, and the AP cervical spine . . . In my own opinion . . . the reason why they are not here is because they showed massive amounts of bullet fragments." "Did you ever hear of anyone connected with the autopsy making any attempts to remove, destroy any of the X-ray material?" "Let me put it this way, gossip is cheap. Everybody has some. I heard some. And sometimes you have to take it with a hill of beans—where it comes from. But I did hear that in a conversation." "When did you hear it in a conversation?" "The next day." "What did you hear?" "That certain pertinent things were taken care of." "Who told you that?" " . . . Nobody told me. I heard it between two officers. High-ranking officers." "Who were the officers?" "One was Ebersol. And one was another radiologist . . . " "To the best of your recollection, who was it who made the statement, Ebersol or the other doctor?" "Ebersol." Custer then identifies the other officer as the captain in charge of the radiology department, Dr. Loy Brown.[122]

Custer is shown an enhancement of the AP view of the skull: "Here's your fragment again." "And you're referring to the large . . . semi-circular fragment?" "Right. Left marker, right orbit, fragments throughout. All I can say is, it's funny how the burn mark gets in the right place. And that's pretty close to what I—my opinion—I believe was an entry wound . . . Air on the right anatomical maxillary sinuses again. Fracture marks throughout the sagimatic, (sic), arch, the mandibular arch, the left anterior portion of the skull, the superior portion of the skull. Fracture marks. Here's that irregular cut mark—what it looks like—appears to me. Snaking fracture marks off to the left anatomical positioning . . . "[123] Custer refers to Ebersol's testimony to the House Committee where he states that there are metal fragments present but they are not bullets. "A metal fragment big enough to be seen has to be a portion of a bullet. Common sense would tell you that. Another thing. When Dr. Ebersol looked at these films—He took basic physics like anybody else did. And why couldn't he see displacement of the anterior portion of the skull, and realize that it had to be coming from the . . . posterior portion of the skull, and realize there had to be force coming from the anterior portion of the skull? He knew that. Now, he's an educated man. He has to know that."[124]

"Earlier in your deposition, you referred to some heat damage on one of the X rays. Do you see any heat damage on this X ray?" "It's right here. You can see it. This is where Dr. Ebersol got it too close to the heat lamp. I stated to him twice, 'Please do not put it too close.' You can see where it started to—" "To wrinkle?" "Curdle, literally. And here, it started to burn. And isn't it funny how where it starts to burn is the area that I suggested was an entry wound." "Now, are you certain that that heat damage took place on this X-ray on the night of November 22nd?" "Yes, sir. I was there, and I saw him do it."[125]

In the next breath they are describing an empty space on the right side of the skull in the X ray in the front. Custer says, "That doesn't set right with me . . . Here's another thing, too, that shows basically this is, more than likely—I'd say 80 to 90 percent—entry wound. See this air down through the sinus area, maxillary sinuses? The only way you get air through the maxillary sinuses is when you have damage to the orbital ridge and the orbital base. Air gets down into the sinuses. The sinuses are right here on the front of the face, on both cheekbones. Your eye orbit sits back in. If you ever have any damage—You get punched in the eye. A lot of times, if this fractures—the orbital ridge, you get an opening that communicates between the sinuses and the eye. And this is why a lot of times they'll take sinus films on a damaged frontal area. And if you see blood or fluid in there, this is where they'll say, 'Well you have an orbital fracture. There's air in the maxillary sinuses.' . . . Extremely important. On the right anatomical side. Extremely important. This is why I don't understand people didn't see this. And look here. Here's another thing . . . Look at the fractures over here . . . On the right side. Right anatomical position. All the fractures are here. And then it gradually snakes out to the lowest anatomical side. This is where all the trauma was right here."[126]

Custer demonstrates that there was a shot from in front to the head, in addition to the shot from behind: "Remember, also, I had stated how a portion of the skull had lifted up and pushed backwards?" "Yes." "Showing that there had to be a force impact this way . . . From the right side, you notice . . . the fragmentation, how it starts to get larger and larger and larger. You have equal and opposite force. Everything being pushed forward. The brain has been pushed back, and it pops the skull out." "So, it's your opinion that the trauma to the head began at the front and moved towards the back of the head?" "Yes, sir. Absolutely."[127] Custer finds that there is no brain in the head when the skull X rays were taken,[128] which seems at variance with the testimony that the X rays were made before any manipulations of the body were performed.

"Where are you identifying the larger wound?" "The larger wound would have to be further back. This one isn't as bad, towards the temporal region. It was open. But the more you went further back, the more destruction you had." Jeremy Gunn asks him: "When you say 'the more destruction', is that consistent with what you were seeing with the X-rays film, where—by what I have been understanding you to say—most of the destruction is towards the front, where it be darker and where there's an absence—apparent absence of bone?" "No. Let me reiterate again. Most of the destruction was towards the occipital area. This area wasn't as bad. You still had the orbital ridge. The frontal forehead was still here. But the further back you got, the worse the destruction became. And the more gaping the hole became."[129]

Then Gunn discovers Dr. David Mantik's "great white patch," where the X rays have obviously been altered, according to Mantik's densitometer tests in the National Archives.[130] Question: "Why is it that on the X rays—and I'm saying this from my perspective as a layman—the film appears to be darker more towards the front and lighter towards the back?" "In other words, you're asking me: Why is this lighter here?" "Why is it lighter with the more apparent bone in the occipital region, and why is there apparently less bone in the frontal and parietal region?"[131]

Where they didn't burn the X rays, a double exposure using light created the "great white patch." "You're missing two." "Now I can tell you that those are the only—the three that you just looked at are the only skull X rays present at the Archives. Are you aware of any other skull X rays?" "There should be at least two more." "And you described those both as oblique X rays; is that correct?" "Or, like you had stated, tangential views." "Tangential. And are you certain that you took those other two X rays on the night of the autopsy?" "Absolutely."[132]

I should add that of all the witnesses, Custer has provided the most acutely accurate descriptions anatomically and historically and left us with the most complete record of those events within his province to know. In addition, he placed his own personal marker in some of the X rays, so as to be able to identify them, until Ebersol caught him and forced him to stop.

In the years immediately following the assassination, it would have been relatively easy to switch evidence in a more loosely controlled environment in the National Archives, as appears to have happened with some of the evidence. If the evidence tends to show that a powerful cabal surrounding President Johnson, Kennedy's successor, was responsible for the assassination of Kennedy, then it would have been a relatively easy matter to control the evidence and substitute materials.

DR. JAMES J. HUMES

Under steady hammering by the counsel for the ARRB, Jeremy Gunn, Dr. Humes admitted that he had written a first draft of the autopsy report and then copied it by hand and destroyed the first draft along with his notes from the autopsy itself. He was unable to explain why he destroyed the notes, which had blood on them, but not the autopsy face sheet drawing and measurement, which also had blood on them. He claimed that he did not want anything with the president's blood on them to get out. Dr. Pierre Finck's notes disappeared completely just after the autopsy.

Humes insisted throughout his interview that the entry of a bullet into the back of the head was near the hairline and to the right, and he did not give any grounds as to the location he gave for it in his autopsy report, saying that the photographs showing the back of the head nowhere showed the bullet hole in the scalp. Humes insisted that the entry hole in the scalp exactly coincided with the hole in the skull,[133] and that the small hole of entry in the skull, assembled when a second piece of bone arrived from Dallas and fit onto the broken skull, showed a con-ing effect on the inside of the skull—indicative of an entry there.

The conflict in the evidence developed in 1968 when a panel of doctors set up by President Johnson's Attorney General, Ramsey Clark, also from Texas, examined the alleged autopsy evidence and concluded that the entry hole was four inches higher on the skull than its placement in the autopsy report. This higher position would allow for a shot from the sixth-floor window, which could exit the head somewhere forward of the entry, but the lower shot made that impossible.

One of the more stunning revelations in the new interviews was the description given by the X-ray technician, Jerrol F. Custer, of now-missing X-rays well documented to have been taken, which showed a disinte-grated bullet in the area of C3/C4 of the neck's vertebrae. This damaged area of the spine fits somewhat with a trajectory from an entry near the hairline to the hole in the anterior neck near the voice box. That hole had been described in Dallas as very small, and could have been from a frag-ment rather than a whole bullet. Bullets don't often go perfectly straight in the body, I am told.

The possibility of a fragment exiting there, which was first described by the Dallas doctors the day of the assassination, would fit a trajectory from a much lower firing position than the sixth-floor win-dow, or one farther away. Accurate shots can be made with sniper's rifles from more than half a mile away.

Humes explained his apparent retreat during a televised public hearing before the HSCA (1978), and to the *Journal of the American Medical Association* (1992) in a response to a written interrogatory from the ARRB, which asked, "Did you believe, at the time you wrote and signed the Autopsy Protocol, that the location of the entrance wound in President Kennedy's skull was 2.5 cm to the right and slightly above the external occipital protuberance, as is stated in the Autopsy Protocol?" "Yes."

As I previously reported, the doctors have been steadfast in their finding that the autopsy photographs, which show the back of the head, do not show the entry wound in the back of the head. Some comment that it is lost in the hair, but one purpose of the photographs was to show the entry hole. The fact that it is not there can lead to only one conclusion: the absolute necessity for the conspiracy to move that wound some four inches higher in order to implicate an assassin who could be linked with the Texas School Book Depository. In addition, I have argued that the apparent change in the attitude of Humes in 1978 was based upon his observations of the alleged autopsy photographs and the distortions that others put on his response. He, along with the other doctors, has been steadfast in insisting that the wounds are not in the right place in this material. I have outlined every scrap of evidence in this regard in my books.

Humes was asked, "During your communications with the House Select Committee on Assassinations, did you ever change your original opinion about the location of the skull entrance wound? If so, what did you conclude about the location of the entry wound?" "Did you ever change your opinion about the location of the entrance wound in the skull? If so, please explain when you changed your opinion and the circumstances that led you to change your opinion." "What is your current belief as to the location of the entry wound in President Kennedy's skull?" to which he responded, "As stated in the autopsy report."

He replied to the rest of the above questions with a short written response, appended hereto: "With regard to your final questions, I make the following response. Both during my testimony before the House Select Committee on Assassinations, and during this deposition I experienced great difficulty in interpreting the location of the wound of entrance in the posterior scalp from the photograph. This may be because of the angle from which it was taken, or the position of the head, etc. It is obvious that the location of the external occipital protuberance cannot be ascertained from the photograph. I most firmly believe that the location of the wound was exactly where I measured it to be in relation to the external occipital protuberance and so recorded it in the autopsy report. After all that was my direct observation in the morgue and I believe it to be far more reliable than attempting to interpret what I believe to be a photograph which is subject to various interpretations."[134] This repeats what Dr. Finck told the HSCA, which can be read in my last book, *Killing Kennedy* (page 37).

This precisely answers all conflicts about the placement of the entry wound, except that it does not show in any photograph or X ray. The weight of the evidence is that there was in fact an entry into the back of the head where they found it during the autopsy, and that this bullet could not have blown out either the back or side of his head, and in fact smashed through the floor of the skull into cervical bone in the neck and disintegrated. The X rays showing this were destroyed. The clear implication is that another shot from in front, striking where Custer and others placed it on the right forehead, did the rest of the explosive and massive damage to the head.

So how did the Clark Panel find that the entry hole into the back of the head was four inches higher than at the autopsy? They made this determination because there was an apparent piece of metal seen on the present X rays allegedly taken at the autopsy, high up on the back of the head at the cowlick, and where there was a corresponding drop of blood or something of that nature on the photos showing the scalp pulled up over the broken-off bone. Custer described to me how Dr. Ebersol asked him to tape bullet fragments to pieces of bone the day after the autopsy and X-ray them[135] (he has now told this story under oath to the ARRB[136]), and it seems clear that these were used to make it appear that a piece of bullet was lodged on the head at that position, though one centimeter below the alleged hole itself, and on the *outer table of the skull*, as the Clark Panel determined years later, too late for anyone to notice the mistake made in the haste to fabricate evidence of a high entry wound that could have come from the sixth-floor window.

One of the key revelations in the new interviews were explanations by Humes and Dr. Boswell of the drawings Boswell made at the autopsy that had marked a very large area, as much as 17 centimeters, as "missing" at the top of the head. Most of this bone showed up when three pieces were brought from Dallas at different times after the autopsy began, and much of the rest was stuck to the scalp when it was reflected back from the head.[137] Their autopsy report stated that an area 10×13 centimeters was missing, mostly in the right parietal area but extending somewhat into the temporal and the occipital in the back of the head.

Humes says that there was very little scalp missing and they could just about close up the skull when it had been reconstructed with a rubber dam put in the back of the head by the morticians after the autopsy. The morticians explained that the only scalp missing was on the very back of the head and that area could not be seen if the coffin was to be opened for viewing.[138] This dovetails with all the testimony of nearly every witness saying that the missing scalp or large hole could not be seen when looking straight at the body on its back. I spent many years interviewing every available witness who confirmed this fact. Humes told the ARRB: "Not as much scalp. There was some scalp missing, but we were able to pretty much close the scalp, skin, when we finished everything. So I can't tell you how much was—but it was not that much skin missing, no."[139]

Humes told the ARRB what he said to the HSCA, that "Did I have the photographs in my hands to look at? No. They had some blow-ups that they were trying to use to demonstrate to the panel, I guess, and I found them very difficult to interpret, to be perfectly candid with you. I had problems with them." He shortly explains that "virtually all" of the photographs were taken at the beginning of the autopsy, except for the ones of the inside of the skull and chest.[140]

The dust-like fragments seen on the X rays on a line across the top of the head from front to back do not relate to either the official entry or exit wounds, but had been described in the autopsy report as describing a line from the low rear head entry hole upwards to the exit wound. This is not at all what is seen in the present-day X ray.

It must be stated that none of those interviewed ventured that the X rays and photos were fake, but they simply found many problems with them. As a matter of logic, it would seem that no one in their position would ever dare come right out with an accusation of forgery, for fear of losing all credibility. We are left to draw our own conclusions after they tell us what is wrong with the material. Only a fool would, upon hearing all the evidence, not believe that the material was altered.

He finds that the cerebellum was " . . . somewhat disrupted . . . but the photographs of the brain show it to you very clearly."[141] The trouble is, they then find problems with the brain photographs. There is a basi-

lar view that apparently was not taken at the autopsy. Humes described
such a photograph taken during the autopsy from below the brain.[142]

Humes explains that the entry hole was found and assembled when
a large piece came in from Dallas, " . . . because it was shelved on the
outer table, and we almost could put it all together, that wound."[143] This
is identical to what he and the other doctors have said all along.

Humes is shown each autopsy view and is asked this question each
time: "Are these the photos that you previously have identified as being
the autopsy photos of President Kennedy?" or "Do you recognize these
as being the original and authentic autopsy photos of President
Kennedy?" "Yes, sir."[144] This "Yes, sir," follows with military precision
in every instance except one when he merely answers "Yes." It seems to
me to be staged, when he calls into question so much with some of the
pictures. Sometimes lengthy explanations then follow in the transcripts
for what the pictures might show, and many questions that have been
pointed out by researchers are brought up.

"Prior to the time that the photographs in View 4 were taken, was
there any cleaning of the hair or scalp of President Kennedy?" "It looks
like there might have been. I can't recall specifically. There was probably still some blood involved there. We may have cleaned that off
slightly. I don't recall."[145] There may have been some cleansing of the
head in Dallas, but it is unlikely, since the skull was like a broken egg
shell and about all that could have been lightly sponged off was the face.
The photographs at the autopsy show a perfectly clean and intact head
of hair in the back. Any knowledge at all of the evidence tells you that
this is not Kennedy's head.

"This is funny—it's a strange way to depict the posterior portion of
the skull, is all I can tell you. There was no significance. It was just a
hole. But it was further down, you see. It wasn't way up there." "I note
here is the external occipital protuberance." "Yes." "Can you describe
generally where there was any missing bone from the posterior portion,
to the best of your recollection?" "There basically wasn't any [bone]. It
was just a hole. Not a significant missing bone."[146]

"Dr. Humes, are you able to identify what you have described previously as an entrance wound in the posterior skull of President
Kennedy on photographs in View 6?" "This the same problem I had at
the Committee (HSCA) hearings . . . I had big difficulty trying to see
which was which among these things, between here and here." The here

and here referred to the apparent spot of blood in the cowlick area, and
the bit of brain matter down near the hairline at the midline of the head.
"I threw these up on a great big screen and said which is what, and I
really had difficulty. I couldn't be sure. I'm disappointed. I was disappointed in that regard. I still have trouble with it." (He is disappointed
because they went to great trouble at the autopsy to take careful pictures,
and they turned out to be next to worthless.) "Are you able to identify on
View 6 the entrance wound?" "Not with certainty, I'm sorry to tell
you."[147]

"This object down near the hairline seems more obviously to be an
artifact of some kind. I don't know what it is,"[148] speaking of an apparent drop of brain matter adhering to the head. Humes has great difficulty,
like every other researcher and witness, orienting the photo of a large
hole in a head as to whether the hole is in the front, side, or back of the
head. He finally opts for it showing the right side.[149]

Of the three photographs that the investigators found to be missing
and Humes remembers having been taken at the autopsy, an extensive
discussion ensues about a photo having been taken of the interior of the
skull showing the beveled edge of the entry hole in the back.[150] Another
missing photo was that taken of the inside of the thorax showing that no
bullet had penetrated there, but that the top of the lung was bruised.[151]
The third was a photograph of the posterior skull entry wound with the
scalp reflected back.[152]

"Am I led to believe that we have not found the photograph from
inside of the posterior portion of the skull?" "You have now seen today
all of the photographs of the skull we had." "I don't know how to explain
it, because we didn't—I don't think we described in anywhere here that
photograph. I'd have to go through the whole list of the photographs to
see, but my recollection is that we took it from both the outside and from
the inside after the brain was removed (View No. 7)."[153]

In November 1966 after the Kennedy family transferred the autopsy
materials to the custody of the National Archives, the doctors were
brought in to inventory and sign a document as to what was there. Some
apparently returned in January 1967, and another document (Exhibit 14)
was produced by the Department of Justice, which was shown to Dr.
Humes, and he does not know who wrote it.[154] An extensive discussion of
the brain photos ensues, starting at about page 202 of the transcript, and
it would appear that they feel that there are two lacerations from front to

back in the brain, but when this seems to lead to the implication that there were two gunshot tracks, Humes retreats. He feels that the force of a bullet creates a shock wave, though he does not call it that, which creates separate lacerations.[155] "Laceration is a bad way to describe it. It's a big disruption. I guess we called it a laceration because that seemed like as good a word as any. But it significantly destroys much of that right cerebral hemisphere." . . . "Do these two lacerations connect to each other?" "I don't know. You can't tell from here."[156] Of course, they had not sectioned (at lease, officially) the brain, so they couldn't know. Humes does say that they had to cut the brainstem in order to remove it.[157] There had been speculation that the brain had already been cut loose by a shot or the force of one. Humes admits that the stem was badly injured. There are several discussions of the cerebellum in these pages, and Humes says, "In this photograph, it would appear the right cerebellum has been partially disrupted, yes."[158]

When shown the X rays, Humes notices right off what Dr. David Mantik calls "The Great White patch," and he is surprised by the large 6.5 mm round fragment of an apparent bullet on the back of the skull in the cowlick area. "Did you notice what at least appears to be a radiopaque fragment during the autopsy?" "I'm not sure what that is or whether that's a defect. I'm not enough of a radiologist to be able to tell you. But I don't remember retrieving anything of that size." He shortly repeats this, and they certainly would have removed any such large metal fragment.[159]

"Was the frontal bone present on—was the frontal bone still intact on the President?" "It was intact, yes. I can't even make it out here, really." "You can't see it there, but it was present?" "It was present, yes, sir."[160] This was the problem pointed out in this book in 1989 when I, a radiologist friend of mine, and Dr. John Lattimer and others thought that a great deal of frontal bone was missing. Some X ray!

"Could we look at the second X ray, please? This will be a right lateral view of the skull, 5-B No. 2. Dr. Humes, can you identify 5-B No. 2 as being an autopsy X ray taken on November 22, 1963?" "I guess so. That's really—it's got some very—it's a peculiar exposure . . . Those were the fracture lines, and it's difficult—I don't know why this is so radiopaque, this whole area." "You're referring to the right frontal area." "What seems to be the frontal portion of it. I don't understand why that is . . . "

"I'd like you to see if you could identify where you understand the entrance wound to have been on the skull, looking at this lateral X-ray." "Well, back in this area." "You're referring to the very low back of the cranium . . . very near to the vertebra; is that correct?" "Well, fairly near, yeah. You can't see it here. I can't see it." "—Where the entry wound was. Of course, that's not showing it in relationship to the midline." Humes responds to Gunn: "No, it does not show it. No. I don't understand this great big void there. I don't know what that's all about."[161]

Humes repeats, toward the end of what will probably be his last day in court, what the entry wound was: "In one of the bone fragments there was a semicircular defect that was not complete, only part of it. And then when we got these fragments, at one margin of it there's something that seemed to match up with that fragment that was still in the skull. My memory's pretty good. . . . I described several metallic fragments along the line corresponding to a line joining the occipital wound with the right supraorbital ridge." "Could you point out for me on X-ray No. 2 where the minute particles of metal in the bone are in relationship to the small occipital wound and the right supraorbital ridge?" "Well, they don't relate at all in this picture, as far as I'm concerned . . . The occipital wound would never be up that high anywhere up there. There's nothing up there." "You're pointing to the top left portion of the brain slightly above.—"[162]

"Are you reasonably certain that there was an X-ray that showed metallic fragments going from a small occipital wound?" "All I know is I wrote it down. I didn't write it down out of whole cloth. I wrote down what I saw." "Does that raise any question in your mind about the authenticity of the X-ray that you're looking at now in terms of being an X-ray of President Kennedy?" "Well, there's aspects of it I don't understand. I don't understand this big void up—maybe a radiologist could explain it. I don't know what this big non-opaque area that takes up half of the skull here, I don't understand that." "Do you remember seeing that on the night of the autopsy?" "No, I don't. That doesn't mean it wasn't there, but I don't remember it."[163] This is pretty stupendous stuff coming from the chief pathologist at the autopsy, when one realizes that it is more than credible and backed up by so much more evidence.

When questioned about whether there was any X-ray or photo taken with a probe inserted into the posterior thorax, Humes responds, "No, absolutely not. I do not have a recollection of such."[164]

Humes is unable to adequately explain the massive discrepancies in the weights of the brain and liver. The brain, after the autopsy, weighed 1,500 grams,[165] more than an average male brain, and yet he describes one quarter of it missing when the body came in. Others said that much more of it was missing. The liver was recorded as weighing 650 grams, a thousand less than normal. Since the brain was not weighed at autopsy as is the custom, but days later when it probably had been switched, one must conclude that the weights of the organs were invented and not taken. Strange, if the intent was to spare the family, when so many describe the scene late in the autopsy as one of gross butchery of the president's body, and a botched one at that.

One of the last things Humes says is, "I wish that the photographs were more graphic and more specifically helpful than they are. I'm disappointed by that, and I didn't find that out with certainty, really, until I got the House Select Committee hearing. I had difficulty. There was a lot of people around, and they were showing and throwing these up, and I really didn't have the time that I had here even today. And I'm somewhat confused today, as you heard. I was even more confused at that point. But, you know, that's spilled milk. There was nothing I could do about those photographs and X-rays, and I just wish they had been more graphic.

"But would I have done anything otherwise differently retrospectively? Not particularly, you know . . . No, it was a very long night that didn't get over until about 5 o'clock in the morning, just by everybody's urging that we be expeditious in our efforts. It was not an experience I'd wish to relive, I'll tell you that . . . I'm still somewhat vague on the precise bottom line of your efforts to do these things, and I hope that they're helpful. But if you ask a person enough questions often enough, you're going to confuse themselves sooner or later and not say the same thing twice. Probably minor variations, but . . . you know the expression in golf: You get paralysis of analysis. You know, you get more information than you can usefully put together. But that's for you to decide, not me. I can't tell."[166]

DR. J. THORNTON BOSWELL

"Was it your impression in 1963 that Dr. Burkley was supervising what was going on in the autopsy room?" "Well, he wasn't supervising very closely. We were acting on certain of his instructions. Initially, Jim (Dr. Humes)—at this time, I can't remember how Jim got his instructions from Burkley. I don't know whether Jim actually went upstairs to see Burkley or whether he came down. I never saw Admiral Burkley in the morgue. But at some point, Jim understood that we were to do a limited autopsy to find—I think the initial things that they told us was that we were to find the bullets, that they had captured the assailant, and that that's all they needed. And Jim argued and said that was—you know, we couldn't do that kind of an autopsy. But we started out just with the idea that we were going to do an external examination and then we were going to do a limited internal examination. But at a point shortly after we started, it was agreed that we would do a complete autopsy. But I don't know how Jim got those instructions, whether he left the morgue and went up to see Burkley or whether Burkley came down or whether he sent a messenger."

"Was it your understanding that the instructions about the scope of the autopsy were, however, coming from Burkley?" "Oh, yes."[167]

The following colloquy is instructive: "Ultimately, did it seem to you as if a complete autopsy had been performed on President Kennedy?" "Well, a generally complete autopsy was done. We did not do some of the more radical things that you do in forensic autopsies, like remove limbs or large portions of spine and that sort of thing. But, otherwise, a complete autopsy was done."

"Did you ever understand that there were any orders or instructions to limit the scope of the autopsy of the brain?" "No." "Did you understand that there were any orders or instructions to limit the autopsy of the organs of the neck?" "No." "Were the organs of the neck dissected?" "Yes."[168] As everyone knows, the latter is a lie, the thyroid was not taken, and the brain was not sectioned. Since these were the two areas that were struck by bullets, they sure weren't on the job. All that cutting for nothing.

Here come the contradictions: "When you referred to the wound in the anterior neck, what was your first impression as to what that wound was?" "I'm not sure what our first impression—oh, we thought that they had done a tracheotomy, and whether or not that was a bullet wound, we weren't sure, initially. It was after we found an entrance wound and then the blood external to the pleura that we had a track, and that proved to be the exit wound; but it was so distorted by the incision, initially we just assumed it to be a tracheotomy."

"Did you reach the conclusion that there had been a transit wound through the neck during the course of the autopsy itself?" "Oh, yes."[169] They had no idea until after the body was gone and the night had passed. It was all invented in their report. Boswell is questioned closely in the next pages about any information that might have come to him from Dallas during the autopsy, and he (and the others) deny that they had heard anything at all about the fact that the doctors in Dallas had all reported a bullet wound in the throat, which they described as a wound of entrance. It was obvious to the doctors that a tracheotomy had been performed.

After describing the scene in the morgue, he is asked, "When the body was first unwrapped, particularly the head, was the brain still present in the cranium?"

"Most of it."

"When you say most of it, approximately how much was there—"

"Well, probably half of one hemisphere was absent. The bullet came in here, went through and exploded, and bone was eviscerated, and the upper surface of that side of the brain was missing."[170]

With regard to the liver, which their record showed was 1,000 grams less than a normal male liver of 1,650 grams, he says, "I don't know how that got down to 650. Average is 1,650, and his was 650."

"So, several of the organs would be under or substantially under what the average weight would be?"

"That's right."

"Did you notice that at the time of the autopsy? Did anyone remark upon that?"

"I don't know. As I say, I don't know whether I ever appreciated that or not, because I did not write those and I didn't measure them— well, I probably did measure them—well, I probably did measure some of these because I think I took the lungs out and maybe the heart." "I note that there's no weight there for the brain. Do you remember whether the fresh brain was weighed?"

"I doubt that it was weighed."

"Why not—"

"Well, I shouldn't say that. It was formalin-fixed. We floated them in formalin and a piece of cloth, and it was taken out, and it probably was weighed. Why the weight is not down here, I don't know."

"Wouldn't that be a fairly important thing to weigh if there were a gunshot wound to the head?"

"Especially with some of it missing, that's true. I don't know why the weight's not down here. I remember taking it out."[171] They are speaking of the autopsy report itself, where these weights are missing or apparently fudged. A brain turned up a few days later, weighing more than an average male brain, and was examined and reported upon in a supplemental autopsy report.

The questions continue about this. "First, you made the statement, as I have it down, that you know that it was weighed at that time. It wasn't clear to me at what time you were saying that it was weighed. At the time of the autopsy or—"

"No."

"—The supplementary examination?"

"The supplementary examination. I'm sure it must have been weighed at the autopsy. I know of no reason why it wouldn't—the scale is right there at the head of the table, and every organ, as it's removed, is weighed. I'm sure it was weighed. Do we not have the weight of the brain in the final autopsy report?"

"There is no weight—in the supplementary report, when it was weighed at that time, there is a weight. But I am aware of no weight prior to the supplementary report."[172]

Boswell says, "Now, as far as the difference in the weights from average and these, I don't know why these are so far—these are really far off, the liver, for instance. The rest of these I wouldn't be too concerned about. They could be very accurate or they could be inaccurate."[173]

Boswell runs counter to the massive weight of evidence that a significant portion of scalp was missing. Even his own autopsy report states that " . . . there is a large irregular defect of the scalp and skull on the right involving chiefly the parietal bone but extending somewhat into the temporal and occipital regions. In this region there is an actual absence of scalp and bone producing a defect which measures approximately 13 cm in greatest diameter."

"What portions of the scalp were missing when you first began the autopsy?"

"Actually, very little. This drawing is somewhat deceptive, but there was . . . "

"When you say 'this drawing,' you're referring to MI 13?"

"MI 13, in that we were able to—the morticians were able to cover this defect completely by using some sort of plastic to cover the brain cavity, because there wasn't much bone to replace the brain cavity. But they were able to use his scalp to almost completely close the wound."

"So it would be fair to say that although there was a very large piece of skull missing, there was very little scalp missing?"

"Right."

"Do you recall whether there were tears or lacerations in the scalp?"

"Right across here and—"

"Approximately across the midline?"

"What I have previously described, post-occipital, and on the left, across the top, and then down to the right frontal area, and then the laceration extended into the right eye."[174]

Both Humes and Boswell were asked to mark the large defect and the entry hole on plastic skulls, and these may be seen in the National Archives. Immediately following the marking of the skull with what Boswell calls "approximate" markings,[175] he is asked, "Would it be your impression that, first, the markings that are contained in the face sheet, Exhibit 1, and in the autopsy protocol are accurate?" "Yes." "So those are accurate. And would it be fair to say that the markings that you have put on the skull are approximate dimensions based upon what you considered to be the accurate markings that are in the autopsy protocol and the face sheet?" "That's true, and these really only indicate sort of the magnitude of the wound and the approximate position of it."[176] So we are left with trooping down to the Archives over the next few centuries until no one cares anymore to see for ourselves what is marked on the plastic skulls. Not that the skulls do not have the centimeter markings that Boswell's drawings have that were made at the autopsy.

"With respect to the photographs, was anything done to the skull or to the hair to prepare it for the photographs? For example, was the hair cleaned at all? Was the hair parted in any way or any skull fragments put in before the photographs were taken?" "Well, photographs were taken at various stages. The scalp was pulled forward in order to demonstrate the wound of entrance. And then the scalp was reflected to show the magnitude of the wound and more or less the direction of the bullet, and then to remove the brain."[177] According to these same doctors, we don't have any wound of entrance showing in the photographs of the back of the head, that is, after we are finished wrestling with the two locations of possible wounds that show in the pictures. In the long run, they are quite clear about this, that the entry hole does not show on the cleaned-up head with the scalp pulled up over the large defect.

"Was the hair cleaned in any way for purposes of the photographs?" "No, I don't think so. There was not a lot of blood, as I remember [author's intervention: What happened to the "mess" that so many described?], and I think he had been pretty well cleaned up in the operating—in the emergency room [in Dallas, where the body was cleaned up]. And I don't think we had to do much in the way of cleansing before we took photographs." "Were any skull fragments put back into place before photographs or before X-rays?" Was the skull reconstructed to make the pictures?

"I think before we took the—ones that came from Dallas were never put back in except to try and approximate them to the ones that were present. But I think all of the others were left intact."

"So, for example, was there a fragment that had fallen out at any point that you then put back into its place before a photograph or X-ray was taken?" "Yes." "What size fragments and where did you place them at the—" "Well, the one that's in the diagram on Exhibit 1, that 10 centimeter piece I'm sure was out at one time or another. And I think maybe some of these smaller fragments down at the base of that diagram also were out at one time or another. But those were all put back."[178] There is no further clarification and the question is not pursued. But the X-ray that shows a big fracture at the top rear of the skull, with bone overlapping bone, has always made me think that this was the piece that Clint Hill brought back and that the skull was put together there for the X-ray.

The invasive procedure that the family was trying to prevent occurred because of the desperation the medical community had about Kennedy's adrenals, the question on the tip of every doctor's tongue: "I was trying to palpate through the diaphragm the adrenals, and I couldn't find them because he didn't have any. And so we talked to Burkley at some point, and we were able to go in and get the kidneys out where the adrenals sit on top of." "So you made a vertical incision that would come down from the sternum—" "Right."[179]

He thought that the brain was removed first, of the organs. "Was it necessary to make any incisions in the scalp in order to remove the brain?" "No." "Was it necessary to saw any of the bones in the cranium?" "No." "Who was it that removed the brain?" "I think Jim Humes did, but I can't be sure of that."[180]

He stated to the ARRB that the two late-arriving pieces of bone were kept out of the body and remained with the specimens as " . . . part of the forensic material that's retained for courts and trials and so forth."[181]

We have now heard on the wire services the bitching of Dr. Finck at the time about his missing notes. Boswell said, "And then Jim took all our collected notes with him to write up the autopsy."[182]

"Jim took the bucket with the brain and whatever else—we had the tissue samples for microscopy. We took all that up to our offices and into Smoky's Office (Captain John H. Stover), and at that time, it was thought that there was some sort of a cabal and that some—you know, anybody was likely to be killed, Johnson or anybody else."[183]

Boswell is then shown the photographs of the president's body, and is asked, "Approximately when during the course of the autopsy were these photographs taken? And by that I mean the beginning, middle, end."[184] "This is the beginning, very beginning. These were initial photographs." In some we see the front of the body and it has not been cut with the "Y" incision. Boswell is asked a standard question with each photo, as are the other witnesses: "To the best of your recollection, are those true and accurate representations of photographs taken at the autopsy of President Kennedy?" In the case of the first photos he was shown, he affirms this.[185] A quite lengthy discussion ensues, which interprets, or tries to interpret, what they are looking at in a photo that explains the pieces of skull and blasted scalp. It is very difficult if not impossible for the rest of us to follow.

Boswell takes responsibility for pulling the huge flap of scalp up over the large defect in the pictures. "I think that I probably was pulling the scalp up." On the same page they discuss the little glob of apparent brain matter or bone near the midline and the hairline. "I have seen that and worried and wondered about it for all these many years. Some people—many people have alleged that to be the wound. I don't think it is."[186] The wound was more to the right, about 2.5 cm, according to the autopsy report. "I think that the entrance wound is up in here someplace.

I'm talking like a couple of centimeters above the hairline and 4 centimeters to the left of the ear." The key thing with this statement is that he still has the entry four inches below where it ended up with the Clark Panel and the HSCA. The doctors will not budge from this, although Humes seemed to budge during the 1978 HSCA public hearings. See the appendix for his clarification in writing; and I was correct in my interpretation in *High Treason* that he had not, in fact, budged.

Boswell places the back wound at T2, one thoracic vertebra above where Burkley placed it in his death certificate.[187]

The eyes are open in the "stare of death" picture, and he says, "I don't think we made any attempt to take the pictures with the eyes open or closed."[188]

"I'd like you to note the semi-triangular shaped marking that goes into the forehead. Does that correspond to the laceration that we previously noted in the second view?" "Yes."[189] This is important because Boswell describes a huge laceration of the scalp from front to back,[190] and this has been commented upon extensively in my *High Treason 2*.

The crucial issue of where the entry hole is comes up again with the sixth view, the "wound of entrance in right posterior occipital region" (corresponding to black and white photos Nos. 15 and 16, and color photos Nos. 42 and 43). Boswell first agrees with the statement, as he does with all the pictures, that it is an " . . . accurate representation of photographs taken during the autopsy of President Kennedy." "In that photograph, is the scalp of President Kennedy being pulled forward?" "Yes." "For what purpose was it being pulled forward?" "In order to take the photograph, because if it wasn't pulled forward, this would just—the scalp would come down and cover the wound of entrance here. And this was necessary to demonstrate the wound here." But what is he pointing at as the entrance?

"Could you identify where on the photograph the wound of entrance was located, please—the wound of entrance in the skull?" "This is the one that I have—photograph that I have had a dilemma about for so many years. This is the white spot that you showed me in the other photograph." "Yes, down near the hairline." "Yeah. And that is not where I thought that the wound of entrance was. This must be the wound of entrance." "You're pointing down to the white marking near the hairline?" "Yeah. I'm trying to find anything up in here, and obviously the photographer was taking this in such a manner to show that. I

can't find anything else. This is in disagreement with this, obviously."
"When you say it's in disagreement, you're referring to Exhibit MI 13,
the Rydberg drawing [the drawings Humes had made for the Warren
Commission]. "Right, because this is more in the midline and lower."
"I'd like to draw your attention in the color photograph to the round, reddish marking just to the right of the ruler, very near the top of the ruler."
"Yes." "Could that round or ovular-shaped marking be the entrance
wound?" "No." Boswell explains that the red mark four inches above
where they placed the entry, which the Clark Panel and others took to be
the entrance wound, is " . . . occurring from beneath with the explosion
of the bullet," and not an entrance wound.[191]

Yet, Boswell is unable to say that the photo is simply a fake even
though he knows there was scalp missing where we now see intact scalp.
"Is there any question in your mind about whether that photograph may
have been changed or altered in any way?"

"Oh, I don't know how they would—how anybody could have done
that. I mean, all the other things I see here, my hairy arm, everything else
looks normal." "Is there anything in that photograph that appears to be
different from how you remember it on the night of the autopsy?" "No,
and I've seen it many times since. I've seen this photograph many times
since then, and it's—I think this was the photograph that was taken
there. It's just that my memory of this apparent lesion—" "Down at the
bottom of the hairline?—was in a different location. But everything else
fits." A bit later, he asks plaintively, "Is there another photograph showing the head wound of entry?"[192]

As for the back of the head missing, he confirms it: "Would the portion as it would appear on this photograph to the left of his right ear all
be the portion of the skull that was missing?" "Yes."[193] He is then shown
the photo of a large hole in someone's head: "I cannot orient this at
all."[194] Neither can almost anyone else. Then the problem becomes more
serious because "I can't identify anything else in here to tell where we
are. This is a different appearance of scalp, but there are other things in
here that I can't identify. This looks like part of the chest flap that's
down here. The hair and the bone—this is skull, I'm sure of that."
"You're pointing to the jagged piece very near the center of the photograph."[195]

Then he seems to deny that the photo showing a large hole in the
bare skull can possibly show the entry, which it was supposed to do. "It

says that there is a missile—or that it's depicting a missile wound of entrance. Do you see where that wound of entrance would be or what you were referring to, at least—" "It couldn't be."? "—as of 1966 [when they inventoried and labeled the pictures] "Couldn't be." "Couldn't be?" "No." He does see that there is a wound of exit indicated by bone beveled on the outer table of the skull.[196] "Would it be your best estimate right now that the description of that photograph from 1966 under entry No. 17 on page 5 would be inaccurate?" "Inaccurate, and I'm not sure about that one either."[197] A couple of months later, another inventory was made—were the photos doctored or switched after the doctors saw them? Jeremy Gunn, struggling, says, "To me as a lay person, it appears as if in November of 1966, view 7 is being described as an entrance wound, and in January of 1967, two months later, it's being described as an exit wound. First, do you have any reason for thinking that my understanding is inaccurate? Is there a switch in how those two photographs are described?" "Yes, I agree, and I have no explanation for that. I think they were both wrong, and I think the reason is that it's just such a terrible photograph."[198]

One wonders why they ever took them. But obviously someone should have checked with the Department of Justice, which had intervened in those years and played such a large role in the inventory of the pictures.

Boswell identifies at least three pictures that are missing: Color photos showing the tunneling of the entry hole into the scalp[199] (and perhaps the same or separate one showing clearly the entry hole into the scalp), one showing the interior of the chest,[200] and one showing the interior of the skull and the entry hole.[201] "Do you remember seeing the photographs themselves or do you remember taking the photographs?" "I've never seen the one of inside of the chest. The one of the skull wound, I thought I remembered seeing it, but I—now, I've seen an awful lot of pictures like in Livingstone's books. Where those came from, I don't know. And whether they're fabricated, some of them, or not—and I may be confusing pictures I've seen that are alleged to be autopsy photographs."[202]

After a long discussion about the damage to the brain, he admits that the bullet struck the head close to the cerebellum and that it was badly "disrupted."[203]

There follows a discussion of the weight of the brain and the fact that they did not weigh it at the autopsy itself, but some days later. Boswell agrees that an average male brain weighs 1,400 grams, and that a third of Kennedy's was gone: "That would mean that the brain . . . would have weighed, fully intact, approximately 2,000 grams."[204] The truth is, they didn't have Kennedy's brain, and the fixative that was used did not add all the weight that we now have to deal with. For a discussion of this, see page 191 of the interview. Gunn comes to the same thought as above: "It seems as if the brain of President Kennedy, even after a large portion of it had been blow away, is much or significantly larger than the average brain. Does anything seem incorrect or unusual to you in those figures or that analysis?" "I don't think so. I would not put too much emphasis on that, I don't think."[205]

Boswell has one interesting thought: "Well, another factor in favor of only one weapon or one shot entering the brain is the reasonably limited destruction of the brain. I mean, even though it's catastrophic, still, look at the intact left lobe and the intact cerebellum."[206] Limited but catastrophic.

They now look at the X rays and study the 6.5 mm fragment that was evidently taped to some skull and re-X rayed in an overlay with the AP we now have in evidence. "Let me draw your attention to a white semicircular marking in what appears to be in the right orbit, and I'll say that's on the left side of the X ray we're looking at it now. Do you see that white apparently radiopaque object?" "Yes." "Do you know what that object is?" "No." "Do you know whether that is an artifact that is just there as part of either the developing process or whether that is a missile fragment?" "No, I can't tell you that. I don't remember the interpretations. I see a lot of metallic-looking debris, X-ray opaque material . . . " "Can you relate that, again, apparently large object to any of the fragments that you removed?" "No. We did not find one that large. I'm sure of that."[207]

Well, that is as clear and startling as one gets with this evidence. Here we have a large piece of metal known to be on the outer table of the skull and thought to be close to the entry hole by the Clark Panel, but nothing like it was seen or removed, which it would have been, at the autopsy. The first public discussion of this was in *High Treason* by the present author.

Boswell is then shown X-ray No. 2, the right lateral view: "Where on the X ray that you're examining would you identify the bullet entrance wound?" "I don't think I can identify the entrance wound." "Do you recall if on the night of the autopsy you were able to identify the entrance wound in any of the X rays?" "No—well, the entrance wound, no. I thought that there was a little bit of metallic material along one transverse process down here near the entrance wound in the back, but I don't see that in this X ray."[208]

He is asked to point out where the entrance wound was, even though it isn't visible on the X ray. This is very interesting: "Has to be this general area right here. The left, left side of the X ray at the base of the skull, just an inch or so behind the vertebra."[209] "I'd like to draw your attention to what appears to be, in my term, sort of a shelf-like disruption of the skull. Do you recall seeing that on the night of the autopsy? I will say, in a very rough inexpert way, it's near the cowlick area, although that's not a medical term . . . Did you observe anything in that area on the night of the autopsy?" "No." (Author's note: this might also be where the large missing piece of the skull was put back in to see how it fit when Clint Hill delivered it from the backseat of the limousine.) "Do you have any understanding as to what that shelf or plate is there?" "I don't know what any of this is. But you're talking about this fractured line right here?" "Yes." "Well, I recognize what that is. That's a depressed fracture."

"Does that depressed fracture correlate in any way to the entrance wound that you observed on the night of the autopsy?" Again, this is where it was placed by the Clark Panel and the HSCA.

"I think it's a long way from it. I think that's quite a ways from the entrance wound."[210]

He is then asked about the apparent trail of dustlike fragments across the top of the head, and he overturns the notion that it is the track of a bullet, probably because it does not relate to any track he knew of, even a second bullet: "At first glance, that looks like a straight line. But then you've got fragments elsewhere in there, and I—that wouldn't be inconsistent with a track, but I think that those have fragmented off at some point where the bullet has hit something really hard and scattered. I don't think traveling through the soft tissue of the brain that tiny fragments are going to just spill off like that . . . I don't think that's a track even though the fact that it's a straight line might suggest that."[211] So what happened to the track of a bullet that was described low down in the skull in the autopsy report? There is a discussion for the next few pages about this, and Boswell again says, "Although I interpret it differently now than whoever did that. I see the line here, but it doesn't connect with the wound of entry, although they say it does there [in the autopsy protocol]."[212]

When Martin Luther King was assassinated, who did the Justice Department turn to first to conduct the autopsy? Dr. Boswell, who bowed out, but said that it was the same Carl Eardley who had them inventory the autopsy materials in 1966-67 (which seems to have some strange records) from Justice. When Eardley tried to rope Boswell into it, Boswell says he told him, "I'm the last one you want to go down."[213] It was Justice who flew Boswell down to New Orleans when Dr. Finck was testifying in Jim Garrison's prosecution (some would say "persecution") of Clay Shaw. Justice paid his hotel bill and plane ticket, groomed him as an expert witness, and then chickened out.[214] It was Eardley who got him to write a letter to him asking for a panel to review the autopsy evidence.[215] Naturally, many of these people were from Texas. The reader might want to look at my article in Jerry Rose's *The Fourth Decade* on the involvement of Barefoot Sanders of Dallas with the autopsy materials during the above inventories. I don't think we have the whole story on this.

About the letter he was asked to write, he said, "He just called me out of the blue and said he thought it was a good idea—said they thought it was a good idea to have an independent panel. I believe that's what it was. Now, I had been talking about this with perhaps him and other people, Jim particularly, that now that all the material was back, that it should be reviewed, if they're not going to. And whether Carl suggested it or whether I convinced him, I'm not sure. But, anyway, he was willing to accept the letter, which he essentially described to me what they wanted, and I wrote it."[216]

Speaking of the Clark Panel, this is the old-boy network at work: "This was the good panel. We met with a couple of panels. This one were all people that, for some reason, Jim and I knew. Not that we had anything to do with selecting them, but these guys—well, we did know Oscar Hunter and Russ Fisher."[217] Russell Fisher was the Chief Medical Examiner of Maryland, who had close relations with the Armed Forces Institute of Pathology. Look him up in *High Treason*. Oscar Hunter was not on the Panel. Again, interestingly, Boswell is read the relative portions of the Panel's findings about the new location of the rear head entry near the top of the head: "Did you have any discussions with members of the Clark Panel about the entrance wound location for the skull wound?" "We had a lot of discussion with them." "Did you understand or did you ever come to believe that the Clark Panel located the entrance wound at a point superior to where you had identified the entrance wound in the autopsy protocol?"

"I never believed this . . . But if you can believe that photograph that we were just looking at, this is not true, because that is way below the point they're indicating."[218]

When asked about autopsy photos that show intact scalp on most of the head, especially in the area most directly affected by the shot, he says, "And what I meant was that the wound in the scalp could be closed from side to side so that it didn't appear that there was any scalp actually—scalp missing."[219] All of a sudden, their own autopsy report and the recollection of every single witness to the head wounds was in a dream world. Every one of these people who saw the head, described scalp missing in the back, but now, on the pictures of someone's very cleaned up head, there is no scalp missing. Everyone from Dallas to the morticians who put the finished head on the pillow in the coffin stated that you could not see the missing scalp when the head was lying flat on a table or a pillow. No hairpiece was used, and no scalp was missing on the top of the head.

They cannot get around Secret Service agent Clint Hill's testimony, remarkable because he was on the trunk of the limousine looking into the backseat, which described a large piece of the back of the president's head lying in the backseat: "The right rear portion of his head was missing. It was lying in the rear seat of the car."[220] As for the shot to Kennedy's back, "Did you see any other wound other than the head wound?" "I saw an opening in the back, about 6 inches below the neckline to the right-hand side of the spinal column."[221]

But key testimony from Boswell is shortly forthcoming. He, as are the other doctors, is adamant that the entry hole was low on the head near the hairline: "Did you at any point ever change your mind about the location of the entrance wound in the skull?" "No."

"Do you know whether Dr. Humes ever changed his position with respect to the location of the entry wound in the skull?"

"I've had a lot of people tell me that he did, before the House committee that he agreed to lower this wound." (Author's note: Boswell meant to say, "raise" the wound, and not lower it. This is clear from the context.)

"You're referring to the skull wound in the back of the head?"

"Yeah, but since I've talked with him since then, he denies that, and I think he now relies on this written report right here (the autopsy report)."[222]

A major point is then cleared up in the evidence with regard to Boswell's drawing on the autopsy face sheet, which marked a large area at the top of the head as "missing": "Were skull fragments missing from this 10-by-17 area space, or does this just mean that there were fractures in the skull from the 10-by-17 space?"

"Most of that space, the bone was missing. There were a lot of small fragments attached to the scalp as it was reflected, but most of that space, the bone was missing, some of which—I think two of which we subsequently retrieved."[223] Boswell describes fractures through much of the skull, which extend into the frontal bone and the eye sockets. He says, "There was actually an explosion in his cranial cavity, and half of the right lobe of his brain disappeared through that cavity and loosened the surface of the membrane there."[224]

Another question was the "10" cm that was on the left side of Boswell's drawing of the "missing" portion at the top of the skull. He says that 60–70 percent of the space is on the right side of the head, with the remainder on the left, " . . . where that bone has been removed."[225] "That was a piece of the skull that was loose. Is that correct?" "Fragmented from the rest of the skull but still attached to the scalp on its under surface."[226]

Boswell is a proponent of the "scrunched up coat" theory, meaning that the hole is far down on his coat because the president had his hand raised, waving at the crowd. Gerald Ford or his handler first thought of this.[227] They all ignored that the bullet hole in the shirt corresponded to both the bullet hole in the coat and the hole in the back as described by Admiral Burkley in his death certificate and shown in the photographs of the back, more or less. "It was really at the base of his neck," Boswell tells us.[228] "It would not be a thoracic vertebra. It would have to be a cervical vertebra."[229] Burkley wrote that the hole was at the level of the third thoracic vertebra.

Shall we discuss the man's credibility? The problem for us "buffs" and other subhumans in the case is to find anything that might be credible and solid, but then where are we fools if we dare point to some apparently solid piece of testimony only to have our judges instantly discredit the witness on the basis of a plethora of many foolish statements.

So we'll go on with Dr. Boswell. It is difficult because I personally (and I was not alone) had to endure at various times abuse, humiliation, and ridicule while trying to get some answers from him. He doesn't dare abuse the federal lawyer who is interrogating him under subpoena.

"When we saw the clothing, we realized that where I had drawn this was—if you looked at the back of the coat, it was in the exact same place. But the coat had been—was all scrunched up like this. And the bullet went through the coat way below where this would be on the body, because it was really at the base of his neck. And the way I know this best is my memory of the fact that—see, we probed this hole which was in his neck with all sorts of probes and everything, and it was such a small hole, basically, and the muscles were so big and strong and had closed the hole and you couldn't get a finger or a probe through it.

"But when we opened the chest and we got at—the lung extends up under the clavicle and high just beneath the neck here, and the bullet had not pierced through into the lung cavity but had caused hemorrhage just outside the pleura. The wound came through and downward just above the thoracic cavity and out at about the thyroid cartilage."[230] I hope you followed that. The bullet entered the neck, came down through the chest, bruised the lung (internal organs can be damaged by body trauma when they bounce off the inside of the body), exited the middle of the throat, and went through John Connally. The "magic bullet theory" is a good name for it.

Boswell is confronted with his own drawing on the autopsy face sheet, which shows the bullet entry six inches down on the back, and the diagram (Warren Commission Exhibit 386) prepared by a Navy artist under Dr. Humes's direction. "If I understand you correctly, you have been suggesting that although the wound as depicted on the diagram in Exhibit 1 may look more as if it's thoracic, you are arguing now or your statement of clarification now would be that it's more in the neck wound. Does the drawing in Exhibit No. MI 13 better demonstrate to your mind where the actual entrance wound was?" "Exactly. Yes."[231] In those days, the Navy trained its doctors in India under qualified Yoga masters who taught them to lie on beds of nails, contortionism, and the art of getting out of a basket while someone played the flute.

Moving rapidly along, they turn to the head wound and establish that the bullet hole of entry was to be found only when a piece of bone arrived from Dallas and they could see that it was beveled in one place and fit on the skull where there was a semicircular hole with interior beveling, meaning a bullet entered there. This is about as solid as he can get, taking into account the passage of thirty-five years. "Could you tell me whether the entrance wound that you identified in the skull was something that appeared like a puncture in a bone with the remainder of the bone surrounding the hole? Or did the hole break off such that you would need other pieces of bone to be brought into place to show the entire periphery of the wound?"

"Yes, I understand it, and I think maybe the photographs that we have explain it. I believe that there was an area of bone intact down here that we could attach this to."[232] That was how they have always described it, as being in two pieces of bone.

Another conundrum in the case is Boswell's idea that the bullet tunneled under the scalp for ¾" before penetrating the skull.[233] But this is denied by Humes.

At first, Boswell denied that they had been ordered to keep their mouths shut after the autopsy, even though they had all signed a silencing order. "I don't think Jim or Pierre or I had any question about being able to say anything we wanted to at any time, except that Jim had promised George Burkley, the President's physician, that we would not discuss the adrenals. And we had to always be very cautious about talking about that and with whom we spoke about it."[234] "Bob Karnei, he was later—when he retired, he was the commanding officer at the AFIP (Armed Forces Institute of Pathology). He spoke with Livingstone, who has written those three books, and he told several different stories about the adrenals, none of which were true."[235]

See Dr. Karnei's interview with me in *High Treason 2*,[236] pages 179–190, with his statement that the president had no adrenals, which had atrophied. Dr. Boswell's chapter follows Karnei's in the same book.

Karnei's statements were corroborated for me by Dr. Lawrence Altman of the *New York Times*.[237] The *Journal of the American Medical Association* confirmed the "virtual absence of adrenal tissue" was " . . . based on interviews with Dr. Karnei and Dr. J. Thornton Boswell, one of the principal pathologists who performed the Kennedy autopsy.

"Although the pathologists had vowed to remain silent about Kennedy's autopsy, they spoke in an interview with CBS in 1967 and again with Dr. Lundberg's journal last May. But in May, they declined to discuss Kennedy's adrenals. Dr. Lundberg said Dr. Boswell agreed to discuss Kennedy's adrenal glands after he was told that Dr. Karnei had disclosed that they were missing and after Dr. James J. Humes, the other principal, released Dr. Boswell from the vow of silence.

"The impact of a full disclosure about Kennedy's adrenal condition on the 1960 presidential election . . . " The rest of Altman's article was about adrenals and politics. Dr. Altman apparently had no interest in discussing or writing about the problems with the statements of the *Journal of the American Medical Association* and their interviews with the autopsy doctors. The main interest in the medical community was the condition of Kennedy's adrenals, and it consumed much of their interest. The adrenal issue served as a convenient dodge to misdirect attention away from the issues we have been writing about.

For the record, if someone missed the point, here the doctor is still trying to castigate Karnei and implies that there were adrenals, and that Karnei or myself lied, forgetting that he confirmed this to Dr. Altman and the *Times*. "But you can't get down into the liver and stomach and so forth. So I was trying to palpate through the diaphragm the adrenals, and I couldn't find them because he didn't have any."[238] At that point, they " . . . made a vertical incision that would come down from the sternum." "Right."[239]

For the sake of history and the paper trail, it is also worth explaining how the Clark Panel came about in 1968: "At some point later on, I was asked by . . . one of the attorneys for the Justice Department that I write them a letter and request a civilian group be appointed by the Justice Department, I believe, or the President, or somebody. And I did write a letter to him, Carl Eardley."[240] It is easy to become a stooge in the military and bureaucracies.

The buck is often passed to the Kennedy family for the botched autopsy. It was they, according to this legend, who limited things and pushed it in haste.

This is not what happened.

* * *

The chain of custody of the autopsy materials, as found in the research of the House of Representatives,[241] is as follows: *At the conclusion of the autopsy on the evening of November 22, 1963, Capt. John H. Stover, Jr., the commanding officer of the U.S. Naval Medical School, gave Secret Service Agent Roy H. Kellerman all the photographic film that the medical photographers had exposed during the autopsy. (1) Additionally, Comdr. John H. Ebersol, the acting chief of radiology, gave Kellerman all the X-ray film. (2) In the early morning hours of November 23, Kellerman delivered this material to Robert I. Bouck, Special Agent in Charge of the Protective Research Division, U.S. Secret Service, which is located at the Executive Office Building, Washington, D.C. (the White House). (3)*

(102) On or about November 27, Bouck instructed James K. Fox of the Secret Service to make arrangements with the Naval Processing Center located in Anacostia, MD, to process both the black and white and the color film. (4) Fox, along with Robert L. Knudsen, Mrs. Kennedy's personal photographer, proceeded to Anacostia that same day. (5) At the Naval Center, Lt. V. Madonia of the U.S. Navy processed both black and white negatives and color positives. (6) Fox returned the materials to Bouck the same day. (7) A few days later, under more instructions from Bouck, Fox made black and white prints from the negatives in the Secret Service laboratory, located at the Protective Research Division, Executive Office Building. (8)

(103) On December 9, Bouck directed Fox to take the color positives back to the Navy photographic laboratory and supervise the processing of enlarged color prints. (9) Fox returned all the color prints and positives to Bouck that evening (10).

(104) Bouck and Edith Duncan, his administrative assistant, kept the photographic film and the X-ray films in a combination lock-safe file in the Protective Research Division of the Secret Service in the Executive Office Building, Washington, D.C. (11) The combination to the safe was known only to Bouck and Duncan. (12) From the early morning of November 23 until the transfer of the materials from the Executive

Office Building in April 1965, the Secret Service maintained custody of the X-ray and photographic films. (13)

Francis X. O'Neill gives us some interesting additional information. He says that Roy Kellerman, who was sitting in the front seat of the limousine and who was very slow to react when the shooting started, told him that he heard Jack Kennedy say, "My God, I've been hit." How did O'Neill know? Kellerman said, "I knew that man. I know his accent better than I know my father's. And there was only one man in that back seat that spoke with a Boston accent. And that was the President."[242]

"In the interview with Arlen Specter, at no time does he say anything about the words spoken by Kellerman . . . Regardless of the terminology, both of them indicate that the President said something in the back seat of that car. And that would have been after the first shot. And there is nothing whatsoever said about that in that particular 302 or in that particular statement which he made." "You're referring to Mr. Specter's summary of the—" "That is correct, yes. There's nothing. And that—to me, that's an extremely important point; that the President himself, after the first shot, said something in the back of the car." "And in what way do you regard that as being significant?"

"Because the single-bullet theory is based on that first bullet coming in the back and coming out through the neck. And it would seem that if it came out through the neck, that it would disturb the vocal cords to a point where the President could not have said something. So, whether or not the President said, 'My God, I've been hit,' or 'I've been hit. Get to the hospital,' or something similar to that, Kellerman did say, on both occasions—The terminology is different, but he did say that he heard the President in the back seat say something—the President say something. 'My God, I've been hit' or 'Get me to the hospital.'

"That, to me, would discount to a large extent the single-bullet theory as put forth by Mr. Specter. And he is the author, as I understand it, of the single-bullet theory. It would seem, to properly inform the members of the Warren Commission of the interview which we had with him, he would have set forth those particular statements."[243] O'Neill explains for several pages alterations in what he and Sibert told Specter, and this certainly shows how the Warren Commission was steered away from what these men knew.[244] We can only imagine how much else was kept from the Commission.

As for the statement in their autopsy report that the doctors reported "surgery to the head area," O'Neill is asked about the large 10 by 6.5 centimeter piece of skull, which was brought from Dallas to Dr. Humes, "who was instructed that this had been removed from the President's skull." "Can you tell me what that means; that it was removed from the President's skull?" "Well, it would be quite evident that if it was shot, it was removed. I mean, when it blow out, that would be removed. Maybe the terminology is what's confusing people. He did not, in any way, indicate to us that he thought that a surgical procedure had been performed to remove that."[245] Sibert has this to say about it: "And that, in particular, there was the statement that Humes made when we first arrived when the body first came in, and they opened the casket. It was wrapped in sheets, a sheet around the body and a separate sheet around the head, which was blood-soaked. But it was either then or when they placed the body on the autopsy table, that Humes made the statement that there's been an apparent tracheotomy and surgery in the head area . . . After the big piece of bone came in from Dallas—which was found in the limousine out in Dallas, a piece of the skull—that if I would have had the presence of mind to ask a question. Of course, things were happening fast, and you had brass and rank there that went to the ceiling. If only I had asked—'Dr. Humes, now that this piece has come in, does this account for your first statement about there being surgery in the head area?' Which didn't occur to me at the time. In Lifton's book, this was a central theme, about surgery in the head area. And looking back, I would say that that's been one thing I've always regretted that I didn't do."[246] A few minutes later he says, "Any statement like this tracheotomy and surgery to the head area, this was voiced by Humes. And we just merely made a note right at the inception of the autopsy as to what was said." "But there definitely was a large cavity and I think this probably accounts for what Humes mentioned at the first about surgery to the head area. I mean, it was just that apparent that there was that much skull missing." His position is that he merely wrote down the language that he heard the doctors use.

During the call the next day from Humes to Dr. Malcolm Perry in Dallas, O'Neill reconstructs it: "And then Perry said, 'Well, how about the bullet wound in the throat?' And I think it was Humes said, 'What bullet wound in the throat?' And they said, 'Well, we performed a tracheotomy over a wound in the throat.' And now place yourself in the position of the autopsy surgeons, to try to explain a completed autopsy on the President of the United States without explaining a bullet wound in the throat."[247] He tells us that when they learned about the new version of the autopsy report, that a bullet was now claimed to have transited the body, "Both Jim and I looked at each other and said, 'No way.' I mean, we sat—I was here; he was there. We had our office together, he and I . . . "[248] And they have been stunned ever since, because they saw and recorded that the numerous attempts to probe the back wound led nowhere, and this has been reported by many at the autopsy. "Did anyone from the FBI ever contact you and ask you any questions about that?" "No." "Did that surprise you—that no one from the FBI ever contacted you about it? About what we can say is an apparent discrepancy between what your report of the autopsy says and what the final autopsy protocol says?" "No, because the Bureau, quite frankly, had faith in us as agents, and believed—I don't know whether they still do to this day or not—that what we said was a fact. And in fact they put it into several reports, even after the information came out relative to it. We were there. We saw. We have no axe to grind. In fact, we were the only people there who had no axe to grind. It wasn't our man who was killed. It wasn't we who were conducting the autopsy and, evidently—how am I going to say this— rephrased some of the things or re-thought some of the things after the body had gone. No. We just reported it as we—as we put it down in black and white."[249]

"There was not the slightest doubt when we left there that the bullet found on the stretcher in Dallas was the bullet which worked its way out through external cardiac massage." They also thought it might be an ice, wax, or plastic bullet. "There was no explanation of it" until they heard that a bullet had been found on the stretcher in Dallas.[250]

Congressman O'Neill described in great detail in this interview the motorcade he rode in from Andrews Air Force Base with the body to Bethesda, removing the casket from the Navy ambulance, taking it into the morgue, opening the casket and seeing the sheet wrappings on the body and " . . . the body itself in these sheets was on another plastic type of a material, which we could only assume was placed under the body to prevent it from oozing blood all over the inside of the casket. Taking the sheet off the President's head, his—the first thing which struck you is, there's a massive wound in the upper right. Back here." "Just so I can say that. When you were pointing to the area above and behind your right ear—" "Yes." "Is that correct?" "That is correct, yeah."[251]

As far as the receipt for the "missile" was concerned, he explains that a Navy corpsman typed it, and Navy terminology for a fragment of any kind that was propelled is "missile," not the language of the FBI.[252] He tells us that the brain was weighed and measured and put into a jar, but half of it was gone.[253] O'Neill was another who did not recall the metal stirrup showing in some autopsy photos, nor does he recall the towel beneath the head.[254]

O'Neill's extensive comments (as are Sibert's similar statements, though with different if not more colorful invective) on now Senator Arlen Specter are rather priceless in American political history, calling him everything from a weasel to a flunky. As with all human affairs, the maggot factor effects the destiny of Pygmies same as it does the worms in a dead dog in the woods.

Jeremy Gunn addressed former FBI man James W. Sibert: "You referred earlier in this deposition to a wound on—I think you said below the shoulders." "Right." "Can you tell me where that wound was, or describe that for me?" "Well that drawing you gave me there, it was below the scapula or the shoulders. And down far below the base of the neck . . . Now Humes, as I recall, didn't give any measurement on that. He did on this piece of skull that was brought in and the fragments. It was below the shoulders and to the right of the midline of the body."[255] If Dr. Humes did not have his notes when he wrote the autopsy report because the Secret Service in fact had them, he may have invented the measurement from the mastoid process behind the ear to the bullet hole in the back for the very reason that the mastoid process was not a fixed body landmark relative to the scapula—and it was a good way to fudge the deal. He didn't have the weight of the brain, so they had to make it up.

Here are some key questions: "Were you at the—in the autopsy room at any time when photographs were being taken?" "No, I don't think I was." "You mentioned it first that you left the room while photographs were taken. I just wanted to make sure that no photos, as far as you're aware, were taken after the procedures—"

"I don't recall any additional photos being taken while I was there."

"After the first round of X-rays was taken, do you recall needing to leave the room again for additional X-rays to be taken—subsequent X-rays?"

"I don't remember being excluded like we were on that first one when X-rays were taken."

"Do you remember any discussion among the doctors about the need for performing additional X-rays during the course of the autopsy?"

"No."

"Did you ever see anyone whom appeared to you to be a photographer at the autopsy?"

"No."[256] This seems awfully strange. The FBI men were there to observe every little thing, and yet they were made to leave the room while X-rays were being taken and, apparently, the photographs. I believe some X-rays continued to be taken at various stages, and yet that is controverted by some of the testimony. If this were true, it would seem that someone did not want the FBI agents to observe the photography and possibly some of the probing. I continue to think that there was some sort of preliminary, hasty, and secret exam before the affair officially started.

Jeremy Gunn says to Sibert: "We have a peculiar situation here, where an autopsy is being rewritten later; and that there are, indeed, two versions. What is not clear . . . is why the FBI did not do something more with this?"[257] The FBI maintained for some months that Kennedy and Connally were hit with separate bullets, and certainly O'Neill and Sibert's autopsy report substantiates this, along with the recent admission from Gerald Ford that he changed the language of the Warren Report[258] to move the bullet wound in Kennedy's back much higher so that a bullet could exit the neck and strike Connally. Sibert was asked what his reaction was when he heard on July 3, 1997 that Ford had done this: "Well, I felt like, 'Thank goodness, that is the answer.' Because I couldn't account for how that wound in the back had been moved up gradually—up to the base of the neck from down below the scapula [author's note: the autopsy report places the entry just above the upper border of the scapula, but some have placed it just below]."

"So, now, based upon what you know from what you observed at the autopsy, do you have any assessment on what happened on November 22nd in Dealey Plaza?"

"Let me say this. And I've said this before. That I won't go so far as to say there was a conspiracy, but I have always had trouble assimilating the single-bullet theory. Seeing where that back wound was, an eyewitness there—12 inches from it, seeing them probe that. And from what I understand, the bullet holes both in the shirt and coat match the bullet wound in the back and with the first location that Humes gave us. And, of course, they tried to say that if he raised his arm up—But if you raise your arm up, you're not going to raise your shirt. It's pinned in there with your belt. Plus the fact that the President wore a back brace, I understand, that was pretty tight, too, which would help to hold down the shirt. And so, I've always had trouble with the single bullet or 'magic' bullet theory."[259]

"The way that the autopsy protocol reads and the conclusions that it reaches, certainly, seem different from some of the things that are in your report that was taken sometime—"

Sibert interrupts: "There were many contradictions, as I said, what it boils down to, you had two autopsy reports. The one that's in the Archives pertaining to what occurred on the night of the 22nd of November with O'Neill and I reporting what happened there. And then you had the other one, the official autopsy report. And you had what O'Neill and I had said repeated in those summary reports that were sent to Dallas, you know, out of Baltimore, by the Liaison Agent assigned to the case there. But then the findings and conclusions contained in the official autopsy report were completely different . . ."[260]

He describes the bungling that followed the autopsy, the fact that he did not know that Humes had called Perry and got a whole new idea about the shot that hit from behind and came out the neck. For that the Clark Panel and the HSCA had to move it much higher on the back to the base of the neck, just as the head wound had to be moved four inches higher later on. "Now, if only they would have called the Bureau, who would have gotten in touch with O'Neill and I through Baltimore, and said, 'We called Parkland. We found out where this tracheotomy was made where a bullet entered and exited. That's a bullet wound. And we've got some changes in the autopsy report."[261] He wanted to know why they didn't call the doctors during the autopsy, or have one of them there from Dallas during it. "We would have held up, probably, dictating our FD 302. We wouldn't have torn up our notes . . . But their official autopsy report would have gone into Bureau reports if we had gone back and interviewed Humes and been given the revised autopsy conclusions. But we had no word at all of these changes being made relative to autopsy conclusions.' "[262]

Nothing here about Humes's Saturday conclusion, about a bullet piercing the body, presumably, based entirely on a speculation having no scientific basis in his autopsy report: "The second wound presumably of entry is that described above in the upper right posterior thorax . . . The missile path through fascia and musculature cannot be easily probed. The wound presumably of exit was that described by Dr. Malcolm Perry of Dallas in the low anterior cervical region. When observed by Dr. Perry the wound measured 'a few millimeters in diameter,' however it was extended as a tracheotomy incision and thus its character is distorted at the time of autopsy."

"Is it surprising to you that someone at the FBI didn't say something to you in December or January when the FBI got a copy of the autopsy report?" " . . . They never mentioned nor did they ever come out like this and say, 'Well, your account sure is in contradiction. It doesn't agree with the other autopsy report.' "

"It appears to us, fairly clear that the FBI consistently agreed with your version of the autopsy. But subsequent FBI documents stayed with that. And the FBI never questioned it." "That is right."[263]

Interestingly, there is a report from Jim Snyder of the CBS Washington bureau that in discussions with his friend, Dr. James Humes, Humes told him of an X ray they took that shows a probe stuck through the neck, entering in the back and coming out the throat. "Humes said one X ray of the Kennedy autopsy would answer many questions that have been raised about the path of the bullet going from Kennedy's back through his throat." When you hear the rest, this probe is going to be a little hard to swallow—kind of like Deep Throat in the Watergate nightmare. Remember that the X-ray technician, Jerrol Custer, described a similar X ray showing a probe through the body, and we heard this from Robert Knudsen. But where is the X ray? Custer said the probe entered at the bullet hole at the base of the neck and exited at the throat. Now we hear that Humes told us that the FBI agents were not actually in the room during the autopsy. "They were kept in an anteroom, and their report is simply wrong. Although initially in the autopsy procedure the back wound could only be penetrated to finger length, a probe later was made—when no FBI men were present—that traced the path of the bullet from the back going downwards, then upwards slightly, then downwards again exiting at the throat. One X-ray photo taken, Humes said, clearly shows the above, as it was apparently taken with a metal probe of some kind that was left in the body to show the wound's path.

"Humes said that a wound from a high power rifle, once it enters a body, causes muscle, etc. to separate and later contract; thus the difficulty in initially tracing the wound's path in the case of Kennedy. Also, once a bullet from a high power rifle enters a body its course can be completely erratic; a neck wound could result in a bullet emerging in a person's leg or anywhere else.

"Humes also said he had orders from someone he refused to disclose—other than stating it was not Robert Kennedy—to not do a complete autopsy. Thus the autopsy did not go into JFK's kidney disease, etc. Humes' explanation for burning his autopsy notes was that they were essentially irrelevant details dealing with routine body measurements, and that he never thought any controversy would develop from his having done this." We also learn that Humes was contemplating a suit against the *Saturday Evening Post* and their writer for the hatchet job they did on his alleged autopsy.[264]

If this story is at all accurate, then my guess that Humes might have fudged the weights and measurements gains credence, since all this sort of detailed stuff was "irrelevant." We are also told that there was essentially no complete autopsy, which flies in the face of the repeated claims by the doctors that they fulfilled the requirements of a complete autopsy. And we now know that they were hot after the adrenals like dogs after a steak and cut the president's belly open for that purpose and that purpose only, though apparently weighing the remainder of his abdominal organs, although possibly with great inaccuracy. Or did they weigh them at all? Clearly, Humes would say the FBI men were not in the room, contrary to all the evidence, if he had something to hide and therefore had to discredit the men behind their backs in a private discussion with Snyder, something he didn't dare do in public.

And were the FBI men there or weren't they? Or were they just dazed with the terrible shock that so many felt, or was Sibert trying to tell us something when he could not recall many events? Somebody is lying at every step and on every question, and I don't think it was these particular FBI men, although I recognize that Sibert and O'Neill could not see everything that occurred at the autopsy and in fact apparently did not. What remains is their strong knowledge that the pictures are inaccurate, wrong, or missing. They did not make up what they wrote they overheard the autopsy doctors say. They had to get it from someplace. But was everyone fudging? Is this the bottom line of modern organized human endeavor: Disorganization? And if Humes burned his notes (and those of Finck too?) because they were irrelevant, did the irrelevant details include the placement of the back entry wound? Did someone tell him, "Oh, you better make something up, because we have to have it? That's why you did the autopsy." But he forgot.

As with the issuance of the Warren Commission's twenty-six volumes of supporting documents, and the same for the HSCA, the media is unable to take the time to study what is actually being released and is mostly dependent upon the statements issued by these agencies. In addition, it takes years of immersion to master just the medical evidence in the JFK case, and it is easy for half-baked theories and authors to interpose themselves in their write-ups of the case. It is interesting that the wire services quoted two authors who are deadly foes of any evidence showing a faked case and forged evidence, and did not quote researchers who have compiled massive evidence of forgery. Until 1989 and the publication of *High Treason*, no one presented a cohesive and comprehensive argument with the evidence for a faked case and forged evidence.

My 1995 book, *Killing Kennedy and the Hoax of the Century*, led directly to the medical interviews conducted by the ARRB soon afterward. This book synthesized the massive evidence in the official record that established the argument for faked autopsy evidence, and also published hundreds of pages from the previously secret documents that were released as a result of the JFK act and the establishment of the ARRB, and independent action of the National Archives.

To see the Military Mind at work, this is what Dr. Humes thinks of us peons and truth seekers: "I continue to be dismayed by the large number of these so-called assassination buffs. In fact, they seem to proliferate. I was also very displeased with the Oliver Stone film, which my children urged me to go see because they said, 'They got some guy that looks like he's 89 years old playing your rôle, and you were 39.' So I did go to see it, and it just seemed to me to be a disservice to the American people. There were so many vague and cloudy implications that were mentioned during it. I just found it mind-boggling. It just disturbed me.

"The other people—who they got an Academy Award for film editing, which they deserved because they took contemporaneous film and blended it with their film, and it really made it look like it was contemporaneous. So I think young people who weren't even born or were in their infancy when this event occurred can be just totally confused by it, such things as that. That really has nothing to do with anything. Apparently, that's artistic license. That's what I understand. But I didn't think it was very helpful to anybody."

"Okay. Thank you very much, Dr. Humes. We appreciate it." Jeremy Gunn said.

"Thank you for the opportunity to be here, and I hope I have not appeared to be evasive, because I had no intention of being evasive . . . "[265]

I appreciate the compliment, and all of us patriots who are so summarily consigned to the untouchable caste and dung heaps of "buffs," for our trouble, await the final destruction of the lies these arrogant *functionaries* have bestowed upon us, forever warping the history of this great nation: The lie in the autopsy report of a transiting bullet through the torso and neck from back to front, the covering up of additional shots striking the president from in front, the lie about the condition of the brain, and failing to openly admit that the autopsy photos and X-rays are frauds. What we got were oblique admissions when they did in fact find fault with this material, but none dare either face or state the truth openly. Like most bureaucrats and timeservers in every government and military in the world, they are thinking of their perks and retirement, and nobody is going to rock the boat where personal interests are concerned.

We can only be grateful for the scraps of truth they have insisted upon with regard to the low position of the entry hole into the head near the hairline and some other bits and pieces. That low entry means John Kennedy was not shot in the head from that sixth-floor window.

So what do you suppose is going to be done about all this? Isn't it time for a legal proceeding of some sort? But it's too late, isn't it?

One must keep in mind that the Assassination Records Review Board was set up to counteract the ideas in the Oliver Stone film *JFK* (if he'd left Jim Garrison out of it, there'd have been no problem, but he had, like Garrison, to hoax it up), but the results are the new witness interviews we now have and are grateful for. One has to look at the political makeup of those on the Board, and statements all along by them that they saw no evidence of conspiracy in the murder. At the time the interviews above were released, the chairman, John Tunheim, stated that the medical evidence showed no indication of a shot from in front. Interesting that a lawyer was qualified to pass on the medical evidence in this fashion. Tunheim, an assistant attorney general of Minnesota, was appointed to the federal bench during this inquiry and had his moment of fame on *Oprah Winfrey* with Marina Oswald and some fool writers pulling the wool over everyone's eyes.

It will be interesting to see what the report of the Board has to say about the medical findings, if anything. As far as the research community is concerned, the JFK case is now on an entirely new level of thought and inquiry, thanks to the work of the ARRB. The focus of questions is now primarily on the authenticity or lack of it in the official evidence and testimony. This is something new in the experience of most of us.

My conclusion is: All the evidence in the case was faked. The proofs for this are many. In fact the accumulating mountain of clues in all the other areas of evidence beside the medical is too massive almost to be believed. It was staring us in the face for thirty-five years. We must now suspend our disbelief and approach the case from an entirely different direction, with an assumption of fabricated evidence. Then it all begins to fit and we can understand the whole picture. In the end, the case was simple once you understood it, but no one did for most of those years, laboring in the garbage pits of history. It is clear that the autopsy doctors lied on key points, as well, but what is the totality of the lie, if even they did not have their own notes to write the autopsy report from? One tragedy is, among many, that so many years have passed and witnesses began to pass away one by one. There was simply not a good enough job done investigating the medical evidence while there was a chance early in the case. The conspirators' main goal was to prevent just that from happening and let the memories of those who knew the truth fade with time. They relied on the passage of time to cover everything up better.

But today each witness makes one big point that gives us a clue, and each often gives a different clue from the next. That's all they dare to do when they might all agree on the position of the entry hole, and the larger hole in the scalp and bone in the back of the head—they can only say so much. But we can now assemble much more of the puzzle as each one gives us a new piece. In those days they used to ruin or kill security risks, and the fear of that still strikes fear into the witnesses, many of whom were in the military.

How much else are they hiding?

1. James W. Sibert interview with the Assassination Records Review Board, Jeremy Gunn, September 11, 1997, p. 145.
2. James Sibert, ARRB, to Jeremy Gunn, September 11,1997, pp. 126–29. See also 130–32 for "I don't recall anything that appeared like that during the autopsy" with regard to Photo No. 44 of a large hole with reflected scalp in someone's skull, which no witness has been able to orient.
3. Sibert, p. 136–7; O'Neill, pp. 34–7, 184–201, 215, 217.
4. Francis X. O'Neill, ARRB September 12, 1997, pp. 158–162.
5. Ibid., pp. 164–166.
6. Ibid., p. 157–8.
7. John T. Stringer, ARRB, July 16, 1996, p. 189.
8. John T. Stringer, ARRB, July 16, 1996, p. 153.
9. John T. Stringer, ARRB, July 16, 1996, pp. 216–218, 221–2.
10. Ibid., pp. 193–5.
11. Ibid., p. 174–5.
12. Ibid., p. 199.
13. Ibid., p. 213.
14. Ibid., pp. 214–216.
15. Ibid., p. 213.
16. ARRB Stringer interview, April 8, 1996 (MD 227).
17. Ibid.
18. Ibid.
19. The quotes from the autopsy reports may be found in *The New York Times* edition of the Warren Report, p. 505.
20. *Killing Kennedy and the Hoax of the Century,* H. Livingstone, Carroll & Graf, 1995, pp. 35 forward.
21. Dr. Pierre A. Finck, testimony to the ARRB, May 24, 1996, pp. 41–5.
22. Dr. Pierre A. Finck, testimony to the ARRB, May 24, May, 1996, p. 41–5.1996, p. 47.
23. Ibid., p. 51.
24. Ibid., pp. 79–87.
25. Ibid., pp. 86–7.
26. Ibid., pp. 98–101.
27. Ibid., pp. 130–134.
28. ARRB deposition with Saundra Spencer, June 5, 1997, (MD 233), p. 6.
29. ARRB interview with Saundra Spencer, December 13, 1996 (MD 233) deposition, June 5, 1997.
30. ARRB interview with Saundra Spencer of December 13, 1996.
31. ARRB Spencer interview of December 13, 1996 (MD 233).
32. Discussion with researcher Kathleen Fitzgerald, August 8, 1998.
33. ARRB Spencer interview of December 13, 1996 (MD 233).

34. ARRB Spencer, December 13, 1996 (MD 233).
35. ARRB Spencer deposition June 5, 1997, p. 28.
36. ARRB Spencer interview Supra.
37. ARRB description of a call from Randolph Robertson, M.D., September 27, 1996, Douglas Horne.
38. HSCA interview with Robert Knudsen, August 11, 1978, p. 5.
39. ARRB interview with Joe O'Donnell, January 29, 1997, conducted by Jeremy Gunn and Douglas Horne on a lead by Gary Aguilar, M.D., (MD 231).
40. ARRB 2nd interview with Joe O'Donnell, conducted by Jeremy Gunn, David Marwell, Dave Montague and Douglas Horne, February 28, 1997.
41. Secret Service statement signed by Kellerman, Bouck, Duncan, Fox, and Kelly in February 1967. Record Number 180-10109-10368, Agency File No. 002631.
42. Outside contact report of Andy Purdy, HSCA, with James K. Fox, August 7, 1978. Fox told Purdy that the black and white film was developed at the Secret Service lab, and the color was done at the Naval Processing Center. Fox said that Robert Knudsen was with him there and in the drying room. Fox checked and there was film on each side of the color film holders, but that some of the black and white was missing. He and Knudsen were sent back by Bouck in 4 to 5 days to have prints made, and there were two women in the drying room who passed out when the pictures came through. He did not help Knudsen put the prints in holders and recalled only one or two sets.
43. Ibid.
44. Knudsen HSCA interview supra, p. 7 and in many other places.
45. Spencer deposition, p. 35.
46. Ibid., pp. 33–42.
47. Ibid., p. 44.
48. Ibid., p. 46.
49. Ibid., pp. 49–51.
50. Ibid., pp. 52–3.
51. Ibid., p. 55.
52. Ibid., pp. 35, 56.
53. ARRB interview with Dennis David, February 14, 1997 (MD 177)
54. Ibid., p. 58.
55. Ibid., p. 58–9.
56. Ibid., pp. 61–2.
57. ARRB interview with Gloria Knudsen, October 8, 1996.
58. HSCA Knudsen interview with Andy Purdy, August 11, 1978, p. 23.
59. ARRB interview with Knudsen's widow and children, May 7, 1996, MD 230.
60. CBS Memorandum, January 10, 1967, from Bob Richter to Les Midgley.
61. HSCA Knudsen interview with Andy Purdy, August 11, 1978, p. 24.
62. Ibid., pp. 31–2.
63. Ibid., p. 33.
64. Ibid., pp. 34–5.
65. Ibid., pp. 39–40.
66. *Killing The Truth*, H. E. Livingstone, 1993, after p. 384. See also the chapter on Diana Bowron, p. 179.
67. Knudsen supra, p. 36.
68. Ibid., p. 41.
69. Ibid., p. 40.
70. Ibid., p. 6.

71. Ibid., p. 5.
72. Ibid., p. 42–3.
73. Ibid., p. 44.
74. Ibid., p. 13.
75. Ibid., p. 45.
76. Ibid., p. 46.
77. Ibid., pp. 46–7.
78. Ibid., p. 47.
79. Ibid., p. 47. Knudsen continues to repeat that he saw this picture of the probes, and another example is on p. 51–3.
80. Ibid., pp. 52–3.
81. 7 HSCA 23 (102). This passage states that Lt. V. Madonnia processed the photos, both black and white negatives and color positives on November 27th, 1963, and a few days later, Fox made black and white prints from the negatives in the Secret Service laboratory at the EOB. On December 9, Fox was again sent to Anacostia where enlarged color prints were made. (103) Evidently, Knudsen was not with him but had knowledge of this.
82. Knudsen HSCA interview supra., p. 16–20.
83. R. E. Boyajian, USMC report to his C.O. of 26 November, 1963.
84. HSCA record No. 180-10109-10310.
85. ARRB interview with Floyd Boring September 19, 1996, (MD 259).
86. ARRB interview with Leonard Saslaw, April 26, 1996 (MD 254) and Saslaw's Affidavit, 15 May, 1995 (MD 74).
87. ARRB interview with Robert Bouck, May 2, 1996 (MD 258).
88. Ibid.
89. Ibid.
90. Report HSCA, pp. 2, 227–235; *High Treason*, H. E. Livingstone, Chapter 8, pp. 127–137. See 11 HSCA 521–530.
91. Knudsen interview supra, p. 26–27.
92. ARRB interview with Robert F. Karnei, M.D., May 21, 1996, (MD 178)
93. ARRB interview with Dr. Robert F. Karnei, Jr., May 21, 1996 by Jeremy Gunn, Tim Wray, and Doug Horne.
94. *High Treason 2*, H. Livingstone, Carroll & Graf, 1992, p. 306.
95. HSCA interview with Thomas Evan Robinson, January 12, 1977, Andy Purdy and Jim Conzelman.
96. *High Treason 2*, H. E. Livingstone, Carroll & Graf, 1992, p. 580: " 'There was one very small hole in the temple area, in the hairline. I used wax in it, and that is all that I had to do. I just put a little wax in it.' 'What side was it on?' 'I can't remember for sure, but I think it was on the right side.' In another interview he told me that the skull was penetrated in two or three more places by shrapnel, which he filled with wax. These places were near the eyes."
97. ARRB interview with Tom Robinson, June 21, 1996.
98. ARRB interview with Tom Robinson, June, 1996 (MD 180).
99. ARRB interview with John Van Hoesen, conducted by Doug Horne, September 26, 1996 (MD 181).
100. ARRB interview with Tom Robinson, June 21, 1996 (MD 180).
101. Ibid.
102. ARRB Sibert Deposition, p. 122.
103. ARRB interview with Earl McDonald, May 14, 1996 (MD 228).
104. 7 HSCA 46, top of page.

105. The "Burn Party," *High Treason 2*, H. E. Livingstone, Carroll & Graf, 1992, pp. 322–326.
106. ARRB interview with Keny Vrtacnik of AFIP, November 13, 1996.
107. *High Treason 2*, H. Livingstone, Carroll & Graf, 1992, p. 311.
108. ARRB interview of Janie B. Taylor, November 24, 1995, with Dave Montague (MD 45).
109. ARRB contact with Nancy Denlea, by Doug Horne, January 13, 1997.
110. Richard Sprague memo for file of March 18, 1977, HSCA file No. 000988, Record Number 180-10086-10295)
111. Knudsen HSCA interview, pp. 18–19.
112. 7 HSCA 32–3.
113. Knudsen HSCA interview, p. 21.
114. Boswell ARRB interview, February 1996 p. 128.
115. ARRB interview with Richard Davis, February 27, 1997 (MD 179).
116. LBJ Library, January 26, 1967.
117. ARRB interview with Velma Reumann (Vogler) October 4, 1996 (MD 234).
118. ARRB interview with Vincent Madonia, June 21, 1996 (MD 232). (See also interview of November 27, 1996)
119. Ibid.
120. Ibid.
121. Custer, ARRB, p. 112, Jeremy Gunn states that the accompanying description of X-ray No. 1 was identified in the 1966 inventory by the doctors as being an "anterior/posterior view of the skull, slightly heat damaged." See the discussion below by Custer saying that the X-ray was deliberately damaged by the radiologist to obscure an entry wound.
122. Jerrol Custer, ARRB, October 28, 1997, p. 167–172.
123. Ibid., p. 183.
124. Ibid., pp. 193–4.
125. Ibid., pp. 114–115.
126. Ibid., pp. 116–117, 120.
127. Ibid., p. 126.
128. Ibid., p. 127.
129. Ibid., p. 138.
130. *Killing Kennedy and the Hoax of the Century* H. E. Livingstone, Chapter 4, "The Forged Autopsy X-rays and Dr. Mantik's Historic Findings," pp. 79–114. "Great White Patch," pp. 84–7, 110, 113, 260, 264.
131. Ibid., p. 139.
132. Ibid., p. 142–3.
133. Ibid., p. 181. "It went right through from the site of the skin wound, when you looked at the wound from the inside and matched them up with the scalp wound." "Did you have any difficulty identifying the scalp entry wound during the time of the autopsy?" "No, I didn't at the time of the autopsy, but the photographs I think create ambiguity. For me they do, much to my displeasure and dismay. I thought they would erase ambiguity rather than create it."
134. Letter of James J. Humes, M.D., March 11, 1996 to the ARRB.
135. *High Treason 2*, H. E. Livingstone, Chapter 10, p. 213.
136. Custer, ARRB testimony, p. 38, 144–5.
137. Humes, ARRB interview of February 13, 1996, p. 82–85.
138. *High Treason 2*, p. 184–5.
139. Humes, ARRB, p. 90.
140. Ibid., pp. 96, 97.
141. Ibid., p. 106.

142. Ibid., p. 147.
143. Ibid., p. 111.
144. Ibid., pp. 155, 157.
145. Ibid., p. 166.
146. Ibid., p. 170.
147. Ibid., pp. 177, 181.
148. Ibid., p. 182.
149. Ibid., beginning on p. 184, the Seventh View.
150. Ibid., p. 192.
151. Ibid., p. 193.
152. Ibid., p. 200.
153. Ibid., p. 195.
154. Ibid., p. 197.
155. Ibid., p. 210.
156. Ibid., p. 207.
157. Ibid., p. 209.
158. Ibid., p. 209.
159. Ibid., p. 213.
160. Ibid., pp. 214–215.
161. Ibid., pp. 216, 218.
162. Ibid., pp. 220–1.
163. Ibid., pp. 222–3.
164. Ibid., pp. 223–4.
165. Autopsy report, and Finck, supra, p. 116–17.
166. Humes, ARRB, pp. 236–40.
167. ARRB, Boswell, pp. 24–26.
168. Ibid., p. 25.
169. Ibid., p. 24.
170. Ibid., pp. 42–43.
171. Ibid., pp. 48–50.
172. Ibid., pp. 51–2.
173. Ibid., p. 52.
174. Ibid., p. 90–1.
175. Ibid., p. 94.
176. Ibid., pp. 94–5.
177. Ibid., p. 97.
178. Ibid., pp. 98–99.
179. Ibid., p. 103.
180. Ibid., p. 104.
181. Ibid., pp. 107–8.
182. Ibid., p. 108.
183. Ibid., p. 109.
184. Ibid., pp. 136, 138.
185. Ibid., p. 139.
186. Ibid., pp. 150–1.
187. Ibid., p. 155.
188. Ibid., p. 159.
189. Ibid., p. 159.
190. Ibid., pp. 139, 142, 159.

191. Ibid., pp. 160–4.
192. Ibid., pp. 164–5.
193. Ibid., p. 167.
194. Ibid., p. 97.
195. Ibid., p. 170.
196. Ibid., p. 173.
197. Ibid., p. 175.
198. Ibid., p. 175.
199. Ibid., p. 177.
200. Ibid., pp. 176–7.
201. Ibid., p. 177.
202. Ibid., p. 178.
203. Ibid., p. 186.
204. Ibid., p. 190.
205. Ibid., pp. 191–2.
206. Ibid., p. 195.
207. Ibid., pp. 196–7.
208. Ibid., p. 198.
209. Ibid., p. 199.
210. Ibid., pp. 199–200.
211. Ibid., p. 201.
212. Ibid., p. 205.
213. Ibid., p. 213.
214. Ibid., pp. 212–213.
215. Ibid., p. 214, and as above.
216. Ibid., pp. 214–5.
217. Ibid., p. 216.
218. Ibid., p. 117.
219. Ibid., p. 60.
220. Warren Commission Hearings, vol. 2, p. 141.
221. Ibid., p. 143.
222. Boswell, p. 62.
223. Ibid., pp. 64–5.
224. Ibid., p. 68. Head damage begins on p. 63.
225. Ibid., p. 69.
226. Ibid., p. 70.
227. Ibid., p. 75.
228. Ibid., p. 75.
229. Ibid., p. 74.
230. Ibid., pp. 75–6.
231. Ibid., pp. 76–7.
232. Ibid., pp. 80–1.
233. Ibid., p. 82 and before, 166.
234. Ibid., p. 11.
235. Ibid., pp. 14–15.
236. *High Treason 2*, H. E. Livingstone, Carroll & Graf, New York, 1992.
237. *The New York Times*, October 6, 1992, science section.
238. Ibid., p. 103.
239. Ibid.

240. Ibid., p. 10.
241. 7 HSCA 23 (100.1) 1979 (House Select Committee on assassinations).
242. ARRB O'Neill deposition, September 12, 1997, pp. 27–8.
243. Ibid., pp. 216–217.
244. Ibid., pp. 11–12, 34–38, 184–201, 215–217.
245. ARRB Francis X. O. Neill deposition, p. 120.
246. ARRB deposition of James W. Sibert, September 11, 1997, pp. 16, 22, 67, 95–6, 98, 158.
247. Ibid., pp. 31–2.
248. Ibid., p. 33.
249. Ibid., p. 34.
250. Ibid., pp. 29–30.
251. Ibid., p. 60. O'Neill says Kennedy's eyes were open, his mouth was in a sort of a grimace, and his hands were up (clenched).
252. Ibid., p. 78.
253. Ibid., p. 116–117.
254. Ibid., p. 152 & 155.
255. ARRB Sibert deposition, p. 74–5.
256. ARRB Sibert deposition, pp. 79–80.
257. Ibid., p. 160.
258. Associated Press story in the Baltimore *Sun*, 3 July, 1997, p. 4A: "Conspiracy theorists seize on Ford change in Warren Report; Entry wound was moved, reinforcing single-bullet theory in JFK assassination."
259. Ibid., p. 161–2.
260. Ibid., pp. 154–5.
261. Ibid., p. 156.
262. Ibid., p. 156–7.
263. Ibid., pp. 158–9.
264. CBS Memorandum, January 10, 1967, from Bob Richter to Les Midgley. Very graciously provided to the author by Roger Feinman.
265. James J. Humes, testimony to the ARRB, February 13,43 1996, pp. 239–240.

ARRB CALL REPORTS/MEETING REPORT

DESCRIPTION OF THE CALL

Date: 11/24/95
Subject: **Interview Of Janie B. Taylor Re:JFK Autopsy Information**

Summary of the Call:

I spoke with retired biologist Janie Taylor today regarding an account she was told regarding the JFK Autopsy. Taylor worked as a biologist at the National Institute of Health (NIH) in 1963. NIH is physically located across the street from the Bethesda Naval Medical Center, where the JFK autopsy was conducted. I informed her of the fact that the secrecy order applicable to people at the autopsy was lifted in 1977.

A man named Clarence Israel (deceased) of Rockville, MD told Taylor that his brother (deceased and no name given) was one of two African-American orderlies present in the autopsy room of the Medical Center the day of the autopsy. Israel said his brother had not mentioned the story to anyone including his wife & daughter who his brother outlived. His brother wanted to insure that his story was known because he was verbally threatened by a guard at the time of the autopsy.

Taylor said that African-Americans during that time period were often ignored and that non-African-American workers in many workplaces would assume that an African-American's presence did not count. She believed that activities were often done in their presence with the perception that the activities would never be reported.

Israel told her **the orderlies saw one doctor was in the autopsy room at the Medical Center who was waiting for some time prior to the arrival of the body and any other physicians. When the body arrived, many people were forced out of the room and the doctor performed some type of mutilation of three bullet punctures to the head area. The doctor was working at a very "hurried" pace and was done within a few minutes, at which point he left the autopsy room.**

Taylor believes she may have Israel's obituary which may provide more information about the family and any other relatives which may know of the story. *I thanked her for her time and told her I would send an information packet and letter to her based on our conversation.*

Taylor's information is:

Mrs. Janie B. Taylor

DESCRIPTION OF THE CALL

Date: 05/07/96
Subject: **Gloria Knudsen Called ARRB**

Summary of the Call:

As she promised Dave Montague on Monday, May 6, 1996, Gloria Knudsen called Dave Montague on May 7, 1996 to discuss her husband's role as White House Photographer in the events surrounding the Kennedy Assassination. I was invited to sit in on the call by Dave Montague.

She began by saying that she and two of her four children (Yvonne Becker and Robert Knudsen) have important things they want to say (about their father's recollections), but that they would all rather do it in person. She preferred meeting with us this week to the middle of next week (which we initially suggested), so Dave Montague and I agreed to a 10:00 appointment this Friday, at ARRB.

She did offer up the following statements about her husband—these are summaries and not a verbatim transcript:

-He worked for five presidents (Truman, Eisenhower, Kennedy, LBJ, and Nixon) as White House photographer;

-She said her husband felt extremely close to President Kennedy, and was emotionally broken by the assassination;

-She said her husband would never lie, was a deep thinker, and was an extremely intelligent person who always carefully measured his words.

Prior to the assassination: Her husband, she says, would have been the president's photographer on the Dallas trip, but injured himself earlier that week when he got a metal splinter in his eye while restoring an antique piece of furniture. As a result, he had the splinter removed a couple of days or so prior to the Texas trip, and had to recuperate, so the "other" photographer (presumably Cecil Stoughton) got to make the trip instead.

Day of the Assassination: While eating lunch at home on the day of the assassination, she and her husband heard about the shooting of the President on the radio. About 3:00 that afternoon, her husband got a telephone call, from the Secret Service she believes, and was ordered to go to Andrews AFB, meet the airplane, and accompany the body to Bethesda. At this point she said that this was all she was going to tell us on the phone, and that the rest would have to wait until Friday, May 10, 1996.

I told her that I had read the transcript of her husband's testimony before the HSCA, and that I was very interested in what she had to say. She then stated that she was still very angry about the fact that the HSCA had promised her husband a copy of the transcript, but that they had never received it. I told her that this document about her husband, and a few others (OCRs), were all open documents which were releasable to the public, and that we would be happy to provide her with copies after she talked with us; this made her very happy. (I briefed David Marwell on this subsequently and received his approval to provide these documents to the Knudsen family after the interview was over.)

She stated her husband had participated in another investigation into the assassination which she thought the public knew nothing about, and said she would bring the letter which invited him to appear in this forum with her on Friday to ARRB. She thought that the letter was received in September, 1988. (Her husband died in 1989.)

I asked if her husband kept any diary or journal, and she said that she thought that he did, and said she would have to look for them. We asked her to do so, and she said she would try.

When briefed subsequently, David Marwell asked that we audio-tape the meeting with the Knudsen family members.

MEETING LOGISTICS

Date: 05/10/96
Agency Name: Witnesses/Consultants
Attendees: Gloria Knudsen and Children Terri and Bob, Jeremy
                        Gunn, Tim Wray, Dave Montague, and Doug Horne
Topic: **JFK Autopsy Photography**

Summary of the Meeting

The surviving wife and two of the four children of official White House photographer Robert L. Knudsen (part-time from 1946–1953, and full-time from 1958–1974) met with ARRB staff at their own request to inform us of recollections passed to them by their father before he died in January 1989. The meeting was audiotaped—duration of recording is one 90-minute cassette, and about 10–15 minutes of cassettee number 2.

All 3 family members recounted that Mr. Knudsen had told them he photographed the autopsy of President Kennedy, and was the only one to do so. All statements henceforth recorded in this meeting report represent summaries of what family members attributed to their father. After dressing in a civilian business suit (normal procedure even though he was a Navy Chief Petty Officer), he reported to the White House for duty on November 22, 1963, and was subsequently directed to meet Air Force One at Andrews AFB and accompany the body of the President to Bethesda. His daughter Terri said her father called in to the White House to ask for instructions before going in; his wife, Gloria, said that he received a call at home from the Secret Service telling him to go in to work. All family members agreed that he had met Air Force One at Andrews, accompanied the official motorcade to Bethesda, and had photographed the autopsy of President Kennedy. He had told them it was the hardest thing he had ever had to do in his life, in the emotional sense, since he reportedly had a brotherly relationship with President Kennedy. All 3 family members said that they did not see their father for 3 days after he left the house (i.e., until after the funeral on November 25, 1963), with the exception of Saturday, November 23, 1963 when they were allowed to view the casket lying in state in the East Room of the White House, where Mr. Knudsen was working that day.

His son, Bob, said he thought his father had ridden in the last car in the motorcade with some Secret Service agents from Andrews to Bethesda, and had entered Bethesda through the back door at the loading dock; he was present and began working at "set up" for the autopsy.

Mr. Knudsen had recounted to family members the following substantive remarks:

-he witnessed and photographed probes inserted in the President's body which left no doubt of the number and direction of bullet trajectories; son Bob thought that his father had described 3 probes in the body (2 in the thorax/neck, and one in the head);

-although none of the family remembers any discussion of type of camera, film, format of film, or number of pictures taken, they all claimed their father told them that he was the only one in the morgue with a camera, and believed he was the only person to photograph the autopsy;

-*the Secret Service took his film from him as soon as he had exposed the various pieces of film*, which he thought strange, since he was personally acquainted with the agent and thought that the agent trusted him;

-the only family member who remembered Mr. Knudsen talk about having developed autopsy film was son Bob, with whom he had been a business partner in the family photography business for approximately 10 years before his death;

-they believed that he had been questioned by Warren Commission staff, but could recall no names or details;

-after he appeared before the HSCA in 1978, he told his family (at different times) that 4 or 5 of the pictures he was shown by the HSCA did not represent what he saw or took that night, and that one of the photographs he viewed had been altered. His son Bob said that his father told him that "hair had been drawn in" on one photo to conceal a missing portion of the top-back of President Kennedy's head;

-Mrs. Gloria Knudsen said that her husband Robert had told her that the whole top of the President's head was gone, and that the President's brain(s) were largely missing (blown out);

-all 3 family members said that although the HSCA had promised a smooth copy of the deposition transcript, they were all (including Robert Knudsen) disturbed by the fact that no smooth copy had ever been received. Subsequent attempts by Robert Knudsen to obtain a copy of the smooth transcript from Congress were unsuccessful, causing him extreme frustration when he was told (at a time not clearly identified) that there was no record of him or his testimony;

-although none of the family members recalled seeing the draft copy of the deposition transcript, when shown Mr. Knudsen's signature on the original copy, they agreed it was his signature, thus substantiating that Mr. Knudsen did at least see the draft;

-all 3 family members agreed that Mr. Knudsen appeared before an official government body again sometime in 1988, about 6 months before he died in January 1989. They all had the impression that it was "on Capitol Hill," and that it may have been a Congressional inquiry of some kind. They were unanimous that Mr. Knudsen came away from this experience very disturbed, saying that 4 photographs were "missing," and that one was "badly altered;" Mrs. Gloria Knudsen used the phrase "severely altered" regarding the one altered photograph when recounting her husband's statements afterwards. She further elaborated that the wounds he saw in the photos shown him in 1988 did not represent what he saw or took. He also told them that some of the details in the room in the background of the photos were "wrong." He had recounted that this experience was a waste of time for him because as soon as he would answer a question consistent with what he remembered, he would immediately be challenged and contradicted by people whom he felt already had their minds made up;

-Mr. Knudsen expressed skepticism with his daughter Terri over the years about the conclusions of the Warren Report in regard to the President's wounds and the manner in which he was shot, because of the observations he had made the night of the autopsy;

-when asked by ARRB staff, all 3 members of the Knudsen family said that their father never spoke with any assassination researchers, and never read any assassination books (with the exception of looking at the pictures in one in 1988 with his son, Bob).

Mrs. Knudsen allowed ARRB staff to peruse Mr. Knudsen's "wheel book," his miniature appointments calendar for 1963, and to copy selected pages from it. Entries on various pages confirmed that Mr. Knudsen was originally scheduled to go to Texas on 21–22 November, 1963 prior to his eye injury the week of the assassination, and also indicated that he was at least aware of who John Stringer was, since Mr. Stringer's name and telephone number were in his wheel book under the "Bethesda" listing.

At the conclusion of the meeting ARRB staff gave each family member a copy of Mr. Knudsen's 1978 HSCA Deposition Transcript, as well as OCRs recorded at the time by HSCA staff after talking to Mr. Knudsen on the phone. Prior to the meeting with ARRB, the family said they had not seen the transcript, and furthermore showed no familiarity with its contents.

The Knudsen family members who met with ARRB staff were very proud of their father's career and his service to the White House, and vouched repeatedly for his trustworthiness, candor and honesty.

DESCRIPTION OF THE CALL

Date: 10/08/96
Subject: **Doug Horne Called Gloria Knudsen**

Summary of the Call:

Following up on a lead from researcher Randy Robertson that Gloria Knudsen may know people who could verify that her husband was present at President Kennedy's autopsy, I called Gloria Knudsen today, as directed by the Head of R & A, in an attempt to pursue Dr. Robertson's possible lead.

Gloria Knudsen said that Dr. Robertson had called to discuss her husband's HSCA deposition transcript, which is now an open-in-full document, and that she had briefly discussed her husband's involvement with events related to the assassination of the President the weekend of November 22–25, 1963, as he had relayed those events to his family. She said that she had become upset after hearing Dr. Robertson cast some doubt on her husband's account that he had been present at, and photographed, JFK's autopsy. As a result, she verified to me that last week she called several former Navy associates of her husband's, in an attempt to find out if anyone he formerly worked with could verify that he photographed the President's autopsy.

Without naming names, or telling me the precise number of her husband's former associates that she called, she said that she spoke last week with some former Navy people who in one case (along with her husband, Robert Knudsen) saw, and in another case helped Robert Knudsen print, photos of President Kennedy's autopsy. She said that these former Navy people said they never directly asked Bob Knudsen whether he had been present at the autopsy, and he never volunteered such information either, but that from certain remarks he had made, and by evaluating the quality of the photographs, these people were of the belief that he may well have been present at the autopsy. When I asked her for the names of these former Navy people, she said that she had promised these people last week not to divulge their names, and consequently would not do so under any circumstances. When I made a second attempt later in the conversation to impress upon her the importance of the ARRB's pursuit of photographic leads pertaining to the autopsy, she again politely but very firmly refused to divulge names, and said that her word of honor was the most important principle at stake here.

She elaborated that one of the former Navy people she called said that he did recall one particular photo which showed the back of the President's head "blown out." I asked her to recall as precisely as she could whether this person said "back of the head" or "top of the head," and she said the person to whom she spoke last week definitely said the "back" of the head was blown out in the photograph he sighted.

She told me that her husband told her on one occasion that he knew who had previously had custody of the autopsy photographs, and that he therefore could deduce who had been responsible for some of them disappearing, but that he was not going to stick his neck out on something this big, because he had a family to protect. She also reiterated her husband's firm belief that the photographs of the back of the head which show it to be intact were forgeries.

She told me that her 3 children had reviewed the transcript of Robert Knudsen's 1978 HSCA testimony, and that one of them, in particular, thought that the first 6 pages of the transcript "did not sound like her father." By this she explained that her husband was a perfectionist about everything, including spelling, and he would not have misspelled the word Annandale, nor would he have misspelled the last name "Stoughton," a man who was his co-worker (Cecil Stoughton, USAF Major) at the White House for years, nor would he have signed a transcript which had these items misspelled without correcting same. She said it was her opinion, and that of her family, that *after* the first 6 pages, the transcript did sound like her husband. She said that Dr. Robertson had mentioned that there was supposed to be an audiotape of her husband's testimony; she told me that if this were true, that she would be very interested in hearing it in order to evaluate (1) whether he said everything on the transcript, and (2) whether he was being totally forthcoming, or withholding information—she said that she would be able to determine a lot by the timber and tone of his voice, if she could hear the tape. I told her I would be glad to look into this matter for her.

She also reiterated that to her knowledge "we never received that transcript from the House Committee"—meaning the deposition transcript dated August 11, 1978, to which her husband's signature (but not a notary public's) is affixed, which was provided to her by the ARRB.

Gloria Knudsen told me that their house was burglarized shortly after the HSCA deposed her husband, and that she had always wondered if there were any connection between the two events.

She somewhat cryptically reminded me that her husband was a man who did not talk much, and who very reliably could keep secrets, and told me that sometimes people in the military are required to "take secrets to the grave" with them, when ordered to do so by competent authority, regardless of what attempts are later made to get them to talk. She told me her husband had impressed upon her that his loyalty was to the Presidency as an office and institution, not to any particular office-holder (without elaborating on what this meant).

I asked Gloria Knudsen if she knew how Dr. Robertson found her, and she said that he told her he got the information from the Review Board. I told her that this was patently untrue—that we were forbidden from violating privacy in this manner and that we had not shared her address or telephone number with anyone, nor had we shared the contents of her ARRB interview with anyone. She said Dr. Robertson also represented himself as the only person with access to the JFK autopsy materials in the Archives, but that she did not believe that. I told her that in reality, the Kennedy family's legal representative had authorized several researchers (of varying beliefs regarding what happened during the assassination) access to the autopsy photographs and X-Rays.

Our conversation ended on a friendly note, but with Gloria Knudsen saying that she thought she had told me enough, and still unwilling to divulge the names of the people who claim to have sighted or developed autopsy photographs of President Kennedy with Robert Knudsen. I closed by asking her to please contact the Review Board if she or her children could remember anything at all about which government agency, entity, or body it was that interviewed or deposed her husband again circa 1988.

BEFORE THE
ASSASSINATION RECORDS REVIEW BOARD

- - - - - - - - - - - - -X

In Re:

PRESIDENT JOHN F. KENNEDY

- - - - - - - - - - - - -X

College Park, Maryland

Thursday, June 5, 1997

The deposition of SAUNDRA KAY SPENCER, called for examination by counsel for the Board in the above-entitled matter, pursuant to notice, at Archives II, 6381 Adelphi Road, College Park, Maryland, convened at 10:00 a.m., before Robert H. Haines, a notary public in and for the State of Maryland, where were present on behalf of the parties:

APPEARANCES:

On behalf of the Assassination Records
Review Board:

T. JEREMY GUNN, ESQ.
General Counsel
Assassination Records Review Board
600 E Street, N.W., Second Floor
Washington, D.C. 20530
(202) 724-0088

ALSO PRESENT:

DAVID G. MARWELL
Executive Director
DOUGLAS P. HORNE
Chief Analyst for Military Records
DAVE MONTAGUE
Senior Investigator

CONTENTS

WITNESS	EXAMINATION
Saundra Kay Spencer	3

[1]   PROCEEDINGS

[2]   MR. GUNN: Would you swear the witness,

[3]   please.
[4]   Whereupon,
[5]   SAUNDRA KAY SPENCER
[6]   was called as a witness, and, having been first
[7]   duly sworn, was examined and testified as follows:
[8]   EXAMINATION
[9]   BY MR. GUNN:
[10]   Q: Would you state your full name for the
[11]   record, please.
[12]   A: Saundra Kay Spencer.
[13]   Q: Ms. Spencer, were you employed in November
[14]   of 1963?
[15]   A: Yes, I was.
[16]   Q: What position did you have in November of
[17]   1963?
[18]   A: I was 1st Class with United States Navy.
[19]   Q: Where did you work at that time?
[20]   A: I worked at the Photographic Center in a
[21]   special unit for the Naval Aide to the President
[22]   for Photography.

Page 4

[1]   Q: When you say the "Photographic Center,"
[2]   what do you mean?
[3]   A: That is a Class A lab, which was the
[4]   central photo lab for the Navy. It's located at
[5]   Anacostia.
[6]   Q: Has this been also known as the Naval
[7]   Photographic Center?
[8]   A: Yes.
[9]   Q: I would like to come back to your position
[10]   in 1963, but if we could go a little bit earlier
[11]   and then we will come back to it later.
[12]   Did you have any formal training in
[13]   photography?
[14]   A: Yes, I entered the basic photography
[15]   school out of recruit training in '57. I also had
[16]   special color school, Rochester Institute of
[17]   Technology and Quality Control, Class B school,
[18]   which is the advanced photography school, a
[19]   cinematography school, a school in recon camera

[20]   systems repair and camera repair.
[21]   Q: Did you take all of those courses during
[22]   the time that you were in the Navy?

[1]   A: Yes.
[2]   Q: Were all of those courses taken prior to
[3]   1963?
[4]   A: No. The A and the B school, and the color
[5]   school was taken prior.
[6]   Q: While you were in the Navy, did you do any
[7]   work other than in the area of photography?
[8]   A: No, it was all photographic related—oh,
[9]   I take that back. I did go for a tour at recruit
[10]   training for women at Bainbridge, Maryland, where I
[11]   was chief drill instructor and swimming instructor.
[12]   Q: Would it be fair to say that for
[13]   approximately six year between 1957 and 1963, that
[14]   your principal area of work was in photography?
[15]   A: Yes.
[16]   Q: Had you had any experience in photography
[17]   prior to the time that you joined the Navy?
[18]   A: Yes, since the time I was about 11 years
[19]   old, dad insisted we have family hobbies, and
[20]   photography was one of them, so I learned
[21]   photography. Then, in my senior year of high
[22]   school, the photographer that was scheduled to do

[1]   our annuals passed away, and so I took over the
[2]   photographic shooting and everything for our school
[3]   annual.
[4]   Q: Prior to 1963, had you had any experience
[5]   with photography of autopsies or of cadavers?
[6]   A: Yes. While I was stationed at a Class D
[7]   lab at Pensacola, Florida, at the Naval Air
[8]   Station, we were responsible for photographing the
[9]   autopsy of student pilots for the Navy that didn't
[10]   quite make it, and we provided 2¼" by 2¼"
[11]   slides for BuMED (Naval Bureau of Medicine and
[12]   Surgery).
[13]   Q: Did you take the photographs yourself?

[14]   A: Yes.
[15]   Q: Did you also develop the photographs?
[16]   A: Yes.
[17]   Q: Approximately, how many persons did you
[18]   take photographs of who were deceased?
[19]   A: Probably around 10, 12 during the two
[20]   years I was on the shooting crew.
[21]   Q: I would like to go now to the Naval
[22]   Photographic Center in 1963. Could you describe in

[1]   just a very general way the structure of the NPC?
[2]   A: Okay. NPC was a three-story building that
[3]   was originally built by Eastman Kodak during World
[4]   War II, on the top floor was the library and the
[5]   color lab primarily.
[6]   The second floor was black and white
[7]   division and some of the office spaces for support.
[8]   The third or the bottom floor dealt primarily with
[9]   motion picture production and TV production. They
[10]   have a sound stage.
[11]   Also on the third floor was the art and
[12]   animation divisions.
[13]   Q: Was there a White House lab or a White
[14]   House section in the NPC building?
[15]   A: Yes. It was located within the color
[16]   division. It was a single room, probably I would
[17]   say about 15 feet by 15 foot with an adjoining 8 by
[18]   10 room, and that was further broken down into two
[19]   color print room, a black and white print room
[20]   with sink, two dryers, and the adjourning room was
[21]   where we had the Calumet color processor. It was a
[22]   small unit and it all had the C-22 process in it

[1]   plus the color print process.
[2]   Q: Was that the area that you worked in?
[3]   A: Yes.
[4]   Q: Do you know why the White House lab was
[5]   located within the color lab?
[6]   A: Most of the work primarily was color at
[7]   that time, so it was just close proximity, we could

[8]   draw our chemistry and stuff from the main lines of
[9]   the color lab.
[10]   The black and white we did was a lot of
[11]   fine development, because they didn't like to use
[12]   flash at the White House, so a lot of it was
[13]   available-light photography. We did the ultra-fine
[14]   development on it, so that was not regularly
[15]   done downstairs in the black and white division,
[16]   and we had a limited amount of black and white that
[17]   we actually produced.
[18]   Q: Do you know of any other lab that
[19]   typically handled White House photography in 1963?
[20]   A: They had two or three photographers that
[21]   were with the motion picture crews, but they worked
[22]   directly for one person. Chief Knudsen would

[1]   usually direct them and what they did was aside
[2]   from anything that we did. They did not have a
[3]   special unit.
[4]   Q: Do you know of any other lab that
[5]   developed still photography in addition to the lab
[6]   where you worked?
[7]   A: To my knowledge, no.
[8]   Q: What was your position in the White House
[9]   lab in November of '63?
[10]   A: I was Petty Officer in Charge.
[11]   Q: Did you have any supervisor who was also
[12]   within the White House lab?
[13]   A: Chief Knudsen was our liaison and
[14]   supervisor from the White House, but we fell also
[15]   under the Office in Charge of the color lab, but
[16]   they pretty much left us alone, did our own thing.
[17]   They gave us a cipher lock on our room and said do
[18]   try to stay awake.
[19]   Q: When you say "they" left you alone, you
[20]   are referring to the color lab itself?
[21]   A: The color lab and the Officer in Charge.
[22]   They would ask periodically if we needed any

[1]   support or anything, and if we needed anything we
[2]   just asked them and we usually got what we needed.
[3]   Q: How many people worked under you in the
[4]   White House lab in November of '63?
[5]   A: It averaged four to five at various times,
[6]   people would come and go as they transferred in and
[7]   out, they were assigned to the Photographic Center,
[8]   and they were then detailed to us.
[9]   Q: During the time that you worked in the
[10]   White House lab, did you ever develop color
[11]   transparencies?
[12]   A: No.
[13]   Q: Did you have the capability of developing
[14]   color transparencies in the White House lab?
[15]   A: No.
[16]   Q: Did the color division, separate from the
[17]   White House lab, have any capability of developing
[18]   color transparencies?
[19]   A: Yes, they did.
[20]   Q: Did you ever work yourself developing
[21]   color transparencies in the color lab at NPC?
[22]   A: Yes.

[1]   Q: When and what kinds of occasions did you
[2]   do that?
[3]   A: When I returned, after I had gone to
[4]   camera repair school, after I had left the
[5]   Photographic Center the first time, I went to
[6]   camera repair school, and then I returned, and at
[7]   that time, they had placed a lot of mechanized
[8]   equipment in, so I started working over there and
[9]   stuff. You don't have any hands-on, but you load
[10]   the reels and put them in the baskets, and it
[11]   travels through until it bumps into the doors.
[12]   Q: Was there a capacity to develop positive
[13]   color transparencies by November of 1963?
[14]   A: Yes.
[15]   Q: Do you know what kinds of film were
[16]   capable of being developed, color transparencies in

[17]   November of '63?

[18]   A: It was the Ektachrome. Anything like

[19]   Kodachrome was sent out to Kodak directly.

[20]   Q: So Kodachrome would be sent to Kodak, but

[21]   Ektachrome could be developed?

[22]   A: Ektachrome could be in-house, and we were

Page 12

[1]   working with E-3, E-4s right around that time.

[2]   Q: You mentioned earlier a person by the name

[3]   of Knudsen. How often did you see Mr. Knudsen?

[4]   A: Not that often. When he needed a back-up

[5]   photographer, we would go over. Usually, most of

[6]   his film come by courier to us or we would go out

[7]   to Andrews to pick up from the courier planes, and

[8]   he would call us on the telephone, usually daily,

[9]   and we would again courier or take his proof prints

[10]   over and drop them off, and we would just get them

[11]   back by courier circled with what he wanted.

[12]   Q: Do you remember who the supervisor of the

[13]   color lab was in November of '63?

[14]   A: Oh, I can picture his face, but I can't

[15]   remember his name. It was a Lieutenant—

[16]   Q: Does the name Vince Madonia ring a bell?

[17]   A: Yes, that's him.

[18]   Q: How often would you interact with Mr.

[19]   Madonia around 1963?

[20]   A: Oh, I would have seen him on a daily

[21]   basis.

[22]   Q: Now I would like to go to November 22nd of

Page 13

[1]   1963, and ask you what you were doing when you

[2]   first heard about the assassination of President

[3]   Kennedy.

[4]   A: I was sitting and color correcting a photo

[5]   of John-John in President Kennedy's office, and it

[6]   came over the NPC radio speaker that the President

[7]   had been shot.

[8]   Q: After you heard that, what did you do?

[9]   A: We just continued to work until we got

[10]   word that they wanted to go ahead and close the NPC

[11] down and move all except our personnel out of the
[12] immediate areas.
[13]   In that time, just about all of D.C. went
[14] into a period of mourning, and I think they
[15] released most people at the agencies and stuff, the
[16] ones directly related to the President, I think
[17] were held on call until we actually found out what
[18] was going on.
[19]   Q: When you say they moved all the personnel
[20] out of NPC except "our area," do you mean the White
[21] House area or the color lab area?
[22]   A: They secured the regular color lab crews

[1] and we stayed.
[2]   Q: So approximately, how many people stayed
[3] when the rest of NPC closed down?
[4]   A: There was about three of us up there.
[5]   Q: Do you remember the names of any of the
[6] other people who stayed?
[7]   A: Carol Bonito was the only one I can
[8] identify. There was a 2nd Class that had come
[9] aboard just recently, but I didn't remember. The
[10] only thing I remember is Kirk was on his name.
[11]   Q: Ms. Spencer, I am going to hand you a
[12] document that has been marked Exhibit No. MD 144,
[13] which appears on its face to be an Enlisted
[14] Distribution and Verification Report.
[15]   It appears to be dated between June of '63
[16] and October of '63. Could you first look at the
[17] document and see whether you are familiar with that
[18] type of document?
[19]   A: The first time I had seen a document like
[20] this is when you had sent me the photocopies of it.
[21]   Q: I would like you to turn, if you would, to
[22] the seventh page where the first name at the top of

[1] the page is Ashton Thomas Larr. Do you see that
[2] page?
[3]   A: Yes.

[4]   Q: Do you see the name Carol Bonito—

[5]   A: Yes.

[6]   Q: —down approximately six names or so?

[7]   A: Yes.

[8]   Q: Is this the Carol Bonito that you were

[9]   referring to just a moment ago?

[10]   A: Yes.

[11]   Q: Could you look through this list—and

[12]   take as much time as you need—to see if you are

[13]   able to identify any other names of personnel who

[14]   were in the White House lab on the days after

[15]   November 22nd of '63?

[16]   A: Look at the 2nd Class, the gentleman I was

[17]   talking about was a 2nd Class. No, I don't see his

[18]   name on there.

[19]   Q: Okay. Let me show you one name and see if

[20]   looks familiar to you. This is on the fourth page.

[21]   The first name at the top of the page appears to be

[22]   Somers, S-o-m-e-r-s, Joseph M. You do see your

[1]   name immediately under there?

[2]   A: Right.

[3]   Q: Do you see the name Stover?

[4]   A: Yes. Somers was in the color lab side.

[5]   Q: But not in the White House area?

[6]   A: No.

[7]   Q: Is that right?

[8]   A: Richard Stover, Smoky Stover was there.

[9]   Strickland was a chief. He was down in the black

[10]   and white division. Usually, in the color lab, we

[11]   had a high number of 1st and 2nd Class and a few

[12]   Airmen and 3rd Class, but they—Leo Marshall was

[13]   the Chief in Charge of the color lab.

[14]   Q: Ms. Spencer, did you have any work after

[15]   November 22nd, 1963, that was related to the death

[16]   of President Kennedy?

[17]   A: Yes. We were requested to develop 4" by

[18]   5" color negatives and make prints of an autopsy

[19]   that was—we were told it was shot at Bethesda

[20]   after the President's body was brought back from

[21]   Dallas.
[22]   Q: I would like to come to that in a minute.

[1]   Prior to that, did you have any other work or
[2]   responsibilities related to the death of President
[3]   Kennedy?
[4]   A: We were trying to put together the prayer
[5]   cards. Mrs. Kennedy had selected a black and white
[6]   photograph, and so we needed a number of them.
[7]   What we did was take four prints, 4" by 5" prints,
[8]   and do the vignetting on those, and then they were
[9]   copied to a master negative, and we took it
[10]   downstairs and put it on the automatic black and
[11]   white printers to print out the required numbers.
[12]   Then, we brought them back and we did not
[13]   cut them here. We brought them to the White House.
[14]   They took them to the printers and evidently they
[15]   were printed and cut there.
[16]   Q: Did you bring with you today some examples
[17]   of those prints that you made?
[18]   A: Yes, I brought just two on a half-sheet.
[19]   MR. GUNN: What I would like to do is mark
[20]   those as Exhibit No. 146, MD 146, and they will go
[21]   into the record as part of that.
[22]   [Exhibit No. MD 146 was marked

[1]   for identification.]
[2]   BY MR. GUNN:
[3]   Q: Do you remember approximately how many of
[4]   these prints you made?
[5]   A: I think the count was supposed to be
[6]   around 10,000, but I am sure we went over.
[7]   Q: What is your best recollection as to when
[8]   you started working on the prints?
[9]   A: It was after the President's body had been
[10]   brought back because Mrs. Kennedy personally
[11]   selected the print. Chief Knudsen told us which
[12]   one, and then we went ahead and pulled it, and
[13]   started the process of producing the—
[14]   Q: President Kennedy's body arrived at

[15]   approximately 6:00 p.m. in Washington, D.C. Does
[16]   that help you determine approximately the time when
[17]   you began work on the black and white prints?
[18]   A: No.
[19]   Q: Do you remember whether it was on the
[20]   evening of November 22nd?
[21]   A: It seems to me like we had gotten word the
[22]   following day, which would have been a Saturday.

Page 19

[1]   Q: So on Friday, November 22nd, 1963, did you
[2]   do any work related to either the funeral of
[3]   President Kennedy or to autopsy photographs that
[4]   you mentioned?
[5]   A: No, we were primarily in a standby
[6]   position.
[7]   Q: Approximately, how long did it take for
[8]   you to work on the black and white prints?
[9]   A: It took most of the day. It seemed to me
[10]   it was late, maybe 2 o'clock in the morning, by the
[11]   time we got them over to the White House after we
[12]   got the indication of which ones we needed to
[13]   print.
[14]   Q: So this would be, then, you worked on them
[15]   on Saturday, November 23rd, until approximately 2
[16]   o'clock in the morning on Sunday, November 24th, is
[17]   that—
[18]   A: I can't remember the day. All I remember
[19]   is that it was after the President's body had been
[20]   taken up to the Rotunda, because as we went to the
[21]   White House, the lines were forming for the
[22]   Rotunda.

Page 20

[1]   Q: Just to make sure that I understand this
[2]   correctly, that you took prints over to the White
[3]   House, the black and white prints, and at that
[4]   time, you noticed lines that were forming to go the
[5]   Rotunda on Capitol Hill?
[6]   A: Yes.
[7]   Q: And at the time that you took the prints
[8]   to the White House, do you remember whether the

[9]   body was at the White House or whether it was at
[10]   Capitol Hill?
[11]   A: It had to be up at the Capitol Rotunda at
[12]   that time.
[13]   Q: Now, a few minutes ago you mentioned some
[14]   work related to the autopsy photographs of
[15]   President Kennedy. When did you first receive
[16]   information that you would be doing some work on
[17]   that issue?
[18]   A: We received a call from the quarterdeck,
[19]   and they said an agent was there, and we were
[20]   supposed to perform, photographic work for him.
[21]   They logged him in and brought him up.
[22]   He had in his hand 4 by 5 film holders, so

Page 21

[1]   I am estimating—he was a large man—so he
[2]   probably had four or five film holders.
[3]   Q: Now, when you say he called from the
[4]   quarterdeck, where was the quarterdeck?
[5]   A: The quarterdeck is on the first floor of
[6]   NPC.
[7]   Q: Do you remember approximately when the
[8]   telephone call happened, which day of the week?
[9]   A: No, I don't.
[10]   Q: Do you remember what you were doing at the
[11]   time that you heard about the telephone call from
[12]   the quarterdeck?
[13]   A: No, I don't. It seemed like it was in the
[14]   morning.
[15]   Q: Were you working on the developing of the
[16]   black and white prints, did it interrupt that, or
[17]   was it before or after?
[18]   A: No, it was after.
[19]   Q: So it was after you had finished the
[20]   prints. Had you done any other work between the
[21]   time that you worked on the black and white prints
[22]   and that you received a call from the quarterdeck?

Page 22

[1]   A: We were finishing up job orders that we
[2]   had, that had been requested from the White House.

[3]   Q: Do you remember the name of the agent who
[4]   came with the film?
[5]   A: No, I don't. The only thing I remember, I
[6]   think he said he was with the FBI.
[7]   Q: Do you remember we spoke earlier, you and
[8]   I spoke on the telephone in December of 1996?
[9]   A: Yes.
[10]   Q: At that time you mentioned the name of an
[11]   agent. Do you remember the name that you used at
[12]   that time?
[13]   A: No, I don't, because I really couldn't
[14]   verify that that was the agent, so I just—he was
[15]   an agent.
[16]   Q: In December of 1996, you spontaneously
[17]   said to us that you recalled the name was Fox, but
[18]   that you weren't certain. Does that ring a bell?
[19]   A: Yes.
[20]   Q: When Mr. Fox or the person came to the
[21]   White House lab, approximately, how many other
[22]   people were working in the lab at that time?

Page 23

[1]   A: Two others.
[2]   Q: Do you remember who they were? Was one
[3]   Ms. Bonito, for example?
[4]   A: Yes, and the 2nd Class. The day crew was
[5]   on. We had two, usually two 2nd Class that worked
[6]   the evening shift.
[7]   Q: Now, when you say that the agent had 4 by
[8]   5 film holders, what do you mean by that?
[9]   A: It means they either used a 4 by 5 press
[10]   camera or a view camera, and a film holder is a
[11]   two-sided container that holds two sheets of film,
[12]   insert it in the camera, pull the dark slide, do
[13]   your photograph, reinsert the dark slide, turn the
[14]   holder over, and you are ready—and pull the dark
[15]   slide, and you are ready for a second shot.
[16]   So there is two sheets of film in each of
[17]   the holders.
[18]   Q: When you refer to a press camera or a view
[19]   camera, are those also known as large format

[20]   cameras?
[21]   A: Yes, large format cameras.
[22]   Q: Now, if I recall correctly, you said that

[1]   your recollection was that he had four or five of
[2]   these duplex film holders, is that correct?
[3]   A: Correct.
[4]   Q: Did the agent speak to you directly or did
[5]   he speak with somebody else?
[6]   A: To me directly.
[7]   Q: What did he ask you to do?
[8]   A: He said he needed the film processed and a
[9]   print of each of them.
[10]   Q: What did you then do?
[11]   A: We took them and then checked our
[12]   chemistry, brought it up to temperature, and
[13]   processed the negatives. We put the negatives in
[14]   the drying cabinet, and when they were completed,
[15]   we brought them out.
[16]   We went into the dark room and made a test
[17]   print on them, which we processed and color
[18]   corrected, and made the final print, at which time
[19]   we took all scraps and anything related to that
[20]   job, and put it in an envelope and gave it to the
[21]   agent, returned his film holders to him.
[22]   Q: Did you keep any material at all related

[1]   to the development of those photographs?
[2]   A: Absolutely not. The agent was very
[3]   specific that he wanted everything, any test scraps
[4]   or anything that we might use.
[5]   Q: What type of film did you develop?
[6]   A: It was a color negative C-22 process.
[7]   Q: Could you describe for me briefly what a
[8]   C-22 process is?
[9]   A: It is a standard color—well, it was a
[10]   standard color negative at the time, and it's a
[11]   three-layer image, reverse image of each of the
[12]   three basic primary colors with a reddish yellow
[13]   masking material that is incorporated into the

[14]   negative to prevent bleedover of the various layers
[15]   when printing.
[16]   Q: Did you develop those negatives in the
[17]   White House lab or did you go into the color lab to
[18]   develop them?
[19]   A: They were processed in the White House
[20]   section in the Calumet Unit in the small off-room.
[21]   We had the color negative processing capability
[22]   plus the print processing.

[1]   Q: When you developed the first test print,
[2]   what kind of paper did you put that onto?
[3]   A: It's the standard color print material.
[4]   Q: Now, you brought with you today a
[5]   photograph of President Kennedy that you said it
[6]   was your understanding was taken approximately two
[7]   weeks before the assassination, is that correct?
[8]   A: Yes, the Black Watch performed at the
[9]   White House, and these were brought to us, so I
[10]   would estimate this print was probably made about a
[11]   week to 10 days prior to the printing of the
[12]   autopsy material, so the chemical content within
[13]   the paper should be fairly close to what the
[14]   autopsy photo chemical content was.
[15]   MR. GUNN: What I would like to do is to
[16]   mark the print that you brought with you as MD No.
[17]   147.
[18]   [Exhibit No. MD 147 was marked
[19]   for identification.]
[20]   BY MR. GUNN:
[21]   Q: Now, for MD 147, if I am understanding you
[22]   correctly, that the paper that Exhibit 147 was

[1]   developed on is the same material as you used for
[2]   the test prints, is that correct?
[3]   A: Yes, at the Photographic Center, when we
[4]   ordered our paper, we ordered an entire run, and
[5]   they cut it to the various sizes that we needed, so
[6]   that we could make a 4 by 5, an 8 by 10, or a 16 by
[7]   20, all from the same color pack, and make them

[8]   totally match, so that that paper should be the
[9]   same batch that was used.
[10]   Q: When you said you made a test print, how
[11]   many test prints did you make of each negative?
[12]   A: The general rule was for us to make a test
[13]   print of each, but I am not sure that we tested all
[14]   of them, because, you know, they were all the same
[15]   subject matter. It was general practice, though,
[16]   to go ahead and prepare one test print of each.
[17]   Q: Do you know whether more than one test
[18]   print was made of any of the negatives?
[19]   A: No.
[20]   Q: That is, there were no prints—
[21]   A: No, there were no—just one test print
[22]   was made of each.

Page 28

[1]   Q: After the color correction, how many
[2]   prints were made of each negative?
[3]   A: One.
[4]   Q: So would it be fair to say that, at
[5]   maximum, there were two prints made of each
[6]   negative?
[7]   A: That is correct.
[8]   Q: And were the final prints also developed
[9]   on the same paper as Exhibit No. 147?
[10]   A: Correct.
[11]   Q: And so you would expect that on the
[12]   original test print, as well as the original color-corrected
[13]   print, there would be the same type of
[14]   markings that are on the back of Exhibit No. 147?
[15]   A: Yes, it should have the same watermarks
[16]   and markings plus the same border pattern.
[17]   Q: When you say the "same watermarks," what
[18]   do you mean?
[19]   A: On the back of all Kodak paper, they print
[20]   their Kodak label, and it changes from year to
[21]   year, but it just says Kodak paper.
[22]   Q: So on the Exhibit No. 147, it appears that

[1]   there is either a delta figure, or appears a delta
[2]   figure, and then Kodak paper, is that what you are
[3]   referring to?
[4]   A: Yes.
[5]   Q: Do you know the difference between a
[6]   negative and an inter-negative?
[7]   A: Yes.
[8]   Q: What is the difference in just a very
[9]   general way?
[10]   A: A negative is an original piece of film.
[11]   An inter-neg is an intermediate negative material
[12]   designed to go from a transparency to a print.
[13]   Q: Would you have been able to tell, at the
[14]   time that you developed the duplex films, whether
[15]   the film was a negative or an inter-negative?
[16]   A: Yes, because the inter-negative cannot be
[17]   processed C-22.
[18]   Q: So that you are certain then that they
[19]   were not inter-negatives that you developed?
[20]   A: No, they were original.
[21]   Q: Approximately, how much time did it take
[22]   between the time that you first saw the 4 by 5

[1]   duplex holders and the time that the agent left?
[2]   A: It takes—it was 30 minutes for the
[3]   processing on the negative, approximately 45
[4]   minutes to dry the negatives, and then the
[5]   printing, the other print process was 18 minutes,
[6]   and then on the drying drums probably about 3
[7]   minutes, so less than two hours.
[8]   Q: Did the agent leave immediately after the
[9]   final prints had been dried?
[10]   A: Yes.
[11]   Q: So he did not stay around and talk at all
[12]   or say anything?
[13]   A: No.
[14]   Q: Did he talk to you at all about where he
[15]   had obtained the photographs?
[16]   A: No. When he gave us the material to

[17]   process, he said that they—had been shot at
[18]   Bethesda and they were autopsy pictures, for us to
[19]   process them and try to not observe too much, don't
[20]   peruse.
[21]   Q: Did he say anything that you now recall
[22]   other than what you have just mentioned?

[1]   A: No. We did sign a chain of evidence
[2]   forms.
[3]   Q: Could you describe that form for me or
[4]   what you recall about that?
[5]   A: It was just a form that everybody that had
[6]   handled the material signed.
[7]   Q: What happened to that form?
[8]   A: The agent took it with him.
[9]   Q: Did you ever have a copy of that form?
[10]   A: No.
[11]   Q: Do you remember whether it was typewritten
[12]   or handwritten?
[13]   A: It was a regular printed form.
[14]   Q: Had you seen forms like that before or did
[15]   it seem as though it was unique for that particular
[16]   situation?
[17]   A: It just was that—what the material, you
[18]   know, film and paper, and he wrote down how many of
[19]   each thing on it, and stuff, and I signed off on
[20]   it.
[21]   Q: Did you use forms like that for your other
[22]   work with the White House?

[1]   A: No.
[2]   Q: Have you ever signed a form like that
[3]   previously?
[4]   A: It pretty much followed like for a
[5]   classified piece of material.
[6]   Q: Did you develop photographs previously
[7]   that had classified information in them?
[8]   A: No, we just treated everything that we got
[9]   as semi-classified and just kept it within the
[10]   unit.

[11]   Q: Was there a reason of which you were aware
[12] for treating most of the material as if it were
[13] semi-classified?
[14]   A: Because the only people that had the right
[15] to release it was the White House.
[16]   Q: After the agent left, did you do any
[17] additional work related to any autopsy photos?
[18]   A: No.
[19]   Q: Did you do any other work related to the
[20] death of the President?
[21]   A: No. At that point, we started to gather
[22] all the negatives and started to make two, 5 by 7's

[1]   of every negative that we had in the library, and
[2]   then we would start to package them and they were
[3]   taken away. They were going to take them to the
[4]   Kennedy Library when it was built. I left before
[5]   that project was completed.
[6]   Q: By the way, approximately, when did you
[7]   leave the NPC for the first time?
[8]   A: Let's see. It was within two or three
[9]   months after the assassination.
[10]   Q: Did you ever see any other photographic
[11] material related to the autopsy in addition to what
[12] you have already described?
[13]   A: Just, you know, when they came out with
[14] some books and stuff later that showed autopsy
[15] pictures and stuff, and I assumed that they were
[16] done in—you know, down in Dallas or something,
[17] because they were not the ones that I had worked
[18] on.
[19]   Q: Do you recall any books that you have seen
[20] with autopsy photographs in them?
[21]   A: I can't quote the titles of them.
[22]   Q: But you have seen commercially published

[1]   books with what appear to be autopsy photos in
[2]   them?
[3]   A: Yes.
[4]   Q: Did you ever hear of any discussion

[5]   related to autopsy photos at NPC?

[6]   A: No.

[7]   Q: So, did you ever discuss the fact that you

[8]   had processed those with Mr. Madonia, for example?

[9]   A: No.

[10]   Q: Did you ever discuss it with anyone else

[11]   your own work?

[12]   A: No.

[13]   Q: Or did you hear of anyone else at NPC who

[14]   had worked on any other autopsy photographs?

[15]   A: No.

[16]   Q: Did you have any opportunity to observe

[17]   the content of the negatives and the prints as you

[18]   were working on them?

[19]   A: Yes, I did.

[20]   Q: Can you describe for me what you saw as

[21]   best you can recollect?

[22]   A: Briefly, they were very, what I consider

Page 35

[1]   pristine for an autopsy. There was no blood or

[2]   opening cavities, opening or anything of that

[3]   nature. It was quite reverent in how they handled

[4]   it.

[5]   Q: If I can just ask for some clarification.

[6]   Do you mean that the body appeared to be clean, had

[7]   been washed? Is that what you are suggesting?

[8]   A: Yes.

[9]   Q: And that was different from what you had

[10]   seen in other autopsy photographs, is that right?

[11]   A: Yes. In other autopsies, they have the

[12]   opening of the cavity and the removing of vital

[13]   organs for weighing and stuff of this nature. The

[14]   only organ that I had seen was a brain that was

[15]   laid beside the body.

[16]   Q: And that was in the photograph of

[17]   President Kennedy?

[18]   A: Yes.

[19]   Q: So there was a brain in the photograph

[20]   beside the body, is that correct?

[21]   A: Well, yes, by the side of the body, but,

[22]   it didn't appear that the skull had been cut,

[1]   peeled back and the brain removed. None of that

[2]   was shown. As to whose brain it was, I cannot say.

[3]   Q: But was it on a cloth or in a bucket or

[4]   how was it—

[5]   A: No, it was on the mat on the table.

[6]   Q: Did you see any people in the pictures in

[7]   addition to President Kennedy, such as bystanders

[8]   or doctors?

[9]   A: I don't remember anybody or any real

[10]   measuring material, instruments, because normally,

[11]   when you are photographing something like that, you

[12]   have gauges in there, so that you can determine

[13]   size and everything.

[14]   Q: Did you see any cards or any

[15]   identification markers that would identify an

[16]   autopsy number or the victim, or something of that

[17]   sort?

[18]   A: I don't remember any.

[19]   Q: Were there any photographs that would show

[20]   the entire body in one frame, do you recall?

[21]   A: It seems like there was a full-length one,

[22]   kind of shot at a 45-degree angle, at a slightly

[1]   high angle.

[2]   Q: Did you see any photographs that focused

[3]   principally on the head of President Kennedy?

[4]   A: Right. They had one showing the back of

[5]   the head with the wound at the back of the head.

[6]   Q: Could you describe what you mean by the

[7]   "wound at the back of the head"?

[8]   A: It appeared to be a hole, inch, two inches

[9]   in diameter at the back of the skull here.

[10]   Q: You pointed to the back of your head.

[11]   When you point back there, let's suppose that you

[12]   were lying down on a pillow, where would the hole

[13]   in the back of the head be in relationship to the

[14]   part of the head that would be on the pillow if the
[15]   body is lying flat?
[16]   A: The top part of the head.
[17]   Q: When you say the "top of the head," now,
[18]   is that the part that would be covered by a hat
[19]   that would be covering the top of the head?
[20]   A: Just about where the rim would hit.
[21]   Q: Are you acquainted with the term "external
[22]   occipital protuberance"?

[1]   A: No, I am not.
[2]   Q: What I would like to do is to give you a
[3]   document or a drawing, and ask you, if you would,
[4]   on this document, make a mark of approximately
[5]   where the wound was that you noticed.
[6]   MR. GUNN: We will mark this Exhibit No.
[7]   148.
[8]   [Exhibit No. MD 148 was marked
[9]   for identification.]
[10]   THE WITNESS: Probably about in there.
[11]   BY MR. GUNN:
[12]   Q: And you have put some hash marks in there
[13]   and then drawn a circle around that, and the part
[14]   that you have drawn, the circle that you have drawn
[15]   on the diagram is labeled as being as part of the
[16]   occiptal bone, is that correct?
[17]   A: Yes.
[18]   Q: Did you see any biological tissue, such as
[19]   brain matter, extruding from the hole that you saw
[20]   in the back of the head?
[21]   A: No.
[22]   Q: Was the scalp disturbed or can you

[1]   describe that more than just the hole?
[2]   A: It was just a ragged hole.
[3]   Q: And it was visible through the scalp, is
[4]   that correct?
[5]   A: Yes.
[6]   Q: Did you see any photographs with the scalp
[7]   pulled back or reflected?

[8]   A: No.
[9]   Q: Did you see any other wounds on the head
[10]   in addition to the one that you have identified?
[11]   A: I don't remember any additional.
[12]   Q: Did you see any photographs that would
[13]   have shown the right profile of President Kennedy's
[14]   head?
[15]   A: I don't remember.
[16]   Q: Did you see any photographs that would
[17]   have shown any wounds in either the neck or
[18]   shoulders or back?
[19]   A: It seems like I seen—there was at the
[20]   base of the neck.
[21]   Q: When you are pointing, you are pointing to
[22]   the front of your neck to the right side?

Page 40

[1]   A: Yes.
[2]   Q: Do you remember approximately how large
[3]   that injury was?
[4]   A: Just about the size of like your thumb
[5]   pressed in.
[6]   Q: About how much time were you able to look
[7]   at the photographs, did you get a good observation
[8]   of them, was it fleeting? How would you describe
[9]   that?
[10]   A: It was—they traveled. You placed them
[11]   on the drum, they would travel around, so after you
[12]   place it on, probably about 15 seconds or so, they
[13]   start under the drum and it rotates around, and
[14]   then they drop off, and you grab them and stack
[15]   them. So probably just 10 or 15 seconds.
[16]   Q: Are your observations based upon the
[17]   prints rather than the negatives?
[18]   A: Yes. Like I said, the negatives have
[19]   masking on them, and you don't see too much on a
[20]   color negative when you are printing.
[21]   Q: And for the prints to dry, that takes
[22]   approximately how long?

[1]   A: Probably about two to three minutes by the
[2] time it goes on, it goes around the drum.
[3]   Q: And that is all entirely on the drum?
[4]   A: Yes.
[5]   Q: So the prints themselves would not hang
[6] from a wire or anything?
[7]   A: No, they have electric drum, and it puts
[8] the ferrotype finish to it. That was before RC
[9] papers when you can air-dry them.
[10]   Q: What is your best recollection of the
[11] approximate size of the wound on the throat that
[12] you identified before?
[13]   A: Just about like that, just like a finger,
[14] half-inch.
[15]   Q: Do you remember whether the wound was
[16] jagged or how that appeared?
[17]   A: No, just—it appeared just indented. It
[18] was, again, clean, pristine, no—you know, it
[19] wasn't an immediate wound, it had some cleaning
[20] done to it or something.
[21]   Q: Were you able to observe any
[22] characteristics of the room in which the

[1] photographs were taken?
[2]   A: No.
[3]   Q: Do you remember what the walls looked like
[4] or whether they—
[5]   A: No, everything basically concentrated
[6] straight on the body. It didn't appear like the
[7] normal medical setting, you know. I don't know
[8] whether they did it in a separate room or they used
[9] special coverings on their tables or what, but I
[10] don't remember, you know, hospital stainless-steel
[11] gleaming or anything, or people running around in
[12] green scrubs or anything.
[13]   It was just, like I said, it looked a very
[14] reverent laid out arrangement.
[15]   Q: What is your best recollection as to how
[16] long after the autopsy you received the

[17]   photographs? Let me try and put it in terms of
[18]   some other events that happened. Do you remember
[19]   whether you developed the photographs before or
[20]   after the funeral, for example?
[21]   A: It was before.
[22]   Q: Before the funeral. But your recollection

[1]   also is that it was after the black and white cards
[2]   had been delivered to the White House?
[3]   A: Right.
[4]   Q: Do you recall whether it was on a Sunday
[5]   or a Monday?
[6]   A: It was sometime over the weekend. It was
[7]   during the day. I believe the body arrived back at
[8]   the White House Saturday morning about 1:00 a.m.,
[9]   so—because we had a black and white photograph
[10]   of it being carried into the White House. It was
[11]   dark, so it would had to have been—the film
[12]   would have had to have been shot by that time.
[13]   MR. GUNN: What I would like to do is ask
[14]   that the autopsy photographs be brought in and have
[15]   you have an opportunity to take a look at those.
[16]   We will take a short break.
[17]   [Recess.]
[18]   BY MR. GUNN:
[19]   Q: Ms. Spencer, what we would like to do is
[20]   to start with the very first view, which
[21]   corresponds to color Nos. 29, 30, and 31.
[22]   Ms. Spencer, could you go to the light box

[1]   and tell me whether you can identify the color
[2]   transparency of View No. 1 and Image No. 29, as
[3]   having seen that before.
[4]   A: No.
[5]   Q: In what respect is the Image No. 29
[6]   different from what you previously saw?
[7]   A: Like I said, there was none of the blood
[8]   and matted hair.
[9]   Q: Can you explain what you mean by that?
[10]   Are you seeing blood and matted hair on Image 29?

[11]   A: On the transparency.
[12]   Q: But that was not present, the blood and
[13]   matted hair was not present—
[14]   A: I don't remember.
[15]   Q: —on the images that you saw?
[16]   A: No.
[17]   Q: Would you describe Image No. 29 as a color
[18]   positive transparency or a color negative?
[19]   A: This is a color transparency.
[20]   Q: Ms. Spencer, could you again look at the
[21]   color transparency and tell me whether, again, you
[22]   are certain that you did not develop color

Page 45

[1]   transparencies of the autopsy of President Kennedy?
[2]   A: No, I did not process any color
[3]   transparencies.
[4]   Q: Let's turn to the print. Can you identify
[5]   the print as being a print that you printed
[6]   yourself at Naval Photographic Center?
[7]   A: I don't believe it is.
[8]   Q: Can you look at the back—turn the light
[9]   on, please—can you look at the back of the print
[10]   and identify whether that is the same type of paper
[11]   as the Exhibit No. 147, that you brought with you
[12]   today?
[13]   A: No, it's not.
[14]   Q: In what respect do you see it as being
[15]   different?
[16]   A: The Kodak logo is smaller.
[17]   Q: So, based upon your experience, would it
[18]   be safe to say that it is your best recollection,
[19]   best understanding, that the print of the autopsy
[20]   that is in the Archives does not correspond with
[21]   the paper that you were using in November of 1963
[22]   at NPC?

Page 46

[1]   A: Correct.
[2]   Q: Could you look again at the image of View
[3]   No. 29? In what respect is the image that you see

[4]   in 29, in the color print, different from what you
[5]   observed on the prints that you made at NPC?
[6]   A: Like I said, the body was pristine, and
[7]   this has dried blood on the support, the ear, and
[8]   the hair.
[9]   Q: Do you recall whether there was a metal
[10]   holder for the head on the images that you
[11]   developed?
[12]   A: I don't remember a metal holder.
[13]   Q: Do you remember what kind of cloth or any
[14]   other material was identifiable in the photograph
[15]   in comparison to what you see on this image?
[16]   A: As I remember it was a darker cloth. This
[17]   appears to be a towel over one of the trays,
[18]   stainless-steel trays.
[19]   Q: Previously, you said that, if I recall
[20]   correctly, that the background in the photograph
[21]   looked different from what you had previously seen
[22]   in terms of—I understood that you said that it

Page 47

[1]   didn't look like a hospital.
[2]   A: Right.
[3]   Q: Could you describe the photograph that you
[4]   see in front of you now, whether that is the same
[5]   sort of background that you noticed in the
[6]   photographs that you developed?
[7]   A: Well, it would be the dark background,
[8]   because normally, when you are doing the autopsies,
[9]   the overhead lights and stuff are on. It appears
[10]   that the lights have been turned off and that they
[11]   were using a flash rather than just overall general
[12]   lighting.
[13]   Q: Do you remember, in the photographs that
[14]   you developed, whether the background was visible,
[15]   such as the walls?
[16]   A: No.
[17]   Q: You don't remember?
[18]   A: I don't remember, but it appeared that it
[19]   was darkened, the room was darkened.
[20]   Q: So, to that extent that the images would

[21]   seem to correspond to what you recollect—
[22]   A: Right.

[1]   Q: —the background would seem to, you don't
[2]   notice any difference?
[3]   A: No.
[4]   MR. GUNN: Just so the record is clear,
[5]   that the one that Ms. Spencer has just been shown
[6]   is the first view, left side of head and shoulders,
[7]   corresponding to color Nos. 29, 30, and 31.
[8]   Could we now see the second view,
[9]   identified in the 1966 inventory as the right side
[10]   of head and right shoulder, corresponding to color
[11]   Nos. 26, 27, and 28.
[12]   BY MR. GUNN:
[13]   Q: Ms. Spencer, have you had an opportunity
[14]   now to look at the second view corresponding to
[15]   color Nos. 26, 27, and 28?
[16]   A: Yes, I have.
[17]   Q: Do those two images correspond to the
[18]   photographs that you developed at NPC in November
[19]   of 1963?
[20]   A: No.
[21]   Q: In what way are they different?
[22]   A: There was no—the film that I seen or

[1]   the prints that we printed did not have the massive
[2]   head damages that is visible here.
[3]   Q: Putting aside the question of the damage
[4]   of the head, does the remainder of the body, the
[5]   face, correspond to what you observed?
[6]   A: No.
[7]   Q: In what way is it different?
[8]   A: The face in the photographs that we did,
[9]   did not have the stress that these photos—on the
[10]   face that these photos show.
[11]   Q: Could you describe a little bit more what
[12]   you mean by that?
[13]   A: The face, the eyes were closed and the
[14]   face, the mouth was closed, and it was more of a

[15]   rest position than these show.
[16]   Q: Could you look at the back of the print
[17]   and see whether that paper corresponds to the image
[18]   that you brought with you today, please.
[19]   A: No.
[20]   Q: It doesn't correspond. So, the paper that
[21]   these prints are printed on is not the paper that
[22]   you were using at NPC in November of 1963, is that

Page 50

[1]   correct?
[2]   A: Correct.
[3]   Q: Could we next look at View 3, identified
[4]   as the superior view of the head corresponding to
[5]   color Nos. 32, 33, 34, 35, 36 and 37.
[6]   Ms. Spencer, have you had an opportunity
[7]   to look at the third view?
[8]   A: Yes, I have.
[9]   Q: Do you those two images, again when you
[10]   are looking at a positive transparency and a print,
[11]   do those correspond to the photographs that you
[12]   developed in November of 1963?
[13]   A: No.
[14]   Q: In what way are they different?
[15]   A: Again, none of the heavy damage that shows
[16]   in these photographs were visible in the
[17]   photographs that we did.
[18]   Q: So, just to make sure that I am
[19]   understanding correctly, previously, in your
[20]   deposition, you described a wound, a small,
[21]   circular wound in the back of the head,
[22]   approximately two inches or so as I recall that you

Page 51

[1]   stated, whereas, these show a much larger injury,
[2]   is that correct?
[3]   A: That is correct.
[4]   Q: Could you once again take a look at the
[5]   paper on which the print is made and tell me
[6]   whether that corresponds to the paper that you
[7]   brought with you today?
[8]   A: No.

[9]   Q: Just so the record is clear, the paper
[10]   does not correspond to the paper that was used in
[11]   November '63 at NPC.
[12]   A: No.
[13]   Q: Is that correct?
[14]   A: That's right.
[15]   Q: Thank you. Could we look at the fourth
[16]   view, which is identified as the posterior view of
[17]   wound at entrance of missile height and shoulder,
[18]   corresponding to color Nos. 38 and 39.
[19]   Ms. Spencer, do you have the fourth view
[20]   in front of you now?
[21]   A: Yes, I do.
[22]   Q: Can you tell me whether those photographs

Page 52

[1]   correspond to the photographs that you developed in
[2]   November of 1963?
[3]   A: No, it does not.
[4]   Q: In addition to what you have already said
[5]   in describing the other photographs, is there
[6]   anything additional in these photographs that
[7]   appears to you to be different?
[8]   A: They are using a measuring device, which I
[9]   don't remember in any of the photographs that we
[10]   produced, and I don't remember any hands on the
[11]   President during any of the shots that we
[12]   reproduced.
[13]   Q: Now, could you look at the place on the
[14]   back of President Kennedy's head that corresponds
[15]   to where you identified a wound in the back of the
[16]   head. Do you see that wound present in these
[17]   photographs?
[18]   A: No, I do not.
[19]   Q: Would this view have shown the wound that
[20]   you previously saw in the photographs of President
[21]   Kennedy's head?
[22]   A: Yes. The wound that I seen would have

Page 53

[1]   been approximately in this area.
[2]   Q: If we described that as very roughly the

[3]   cowlick area, would that be fair to say?
[4]   A: Yes.
[5]   Q: Could we look at the fifth view now,
[6]   described as the right anterior view of head and
[7]   upper torso including tracheotomy wound, color Nos.
[8]   40 and 41.
[9]   Let me try the first question as being
[10]   whether the paper on the print matches the paper
[11]   that you brought with you to the deposition today.
[12]   A: No, it does not.
[13]   Q: Ms. Spencer, could you look at the wound
[14]   in the throat of President Kennedy and tell me
[15]   whether that corresponds to the wound that you
[16]   observed in the photographs you developed?
[17]   A: No, it does not.
[18]   Q: In what way are they different?
[19]   A: This is a large, gaping gash type.
[20]   Q: That is, in the fifth view, it's a large,
[21]   gaping gash, is that correct?
[22]   A: Yes. In the one that we had seen, it was

Page 54

[1]   on the right side, approximately half-inch.
[2]   Q: Is the wound in a different location or is
[3]   it just a larger wound on the throat?
[4]   A: It could be just a larger wound.
[5]   Q: Is there anything else that you can
[6]   identify in these images that are different from
[7]   what you observed in November of 1963, on the
[8]   photographs you developed?
[9]   A: Right. None of the flooring was showing
[10]   or anything of that nature. I don't remember any
[11]   floor. I don't remember any extremely high angles
[12]   like this.
[13]   Q: Can we turn to the sixth view described as
[14]   the wound of entrance in right posterior occipital
[15]   region corresponding to color Nos. 42 and 43.
[16]   Ms. Spencer, is there any differences that
[17]   you noticed between the sixth view, that is now
[18]   present before you, and those photographs that you
[19]   saw in November of 1963?

[20]   A: Yes. They are again using measuring
[21]   devices that were not in the pictures that we did.
[22]   The section that appears to be the skull weight,

[1]   the side is not there, and again, there are hands
[2]   in the background. This is not a photograph that
[3]   was in the set that we produced.
[4]   Q: In terms of the locations of the wound, do
[5]   you see any differences or similarities with those
[6]   that you developed in November 1963?
[7]   A: No, there is no similarity.
[8]   Q: Could we look now at the seventh view
[9]   described as missile wound at entrance and
[10]   posterior skull following reflection of scalp
[11]   corresponding to color Nos. 44 and 45.
[12]   Ms. Spencer, in November of 1963, did you
[13]   see any images corresponding to the seventh view
[14]   that you have in front of you now?
[15]   A: No.
[16]   Q: Are you able to identify what that view
[17]   is?
[18]   A: It appears to be the opening of the
[19]   cavity, top of the head, with the brain removed.
[20]   Q: Could you look once again at the paper for
[21]   the color print and tell me whether that is the
[22]   paper that you were using in 1963 at the NPC?

[1]   A: No, it is not.
[2]   Q: Can we take a look at the eighth view,
[3]   please. The eighth view is described as the
[4]   basilar view of brain, corresponding to color Nos.
[5]   46, 47, 48, and 49.
[6]   Ms. Spencer, during your testimony, you
[7]   said that you had seen an image with the brain
[8]   present next to the body. Is Image No. 8 the view
[9]   that you saw previously?
[10]   A: No.
[11]   Q: Did you see any work in November of 1963
[12]   that resembled the view that you are being shown
[13]   now?

[14]   A: No, I did not.
[15]   Q: Could you look at the paper for the color
[16]   print and tell me whether that is the paper that
[17]   you were using in November of 1963?
[18]   A: No, it is not.
[19]   MR. GUNN: I think we don't need to take a
[20]   look at the ninth here, which is the superior area
[21]   over the brain.
[22]   BY MR. GUNN:

Page 57

[1]   Q: Ms. Spencer, you have now had an
[2]   opportunity to view all of the colored images, both
[3]   transparencies and prints, that are in the
[4]   possession of the National Archives related to the
[5]   autopsy of President Kennedy.
[6]   Based upon your knowledge, are there any
[7]   images of the autopsy of President Kennedy that are
[8]   not included in those views that we saw?
[9]   A: The views that we produced at the
[10]   Photographic Center are not included.
[11]   Q: Ms. Spencer, how certain are you that
[12]   there were other photographs of President Kennedy's
[13]   autopsy that are not included in the set that you
[14]   have just seen?
[15]   A: I could personally say that they are not
[16]   included. The only thing I can determine is that
[17]   because of the pristine condition of the body and
[18]   the reverence that the body was shown, that—this
[19]   is speculation on my part—that perhaps the
[20]   family had the second set shot and developed as
[21]   possible releases if autopsy pictures were
[22]   demanded, because at that time, Mrs. Kennedy was

Page 58

[1]   attempting to keep all sensationalism out of the
[2]   funeral and maintain the President's dignity and
[3]   name.
[4]   Q: Are you able to—let's start with a
[5]   conjecture as to whether the photographs that you
[6]   developed, and the photographs that you observed
[7]   today, could have been taken at different times?

[8]   A: I would definitely say they were taken at
[9]   different times.
[10]   Q: Is there any question in your mind whether
[11]   the photographs that you saw today were photographs
[12]   of President Kennedy?
[13]   A: There is not doubt they are pictures of
[14]   President Kennedy.
[15]   Q: Is there any doubt in your mind that the
[16]   photographs that you saw in November 1963 also were
[17]   of President Kennedy?
[18]   A: No, that was President Kennedy, but
[19]   between those photographs and the ones that we did,
[20]   there had to be some massive cosmetic things done
[21]   to the President's body.
[22]   Q: Do you have an opinion as to whether the

Page 59

[1]   photographs that you developed in 1963 were taken
[2]   before or after the photographs that you observed
[3]   today?
[4]   A: I would say probably afterwards.
[5]   Q: So you would think that the photographs
[6]   that you developed were taken after reconstruction
[7]   of the body?
[8]   A: Yes.
[9]   Q: In the photograph that you saw in November
[10]   of 1963, with the brain lying next to the body,
[11]   were you able to observe whether there had been any
[12]   damage to the brain?
[13]   A: No, it was not damaged as this brain, as
[14]   the brain on these photographs were.
[15]   Q: When you say "these photographs," you
[16]   means that we just saw today?
[17]   A: The ones that we just viewed.
[18]   Q: Ms. Spencer, before we started I said that
[19]   I would give you an opportunity to add anything if
[20]   you have any additional statement that you would
[21]   like to make, and I will just give you that
[22]   opportunity now.

Page 60

[1]   A: I had brought along a photograph that was
[2]   reproduced approximately 10 days prior to the time
[3]   that we printed the autopsy photographs that we
[4]   produced at NPC, and because of the watermark and
[5]   stuff on it does not match those that I viewed, and
[6]   NPC bought all of a run, which meant every piece of
[7]   paper within the house would have the same
[8]   identical watermarking and logo on it, I can say
[9]   that the paper was not a piece of paper that was
[10]   processed or printed out of the Photographic Center
[11]   within that time frame.
[12]   Like I said, the only thing I can think of
[13]   is that a second set of autopsy pictures was shot
[14]   for public release if necessary.
[15]   MR. GUNN: Ms. Spencer, thank you very
[16]   much. We appreciate your time in coming all the
[17]   way from Missouri. Thank you very much.
[18]   THE WITNESS: I wish I could have
[19]   identified them for you.
[20]   MR. GUNN: Thank you.
[21]   [Off the record.]
[22]   BY MR. GUNN:

Page 61

[1]   Q: Ms. Spencer, there is one other question I
[2]   would like to ask you about, and this is in
[3]   reference to a document that is labeled Exhibit MD
[4]   121, that appears on its face to be a cover sheet
[5]   and a memorandum signed by James Fox dated February
[6]   16, 1967.
[7]   After we concluded the deposition, I
[8]   showed you a copy of this document. Did you have
[9]   an opportunity to read that?
[10]   A: Yes, I did.
[11]   Q: Can you tell me, if you wouldn't mind
[12]   going through the document, and telling me anything
[13]   that you perceive in the document either to be
[14]   accurate, that is, as you recall, or inaccurate and
[15]   different from what your own recollection is?
[16]   A: Okay. During the time that I saw Agent

[17]   Fox, he did not have any black and white film with
[18]   him. The only thing he had in his possession was
[19]   color film, and he remained with us while we
[20]   processed it and printed it. It was not printed on
[21]   different days.
[22]   Q: Mr. Fox says that this happened on

[1]   November 27th, 1963, which would be approximately
[2]   five days after the assassination.
[3]   Does that correspond with your
[4]   recollection as to when he came to—or when an
[5]   agent came to the NPC?
[6]   A: No. My recollection was before the burial
[7]   of President Kennedy.
[8]   Q: And in the statement by Agent Fox, he
[9]   refers to color positives. From what you have said
[10]   before, that would not be—
[11]   A: No.
[12]   Q: —correspond with what you yourself
[13]   observed, is that correct?
[14]   A: Right. The only thing that we processed
[15]   was color negative material.
[16]   Q: Mr. Fox also refers to going with Chief
[17]   Robert Knudsen. You knew Mr. Knudsen, is that
[18]   correct?
[19]   A: Yes. Chief Knudsen was our liaison boss
[20]   between the White House and the Photographic
[21]   Center, he was not with the agent when the agent
[22]   came, and if he was in the building, he would have

[1]   come up.
[2]   Q: So to the extent that Mr. Fox is correct
[3]   in what he makes on the statement, this is not the
[4]   event that you yourself witnessed, would that be
[5]   fair to say?
[6]   A: That is correct.
[7]   MR. GUNN: Thank you very much.
[8]   [Signature not waived.]
[9]   [Whereupon, at 11:40 a.m., the deposition
[10]   was concluded.]

[1]   Written Interrogatories to supplement the oral
[2]   deposition of Dr. James Joseph Humes.
[3]   In the Autopsy Protocol, the skull entry
[4]   wound was described as follows:
[5]   "Situated in the posterior scalp
[6]   approximately 2.5 cm. laterally to the right and
[7]   slightly above the external occipital protuberance
[8]   is a lacerated wound measuring 15 ¥ 6 mm."
[9]   (Autopsy Protocol, p. 4.)
[10]   The Forensic Pathology Panel of the House
[11]   Select Committee on Assassinations reported the
[12]   following exchange from September 16, 1977:
[13]   "Dr. Petty: I'm looking at No. 2, X-ray
[14]   No. 2. Is this the point of entrance that I'm
[15]   pointing to?
[16]   Dr. Humes: No.
[17]   Dr. Petty: This is not?
[18]   Dr. Humes and Boswell: No.
[19]   Dr. Petty: Where is the point of
[20]   entrance? That doesn't show?
[21]   Dr. Humes: It doesn't show. Below the
[22]   external occipital protuberance.

[1]   Dr. Petty: It's below it?
[2]   Dr. Humes: Right.
[3]   Dr. Petty: Not above it?
[4]   Dr. Humes: No. It's to the right and
[5]   inferior to the external occipital protuberance.
[6]   [Dr. Humes then shown photo 42 (the "wound
[7]   of entrance in right posterior occipital region").]
[8]   Dr. Petty: Then this is the entrance
[9]   wound? The one down by the margin of the hair in
[10]   the back?
[11]   Dr Humes: Yes, sir."
[12]   (Vol. 7, p. 246 of the House Select
[13]   Committee on Assassinations Appendices to the
[14]   Investigation of the Assassination of President
[15]   John F. Kennedy.)
[16]   The following was taken from your sworn

[17]   testimony to the House Select Committee on
[18]   Assassinations on September 7, 1978, while being
[19]   shown the Ida Dox drawing (Figure 13):
[20]   "[I]t is obvious to me as I sit here now
[21]   with [this] markedly enlarged drawing of the
[22]   photograph that the upper defect to which you

[1]   pointed or the upper object is clearly in the
[2]   location of where we said approximately where it
[3]   was, above the external occipital protuberance;
[4]   therefore I believe that is the wound of
[5]   entry.". . . .
[6]   "[T]he object in the lower portion, which
[7]   I apparently and I believe now erroneously
[8]   previously identified before the most recent panel,
[9]   is far below the external occipital protuberance
[10]   and would not fit with the original autopsy
[11]   findings." (Vol. 1, p. 327.)
[12]   The House Select Committee on
[13]   Assassinations reported that you changed your
[14]   opinion on the location of the entry wound.
[15]   "The panel concludes unanimously that the
[16]   head entrance wound was located approximately 10 cm
[17]   above the EOP and slightly to the right of the
[18]   midline . . . [W]hile testifying before this committee,
[19]   Dr. Humes, the chief autopsy pathologist, changed
[20]   his earlier testimony and supported the panel's
[21]   conclusion as to the location of the wound." (Vol.
[22]   7, p. 176.)

[1]   Mr. Gerald Posner, author of the book
[2]   "Case Closed," reported in Congressional testimony
[3]   that:
[4]   "It was the work of [the HSCA] that had
[5]   the two autopsy physicians change their mind, that
[6]   they had been mistaken about the placement of the
[7]   wound, here [slightly above the hairline], and that
[8]   it is in fact correctly placed 4 inches higher
[9]   [near the "cowlick" area]. I have spoken to them
[10]   about this and they have confirmed their change of

[11]   testimony that they gave before the House Select
[12]   Committee on Assassinations."
[13]   (Posner testimony, Hearing before the
[14]   Legislation and National Security Subcommittee of
[15]   the Committee on Government Operations, House of
[16]   Representatives, dated November 17, 1993, 112–113.)
[17]   Please answer the following
[18]   interrogatories under oath. Please feel free to
[19]   attach additional pages to your answers. Your
[20]   answers may be handwritten.
[21]   Interrogatory 1: Did you believe, at the
[22]   time you wrote and signed the Autopsy Protocol,

Page 5

[1]   that the location of the entrance wound in
[2]   President Kennedy's skull was 2.5 cm to the right
[3]   and slightly above the external occipital
[4]   protuberance, as is stated in the Autopsy Protocol?
[5]   Interrogatory 1 answer:
[6]   Yes.
[7]
[8]
[9]
[10]
[11]
[12]
[13]
[14]
[15]
[16]
[17]

Page 6

[1]   Interrogatory 2: During your communi-
[2]   cations with the House Select Committee on
[3]   Assassinations, did you ever change your original
[4]   opinion about the location of the skull entrance
[5]   wound? If so, what did you conclude about the
[6]   location of the entry wound?
[7]   Interrogatory 2 answer:
[8]   See accompanying letter.
[9]

[10]
[11]
[12]
[13]
[14]
[15]
[16]
[17]
[18]
[19]
[20]

[1]   Interrogatory 3: Did you ever change your
[2]   opinion about the location of the entrance wound in
[3]   the skull? If so, please explain when you changed
[4]   your opinion and the circumstances that led you to
[5]   change your opinion.
[6]   Interrogatory 3 answer:
[7]   See accompanying letter.
[8]
[9]
[10]
[11]
[12]
[13]
[14]
[15]
[16]
[17]
[18]

[1]   Interrogatory 4: What is your current
[2]   belief as to the location of the entry wound in
[3]   President Kennedy's skull?
[4]   Interrogatory 4 answer:
[5]   As stated in the autopsy report.
[6]
[7]
[8]
[9]
[10]

[11]
[12]
[13]
[14]
[15]
[16]

FILE COPY

James J. Humes, M.D.
5 Spy Glass Lane
Ponte Vedra Beach, FL 32082
(904) 285-6541
Fax (904) 273-8571

March 11, 1996.

T.Jeremy Gunn,
Assassination Records Review Board,
600 E. Street NW, 2nd Floor, Washington, DC, 20530.

Dear Mr. Gunn,

      I am returning herewith the transcript of my deposition before the Board on Feb. 13,1996. In my review I found the following minor errors:

      Page 22. l.21 "Peter" shoulg be "Pierre".
      Page 32, l1 "Picture" should be "Pictures".
      Page 43, l5 "Roof" should be "Windshield".
      Page 62, l 10 "thera—" should be "therapists".
      Page 80, l15 "to" should be "on"
      Page 120, l 10 delete the "s" in anywheres.

      With regard to the changes which you have suggested in the printed transcript, I agree with all of them.

      With regard to your four final questions, I make the followinmg response. Both during my testimony before the House Select Committee on Assassinations, and during this disposition I experienced great difficulty in interpreting the location of the wound of entrance in the posterior scalp from the photograph. This may be because of the angle from which it was taken, or the position of the head, etc. It is obvious that the location of the external occipital protuberance cannot be ascertained from the photograph. I most firmly believe that the location of the wound was exactly where I measured it to be in relation to the external occipital protuberance and so recorded it in the autopsy report. After all that was my direct observation in the morgue and I believe it to be far more reliable than attempting to interpret what I believe to be a photograph which is subject to various interpretations

      I appreciated your courteous manner in conducting the deposition and will be available if I can be of further assistance.

                          Sincerely

ARGUMENTS FOR
ZAPRUDER FILM ALTERATION

By David Mantik, M.D., Ph.D.

1. The inter-sprocket areas of the Zapruder film (especially after about Z-240) are darker than the central image (the one that appears on the screen). That phenomenon is not typical of 8 mm film—in fact, it is not seen in the inter-sprocket areas on the "home movie" track of the Zapruder film, nor before about Z-240.

2. In the upper one-third (approximately) of the inter-sprocket area is a superimposed image after about Z-310. The image is of a motorcycle front fender and tire definitely on the right side of the car. This phenomenon is not expected for 8 mm film. It does not occur in the earlier portion of the motorcade sequence, nor does it occur on the "home movie" portion. Is it mere coincidence that this occurs just before "the head shot"?

3. After these many decades there is still no satisfactory explanation for the head snap that is seen immediately after frame Z-313. Recent ballistics experiments, independently by Dough DeSalles, MD and by Arthur Snyder, PhD, have failed to find convincing evidence of such a head snap (either forward or backward). Itek's analysis many years ago for the HSCA offered mathematical proof that a frontal bullet lacked the required energy for this effect. Even after correcting their anatomic assumptions, I have found that their conclusion is essentially correct. The neuromuscular reaction is still supported by David Belin and other laymen but it has no support in the scientific community. Furthermore, it has never been publicly supported by anyone from the appropriate specialty—the neurosciences. If, however, frames were (uniformly) removed from the Zapruder film over a fairly long sequence, then all movements would be correspondingly accelerated; a slow posterior drift of the head might well be converted into a head snap. The eyewitness testimony is unanimous that the backward motion of the head was indeed slow.

4. There is near unanimity among eyewitnesses that the presidential limousine either stopped or slowed abruptly during the head shots. That is not seen in the extant Zapruder film. Careful analysis by

Alvarez of the limousine's speed does indicate a slowing from about 12 to 8 mph. This modest change, however, appears inconsistent with the eyewitness reports. Many, including James Hargis, the motorcycle man on the left side of the limousine, report that the vehicle actually stopped. Hargis, in fact, estimated that it stopped for about half a second.

5. The different movie films of the assassination actually may not agree with one another as well as is widely believed. Doug Mizzer (*Killing Kennedy*, p. 138) has pointed out an apparent discrepancy between the Zapruder and Nix films. Clint Hill testified that he grabbed Jackie and put her back into her seat (2 H 138–9). In the Nix film, Hill gets both feet onto the limousine and puts one hand on each of Jackie's shoulders. He even seems to be hugging her head and shoulders as he pushes her back into the seat. But the Zapruder film shows that he only reached out and perhaps barely touched her outstretched hand when she turned and climbed back into the seat.

6. Several eyewitnesses saw tissue debris fly posteriorly after the head shots. On still frames used during their work, the surveyors are confident they saw large blobs of debris leaving JFK's head, going to the rear. This appeared on at least three frames. That is not seen in the extant film. Experiments with melons (and human skulls, too) by a number of scientists (John Lattimer, Luis Alvarez, Doug DeSalles, Arthur Snyder) clearly show debris in the air for *many* frames after the initial impact.

7. On Z-28, Roy Schaeffer has identified a sharp, clearly defined + near the center of Elm Street. I have discovered another one on Z-308 (good resolution is required). There is no current explanation for how these could have materialized. Were these used as register marks during the (clandestine) editing process?

8. Dan Rather, in a very early viewing of the film, described seeing blood on John Connally's shirt front. That is no longer seen. He also described JFK going forward, not backward.

9. In the Muchmore movie film, the right tail light is obviously on for at least nine successive frames—it may be longer, but the tail light is obscured before and after this sequence. This is powerful evidence that the brakes were on during the critical period during which eyewitnesses described the slowing of the limousine.

10. Z-316 to 323 shows the motorcycles overtaking the limousine. This would not be expected for a uniform motorcade speed through

Dealey Plaza (as the extant Zapruder film suggests), but would be expected if the limousine had unexpectedly slowed or stopped.

11. In Z-302, three background figures are quite out of focus, while the limousine and its occupants are well defined. In the very next frame, on the other hand, all three background figures are suddenly well defined, while the limousine image remains nearly constant. The same situation occurs in Z-314–315 for the solitary background figure. This is, at the very least, a most uncommon optical phenomenon.

12. The reverse phenomenon occurs in Z-307 to 308. Furthermore, the image of Jean Hill is suddenly doubled in Z-308, while no other images are doubled in this same frame—not even the motorcycle windshield directly in front of her. Film vibration cannot be the explanation, since the windshield is a single image.

13. In Z-312 there is a double image of Mary Moorman's face, but only a single image of the motorcycle windshield. In the very next frame the windshield is doubled. In Z-314 it is single again, then doubled again in Z-315, and then single in Z-316.

14. The first re-enactment in Dealey Plaza (early December, 1963) clearly describes (and diagrams) a shot at about Z-276 and another at about Z-358 [See page 243 in *Whitewash II* by Harold Weisberg.] Marler has located documentary support (CE 2111) for this view as well. There is also surprisingly strong evidence that the initial survey measurements were subsequently altered, possibly to eliminate evidence for these widely separated shots.

15. The eyewitnesses are remarkably consistent in describing two separate head shots, easily separated in time and space. These witnesses describe no backward head snap. Instead, they recall a slow backward drift, with the head becoming *erect* after the first head shot. Then another shot (or shots) were heard. The movement that struck almost all of them was a sudden *forward* lurch. A good example of this class is Clint Hill, who begins running forward right after Z-313; but he reports hearing another shot just as he reaches the limousine—clearly long after Z-313. He even describes this latter shot as removing a portion of JFK's head. The extant Zapruder film shows only one obvious head shot at about Z-313—with no forward lurch. A second head shot after Z-313 would also explain the apparent absence of an occipital defect immediately after Z-313. This eyewitness evidence was presented at a meeting in Dallas in November, 1996.

16. Noel Twyman interviewed Erwin Schwartz, who was Zapruder's business partner. Schwartz says that he viewed the original Zapruder film about 15 times during that initial weekend. He saw tissue debris flying to the rear, something not seen on the extant film. He does not report a head snap, but rather describes Jackie as lifting JFK's head upward and backward (presumably in order to see his face better). He also describes JFK's head as twisting to the left with a head shot, something also not seen on the extant film. The comments of Jean Hill and Mary Moorman may be consistent with this head rotation. The HSCA had previously noted that such head rotation may sometimes occur with head shots (7 HSCA 171).

17. From the Robert Hughes movie film taken earlier in the motorcade, Roy Schaeffer and Mike Pincher have determined the blinking rate for the emergency lights on the front of the presidential limousine. They have compared this pattern to frames Z-133 to 238 of the Zapruder film, and found a substantial disruption of the pattern that would have been expected. If film editing had occurred, however, this disruption would naturally be expected.

18. The Muchmore film may provide better evidence of limousine slowing than the Moorman photograph: There are more images, but even more importantly, it does not suffer the drawbacks of proximity and perspective that are evident in the Moorman photograph. By examining the Muchmore frame shortly before Z-313, as printed in Groden (p. 33) the reader may draw his own conclusions. Note the reflected highlights on the rear of the near motorcycle: they are distinctly blurred. So is the image of the tire and the rear fender. For comparison, look at the limousine. On the rear tire, the whitewall trim seems quite well defined—as compared to the motorcycle tire. Also, examine the limousine right rear taillight and immediately adjacent fender. Again, this seems better defined than the motorcycle fender. In addition, compare the clarity of the limousine hand grip (seen against the background grass) to the rim of the motorcycle windshield. All of this is consistent with a very slow limousine speed. Note that the foreground characters are seen quite clearly, implying that the camera tracking is quite slow at this time. Even the closest female figure on the far right is not blurred, because of her proximity to the camera. Since the limousine image is clearer than the motorcycle, we know that the camera is preferentially tracking the limousine. And, since the bystanders are well seen, the log-

ical conclusion is that the limousine speed is much closer to that of the bystanders (zero) than to the motorcycles. I have also viewed all of the adjacent frames in the Muchmore film with a loupe and cannot avoid the same conclusion there—the limousine is hardly moving. This deceleration appears to begin shortly after Z-300, just as Alvarez said. Simply from qualitative appearances, however, this deceleration appears to be much larger than he suggested, with a final speed much less than his 8 mph.

19. Weatherly, in an insightful analysis (*Killing Kennedy*, pp. 371–381) takes Alvarez's work a step further and raises new and curious issues related to image streaking (vector analysis). For example, between Z-193 and Z-194 the camera moves to the left. This is easily determined by simply looking at the right edge of the frame—the image shifts with respect to the frame edge, presumably as a result of uneven camera movement (tracking). As Alvarez noted, such a movement should produce streaking—of the background figures, the sign, and the closer bystanders. But none of this is seen—it is all quite paradoxical. Based on this, Weatherly proposes that this is a composite scene. This is a remarkably simple and powerful argument. It is difficult to avoid this conclusion.

Meanwhile, in Z-194 and Z-195 the motorcade occupants appear unchanged, but both the *background and foreground* are very fuzzy in Z-195—quite different from Z-194. He notes that this phenomenon occurs repeatedly throughout the film—one part of a frame changes a great deal while another part stays the same. This could occur if the frame were a composite. Any other explanation runs into trouble.

Between Z-198 and Z-199 the camera obviously moves to the left— note the disappearance of the tree trunk at the right edge. As a result of this, some streaking should be seen in Z-199—unless Zapruder knew how to stop moving when the shutter opened! But no streaking is seen— not even on tiny highlights (observe the background for these). Weatherly again concludes that different parts of the frame indicate two incompatible actions for the camera. In both cases, a composite scene is the simplest explanation.

Weatherly also notes similar problems in Z-206 to Z-207. He adds one more significant point: No frames between Z-166 and Z-216 were published by *LIFE* in late November, so no composite frames had to be completed by then.

Between Z-302 and Z-303 the camera moves quite uniformly with the limousine—i.e., it tracks well. The evidence for this is that the bright reflection in front of the windshield appears in the same place (at the right edge of both frames). In Z-302, Jean Hill and Mary Moorman (standing) are very fuzzy, but in Z-303 they are extremely clear. Even if it is conceded that the camera tracked normally before Z-303, then stopped when the shutter opened, and then tracked well again when the shutter closed, the lack of blurring on the motorcade is still inexplicable.

Similar comments apply to Z-308 to Z-311 for Moorman and Hill. And more paradoxes occur in Z-313 to Z-315. In Z-315, note the double image of the windshield. Weatherly interprets this data to mean that frames have been excised from the head shot sequence, possibly to remove incriminating evidence of a frontal head shot. Any reader with a logical bent for objective data is advised, in the strongest terms, to review Weatherly's analysis. It is beautifully simple and the conclusions are inescapable.

20. At the University of Michigan, an experiment with an unexpected result was performed in 1971. Elizabeth Loftus summarizes this work in *Eyewitness Testimony* (1996). Her book won the National Media Award for Distinguished Contribution from the American Psychological Foundation. The book jacket says what you would expect it to say—it implies that eyewitness testimony is unreliable. However, Table 3.1 on page 27 tells quite another story. The data cited are from J. Marshall, et al., *Harvard Law Review* 84: 1620–1643. A total of 151 observers were shown a two minute movie in color and sound—with a fairly complex set of actions. The researchers identified about 900 items present in the film that could have been mentioned. The observers were interviewed immediately after the viewing; they were urged to recount, in all possible detail, what they had seen. The researchers then assessed these responses based on accuracy, completeness, and saliency. Accuracy and completeness were determined by what was actually seen in the film. Saliency, however, was determined, not by the researchers, but rather was defined internally—i.e., by the responses of the observers themselves. Specifically, if an item was described by over 50% of the observers, it was considered highly salient.

Marshall, et al. then graphed the accuracy and completeness of the responses vs. saliency, as follows.

Saliency	Accuracy	Completeness
0	61	64
1–12	78	81
13–25	81	82
26–50	83	92
51–100	98	98

In view of all that has been said about eyewitness *unreliability*, this data is quite astonishing—if over 50% of the witnesses considered an item to be salient, then they were 98% accurate and 98% complete! In other words, an individual witness had only a 2% chance of being wrong if he or she was reporting a salient item. Did the HSCA consider this? What does this tell us about the many witnesses (48 individual witnesses, according to Vince Palamara) who saw the limousine stop? It is noteworthy that this study was published in 1971, years before the HSCA even came into existence. It is doubtful that Blakey had taken time to read this report.

MEMO FOR FILE

Date: February 28, 1998
To: National Archives and Records Administration
NNPS
Archives II, College Park, Maryland
Subject: Review of the "Zapruder" film copies by H. E. Livingstone
From: Harrison E. Livingstone, private citizen.

We examined most or all of the 8mm copies of the Zapruder film held by NARA during a number of visits in January and February this year. Accompanying me were my colleagues Doug Mizzer, Daryll Weatherly, and Officer Matthew Branham, Baltimore City Police. We are preparing a series of charts with measurements and other data on each of the films.

1) We found several films with the number 0186 printed on their leaders. This number was not punched through except in one case, (Secret Service No. 2; 87.010) and were otherwise printed on the film from original perforated copies, presumably, indicating that these films are not the copies made by Jamieson in Dallas on November 22, 1963. Also, they do not have the number "0183" printed on them, which, according to an affidavit made by Kodak November 22, 1963, they should have *in addition to the later numbers*. They are not the Jamieson copies because they have no sprocket hole images in the motorcade and Dealey Plaza sequences and the film is entirely black to the left of the "septum." Jamieson insists that the contact printing process used by his technician, Marshal Collier, would have copied all of the intersprocket areas we know are on the original film and which are on the present copies of the "home movie" which Zapruder took shortly before on the same roll of film. This film is documented by NARA as having been made by Life and given to the Secret Service. Why would they do this when they had two of Jamieson's copies? Both originals appear to have been substituted for by the two made by Life. Did the Secret Service damage them? The bottom line is that the disappearance of the Jamieson copies makes it impossible to compare the intersprocket areas with the "camera original" film.

2) One film, titled "Secret Service Copy No. 1" (87.010) had the number 0183 printed out, but not punched through. This purports to be a copy made from the original but is not a first generation copy because

the sprocket areas, as in the above films, are completely black. This film is also documented as having been made by Life and was evidently given to the Secret Service. It lacks later numbers in the sequence, so the actual pedigree of this film is greatly in doubt. There is a physical splice at Z 133 but none at 207, indicating it is a multi generation made from the original before it was damaged by Life.

3) The single film spoke of in Item 1 above which had the perforated numbers "0186" (Secret Service No. 2; (87.010) is not authentic because the black strip of film with the perforated numbers is spliced into the middle of the film between the motorcade and three people in Dealey Plaza segments, and the rest of the film containing assassination sequences does not have intersprocket area images.

4) Documentation provided to me by the Assassination Records Review Board from Eastman Kodak in Dallas dated November 22, 1963 (possible postdated) indicates that the number 0183 was punched through the camera original film *before* it went to Jamieson to be copied. Jamieson Film Company made an affidavit on the same day stating "And that the end of the processed film carried the identification number: 0183" which was printed onto the said duplicate copies. The later statement is of great importance because it means that the three Jamieson copies would have *both* 0183 *printed* on them, and one of the three numbers: "0185" "0186" or "0187" punched through them when the contact prints were processed at Kodak. We saw no such film at NARA.

5) Doug Mizzer discovered, in his study of home movies made by his father with a similar 8mm or Double 8 camera in the early Sixties, that there is a "fade in" and a "fade out" between scenes extending some three frames. We do not know what make camera was used. As a result of his study, we found that the first frame is overexposed in nearly all the films where a new sequence begins, with one notable exception: the motorcade's appearance at 133. This may be a major indication that many frames were removed at a time when there is evidence that the limousine was stopped just after making the turn onto Elm. The driver admitted to moving at only 3–4 mph, and the brake light is on in the Towner film, which does not appear to be attributable to sunlight, as is the apparent lighting of the left brake light later on when the car is near Zapruder.

6) Another problem surfaces when we consider that there are a number of home movie strips of film in the NARA inventory in excess of the three that Jamieson copied. How can we have all of them showing intersprocket area images? Technically, we can't have more than three, and each of them are spliced to motorcade sequences which have no intersprocket images at all.

7) I have studied C. Mayn's report of 21 December, 1995 concerning his technical review of the "camera original" Zapruder film. He does not find or does not mention the perforated identification number "0183" placed on the film in Dallas. He assumes that the camera original would contain an image covering the entire intersprocket area from the aperture, but we do not know if this is entirely true because it is controverted by the images we have on the home movie. He may or may not be correct, but it seems to me that the intersprocket areas we have on the home movies, in your inventory, which is greatly at variance with the total lack of images in the motorcade sequence intersprocket areas on the *same* film strips would tend to indicate that the opposite of what he says about the operation of film printers is true. That is, the home movie may be more accurate a representation, and it only shows the area half filled up towards the left side, but the edge printing is there.

Therefore, it may be impossible for the "camera original" film presently in possession of the Archives to be an original film because the intersprocket areas are at radical variance with those of the "home movie" in two major respects. a) the home movie lacks any evidence of ghost images in the upper right area adjoining the upper sprocket hole, and b) because the home movie intersprocket area of images carried over from the central frame area are perfect continuations of the central frame image, except for a "septum" dividing them, but only cover the right half of the intersprocket area. The area leading to the left edge and edgeprinting on all home movie copies we examined was black. The slides made from the "camera original" by Life and also reproduced by the Warren Commission in Vol. 18 of the Hearings, show a complete image all the way to the left edge, but with no septum. This image, however, has an upper area and a lower area, both comprising about half of the intersprocket area. The upper area is light, in contradistinction to the lower area which is dark. It is in this upper area where a "ghost image" appears in two separate long segments of the film as seen in the slides and in Vol. 18 of the Hearings of the WC. In the first appearance, we see the image of a motorcycle that must have been on the right rear fender of the car (because we see the entire front wheel and windshield) but which never appears in the central frame itself. The second instance appears much later in the film, and occurs between frames 437 and ends at 458, if I'm not mistaken. The strange thing about this phenomena toward the end of the slides (is this the end of the film? We have slides through Z 483) is that all the intersprocket areas are black and without images from Z 413, except for the small window of pictures in the 21 frames or so above described in the upper right corner of the inter-sprocket area beneath the sprocket hole.

Without the technical experience to comment on this, I will state that it appears that this is evidence of tampering of some kind and Life should be asked if they have an explanation. It is suspicious or sinister in that gunman may have been in the storm drains on the bridge facing the approaching car and this is the area that may be blacked out in the film, if they would have been photographed as the camera panned to the bridge. If the film was blown up and reframed, it might have eliminated activity on top of the bridge near the shooters.

How could the intersprocket area be black and yet have an image in that one area for 21 frames, and throughout the rest of the film have a full image taking up all of the area in the motorcade sequence, and only the right half in the home movie?

It is our belief that the "original film," if it corresponds to the slides in the Archives, is a blown up version of the film which accounts for the complete filling up of the intersprocket area with a continuation of the central image, and that the film has been reframed. What the purpose of is hard to fathom, except to eliminate peripheral data. Of course, it is my personal belief that scenes have been removed and the film altered with retouching and composited frames, as vector analysis conducted by Daryll Weatherly indicates. Enlarging the frames and reframing them might be a method of better concealing such alterations.

Apparent reframing is particularly evident as the limousine emerges from behind the Stemmons Freeway sign and the car and occupants all but disappear in the film.

There is no doubt that additional copies were made on November 22, 1963. Furthermore, it is inconceivable that the Secret Service, which had constructive possession or a chain of evidence on this film throughout most of November 22, 1963, would have ever given up possession of the original to Abraham Zapruder. I cannot imagine any law enforcement agency doing that, and in fact, they demonstrated throughout that day and succeeding days that they would seize any and all photographic evidence and keep it for a period of time, perhaps copying much of it, before returning it—if at all. The most important film of the assassination described in CD 298 as the "Nix" film but in fact that of Beverly Oliver, was never returned.

Autopsy X-Rays
Numbering Supplied by November 10, 1966 Inspection

No.	Description from Inventory
1	Anterior - Posterior View of the Skull, Slightly Heat Damaged
2	Right Lateral View of the Skull, With Two Angle Lines Overdrawn on the Film (8"x10" Film)
3	Lateral View of the Skull (8"x10" Film)
4	X-Ray of 3 Fragments of Bone With the Larger Fragment Containing Metallic Fragments (8"x10" Film)
5	X-Ray of 3 Fragments of Bone With the Larger Fragment Containing Metallic Fragments (8"x10" Film)
6	X-Ray of 3 Fragments of Bone With the Larger Fragment Containing Metallic Fragments (8"x10" Film)
7	Anterior - Posterior View of the Abdomen (14"x17" Film)
8	Anterior - Posterior View of the Right Shoulder and Right Chest (14"x17" Film)
9	Anterior- Posterior View of the Chest (14"x17" Film)
10	Anterior - Posterior View of the Left Shoulder and Left Chest (14"x17" Film)
11	Anterior- Posterior View of the Abdomen and Lower Chest (14"x17" Film)
12	Anterior - Posterior View of Both Femurs including Both Knee Joints (14"x17" Film)
13	Anterior - Posterior View of the Pelvis. There is a Small Round Density of Myelogram Media Projected Over the Sacral Canal (14"x17" Film)
14	Anterior- Posterior View of Lower Pelvis, Hips, and Upper Femurs (14"x17" Film)

Autopsy Photographs
Numbering Supplied by November 10, 1966 Inspection

View	Description from Inventory	B & W Numbers	Color Numbers
1st	"left side of head and shoulders"	1, 2, 3, 4	29, 30, 31
2nd	"right side of head and right shoulder"	5, 6	26, 27, 28
3rd	"superior view of head"	7, 8, 9, 10	32, 33, 34, 35, 36, 37
4th	"posterior view of wound of entrance of missile high in shoulder	11, 12	38, 39
5th	"right anterior view of head and upper torso, including tracheotomy wound"	13, 14	40, 41
6th	"wound of entrance in right posterior occipital region"	15, 16	42, 43
7th	"missile wound of entrance in posterior skull, following reflection of scalp"	17, 18	44, 45
8th	"basilar view of brain"	19, 21, 22	46, 47, 48, 49
9th	"superior view of brain"	20, 23, 24, 25	50, 51, 52

ADDENDUM   559

JFK ASSASSINATION SYSTEM

IDENTIFICATION FORM

AGENCY INFORMATION

                    AGENCY : FBI
           RECORD NUMBER : 124-10018-10310

        RECORDS SERIES :
HQ

AGENCY FILE NUMBER : 62-109060-1431

DOCUMENT INFORMATION

             ORIGINATOR : FBI
                    FROM : BELMONT, A. H.
                      TO : TOLSON

               TITLE :

                    DATE : 11/22/63
                   PAGES : 2

               SUBJECTS :
EVIDENCE, RIFLE, BULLET, CARTRIDGE CASE, REVOLVER, TRANSPORT TO WDS,
ADMIN INSTR

       DOCUMENT TYPE : PAPER, TEXTUAL DOCUMENT
      CLASSIFICATION : U
        RESTRICTIONS : OPEN IN FULL
      CURRENT STATUS : O
DATE OF LAST REVIEW : 10/26/92

     OPENING CRITERIA :

           COMMENTS :

Box 7   Sec 18

NAL FORM NO. 10
1962 EDITION
A GEN. REG. NO. 27   5010-106

UNITED STATES GO RNMENT

Memorandum

Mr. Tolson   DATE: **November 22, 1963**

FROM :   A. H. Belmont

SUBJECT: **ASSASSINATION OF PRESIDENT JOHN F. KENNEDY
NOVEMBER 22, 1963, DALLAS, TEXAS**

I talked to SAC Shanklin in Dallas. He said arrangements have been made with Carswell Air Force Base to fly one of our Agents up to Washington with the rifle that was recovered by the police together with the fragments of the bullet taken from Governor Connelly and the cartridge cases. I told SAC Shanklin that Secret Service had one of the bullets that struck President Kennedy and the other is lodged behind the President's ear and we are arranging to get both of these. I told him to notify us when the gun will reach Washington so we can have the Laboratory standing by.

I told Shanklin that it appeared the rifle was highly important particularly as Oswald is making no admissions and leads should be set out to immediately check this rifle as well as the telescope sight. Shanklin said this was being done. I told Shanklin to also see if the police want us to make a ballistics test on the pistol which shot the police officer and if so to forward the pistol and the bullets to us for examination. I told Shanklin if the police don't want to release the pistol to us, he should find out all about it; that is, make, caliber, how many bullets were fired, etc.

Shanklin said that he realized that it was extremely important to locate and interview the co-workers of Oswald and any people that knew him in order to account for his whereabouts and actions, and he said this is being done.

I told Shanklin that President Johnson has been in touch with the Director and wants to be sure we are on top of this case and is looking to the FBI solving the case. It is, therefore, imperative that we do everything possible in this case. Shanklin understood.

Shanklin was advised that we are sending out another teletype to all offices instructing that any allegations or leads pertaining to the assassination must be run out on an urgent basis and the Bureau and Dallas, office of origin, advised.

1 - Mr. Sullivan   1 - Mr. DeLoach
1 - Mr. Mohr   1 - Mr. Conrad

AHB:cfs
(8)

53 DEC 11 1963

94

- - -

Memorandum to Mr. Tolson
RE: ASSASSINATION OF PRESIDENT JOHN F. KENNEDY

   In view of the fact a number of leads are
developing in Dallas and it is necessary to conduct
numerous interviews at one, I told Shanklin we would
send in an additional 20 Agents, four stenographers
and ten cars. The Administrative Division is handling
this tonight.

- - -

-2-

File No. _89-43-1A 281_

Date Received _4-24-69_

From _New Orleans_
(Name of Contributor)

_____
(Address of Contributor)

By _Ses. 9001_
(Name of Special Agent)

To Be Returned   Yes ☐

No ☐

Description: _Photos of bullet claimed to have been removed from Pres. Kennedy._

Recent photos of the windshield of the President's limousine taken in its box at the National Archives showing an apparent fragment or bullet hole. (*This page and two pages following.*)

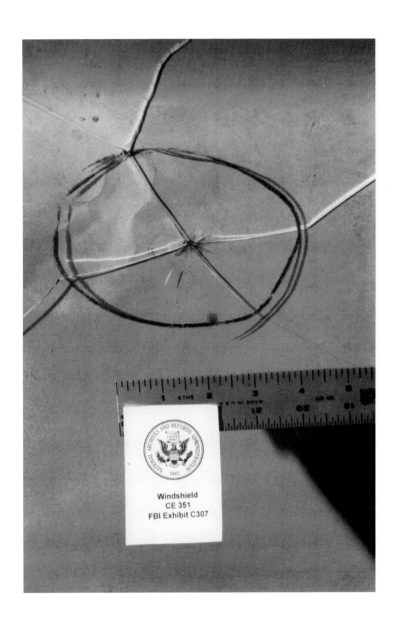

Windshield
CE 351
FBI Exhibit C307

Windshield
CE 351
FBI Exhibit
C307

BIBLIOGRAPHY AND AUTHOR INDEX

Abbreviations used for citations:

3H67: Vol 3. p. 67 Appendix or Hearings of the Warren Report.

3HSCA 422: Vol 3. p. 422 Appendix to the Report of the House Select Committee on Assassinations, or Assassinations Committee. 12 vols. JFK; 13 vols. King.

WR: Warren Report *(NY Times* edition used here unless otherwise stated) Report – Report of the Assassinations Committee. Also New York: Bantam 1979.

CD – Commission Document
CE – Commission Exhibit

Investigation of the Assassination of President John F. Kennedy, Book 7.

Final Report of the Select Committee to Study Governmental Operations with Respect to Intelligence Activities, U.S. Senate 1976 Recommended reading.

Report to the President by the Commission on CIA Activities Within the United States (The "Rockefeller Commission") also Manor Books, New York, 1976.

SICROFA – *Senate Intelligence Committee Report on Foreign Assassinations* "Alleged Assassination Plots Involving Foreign Leaders." Recommended reading.

Anson, Robert Sam, *They've killed the President,* New York: Bantam 1975. Recommended reading for the novice.

Ashman, Charles, *The CIA-Mafia Link.* New York: Manor Books 1975.

Bishop, Jim, *The Day Kennedy Was Shot.* New York: Funk & Wagnalls 1968; Bantam, 1969.

Blumenthal, Sid, with Harvey Yazigian, *Government by Gunplay, Assassination Conspiracy Theories From Dallas to Today.* New York: Signet 1976. Recommended reading.

Bowart, William, *Operation Mind Control, Our Secret Government's War.*

Against Its Own People, New York: Dell Recommended reading.
Buchanan, Patrick, *Who Killed Kennedy,* New York: Putnam 1964; London: Secker, Warburg, 1964, New York; MacFadden, 1965.

Canfield, Michael, with Alan J. Weberman, *Coup d'Etat in America. The CIA and the assassination of John F. Kennedy.* New York: Third World Press 1975.

The Continuing Inquiry (TCI) journal of assassination research, monthly. No longer published.

Curry, Jesse, *JFK Assassination File,* 1969 American Poster & Printing Co. Inc. 1600 S. Akard. Dallas, Texas 75215.

Echoes of Conspiracy 1525 Acton St., Berkeley, CA 94702 (Paul Hoch) A Journal of Assassination Research.

Fensterwald, Bernard, *Assassination of JFK by Coincidence or Conspiracy?* Zebra Books: New York 1977 Committee to Investigate Assassinations (CToIA) Recommended reading.

Flammonde, Paris, *The Kennedy Conspiracy: An Uncommissioned Report on the Jim Garrison Investigation.* New York: Meridith 1969.

Fox, Sylvan, *The Unanswered Questions About President Kennedy's Assassination,* New York: Award Books, 1965 and 1975.

Garrison, Jim, *A Heritage of Stone,* New York: Putnam, 1970, Berkeley 1972. Recommended reading for all Americans.

Best Evidence, By David Lifton, MacMillan, 1980, NYC.; Carroll & Graf, 1988, NYC

Hepburn, James (pseudonym, author unknown, but thought to be French Intelligence and American sources, by William Turner.) *Farewell America* Frontiers Publishing Company 1963, Vaduz, Liechtenstein, Printed in Canada and Belgium, but this is a fictitious publishing company. Some books available from William Turner: San Rafael, CA. Recommended reading: A very important book. The book was written by someone with an intimate knowledge of the CIA and the United States.

Hinckle, Warren and Turner, William *The Fish is Red,* New York: Haper and Row 1981.

Hougan, Jim, *Spooks, The Haunting of America – The Private Use of Secret Agents,* New York: William Morrow, 1978. Recommended reading.

Jones, Jr. Penn, *Forgive My Grief* vols. I-IV. Rt3, Box 356, Waxahachie, TX. 75165 Recommended reading.

Kantor, Seth, *Who Was Jack Ruby?* New York: Everest, 1978.

Manchester, William, *The Death of a President:* November 20-25, 1963. New York: Harper & Row, 1967: Popular Library 1968.

Marchetti, Victor & John D. Marks, *The CIA and the Cult of Intelligence.* New York: Knopf 1974. Recommended reading.

Marks, John, *The Search For The Manchurian Candidate.* New York: Times Books 1979. Recommended reading.

Meagher, Sylvia, *Accessories After the Fact: The Warren Commission, the Authorities, and the Report,* New York: Bobbs-Merrill, 1967: Vintage, 1976. Recommended reading.

Subject Index to the Warren Report and Hearings and Exhibits. New York: Scarecrow Press 1966: Ann Arbor: Michigan University microfilms 1971.

Miller, Tom, The Assassination Please Almanac, Chicago: Henry Regnery Co. 1977 A reference to people and events.

Model, Peter & Groden, Robert *JFK: The Case For Conspiracy,* New York: Manor Books 1967. Recommended reading – a very important book.

Noyes, Peter, *Legacy of Doubt.* New York: Pinnacle Books, 1973, 275 Madison Avenue New York, N.Y., 10016.

Oglesby, Carl, *The Yankee and Cowboy War,* Mission, Kansas: Sheed, Andrews and McNeel, 1976.

Oswald, Robert with Myrick and Barbara Land, Lee: *A Portrait of Lee Harvey Oswald,* New York: Coward-McCann 1967.

O'Toole, George, *The Assassination Tapes: An Electronic Probe Into the Murder of John F. Kennedy and the Dallas Cover-up.* New York: Penthouse Press 1975.

Popkin, Richard H. *The Second Oswald,* New York: Avon Books 1966.

Prouty, L. Fletcher, *The Secret Team. The CIA and Its Allies in Control of the United States and the World,* New York Prentice Hall 1973 Recommended reading, a very important book.

Roffman, Howard, *Presumed Guilty.* Fairleigh Dickinson University Press 1975; Associated University Presses, Inc. Cranbury, New Jersey, London England. An important book.

Sauvage, Leo, *The Oswald Affair: An Examination of the Contradictions of the Warren Report,* Cleveland: World Publishing Co. 1966.

Scheflin, Alan W. & Upton Jr. Edward, *The Mind Manipulators London:* Paddington Press Ltd. 1978. Recommended reading.

Scott, Peter Dale, *Crime and Cover-Up, the CIA, the Mafia, and the Dallas -Watergate Connection:* Westworks 1977 P.O. Box 2071, Berkeley, CA 94702. Recommended reading.

Scott, Hoch, Stetler: Peter Dale Scott, Paul Hoch, Russel Stetler: *The Assassinations, Dallas and Beyond, a Guide to Cover-Ups and Investigations,* Vintage Books 1976: Random House, New York. Recommended reading.

Schlesinger, Arthur, *A Thousand Days: John F. Kennedy in the White House* Boston: Houghton-Mifflin Co. 1965. *Robert Kennedy and His Times,* Boston: Houghton-Mifflin 1978.

Sculz, Tad, *Compulsive Spy, The Strange Career of E. Howard Hunt.* New York: Viking 1974.

Shaw, Gary, *Cover-up: The Governmental Conspiracy to Conceal The Facts About the Public Execution of John Kennedy,* 1976; write Cover-Up, P.O. Box 722, 105 Poindexter, Cleburne, Texas 76031 Recommended reading.

Sorenson, Theodore, *The Kennedy Legacy,* New York: New American Library 1970.

Summers, Anthony, *Conspiracy,* New York: McGraw Hill 1980 Recommended reading.

THE THIRD DECADE, A Journal of Research On The John F. Kennedy Assassination, published by Prof. Jerry Rose at the State University College, Fredonia, New York, 14063. $15 for one year, $26 for two years, and $36 for three years. At this time (1987) this seems to be the best journal published in the field.

Thompson, Josiah, *Six Seconds in Dallas. A Microstudy of the Kennedy Assassination (revised)* New York: Berkley Publishing Corp. 1967, 1976. Bernard Geis Associates 1967. Recommended reading; an important book, though it contains some silly ideas with respect to the wounds.

Thornley, Kerry, *Oswald,* Chicago: New Classics House 1965.

Turner, William & Christian, John G. *The Assassination of Robert Kennedy – A Searching Look at the Conspiracy and Cover-Up 1968-1978.* New York: Random House. 1978. Recommended reading.

Weisberg, Harold, *Whitewash,* Vols. I-IV; write Weisberg at 7627 Old Receiver Rd., Frederick, MD., 21701 *Whitewash,* Vols I & II New York: Bell, 1966, 1967. *Oswald in New Orleans, New York:* Canyon 1967, subtitled *The Case for Conspiracy with the CIA. Post-Mortem* self-published 1975, address above. A very crucial book.

Weissman, Steve, *Big Brother and the Holding Company. The World Behind Watergate,* Palo Alto: Ramparts Press 1974. Recommended reading.

Wilber, Charles, *Medicolegal Investigation of the President John F. Kennedy Murder,* Charles C. Thomas, Publisher, Springfield, Illinois. Very important study, but the author wrote me admitting that he missed the main point of the head wounds.

Wise, David, and Thomas B. Ross, *The Invisible Government. The CIA and U.S. Intelligence.,* New York; Random House 1964, Vintage 1974 Recommended reading. *The Espionage Establishment,* New York. Random House 1967, Bantam 1968. Recommended reading.

There are many other books on the subjects of assassination and intelligence, but these are the most important. The appendix to the Report of the Assassinations Committee is crucial to study the case, but only 20 sets were printed for libraries and the public.

SOURCES AND NOTES

This book was written under appalling strains, and the following may not be as perfect as the authors would like. In some cases secondary sources have been used. One reason for this is the authors' intent to give full credit for the basic research of many others who would go unmentioned if only primary sources were used. The reader must be aware that neither the Warren Report and its appendices, nor the Report of the Assassinations Committee and its appendices, a total of 55 volumes, were indexed. This meant that an immense amount of work was involved just to find a reference or testimony, which ordinarily would have been unnecessary.

Source books are sometimes abbreviated below, and the full titles may be found in the bibliography. The following abbreviations are used in reference to citations from official reports.

Warren Commission Report: WR; (sometimes R, by other writers, but not in this book).

Citations referring to the 26 volumes of Hearings and Exhibits accompanying the Warren Report are referred to by volume and page – e.g. 6 H 33. The H refers to "Hearings." (CE means Commission Exhibit, and CD means Commission Document. This is also written VI. 33 by others. CD 16.5 means Commission Document 16, page 5).

Citations from the Report of the House Select Committee on Assassinations (HSCA) are given as HSCA Report p. 12. Citations from the 12 Kennedy volumes of Hearings and Appendices of the House Select Committee on Assassinations are referred to by volume and page number: 4 HSCA 354. Other writers have used this notation: HSCA V.050. The HSCA Report is abbreviated R herein.

The most frequently used style of notations by scholars is in this style: 6 H 33, and 5 HSCA 253.

Autopsy photographs courtesy Mark Crouch, via David S. Lifton. Original Source: James K. Fox, U.S. Secret Service.

Introduction

NOTE
1. Josiah Thompson's *Six Seconds in Dallas,* Appendix A; HSCA Report p. 87; The statements in this paragraph are amplified throughout this book, with cited evidence.
2. R 1 (HSCA Report p. 1).
3. WR 37-8 (Warren Report – *New York Times* Edition).
4. State of Louisiana v. Clay Shaw, 1969.
5. WR 502.
6. WR 110-112.
7. Shaw 4; Thompson 12, 32, 44, etc...; 7 HSCA 199-203; See index under "single bullet theory" in both Wilber, and Weisberg's *Post Mortem* for important discussions.
8. Shaw 6; The Commissioners are quoted elsewhere in this book. Directly after Congressman Hale Boggs – one of the Warren Commissioners – stated that he did not agree with their findings, he died in a mysterious plane crash in Alaska. Neither the plane nor his body were ever found; Epstein, p. 150, Weisberg in *Whitewash IV* p. 22.
9. Wecht in Thompson's book p. 361; 7 HSCA 1-18, in particular p. 17 for an official critique; pp. 43-51 (authentication of photos and X-Rays); pp. 181-194 (critique of the autopsy); 199-203 (dissent of Dr. Cyril Wecht: Single Bullet Theory). All & HSCA should be studied closely, as well as Dr. Charles Wilber's book. Among the leading authorities on the wounds are Wecht, Wilber, and Weisberg.
10. See Chapter 3 herein and extensive discussion in that chapter; Thompson 57-8.
11. Supra; CD 5, CD 7, 2 H 93, 2 H 127, 24 H 542, 2 H 81, 18 H 744, 2 H 143, 5 H 59-60, 5 H 160, 18 H 89-90; 7 HSCA 262 (Humes' most recent statement, quoted in Chapter 3, p. 97).
12. Thompson xiii; 16 H 987, and see Wecht, Wilber, and Weisberg.
13. 7 HSCA 181-194; Wilber and Wecht are leading authorities on this.
14. 2 H 351 and discussion in chapter.
15. 7 HSCA 243-265.
16. 7 HSCA 243-265 (p. 251-2); and extensive discussion in the first three chapters of this book; Maryland State Medical Journal: March 1977 pp. 69-77 "1968 Panel (Ramsey Clark) Review of Photographs, X-Ray Films, Documents and Other Evidence pertaining to the Fatal Wounding of President John F. Kennedy."; *Postmortem* index under Autopsy Review Panel.
17. 7 HSCA 115 (308) quoted at top of Chapter One herein, and testimony of Humes and Boswell & HSCA 251-256, 247, and in Chapter One p. 45, and Three, p. 90 of this book, with the autopsists' later denial following.
18. Garrison 196-201, also in Shaw 195-197; 7 HSCA 13-14; Thompson ix-x, Wilber.
19. 2 H 93 and ibid. Extensive discussion in this book.
20. Note 15 supra.
21. Ibid. Compare pictures of back wounds on pp. 255 I HSCA & I HSCA 186. Head wounds: I HSCA 255 (from WR drawings reproduced in this book) & 234-251-2. This is discussed extensively in the following chapters. See also Wilber and *Postmortem* on the head wounds and the Clark Panel.
22. Weitzman affidavit in *Rush to Judgement* (Fawcett ed.) p. 348; also 24 H 228; 7 H 108 and further discussion and evidence later in this book.
23. Shaw on Ford: p. 216-218, Gerald Ford *Portrait of the Assassin.* Confirmation hearings for Ford's appointment to the Vice-Presidency, where his act of publishing information from the secret transcripts of the WC was at issue, and his sworn testimony is inconsistent. The CIA was shocked at his book: CIA 994-937; CIA 1289-1019 (Mary Ferrell's index). Allegation concerning Oswald's possible intelligence background was first discussed at the secret January 22, 1964 meeting of the Commission. See the *New Republic* September 27, 1975 for exerpts from the secret transcripts.
24. Summers 90-1; 93; 150-1; 153; 172-80; 294-6; 306; 313-14; 159; 295-7; 217: CIA Oswald's

files: 132, 381-92, "201" File on Oswald 163-70, 171, 558n 56, 169; see also Garrison on Oswald, & HSCA Report 139-146; 185-225; and Anson (index under Oswald: "intelligence community and –); see also Steve Parks in the *Baltimore Sun*, Nov. 21, 1976 section K p. 1; Weisberg: *Oswald in New Orleans. The Fish is Red* by Hinckle and Turner.

25. Fensterwald 87, 83, 84, 92-3; The transcript was published in the *New Republic* September 27, 1975 p. 30; Meeting of December 5, 1963; See also January 27, 1964 transcript in Harold Weisberg's *Whitewash IV*, p. 72.

26. See the chapter on Deaths in this book; also Penn Jones Jr. *Forgive my Grief*, Vols I-IV; *Accessories After the Fact*, by Sylvia Meagher, Random House 1967, Vintage 1976 p. 298-302; Anson on deaths; and 4 HSCA 453-468.

27. *The Scavengers and Critics of the Warren Report*, Lewis & Schiller. See William Turner's comment on this book in *Forgive My Grief II*, p. 156.

28. CIA Directive of April 11, 1967; *NY Times* Dec. 26, 1977.

29. See note 23.

30. Conversations with Victor Marchetti, Steve Parks, and notes above.

31. Report p. 1 (C).

32. Report p. 65-93.

33. Groden; 6 HSCA 296-310.

34. Report 81.

35. FBI memo (dated April 4, 1967) of LBJ's comment to Marvin Watson, relayed to Cartha DeLoach, Senate Intelligence Committee Final Report 1976, Vol. 6, p. 182; See Fensterwald pp. 124-5.

36. See Groden's book, and extensive discussion herein; Thompson p. 125-131; 7 H 518 Altgens: 2 H 141; see later chapters in this book for discussion and evidence herein; Shaw, Model-Groden *JFK: The Case for Conspiracy.*

Chapter 1

1. Dan Christensen's two articles in *Miami Magazine*, 1976, reprinted in *The Continuing Inquiry*, February and March, 1977 issues CD 137.120; CD 1347.121; CD 20.24; 3 HSCA 447, Report p. 234n3, 232; *The Assassinations, Dallas and Beyond*, edited by Peter Dale Scott, Paul L. Hoch and Russell Stetler, Vintage (Random House) 1976, pp. 7, 117-8, 128-34; *Conspiracy*, by Anthony Summers, McGraw-Hill, 1980 p. 427-30 on the plots in Miami and Chicago and concerning Milteer, p. 606-7n127; HSCA Report p. 231-2, 636; CD's 1347/20p4; Concerning the Chicago plot reported by Bolden and his sad fate, Report 231-2, 636; *Coincidence or Conspiracy*, by Bernard Fensterwald, Zebra Books, New York, 1977, p. 560-2, *New York Herald Tribune*, May 22, 1964; "The Plot to Kill JFK in Chicago", *Chicago Independent*, Nov., 1975; 26 H 441; 26 H 662-3; 5 H 454-55, 457; CD 997; CD 1112.

2. Curry p. 1. See *Farewell America*; Anson, p. 17; Shaw 167-70.

3. Shaw 168. Curry 19, 20.

4. Shaw, 199; Manchester 198-9 (*The Death of a President*).

5. Jones III, p. 85; Jones IV 114.

6. "Hepburn", page 300, note 11; Report 235; Model-Groden 163.

7. Emory Roberts gave the order not to move. 18 H 749; Shaw 175, picture on p. 124. The Altgens photograph shows that the guards did not move at all, but turned to look in response to the shots.

8. Secret Service agent Clint Hill testified that Mrs. Kennedy was grabbing after a piece of the skull. He repeated this on *Sixty Minutes.*

9. Clint Hill 6 H 290-2.

10. Harper Bone CD 5, Weitzman: 7 H 107; Thompson p. 130; picture 7 HSCA 123-4. Denial as occipital: 7 HSCA 123 report of Dr. J. Lawrence Angel, saying it was parietal; but he himself was not in fact able to identify the bone properly.

11. Weisberg *Postmortem* 380; Shaw 23; compare with the official edited version 5 H 178-81.

12. Jesse Curry *JFK Assassination File*, p. 32.
13. Ibid p. 34; discussion in the first three chapters herein.
14. Ibid p. 30.
15. Shaw p. 199; Manchester 198-9.
16. Jim Bishop 195; Manchester 168; Bishop: *The Day Kennedy Was Shot*.
17. Dallas Police Radio Tapes, 11-22-63; Shaw, page 199.
18. Shaw, page 199; Manchester, pages 193-5, 224.
19. Shaw, page 200; Theodore White *The Making of a President*, page 2.
20. Manchester, page 224.
21. Shaw, page 200.
22. Shaw, page 199; Bishop, page 271.
23. Shaw, page 198; Bishop, page 203.
24. Curry, page 17.
25. O'Toole, pages 150-5; Shaw, page 194; Summers, page 92.
26. Report, page 228.
27. Prouty interview in *Gallery*, 11-75; similar definition at beginning of *The Secret Team*, page 2.
28. Jones III, page 53.
29. 20H489, Jones III, page 54.
30. *Farewell America*, 358-9, 296; Shaw 175 on Greer's looking back. This is clear in the Zapruder film. Manchester 157. Picture of Greer laughing is on page 124 of Thompson.
31. 7 H 535; Anson 28.
32. 18 H 722-99; Anson 28.
33. 19 H 492; Anson 28.
34. Tramps: Shaw and Harris discussion p 82-97.
35. See *Coup d'Etat in America* for a discussion and pictures of the tramps. The authors claimed that the pictures were of Howard Hunt and Frank Sturgis of Watergate fame, among others. Also see Shaw and Harris p. 83, 89, 100 and 3 Jones 91-4 for pictures, and S & H's discussion pp. 82-97.
36. Warren Report 141-2; 7 H 439; Meagher 73-4; Anson p. 30 for description of Officer Marion Baker and Roy Truly.
37. See Chapter 12 in this book; and *Six Seconds in Dallas,* by Josiah Thomson, p. 36, 83, 102, 170, 258, 373, 377-8 for the speed of operating the rifle.
38. Report 147-52; Anson 30-8, p. 37; CE 1974 p. 59 for description of Tippit's killer.
39. 22 H 632-86; Anson 30-1.
40. 6 H 443-4, Meagher 264; for description of Tippit murder, see Anson 346 & in Chapter 13 of this book.
41. For a good account of the struggle over the body between the President's party and local officials, see *Death of a President,* by William Manchester, Harper & Row, 1967., p. 297-307; Anthony Summers says in *Conspiracy* (p. 42), McGraw-Hill 1980, that the Secret Service took the body at gunpoint. See his note on 528: McKinley *op.cit.* p. 120; and he cites an interview with Dr. Robert Shaw, 1978.
42. Jesse Curry, *JFK Assassination File* p. 122.
43. Keeton: *The Continuing Inquiry* (TCI) February, 1978, p. 12.

Chapter 2

1. Livingstone interview, tape JFK Library.
2. Notes of the *Boston Globe*, JFK Library.
3. WR p. 68.
4. Assassinations Committee Report p. 41.
5. 7 HSCA 37.
6. 7 HSCA 115.
7. 7 HSCA 122.

8. 7 HSCA 38.
9. Order reproduced in *Postmortem* p. 303; Shaw 198.
10. 7 HSCA 114.
11. 1 HSCA 329.
12. WR 502 (*New York Times* Ed.); *Postmortem* p. 514-515.
13. 2 H 360.
14. *Globe* interview.
15. 7 HSCA 118.
16. 7 HSCA 246,249, 250 "So, in that case this exit wound is really in the frontal – it's in front of that notch there – it's in the frontal..." (Dr. Angel interviewing the autopsists.) p. 251 "placing the outshoot wound in the right frontal bone...".
17. See note 9. This book repeats the text later on.
18. 7 HSCA 108.
19. *Postmortem* p. 515, for the handwritten copy of the autopsy report.
20. *Maryland State Medical Journal,* March, 1977.
21. CE 392 (17 H 11-12) Wilber p. 76; 184, *Postmortem* 376. Discussion in the following chapters.
22. *The Washington Post,* George Lardner Jr. June 18, 1979.
23. 1 HSCA 147 testimony of the artist; the *Globe* team also saw the pictures and published June 21, 1981 that it was a "tracing." Our own visual inspection shows that it is a tracing. Also 1 HSCA 325.
24. 7 HSCA, 246 & 251, 115 (308). *Postmortem* see index under Autopsy Review Panel; *Maryland State Medical Journal,* March, 1977 pp. 69-77.
25. CE 392 (8 H and WR 516).
26. CE 392 ibid.
27. 6 H 20.
28. 6 H 136.
29. 6 H 33.
30. 17 H 33, 36.
31. November 18, 1979, p. K-3, *Baltimore Sun* by Steve Parks. McClelland spoke to the *Sun's* Jeff Price, but is not mentioned by name, in the article "The Bullets also Destroyed our Confidence". They sure did.
32. June 21, 1981 by Ben Bradlee, Jr. Nils Bruzilias worked on it with Ben, and went to Dallas with him. Steve Kurkjian, their boss, was also involved. The *Globe* undertook the effort after listening to a bit of my tapes of the doctors, after at first ridiculing the evidence I took. When they studied it, they got on the next plane just about, to try to disprove us. "I want this story bad," Bradlee told me. He is the son of the famous Ben Bradlee of the *Washington Post,* and they consulted with him and Bob Woodward on the story. Bradlee wrote a fine book about the ambush of some policemen and the frame-up of a patsy. His father, who helped remove Richard Nixon from office as President, wrote *Conversations with Kennedy.* I am grateful for the work that the *Globe* people contributed to this investigation, and for turning it over to me. I earned it.
33. Picture of the alleged fragment on p. 123-4 of 7 HSCA, Wilber 210; size 7 cm X 5.5 cm; *Postmortem* 80-81; CD 1250: 1-3 and CD 1269: 1-7.
34. WR p. 69.
35. *Globe* June 21, 1981. The author has placed in the JFK Library in Boston the tapes and summaries of the *Globe's* work: Their tapes of the doctors and nurses. The tape and summary of Dulany is in the JFK Library, and I have since talked with him, verifying this.
36. 21 H 216.
37. *Globe* as above in n 35.
38. 6 H 56, 6 H 53.
39. n 35.
40. *Globe* as in n 35.
41. Ibid; I have placed his letter to me in the JFK Library.
42. 6 H 71; 17 H 31.

43. 6 H 65.
44. 24 H 212.
45. *Globe* summary and tape.
46. TCI, October, 1980.
47. 6 H 40-1.
48. TCI, October, 1980, Author's tape JFK Library.
49. *Globe* summary and tape, chart of 1-10.
50. TCI, October, 1980, Author's tape – JFK Library.
51. *Globe* summary.
52. TCI, October 1980: Author's interview and tape in the JFK Library.
53. 17 H 15; 6 H 48; 6 H 246; WR 492.
54. TCI, October, 1980, Author's tape – JFK Library.
55. *Sun* article, November 18, 1979 supra.
56. 3 H 372. 17 H 4.
57. 6 H 11.
58. *Globe* chart of 1-10 and summary (See Appendix).
59. 7 HSCA 115, pp. 246, 251. Nurses Nelson, Hutton (Gustafson). The nurses who washed and wrapped the body would know best, and were with the body the longest. But see discussion in 7 HSCA 122 (320).
60. Letter to the author, April 1, 1981: JFK Library.
61. 7 HSCA 286-7.
62. *Sun* article, November 18, 1979; *Globe* summary and chart of 1-10.
63. 7 HSCA 295.
64. 6 H 3.
65. 7 HSCA 278.
66. *Globe* summary, 5.
67. *Globe*, June 21, 1981; tape and summary – JFK Library.
68. *TCI*, October 1980; Author's tape – JFK Library.
69. *Globe tape of Akin.*
70. *TCI*, Octoer, 1980; Author's tape – JFK Library.
71. *Globe* interview, and synopsis – JFK Library.
72. 6 HSCA 299. See also Stanley Keeton in *TCI*, December, 1977, January and February, 1978: "The Autopsy Photographs and X-Rays of President Kennedy; A Question of Authenticity". Also *TCI*, October, 1979, by Jack White: "Can a Photograph Lie?".
73. Author's tape in JFK Library.
74. 2 H 141.
75. 2 H 124.
76. 2 H 81.
77. 7 HSCA 246.
78. 7 HSCA 251.
79. *St. Louis Post-Dispatch,* December 1, 1963.
80. Sept. 1977. Jerry Policoff.

Chapter 3

1. Report 43.
2. Shaw p. 41; Dr. Wecht 1 HSCA 332, 7 HSCA 199 and the Committee's reply on p. 210. There are many other dissenters.
3. Report p. 44.
4. Model-Groden Zapruder frame 274 on p. 131.
5. April, 1978 *The Continuing Inquiry,* reprinted from *Maryland State Medical Journal*, October 1977.
6. Report 44.

7. 8 WC Hearings CE 392 (WC Report 516) , Wilber 75, 77; Jenkins p. 491-2 *NY Times* edition of Warren Report.
8. 2 H 376; 2 H 374-5.
9. 4 H 104, 124, 127; Thompson p. 97. Note that the doctors removed a fragment from the thigh of Governor Connally that has apparently been lost. 4 H 125 – Gregory. See Thompson p. 228. Fragments appear in the chest X-rays, and all of them together could not come from CE 399. Also wrist fragments. 6 H 111 (Shires, Thompson p. 196-207) (paperback).
10. Shires 6 H 108, 92. Connally 4 H 132-3.
11. 4 H 113.
12. 4 H 135-36; Thompson 80-104.
13. 1 HSCA 43-4; Curry 103. Countless others agree.
14. Curry.
15. 2 H 382.
16. Report 44.
17. 6 H 85, 4 H 104.
18. Report 44.
19. Thompson 206, Marshal Houts: *Where Death Delights,* 62-3 (Coward McCann, 1967).
20. 6 H 128ff; *Whitewash I,* p 161-2, 171; Little boy's (Ronald Fuller) stretcher, Thompson p. 214. See his index: Stretcher Bullet.
21. 2 H 412.
22. Report 44.
23. Shaw 6.
24. Epstein: *Inquest* 149, Viking Press; Weisberg Whitewash IV p. 21.
25. Epstein op. cit. p. 150.
26. Letter of 4/4/67.
27. Thompson 58-67; Wilber 177-206.
28. Ibid & WC testimony supra.
29. Ibid.
30. Ibid.
31. Wilber p. 187 for a chart of the witnesses' positions.
32. Report 45.
33. Ibid.
34. Ibid.
35. Report 45-6.

Chapter 4

1. Report p. 80.
2. Ibid. It is important to study comments on neutron activation analysis in *Postmortem* (see index), Wilber pp. 171, 173 (and index) NAA update TCI Oct., 1980, p. 13-15 and November, 1976 TCI article by Emory Brown.
3. Report p. 80.
4. Ibid.
5. WR Report firearms expert Robert Frazier said "there did not necessarily have to be *any* weight loss to the bullet" (3 H 430). See p. 199 Thompson; and p. 15 TCI, October, 1980; Curry p. 88 for pictures of the recovered fragments.
6. Thompson 199; 6 H 111; 6 H 382; 2 H 374-6; the weights of the fragments may be found in 5 H 72, 6 H 106; 111; 4 H 113; Dr. Guinn testified before the HSCA, lists the weights of the fragments, and his testimony appears in 1 HSCA 491; his report is on p. 506. In particular, note p. 511. Based on Warren Commission findings, this seems to be a fantasy. The specimens tested by NAA are listed on p. 513-15. The weights are given on p. 517. George Lardner Jr. of the *Washington Post* questioned Dr. Guinn after he testified and Dr. Guinn said that some

key fragments were missing and that the fragments he tested were not the same as the ones tested by the FBI in 1964.

7. Report p. 80.
8. As cited.
9. Summers 533 n 11; TCI p. 15, October, 1980, for Nurse Bell's drawings of the fragments.
10. 7 HSCA 366 n.
11. (CE 841) 1 HSCA 515.
12. (CE 569) 1 HSCA 515.
13. *Postmortem* p. 319, 321, 411; Wilber 172; and note 2 above.
14. Report p. 43-4. Dr. Pierre Finck's testimony in the trial of Clay Shaw, State of Louisiana v. Clay Shaw. This chapter deals elsewhere with the fragments and this question and is specifically sourced. Summers p. 533 n 11.
15. 2 H 353; June 1980 TCI (p. 5-7); *Postmortem* 191; Wilber 164, 208.
16. 2 H 359.
17. 2 H 353.
18. 7 HSCA 281.
19. Humes' testimony 2 H 361; Finck, Lt. Col. Pierre: Testimony in Louisiana v. Shaw 198-059; 1426- (30), Section C., Criminal Court, Parish of New Orleans, LA. 1969. Interview with Art Smith in July, 1978 *Continuing Inquiry,* he seems to indicate that there were no fragments showing in the X-rays: "If it was metallic, it should have shown on the X-rays."
20. *Maryland State Medical Journal,* March 1977, p. 74.
21. TCI April 1978 reprint of his article in Maryland State *Medical Journal,* October, 1977.
22. Interview with Dr. Ebersole in July 1978, TCI p. 1.
23. 7 HSCA p.283.
24. Feb 1978 TCI.
25. 2 H 361.
26. Meagher p. 149.
27. TCI July 1978.
28. Ibid.
29. TCI June 1980 p.5-6. Gary Mack and others demonstrate that X-ray No. 2 is reversed and we are actually looking at the left side of the head. The reader may look at these X-rays in 1 HSCA p. 239 and 7 HSCA p. 110.
30. 7 HSCA p. 282.
31. 1 HSCA pp. 243-44 and 7 HSCA pp. 109, 111.
32. Roffman *Presumed Guilty* p. 115. Clark Panel Report.
33. Ibid p. 115.
34. Ibid p. 116.
35. Ibid p. 116.
36. Ibid p. 109.
37. Ibid p. 122.
38. Ibid p. 109.
39. Ibid p. 118. Thompson p. 110.
40. Ibid p. 119.
41. 3 H 414.
42. Roffman p. 120.

Chapter 5

1. 6 HSCA 225. For a full discussion of the forensic autopsy, critique and procedure, see Wilber Appendix A p. 259; Weisberg *Postmortem* p. 162-201, and his index under X-rays and Photographs, autopsy.
2. 1 HSCA 219-224; WR 500-504.
3. WC Executive Session transcript of January 21, 1964.

4. *Postmortem* p. 555.
5. 16 H 979; 981 (Humes).
6. Shaw p. 78; XVII H 48; *Postmortem* p. 524-5, 559.
7. *Postmortem* p. 303; Shaw 198.
8. *Post Dispatch* December 18, 1963.
9. 1 HSCA 222, ibid. Wilber 97, 100, 112.
10. Wilber 187.
11. 16 H 979, 981 (Humes).
12. 17 HSCA 17 H 29; 3 H 368; 6 H 56, Wilber 97.
13. Garrison 198; Thompson ix; Shaw 195-7; Wilber 256.
14. 2 H 93.
15. 1 HSCA 232
16. Shaw 75.
17. 7 HSCA 264.
18. Waukegan, Illinois *News-Sun*, May 1, 1975 (See Appendix).
19. Garrison 194-5.
20. 1 HSCA 222 and WR.
21. 7 HSCA 246.
22. The picture of the back of the head may be seen in 1 HSCA 234; 7 HSCA 104; Summers 254; Bantam edition of the Report of the Assassinations Committee. These are all copies of the same picture.
23. 7 HSCA 251.
24. Shaw 65.
25. WR p. 501; 1 HSCA 221.
26. 1 HSCA 323-332 (p. 327).
27. Ibid.
28. 1 HSCA 329.
29. Humes WC testimony.
30. 1 HSCA 330.
31. 7 HSCA 262.
32. 6 HSCA 226 n 1.
33. 6 HSCA 226-7.
34. 6 HSCA 303.
35. 6 HSCA 223.
36. 6 HSCA 232.
37. *Maryland State Medical Journal* March 1977.
38. Report p. 41.
39. Ibid.
40. Report p. 42.
41. 7 HSCA 41 (179); p. 50; Wilber 239, 233; see index of *Postmortem* under Autopsy pictures and X-rays; dissent of Cyril Wecht 7 HSCA 199-203.
42. 7 HSCA 46.
43. Report p. 43.
44. 6 HSCA 299.
45. *Washington Post*, June 18-19, 28, 1979, and conversations with staff, R. Groden, Fletcher Prouty (taped, in JFK Library).
46. Conversations with Fletcher Prouty above, confirmed by Steve Parks of the *Baltimore Sun*.
47. Jim Hougan in January 1980 *Harpers*: "The McCord File".
48. Report p. 43.
49. Report p. 43.
50. 7 HSCA 254. Referring to the newly evident entry wound in the cowlick area, Dr. Humes says, "I just don't know what it is, but it certainly was not any wound of entrance".
51. Report 43. Wecht's dissent: 7 HSCA 199.
52. 7 HSCA p. 287.

53. 7 HSCA p. 295.
54. 7 HSCA p. 278.
55. Thompson 368; 2 H 351.
56. 7 HSCA 10 (57). Stringer stated that a Federal agent exposed the film.
57. Charles Wilber, M.D.: *A Medicolegal Investigation of the President John F. Kennedy Murder*, pages 255-58.
58. *Postmortem* 308-09.
59. Sibert & O'Neill p. 2, TCI Feb. 1978.
60. Thompson p. xi & xii.
61. Keeton in TCI, Feb. 1978.
62. Ibid.

Chapter 6

1. Thompson 17: Model-Groden 124-157.
2. Model-Groden 139.
3. Shaw 33n. Rather was privately shown the film on the night of November 23, 1963, after which he narrated it on TV without showing it. The film remained in a vault until 1969.
4. Shaw 124 (photgraphs.).
5. Report as cited above. (p.34) 7HSCA366n; IHSCA515.
6. As above, testimony of Dr. Guinn and report IHSCA 491. Guinn told George Lardner of the *Washington Post* that the two fragments from the brain he was given did not weigh the same as any of the four tested by the FBI, and the two he was given from Connally's wrist did not weigh the same as the three tested by the FBI.
7. Report 158-9; Seth Kantor, Shaw. There are published photos of Ruby at Parkland: back cover of Jones' *Forgive by Grief III*. Wilma Tice was also a witness.
8. Quoted from *Six Seconds in Dallas* by Josiah Thompson, p. 229. Also in Scott, Hoch. *The Assassinations, Dallas and Beyond*, p. 220, note. See his Index under Stretcher Bullet.
9. Thompson and Wecht, p. xii-xiii.
10. Thompson xiii.
11. Wecht: *Modern Medicine*, Nov. 27, 1972.
12. Thompson 17.
13. See Summers' *Conspiracy*, pp. 182-187. Earl Golz in the *Texas Observer*, November 25, 1983 (Cover-Ups, p. 7, March 1984).
14. Gore Vidal in the *New York Review of Books* "The Art and Arts of Howard Hunt", Dec. 13, 1973.
15. *Senate Watergate Committee Report*, GPO edition p. 129. *Coincidence or Conspiracy*, by Bernard Fensterwald, p. 523.
16. Published at the State University of New York, Fredonia, N.Y., 14063.
17. Report 54n9.
18. Report 221.
19. Report 200.
20. Report 223.
21. 4HSCA211, 4HSCA11.
22. "National Archives – Security Classification Problems Involving Warren Commission Files and Other Records"; Hearings before the House Subcommittee on Government Information, 1976.
23. Ibid.
24. *Washington Post*, Nov. 26, 1976.
25. New Orleans Police report January 12, 1968. *New Orleans Times-Picayune*, Jan. 12, 1968.
26. Shaw 53-4; *Forgive My Grief IV* p. 155; *Who was Jack Ruby* p.207-8.
27. *Cover-Up*, Gary Shaw and Larry Harris, p. 54-6.
28. Note 22 *supra*.
29. Note 22 *supra*.

30. Note 22 *supra*.
31. Note 22 *supra*.
32. Note 22 *supra*.
33. Note 22 *supra* and Shaw 51.
34. Note 22 *supra*.
35. Note 22 *supra*.
36. Note 22 *supra*.
37. Note 22 *supra*.
38. Note 22 *supra*.
39. Note 22 *supra*.
40. O'Toole, p. 38.
41. Shaw 72-4.
42. *Washington Post*, June 18, 19, 1979.
43. Report p. 50n8.
44. Report, p. 195.
45. Story by Earl Golz, March 1984, p. 7; *Cover-Ups*, p. 6, December, 1982.
46. National Academy of Sciences Report of the Committee on Ballistics Acoustics, May 14, 1982, log p. 71.

Chapter 7

1. 4 HSCA 453-468.
2. 4 HSCA 465.
3. 4 HSCA 466.
4. 4 HSCA 467.
5. 4 HSCA 467.
6. Livingstone's conversations with the Chairmen, transcribed. See p. 10 357 of *Congressional Record* for September 17, 1976, when the Committee was established by overwhelming vote to investigate the murders. Ms. Dickinson says "... and perhaps we can get at some of the facts and questions that have been raised such as the unnatural deaths of certain of the people connected with the assassination, incidents that seem to be continuing right up to now as for instance, the recent murder of Roselli a month or two ago". Downing's presentation follows, and is most important for researchers. Roselli was talking to Jack Anderson, but Anderson did not grasp what Roselli was trying to tell him. The latest on this was in *Parade* by Anderson and Robert Blakey, November 16, 1980, and a total lie as to the findings of the Committee.
7. Summers 502-3.
8. 4 HSCA 467.
9. 4 HSCA 468.
10. Summers 499.
11. See the important *Gallery* article on DeMohrenschildt by Willem Oltmans, April 1978.
12. 4 HSCA 468.
13. May 11, 1978 *Fort Worth Star-Telegram*. TCI May 1978.
14. Curry 133.
15. Shaw 101; Summers 84-5. *Farewell America* p. 339 n 30; Model-Groden 278.
16. Shaw 72-74; Jones IV 20, 13, 36, 172.
17. Craig was mentioned by Chairman Downing when the Committee was set up, on p. 10 360 of the *Congressional Record* for September 17, 1976 under "The Murder Weapon" when Craig said the rifle they found was a Mauser, Downing says "Any individual, regardless of his experience in firearms, can clearly see it is an Italian rifle because stamped clearly on the rifle are the words 'Made in Italy' and 'Cal. 6.5'. It is unlikely that two police officers upon close inspection would have made such a case of mistaken identification". Even the CIA report of November 25 says it was a Mauser. As to Craig, see Jones III p. 15, 29, 30, 31, 33-37, 64,

79, 80, 86, 88, 90 (on other side of picture of Craig on 89), *90, Vol. IV 31, 33, 148-9. Fensterwald 440-3; Shaw 26-8.

18. Jones III p. 90.
19. Shaw 110; 10 H 353; Jones II p. 37.
20. Shaw 110.
21. Shaw 90.
22. Shaw 90.
23. Shaw 90.
24. Shaw 90.
25. Shaw 90.
26. Epstein: *Inquest* p. 150; Shaw 6; *The Washington Post,* Jan. 20, 21, 1975; Fensterwald 96-105.
27. Shaw 10-11. 6 H 284.
28. Jones II p. 27.
29. Meagher: *Accessories After the Fact,* p. 299; see p. 300 for chronology of the deaths. Also Anson 67-7.
30. Jones III p. 28, 57.
31. Jones III p. 57.
32. See Garrison's *Playboy* interview, October 1967; Summers 498; a most crucial character connected to Marcello & CIA.
33. Anson – many references in index; Garrison, same, and "Hepburn".
34. "Hepburn" *Farewell America* p. 335; Also Marchetti; Fensterwald 295-305 and other references; as CIA p. 298 (Marchetti relating Helms' admission).
35. Fensterwald 309-314.
36. Jones III p. 57.
37. Jones III p. 81.
38. Jones III p. 81.
39. Fensterwald 303-4. Miami PD Homicide Report February 13, 1967.
40. Ibid.
41. Jones III, p. 28.
42. Jones III, p. 57.
43. Anson 140-1; 12 H 350.
44. 4 HSCA 466; Meagher 299.
45. 4 HSCA 466; Meagher 299.
46. Jones I p. 5-6; Meagher 299; Anson 66-7; Fensterwald 578-9.
47. Ibid; *San Francisco Chronicle,* April 24, 1964; Fensterwald 578.
48. Ibid; *Dallas Times Herald,* September 22, 1964; Fensterwald 578.
49. Ibid; see Fensterwald 56, 66, 284.
50. Ibid.
51. Ibid; Fensterwald 56: Fabrication of Ruby's motive.
52. Jones IV p. 116; see Summers chapter "The Good Ole Boy", p. 454, on Ruby, also *Who Was Jack Ruby* by Seth Kantor.
53. Fensterwald 579-80. The Warren Commission said Killam had knowledge of possible links between Oswald and Ruby CE 2882; WR GPO ED 363; March 17-18, 1964 Pensacola Police Department reports; Anson 66; Jones I p. 8, 10, 24; Shaw 113, 164.
54. Jones I p. 24; *If You Have a Lemon, Make Lemonade,* Warren Hinckle p. 238, 240. Jones II, p. 12-13.
55. Ibid.
56. Anson 66; Meagher 293-297; party: Jones II p. 6; Shaw 112 p. 5 for Warren Com. testimony on party.
57. Meagher 293-7.
58. As above.
59. II Jones 16-18; *Assassination Please Almanac* p. 13, 15; Meagher 299; 4 HSCA 467; Shaw 112.
60. Meagher 299; Anson 66; Jones I, p. 174.; TCI Feb 1977, p16; Shaw 113. A.k.a. Karin Carlin.

(Texas Attorney General Investigation of the Assassination of JFK, Vol. XIV). Meagher says she died in 1964.

61. 4 HSCA 466.
62. Oswald's landlady's sister, Bertha Cheek, was a friend of Jack Ruby, Jones I p. 92 (She testified to the Warren Commission). On police car coming by: Jones I p. 171; Shaw 99; 6 H 443-4.
63. Ibid. Jones I p. 172; 6 H 443-4.
64. Shaw 101. Jones II p. 113. Jones II p. 114 (Mrs. Roberts knew Burnley). Ruby and Alexander: Kantor 57, 113-6, 119, 125, 126, 182.
65. Jones II p. 4, 6, 7, 35.
66. Jones I p. 174.
67. Shaw 14; 16 H 959; 2 H 196.
68. Jones II p. 27.
69. Shaw 14; 16 H 959; 2 H 196.
70. Shaw 13.
71. Shaw 12; Summers 74, 110; 24 H 522, see his note p. 535; al2 HSCA 4.
72. *Congressional Record*, Sept. 17, 1976 p. 10, 358, Downing. See also the scurillous article by Chief Counsel Blakey who succeeded Downing and Sprague, in *Parade*, Sunday, November 16, 1980, with accompanying piece by Anderson, falsifying the findings of the Committee. The article says "How sound was our conclusion that organized crime was responsible for the assassination of the President?" This is repeated throughout the article. The Committee found no such thing. See Summers on Roselli and Giancana et al pp. 500-505. Also Fensterwald, *Shaw 171-3; Anson 303-331; *Farewell America,* 89-104; Government by Gunplay "Richard Nixon and Organized Crime" p. 130 (Jeff Gerth). See 9 HSCA on Organized Crime. Report HSCA "The Committee believes... that the national syndicate of organized crime, as a group, was not involved in the assassination of President Kennedy, but that the available evidence does not preclude the possibility that individual members may have been involved: (p. 1) see Anderson's true hate for JFK in *Parade*, November 20, 1977.
73. *Parade*, November 16, 1980 – Anderson admits that his informant is Roselli, p. 5. Also in *Washington Post*, September 9, 1976.
74. Ibid. Also Summers 502.
75. See "New Mafia Killer: a Silenced .22" in *Time*, April 18, 1977; "Mysteries of Giancana's Slaying", *New York Times*, in *San Francisco Chronicle*, April 14, 1976 and "Generous Treatment of a Mafia Boss", same, page 6; and May 6, 1976 p. 6 the CIA, the White House, and the Mafia from p. 1 "Strange Bedfellows" from Howard Kohn in *New York Times*.
76. Jones II, p. 20.
77. Jones II, p. 20.
78. *Farewell America*, p. 349; Shaw 57, 111; Jones II, p. 22; independently verified by Summers, p. 576 n 83; 10 HSCA 199-204.
79. Shaw 20, 21; 12 H 284.
80. *If You Have a Lemon, Make Lemonade*, Warren Hinckle p. 211; Summers 492 Ruby died "just as New Orleans D.A. Jim Garrison was reopening the Kennedy case"; *and* Ruby's conviction had just been overturned and he had won a new trial: Model-Groden p. 259; Ruby was denied medical attention: Model-Groden p. 39; Ruby's famous letter smuggled from jail said that LBJ was behind the plot, and he told reporters that (Summers 492): there was indeed a conspiracy, during jail transfers. His unlisted phone number was in Oswald's notebook: Garrison *Playboy*, October, 1967, p. 174-6. There is massive evidence that they knew each other. Ruby would have been retried outside of Dallas where he could talk more freely. His friend D.A. Bill Alexander said that no one proved that you could not cause cancer by injection. Ruby believed he was being given cancer. He was not examined until too late. He died of cancer, and a blood clot; See Meagher on this, pp. 452-4.
81. They seemed to have Ralph Paul in common, at least: Summers 602 n 117; 12 HSCA 36-42; Officer Olson's testimony to WC Jones I p. 87, that they knew each other. On Olson and Ruby see Fensterwald 416-420, 430. Summers see p. 601 n 115-116.

82. WR 591 *New York Times* Ed. See other "speculations and rumours" in that section.
83. Jones III p. 15.
84. Shaw 112, 113; Jones II p. 3, 4; Summers 543 n 30; 25 H 731; 11 H 437-435.
85. Ibid.
86. Shaw 112.
87. Ibid; Meagher 299.
88. The *News-Sun*, Waukegan, Illinois, May 1, 1975; Jones III, p. 95.
89. Jones II, 23-4; *Farewell America* 339.
90. Summers 508. See extensive testimony in 10 HSCA 37-52.
91. Fensterwald 440-4.
92. Fensterwald 441; also Anson 77; there are many references to Craig in Shaw and Jones, who knew him.
93. Dallas P.D. Homicide Bureau Report, May 15, 1978. It should be clear that the pattern of deaths and the violence among them shows a clear pattern of conspiracy. For the same reason, any evidence in this case which can be questioned and is not beyond reproach, indicates fabrication, taken with the deaths and the nature of the questioned evidence and why it is questionable. This goes for the pattern of missing evidence, and the cover-up, the fact that many persons can openly lie, as in the November 16, 1980 *Parade* article changing the findings of the HSCA. A long, important article on Roselli's death, *New York Times*, p. 1, Feb. 25, 1977 (Gage). These many deaths were never really looked into properly, and their pattern was ignored. The Committee's manner of dealing with them demonstrates the co-option of the Committee by the conspirators. For more on the deaths of Nicoletti, Roselli, Giancana, Bompensiero, see "The Deadly Kennedy Probe: Execution For the Witnesses" in *Rolling Stone* June 2, 1977; *New York Times Magazine,* October 2, 1977. DeMohrenschildt, see new accounts on April 2, 1977, *Time Magazine*, April 11, 1977, p. 20.
94. Scott, Hoch p 283. Shaw 92n.
95. Scott, Hoch 293. FMG III p. 46-7. Flammonde 115. Fensterwald 476.
96. FMG IV p.173-4.
97. Scott, Hoch 283.
98. Summers 500.
99. Summers 506; *Ft. Worth Star Telegram* Nov 10, 1977 article by Jim Marrs, and *Washington Post* same day (reprinted in TCI).
100. Summers 450-507.
101. Summers 451.
102. 4 HSCA 467.

Chapter 8

1. Report 235: "Hepburn" in *Farewell America*, pp. 294-301; "The Secret Service at Dealey Plaza," by Patricia Lambert, *The Third Decade*, March 1985.
2. "Hepburn", page 299.
3. "Hepburn", page 299, notes 10 and 301.
4. CE affidavit 14-15.
5. "Hepburn", page 297.
6. Report, page 227.
7. Report, page 233 (This referred to SS Agent Abraham Bolden's suppressed report of the Chicago plot (see Report p. 236 on Echevarria and Mosley); and the Miami-Milteer recordings.
8. Report, page 235.
9. Report, page 235.
10. *Fort Worth Star Telegram.* May 25, 1984; in *Cover-ups!*, story by Jim Marrs, Nov., 1982, and May, 1984.

11. Jim Marrs in the *Dallas Morning News*, Sept. 5, 1982, reprinted in *The Continuing Inquiry*, Nov. 1982.
12. 11HSCA521.
13. 11HSCA522.
14. 11HSCA526.
15. 11HSCA527.
16. 11HSCA528.
17. 11HSCA529.
18. 11HSCA530.
19. Fensterwald 237.
20. *Washington Post*, September 16, 1973.
21. Fensterwald, 237.
22. Prouty, *The Secret Team* is an important book in our history. This quote was from Prouty's article "An Introduction to the Assassination Business" in *Gallery*, p. 86-87. I don't have the year. See also his articles "The Greatest Cover-Up", See also his articles "The Betrayal of JFK Kept Fidel Castro in Power", *Gallery*, February 1978; "How the CIA Controls President Ford", "The Guns of Dallas", in *Gallery*. These are important articles.
23. Curry, page 10.
24. Shaw 194; 4H318; XI HSCA 521.
25. "The Final Investigation: The HSCA and Army Intelligence," by Paul Hoch in *The Third Decade*, July, 1985. See also Shaw 194.
26. Jones IV, pages 50-51.
27. Secret Service Regulations.
28. Report, page 183. There was extensive evidence of men showing Secret Service identification in Dealey Plaza at the time of the shooting, scaring people off from certain areas or people. ("Allegation a Secret Service agent was on the grassy knoll", p. 183). Shaw 175. Thompson 163-4, 186, 247-9; and elsewhere. This is well documented.
29. Report 227-236. See also Prouty on this.
30. Model-Groden, 141.
31. Shaw, 43.
32. Shaw, 43; 5H105.
33. Curry 15.
34. Curry 12; 11HSCA526.
35. "Hepburn" *Farewell America* 293-301; also Prouty at length in above articles note 85. Report, on Secret Service "was deficient in the performance of its duties" p. 227. Anson 55-7. Curry also criticizes the Secret Service. See 11HSCA "The Motorcade" ("Politics and Presidential Protection") p. 505. Why did they choose that title? Shaw 173-6.
36. Model-Groden 161. See also "Slaughter" in *Farewell America*, p. 351-363.
37. Model-Groden 161.
38. Prouty "The Guns of Dallas" *Gallery* 10-75. See similar statement in his *The Secret Team*, p. 416, end of Chapter 22. "The Guns of Dallas" by Fletcher Prouty, *Gallery* 10-75 is perhaps the most important discussion of this whole subject.
39. *New York Herald Tribune*, May 22, 1964; Fensterwald p. 560-2; HSCA Report 231-2, 636; Anson 55, 57; Summers 428.
40. Scott, p. 35 and p. 67 n145; CD 87, SS 533.1-2; cf 1 H 471- 72).
41. Scott p. 35; U.S. Cong., House, Committee on Banking and Currency, *The Penn Central Failure and the Role of Financial Institutions*, Staff Report, 91st Cong., 2nd Sess. (Washington GPO 1970) Part III, p. 30; Great Southwest Corporation Control (in late 1963) "was tightly centered in the Rockefeller and Wynne families."
42. (CD 470.24).
43. Congressional Record, Jan. 26, 1965, p. 1313; U.S., Cong., Senate, Committee on Rules, *Construction of the District of Columbia Stadium, Hearings*, 88th Cong., 2nd Sess. (GPO 1964) pp. 859-87. Bobby Baker Hearings, pp 987 ff.;Scott 35.
44. Scott 36; Isaac Don Levine Conference, May 28, 1964.
45. Scott 36; CD 1039; CD 360.47, 49; CD 106.251; 2 H 20.

Chapter 9

1. O'Toole/see PSE chart of Oswald at end of his book.
2. *JFK Assassination File*; Dallas Police Chief, Jesse Curry, p. 133.
3. Report p. 41.
4. Jim Garrison: "Guilt of the Great Society," speech, Nov. 14, 1967, Los Angeles.
5. For the chronology, see Robert Sam Anson's account: *They've Killed The President*; The Warren Report.
6. (Jonathan Marshal, *San Jose Mercury News*, November 20, 1983,).
7. Summers p. 126, 469, 492; "Examination of Jack Ruby, Werner Tuteur, M.D. See also Jack Ruby's letter from jail, in *Ramparts*, Feb 1967, p. 26, and in TCI.
8. Jerry Rose in *The Third Decade*, March 1987, p. 20, Nov. 1986. See Gore Vidal's "The Art and Arts of E. Howard Hunt," *The New York Review* Dec 13, 1973.
9. Report, page 52.
10. Report, page 52.
11. Report, page 55, note 11. Scott Crime and Cover-Up, p. 35-38.
12. Report, page 52.
13. *The Kennedy Assassination and the Viet Nam War*, Peter Dale Scott in Scott, Hoch p. 406 and in *Government by Gunplay*, p. 152; O'Donnel & Powers in *Johnny We Hardly Knew Ye*. See the extensive discussion of this in Chapter 19 of this book.
14. Report, page 53; Summers 76-9.
15. Jesse Curry 61-2, and as elsewhere in this book. WR 132. See TCI, Feb. 1981, p. 1-7, by Wallace Milam.
16. Report, page 54; O'Toole 11-40 on rifle.
17. O'Toole 19, WR 123; Summers 100.
18. WR 139-147.
19. Report, page 54.
20. Report, page 54; see long discussion 6HSCA138-225; 6HSCA295.
21. Report, page 55.
22. Report, page 56.
23. Report, page 56-57; WR 130.
24. Summers 101-2. See O'Toole on rifle.
25. Summers 101-2. O'Toole, Shaw.
26. Report, page 57.
27. Summers 108-9.
28. Summers 108; ZH 168-176 (Rowland) JFK Doc #13074 (Walthers); CE2089 pp. 35-6 (Henderson).
29. Summers 105, 541n25; WR 518 "The Paraffin Test". See WR Appendix X "Expert Testimony" concerning the rifle, finger prints, bullets, etc..., also *New York Times* Ed. p. 507, and "The Assassin" p. 113 for the Curtain rods story, palmprints, the sack. Postmortem, 408, 437-440, 445-7, 451, 470-1, 606-7, 624-5 (Parrafin Tests).
30. Report, page 58.
31. Feb. 1981 TCI p.2; WR pp. 151-2.
32. Scott, Hoch 28; Anson "Marksmanship": 50, 61, 65, 77, 141, 143, 144; WR on rifle's marksmanship, p. 177.
33. Thompson 377-8; O'Toole 27-8. WR 180.
34. 3H407.
35. Anson 62-3, 64; Stuckey Exhibit 3; 2H408; 5H610.
36. Report, page 59.
37. Report, page 59n.
38. O'Toole 144.
39. O'Toole 145.
40. WR 161; See Sylvia Meagher in Scott, Hoch: The Murder of Tippit.
41. Report, page 59. See 12HSCA "Oswald-Tippit Association".

42. See Meagher above; Summers 121-7.
43. Report, page 59.
44. Summers p. 100, 541n28; See WR *New York Times* Ed 538 "Hairs and Fibers", particularly p. 542, 543.
45. Dallas Police Tapes; Summers 119. Investigation of a Homicide, Dallas Police Tapes Channel One, p. 335: "I got an eye-ball witness to the get-away man... he was apparently armed with a 32 dark finish automatic pistol..." p. 337; 550 car 2 reports "The shells at the scene indicate the suspect is armed with an automatic, a 38, rather than a pistol". The first call saying Tippit had been shot came at 1:16 p.m., hardly enough time for Oswald to have gotten to the scene (p. 326). Oswald had a revolver, they say.
46. Summers 124.
47. Summers 114, and WR 339 for Oswald's landlady, Mrs. Robert's possible connection to Ruby.
48. Summers 114-117; Meagher p. 55 in Scott, Hoch.
49. Report, page 60.
50. Report, page 61.
51. *New York Times* ed 283 (Warren Report); 4 HSCA 38, 42, 46, 56.
52. Festerwald 232-4; Summers 369.
53. Photo of I.D. in Curry p. 108.
54. Jones IV, p. 111.
55. Conversation with Earl Golz of the *Dallas Morning News.*
56. Report, p. 218-19; Summers 361-2; 467-8.
57. Summers 298; 370.
58. Summers 361-2; 467-8.
59. Summers 364; 467-8.
60. Summers 361-2; 467-8.
61. Summers 364; 467-8.
62. Fensterwald 235.
63. *Washington Post*, January 19, 1970.
64. Anson, *They've Killed the President* p. 216 pb edition; Earl Golz in *Dallas Morning News,* 1975 (exact date lost); AP Nov 14, 1976; Fensterwald *Coincidence or Conspiracy* p. 383, 396 (for the actual photographs: p. 398-9).
65. 3 HSCA: Azcue 127-194; Castro 197-322; Silvia Duran (Tirado) 6-119.
66. 3 HSCA 136.
67. 3 HSCA 206.
68. *Washington Post* Nov 26, 1976, by Ronald Kessler – an important article.
69. Ibid Nov 27, 1976, Nov 13, 1976; Jack Anderson Nov 19, 20, 1977.
70. Showtime cable TV: "On Trial: Lee Harvey Oswald." Nov 21- 22, 1986. See *Echoes of Conspiracy* Dec 8, 1986.
71. Phillips: *The Night Watch*, p. 124; Summers p. 384.
72. O'Toole 150.
73. O'Toole 151; Shaw 194.
74. O'Toole 165.
75. O'Toole 165; *Accessories After the Fact*, Sylvia Meagher, p. 198, 185-91, and all of Ch. 6; See also Paul Hoch's article in *The Third Decade*, "The Final Investigation?" July, 1985, p. 2. On Army Intelligence and the Hidell name.
76. O'Toole 165.
77. O'Toole 166.
78. Shaw 193-4.
79. Shaw 194.
80. Jones I p. 156. Surry printed and distributed the "Wanted For Treason" pamphlets against JFK; Shaw 167.
81. Above. WR 298.
82. Shaw 194; CD 354; Thompson 312.
83. 5H57; Shaw 194.

84. Anson 175; 5H57.
85. Shaw 194. See also CE 709, 22H156-7, 4H180-1.
86. (Jonathan Marshall, November 20, 1983, in the *San Jose Mercury News*. Marshall is the publisher of *Parapolitics/USA*, a newsletter for investigative reporters).
87. "National Archives – Security Classification Problems Involving Warren Commission Files and Other Records," Hearings before the House Subcommittee on Governmental Information, 1976; Fensterwald 296.
88. Fensterwald 298-9; 464; 452-3.
89. Helm's testimony cited above, 4HSCA, note 87 p. 212; Fensterwald 193-203.
90. Summers 512.
91. Jones III, page 30.
92. Jones III, page 31.
93. Jones III, page 29.
94. Shaw 27.
95. Ibid and Jones III page 33.
96. Jones III, page 37.
97. Jones III, page 35, 100.
98. *Cover-Ups*, #16, p. 3.
99. Model-Groden 258, *Farewell America*, page 339 note 30.
100. It was described as a bank vault, and the man was in fact starved. Testimony of Nosenko 2 HSCA 441-481; Testimony of John Hart about Nosenko 2 HSCA 487; on Nosenko's treatment see p.483, 489; from 437 to end. Fensterwald p. 224; 12 HSCA 525-635 for conditions of detention. HSCA Report 101-2; 3 HSCA 581, 620-1, 623-4, 639; 4 HSCA 20-245.
101. 12 HSCA 186, 132. (The whole ms is from pp 70-315.).
102. 12 HSCA 153, 171.
103. Anson 191; Warren Report p. 652-3.
104. Anson 193.
105. Anson 193.
106. Anson 194.
107. Anson 210.
108. Meagher 377-387.
109. 10 HSCA 83; Summers 445-6, 450.
110. *Playboy* article by Jim Hougan, "Prelude to Watergate: The Plot to Wreck the Golden Greek."(Date lost).
111. Ugarte Alvarado, Gilberto: 11 HSCA 162-3.
112. Summers p. 594 n 101.
113. 10 HSCA 44-5; for Veciana report see p. 37. Report p. 135; Summers.
114. Report p. 135; Summers.
115. *Washington Post* Jan 20, 1977.
116. Ibid.

Chapter 10

1. Cpt. Will Fritz' testimony, CE.
2. 6HSCA140; Model-Groden 174-6.
3. 6HSCA146.
4. 6HSCA2n.
5. 6HSCA220.
6. 6HSCA221.
7. 6HSCA162.
8. 6HSCA163.
9. 6HSCA295.
10. 6HSCA221-2.
11. 6HSCA161.
12. 6HSCA162.
13. 6HSCA162.
14. 6HSCA163.
15. 6HSCA146.
16. 6HSCA146.
17. 2HSCA340.
18. 2HSCA344.
19. 2HSCA344.
20. 2HSCA345.

21. 2HSCA346; 6HSCA295.
22. 2HSCA346.
23. 2HSCA338-9.
24. 2HSCA335.
25. 6HSCA221.
26. 6HSCA220.
27. 6HSCA222.
28. 6HSCA224.

29. 2HSCA336.
30. 6HSCA222.
31. Model-Groden 193.
32. 6HSCA203.
33. 6HSCA177.
34. 2HSCA320.
35. 2HSCA323.
36. 2HSCA325

Chapter 11

1. Report p. 60.
2. *Dallas Morning News*, April 11, 1963; *NY Times*, April 12, 1963.
3. Report 98n 4.
4. Summers 563n65: see picture of bullet 7HSCA390 fig 14 .
5. Report 60. The initials scratched on the original bullet were also missing, (O'Toole 31,32). Shaw 44-47; Summers 244.
6. Curry 113.
7. Shaw 47; Summers 244.
8. Report 55n.
9. Shaw 44; 11H294-5.
10. "Automatic" –23 H 868, 870 for transcript of Hill's report; For only one bullet given to FBI: 3H 474 (Cunningham); three more bullets: 3 H 471; for cartridge cases not listed by the police: 24 H 260, 131-5, 262, 117; For Officer Poe with regard to his marking the cases: 3 H 49, Poe and FBI 7 H 66, 24 H 415: testimony of Ronald Simmons, Army ballistics expert on the Benavides shells, see 3 H 449; 7 HSCA 377, HSCA Report 59 says that all 4 cartridge cases found were fired from Oswald's revolver, but then says that since his gun had been modified, it was not possible to determine if any of the bullets found had been fired from the gun. WR 559; Summers 117-8 and his Chapter 136 concerning the Tippit slaying.
11. Meagher; The Murder of Officer Tippit. Curry 96; Summers 118; WR 161.
12. WR 160.
13. WR 160-1; Report of the FBI Lab in Curry 96.
14. Curry 96.
15. Model-Groden 80-86, O'Toole 21, 27, Anson 75-8. Summers 76-8.
16. CE5.
17. Pictures Shaw p. 72-4. These also appear in Jones IV.
18. 7H555; 21H476: Shaw picture 123.
19. Shaw 144.
20. Shaw picture 124: CD1546.
21. See photos above; police car over mark: Shaw 123.
22. Conversations with Dr. James Barger.
23. SS Clint Hill testimony p. 8 of this book, WC.2H144.
24. Garrison.
25. *The Baltimore Sun*, May 1 & May 8, 1977, about Howard Donahue: *The Sun Magazine*.
26. P. 249, Charles Wilber M.D.
27. 6HSCA63, 107: 2HSCA322 (White testimony) on rifles. 3418-344. On rifle length. Anson 76. The gun ordered from Klien's "was 36", and the one found in the TSBD was 40. Roffman "The rifle in the Building" p. 151-174 of *Presumed Guilty.*.
28. Report p. 50n8.
29. Model-Groden 141 (study this whole section.).
30. WR *NY Times* ed. 101.
31. Report p. 80.
32. 2HSCA4; Report 45-6, 47, 80n16, 83; note blur analysis in Appendix E of Thompson, p. 373.

33. Report 80.
34. Model-Groden p. 142.
35. Model-Groden p. 143.
36. Model-Groden p. 143.
37. Model-Groden p. 143.
38. Carl Bernstein's "The CIA and the Media" in *The Rolling Stone.*
39. Model-Groden p. 143-6.
40. Model-Groden p. 142.
41. Model-Groden p. 147.
42. 8HSCA Barger Report, and conversations with Barger, Groden. The heterodyning at Z 226 is well known among staff of the committee, and researchers.
43. Model-Groden p. 147.
44. O'Toole 23. See Thompson 377-8 & Thompson 36 on rifle tests. Oswald's Rifle Capability in *Presumed Guilty* p. 225-247.
45. WR *NY Times* Ed: p. 355 (CE 900.) Full picture is on p202-3 of *Whitewash. The Report on the Warren Report* by Harold Weisberg.
46. Model-Groden 150.
47. 1 HSCA 333.
48. Report p. 80.
49. Ibid p. 81.
50. Report p. 80 n. For the quote which follows see Report p. 47; 6 HSCA 14-31.
51. Report p. 83.
52. Report p. 83.
53. Report p. 83.
54. WR 101; Thompson, Curry p. 100.
55. Report p. 80.
56. Report p. 83.
57. Report p. 83.
58. Report p. 83.
59. Report p. 81-2.
60. Report p. 82.
61. Report p. 82.
62. 1 HSCA 333. See discussion in Wilber 252-3, 142; Wecht's dissent 7 HSCA 199 to the findings of the panel, etc... (Appendix).
63. 1 HSCA 42-3, 54 etc... Thompson 80-104; 4 H 132-3; 135-6.
64. See Wecht's statement on the changing of his testimony by the Rockefeller Commission in Scott, Hoch p. 519 and Shaw p. 29.
65. Report p. 81.
66. Ibid.
67. Ibid.
68. Shaw tells the story of the film taken from the "Babushka Lady," she says by FBI agent Regis Kennedy, who died suddenly at the moment the Committee wanted to talk to him, p. 51-4. Summers 506 on Kennedy.
69. Model-Groden 291. 6HSCA126-131: 296;.
70. Shaw vii. Thompson Appendix A p. 316, 12HSCA1 "Conspiracy Witnesses in Dealy Plaza" Report p87.
71. Model-Groden p.153 Report p. 85; "...Image inhancement techniques successfully established the presence of a human head visible among the leaves of the bush in Zapruder's field of view... he was not, as had been alledged, in a position to have been a hidden gunman.".
72. Report, page 48.
73. Report, page 82.
74. Report, page 47.
75. Report, page 47, note 7.
76. Report, page 49.

77. Summers 74-5.
78. 6HSCA308-9; 6HSCA115-121; Report 49; As to use of the scope and shortening of required time to load, aim and fire the rifle, see Report p. 83, 12HSCA1.
79. Summers 74; 24H522; with Earl Golz. 12HSCA4 Study whole.
80. Summers 73; 12HSCA3 sec. in 12: Conspiracy Witnesses in Dealey Plaza 1-32.
81. Summers 73; 12HSCA4.
82. Summers 76 (Melzer, also in Gallery, July 1979; See Vol.6 HSCA pp. 108-138 on the photos and films.
83. Report, page 49.
84. Report, page 50.
85. Report, page 51; Model-Groden 29.
86. 24H228; Thompson 277.
87. National Archives.
88. Report, page 50, note 8.
89. Report 43.
90. Wilber 210.
91. Dr. Robert McClelland's report, CE 392, Warren Report page 527.
92. 6 H 48.
93. *Philadelphia Sunday Bulletin,* November 24, 1963.
94. *The New York Times* of November 23, 1963.
95. 6 H 74.
96. 6 H 338, 292, 294; 2 H 141; 22 H 662.
97. Curry: *JFK Assassination File* p. 30.
98. CD 5; WR 7 H 107; Thompson P. 130.
99. 7 H 107.
100. 6 H 388.
101. See Model-Groden.
102. See Thompson Appendix A; Introduction to *Cover-Up* by Shaw, Harris.
103. WFAA-TV video tape PKT-24.
104. Thompson, Wilber, Warren Hearings.
105. Wilber.
106. Anson 77 and note. Anson tells us that Deputy Sheriff Roger Craig confirmed that it was a 7.65 Mauser. This note is very important, as it suggests that the shells were planted in the TSBD also, and that the above was stamped on the rifle.
107. Thompson for pictures of the dent pl92 (CE543) see 192-3.
108. (7H404) and Thompson above; Curry 89.
109. Thompson 192-6; See 7 HSCA 383, 371.
110. Report p50 "The rifle Boone found..." See 7HSCA372 paragraph 161-3.
111. Garrison 195.
112. Summers 66.
113. Shaw 76.
114. Letter from Hoover to Rankin dated 7-18-64; Shaw 76-7 Also in *Modern Medicine* 10-28-74.
115. Shaw 77.
116. Shaw 76.
117. Shaw 76.
118. Shaw 76 *Modern Medicine* 10-28-74.
120. Shaw 75; 6 HSCA 11 (60); pl2 (66)-(67).
121. 7 HSCA 15-16.
122. O'Toole 240.
123. Shaw 101. Officer Roy Vaughn brought a suit about this by his attorney James Niell, with whom we have talked. Several police made affidavits that Asst. Chief of Police Charles Batchelor brought Ruby in on the elevator.
124. Curry 15, 124-6.
125. Author's discussion with James Niell, Vaughn's attorney.

126. Report 157; Shaw 101n.
127. As related to the author by Reporter and former aide to Lyndon Johnson, Tom Johnson, from his notes taken when he spoke to Ruby.
128. Ibid; Model-Groden 53; see Curry.
129. Penn Jones, Jr. 4 FMG 114; 3 FMG 85.
130. *Dallas Morning News.*
131. Shaw 101.
132. O'Toole 102; Shaw 99-101 (study closely).
133. Shaw 101.
134. Curry 159.
135. Shaw 99-101.
136. Shaw 101.
137. O'Toole 145.
138. Ibid.
139. 12 HSCA 262.

Chapter 12

1. HSCA Report p. 1.
2. HSCA Report p. 65.
3. HSCA Report p. 67.
4. HSCA Report p. 66 n 1.
5. HSCA Report p. 67-8.
6. HSCA Report p. 68.
7. HSCA Report p. 68.
8. HSCA Report p. 68.
9. HSCA Report p. 68.
10. HSCA Report p. 68.
11. HSCA Report p. 68.
12. HSCA Report p. 68.
13. HSCA Report p. 68-9.
14. HSCA Report p. 69.
15. HSCA Report p. 69.
16. 6 HSCA 298 and 306.
17. HSCA Report p. 71.
18. 2 HSCA 63.
19. Report p. 74.
20. Report of Dr. Barger, see HSCA Vol. 5, Vol. 2, Vol. 8. Dr. Barger stated to me that "all six impulses are ten decibels above any other background noise". See 8 HSCA 78, 0. 55. See p. 43 and Findings on p. 49-50. See Dr. Barger's letter in the appendix.
21. Conversations with staff.
22. Report p. 80.
23. Sept. 1984 *Cover-Ups.*
24. Radio Log reproduced by the Ramsey Panel, *Report of the Committee on Ballistics Acoustics,* National Academy of Sciences, May, 1982 p. 71; TCI August, 1978 reprint of *Dallas Morning News* article by Earl Golz of August 11, 1978.
25. *Dallas Morning News* September 13, 1978; TCI p. 8-9, Sep 1978.
26. *Cover-Up* by Gary Shaw picture and story p. 118. Photo by Phil Willis.
27. Gary Mack in TCI, March, 1981.
28. Dallas Times Herald, Dec 2, 1980.
29. *The Continuing Inquiry* (TCI) November 1981.
30. Report, p. 483.
31. 8 HSCA 70; Feb 1981 TCI; 23 H 832.

32. Mack p. 15 TCI Feb 1981.
33. 8 HSCA 11-112.
34. Mack in TCI August 1981.
35. TCI Sept. 1981. For a more precise and technical refutation of the Vaughn, Barber, and Alvarez analysis, see p.3 of the Sept. 1981 TCI; and "A Brief Rebuttal to the Ramsey Report," by Anthony Marsh, in *The Third Decade,* January, 1986.
36. 3 HSCA 567.
37. March, 1981 *The Continuing Inquiry.*
38. *Cover-Ups* # 18, Sep 1984.

Chapter 13

1. 11HSCA541-549.
2. 11HSCA541.
3. 11HSCA543.
4. 11HSCA542.
5. 11HSCA543.
6. 11HSCA544.
7. 11HSCA544.
8. 11HSCA545.
9. 11HSCA546.
10. 11HSCA546.
11. 11HSCA546.
12. 11HSCA549.
13. 12HSCA35-47.
14. 12HSCA36.
15. 12HSCA37.
16. 12HSCA38.
17. 12HSCA39.
18. 12HSCA39.
19. 12HSCA40.
20. 12HSCA40.
21. 12HSCA40.
22. 12HSCA41.
23. 12HSCA41-2.
24. 12HSCA41-2.
25. Ibid.
26. Ibid. Summers 475; 9HSCA978.
27. "Jack Ruby's pockets and the trunk of his car served as his bank". Warren Report, p. 704. *New York Times* Ed. 9HSCA2-7: "$3,000 on him"; See Kantor 18; HSCA Report 156; WR p. 797; *Dallas Morning News,* October 12, 1978; Kantor 24; 23H117, 303.
28. WR *NY Times* ed. p. 367; p. 613-14; CH1150; 22H180; Anson 160.
29. Shaw 23-4.
30. *Crime and Cover-up*, Peter Dale Scott, Westworks, p. 35.
31. *The Nelson Rockefeller Report to the President*, Manor Books, June 1975, 251-269.
32. *Crime and Cover-Up*, Peter Dale Scott, Westworks, p. 34; 9H202.
33. Scott p. 11.
34. Model, Groden 256; Scott: From Dallas to Watergate: "Overlapping Conspiracies;" See also "Strange Bedfellows: The Hughes-Nixon-Lansky Connection: The Secret Alliances of the CIA From World War II to Watergate" by Howard Kohn, *Rolling Stone,* May 20, 1976; "The Puppet, Uncovering the Secret World of Nixon, Hughes and the CIA," by Larry DuBois and Laurence Gonzalez, *Playboy*, October, November issues, 19.
35. 4 Jones 114, 3 Jones 85.

36. Scott 45.
37. Scott 45; 14 H 459.
38. Scott 37.
39. Ibid.
40. Scott 35; CD470.24.
41. Scott 36.
42. Jones III, p. 101.
43. Curry *JFK Assassination File*, p. 61.
44. Shaw 100-101; O'Toole 164.
45. 10HSCA37-52; Summers 390-2, 417, 508-14, 586n91, 347-8, 356-8, 546n34, 353-62; *The Continuing Inquiry*, August 1979, by Gary Shaw "The Dallas Mystery Man". Shaw says he thinks that Bishop is Michael Victor Mertz, whom he thinks is also QJ/WIN, the Executive Action executioner for the CIA.
46. 10 HSCA 37.
47. 10 HSCA 41.
48. 10 HSCA 37-52; Report 135-7.
49. 10 HSCA 41.
50. Report 136n23; 10HSCA48 (176) tells us that Howard Hunt referred to Phillips as "Knight" in his book on the Bay of Pigs. On June 16, 1980, Anthony Summers, author of *Conspiracy*, confronted Phillips with the accusation on the Tom Brokaw NBC Today Show. Phillips vehemently denied the accusation and subsequently sued a British publisher of excerpts from Summers' book and received a "substantial amount" in settlement.
51. They worked together. 10HSCA42, Summers 508.
52. Alluded in Summers 339; Report 143; Jones IV p. 11-12; also Report 170; 10HSCA108.
53. Fensterwald 226. When Banister died, they found a stack of Oswald's FPCC pamphlets in his office. All these people are intertwined: Hunt, Sturgis, Banister, Ferrie, Oswald, Ruby. See also HSCA Report on 544 Camp St., 143-6; 10HSCA123.
54. Fensterwald 226; Summers.
55. Scott, Hoch 371; Fensterwald 366-7; *Washington Post*, August 1st, 1963; Garrison, Summers.
56. Summers 260-1.
57. 448 (Summers); 10HSCA176 (146). Jack Anderson has written about Sturgis for a long time, who's picture was on the cover of *Parade* about 1960, for an Anderson article about this soldier of fortune. Surely he knew his background, and the accusations that Sturgis might have been involved in the assassination. We wonder, therefore, at Anderson's pushing of his thesis that Organized Crime killed the President.
58. Summers 352-3; 10HSCA37-52; Report 135.
59. Report 112; Summers 351, 449; Fensterwald.
60. Report 142-3.
61. Anson 122, 376; Fensterwald 298-9.
62. Report 145.
63. Scott, Hoch 284.
64. Scott, Hoch 286; see 10HSCA123-132 on 544 Camp St.; 10HSCA 109; Report 144 "The Committee... developed information that in 1961, Bannister, Ferrie, and Archacha were working together in the anti-Castro cause." See pp. 139-147.
65. Summers 324-5.
66. Summers 508.
67. WBA-TV Fort Worth (JFK Library) MR 74-52:1 (tape) Tom Webb; O'Toole 17.
68. Summers "The Curtain Rod Story" p. 101; O'Toole 168-88, 190-2, 195-206, 225, 42, 169.
69. O'Toole 42, 169, 171, 173-188, 201-2, 206; O'Toole 168.
70. O'Toole 205.
71. O'Toole 204. See Meagher's "The Vanished Mauser" p. 95 in *Accessories after the Fact*.
72. O'Toole 204.
73. O'Toole 168.
74. 3 Jones 56.

75. Ibid; *Dallas Morning News,* April 18, 1969.
76. See Peter Dale Scott's important article in *Ramparts,* November 1973, reprinted in *The Assassinations, Dallas and Beyond,* 357.
77. Robert Oswald testimony to the WC; III Jones, p. 78.
78. Jones IV 27.
79. Jones IV 27, 155.
80. Jones IV 11; 155.
81. 10 HSCA 106.
82. Jones IV p. 173-4.
83. Model-Groden 213.
84. *Coincidence or Conspiracy,* by Bernard Fensterwald, p. 128. "Strange Bedfellows: The Hughes-Nixon-Lansky Connection: The Secret Alliances of the CIA From World War II to Watergate" by Howard Kohn, *Rolling Stone,* May 20, 1976.
85. Drew Pearson and Jack Anderson, *U.S.A., Second Class Power* (New York: Simon and Schuster, 1958), pp. 281-2; Fensterwald, p. 128.
86. "The White House, the Teamsters and the Mafia," by Bill Hazlitt and Jack Nelson, The Los Angeles Times, Miami *Herald,* June 3, 1973; Fensterwald p. 129.
87. *The White House Transcripts, New York Times* edition (New York: The Viking Press, 1973) p. 146. Fensterwald, p. 129-30.
88. Fensterwald, p. 131-2.
89. Ibid.
90. Summers 275.
91. Summers 274; *N.Y Times* 10-24-52; Warren was a Republican.
92. Summers 275; International Teamster Feb 1959; See "The Mafia, the CIA, and the Kennedy Assassination," Milton Viorst, *Washingtonian* 1975; see Shaw on Nixon and Hoffa.
93. 14H444; Fensterwald 280-3; Summers et al.
94. Shaw 54; Warren Report 792,3.
95. WR 5H-; Ruby and Organized Crime HSCA Report 149; 9HSCA.
96. *Philadelphia Bulletin,* January 3, 1967, p. 3. See article by former Dallas County Jail doctor, John D. Callahan concerning Ruby's medical treatment or lack thereof, in *Argosy,* Sept. 1967; See 2 Jones 168-9; Meagher 452-3. Ruby died Jan. 3, 1967.
97. 5H206; "Alfred was killed in a taxi in New York." Warren said. The Warren Commission transcribed Alfred McLane as Mark Lane; 5H205; see Scott 45.

Chapter 14

1. Report 180.
2. Bowart, *Operation Mind Control,* p. 201-3.
3. "In fact, DeMohrenschildt knew Oswald better than anyone else alive, except perhaps for Oswald's wife, Marina..." George McMillan in *The Washington Post,* April 3, 1977. The McMillans are *not* recommended reading in this case, but this is an accurate statement. See Warren Report, *New York Times* edition pp. 238-9, 261-2, 371, 376-7, 393-4, 638-640, 642, 645.
4. On background 12 HSCA 49-; Fensterwald 212-14, 38;. Summers "Hepburn" 334 5n.
5. 12 HSCA 61.
6. 12 HSCA 61; WR on Ruth Paine; Marina Oswald lived with Ruth Paine. The Paines' phone was tapped and they were (Warren Commission Document 206) heard to say that "he felt sure that LEE HARVEY OSWALD had killed the President but did not feel OSWALD was responsible, and further stated, "We both know who is responsible" (Fensterwald 216). Jones 118-121. Ruth Paine got Oswald the job at the Depository: Jones IV p. 1. Lesbian affair between Marina and Ruth: Model-Groden p. 228. Garrison 93, 133-4 for possible CIA connections. "... I am of the opinion that Mr. Ruby did in fact know Lee Harvey Oswald prior to Sunday, November 24, 1963, and that he was in my opinion paid to silence Lee Harvey Oswald...

I still do not know why or how, but *Mr. and Mrs. Paine* are somehow involved in this affair." Testimony of Robert Oswald to Allen Dulles of the Warren Commission.

7. 12 HSCA 49.
8. Summers 223.
9. 12 HSCA 52.
10. 12 HSCA 53; note 3 above: DeMohrenschildt taking the Oswalds to a party at the home of Admiral Chester Bruton 12 HSCA 62.
11. 12 HSCA 53-4.
12. 12 HSCA 54.
13. 12 HSCA 56-7.
14. 12 HSCA 60-1.
15. 12 HSCA 57.
16. 12 HSCA 60 (174).
17. 12 HSCA 60-1.
18. 10 HSCA p. 42 (147) 43- (on Veciana) concerning Kail. Summers 249, 509; See Joanne Braun in TCI, Sept 1981, p 14-15; Anson 241; Meagher 385; CE 2943; CE 3108; 26 H 629-630; 14 H 347-8; *Washingtonian* p 177, 184.
19. Bowart *Operation Mind Control*, p. 203 and Willem Oltmans *Atlas*, May 1977; *Gallery*, April 1978 p. 41. The DeMohrenschildt ms is in 12 HSCA p. 69, or that which purports to be. Very nicely typed, and boiler plate.
20. *Farewell America* p. 251-2; Fensterwald 271-5; Jones II p. 8.
21. *Farewell America* p. 245-252; Fensterwald 271-5; Shaw 167; Jones III p. 5, 8, 22-7.
22. Warren Commission Exhibit 2980; Fensterwald 272.
23. Warren Commission Exhibit 2270; Fensterwald 272, 291-2.
24. Warren Commission Documents 385, 401; Fensterwald 444. Both Braden's photo of being arrested and the arrest records are missing from the Archives (Fensterwald p. 446). Shaw 85.
25. Also known as Eugene Hale Brading previously; see Peter Noyes *Legacy of Doubt*, on Braden/Brading.
26. Penn Jones: *The Continuing Inquiry,* Feb. 22, 1977 p. 8: This could also be to E. Howard Hunt, as he put together the anti-Castro Cuban Revolutionary Committee, which had an H.Q. at 544 Camp Street in N.O., the same address Oswald operated his H.Q. The note was also widely printed in newspapers and authenticated by handwriting analysis. As elsewhere quoted herein, Dan Rather, asks if Howard Hunt knew Oswald. All these people were tied together.
27. Fensterwald 573.
28. Fensterwald and *Drew Pearson Diaries*, pp. 228-9 1974 Holt, Rhinehart.
29. Fensterwald 573.
30. Fensterwald 574; for Moore and DeMohrenschildt see 12 HSCA 54.
31. Fensterwald 574.
32. Fensterwald 235-40.
33. 10 HSCA 147: "The Evolution and Implications of the CIA-Sponsored Assassination Plots Against Fidel Castro". This is an important paper. Note in particular data on Frank Sturgis on p. 176.
34. *Farewell America* 245; See also Scott on oilmen.
35. *Farewell America* 249.
36. *Farewell America* 250.
37. *Farewell America* 251.
38. For this story see *If You Have A Lemon, Make Lemonade* by Warren Hinckle (Putnam, 1974). Bantam Ed. pp. 266-; "Whoever James Hepburn was, he had reliable sources of information about the inner workings of American Intelligence" (p. 269).
39. *Farewell America* p. 251-2; also in Fensterwald 575, Shaw 167.
40. Jones I p. 156; See 5 H 420, etc...
41. See House Hearings on FBI Oversight 94th Congressional Serial No. 2 Part 3 on the "Circumstances Surrounding Destruction of the Lee Harvey Oswald Note"; testimony of Hosty on p. 124; Shaw 179 and many other references. Report on dest. of note 195.

42. CE 3108.
43. 14 H 345-353; Anson 240-1. See note 18 above.
44. *Farewell America* 360.
45. See Harold Weisberg *Oswald in New Orleans*; 10 HSCA "Lee Harvey Oswald in New Orleans." Anson; Shaw, Garrison, Summers.
46. Summers 300; Report on Oswald in New Orleans; p.139-146.
47. Ibid.
48. Summers ibid and 343. Report 143 on 544 Camp Street. Senator Schweiker told Summers "it means for the first time in the whole Kennedy assassination investigation we have evidence which places at 544 Camp Street intelligence agents, Lee Oswald, the Mob, and anti-Castro exiles. It puts all these elements together in a way that has never been done before." This is a key to the case.
49. Fensterwald 225-7, Ward's assistant, Hugh Ward, was killed in a plane crash just before Garrison could question him, along with the Mayor of New Orleans, Delessups Morrison, ten days from Bannister's death (Jones III p. 47). (See *Playboy* interview with Garrison October 1967). Another of Bannister' associates, Maurice Brooks Gatlin Sr. was defenestrated (Wm. Turner in *Ramparts*, January 1963, p. 48). See Anson.
50. Summers 301 "O.K. Carlos, if you want to hit me, hit me".
51. Anson 180; 4 H 432; 17 H 758; Report 191.
52. Summers 302.
53. Summers 295-6 for quotes. See also 292, 142, 391.
54. CBS Reports, The American Assassins, Part II, November 26, 1975; Summers 131.
55. Kantor *Who Was Jack Ruby?* p. 47; many other references: Summers 480.
56. Summers 468; 459-; "In 1959, while Jack Ruby was an informant for the FBI..." Congressman (later Chairman of the Assassination Committee) Thomas Downing, September 17, 1976; Cong. Record p. 10,359; Fensterwald 273-284.
57. Quoted from *Accessories After The Fact*; Sylvia Meagher p. 376-387 from Haynes Johnson *The Bay of Pigs* p. 76. See Report on Cuban feelings towards Kennedy p. 132; See "The Betrayal of JFK Kept Fidel Castro in Power" by Fletcher Prouty, *Gallery*, February 1978. "Why had the CIA destroyed its own operation? ...The CIA had signaled Kennedy that his political fate was under CIA control, just as was Eisenhower's in the U-2 incident." Prouty was the liaison between CIA and GCS.
58. Fensterwald 235-240.
59. Senate Intelligence Committee Report on Foreign Assassination Plots p. 74; See Report HSCA on CIA-Mafia plots etc... p. 109-117.
60. Senate IC Report ibid 94-5.
61. Ibid p. 94-6.
62. Ibid p. 97.
63. Ibid; Fensterwald 236.
64. Fensterwald 160-1 (in 1965) and Senate Int. Com. Report ibid 89-90; Fensterwald p. 238.
65. Fensterwald 513; J. Anthony Lukas *Nightmare* (Viking, 1976) p. 278-. Senate Watergate Committee.
66. Senate Intelligence Committee Report on Foreign Assassination Plots 133. See from p. 108-124; Fensterwald 166-7 and from p. 155-174.
67. Senate Intelligence Committee Report p. 84, 132; Fensterwald 166.
68. Ibid 102-3.
69. Ibid 133.
70. Ibid 134.
71. Fensterwald 236.
72. Sorenson (Bantam) 334; see also Prouty cited above note 58.
73. Sorenson 335; see also Wise and Ross *The Invisible Government*, account of the Bay of Pigs Operation.
74. Sorenson 336; Fensterwald 238-9.
75. Sorenson 335.

76. Sorenson 338.
77. Sorenson 342.
78. Fensterwald 237, *Washington Post*, September 16, 1973.
79. Fensterwald 237-8.
80. Fensterwald 238.
81. Fensterwald 238.
82. Fensterwald 238.
83. Senate Int. Committee ibid 85-6; Fensterwald 240.
84. "Helms said the CIA's general position was that it should forward information to the Commission only in response to specific requests". (HSCA Report p. 253); see pp. 252-5. Helm's testimony: 4 HSCA. Helms was Hunt's close friend and idol: Summers 510-512.
85. Fensterwald 517; *True* August 1974; see the long interview of Mike Canfield with Frank Sturgis in *Coup d'Etat in America* appendix. "... I've done a lot of things. I've been on assassination attempts... (p. 230)" "Hey I can show you clippings where they say I was involved in the assassination of President Kennedy..." (p. 235). Sturgis was investigated by the Watergate Committee Concerning the assassination, and questioned by the FBI in 1963 about it. Canfield asks him if other people in the CIA might have done it: "The CIA had a lot of different factions, some of which I didn't trust" (p. 235-6). This book is about Hunt's possible involvement. Further extensive discussion of Hunt's possible involvement may be found in Prouty's articles in *Gallery*: "The Greatest Cover-Up" and why they had to pay off Hunt after the Watergate Break-In; and that Nixon had used Hunt or vice-versa to set up Kennedy by destroying its own operation, that is Cabell, Hunt, Nixon, as in note 58 above, in "The Betrayal of JFK Kept Fidel Castro in Power" (*Gallery*, February 1978). See Prouty's "An Introduction to the Assassination Business." We believe that this is what the Watergate was all about.

Chapter 15

1. Summers 254; Shaw 55; Fensterwald.
2. Shaw 54.
3. Scott 42; Hunt *Give Us This Day* 38; Fensterwald 513-519, *True* 8/1974.
4. Tad Szulc *Compulsive Spy* 74.
5. Shaw 54; The Lou Staples Show, KRLD Radio (Dallas), June 27, 1975. CE 279.
6. CD 279 -"Assassination of Jose Remon, Panama."; Shaw 55.
7. Drew Pearson and Jack Anderson: *U.S.A. - Second Class Power,* (NY, Simon & Shuster, 1958, pp. 281-2; Fensterwald p. 128.
8. *NY Times*, May 3, 4, 1976 (reprinted in *San Francisco Examiner*, and other magazines).
9. WR *Times* ed. 707-8 & Ch VI; Summers 460.
10. Fensterwald 133.
11. *Legacy of Doubt* Peter Noyes.
12. Fensterwald 288 (note 81 p374).
13. Fensterwald 506.
14. Ibid 288.
15. Ibid 288.
16. Report 171.
17. Report 174.
18. Fensterwald 505; 10HSCA 176.
19. Fensterwald 511.
20. Szulc 96, 99.
21. Report 181.
22. Report 181.
23. Jones III 83.
24. Shaw 186; Jones III p. 83.

25. Fensterwald 32.
26. Senate Intelligence Committee Ass. Plots; Report HSCA 112; See the important section "CIA Plots Against Castro" 10HSCA which discusses the retaliation theory, the Anderson articles, and many other issues.
27. *The Assassinations, Dallas and Beyond,* edited by Peter Dale Scott, Paul L. Hoch, and Russell Stetler) p. 404.
28. Report 132 (129); Much of 10HSCA deals with the Cubans.
29. Fensterwald on Hale Boggs (of the Warren Com.) and Hoover 100-101; Shaw on Hoover 175-184.
30. Szulc 129.
31. Scott, Hoch 397.
32. Fensterwald 524-6.
33. Fensterwald 534.
34. Scott 400.
35. Ibid 401.
36. Summers 271.
37. Scott, Hoch 397-405.
38. Summers 271 & refs on 569. This has been well documented. 10HSCA 187 (207) tells us that the plots were apparently concealed from RFK; (to p.189).
39. Fensterwald 32. There are many discussions of Kennedy's severe problems with the CIA.
40. Fensterwald 155-171; Senate Int. Com *Report on Foreign Assassinations* 129; 10HSCA 187; *NY Times* 3-10-69, Hersh:10-20-69 Mankiewicz.
41. Summers 270; Szulc "Cuba On Our Mind" in *Esquire* Feb 74.
42. Summers 271.
43. CBS Radio Aug 10, 1973; Fensterwald 535.
44. WC Doc 395; Fensterwald 507.
45. Ibid 541.
46. Ibid 88.
47. Ibid 547.
48. Ibid 89.
49. Ibid 91.
50. Ibid 542.
51. Ibid 542-3.
52. Ibid 543.
53. Ibid 543.
54. *Washington Post* June 28, 1979 and *Baltimore Sun* same or next day.
55. Fensterwald 544.
56. Ibid 545; Epstein, *Inquest.*
57. Shaw 216-18.
58. Fensterwald 548.
59. Ibid 548.
60. Ibid 549.
61. Ibid 549.
62. Ibid 538.
63. Ibid 539.
64. Ibid 510 June 23, 1972 White House transcript between Haldeman and Nixon.
65. *The Ends of Power* p. 68-9.

Chapter 16

1. *San Francisco Chronicle,* June 24, 1976. See also May 14 *Examiner,* and Tad Szulc in the *Oakland Tribune,* May 28, 1976, and Tribune article of May 19, 1976.
2. *San Francisco Chronicle,* Sept. 11, 1976.

3. *Oakland Tribune*, Sept. 17, 1976. Congressman Thomas Downing in the Congressional Record, p. H 10357 for Sept. 17, 1976.
4. Jerry Polikoff in *Gallery*, p. 62-6, July, 1979.
5. Jeff Goldberg in *Inquiry*, p. 13, reprinted in TCI March 1980.
6. Wayne Chastain, PNS in *San Francisco Sunday Examiner and Chronicle*, Oct. 10, 1976 p. 26 Sec A, "Did Lawmen Set Up King?" and Nov. 28, 1975 AP "King's Widow Thinks U.S. Plotted Death."
7. Congressman Downing's Resolution 432 went in on April 30, 1975 and asked only that JFK's death be examined. Resolution 1540 was introduced by Gonzalez, Downing, and Fauntroy on Sept. 14, 1976, and was passed.
8. For overviews of the Investigation, see "A Great Show, A Lousy Investigation," by Jerry Polikoff and William Scott Malone in *New Times*, Sept. 4, 1978; "The Assignment of G. Robert Blakey," by R. E. Sprague, printed in *People and the Pursuit of Truth*, and in TCI March, 1981; and the excellent *Gallery* insert of July, 1979.
9. *NY Times* Jan 2, 1977 story by David Burnham, and very many stories in the *Philadelphia Inquirer* in 1973.
10. Gary Mack in *Coverups!*, February, March and April, 1983 Issues. Also, Earl Golz *Dallas Morning News*, Nov. 23, 24, 1975.
11. August 3, 1976 United Press.
12. December 10, 1975 United Press.
13. *San Francisco Examiner* May 14, 1976.
14. *The Final Days*, B. Woodward and C. Bernstein, Sacker & Warbuck, London, 1976, p. 269, 307.
15. Wilmington, Delaware *News Journal* August 20, 1978. AP August 22, 1978.
16. *Saturday Evening Post*, Jules Witcover, Feb. 25, 1967; WC Report GPO edition pp 187-89; WC Exhibit 1973; William Manchester, *The Death Of A President*, New York, Harper & Row, 1967, p. 117; *Coincidence or Conspiracy*, by Bernard Fensterwald, p. 530; Missing from the National Archives is a letter of the FBI June 29, 1964 about Richard Nixon, contents unknown (Hearings before the House Subcommittee on Government Information 1976).
17. *Gallery*, July, 1979 p. 84-28.
18. *Senate Watergate Committee Report* p. 126-7; *Coincidence or Conspiracy?* p. 526.
19. *Washington Post*, Sept. 21, 1975; *Coincidence or Conspiracy?* p. 524-5.
20. *News-Herald*, week of June 9-15, 1976.
21. *NY Daily News*, Sept. 20, 1977; also *NY Post* March 31, 1977; *NY Daily News*, Nov. 3, 4, 1977.
22. *NY Daily News*, Nov. 3, 1977.
23. 10 HSCA 93, Note 67.
24. *Sun-Sentinel*, Nov 26, 1963; WC Document 59.
25. *The Assassination Tapes*, George O'Toole, Penthouse 1975 p. 120-9.
26. *NY Times*, Sept 22, 1975; See also *Washington Post* Nov. 13, 26, 27, 1976.
27. *Washington Post*, Nov. 26, 1976.
28. *NY Times Magazine*, July 15, 1979.
29. *National Review*, April 27, 1979.
30. *They've Killed the President*, Robert Sam Anson.
31. Sept. 9, 1976; See also Anderson's stories of Jan. 19, "Mystery Witness in JFK Inquiry," and Jan. 20, 1977: "CIA Tied to False Oswald Story."
32. *Washington Post*, Nov. 28, 1976.
33. ibid.
34. Jack Anderson in the *Washington Post*, Sept. 9, 1976.
35. December 27, 1976.
36. *NY Times*, January 28, 1977.

Chapter 17

1. "Investigations That Were Bound to Fail," by Jerry Policoff, *Gallery*, 1979.
2. "The Reasons For The Firing of the Chief Counsel and Staff Director": Congressional Record for Feb. 16, 1977, Vol. 123, No. 27, statement by Congressman. Gonzalez. Note other citations hereafter.
3. For comments on this, see the *L.A. Times* Jan. 17, 1977 editorial "Inquiry: the Signs Aren't Good"..."Some of the proposed investigative techniques have stirred objections. One is the use of hidden electronic transmitters to secretly record the remarks of potential witnesses; this is a thoroughly bad proposal that, if implemented, would invade the constitutional rights of the subject of inquiry."; See comments by Congressman Don Edwards on this Jan. 11, 1977, p. 2 in the *Washington Post* by George Lardner, Jr., and by Jeremiah O'Leary in the *Washington Star; NY Times* Jan. 6, 1977 by David Burnham.
4. *People Magazine*, Jan. 20, 1977.
5. San Antonio *Express-News*, March 6, 1977.
6. *Washington Star*, Oct. 4, 1976 by Bill Choyke.
7. *Washington Post*, Dec. 2, 1976.
8. *Philadelphia Inquirer*, Dec. 6, 1976.
9. *Los Angeles Times*, Jan. 17, 1977.
10. *Baltimore Sun*, March 27, 1977.
11. *Washington Post*, Jan. 11, 1977.
12. Gonzalez in the Congressional Record for Feb. 16, 1977.
13. *Newsweek*, Feb. 21, 1977.
14. George Lardner, Jr. in the *Washington Post*, Jan. 25, 1977.
15. *Washington Post*, Jan. 12, 1977.
16. *The Washington Post*, Feb. 11, 1977.
17. The San Antonio *Express-News*, March 6, 1977, p. 3A.
18. *Rolling Stone* "Execution for the Witnesses," by Howard Kohn; "Has the Mafia Penetrated the F.B.I.?" by Nicolas Gage in the *NY Times Magazine*, Oct. 2, 1977, and Gage in the *NY Times*, "Roselli Called a Victim of Mafia Because of His Senate Testimony," Feb. 25, 1977; *L.A. Times*, Dec. 15, p. 16, 1976 by Norman Kempster: "Assassination Probe will Study Slayings of Giancana, Roselli for Possible Link."
19. *Washington Post*, April 6, 1977.
20. *New Times*, Sept. 4, 1978, "A Great Show, a Lousy Investigation," by Jerry Policoff and William Scott Malone.
21. *Washington Post*, Dec. 1975.

Chapter 18

1. *Inquiry*, "Waiting for Justice," by Jeff Goldberg, reprinted in *The Continuing Inquiry*, March, 1980. See also Jerry Policoff "A Great Show, a Lousy Investigation," in *New Times*, Sept. 4, 1978; and the major *Gallery* insert of July, 1979. Also former staff member Gaeton Fonzi's considerable comment on the workings of the Committee in the famous *Washingtonian* article of Nov. 1980 (sent to co-author Livingstone by Ben Bradlee, Jr.).
2. 1 HSCA 43-4, 10-60.
3. 1 HSCA 44.
4. 1 HSCA 43.
5. 1 HSCA 61-140.
6. 1 HSCA 129.
7. 1 HSCA 124.
8. 1 HSCA 148, and to 381.
9. *LA Times*, Aug. 1, 1979. This was Dr. Michael Baden, who may actually have been fired

because of his statements in this case; and *Gallery*, p. 75-19, July 1979, concerning Dr. Werner U. Spitz, and selling organs from corpses, etc.
10. AP of Sept. 7, 1978; Dr. Michael Baden 1 HSCA 180-323.
11. 1 HSCA 327.
12. 2 HSCA 142.
13. 3 HSCA 561-98.
14. 4 HSCA 5-250, Report 612; 11HSCA.
15. On misleading testimony, 11 HSCA 64.
16. 5 HSCA 346-77.
17. *Washington Post*, March 24, 1977.
18. *NY Times*, Feb. 25, 1977.
19. *The Don*, William Brashler, Harper and Row, New York, 1977, p. 324.
20. *Seven Days*, Sept. 8, 1978.
21. See Dr. Cyril Wecht's articles in *The Journal of Legal Medicine*, "Why is the Rockefeller Commission So Single-Minded About a Lone Assassin in the Kennedy Case?" July/August 1975; and in *Juris*, Duquesne University School of Law, Dec., 1975, "A Post-Mortem On The 'Warrenfeller' Commission."
22. 1 HSCA 333. See also his dissent in 7 HSCA 199-209.
23. Ibid.
24. Ibid.
25. 1 HSCA 337.
26. Ibid.
27. 1 HSCA 491-505, 553-67; Report 506-52.
28. *Conspiracy*, Anthony Summers, p. 65-7, 69, 532 n. 7.
29. AP, April 1, 1977 and the *Baltimore Sun*.
30. AP, Dec. 6, 1977; *Washington Post*, Jan 5, 1977.
31. Report 198-200.
32. *The Continuing Inquiry*, Feb. 1977, and Mary Ferrell's comment therein, Oct. 1978.
33. *Washington Post*, June 18, 19, 28, 1979; *Washington Star*, June 20, 1979 p. A-17; *NY Post*, June 18,.1979., p. 5.
34. *Washington Post*, June 19, 1979.
35. *NY Times*, Nov. 1978. (date lost.).
36. 1 HSCA 344.
37. *Washington Post*, Dec., 1978.
38. Report 156-7; 4 HSCA 602-3; *Atlanta Constitution*, Jan. 3, 1979.
39. *The Baltimore Sun*, Nov. 18, 1979.
40. *The Washingtonian*, Nov. 1980, "Who Killed JFK?" by Gaeton Fonzi.
41. Ibid.
42. Ibid.
43. Ibid.

Chapter 19

1. "Assassination Plots Described by Liddy", *New York Times*, 1980; *Will*, by Gordon Liddy; *Give Us This Day*, by Howard Hunt; *Compulsive Spy*, by Tad Szulc – about Hunt; interview with Colson in *Argosy*, March, 1976; *Crime and Cover-Up: The CIA, The Mafia, and The Dallas-Watergate Connection*, by Peter Dale Scott; and extensive material in Fensterwald's *Assassination of JFK, Coincidence or Conspiracy?* Final chapter of this book as well. *Government by Gunplay*, edited by Sid Blumenthal (Signet), articles "Richard M. Nixon and Organized Crime", by Jeff Gerth. Numerous excellent articles can be found in *Big Brother and the Holding Company.*
2. Model-Groden 155; "An Introduction to the Assassination Business," by Col. Fletcher Prouty, *Gallery*.

3. "The White Hand," by Ernest Volkman and John Cummings in *Penthouse*, describes "Over 1000 CIA-trained killers have formed their own Murder, Inc., in Latin America – and now even the CIA is worried that this independent terror network is permanently out of control."
4. *High Treason*, by Albert E. Kahn, The Hour Publishers, Groton on Hudson, NY 1950, pp. 204-211 for description.
5. "The CIA and the Media," by Carl Bernstein in *The Rolling Stone*, detailed extensive covert use of publishers and newspapers in the United States; "The Media and the Murder of John Kennedy," by Jerry Policoff; "The American News Media and the Assassination of President John F. Kennedy: Accessories After the Fact," by Richard E. Sprague, *Computers and Automation*, June 1973.
6. Victor Marchetti in *Gallery*, July, 1979, p. 84-28.
7. "Alleged Assassination Plots Against Foreign Leaders," Interim report of the *Select Committee to Study Governmental Operations with Respect to Intelligence Activities, The United States Senate*, GPO Nov 20, 1975, and Final Report thereof, April 23, 1976.
8. House Select Committee on Assassinations, Report, p. 1.
9. n7 above; Fensterwald *Coincidence or Conspiracy*, pp 327- 338.
10. For history of Ruby, see Robert Sam Anson, *They've Killed the President*, 226-42, 309, 322, 328; Seth Kantor, *Who Was Jack Ruby?*, and Criminal associations in the work of the HSCA.
11. Anson p. 324.
12. See "The Kennedy Vendetta," by Taylor Branch and George Crile III, *Harpers*; "The Kennedy Imprisonment," *The Atlantic Monthly*, January and February 1982.
13. Victor Navasky, *Kennedy Justice* (New York: Athenium, 1971), p. 44.
14. Fensterwald, p. 533.
15. Jeb Stuart Magruder, *An American Life*, (NY, Athenium, 1974) p. 178.
16. Fensterwald, p. 534; Senate Intelligence Committee Final Report, Book IV, p. 136.
17. Fensterwald, p. 535; *True*, August, 1974.
18. CBS Radio commentary August 10, 1973.
19. Fensterwald p. 527.
20. Shaw p. 54.
21. Fensterwald p. 524 and 534. Senate Intelligence Committee Final Report, Book IV, P. 136. United Press, Sept. 23, 1975.
22. *A Heritage of Stone*, Jim Garrison, (Putnam, NY, 1970).
23. Fletcher Prouty, *The Secret Team*, p. 416.

Chapter 20

1. *The Secret Team* p. 8 (Fletcher Prouty).
2. General Thomas Lane *The Leadership of President Kennedy* p. 27.
3. *The Secret Team* p. 390.
4. Lane p. 27.
5. Lane 27.
6. Ibid 27.
7. Ibid 28.
8. Ibid 30.
9. Ibid 30.
10. Ibid 28.
11. Ibid 28; For an account see Fletcher Prouty "The Betrayal of JFK Kept Fidel Castro in Power" *Gallery* Feb 1978 concerning the air strikes. Again see Wise and Ross in *The Invisible Government* on this and the Bay of Pigs.
12. Lane 28.
13. Ibid 29.
14. Ibid 30.
15. Ibid 26.

16. Ibid 30-1.
17. Ibid 30.
18. Hepburn *Farewell America* 268 Kennedy quote on Vietnam. See the *Pentagon Papers*, which are not honest.
19. Prouty 392.
20. Ibid 417.
21. Ibid 418.
22. Jim Hougan *Spooks*.
23. Prouty 104.
24. Ibid 113.
25. Ibid 115.
26. Ibid 115.
27. *Gallery* Feb 1978 cited above.
28. Lane 30.
29. Prouty 116.
30. Ibid 117.
31. Ibid 118.
32. Ibid 118.
33. Ibid 119.
34. Ibid 120.
35. Ibid 212.
36. Lane introduction *The Leadership of President Kennedy.*
37. Ibid 37.
38. Ibid xi.
39. Ibid 39.
40. Ibid 41.
41. Ibid 42.
42. Ibid 34.
43. Prouty.
44. Ibid 2-3.
45. Ibid 4.
46. Ibid 6.
47. Ibid 4.
48. Ibid 6-5.
49. Ibid 5.
50. Ibid 5.
51. Ibid 97.
52. Ibid 419.
53. Ibid 101.
54. Ibid 321.
55. Ibid 321.
56. Ibid 396.
57. Ibid 401-3.
58. Ibid 404.
59. Ibid 405.
60. Ibid 405.
61. Ibid 423.

Acoustic evidence, 111, 344
  Aschkenasy and Weiss findings, 214,
    224-225
  Bolt, Berenek and Newman, 207-209,
    212, 213-214, 218, 219, 220, 222
  Carillons, 214-215, 220
  Dictabelt recording, 6-7, 14, 106, 184,
    193, 207-208, 329, 333-334, 335-
    336
    channels, 212, 217, 217-219, 222-
      223
    copies, 212, 222-223
    editing of, 222, 223-224
    Decker statement, 212, 216-218,
      220-221
      Steve Barber's discovery,
        216-217, 218-219, 223
    echo analysis, 209-211, 214, 215,
      338-339
    hum tones, 212, 223
    original, 206, 212, 223
  FBI, 211, 215-216, 219-220, 227
    secret report, 219-220
  House Select Committee on
    Assassinations (1976) findings,
    185, 187, 189, 206, 207, 208, 216,
    329, 330, 333-334, 335-336,
    339, 343-344
    FBI reaction, 212, 215-216,
      219-220
  Indications of more than one shot,
    207-208, 209, 210, 211, 212, 224,
    329
  Pate tape, 206
  Timing of gunshots, 187, 189, 190,
    192, 209-210, 218, 219, 224
  Zapruder film synchronisation, 185,
    188, 189, 211, 224-225, 293-294,
    311, 323
Air Force
  Aircraft
    Air Force One, 17, 35
    Air Force Two, 239
    carrying Cabinet members to Japan,
      12, 17
  Andrews Air Force Base, 239
  Atsugi Air Force Base, 5, 139, 164, 236
  Keneohe Air Force Base, 236, 237
  Tachikawa Air Force Base, 237
Aircraft
  Accidents
    Carol Tyler, 276
    E. Howard Hunt's wife, 279
    Hale Boggs, 116

    John M. Crawford, 250-251
    See also Air Force
Amsterdam, 141
Army Intelligence, 134, 159-160, 260
Assassination plots, 133, 278-279, 280,
  300-301, 354
  Against Fidel Castro, 122, 133, 143(n),
    263, 267-269, 270-271, 272, 273,
    277, 280, 281, 301
  Against George Wallace, 104(n), 294,
    295, 332, 353
  Against John F. Kennedy, 11(n), 129,
    136-137
  See also Murder plots
Assassination warnings
  Abraham Bolden, 11(n), 136-137
  Rose Cherami, 122
Assassinations
  John F. Kennedy. See Dallas; Kennedy,
    John F.
  Jose Antonio Remon, 273
  Martin Luther King, 3, 110, 292,
    293-295, 312, 334, 335, 340, 353
  Ngo Dinh Diem, 280, 299, 364,
    382-383
  Robert Kennedy, 104, 294
  See also Murders
Assassins, 155, 367
  See also Gunmen; Suspects
    (Assassination)
Assassin's window, 65, 121, 135, 139,
  149-151, 185, 195-196, 227, 228
  Trees, 187, 189
Automatic Gain Control, 213-214, 215
Autopsists, 228-232 passim
  Intimidation, 29, 50, 67, 76, 83
  Testimony re: headwounds, 25, 26-27,
    29-33, 49-53, 65, 66-67, 70,
    83-87, 88, 197, 199, 230
Autopsy
  FBI report, 81-82, 97(n), 201
  Film, 75, 107, 228
  Lee Harvey Oswald, 296(n)
  Procedures, 21, 79-81, 82, 85, 87-88,
    107, 227, 228, 230
  Suspected presence of William Pitzer,
    51
Autopsy report, 3, 22, 229
  Alteration by George Burkley, 95, 229
  Brain, 3, 79
  Face sheet, 96, 197
  Headwound, 30, 197
  Neck, 79-81, 83
  News leak, 78

Original notes, 73, 75-76, 87-88, 95-96
Photographic evidence, 3, 4, 7-8, 16,
    25-53, 31, 71-72, 74-75, 75, 81,
    84, 87, 88-95, 97-98, 229, 230,
    232, 242, 323-324, 340
    Groden analysis, 47, 88-89, 92,
        323-324, 333, 341-342
    missing, 102-103, 230
    theft, 32, 92, 107
    X-rays showing bullet fragments,
        62-72
    See also Autopsists; Wounds

Backyard photographs, 89, 146, 148-149,
    171-180, 258
    Dallas Police Department, 202
    Marina Oswald's testimony, 180
    Newspapers, 171, 179
    Rifle, 149, 175-176, 180
    Robert Groden's testimony, 173, 176
    Shadows, 148, 177-179
Bagman, 18
Ballistic evidence
    Bullets, 227-228
        atomic structure, 64-65
        CE399 (Pristine), 55, 58, 102, 190,
            226, 228, 329-330
        found during autopsy, 81-82, 201,
            231
        found in grass, 114, 183-184
        found near railroad tracks, 331
        fragments, 2, 55, 56, 57, 60,
            62-63, 62-72, 102, 190, 227,
            229-230, 331
            collar shaped, 69, 71
            missing, 60, 64, 71, 331
        military jacketed, 60-61, 63, 66,
            69, 71, 227
    Marks on sidewalk, 101-102, 183, 184,
        186
    Missing, 104, 105, 107-108, 183-184,
        338
    Neutron activation analysis, 60, 62,
        64-65, 200-201, 331
    Nitrate tests, 151
    Spectrographic analysis, 106, 201, 250,
        285-286
    Texas School Depository Building,
        107, 190, 199, 199(n),
        204, 207, 228
    Tippit murder, 152-153, 182-183
    Walker shooting, 181-182
    See also Gunmen; Gunshots; Handguns;
        Magic bullet theory; Rifles

Bay of Pigs, 133, 165(n), 251-252, 263,
    266-270, 272, 355, 369-371, 377, 384
    Investigation by Robert Kennedy, 374-
        375
    Richard Nixon, 244, 251-252, 272,
        296-297, 365
Berlin Wall (Nixon advisors), 361-362
Bethesda Naval Hospital
    William Pitzer, 50, 51, 52, 83, 92, 124
    See also Autopsists; Autopsy; Autopsy
        report
Blakey's Problem, 208
Bone fragments, 15, 27, 37, 198
Boston Globe report (June 1, 1981), 41-44

Cameras
    Autopsy, 88
    Lee Harvey Oswald
        Imperial Reflex, 148, 176
        Minox, 108
        Minox lightmeter, 108
Camp Street (New Orleans), 266
Carillons, 214-215, 220
Cars
    Dealerships, 164
    Dealey Plaza
        Rambler stationwagon, 114, 121,
            161-162
    Grassy Knoll
        Chevrolet Impala (1961), 116
        Ford (black), 116
        Oldsmobile stationwagon, 116
    Lee Harvey Oswald, 114, 161-162, 164
    Tippit murder
        Ford (red), 239-240
        Plymouth (red), 238-239
    Walker shooting
        Chevrolet (1957), 181-182
    See also Limousine
CIA
    Antonio Veciana, 124, 166, 246-248,
        249
    Assassination plots, 59, 272-281
        passim, 286, 298-301
    Attacks on Cuba, 248, 272-273, 274,
        276-281
        See also Bay of Pigs
    Clay Shaw, 125
    Connection with Oswald, 142,
        248-249, 300-307
        file, 93(n), 104
    Covert operations, 351, 368-369,
        373-378, 383
    David Atlee Phillips, 147-158, 167,

168, 246-247, 302, 303, 307
Funds, 377
George DeMohrenschildt, 259-262
Harry S. Truman, 383
Mafia involvement, 267-269, 272, 275,
    277, 280, 326-328,
    356-357
Marina Oswald, 137, 244
No-Name Key Group, 356
Operation 40, 300
Operation Chaos, 309
Operation Desktop, 377
Power, 293
Relationship with John F. Kennedy,
    267, 276-281, 355-356.
    See also Bay of Pigs
Relationship with the Press, 291-292
Ruby, Jack, 119
Special Group 54-12, 272
Time Inc., 186
Vietnam War, 366
Warren Commission, 5, 58, 299, 302,
    325
Clandestine operations. See Covert action
    capabilities
Clark panel, 4, 31-32, 50, 84, 90, 94, 283
Bullet fragments, 66-67, 68, 71
Clinton (Louisiana), 248
Clothing evidence, 228
John Connally, 57, 103
Kennedy, John F., 54, 81, 96
Lee Harvey Oswald, 153-154
Rifle, 153-154
Suspects in Texas School Book
    Depository, 153
Club, The. See Secret Team
Code book, 17
Coffin, 21, 35
Committee on Ballistic Acoustics. See
    Ramsey Report
Communism, 22, 351-352, 359, 377
Connally, John, 232, 249, 276
Position in limousine, 12
Testimony re: gunshots, 55, 56,
    190-191, 226, 322-323
Wounds, 2, 13, 14, 54-57, 62-63, 65,
    187, 193, 194, 228, 331
    bullet fragments, 2, 55, 56, 64-65,
    227, 62063
    clothing evidence, 57, 103
Zapruder film, 187, 190-191
Conspiracy, 354-355, 364-365
House Select Committee on
    Assassinations (1976), 6, 110-111,

206-208, 216, 303-304, 319, 321,
    324, 333-342, 344
government involvement, 275-276,
    335
intelligence agencies, 275-276
mafia involvement, 335, 335(n)
Martin Luther King, 292, 294-295,
    334, 340
military involvement, 275-276
Warren Report, 226-227, 231, 322, 338
See also Secret Team
Counterinsurgency, 374, 377
County Records building, 184
Covert action capabilities, 21, 133,
    351-352, 367, 368-369, 373-378, 383
Craniotomy
Lee Harvey Oswald's autopsy, 296(n)
Cuba, 355, 360, 384-385
Attacks by CIA, 247, 248, 355-356
Embassy in Mexico, 157-158, 164,
    166, 167-168, 246, 302-304, 325
Hoover memo re: Mexico City, 305-308
See also Bay of Pigs; Name Index:
    Castro, Fidel
Cuban exiles, 18, 142, 165-166, 266-267,
    296-297, 356, 364-365
Alpha 66, 166, 247, 248
Cellula Fantasma, 247
Kennedy assassination threats, 11(n),
    136-137
Cuban missile crisis, 355, 384-385
Curtain rods, 150, 175, 249-250

Dallas, 11-12
County Records building, 184
Dallas County Jail Building, 162
Dallas Textile building, 160, 185, 210,
    262
Elsbeth Street, 18, 155, 158, 160
North Beckley Avenue, 119
Power structure, 133, 262-264
Railroad overpass/underpass, 19,
    101-102, 184, 210
Right wing extremists, 11-12, 203. See
    also Right wing extremists
Stemmons Freeway, 132, 213, 214
Telephone system, 17
See also Grassy Knoll; Motorcade;
    Parkland Hospital; Texas School
    Book Depository
Dallas Police Department
Backyard photographs, 178
Car outside Oswald's home, 20, 120,
    203

Implication in frame-up of Oswald,
   202-205, 245-246
Involvement in investigation, 18, 245,
   344
Jack Ruby, 202-203, 339
Lee Harvey Oswald, 158-159, 160,
   161-163
Motorcade security arrangements,
   131-132, 162-163
Radio communications jammed, 17,
   132
Radios, 213-214, 215
See also Acoustic evidence: Dictabelt
   recording; Motorcycle officers
Dealey Plaza. See Grassy Knoll; Gunmen;
   Motorcade; Texas School Book
   Depository
Death certificate, 85, 96, 197, 229
Deaths
   FBI personnel, 122, 125-126, 332
   See also Assassinations; Murders;
      Witnesses: Deaths
Defectors
   Lee Harvey Oswald, 6, 140-143
   Yuri Nosenko, 163, 283, 325
Defense Intelligence Agency, 17, 236, 351
Diaries, 103-104, 143, 163
Disinformation
   Hoover memo re: Mexico City, 305-308

Elsbeth Street (Dallas), 18, 155, 158, 160
Evidence
   Destroyed
      autopsy film, 75, 107, 228
      autopsy report original notes, 75,
         95
      bullet marks, 184
      John Edward Pic records, 236
      manholes, 102, 184
   Fabricated, 101-109, 226-232 passim
   Ignored, 21, 26, 29-31, 90, 226-227
      Lee Bowers' testimony, 116-117
      Seymour Weitzman's testimony re:
         rifle, 196-197
   Missing, 101-109, 161, 226-232
      passim, 286
      autopsy camera, 88
      autopsy microscopic slides, 71, 102
      autopsy photographs and X-rays,
         71-72
      brain, 3, 102, 197, 228
      bullet found in grass, 183-184
      Dictabelt original recording, 206
      Mexico City transcripts, 104-105,

         167-168, 302-303, 305-309
      military files, 160
      military investigation report,
         235-238, 237
      Moorman photograph, 106
      Oliver film, 363
      Oswald camera, 108
      Oswald interrogation records, 162
      traffic sign, 105
   National Archives, 85
      classified material, 90-91
      Dictabelt recording, 206
      John F. Kennedy's brain, 3, 102,
         197, 227, 228, 330
      Missing documents, 104-106, 161,
         286
      Rifles, 175, 196-197
   Planted, 226-232 passim. See also
      Backyard photographs; Magic
      bullet theory; Rifles
      handguns, 152-153
      Hidell identification, 158-159, 159,
         245-246
      letters from Cuba, 166
      palmprint on rifle, 146-147
      rifles, 63
      spent cartridges in Texas School
         Book Depository, 107, 190,
         199, 199(n), 204, 207, 228
   Tampered with. See also Autopsy report
      Dictabelt recording, 212, 222,
         223-224
      rifles, 175, 196-197
      testimonies, 114, 162, 191, 191(n),
         226
         Boston Globe Report, 41-44
      Walker shooting, 181-182
      Zapruder film, 185-187
   See also Acoustic evidence; Ballistic
      evidence; Clothing evidence;
      Forgeries; Impersonations of Lee
      Harvey Oswald; Photographic
      evidence
Exhumation, 295-296, 296(n)
Eyewitnesses, 227, 304
   Clint Hill, 14-15, 16, 48, 127, 198
   Frontal wound, 14-15, 16, 197-198,
      199
   Grassy Knoll, 116-117, 160
   Ike Altgens, 187
   Jacqueline Kennedy, 15-16, 84
   John Connally, 187, 190-191, 226,
      322-323
   Nellie Connally, 187, 191, 322

Railroad overpass, 19
Tippit murder, 123-124, 153-154
See also Autopsists; Films; Parkland
    Hospital: Personnel; Witnesses

FBI, 18, 59, 166, 221
    Acoustic evidence, 211, 215-216,
        219-220, 227
        secret report, 219-220
    Autopsy evidence, 74, 81-82, 97(n)
    Bullet found by railroad tracks, 331
    Bullet found in grass, 114, 183-184
    COINTELPRO, 309(n), 335
    Cooperation with Warren Commission,
        132
    Deaths of high level personnel, 122,
        125-126, 332
    George DeMohrenschildt, 261
    H.L. Hunt, 263, 264
    Hoover memo re: Mexico City, 305-308
    Intimidation of witnesses, 121
    Involvement in assassination, 265
    Martin Luther King, 99-100, 335
    Minox camera / lightmeter, 108
    Pate tape recording, 206
    Reaction to acoustic findings of House
        Select Committee on Assassinations
        (1976), 212, 215-216, 219-220
    Reactions to critics, 116
    Reenactments, 78
    Report on assassination, 77, 97(n), 106,
        232
    Warren Report, 5
    Zapruder film, 101
Films, 46-47, 105, 192
    Autopsy, 75, 107, 228
    Bronson, 195, 197
    Hughes, 196
    KXAS-TV News, 220
    Muchmore, 197
    Nix, 192, 197
    Oliver, 105, 363
    See also Zapruder film
Fingerprints, 146-147, 149-150
    Cards signed in New Orleans, 147
    Oswald's handgun, 153
    Texas School Book Depository, 105
Florida, 355, 356, 364
    See also Miami
Forgeries, 103-104
    John F. Kennedy (Lifton theory of
        medical forgery of the body), 34-35
    Oswald's diaries, 103-104, 143, 163
    Palmprint, 146-147
    Signatures, 104, 145, 147-148, 179

See also Autopsy report: Photographic
    evidence; Evidence; Backyard
    photographs
Freedom of Information Act, 286
Funeral, 21-22

Gambling syndicates. *See* Mafia
Garrison probe, 4, 79-81, 117, 125, 161,
    213, 249, 262-263, 270, 356
    Deaths of witnesses, 107, 117-118
Grassy Knoll, 6-7, 14, 188, 331
    Acoustic evidence, 208, 222, 338-339
    Gunmen, 116-117, 117(n), 160, 188,
        192-193, 198, 208, 210-211,
        224-225, 333, 336, 338-339
    Secret Service, 19, 137, 160
    Testimony of witnesses, 116-117, 160
Gray Audograph, 218-219
Guatamala, 355
Gunmen, 7, 19, 116-117, 193, 217,
    224-225, 226, 365-366
    Frank Sturgis, 281, 301
    Harry Weatherford, 162
    House Select Committee on
        Assassinations findings, 58, 60,
        206, 338, 366
    Locations
        County Records Building, 184
        Dallas County Jail Building, 162
        Dallas Textile building, 160, 185,
            210
        Grassy Knoll, 116-117, 117(n),
            160, 188, 192-193, 198, 208,
            210-211, 224-225, 333, 336,
            338-339
        Manholes, 101, 184, 188, 192, 210
        Overpass/underpass, 101-102, 184,
            210
        Texas School Book Depository,
            114, 120, 135, 139, 149-151,
            151, 153, 185, 189, 194,
            195-196, 224, 227, 228
    Secret Service evidence, 128
    Warren Commission findings, 58-59,
        365
    See also Ballistic evidence; Gunshots;
        Oswald, Lee Harvey; Rifles
Guns. *See* Handguns; Rifles
Gunshots, 6-7, 106, 183-185
    FBI report, 232
    House Select Committee on
        Assassinations (1976), 207-208
    Number, 227
        Bolt, Beranek and Newman report,
            207-209

House Select Committee on
Assassinations (1976), 185, 187,
188-189, 190-192, 207-208
independant findings, 193-194
indications of more than four,
207-208, 209, 210, 211, 212,
224, 329
John Connally's testimony, 55, 56,
190-191, 226, 322-323
seventh, 210
Warren Report, 186, 189, 193, 206
Testimony of John Connally, 190-191,
322-323
Timing, 20, 187, 189, 190, 192, 208,
210, 211, 218, 219, 224
Trajectory analysis, 71, 188, 192,
193-194, 227
Warren Report, 207
See also Zapruder film

Handguns
Giancana murder, 122, 328
Jack Ruby, 203
Lee Harvey Oswald, 144, 152-153,
154, 205
Tippit murder, 118, 152-153, 154,
204-205
Use in Kennedy assassination, 14, 184,
185
See also Rifles
Harper fragment, 15, 37, 198
Hawaii, 235-238
Head wounds. See Wounds: Head
Heterodyning effect, 186, 210
V for Victory, 109
Hidell, Alek J.. See Oswald, Lee Harvey
House Select Committee on Assassinations
(1976), 310-321
Acoustic evidence, 185, 187, 189, 206,
207, 208, 216, 329, 330, 333-334,
335-336, 339, 343-344
Autopsy evidence, 3, 4
authentication, 73-98 passim
medical opinion, 25-33, 40, 43,
44, 49, 50, 52-53
Ballistic evidence, 63, 181-193 passim,
322-325, 329-331
bullet fragments, 62-67, 68
CIA, 294, 310, 314-315
Establishment, 291-295
Findings, 334-335, 339-340, 344-345
conspiracy, 6, 110-111, 206-208,
216, 303-304, 319, 321, 324,
333-342, 344
government involvement,

275-276, 335
intelligence agencies, 275-276
mafia involvement, 335,
335(n)
military involvement, 275-276
Grassy Knoll sniper, 6, 338-339
Jack Ruby, 203
Lee Harvey Oswald, 139, 140, 143-168
passim, 340-341
Marina Oswald, 144
Medical panel, 324
Mexico City, 157-158, 164, 168, 304,
307-308
Mysterious deaths project, 111-126
Photographic evidence
Backyard photottgraphs, 172-180
Groden report, 47, 92, 92(n),
323-324, 341-342
Rifles, 145-149, 196-197, 199-201
Secret Service conduct, 129-132, 134
Single bullet theory, 54-61, 330-331
Texas School Book Depository,
149-152
Tippit murder, 152-154, 205, 238-240

Impersonations of Lee Harvey Oswald, 143
Austin (Texas), 164
Dallas, 114-115, 164-165, 281
Mexico City, 155-158, 164, 304-305,
341
Inner government. See Secret Team
Intelligence agencies, 275-276, 335, 365,
373
Covert action capabilities, 21, 133,
321-352, 351, 367, 368-369,
373-378, 383
Senate Intelligence Committee, 112,
122, 263, 266, 267-269, 270-271,
364
See also Army Intelligence; CIA; FBI;
Office of Naval Intelligence; Secret
Service
Intimidation. See Witnesses
Investigations, 293
See also Clark Panel; Garrison probe;
House Select Committee on
Assassinations (1976); Military
investigations; Senate Intelligence
Committee; Warren Report
Iran-Contra hearings, 351
Iranian revolution, 352

Japan
Atsugi Air Force Base, 5, 139, 164, 236
Cabinet members en route, 12, 17

Lee Harvey Oswald's military service, 139
Military investigation of assassination, 235-238
Tachikawa Air Force Base, 237
Joint Chiefs of Staff, 18, 375, 379-380, 384

Kennedy, John F., 359
Body, 21
Lifton theory, 34-35
removal by Secret Service, 21, 229
Brain, 3, 25, 36, 102, 197, 227, 228, 330
CIA, 267, 276-281, 355-356. See also Bay of Pigs
Death certificate, 85, 96, 197, 229
Funeral, 21-22
Policies
domestic
civil rights, 359
education, 373-374
mafia, 253, 357, 358, 360
oil depletion allowance, 360
steel companies, 360
foreign, 8, 133, 145
Cuba, 277, 280, 355-356, 359, 360, 384-385. See also Bay of Pigs
Soviet Union, 355, 360, 366
military, 360, 366, 369-373, 372, 377-381. See also Bay of Pigs; Vietnam War
National Security Action Memorandums, 373-378, 383, 384
Reasons for his assassination, 8, 145, 355-361, 382
Secret Team and, 350
See also Autopsy report; Parkland Hospital: Medical treatment of John F. Kennedy; Wounds
King assassination, 3, 110, 292, 293-295, 312, 334, 335, 340, 353

Lacombe (Louisiana), 248
Lake Pointchartrain (Louisiana), 142, 355, 356
Lightmeter, 108
Limousine, 106
Bubble, 128, 131
Bullet fragments, 64, 65, 68, 70-71, 338
Driver, 12, 13, 19, 48, 127
Position in motorcade, 135
Rebuilding, 75

See also Motorcade
Louisiana, 364
Albert Guy Bogard's death, 115
Clinton, 248
Hale Boggs, 116
Lacombe, 248
See also New Orleans
Mafia, 122, 130, 251
Assassination plots against Fidel Castro, 267-269, 270-271, 272, 277, 280-281
Involvement in John F. Kennedy assassination, 325-328, 335, 335(n), 357, 358, 364-365
Involvement with CIA, 267-269, 272, 275, 277, 280, 326-328, 356-357
Jack Ruby and, 240, 273, 274-275, 328, 357-358
Kennedy family, 267, 274-275, 280-281, 326, 327, 357-358, 360-361
Richard Nixon and, 252-254, 274, 277
Magic bullet theory, 54-61, 191, 226, 324-325
Deformation of bullet, 56, 57, 60-61, 329-331
Finding of bullet (CE 399), 58, 102
Neutron activation analysis, 60, 62, 64-65, 201
Zapruder film, 186
Mail order purchase of guns, 144, 145, 147, 159, 180
Manholes, 101, 184, 188, 192, 210
Marine Corps, 235-238
Media. See Press
Medical opinions
Clark panel, 4, 31-32, 66-67, 68, 71, 84, 90
House Select Committee on Assassinations medical panel, 324
See also Autopsists; Autopsy report; Parkland Hospital: Personnel
Mexico
H.L. Hunt, 264-265
Mexico City, 6, 105, 155-158, 164, 166, 275, 302-305, 325, 340-341
CIA, 167-168
Missing transcripts, 104-105, 167-168, 305-309
Miami
Police
Milteer assassination plot, 11(n), 137
Santos Trafficante, 130, 275, 325-327, 357, 364

Microphones, 16, 132, 210, 212, 213, 214, 215
Military
    Army Intelligence, 134, 159-160, 260
    Files on Oswald, 140
    Immediate response to assassination, 17-18
    Involvement in assassination, 275, 335, 365, 367
    Office of Naval Intelligence, 5, 104, 139, 249
    Pentagon Papers, 22, 376, 382
    Relationship with John F. Kennedy, 360, 369-373, 377-378, 378-380
        National Security Action Memorandums, 373-378, 383, 384
    Right wing extremists and, 359
    Special Group 54-12, 272
    See also Air Force; Bay of Pigs; Navy; Pentagon; Vietnam War; War Party
Military investigations, 235-237
Milteer assassination plot, 11(n), 137
Missing evidence
    Bullet picked up in grass, 114, 183-184
Moorman photograph, 106, 210-211
Morse code signal, 109, 213
Motorcade, 12-16, 19, 214
    Police radio, 17
    Route, 130-131, 134-135
    Security arrangements, 128-132, 133-136, 159-160, 162
    See also Limousine; Motorcycle officers
Motorcycle officers, 16, 17, 19, 128-129, 131-132, 135, 198
    Leave motorcade, 132, 135
    Open microphone, 16, 132, 210, 212, 213, 214, 215
Motorola radios, 213-214
Movie theater. See Texas Theatre
Murder plots
    Against J. Edgar Hoover, 364
    Against Jack Anderson, 363-364
    See also Assassination plots
Murders
    J.D. Tippit, 20, 120, 122-123, 145, 152-153, 154, 182-183, 204-205, 238-240
    John Roselli, 112, 121-122, 327
    Lee Harvey Oswald, 113-114, 163, 245
    Sam Giancana, 112, 121-122, 328
    William Pitzer, 50, 51, 52, 83, 92, 124
    See also Assassinations; Deaths; Witnesses: Deaths

My Lai massacre, 385
Mysterious deaths project, 111-126

NAS. See Ramsey Report
National Science Foundation. See Ramsey report
National Security Action Memorandums (NSAMs), 373-378, 383, 384
National Security Agency, 381
National Security Council, 351, 381
Navy, 67
    See also Autopsists; Autopsy; Autopsy report; Bethesda Naval Hospital; Office of Naval Intelligence
Nazi doctrines, 241, 362-362
    See also Right wing extremists
Neutron activation analysis, 60, 62, 64-65, 200-201, 331
New Orleans, 116, 156, 164
    Anti-Castro movement, 265
    Camp Street, 266
    Coroner Nicholas Chetta, 117, 118
    Guy Banister's death, 133
    Lake Pontchartrain training camp, 142, 355, 356
    Mafia, 118
    Mayor DeLesseps Chep Morrison, 125
    Police, 161
    See also Garrison probe
Newspapers
    in Backyard photographs, 171, 179
Nitrate tests, 151
NSAMs. See National Security Action Memorandums
Nuclear Test Ban Treaty, 366

Office of Naval Intelligence, 5, 249
    Connection with Lee Harvey Oswald, 104, 139
Oil depletion allowance, 263, 360
Oil interests, 242, 260, 262, 263-264, 274, 276, 359, 381
Operation 40, 300
Operation Chaos, 309
Operation Desktop, 377
Organized crime. See Mafia
Oswald, Lee Harvey, 4-5, 18, 130, 138-139, 221, 275, 281, 328
    Addresses
        Camp Street (New Orleans), 266
        Elsbeth Street (Dallas), 18, 155, 158, 160
        North Beckley Avenue (Dallas), 119

Aliases
  Alek J. Hidell, 145, 158-159, 245-246
Arrest, 106-107, 113-114, 138, 158-159, 161, 162, 178, 204
  interrogation, 105, 107, 162, 178
Attitude towards John F. Kennedy, 138, 152, 155, 163
  motives for assassination, 155
Autopsy, 296(n)
Backyard photographs, 89, 146, 148-149, 171-180, 258
Camera, 108, 148, 176
Cars, 114, 161-162, 164
CIA connections, 93(n), 118, 142, 303, 331-332
Clothing, 153-154
Craniotomy, 296(n)
Cuban exile connections, 142, 246-248, 265-266
Death, 113-114, 138, 163, 245
Defection to Soviet Union, 6, 140-142
  return to United States, 140, 141-143
Diaries, 103-104, 143, 163
Exhumation, 295-296
Frame-up, 5, 156, 158-159, 160, 166-167, 181, 202-205, 300-305. See also Evidence
Government agent, 5, 6, 104, 106(n), 113, 139-143, 148, 159, 248-249, 251, 259, 266
Guns, 63, 139, 143, 144, 145-149, 159, 175, 180, 203
  Tippit murder, 182-183, 204-205
  Walker shooting, 181
Intellectual level, 163-164, 257
Marksmanship, 151, 189
Mexico City, 6, 105, 155-158, 164, 166-168, 246-247, 275, 302-305, 325, 340-341
Military service, 6, 139-141, 142, 151
  Atsugi Air Force Base, 5, 139, 164
  discharge, 140, 142
Money, 142, 241
Nitrate tests, 151
Physical description, 164, 165, 173, 304
Relationship with Clay Shaw, 248
Relationship with David Ferrie, 248, 249, 251
Relationship with Frank Sturgis, 281, 300-301
Relationship with George DeMohrenschildt, 138, 163, 176,
  180, 242, 257, 258
Relationship with Guy Banister, 266
Relationship with Jack Ruby, 113, 143(n), 154
  witnesses, 105, 117, 118, 119, 122, 138-139
Relationship with James Hosty, 108, 160, 265
Russian language, 113, 139, 163-164
Signatures, 104, 145, 147-148, 179
Soviet Union, 6, 140-143
Tax returns, 241
Taxi driver (alleged), 120
Texas School Book Depository, 20, 146, 149-151, 152, 153, 158, 250
Tippit murder, 20, 182-183, 204-205, 238-239
Violent behavior, 154, 181, 258
Warren Report, 2, 115, 119, 139-140
See also Impersonations of Lee Harvey Oswald
Overpass/underpass, 19, 101-102, 184, 210

Palmprint, 146-147
Panama, 273
Parkland Hospital, 16
  Medical treatment of John Connally, 56
  Medical treatment of John F. Kennedy
    drainage tubes in chest, 55, 77, 230
    evidence of surgery to temple area, 67, 227
    tracheotomy, 3, 59-60, 79, 82
  Personnel
    testimony re: headwounds, 25-27, 28, 32, 33, 35-46, 76
    testimony re: John Connally's wounds, 56-57
    testimony re: throat wounds, 59-60, 79, 82
  Presence of Jack Ruby, 102, 228, 339
  Removal of body, 21, 229
Pate tape, 206
Pentagon, 360, 366, 372, 377-378, 381
  Defense Intelligence Agency, 17, 236, 351
  See also Bay of Pigs; Military; Vietnam War; War Party
Pentagon Papers, 22, 376, 382
Photographic evidence, 323-324
  Altgens' photograph, 187
  European experts, 89, 172, 173, 177-178
  Films, 46-47, 105, 192, 195, 196, 197, 363
  Grassy Knoll sniper, 6-7

Missing, 105, 106, 107, 363
Mooreman photograph, 210-211
Tramp photographs, 19-20, 123, 298
Walker shooting, 182
See also Autopsy report: Photographic
    evidence;Backyard photographs;
    Zapruder film
Planes. *See* Aircraft
Police
    Miami, 11(n), 137
    New Orleans, 161
    Violence, 352-353
    See also Dallas Police Department
Power Control Group. *See* Secret Team
Press, 289, 354
    Bus, 135-136
    CIA and, 291-292
    Early news reports, 17, 41, 78, 250
       FBI report, 77
       Time-Life, 77
    Telephone, 17
Pristine bullet. *See* Magic bullet theory

Radical right politics. *See* Right wing
    extremists
Radios
    Dallas Police Department, 17, 213-214,
    215
       heterodyning effect, 109, 186, 210
       open microphone, 16, 132, 210,
          212, 213, 214
       V for Victory, 109, 213
    Jim Hicks, 213
    See also Dictabelt recording
Railroad overpass/underpass, 19, 101-102,
    184, 210
Ramsey report, 212, 213, 214, 215,
    222-223
Reconstruction (1978)
    Echo analysis, 209-211
Recordings. *See* Acoustic evidence; Films
Records building, 184
Researchers
    Harassment, 5
Rifles, 4-5, 117, 117(n), 212-213, 249-250
    Blanket and clothing fibers, 146, 154
    Lengths, 150, 175, 184-185
    Mannlicher-Carcano, 4, 62, 63, 77,
       108, 144, 145-149, 159, 183
       evidence of recent firing, 190
    Mausers, 63, 108, 124, 196-197, 199-
       200
    National Archives, 175, 196-197
    Photographs, 175, 180, 196
    See also Ballistic evidence; Gunshots;
       Handguns

Right wing extremists, 125, 156(n), 163,
    203-204, 240, 255, 262-271, 293, 353-
    354, 358-359, 364-365
    Dallas, 11-12, 203
    Edwin A. Walker, 144, 154, 181-182,
       255, 264-265, 379
    H.L. Hunt, 130, 163, 203, 262-265,
       274, 332
    Jack Lawrence, 115-116
    William Alexander, 120, 203, 204, 249
    See also Cuban exiles
Rockefeller Commission, 191(n), 242, 295,
    299
Ruby, Jack, 20, 105, 130
    Arms smuggling, 118, 203, 260, 265
    Associates, 115, 118-119, 120, 238,
       240-241, 245, 251, 274
       political, 243-244
    CIA, 119
    Conspiracy, 203, 254-256
    Cuba, 273-274, 328
    Dallas Police Station, 202-203, 339
    Death, 122
    International Brotherhood of
       Teamsters, 253-254
    Mafia, 240, 251, 273, 274-275, 328,
       357-358
    Money, 241
    New trial, 122
    Oswald murder, 113-114, 163,
       202-203, 245, 339
    Presence in Parkland Hospital, 102,
       228, 339
    Pristine bullet, 228
    Relationship with David Ferrie, 105
    Relationship with J.D. Tippit, 20, 122-
       123, 238, 240
    Relationship with Oswald, 113, 143(n),
       154
       witnesses, 105, 117, 118, 119,
          122, 138-139
    Relationship with Richard Nixon, 254
    Warren Commission interview, 243,
       254-256, 284

Scalp flap theory, 33-34, 42
Secret Service, 18, 128, 220
    Accidental shooting (possible) of John
       F. Kennedy, 184
    Autopsy evidence, 74, 75, 76
    Cooperation with Warren Commission,
       132, 136-137, 226
    Handling of evidence, 226
    Marina Oswald, 137, 244
    Motorcade, 14, 127-137

Party (night prior to assassination), 11, 12, 129-130
Presence on Grassy Knoll, 19, 137, 160
Presidential guards, 11, 12, 127, 129-130
Removal of body, 21, 229
Testimony re: gunshots, 184
Testimony re: headwounds, 48-49
Secret Team, 6, 8, 18-19, 21, 22, 51, 133, 134, 136, 349-386 *passim*
Definition, 18-19, 293, 350, 351
Effects on Presidency, 350, 361, 367
John F. Kennedy and, 350
Select Committee on Assassinations. *See* House Select Committee on Assassinations (1976)
Senate Intelligence Committee, 112, 122, 263, 266, 267-269, 270-271, 364
Sewers. *See* Manholes
Shadow government. *See* Secret Team
Shaw murder trial, 4, 79-81, 107, 249
See also Garrison probe
Single bullet theory. *See* Magic bullet theory
Situation Room, 17
Snipers. *See* Gunmen
Sniper's nest. *See* Assassin's window
Southeast Asia, 369, 380, 381
See also Vietnam War
Soviet Union, 355, 360
Defection of Lee Harvey Oswald, 6, 140-143
Embassy in Mexico City, 157, 158, 163, 164, 167-168, 302-304
Nuclear Test Ban Treaty, 366
Spectrographic analysis, 106, 201, 250, 285-286
Steel industry, 360
Stemmons Freeway, 132, 213, 214
Stock exchange, 241
Stockade fence. *See* Grassy Knoll
Suspects (Assassination), 19-20, 104
David Ferrie, 117-118
Jack Lawrence, 115-116
Jim Braden, 104, 262
Tramps, 19-20, 104, 123, 155, 298
See also Gunmen; Oswald, Lee Harvey

Tax returns, 241
Telephone system
Dallas, 17
Washington, 16-17
Texas School Book Depository, 20, 63, 189-190, 250
Employees, 158
Evidence
bullet fragments, 190

fingerprints, 105
paper sack, 146, 149-150
spent cartridges, 107, 190, 199, 199(n), 204, 207, 228
Presence of Oswald, 20, 146, 149-151, 152, 153, 158, 250
Presence of suspected assassins, 114, 120-121, 153, 189, 194, 195-196
Roof, 194
Suspects running from building, 114, 120-121
See also Assassin's window
Texas Theatre, 20-21, 126, 145, 152, 154, 204, 239
Third World countries, 381, 382
Guatamala, 355
Panama, 273
See also Cuba; Southeast Asia; Vietnam War
Tippit murder, 20, 120, 122-123, 145, 182-183, 204-205, 238-240
Weapon, 118, 152-153, 154, 204-205
Witnesses, 123-124, 153-154
Tracheotomy, 3, 59-60, 79, 82
Traffic sign, 105
Tramp photographs, 19-20, 123, 298
Triple underpass. *See* Overpass/underpass

V for Victory signal, 109, 213
Vietnam War, 145, 242, 299, 366-367, 372, 381, 382-383, 385
Covert actions, 369
Ngo Dinh Diem assassination, 280, 299, 364, 382, 383
Withdrawal of troops, 8, 145, 351, 366

Walker shooting
Ballistic evidence, 181-182
Lee Harvey Oswald's involvement, 144
Photographic evidence, 182
War Party, 8, 349-386 *passim*
Warren Commission, 163, 276, 295
Composition, 1-2, 58
Critics, 5
Jack Ruby interview, 243, 254-256
Relationship with CIA, 5, 58, 299
Relationship with FBI, 132
Relationship with Secret Service, 132, 136-137
Warren Report, 209, 226-227, 231
Acoustic evidence, 206, 207
Alterations of testimonies, 47, 114, 162, 226
Altgens' photograph, 187
Autopsy evidence, 22, 73-98 *passim*, 228-229

Ballistic evidence, 189, 193
Bullet fragments, 62, 64, 70-71
Conspiracy findings, 226-227, 231, 322, 338
Lee Harvey Oswald, 2, 115, 119, 139-140
Marina Oswald, 144
Mexico City, 155-158
Mexico City transcripts, 167, 168
Oswald leaving Dealey Plaza, 161
Oswald's motives, 155
Rifle, 145-148, 199-201
Single bullet theory, 1-3, 54-61
  lack of unanimity, 58-59
Texas School Book Depository, 149-151
Tippit murder, 123, 205
Zapruder film, 101, 185-186
Warrenfeller Report, 215
Washington
  Situation Room, 17
  Telephone system, 16-17
Watergate, 242, 253, 268, 272-287, 297-298, 349, 361
  Tapes, 207, 286-287, 363
Weapons. *See* Handguns; Rifles
White House
  Situation Room, 17
White supremacists, 353, 358-359
Witnesses, 227
  Alteration of testimonies, 47, 84, 107, 114, 121, 162, 191, 226-232 *passim*
    Boston Globe report, 41-44
  Deaths, 5, 7, 10, 21, 111-126, 250-251, 279, 318-319, 327, 328, 352-353
    Pitzer, William Bruce, 50, 51, 52, 83, 92, 124
  Intimidation, 5, 29, 30, 77, 83, 103, 105, 107, 121, 136, 229, 249
    court martial threats, 29, 31, 50, 67, 111, 229
  Tippit murder, 118, 123-124, 153-154
  See also Autopsists; Eyewitnesses; Films; Parkland Hospital: Personnel

Wounds, 2, 3, 8, 227-232
  Back, 55, 76-77, 78, 81, 82, 85, 97, 226, 228, 230, 336-337
    clothing evidence, 54, 81, 96
  Back of neck, 65-66, 81, 230
  Bullet fragments, 65-72
  Head, 28(illus.), 83-87, 88, 94, 197-199, 211, 227-228, 229, 230
    Scalp flap theory, 33-34, 42
    testimony of autopsists, 25, 26-27, 29-33, 49-53, 65, 66-67, 70, 83-87, 88, 197, 199, 230
    testimony of Cyril Wecht, 187-188
    testimony of eyewitnesses, 187, 197-198
    testimony of Jacqueline Kennedy, 15-16, 84
    testimony of Parkland Hospital personnel, 25-27, 28, 32, 33, 35-46, 76, 94, 198
    testimony of Secret Service agents, 14-15, 48-49, 78
    testimony of William Greer, 48
    trajectories of body matter, 14-15, 16, 197, 198, 199
  Throat, 3, 39, 59-60, 67, 79, 82, 83, 86, 96, 186, 200, 226, 229
  See also Zapruder film
Wounds (John Connally), 54-57, 226
  bullet fragments, 2, 55, 56, 62-63, 64-65, 227

X-rays. *See* Autopsy report: Photographic evidence

Zapruder film, 7, 8, 13-14, 46-47, 56, 101
  Acoustic tape synchronisation, 185, 188, 189, 211, 224-225, 293-294, 311, 323
  Blur (jiggle) analysis, 185, 188
  John Connally's wounds, 187, 190-191
  Motorcycle officer, 132, 135
  Optical enhancement, 293-294, 311
  Tampered with, 101, 185-187, 198
  Time Inc., 185, 186, 198

ZR/RIFLE. *See* CIA: Assassination plots

Aerospace Corporation, 172
Agnew, Spiro, 5, 242, 295
Akin, Gene, 38-39, 45
Albert, Carl, 295
Alch, Gerald, 314
Alexander, William, 120, 203, 204, 249
Alpha 66, 166, 247, 248
Altgens, Ike, 187
Alvarado, Gilberto Ugarte, 166
AM/LASH. *See* Cubela, Rolando
American Constitution Party, 358
American Fact-Finding Committee, 12
American Friends Service Committee, 352
Anderson, Jack, 122, 167, 252, 263, 273, 307-308, 327
    Frank Sturgis and, 278, 280
    Plot to murder, 279, 299, 363-364
Anderson, John, 311
Andrews Air Force Base, 239
Angleton, James, 286, 309(n)
Anson, Robert Sam, 164, 165, 358
Arnold, Carolyn, 150-151
ARTICHOKE, 347
Artime, Manuel, 268
Aschkenasy, Ernest, 214, 224-225
Aspin, Les, 291-292
Atomic Energy Commission, 250
Atsugi Air Force Base, 6, 139, 164, 236
Attwood, William, 277
Aubrey, H.E., 237
Austin's Barbecue, 240
Azcue, Eusebio, 157, 325, 341

Babushka Lady. *See* Oliver, Beverly
Baden, Michael, 87-88, 188, 324
Bader, William, 186
Baker, Bobby, 137, 243, 276
Baker, Marrion L., 131, 151
Baker (motorcycle policeman), 131, 151
Ball, Joseph, 105, 117, 162, 283
Banister, Guy, 133, 248, 249
    Death, 124-125, 133
    Involvement in assassination, 161
    Relationship with Lee Harvey Oswald, 147, 148, 156, 266, 364
Barber, Steve, 216-217, 218-219, 223
Barger, James, 207, 209, 212, 213, 214, 218, 329
Barker, Bernard, 251, 275
Bashour, Fouad, 39
Batchelor, Charles, 134, 135, 162-163, 202, 203, 339
Batista, Fulgencio, 274, 356
Bauman, Robert E., 317-318

Baxter, Charles, 39
Behn, Jerry, 128
Belin, David
    House Select Committee on Assassinations (1976), 304
    Rockefeller Commission, 191, 191(n), 242, 295, 299
    Warren Commission, 105-106, 114, 179, 204, 303, 305
Bell, Audrey, 64
Bell, Griffin, 317
Bell Telephone Acoustics & Speech Research Laboratory, 206
Bellah (motorcycle policeman), 19
Belmont, Alan H., 147
Benairdes, Edward, 112
Benevides, Domingo, 239-240
Benevides, Edward, 123-124
Bennett, Glenn, 78
Bentley, Paul, 158-159
Bernstein, Carl, 284
Bethesda Naval Hospital. *See* Pitzer, William Bruce; Subject index: Autopsists; Subject index: Autopsy; Subject index: Autopsy report
Bickley, Alex, 202-203
Billings, Richard, 189, 210, 211, 335(n), 345
Binion, Bennie, 130
Bishop, Jim, 17-18
Bishop, Maurice, 166, 167, 168, 246-248, 260
    See also Phillips, David Atlee
Bissell, Richard, 267, 355, 370, 375, 380
Black Legion, 353, 353(n)
Blahut, Regis, 92, 107, 332-333, 341
Blakey, G. Robert, 111, 212, 216, 217, 298-299, 310, 319-321, 335(n), 344-345
    Autopsy photographic evidence, 93, 332, 333, 340, 343
    Gunshots, 189, 208, 225
    Robert Kennedy, 12, 294
Bobby Baker Set, 243
Bogard, Albert Guy, 112, 114-115, 164
Boggs, Hale, 58, 59, 112, 116, 320
Boggs, Lindy, 320
Bolden, Abraham, 11(n), 136-137
Bolt, Beranek and Newman, 207-209, 212, 213, 214, 218, 219, 220, 222
Boone, Eugene, 124, 199(n)
Bosch, Orlando, 300
Boswell, Thornton, 25, 30, 49-52, 56, 67, 70, 86, 93, 199, 230

Bouck, Robert, 201
Bouvier family, 258
Bowen, Howard, 155
Bowen, John (Jack), 155-157
Bowers, Lee, Jr., 112, 116-117
Bowles, Jim, 109, 213, 214, 217, 223
Bowman, Mrs., 240
Bowron, Diana, 36
Boyle, Tony, 313
Braden, Jim, 104, 160, 162, 262, 274, 275
Brading, Eugene Hale. See Braden, Jim
Bradlee, Ben, Jr., 33, 37, 38, 40-41, 42, 343
Bradley, Edgar Eugene. See Braden, Jim
Brantly, Roy, 203
Braun, Joanne, 260
Brehm, Charles, 198
Bremer, Arthur, 103, 104(n), 332
Brewer, Dennis, 19
Brezhnev, Leonid, 360
Bringuier, Carlos, 265-266
Bronson, Charles L., 195
Brooten, Kenneth, 336-337
Brown, Earl, 214
Brown, L. Dean, 292
Bull Pen, 240
Bundy, McGeorge, 17, 370, 371
Bunge Corporation, 241
Burke, Yvonne, 312
Burkley, George, 75, 85, 95, 96, 201
Burnham, David, 312, 315
Bush, George, 306
Butler, George, 163
Byars, Billy, 243
Byrd, Chief, 202

Cabana Motel, 274
Cabell, Charles, 133, 251, 262, 263, 267, 269, 270-271, 368, 376
Cabell, Earle (mayor), 133, 138, 245, 262
Cain, Wofford, 243
Califano, Joseph, 362
Camp Smith, 235-238
Campisi, Joseph, 240
Canfield, Michael, 298
Capone, Al, 357
Carlin, Karen Bennett. See Norton, Teresa
Carousel Club, 105, 115, 251
Carousel Hotel, 276
Carr, Richard Randolph, 121
Carrico, James, 43-44, 94
Carroll, Bob, 204
Carter, Jimmy, 361
Carter, John, 119

Caster, FNU, 260, 265
Castorr, Robert, 260
Castro, Fidel, 297, 305, 360
    Assassination plots against, 122, 133, 143, 263, 267-269, 272, 274, 280, 299, 300-301, 326, 328, 356, 357
    Testimony for House Select Committee on Assassinations (1976), 157, 325
Cellar (bar), 12, 129-130
Cellini, Dino, 130
Cellula Fantasma, 247
Chaney, James, 199
Chaos, Operation, 309
Charles, Joseph Clemard, 260
Charles, Pedro, 166
Chase, Norman, 65, 66, 67
Cherami, Rose, 122
Chesher, Bill, 112, 117
Chetta, Nicholas, 112, 117, 118
Chotiner, Murry, 252, 273 4
Choyke, Bill, 314-315
Church, Frank, 273
Civello, Joe, 274
Clark, Kemp, 26, 36
Clark, Ramsey, 4, 32, 250
    See also Subject index: Clark panel
Clifton, Chester, 18
Cline, Ray, 292
Coe, John I., 84
Cohen, Jacob, 72
Cohen, Jerry, 214
Cohen, Mickie, 252
Cohn, Roy, 263
COINTELPRO, 309(n), 335
Colby, William E., 291-292
Coleman, William, 282
Collins Radio Co., 239
Colony Club, 105
Colson, Charles, 252, 281-282, 332, 362
Committee on Ballistic Acoustics
    Ramsey Report, 212, 213, 214, 216, 222-223
Committee to Investigate Assassinations, 283
Committee to Re-Elect the President, 278, 285, 298, 363
Connally, John. See Subject index: Connally, John
Connally, Nellie, 187, 191, 322
Connel, Mrs. C.L., 265
Cook, Austin, 240
Cooke, Leon, 357
Cooper, John, 58, 59
Cooper, Marion, 273

Cornwall, Gary, 86-87
Cox, Archibald, 106(n), 284
Craig, Roger, 114, 121, 123, 124, 161, 162
Crawford, John M., 250-251
Cuban Revolutionary Council, 142, 265
Cubela, Rolando, 248, 276-277, 325
Curry, Jesse, 16, 18, 22, 56, 113, 133-134,
    138-139, 182, 183, 189, 198, 203, 245
    Dictabelt recording, 213, 217-218,
    219, 220-221
Cushman, Robert, 252, 273

Dalitz, Mo, 274
Daniels, Napoleon J., 202, 203
David, Dennis, 229-230
Davis, Joseph H., 49, 84
Davis, Red, 202
Day, J.C., 147
Dean, John, 279, 282
Dean, Patrick, 242
DeAngelis, Tino, 241
Decker, William, 161, 162, 213, 254, 255
    Dictabelt recording, 212, 216-218,
    220-221
Deep Throat, 282
DeGaulle, Charles, 128
Del Charro Set, 243
Del Mar Racetrack, 243
del Valle, Aladio, 118
Delaney, Gil, 67
Delaune, Henry, 117
Delilah. See Walle, Marilyn April
DeLoach, Cartha D., 59
DeMohrenschildt, George, 138, 163, 205,
    242, 245, 250, 257-262
    Backyard photographs, 176, 180, 258
    Haiti, 257, 258, 259-260, 261
    Money, 241
    Suicide, 112-113, 258, 261, 262, 319
DeMohrenschildt, Jeannie, 113, 261-262
Denius, Franklin, 243
Desktop, Operation, 377
Devine, Sam, 311, 318, 320
Dickerson, Nancy, 385
Diehl, Kemper, 318
Diem. See Ngo Dinh Diem
Dillon, Douglas, 370
Dobbs House, 238
Dodd, Christopher, 7, 188, 189-190, 196,
    218
Dolan, James, 275
Dolan, Joe, 45
Donovan, Gay, 111
Dorfman, Allen, 253

Douglas, William O., 372-373
Dowling, Ada, 238
Downing, Thomas, 121-122, 292-293, 294,
    296, 297, 304, 313, 314, 315, 316
Downtown Lincoln Mercury, 114-116, 251
Dox, Ida, 32
DRE. See Cuban Revolutionary Council
Dryer, Joseph, 257, 259, 260
Duff, William McEwan, 265
Dulany, Richard, 37, 40
Dulles, Allen, 166(n), 267, 377
    Bay of Pigs, 165, 355, 370, 371, 375
    Warren Commission, 5, 30-31, 58,
    158, 375
Duran, Sylvia, 164, 303, 307
Duvalier, Francois (Papa Doc), 257

Ebersole, John H., 65-66, 67
Eddowes, Michael, 295-296
Edgar, Robert W., 112
Edwards, Don, 316
Edwards, Sheffield, 267, 269
Ehrlichman, John, 283, 297-298, 361
Eisenhower, Dwight D., 243, 272, 350,
    368, 369
El Chico Restaurant, 238
Ellis (motorcycle policeman), 19
Ellsberg, Daniel, 283, 364
Epstein, Edward J., 163, 258, 296

Fair Play for Cuba Committee, 142, 156,
    249, 266, 275
Fauntroy, Walter, 318, 340
Feeney, Rick, 316
Fensterwald, Bernard, 252, 270, 274, 283,
    286, 314-315, 362
Ferrell, Mary, 162
Ferrie, David, 105, 117-118, 161, 248-249,
    251, 274, 275, 313, 364
    Relationship with Jack Ruby, 105
Fillinger, Halpert, 69, 70
Finck, Pierre, 4, 27, 30, 56-57, 67, 79-81
Fiorini, Frank. See Sturgis, Frank
Fisher, Russell, 31-32, 84, 283
Fitzgerald, Desmond, 248, 276-277
Fitzsimmons, Frank, 253, 274
Fogelson, E.E., 243
Folsom, Allison G., 139
Fontainebleau Hotel, 278-280
Fonzi, Gaeton, 163, 345
Ford, Gerald, 2, 4-5, 5, 58, 77, 191(n),
    231, 242, 262, 284, 299, 325
    Jack Ruby interview, 254-256, 284
Forty (40), Operation, 300

Fox, Mr., 274
Frazier, Buell, 150, 175, 249-250
Frazier, Robert, 70
Freeman, H.D., 132
Fritz, Will, 107, 161, 162, 245
Fromm, Joseph, 292
Fulbright, William, 370, 383-384

Gannaway, W. Patrick, 158
Garner, Darrell Wayne, 119, 123
Garrick (motorcycle policeman)
Garrison, Jim, 83, 200
    See also Subject index: Garrison probe
Gatlin, Maurice Brooks, 125
Gaudet, William George, 156
Gener, Macho, 326
Genzman, 175
Giancana, Sam, 112, 121-122, 268,
    280-281, 326, 327, 357
Giesecke, Adolphe, 25-26, 40, 42, 197
Glomar Explorer, 377
Goldberg, Jeff, 344
Goldsmith, Michael, 175-176, 177
Goldstein, David, 112, 118
Golz, Earl, 101-102, 213, 214
Gonzalez, Henry, 293, 304, 313-318, 320,
    328
Gonzalez, Virgilio, 374
Gray (motorcycle policeman), 19
Great Southwest Corporation, 137, 242,
    244, 245
Greer, William, 12, 13, 19, 48, 127
Gregory, Charles F., 56
Gregory, Dick, 294, 354
Griffin, Burt, 242
Groden, Christine, 294
Groden, Robert, 46-47, 225
    Autopsy photographs, 47, 88-89, 92,
        323-324, 333, 341-342
    Backyard photographs, 173, 176, 179
    Zapruder film, 8, 46-47, 82, 190, 191,
        224-225, 293-294
Grosse, John, 156
Grossman, Robert, 26, 31, 44, 46
Guinn, Vincent, 60, 64, 102, 200, 331
Gustafson, Patricia (Hutton), 37

Haig, Alexander, 272
Haldeman, H.R., 282, 286-287, 297-298,
    361
Hallet, Oliver, 17
Hamilton, Edward J., 278, 279
    See also Hunt, E. Howard; Sturgis,
        Frank

Hargis, Bobby, 16, 198
Harper, Billy, 198
Harrelson, Charles, 123
Harris, Larry, 58-59, 114
Harris, Mrs., 131
Harvey, William, 268, 269
Haseltine, Nat, 78
Haygood, Clyde A., 131
Helms, Richard
    CIA, 93, 161, 163, 249, 261, 268,
        283, 325
    House Select Committee on
        Assassinations (1976), 271, 325
    Warren Commission, 93, 125(n), 163,
        294
    Watergate, 155, 297-298
Helperman, Sammy, 298
Helpern, Milton, 57-58
Henchcliffe, Margaret. See Hood, Margaret
Henderson, Ruby, 151, 195
Hepburn, James, 128, 264-265
Hess, Jacqueline, 111-113, 126
Hicks, James, 105
Hicks, Jim, 157, 213
Hidell, Alek (Oswald alias), 145, 158-159,
    245-246
Hill, Clint, 14-15, 16, 48, 127, 198
Hill, Gerald, 152-153, 154, 158-159, 182,
    204-205, 246
Hiss, Alger, 361
Hitler, Adolph, 362
Ho Chi Minh, 360
Hoffa, Jimmy, 103, 112, 133, 243, 253,
    357
Holland, S.M., 199
Holm, Mike, 294
Hood, Margaret (Henchcliffe), 39, 60
Hoover, J. Edgar, 64, 135, 141, 200, 201,
    203, 243, 250,
    265, 278, 305, 360, 364, 375
    Blackmail of government members, 100
    Dallas, 12
    Martin Luther King, 99-100
Hosty, James, 108, 160, 265
Hougan, Jim, 92, 122, 374
Houston, Lawrence, 281
Howard, Thomas Hale, 112, 118-119
Huber, Oscar, 197
Huff, Larry, 235-237
Hughes, Howard, 133, 263, 268, 270, 327,
    377
Hughes, Robert
    Film, 195, 196
Humes, James, 25, 30-31, 49-52, 55-56,

65, 66-67, 73, 74, 75-76, 79, 82,
83-88, 93, 201, 324
Hunt, E. Howard, 92, 103, 133, 161, 165,
242, 332, 364
Anti-Cuban involvement, 251, 268,
273, 277-278, 369
Dallas, 298-299
Role in assassination plots, 247, 272,
273, 275, 281, 295, 299, 364
Watergate, 279, 281, 297-298, 333
Wife, 279
Hunt, H.L., 112, 130, 163, 203, 262-265,
274, 332
Hunt, Jackie, 45
Hunter, William, 112, 118-119
Hutton, Patricia. See Gustafson, Patricia
Hyde, William Avery, 257, 259

Ingram, Hiram, 123
International Anti-Communist Brigade, 281

Jacks, Hurchel, 75
Jackson, C.D., 244
Jackson, Murray James, 238
Jaggers-Chiles-Stoval, 140, 155, 156
Jaworski, Leon, 106, 106(n), 284
Jenkins, Marion, 39-40, 42-43, 55, 76-77,
197
Jenner, Albert, 285
Johnson, Clyde, 112, 118
Johnson, Guy, 249
Johnson, Lyndon Baynes, 14, 17, 35, 130,
243, 263, 266, 270-271, 308
Belief in conspiracy, 7, 59, 297, 365
Dallas Police Department investigation,
162, 245
Relationship with John F. Kennedy,
276
Secret Team and, 136, 361, 366-367,
382
Johnson, Tom, 203
Jones, Penn, Jr., 114, 134, 243
Jones, Ronald Coy, 37
Just, Ward, 292

Kail, Sam, 260
Kantor, Seth, 339
Karamessines, Tom, 298
Katzenbach, Nicolas, 221
Keeton, Stanley, 22, 66, 96-98
Kellerman, Roy, 48, 81, 128
Kelly, Thomas, 129
Keneohe Base, 236, 236-237, 237
Kennedy, Edward, 276, 280, 286, 353

Kennedy, Jacqueline, 35
Testimony, 15-16, 84
Zapruder film, 14-15, 197
Kennedy, John F.. See Subject Index:
Kennedy, John F.
Kennedy, Regis, 105, 125, 363
Kennedy, Robert, 8, 128, 282, 384
Anti-Mafia campaign, 274, 326, 327,
357-358, 360-361
Assassination, 294, 353
Bay of Pigs investigation, 374-375
CIA assassination plots, 268, 278-279,
280
Cuba, 277
Kenney, Admiral, 81
Kenney, George C., 264
Kerr, Bob, 113
Kersta, Lawrence, 206
Kessler, Ronald, 116, 302
Khrushchev, Nikita, 355, 360
Kilgallen, Dorothy, 112, 119
Killam, Thomas Henry (Hank), 112, 119
Killam, Wanda Joyce, 119
King, Coretta, 100, 293, 294-295
King, Martin Luther, 3, 110, 293, 312, 353
Conspiracy evidence, 292, 294-295,
334, 340
FBI, 99-100, 335
Kirkwood, Pat, 12, 129-130
Kissinger, Henry, 361, 386
Kliens. See Subject index: Mail order
purchase of guns
Klindienst, Richard, 361
Koethe, Jim, 112, 118
Kohly, Mario Garcia, Sr., 297
Kohn, Howard, 273
Kopechne, Mary Jo, 276, 280
Krogh, Egil, 361, 363
Ku Klux Klan, 353, 358
Kupcinet, Karyn, 122
KXAS-TV, 220

La Costa Country Club, 253, 274
Lancelot, Jacqueline, 257, 259-260
Lane, Mark, 314, 315
Lane, Thomas, 369, 371-373, 376, 379-380
Lansky, Meyer, 130, 243, 273-274
Lanz, Pedro Diaz, 300
Lardner, George, Jr., 117, 312, 313, 314,
316, 317, 338
Lattimer, John, 94, 228
Lawrence, Jack, 115-116
Lawrence, Perdue W., 131
Lawson, Winston, 131-132, 134, 135

Lawyers for Nixon-Agnew, 242
Lee, James Bradlee. *See* Braden, Jim
Lemnitzer, Lyman L., 370, 377, 384
Lester, Dick, 331
Levens, FNU, 112, 118
Levine, Isaac Don, 137, 244
Lewis, David L., 249
Liddy, Gordon, 279, 281, 362, 364
Liebeler, Wesley, 282
Lifton, David, 32-35
Lincoln, Abraham, 12, 353
Little Lynn. *See* Norton, Teresa
Livingstone, Harrison, 291, 293, 340-342, 343
Loeb & Rhodes, 259
Long, Rowland, 69
Long, Steve, 340, 341
Lopez, Edwin J., 157-158
Loquvam, George S., 49
Lorenz, Marita, 281, 300-301
Lowenstein, Allard, 353
Luce, Clare Booth, 165-166
Luce, Henry, 165
Lumpkin, George, 131

MacArthur, Douglas, 360
MacDonald, Betty Mooney, 119-120, 123
Mack, Gary, 38, 65, 67, 207, 211, 212, 218, 220, 222
Magruder, Jeb Stuart, 278, 279, 362
Maheu, Robert, 133, 268, 270, 326, 327, 357
Malone, William Scott, 319, 325
Manchester, William, 363
Mansfield, Mike, 355
Marcello, Carlos, 103, 248, 274-275, 280-281, 327, 357, 364
Marchetti, Victor, 125, 161, 249, 251, 298, 356
Marks, John, 380
Marrs, Jim, 130, 261
Marshall, George, 380
Martin, B.J. (motorcycle policeman), 198
Martin, Frank, 122
Martin, Jack, 161
Martin, James Herbert, 244, 245
Martin, Ralph, 382
Martino, John, 126
Mather, Carl, 238-239
Mathews, Russell D., 123
Matlack, Dorothy, 259-260
Maury, John, 292
McBride, G.C., 19
McCamy, Calvin, 325

McCandless, Robert, 315
McCarthy, Joseph, 263
McClellan Committee, 253
McClelland, Robert, 32, 36-37, 38, 39, 59
McClendon, Gordon, 256
McCloy, John, 58, 74, 227, 284
McCone, John, 268, 305, 308
McCord, James, 92, 279, 282, 283, 314, 333
McGann, Beverly. *See* Oliver, Beverly
McGann, George, 105, 123
McHugh, Godfrey, 35
McKenzie, William A., 244-245
McLain, Alfred. *See* McLane, Alfred E.
McLain, H.B., 212, 214
McLane, Alfred E., 243, 256
McLeney, William, 248
McNamara, Robert, 18, 145, 366, 367, 369, 370, 382, 383
McVicker, John A., 141
McWillie, Lewis, 130, 243, 274
Meagher, Sylvia, 67
Mendoza, Charles, 261-262
Mercer, Julia, 117, 117(n)
Meyers, Lawrence, 274
Miami Beach First National Bank, 278
Milteer, Joseph, 11(n), 358
Minh, Ho Chi. *See* Ho Chi Minh
Minutemen, 264, 358
Mitchell, John, 253, 278, 285-286
Mitchell, Martha, 253, 279
MK/CHILD, 294
MK/ULTRA, 347
Model, Peter, 179
Moffitt (pilot), 237
Moon, Marilyn Magyar. *See* Walle, Marilyn April
Mooney, Luke, 196, 204
Mooney, Nancy Jane. *See* MacDonald, Betty Mooney
Moore, J. Walton, 113, 258-259, 260
Moorman, Mary, 106
Moreell, Ben, 379
Morgan, Roger C., 235-237
Morrison, DeLesseps Chep, 125
Morrow, Robert, 275, 296-297
Moyers, Bill, 131, 221
Muchmore, Marie
    Film, 197
Murchison, Clint, 12, 130, 203, 242, 243, 245, 250, 262

National Archives Dictabelt recording, 206
    John F. Kennedy's brain, 3, 102, 197, 227, 228, 330

Missing documents, 105-106, 162, 286
Rifles, 175, 196-197
National Science Foundation
Ramsey report, 212, 213, 214, 215,
222-223
National States Rights Party, 358
Nelson, Doris, 38
Newman, Larry, 382
Ngo Dinh Diem, 280, 299, 364, 382, 383
Ngo Dinh Nhu, 382-383
Nichols, John, 66
Nicoletti, Charles, 319
Niell, James, 202, 203
Nikel, Herman, 292
Nitti, Frank, 357
Nix, Orville, 192
Nixon, Donald, 252
Nixon, Richard, 5, 104(n), 105, 165, 244,
280, 332, 333, 349, 353, 361, 381
Attitude toward John F. Kennedy, 244,
253
Bay of Pigs, 244, 251-252, 272,
296-297, 365
Covert operations, 251, 272
Dallas, 12, 203, 243, 244, 298, 363
Mafia, 252-254, 277
Oil interests, 242, 252, 262, 360, 381
Relationship with Jacob Rubenstein
(Jack Ruby), 254
Role in assassination plots, 272, 273,
274
Secret Team, 350, 355, 363
Vietnam war, 381, 385-386
Watergate, 106(n), 133, 281-287, 297-
298
No-Name Key Group, 356
Norton, Teresa, 112, 120
Nosenko, Yuri, 163, 283, 325
Noyes, Peter, 274

Odio, Sylvia, 165, 282, 345
O'Donnell, Kenneth, 35, 366
Oglesby, Carl, 344
Oliver, Beverly, 105, 115, 251, 363
Onassis, Aristotle, 165
O'Neill, Francis X., 81-82, 97(n), 201
O'Neill, Thomas P. (Tip), 313, 318, 366
Osborne, Albert. See Bowen, John (Jack)
Osborne, Albert Alexander. See Bowen,
Howard
Osborne, David, 201
Osborne, Howard, 155(n)
OSS, 383
Oswald, Lee Harvey. See Subject Index:
Oswald, Lee Harvey

Oswald, Marguerite, 141
Oswald, Marina, 138, 141, 144, 160,
179-180, 182, 245, 257, 325
Backyard photographs, 180
Secret Service connection, 137, 242,
244
Testimony coached, 244-245
Oswald Robert, 251
O'Toole, George, 152-153, 158-159, 202,
250, 301

Paine, Michael, 146
Paine, Ruth, 108, 146, 161, 250, 257-258
Paisley, John Arthur, 163, 283-284
Paisley, Marianne, 283
Parkland Hospital. See Subject index:
Parkland Hospital
Parks, Steve, 41, 139, 249, 343
Pate, Sam, 206, 238
Patrick, Lenny, 253
Patterson, Oliver, 319
Paul, Ralph, 240
Pawley, William, 126
Pearson, Drew, 252, 273
Pellicano, Anthony, 213
Pennington, Joe, 273
Pepsico, 244
Perrin, Nancy. See Rich, Nancy Perrin
Perrin, Robert, 117, 118
Perry, Malcolm, 16, 40-41, 43, 45, 59-60,
79, 94, 198
Peters, Paul, 38
Petty, Charles S., 49, 83-84, 296
Phillips, David Atlee, 157-158, 167, 168,
246-247, 302, 303, 307
See also Bishop, Maurice
Pic, John Edward, 236
Pickford, J.A., 239
Pitzer, William Bruce, 50, 51, 52, 83, 92,
124
Policoff, Jerry, 319, 325
Porter, William, 292
Powell, James, 160
Powell, John, 195
Powers, Dave, 35, 366
Presser, Jack, 253
Preyer, Richardson, 311, 318, 320, 323,
336, 340, 340-342
Price, Jeff, 41
Prio, Carlos, 125
Prouty, Fletcher, 8, 17, 18-19, 21, 47-48,
121, 128, 133, 134, 136, 351, 367,
368-385 passim
Provenzano, Anthony, 253
Prusakova, Ilya, 141

Purdy, Andy, 294
Puterbaugh, Jack, 134

Quiroga, Carlos, 249

Raikin, Spas, 165
Ramsey, Norman, 212, 216, 218
Randle, Linnie, 250
Rankin, J. Lee, 75-76, 96-97, 136, 147, 282
Rather, Dan, 77, 101, 281, 362
Ray, James Earl, 314, 325, 334
Rayburn, Sam, 130
Reagan, Ronald, 351
Rebozo, Bebe, 252, 277
Redlich, Norman, 137
Remon, Jose Antonio, 273
Repphert. Ralph, 184
Revill, Jack, 107, 158, 160
Reynolds, Warren, 119, 122
Rhyne, Charles, 284-285
Rich, Nancy Perrin, 118, 260, 264, 265
Richardson, Eliot, 106(n), 284
Richardson, Syd, 262, 276
Rivera, Geraldo, 294
Roberts, Carson A., 235
Roberts, Delphine, 149
Roberts, Earline, 112, 120
Roberts, Emory, 14
Rockefeller, John D., 263, 353
Rockefeller, Nelson, 191, 191(n), 242, 324
Rockefeller family, 58, 237, 242, 244, 361
Rodino, Peter, 285
Roffman, Howard, 68-70
Rose, Gus, 108
Rose, Jerry, 104
Roselli, John, 112, 121-122, 133, 268, 275, 308, 326, 327, 328, 357
Rosen (FBI), 147
Rowland, Arnold (Mr. and Mrs.), 121, 151, 195-196
Rowley, James, 128
Rubenstein, Jacob (Jack). See Subject Index: Ruby, Jack
Ruby, Jack. See Subject Index: Ruby, Jack
Ruiz, 246
Rusk, Dean, 17, 270, 370, 371
Russell, Harold, 112, 120
Russell, Lew, 314
Russell, Richard, 58-59, 156, 266

Salinger, Pierre, 17
Schorr, Daniel, 179, 299
Schweiker, Richard, 168, 247, 266, 291, 297, 306
Scott, Peter Dale, 242, 251, 299, 300
Selzer, Robert, 196

Senator, George, 115, 118
Shaffer, Charles, 282
Shah of Iran, 252
Shanklin, J. Gordon, 108
Shaw, Clay, 125, 161, 248, 249, 251
   See also Subject Index: Shaw murder trial
Shaw, Gary, 58-59, 114, 200-201, 202, 363
Shaw, Robert, 56, 57
Sheehan, Neil, 22
Sherman, Mary, 117, 118
Shires, George, 56
Sibert, James W., 81-82, 97(n), 201
Silkwood, Karen, 312(n)
Similas, Norman, 197
Simmons, James L., 19
Sirhan Sirhan, 104, 294
Sirica, John H., 207
Sisk, B.F., 293
Smathers, Frank, 278
Smathers, George, 276, 278, 280
Smith, Mrs. Earl T., 119
Smith, Art, 67
Smith, Merriman, 17
Smith, Robert, 107
Smith, Sergio Archacha, 249
Sorenson, Theodore, 269, 308
Sorrels, Forrest, 128, 130-131, 134, 135
Special Group 54-12, 272
Specter, Arlen, 2, 55-56, 73-74, 226, 242, 285, 313, 315
Sprague, Richard A., 295, 310-319, 320
St. Clair, James, 285
Stevenson, Adlai, 12, 370
Stewart, David, 45
Stokes, Louis, 157, 211, 223, 275, 312, 313, 319, 320, 325-327, 329, 335-336, 340
Stover, John, 74, 76
Sturgis, Frank, 278, 362
   Anti-Cuban involvement, 142, 246, 247, 248, 251, 274
   Mafia, 248, 275
   Oswald connection, 272, 281, 300, 301
   Role in assassination plots, 271, 272, 281, 299, 300, 308
   John F. Kennedy, 281, 300-301
   Watergate, 279-280
Sullivan, William, 125-126, 286-287, 332
Summers, Anthony, 7, 200, 247
Surrey, Robert A., 160, 264, 265
Sutton, Horace, 278
Sweatt, Allen, 106
Szulc, Tad, 280

Tachikawa Air Force Base, 237

Tague, James, 2, 14, 184, 190, 193, 207
Tatum, Jack Ray, 240
Taylor, Maxwell, 269, 366, 367, 377-378, 379, 383
Teamsters, International Brotherhood of, 242, 243, 253-254
Texas School Book Depository. *See* Subject index: Texas School Book Depository
Texas Theatre, 126, 145, 152, 154, 204, 239
Thomas, Helen, 253
Thompson, Frank, 316
Thompson, Josiah (Tink), 95, 102
Thompson, Malcolm, 89, 172, 173, 177-178
Thomson, Edward K., 244
Three States Oil and Gas, 343
Time Inc., 101, 244, 325
    Zapruder film, 185, 186, 198
Tippit, J.D., 20, 120, 122-123, 145, 153-154, 204-205, 238-241
    Murder weapon, 118, 152-153, 154, 182-183, 204-205
    Oswald connection, 20, 182-183, 204-205, 238-239
Tolson, Clyde, 59
Tomlinson, Darrell, 58, 102
Tonahill, Joe, 256
Trafficante, Santos, 103, 130, 275, 325-327, 357, 364
Treasury Department, Protective Reasearch Section, 201
Tropicana Casino, 274
Truehart, William, 292
Trujillo, Rafael, 280
Truly, Roy, 151
Truman, Harry S., 368, 383
Turner, Bill, 264
Tuteur, Werner, 143
Tydings, Mrs. Millard, 252
Tyler, Carol, 276

Ugarte, Gilberto, Alvarado. *See* Alvarado, Gilberto Ugarte
Underhill, Gary, 124
University of California Image Processing Institute, 172

Van Fleet, James, 264
Vaughn, Roy, 202-203
Vaughn, Todd, 218-219
Veciana, Antonio, 124, 166, 246-248, 249
Vesco, Charles, 252
Veterans Administration, 164
Vidal, Gore, 103

Walker, Edwin, 144, 154, 181-182, 255, 264-265, 379
Wallace, George, 104(n), 294, 295, 332, 353
Walle, Marilyn April, 112, 119-120
Walther, Carolyn, 121, 151, 195
Walthers, Buddy, 114, 183
Ward, Hugh, 125, 248
Warren, Earl, 226, 253
    Jack Ruby, 254-256
Warren, Edward. *See* Hunt, E. Howard
Weatherford, Harry, 162
Webb, Thomas, 243
Weberman, A.J., 298
Wecht, Cyril, 85, 91, 93-94, 187-188, 191-192, 284, 329-330, 337
Wedemeyer, Albert, 264
Weeden, Ronny, 123
Weems, George, 283
Weisberg, Harold, 58-59, 65, 85(n), 90-91, 95, 200, 201, 285-286, 337
Weiss, Mark, 214, 224-225
Weitzman, Seymour, 124, 196-197, 198, 199-200
West, Jean, 274
Whaley, William, 112, 120
White, Jack, 175-176, 178, 180, 184-185, 220-221
White, Pete, 244
White, T.F., 239
White Citizen's Council, 358
White Hand, 354
Whitmeyer, George, 159-160
Wilber, Charles, 65, 90, 95-96, 132, 184, 197, 199, 231
Wilcott, James B., 331-332
Willis, Philip, 186
Wise, Wes, 238, 239
Wiseman, John, 106
Wisner, Frank, 270
Wofford, Harris, 8
Wood, John H., Jr., 123
Woods, Rose Mary, 284-285
Woodward, Bob, 282, 284
Worrell, James R., 112, 120
Wright, O.P., 58
Wynne, Bedford, 243
Wynne, Jaffe & Tinsley, 244
Wynne family, 137, 242, 244, 245

Yablonski, Jock, 313
Yaras, David, 254
Yarborough, Ralph, 14, 128

Zapruder, Abraham, 13, 184, 188
    See also Subject Index: Zapruder film